READINGS IN
PHILOSOPHY

EDITED BY

JOHN HERMAN RANDALL, JR.

JUSTUS BUCHLER

EVELYN SHIRK

THIRD EDITION

BARNES & NOBLE BOOKS

A DIVISION OF HARPER & ROW, PUBLISHERS

New York, Evanston, San Francisco, London

*the text of this book is printed
on 100% recycled paper*

First BARNES & NOBLE BOOKS edition published 1972.

LIBRARY OF CONGRESS CATALOG CARD NUMBER: 72–157316

STANDARD BOOK NUMBER: 06–460059–9

PREFACE

The Preface of the earlier editions stated, in part:

This book of readings has been prepared especially for those who have not previously studied philosophy. The scope of its contents will, we hope, also make it serviceable to readers and courses of a more advanced status or in fields cognate to philosophy.

The choice of materials has been determined by criteria for individual selections and for the selections considered as a body. To justify inclusion of an individual selection, we felt that an affirmative answer should be given to each of the following questions: Does it make interesting reading for an inquiring layman? Is it digestible by such a reader after a reasonable degree of concentration on his part, and is it free from insuperable technical matter? Does it raise or reveal problems and excite philosophic thinking? With respect to the selections considered collectively, the questions asked were: Do they represent a sufficiently wide range of problems? Do they represent a sufficient diversity of historically important viewpoints? Do they represent the major branches of philosophic study?

It is necessary to emphasize that this volume is interested primarily in selections as such rather than in writers, in utility to the student rather than in deference to formal schools of thought, in philosophic suggestiveness rather than in homage to persons or ages. On the other hand, it is hardly necessary to emphasize that in consequence of its varied aims this collection could not possibly or desirably have been representative in all respects.

Apart from the occasional addition in editorial brackets of an explanatory synonym, a translation of a foreign phrase, or a note, we have avoided guides, commentaries, or introductions. Our aim in this respect has been not only to allow space for the maximum amount of material but to leave the selections absolutely free for independent interpretation by reader or teacher and for adaptation to special or limited uses. . . .

We wish to thank Herbert W. Schneider, Ernest Nagel, James Gutmann, Benjamin N. Nelson, and Fred W. Householder, Jr., for the comments or suggestions they have offered.

In the present revised edition seven new selections have been added, considerably augmenting the variety of the book. Two of the older selections have been dropped, in the belief that their meaning was too dependent upon a context that could not be provided. Two other selections have been abbreviated, in the interest of greater clarity and directness. New titles have been given to six of the selections. Fresh attention has been devoted to the order of the readings, aiming to achieve more provocative contrast and comparison for those who prefer to read in sequence.

Readers who seek systematic discussion of philosophic viewpoints and problems are referred to the volume *Philosophy: An Introduction,* also published in the present series. That book and this one, we believe, achieve most when used together.

We wish to thank Richard G. Garrett for his comments on the previous editions.

About the Authors

John Herman Randall, Jr. is Frederick J. E. Woodbridge Professor Emeritus of Philosophy in Columbia University. Among his books are *The Making of the Modern Mind, Nature and Historical Experience, Aristotle,* and *The Career of Philosophy.*

Justus Buchler, formerly Johnsonian Professor of Philosophy in Columbia University, is Distinguished Professor of Philosophy in the State University of New York at Stony Brook. Among his books are *Toward a General Theory of Human Judgment, Nature and Judgment, The Concept of Method, and Metaphysics of Natural Complexes.*

Evelyn Shirk is Professor of Philosophy in Hofstra University. She is author of *The Ethical Dimension, Adventurous Idealism: The Philosophy of Alfred Lloyd,* and (with E. Kronovet) *In Pursuit of Awareness.*

TO THE READER

The best way to discover and achieve philosophic thinking is to come into direct and living contact with it. Each of the following selections deals with an issue which is of that basic, foundational character known as philosophical. It might be more accurate to say that in the discussion of its main problem each selection raises many others, which the reader who has developed the philosophic habit of thought gradually comes to discriminate. Often the same problem will turn up in more than one writer and a similar or a sharply contrasting viewpoint will emerge.

The reader will want to know what it is that he is *not* to expect in a book of this kind. To begin with, he is not to suppose that he will discover every possible problem of philosophy, every possible treatment of any one problem, or every possible school of thought. It is likely that almost any issue he meets either has been or could be approached from some other philosophic viewpoint. The searching, ever-critical character of philosophy makes this inevitable. In a book of this kind it is naturally most useful to be able to find out how different rather than how fundamentally similar philosophic theories and analyses and formulations can be. Further, it must not be supposed that any selection is a key to or a summary of its writer's entire thought. This may or may not be so; but a selection is best read for what it actually says or implies.

The reader *may* truthfully assume that he has before him an array containing many outstanding names in the history of philosophy; that the issues here open to his experience are typical and multifarious; and that the reading of these selections requires no technical philosophic equipment. He may wonder why the selections are not listed in chronological order. The answer is that since this book does not aim primarily to exhibit the history of philosophy, such an order would be inappropriate and even misleading. The period of composition for each selection has been indicated. Every historical product reflects its time and circumstances, and a philosophy interprets and analyzes the age it knows. But philosophy is able also to transcend specific times and circumstances, and in recognition of this truth a chronological arrangement has been ignored.

If the reader further wonders why the selections are arranged in just the order that they are, the answer is that this order promised to be suggestive but that little harm can come from his adopting another more manageable or useful to him. A deliberate attempt has been made to avoid a fixed and rigid pattern among the selections. They have been so chosen that many patterns can and should emerge. Philosophic problems, however different and unrelated they may seem, often have important bearing on one another. Sharply to segregate ideas or subjects would be to risk concealing this potential interrelation, the perception of which is one kind of fruitful philosophizing.

One who succeeds in understanding another's thought will not be content with swallowing it bodily. The reader of philosophy is himself, perforce, a philosopher, and in so far, a critic. The strongest of thinkers is not exempt from criticism of one kind or another; and at the same time, any worth-while thinker of whatever persuasion can offer something of value. The better the critic the better and larger his imagination. It is much more difficult to weigh and understand than to admonish.

There is no royal road to any of the intellectual disciplines, and certainly not to philosophy. The chances are that even when free of unduly technical elements a piece of philosophic thought will make difficult reading. The selections in this book vary in difficulty, but all of them require sustained attention. On the other hand, it is not wise to become discouraged if passages or ideas prove obstinate. Reflection has ways of ironing itself out or of discovering the means to that end. And it is unlikely that the student will be content with a single reading of any selection.

Once conversant with the philosophic temper, the student's urge is to put his own intellectual convictions in better order. Faced with different ways of thinking, different answers to problems, and different ways of viewing the universe, his complaint may be that he is now "confused" where once he was not. Perhaps it is small comfort to him to be told that this is a sign of progress and that his uncertainties have arisen precisely because his previous ideas have not stood up. The ancients were fond of saying that philosophy begins in wonder. Having opinions, cherishing convictions, is a requirement of sanity. But pitfalls threaten the philosophic attitude: seeking immediate answers, taking refuge in easy dogmas, worshipping finality for its own sake. The reader who has no fear of ideas, or of the doubts they can engender, will heed Plato's advice, simply to follow the argument wherever it may lead.

TABLE OF CONTENTS

PART ONE

Emphasis on

PHILOSOPHIC CRITICISM, DEFINITION, AND ANALYSIS

1

EUTHYPHRO *

by

PLATO

(B.C. 427–347)

Euthyphro. Why have you left the Lyceum, Socrates? and what are you doing in the porch of the King Archon? Surely you can not be engaged in an action before the king, as I am.

Socrates. Not in an action, Euthyphro; impeachment is the word which the Athenians use.

Euth. What! I suppose that some one has been prosecuting you, for I can not believe that you are the prosecutor of another.

Soc. Certainly not.

Euth. Then some one else has been prosecuting you?

Soc. Yes.

Euth. And who is he?

Soc. A young man who is little known, Euthyphro; and I hardly know him: his name is Meletus, and he is of the deme of Pitthis. Perhaps you may remember his appearance; he has a beak, and long straight hair, and a beard which is ill grown.

Euth. No, I do not remember him, Socrates. And what is the charge which he brings against you?

Soc. What is the charge? Well, a very serious charge, which shows a good deal of character in the young man, and for which he is certainly not to be despised. He says he knows how the youth are corrupted and who are their corruptors. I fancy that he must be a wise man, and seeing that I am anything but a wise man, he has found me out, and is going to accuse me of corrupting his young friends. And of this our mother the state is to be the judge. Of all our political men he is the only one who seems to me to begin in the right way, with the cultivation of virtue in youth; he is a good husbandman, and takes care of the shoots first, and clears away us who are the destroyers of them. That is the first step; he will afterwards attend to the elder branches; and if he goes on as he has begun, he will be a very great public benefactor.

* [The complete dialogue, translated by Benjamin Jowett (1871).]

Euth. I hope that he may; but I rather fear, Socrates, that the reverse will turn out to be the truth. My opinion is that in attacking you he is simply aiming a blow at the state in a sacred place. But in what way does he say that you corrupt the young?

Soc. He brings a wonderful accusation against me, which at first hearing excites surprise: he says that I am a poet or maker of gods, and that I make new gods and deny the existence of old ones; this is the ground of his indictment.

Euth. I understand, Socrates; he means to attack you about the familiar sign which occasionally, as you say, comes to you. He thinks that you are a neologian, and he is going to have you up before the court for this. He knows that such a charge is readily received, for the world is always jealous of novelties in religion. And I know that when I myself speak in the assembly about divine things, and foretell the future to them, they laugh at me as a madman; and yet every word that I say is true. But they are jealous of all of us. I suppose that we must be brave and not mind them.

Soc. Their laughter, friend Euthyphro, is not a matter of much consequence. For a man may be thought wise; but the Athenians, I suspect, do not care much about this, until he begins to make other men wise; and then for some reason or other, perhaps, as you say, from jealousy, they are angry.

Euth. I have no desire to try conclusions with them about this.

Soc. I dare say that you don't make yourself common, and are not apt to impart your wisdom. But I have a benevolent habit of pouring out myself to everybody, and would even pay for a listener, and I am afraid that the Athenians know this; and therefore, as I was saying, if the Athenians would only laugh at me as you say that they laugh at you, the time might pass gaily enough in the court; but perhaps they may be in earnest, and then what the end will be you soothsayers only can predict.

Euth. I dare say that the affair will end in nothing, Socrates, and that you will win your cause; and I think that I shall win mine.

Soc. And what is your suit? and are you the pursuer or defendant, Euthyphro?

Euth. I am pursuer.

Soc. Of whom?

Euth. You will think me mad when I tell you whom I am pursuing.

Soc. Why, has the fugitive wings?

Euth. Nay, he is not very volatile at his time of life.

Soc. Who is he?

Euth. My father.

Soc. Your father! good heavens, you don't mean that?

Euth. Yes.

Soc. And of what is he accused?

Euth. Murder, Socrates.

Soc. By the powers, Euthyphro! how little does the common herd know of the nature of right and truth. A man must be an extraordinary man and have made great strides in wisdom, before he could have seen his way to this.

Euth. Indeed, Socrates, he must have made great strides.

Soc. I suppose that the man whom your father murdered was one of your relatives; if he had been a stranger you would never have thought of prosecuting him.

Euth. I am amused, Socrates, at your making a distinction between one who is a relation and one who is not a relation; for surely the pollution is the same in either case, if you knowingly associate with the murderer when you ought to clear yourself by proceeding against him. The real question is whether the murdered man has been justly slain. If justly, then your duty is to let the matter alone; but if unjustly, then even if the murderer is under the same roof with you and eats at the same table, proceed against him. Now the man who is dead was a poor dependent of mine who worked for us as a field laborer at Naxos, and one day in a fit of drunken passion he got into a quarrel with one of our domestic servants and slew him. My father bound him hand and foot and threw him into a ditch, and then sent to Athens to ask of a diviner what he should do with him. Meantime he had no care or thought of him, being under the impression that he was a murderer; and that even if he did die there would be no great harm. And this was just what happened. For such was the effect of cold and hunger and chains upon him, that before the messenger returned from the diviner, he was dead. And my father and family are angry with me for taking the part of the murderer and prosecuting my father. They say that he did not kill him, and if he did, the dead man was but a murderer, and I ought not to take any notice, for that a son is impious who prosecutes a father. That shows, Socrates, how little they know of the opinions of the gods about piety and impiety.

Soc. Good heavens, Euthyphro! and have you such a precise knowledge of piety and impiety, and of divine things in general, that, supposing the circumstances to be as you state, you are not afraid that you too may be doing an impious thing in bringing an action against your father?

Euth. The best of Euthyphro, and that which distinguishes him, Socrates, from other men, is his exact knowledge of all these matters. What should I be good for without that?

Soc. Rare friend! I think that I can not do better than be your disciple, before the trial with Meletus comes on. Then I shall challenge him, and say that I have always had a great interest in religious questions, and now, as he charges me with rash imaginations and innovations in religion, I have become your disciple. Now you, Meletus, as I shall say to him, acknowledge Euthyphro to be a great theologian, and sound in his opinions; and if you think that of him you ought to think the same of me, and not have me into court; you should begin by indicting him who is my teacher, and who is the real corruptor, not of the young, but of the old; that is to say, of myself whom he instructs, and of his old father whom he admonishes and chastises. And if Meletus refuses to listen to me, but will go on, and will not shift the indictment from me to you, I can not do better than say in the court that I challenged him in this way.

Euth. Yes, Socrates; and if he attempts to indict me I am mistaken if I don't find a flaw in him; the court shall have a great deal more to say to him than to me.

Soc. I know that, dear friend; and that is the reason why I desire to be your disciple. For I observe that no one, not even Meletus, appears to notice you; but his sharp eyes have found me out at once, and he has indicted me for impiety. And therefore, I adjure you to tell me the nature of piety and impiety, which you said that you knew so well, and of murder, and the rest of them. What are they? Is not piety in every action always the same? and impiety, again, is not that always the opposite of piety, and also the same with itself, having, as impiety, one notion which includes whatever is impious?

Euth. To be sure, Socrates.

Soc. And what is piety, and what is impiety?

Euth. Piety is doing as I am doing; that is to say, prosecuting any one who is guilty of murder, sacrilege, or of any other similar crime —whether he be your father or mother, or some other person, that makes no difference—and not prosecuting them is impiety. And please to consider, Socrates, what a notable proof I will give you of the truth of what I am saying, which I have already given to others:—of the truth, I mean, of the principle that the impious, whoever he may be, ought not to go unpunished. For do not men regard Zeus as the best and most righteous of the gods?—and even they admit that he bound his father (Cronos) because he wickedly devoured his sons, and that he too had punished his own father (Uranus) for a similar reason, in a nameless manner. And yet when I proceed against my father, they are angry with me. This is their inconsistent way of talking when the gods are concerned, and when I am concerned.

Soc. May not this be the reason, Euthyphro, why I am charged with impiety—that I can not away with these stories about the gods? and therefore I suppose that people think me wrong. But, as you who are well informed about them approve of them, I can not do better than assent to your superior wisdom. For what else can I say, confessing as I do, that I know nothing of them. I wish you would tell me whether you really believe that they are true?

Euth. Yes, Socrates; and things more wonderful still, of which the world is in ignorance.

Soc. And do you really believe that the gods fought with one another, and had dire quarrels, battles, and the like, as the poets say, and as you may see represented in the works of great artists? The temples are full of them; and notably the robe of Athene, which is carried up to the Acropolis at the great Panathenaea, is embroidered with them. Are all these tales of the gods true, Euthyphro?

Euth. Yes, Socrates; and, as I was saying, I can tell you, if you would like to hear them, many other things about the gods which would quite amaze you.

Soc. I dare say; and you shall tell me them at some other time when I have leisure. But just at present I would rather hear from you a more precise answer, which you have not as yet given, my friend, to the question, What is "piety?" In reply, you only say that piety is, Doing as you do, charging your father with murder?

Euth. And that is true, Socrates.

Soc. I dare say, Euthyphro, but there are many other pious acts.

Euth. There are.

Soc. Remember that I did not ask you to give me two or three examples of piety, but to explain the general idea which makes all pious things to be pious. Do you not recollect that there was one idea which made the impious impious, and the pious pious?

Euth. I remember.

Soc. Tell me what this is, and then I shall have a standard to which I may look, and by which I may measure the nature of actions, whether yours or any one's else, and say that this action is pious, and that impious.

Euth. I will tell you, if you like.

Soc. I should very much like.

Euth. Piety, then, is that which is dear to the gods, and impiety is that which is not dear to them.

Soc. Very good, Euthyphro; you have now given me just the sort of answer which I wanted. But whether it is true or not I can not as yet tell, although I make no doubt that you will prove the truth of your words.

Euth. Of course.

Soc. Come, then, and let us examine what we are saying. That thing or person which is dear to the gods is pious, and that thing or person which is hateful to the gods is impious. Was not that said?

Euth. Yes, that was said.

Soc. And that seems to have been very well said too?

Euth. Yes, Socrates, I think that; it was certainly said.

Soc. And further, Euthyphro, the gods were admitted to have enmities and hatreds and differences—that was also said?

Euth. Yes, that was said.

Soc. And what sort of difference creates enmity and anger? Suppose for example that you and I, my good friend, differ about a number; do differences of this sort make us enemies and set us at variance with one another? Do we not go at once to calculation, and end them by a sum?

Euth. True.

Soc. Or suppose that we differ about magnitudes, do we not quickly put an end to that difference by measuring?

Euth. That is true.

Soc. And we end a controversy about heavy and light by resorting to a weighing-machine?

Euth. To be sure.

Soc. But what differences are those which, because they can not be thus decided, make us angry and set us at enmity with one another? I dare say the answer does not occur to you at the moment, and therefore I will suggest that this happens when the matters of difference are the just and unjust, good and evil, honorable and dishonorable. Are not these the points about which, when differing, and unable satisfactorily to decide our differences, we quarrel, when we do quarrel, as you and I and all men experience?

Euth. Yes, Socrates, that is the nature of the differences about which we quarrel.

Soc. And the quarrels of the gods, noble Euthyphro, when they occur, are of a like nature?

Euth. They are.

Soc. They have differences of opinion, as you say, about good and evil, just and unjust, honorable and dishonorable: there would have been no quarrels among them, if there had been no such differences—would there now?

Euth. You are quite right.

Soc. Does not every man love that which he deems noble and just and good, and hate the opposite of them?

Euth. Very true.

Soc. But then, as you say, people regard the same things, some as just and others as unjust; and they dispute about this, and there arise wars and fightings among them.

Euth. Yes, that is true.

Soc. Then the same things, as appears, are hated by the gods and loved by the gods, and are both hateful and dear to them?

Euth. True.

Soc. Then upon this view the same things, Euthyphro, will be pious and also impious?

Euth. That, I suppose, is true.

Soc. Then, my friend, I remark with surprise that you have not answered what I asked. For I certainly did not ask what was that which is at once pious and impious: and that which is loved by the gods appears also to be hated by them. And therefore, Euthyphro, in thus chastising your father you may very likely be doing what is agreeable to Zeus but disagreeable to Cronos or Uranus, and what is acceptable to Hephaestus but unacceptable to Here, and there may be other gods who have similar differences of opinion.

Euth. But I believe, Socrates, that all the gods would be agreed as to the propriety of punishing a murderer: there would be no difference of opinion about that.

Soc. Well, but speaking of men, Euthyphro, did you ever hear any one arguing that a murderer or any sort of evil-doer ought to be let off?

Euth. I should rather say that they are always arguing this, especially in courts of law: they commit all sorts of crimes, and there is nothing that they will not do or say in order to escape punishment.

Soc. But do they admit their guilt, Euthyphro, and yet say that they ought not to be punished?

Euth. No; they do not.

Soc. Then there are some things which they do not venture to say and do: for they do not venture to argue that the guilty are to be unpunished, but they deny their guilt, do they not?

Euth. Yes.

Soc. Then they do not argue that the evil-doer should not be punished, but they argue about the fact of who the evil-doer is, and what he did and when?

Euth. True.

Soc. And the gods are in the same case, if as you imply they quarrel about just and unjust, and some of them say that they wrong one another, and others of them deny this. For surely neither God nor man will ever venture to say that the doer of evil is not to be punished:—you don't mean to tell me that?

Euth. That is true, Socrates, in the main.

Soc. But they join issue about particulars; and this applies not only to men but to the gods; if they dispute at all they dispute about some act which is called in question, and which some affirm to be just, others to be unjust. Is not that true?

Euth. Quite true.

Soc. Well then, my dear friend Euthyphro, do tell me, for my better instruction and information, what proof have you that in the opinion of all the gods a servant who is guilty of murder, and is put in chains by the master of the dead man, and dies because he is put in chains before his corrector can learn from the interpreters what he ought to do with him, dies unjustly; and that on behalf of such an one a son ought to proceed against his father and accuse him of murder. How would you show that all the gods absolutely agree in approving of his act? Prove to me that, and I will applaud your wisdom as long as you live.

Euth. That would not be an easy task, although I could make the matter very clear indeed to you.

Soc. I understand; you mean to say that I am not so quick of apprehension as the judges: for to them you will be sure to prove that the act is unjust, and hateful to the gods.

Euth. Yes indeed, Socrates; at least if they will listen to me.

Soc. But they will be sure to listen if they find that you are a good speaker. There was a notion that came into my mind while you were speaking; I said to myself: "Well, and what if Euthyphro does prove to me that all the gods regarded the death of the serf as unjust, how do I know anything more of the nature of piety and impiety? for granting that this action may be hateful to the gods, still these distinctions have no bearing on the definition of piety and impiety, for that which is hateful to the gods has been shown to be also pleasing and dear to them." And therefore, Euthyphro, I don't ask you to prove this; I will suppose, if you like, that all the gods condemn and abominate such an action. But I will amend the definition so far as to say that what all the gods hate is impious, and what they love pious or holy; and what some of them love and others hate is both or neither. Shall this be our definition of piety and impiety?

Euth. Why not, Socrates?

Soc. Why not! certainly, as far as I am concerned, Euthyphro. But whether this admission will greatly assist you in the task of instructing me as you promised, is a matter for you to consider.

Euth. Yes, I should say that what all the gods love is pious and holy, and the opposite which they all hate, impious.

Soc. Ought we to inquire into the truth of this, Euthyphro, or simply to accept the mere statement on our own authority and that of others?

Euth. We should inquire; and I believe that the statement will stand the test of inquiry.

Soc. That, my good friend, we shall know better in a little while. The point which I should first wish to understand is whether the pious or holy is beloved by the gods because it is holy, or holy because it is beloved of the gods.

Euth. I don't understand your meaning, Socrates.

Soc. I will endeavor to explain: we speak of carrying and we speak of being carried, of leading and being led, seeing and being seen. And here is a difference, the nature of which you understand.

Euth. I think that I understand.

Soc. And is not that which is beloved distinct from that which loves?

Euth. Certainly.

Soc. Well; and now tell me, is that which is carried in this state of carrying because it is carried, or for some other reason?

Euth. No; that is the reason.

Soc. And the same is true of that which is led and of that which is seen?

Euth. True.

Soc. And a thing is not seen because it is visible, but conversely, visible because it is seen; nor is a thing led because it is in the state of being led, or carried because it is in the state of being carried, but the converse of this. And now I think, Euthyphro, that my meaning will be intelligible; and my meaning is, that any state of action or passion implies previous action or passion. It does not become because it is becoming, but it is becoming because it comes; neither does it suffer because it is in a state of suffering, but it is in a state of suffering because it suffers. Do you admit that?

Euth. Yes.

Soc. Is not that which is loved in some state either of becoming or suffering?

Euth. Yes.

Soc. And the same holds as in the previous instances; the state of being loved follows the act of being loved, and not the act the state.

Euth. That is certain.

Soc. And what do you say of piety, Euthyphro: is not piety, according to your definition, loved by all the gods?

Euth. Yes.

Soc. Because it is pious or holy, or for some other reason?

Euth. No, that is the reason.

Soc. It is loved because it is holy, not holy because it is loved?

Euth. Yes.

Soc. And that which is in a state to be loved of the gods, and is dear to them, is in a state to be loved of them because it is loved of them?

Euth. Certainly.

Soc. Then that which is loved of God, Euthyphro, is not holy, nor is that which is holy loved of God, as you affirm; but they are two different things.

Euth. How do you mean, Socrates?

Soc. I mean to say that the holy has been acknowledged by us to be loved of God because it is holy, not to be holy because it is loved.

Euth. Yes.

Soc. But that which is dear to the gods is dear to them because it is loved by them, not loved by them because it is dear to them.

Euth. True.

Soc. But, friend Euthyphro, if that which is holy is the same as that which is dear to God, and that which is holy is loved as being holy, then that which is dear to God would have been loved as being dear to God; but if that which is dear to God is dear to him because loved by him, then that which is holy would have been holy because loved by him. But now you see that the reverse is the case, and that they are quite different from one another. For one is of a kind to be loved because it is loved, and the other is loved because it is of a kind to be loved. Thus you appear to me, Euthyphro, when I ask you what is the essence of holiness, to offer an attribute only, and not the essence—the attribute of being loved by all the gods. But you still refuse to explain to me the nature of piety. And therefore, if you please, I will ask you not to hide your treasure, but to tell me once more what piety or holiness really is, whether dear to the gods or not (for that is a matter about which we will not quarrel). And what is impiety?

Euth. I really do not know, Socrates, how to say what I mean. For somehow or other our arguments, on whatever ground we rest them, seem to turn round and walk away.

Soc. Your words, Euthyphro, are like the handiwork of my ancestor Daedalus; and if I were the sayer or propounder of them, you might say that this comes of my being his relation; and that this is the reason why my arguments walk away and won't remain fixed where they are placed. But now, as the notions are your own, you must find some other gibe, for they certainly, as you yourself allow, show an inclination to be on the move.

Euth. Nay, Socrates, I shall still say that you are the Daedalus who sets arguments in motion; not I, certainly, make them move or go round, for they would never have stirred, as far as I am concerned.

Soc. Then I must be a greater than Daedalus; for whereas he only made his own inventions to move, I move those of other people as well. And the beauty of it is, that I would rather not. For I would give the wisdom of Daedalus, and the wealth of Tantalus, to be able to detain them and keep them fixed. But enough of this. As I perceive that you are indolent, I will myself endeavor to show you how you might instruct me in the nature of piety; and I hope that you will not grudge your labor. Tell me, then,—Is not that which is pious necessarily just?

Euth. Yes.

Soc. And is, then, all which is just pious? or, is that which is pious all just, but that which is just only in part and not all pious?

Euth. I don't understand you, Socrates.

Soc. And yet I know that you are as much wiser than I am, as you are younger. But, as I was saying, revered friend, the abundance of your wisdom makes you indolent. Please to exert yourself, for there is no real difficulty in understanding me. What I mean I may explain by an illustration of what I do not mean. The poet (Stasinus) sings—

"Of Zeus, the author and creator of all these things,
  You will not tell: for where there is fear there is also reverence."

And I disagree with this poet. Shall I tell you in what I disagree?

Euth. By all means.

Soc. I should not say that where there is fear there is also reverence; for I am sure that many persons fear poverty and disease, and the like evils, but I do not perceive that they reverence the objects of their fear.

Euth. Very true.

Soc. But where reverence is, there is fear; for he who has a feeling of reverence and shame about the commission of any action, fears and is afraid of an ill reputation.

Euth. No doubt.

Soc. Then we are wrong in saying that where there is fear there is also reverence; and we should say, where there is reverence there is also fear. But there is not always reverence where there is fear; for fear is a more extended notion, and reverence is a part of fear, just as the odd is a part of number, and number is a more extended notion than the odd. I suppose that you follow me now?

Euth. Quite well.

Soc. That was the sort of question which I meant to raise when asking whether the just is the pious, or the pious the just; and whether there may not be justice where there is not always piety; for justice is the more extended notion of which piety is only a part. Do you agree in that?

Euth. Yes; that, I think, is correct.

Soc. Then, now, if piety is a part of justice, I suppose that we inquire what part? If you had pursued the injury in the previous cases; for instance, if you had asked me what is an even number, and what part of number the even is, I should have had no difficulty in replying, a number which represents a figure having two equal sides. Do you agree?

Euth. Yes.

Soc. In like manner, I want you to tell me what part of justice is piety or holiness; that I may be able to tell Meletus not to do me injustice, or indict me for impiety; as I am now adequately instructed by you in the nature of piety or holiness, and their opposites.

Euth. Piety or holiness, Socrates, appears to me to be that part of justice which attends to the gods, as there is the other part of justice which attends to men.

Soc. That is good, Euthyphro; yet still there is a little point about which I should like to have further information, What is the meaning of "attention"? For attention can hardly be used in the same sense when applied to the gods as when applied to other things. For instance, horses are said to require attention, and not every person is able to attend to them, but only a person skilled in horsemanship. Is not that true?

Euth. Quite true.

Soc. I should suppose that the art of horsemanship is the art of attending to horses?

Euth. Yes.

Soc. Nor is every one qualified to attend to dogs, but only the huntsman.

Euth. True.

Soc. And I should also conceive that the art of the huntsman is the art of attending to dogs?

Euth. Yes.

Soc. As the art of the oxherd is the art of attending to oxen?

Euth. Very true.

Soc. And as holiness or piety is the art of attending to the gods?— that would be your meaning, Euthyphro?

Euth. Yes.

Soc. And is not attention always designed for the good or benefit of that to which the attention is given? As in the case of horses, you may observe that when attended to by the horseman's art they are benefited and improved, are they not?

Euth. True.

Soc. As the dogs are benefited by the huntsman's art, and the oxen by the art of the oxherd, and all other things are tended or attended for their good and not for their hurt?

Euth. Certainly, not for their hurt.

Soc. But for their good?

Euth. Of course.

Soc. And does piety or holiness, which has been defined as the art of attending to the gods, benefit or improve them? Would you say that when you do a holy act you make any of the gods better?

Euth. No, no; that is certainly not my meaning.

Soc. Indeed, Euthyphro, I did not suppose that this was your meaning; far otherwise. And that was the reason why I asked you the nature of this attention, because I thought that this was not your meaning.

Euth. You do me justice, Socrates; for that is not my meaning.

Soc. Good: but I must still ask what is this attention to the gods which is called piety?

Euth. It is such, Socrates, as servants show to their masters.

Soc. I understand—a sort of ministration to the gods.

Euth. Exactly.

Soc. Medicine is also a sort of ministration or service, tending to the attainment of some object—would you not say health?

Euth. Yes.

Soc. Again, there is an art which ministers to the ship-builder with a view to the attainment of some result?

Euth. Yes, Socrates, with a view to the building of a ship.

Soc. As there is an art which ministers to the house-builder with a view to the building of a house?

Euth. Yes.

Soc. And now tell me, my good friend, about this art which ministers to the gods: what work does that help to accomplish? For you must surely know if, as you say, you are of all men living the one who is best instructed in religion.

Euth. And that is true, Socrates.

Soc. Tell me then, oh tell me—what is that fair work which the gods do by the help of us as their ministers?

Euth. Many and fair, Socrates, are the works which they do.

Soc. Why, my friend, and so are those of a general. But the chief of them is easily told. Would you not say that victory in war is the chief of them?

Euth. Certainly.

Soc. Many and fair, too, are the works of the husbandman, if I am not mistaken; but his chief work is the production of food from the earth?

Euth. Exactly.

Soc. And of the many and fair things which the gods do, which is the chief and principal one?

Euth. I have told you already, Socrates, that to learn all these things accurately will be very tiresome. Let me simply say that piety is learning how to please the gods in word and deed, by prayers and sacrifices. That is piety, which is the salvation of families and states, just as the impious, which is unpleasing to the gods, is their ruin and destruction.

Soc. I think that you could have answered in much fewer words the chief question which I asked, Euthyphro, if you had chosen. But I see plainly that you are not disposed to instruct me: else why, when we had reached the point, did you turn aside? Had you only answered me I should have learned of you by this time the nature of piety. Now, as the asker of a question is necessarily dependent on the answerer, whither he leads I must follow; and can only ask again, what is the pious, and what is piety? Do you mean that they are a sort of science of praying and sacrificing?

Euth. Yes, I do.

Soc. And sacrificing is giving to the gods, and prayer is asking of the gods?

Euth. Yes, Socrates.

Soc. Upon this view, then, piety is a science of asking and giving?

Euth. You understand me capitally, Socrates.

Soc. Yes, my friend; the reason is that I am a votary of your science, and give my mind to it, and therefore nothing which you say will be thrown away upon me. Please then to tell me, what is the nature of this service to the gods? Do you mean that we prefer requests and give gifts to them?

Euth. Yes, I do.

Soc. Is not the right way of asking to ask of them what we want?

Euth. Certainly.

Soc. And the right way of giving is to give to them in return what they want of us. There would be no meaning in an art which gives to any one that which he does not want.

Euth. Very true, Socrates.

Soc. Then piety, Euthyphro, is an art which gods and men have of doing business with one another?

Euth. That is an expression which you may use, if you like.

Soc. But I have no particular liking for anything but the truth. I wish, however, that you would tell me what benefit accrues to the gods from our gifts. That they are the givers of every good to us is clear; but how we can give any good thing to them in return is far from being equally clear. If they give everything and we give nothing, that must be an affair of business in which we have very greatly the advantage of them.

Euth. And do you imagine, Socrates, that any benefit accrues to the gods from what they receive of us?

Soc. But if not, Euthyphro, what sort of gifts do we confer upon the gods?

Euth. What should we confer upon them, but tributes of honor; and, as I was just now saying, what is pleasing to them?

Soc. Piety, then, is pleasing to the gods, but not beneficial or dear to them?

Euth. I should say that nothing could be dearer.

Soc. Then once more the assertion is repeated that piety is dear to the gods?

Euth. No doubt.

Soc. And when you say this, can you wonder at your words not standing firm, but walking away? Will you accuse me of being the Daedalus who makes them walk away, not perceiving that there is another and far greater artist than Daedalus who makes them go round in a circle; and that is yourself: for the argument, as you will perceive, comes round to the same point. I think that you must remember our saying that the holy or pious was not the same as that which is loved of the gods. Do you remember that?

Euth. I do.

Soc. And do you not see that what is loved of the gods is holy, and that this is the same as what is dear to them?

Euth. True.

Soc. Then either we were wrong in that admission; or, if we were right then, we are wrong now.

Euth. I suppose that is the case.

Soc. Then we must begin again and ask, What is piety? That is an inquiry which I shall never be weary of pursuing as far as in me lies; and I entreat you not to scorn me, but to apply your mind to the utmost, and tell me the truth. For, if any man knows, you are he; and therefore I shall detain you, like Proteus, until you tell. For if you had not certainly known the nature of piety and impiety, I am confident that you would never, on behalf of a serf, have charged your aged father with murder. You would not have run such a risk of doing wrong in the sight of the gods, and you would have had too much respect for the opinions of men. I am sure, therefore, that you know the nature of piety and impiety. Speak out then, my dear Euthyphro, and do not hide your knowledge.

Euth. Another time, Socrates; for I am in a hurry, and must go now.

Soc. Alas! my companion, and will you leave me in despair? I was hoping that you would instruct me in the nature of piety and impiety, so that I might have cleared myself of Meletus and his indictment. Then I might have proved to him that I had been converted by Euthyphro, and had done with rash innovations and speculations, in which I had indulged through ignorance, and was about to lead a better life.

2

ARE THERE ABSOLUTE VALUES? *

by

MORITZ SCHLICK
(1882–1936)

1. The Theory of Objective Values

The opinion we have to examine may best be expressed negatively in the assertion that the moral value of a disposition cannot in any way be grounded in feelings of pleasure. Value is something wholly independent of our feelings, something pertaining to valuable objects, in a definite amount and degree, quite independently of the way in which we react emotionally to them, and to whether anyone acknowledges the value or not. Pleasure, to be sure, is a value, but only one among many, and obviously not the highest. Often it is admitted that the valuable produces feelings of pleasure in the observer, but this fact is supposed to have nothing to do with the *essence* of the value, but is, in a sense, accidental. I say "in a sense," for many who hold this view do not wish, I believe, to deny that perhaps the generation of feelings of pleasure in the presence of something valuable is a natural law, and that a causal connection exists between the two. But they say that this is quite unessential, that if it were not so it would make no difference to the value of the valuable thing; this value would exist even if the law of nature read: "The idea of the valuable thing is quite indifferent to all men," or "extremely annoying" or "horrible."

* [Most of Chapter V, from *Problems of Ethics* by Moritz Schlick, Dover Publications, Inc., New York, first published in 1939. Reprinted through the permission of the publisher.]

The role played in ethics by this theory of the objectivity of value is too well known to require one to dwell upon it. It proclaims the existence of a system of values, which, like the Platonic ideas, constitutes a realm independent of actuality, and in which is exhibited an essential order of such a nature that the values compose a hierarchy arranged according to higher and lower. And its relation to reality is only established by the moral command, which runs, approximately, "Act so that the events or things produced by your actions are as valuable as possible."

The criticism which we make of this view is extremely simple. Its main lines are prescribed by our philosophical method. We ask *first*, "What does the word value *mean*?" or, which comes to the same thing, "What is the meaning of an assertion which ascribes a certain value to any object?" This question can be answered only by stating the method of determining the truth of a value judgment; that is, one must state exactly under what empirical conditions the proposition "This object is valuable" is true, and under what conditions it is false. If one cannot state these conditions, then the proposition is a meaningless combination of words.

Thus we ask the philosopher, "How do you recognize the value of an object?" And since no one is here to answer (the author writes these lines in deep seclusion on the rocky coast of the Adriatic Sea) we shall search for the usual and possible answers together.

2. *Pleasure as the Criterion of Objective Value*

(*a.*) In case anyone (I do not know whether there is any such person) should answer that values are in fact to be recognized only in feelings of pleasure which valuable things awaken in us, and that also the rank of the value is disclosed to us only by means of the intensity of the corresponding feeling, and that in addition there is no other criterion of the existence and rank of the value, yet that nevertheless the value does not *consist* in the activity of producing pleasure, but is something else, then we must accuse him of logical nonsense. However, we do it very unwillingly, for factually we do not find anything to dispute regarding the consequences of his theory. The nonsense consists in the fact that with respect to all *verifiable* consequences his view is in complete agreement with our own (that "value" is nothing but a name for the dormant pleasure possibilities of the valuable object), but despite this he asserts that they are different. The proposition that "to be valuable" means something quite different from "to bring pleasure" presupposes that there is some property which belongs only to the valuable, and not to the pleasure-bringing: the assertion becomes senseless if pleasure-produc-ing is the *only* characteristic of the valuable. If we should peacefully grant the existence of "objective" value, this would be nothing but a contentless addition. Everything would remain as if it were essen-tially subjective, for we would be able to make an assertion about it only because of its pleasure consequences, as is also the case accord-ing to our own view.

I add that from the criticized standpoint every feeling of pleasure must be interpreted as the sign of an objective value. If this held only in certain cases, but not in others, we should have to be able to say how the cases differed, and this would require a new criterion and the rejection of the original one, which was simply pleasure. The advocate of objective values requires, then, an empirical criterion of value which cannot be identical with pleasure.

3. *Objective Criteria of Value?*

(*b.*) It is natural to want to give an objective criterion for objec-tive values—just as we recognize that an animal is a camel by the fact that it has two humps, concerning whose existence one can convince himself by sense-perception. Sense-perception, whose value as a criterion for objectivity has often been disputed in epistemolog-ical considerations, may be unhesitatingly accepted as the judge in our problem, as in all questions of daily life. Hence if value could be seen or touched as can a camel's hump, ethics would have no occasion to discuss its nature. But since this is not so, one seeks some objec-tive fact which shall serve as the sign of values; and thus one asserts, for example, "Whatever furthers the progress of evolution is valu-able," or, "Whatever contributes to the creation of spiritual posses-sions, for example, works of art, and science, is valuable," or similar statements. If I am not mistaken, Wilhelm Wundt in his ethics of objective spiritual products made such an attempt.

We feel at once what is wrong in such attempts. Even if one should succeed in finding a formula which fitted everything generally con-sidered to be valuable, such a formula, it seems to me, would always appear to be circular. Since, for example, what a "spiritual possession" is, what shall pass for an "upward evolution" (as opposed to down-ward) can only be determined by comparison with some standard. It cannot itself determine the standard. And if, in order to escape the circle, one arbitrarily establishes what should be understood by spir-itual possessions, and things of the sort, this determination would be arbitrary; at best one would have produced the definition of a con-cept, based upon opinion, which one decides to call "value"; but this would not offer a criterion for *that* which we all *mean* when we use the word "value."

A fundamental error lies at the basis of the whole attempt: it consists in seeking value distinctions in the objective facts themselves, without reference to the acts of preference and selection, through which alone value comes into the world.

4. *Subjective Criteria of Value*

(*c*.) Thus there remains no alternative to locating the characteristic of value once more in an immediate datum and to finding the verification of a proposition concerning value in the occurrence of a definite experience. Our own criterion is of this sort: the corresponding experience is simply the feeling of pleasure . . . the *essence* of value is completely exhausted by it. The opposing theory of absolute value cannot, as was shown in (*a*.), use pleasure as the characteristic of value; it must therefore assert the occurrence of a wholly different experience which indicates the existence of a value. This is, in fact, if I understand them rightly, the opinion of the noteworthy representatives of that theory (of Brentano, and the schools following him). According to them we possess the capacity of determining the existence of a value in much the same way as we are acquainted with the presence of a material object by means of perception. The role here played by sensation is there taken over by a specific experience, which one may call the feeling or experience of value, insight, or what not; without of course contributing anything to a closer description by this naming. In any case, it is always something ultimate, unanalyzable, which must appear when a value judgment is verified, and which one either has or does not have, concerning which therefore there can be no further discussion.

What should we say regarding this theory? In so far as it asserts the existence of a special datum of consciousness, a "value-experience," any disagreement would be senseless, for each person alone can know what he experiences. One could simply accept or reject the theory wihout any proof. (I personally could not accept it, because I do not succeed in distinguishing between the feeling of pleasure that I have when I hear "Don Juan" or see a noble face or read about the personality of Abraham Lincoln, and an elementary value-experience which, according to that view, must first assure me that what gives me joy is also a *value*.)

But the theory asserts not only the existence or occurrence of a certain datum of consciousness, but asserts further that this informs me of something objective, independent of me, that it guarantees for me the existence of an absolute value. Does this assertion also not require vertification? That the criterion is finally found in a datum of consciousness, that is, in the realm of the "subjective," would not in itself be suspicious; for this cannot be avoided, and the example of perception teaches us that "subjective" sensations can lead us to objects whose independence of us, and objectivity, leave for all practical purposes nothing to be desired. And in ethics we are concerned with practical knowledge in the significant sense. But the sensations are able to carry out that performance only because they obey very definite *laws*. The play of perceptions, however colorful it be, exhibits a very definite regularity, which is expressed by the fact that we are able to make verifiable predictions concerning the occurrence of sensations. (Regularity does not indicate something objective, but is itself objectivity.) If something of the sort held of the hypothetical value-feelings, as holds for sensations; if value propositions cohered in a consistent system, as do the propositions about perceptions, *then* value-feelings could guarantee objective values. But that is not the case. The chaos of valuations is proverbial, and there is no hope of putting value theory, ethics and aesthetics, on a level with physics, which would otherwise be easy.

Thus there is no possibility of passing from elementary value-experiences to the justification of objective absolute values. But if one says that the justification lies already contained within the experience itself I can only answer that I cannot imagine how such an assertion would be verified, and that therefore I do not know what it means.

5. *Do Value Judgments Have the Validity of Logico-Mathematical Propositions?*

(*d.*) Perhaps many hold the comparison of absolute values to objective material bodies to be improper, because the realm of values seems incomparable to gross physical reality. At least we hardly ever find the analogy to perception drawn.† Instead of it, the more often, another, that is, the value-propositions are compared to the propositions of logic or mathematics, and explained by means of them. Neither deals with "actual" objects, and the validity of both is of the same sort. In the example of logic or mathematics we see best, it is supposed, how it is possible, despite the subjectivity of our experience of evidence, to arrive at what is intrinsically valid, absolute, and existing independently of any assent or any act of thought or feeling. The law of contradiction, and the proposition "Two times two equals four" hold simply, whether anyone thinks and understands

---

† Nevertheless the advocates of absolute values often say that these are *intuitively* known, and their whole outlook is thus called "intuitionism," a term in use in particular among English writers. But intuition signifies something similar to perception.

them or not. As here with absolute truth, so there with absolute value. The notion of the objectivity of value is usually made plausible in this way (for example, see Nicolai Hartmann, *Ethics*), and generally it remains the *only* way.

But, however misleading the argument is, our comparison with perception and its objects is a thousand times better, even from the standpoint of the absolutist theory. A comparison of any propositions with those of logic (which in this context also include the mathematical) always leads to nonsense; for logic is simply not comparable to anything (I hope I may be forgiven this somewhat paradoxical statement, but the way in which even today the essence of logic is misunderstood demands forthright criticism). This is not the place for me to expand this point; I note briefly only that the propositions of logic and the so-called propositions of mathematics are tautologies, or tautology-like forms, that is, they express nothing whatever (they are merely rules for the transformation of propositions). It is to this alone that they owe their absolute (independent of every experience) truth, which is really only a meaningless limiting case of truth. Thus in logic it is not as, according to the hopes or statements of the absolutists, it should be in value theory: namely, that here, in some sense, there is a realm of non-actual essences, independent of us, but ready to be recognized by us at any time, or, perhaps, in the case of values, to be realized. Logical propositions furnish us with no knowledge whatever, they express no facts, and teach us nothing about what exists in the world, or how anything does or should behave in the world Thus if the value-propositions were similar to them it would only follow that they too were mere tautologies, in all strictness saying nothing; a consequence that would certainly cause us to wish value-propositions to have as little similarity as possible to those of logic. Judgments about value ought to tell us just what is most important.

Tautological propositions can be formed about anything, and of course, about values. When, for example, I write the proposition: "If the value A is greater than the value B, then the value B is smaller than the value A," I have clearly said in this true proposition nothing at all about values, but have merely shown the equivalence of two different modes of expression. Indeed the proposition is not a proposition of value theory, but belongs to logic. And so it is always: whenever I come upon a proposition that is true independently of every experience, I am in the realm of logic. Only the propositions of logic, and all of them, have this character. In this lies their peculiarity, which I spoke of before.

Thus also in a comparison with logic and mathematics we fail to find a verifiable meaning in propositions about absolute values. . . .

7. *The Emptiness of the Hypothesis of Absolute Values*

Thus we come to the second argument against objective values, which is quite conclusive, and which frees us from and raises us above the hair-splitting that we, perhaps, began to feel in the line of thought of the first argument. This . . . simply asked for the *meaning* of so-called absolute value judgments, and concluded that none could be shown, however one tried.

But now let us assume that the desired meaning has been found, so that we are able to determine in some way that there is a hierarchy of objective values wholly independent of our feelings. We now consider "value" to be a property of objects, qualifying them in various forms (for example, beautiful, good, sublime, and so forth) and in different degrees. All these possible properties together form a system, and in each case [it] is unambiguously determined which of these properties a specific object has, and to what degree; thereby assigning to it a definite position in the system of the value hierarchy.

Good, we say, let it be so! What follows? What have we to do with that? *How does it concern us?*

The only interest we could take in this realm of values would be a purely scientific interest; that is, it might be of interest to an investigator that the things in the world, in addition to other properties, also have these, and by means of them can be ordered in a certain way; and he might devote much labor to the description of this system. But for life and conduct this arrangement would be no more important than, say, the arrangement of the stars in the order of their magnitudes, or the serial arrangement of objects according to the alphabetical order of their names in the Swahili language.

This is no exaggeration or misrepresentation, but is actually the case. To my question, "What do these objective values mean to me?" the absolutist answers, "They constitute the guiding lines of your conduct! In setting up your goals of action you should prefer the higher to the lower." If I then ask, "Why?" the absolutist simply cannot give any answer. This is the decisive point, that because of his thesis of the independence of values, the absolutist has cut himself off from all possibility of giving any other answer to my question, "What happens if I don't do it?" than "Then you don't do it, that is all!" Should he answer, "In that case you are not a good man," then we should note that this answer is relevant and can influence my action only if I desire, or have reason to desire, to be a "good man," that is, only if it is presupposed that certain feelings are connected with that concept. And just such a presupposition may not be made by the absolutist; he may not say, "You will be more highly respected as a good man, you will lead a happier life, you will have a better conscience, you will be more at peace with yourself," and so forth; for in doing so he appeals to my feelings, as though the value were really binding upon me only because it brought me joy; and this doctrine is expressly repudiated. Even though in every way it were pleasant to me to be a scoundrel, and if I had the cordial respect of others, genuine peace in my soul, and pure inner joy as a result (imagine this in a lively manner, though it is difficult to do so, because the fact is otherwise), if, thus, my life were more agreeable, exalted and happier because of my failure to obey the moral laws, still the absolutist would have to say, "Yet you must obey them, even though you become · extremely unhappy." Whether happy or unhappy, pleasant or unpleasant, all this has, for the intuitionist, absolutely nothing to do with moral value—which has been emphasized by no one more sharply than by Kant. But in these philosophers we still always find a hidden appeal to the feelings, even though it consist only in the use of certain honorific terms, like "honorable" itself.

Perhaps the philosopher is even proud that he cannot answer the question, "What do absolute values mean to me? What happens if I pay no attention to them?" Perhaps he even despises our question. If so, we answer his proud silence with the statement that in all seriousness we simply have no concern with such values, to which it makes no difference whether we are concerned with them or not, whose existence has no influence upon our peace of mind, our joy or sorrow, upon all those things that interest us in life. Indeed we *cannot* be concerned with such "values," for . . . only those objects can arouse our volition which in some way or other arouse feelings of pleasure or pain in us. They would not be values for us.

Thus we conclude: if there were values which were "absolute" in the sense that they had absolutely nothing to do with our feelings, they would constitute an independent realm which would enter into the world of our volition and action at no point; for it would be as if an impenetrable wall shut them off from us. Life would proceed as if they did not exist; and for ethics they would not exist. But if the values, in addition to and without injuring their absolute existence, also had the property or power of influencing our feelings, then they would enter into our world; but only in so far as they thus affected us. Hence values also exist for ethics only to the extent that they make themselves felt, that is, are relative to us. And if a philosopher says, "Of course, but they *also* have an absolute existence," then we know that these words add nothing new to the verifiable facts, that therefore they are empty, and their assertion meaningless.

3

TWO MEDITATIONS *

by

RENÉ DESCARTES

(1596–1650)

MEDITATION I

OF THE THINGS WHICH MAY BE BROUGHT WITHIN THE SPHERE OF
THE DOUBTFUL

It is now some years since I detected how many were the false
beliefs that I had from my earliest youth admitted as true, and
how doubtful was everything I had since constructed on this basis;
and from that time I was convinced that I must once for all seriously
undertake to rid myself of all the opinions which I had formerly
accepted, and commence to build anew from the foundation, if I
wanted to establish any firm and permanent structure in the sciences.
But as this enterprise appeared to be a very great one, I waited until I had attained an age so mature that I could not hope that at
any later date I should be better fitted to execute my design. This
reason caused me to delay so long that I should feel that I was
doing wrong were I to occupy in deliberation the time that yet remains to me for action. To-day, then, since very opportunely for
the plan I have in view I have delivered my mind from every care
[and am happily agitated by no passions] and since I have procured
for myself an assured leisure in a peaceable retirement, I shall at
last seriously and freely address myself to the general upheaval of
all my former opinions.

* [The entire first and second of the *Meditations* (1641). Translated from
the Latin by E. S. Haldane and G. R. T. Ross in *The Philosophical Works of
Descartes* (1912). By kind permission of the Macmillan Co. and the Cambridge
University Press.]

Now for this object it is not necessary that I should show that all of these are false—I shall perhaps never arrive at this end. But inasmuch as reason already persuades me that I ought no less carefully to withhold my assent from matters which are not entirely certain and indubitable than from those which appear to me manifestly to be false, if I am able to find in each one some reason to doubt, this will suffice to justify my rejecting the whole. And for that end it will not be requisite that I should examine each in particular, which would be an endless undertaking; for owing to the fact that the destruction of the foundations of necessity brings with it the downfall of the rest of the edifice, I shall only in the first place attack those principles upon which all my former opinions rested.

All that up to the present time I have accepted as most true and certain I have learned either from the senses or through the senses; but it is sometimes proved to me that these senses are deceptive, and it is wiser not to trust entirely to any thing by which we have once been deceived.

But it may be that although the senses sometimes deceive us concerning things which are hardly perceptible, or very far away, there are yet many others to be met with as to which we cannot reasonably have any doubt, although we recognise them by their means. For example, there is the fact that I am here, seated by the fire, attired in a dressing gown, having this paper in my hands and other similar matters. And how could I deny that these hands and this body are mine, were it not perhaps that I compare myself to certain persons, devoid of sense, whose cerebella are so troubled and clouded by the violent vapours of black bile, that they constantly assure us that they think they are kings when they are really quite poor, or that they are clothed in purple when they are really without covering, or who imagine that they have an earthenware head or are nothing but pumpkins or are made of glass. But they are mad, and I should not be any the less insane were I to follow examples so extravagant.

At the same time I must remember that I am a man, and that consequently I am in the habit of sleeping, and in my dreams representing to myself the same things or sometimes even less probable things, than do those who are insane in their waking moments. How often has it happened to me that in the night I dreamt that I found myself in this particular place, that I was dressed and seated near the fire, whilst in reality I was lying undressed in bed! At this moment it does indeed seem to me that it is with eyes awake that I am looking at this paper; that this head which I move is not asleep, that it is deliberately and of set purpose that I extend my hand and perceive it; what happens in sleep does not appear so clear nor so distinct as does all this. But in thinking over this I remind myself that on many occasions I have in sleep been deceived by similar illusions, and in dwelling carefully on this reflection I see so manifestly that there are no certain indications by which we may clearly distinguish wakefulness from sleep that I am lost in astonishment. And my astonishment is such that it is almost capable of persuading me that I now dream.

Now let us assume that we are asleep and that all these particulars, e.g. that we open our eyes, shake our head, extend our hands, and so on, are but false delusions; and let us reflect that possibly neither our hands nor our whole body are such as they appear to us to be. At the same time we must at least confess that the things which are represented to us in sleep are like painted representations which can only have been formed as the counterparts of something real and true, and that in this way those general things at least, i.e. eyes, a head, hands, and a whole body, are not imaginary things, but things really existent. For, as a matter of fact, painters, even when they study with the greatest skill to represent sirens and satyrs by forms the most strange and extraordinary, cannot give them natures which are entirely new, but merely make a certain medley of the members of different animals; or if their imagination is extravagant enough to invent something so novel that nothing similar has ever before been seen, and that then their work represents a thing purely fictitious and absolutely false, it is certain all the same that the colours of which this is composed are necessarily real. And for the same reason, although these general things, to wit, [a body], eyes, a head, and such like, may be imaginary, we are bound at the same time to confess that there are at least some other objects yet more simple and more universal, which are real and true; and of these just in the same way as with certain real colours, all these images of things which dwell in our thoughts, whether true and real or false and fantastic, are formed.

To such a class of things pertains corporeal nature in general, and its extension, the figure of extended things, their quantity or magnitude and number, as also the place in which they are, the time which measures their duration, and so on.

That is possibly why our reasoning is not unjust when we conclude from this that Physics, Astronomy, Medicine and all other sciences which have as their end the consideration of composite things, are very dubious and uncertain; but that Arithmetic, Geometry and other sciences of that kind which only treat of things that are very simple and very general, without taking great trouble to ascertain whether they are actually existent or not, contain some measure of certainty and an element of the indubitable. For whether I am awake or asleep, two and three together always form five, and the square can never have more than four sides, and it does not seem possible that truths so clear and apparent can be suspected of any falsity [or uncertainty].

Nevertheless I have long had fixed in my mind the belief that an all-powerful God existed by whom I have been created such as I am. But how do I know that He has not brought it to pass that there is no earth, no heaven, no extended body, no magnitude, no place, and that nevertheless [I possess the perceptions of all these things and that] they seem to me to exist just exactly as I now see them? And, besides, as I sometimes imagine that others deceive themselves in the things which they think they know best, how do I know that I am not deceived every time that I add two and three, or count the sides of a square, or judge of things yet simpler, if anything simpler can be imagined? But possibly God has not desired that I should be thus deceived, for He is said to be supremely good. If, however, it is contrary to His goodness to have made me such that I constantly deceive myself, it would also appear to be contrary to His goodness to permit me to be sometimes deceived, and nevertheless I cannot doubt that He does permit this.

There may indeed be those who would prefer to deny the existence of a God so powerful, rather than believe that all other things are uncertain. But let us not oppose them for the present, and grant that all that is said of a God is a fable; nevertheless in whatever way they suppose that I have arrived at the state of being that I have reached—whether they attribute it to fate or to accident, or make out that it is by a continual succession of antecedents, or by some other method—since to err and deceive oneself is a defect, it is clear that the greater will be the probability of my being so imperfect as to deceive myself ever, as is the Author to whom they assign my origin the less powerful. To these reasons I have certainly nothing to reply, but at the end I feel constrained to confess that there is nothing in all that I formerly believed to be true, of which I cannot in some measure doubt, and that not merely through want of thought or through levity, but for reasons which are very powerful and maturely considered; so that henceforth I ought not the less carefully to refrain from giving credence to these opinions than to that which is manifestly false, if I desire to arrive at any certainty [in the sciences].

But it is not sufficient to have made these remarks, we must also be careful to keep them in mind. For these ancient and commonly held opinions still revert frequently to my mind, long and familiar custom having given them the right to occupy my mind against my inclination and rendered them almost masters of my belief; nor will I ever lose the habit of deferring to them or of placing my confidence in them, so long as I consider them as they really are, i.e. opinions in some measure doubtful, as I have just shown, and at the same time highly probable, so that there is much more reason to believe than to deny them. That is why I consider that I shall not be acting amiss, if, taking of set purpose a contrary belief, I allow myself to be deceived, and for a certain time pretend that all these opinions are entirely false and imaginary, until at last, having thus balanced my former prejudices with my latter [so that they cannot divert my opinions more to one side than to the other], my judgment will no longer be dominated by bad usage or turned away from the right knowledge of the truth. For I am assured that there can be neither peril nor error in this course, and that I cannot at present yield too much to distrust, since I am not considering the question of action, but only of knowledge.

I shall then suppose, not that God who is supremely good and the fountain of truth, but some evil genius not less powerful than deceitful, has employed his whole energies in deceiving me; I shall consider that the heavens, the earth, colours, figures, sound, and all other external things are nought but the illusions and dreams of which this genius has availed himself in order to lay traps for my credulity; I shall consider myself as having no hands, no eyes, no flesh, no blood, nor any senses, yet falsely believing myself to possess all these things; I shall remain obstinately attached to this idea, and if by this means it is not in my power to arrive at the knowledge of any truth, I may at least do what is in my power [i.e. suspend my judgment], and with firm purpose avoid giving credence to any false thing, or being imposed upon by this arch deceiver, however powerful and deceptive he may be. But this task is a laborious one, and insensibly a certain lassitude leads me into the course of my ordinary life. And just as a captive who in sleep enjoys imaginary liberty, when he begins to suspect that his liberty is but a dream, fears to awaken, and conspires with these agreeable illusions that the deception may be prolonged, so insensibly of my own accord I fall back into my former opinions, and I dread awakening from this slumber, lest the laborious wakefulness which would follow the tranquillity of this repose should have to be spent not in daylight, but in the excessive darkness of the difficulties which have just been discussed.

MEDITATION II

OF THE NATURE OF THE HUMAN MIND; AND THAT IT IS MORE EASILY KNOWN THAN THE BODY

The Meditation of yesterday filled my mind with so many doubts that it is no longer in my power to forget them. And yet I do not see in what manner I can resolve them; and, just as if I had all of a sudden fallen into very deep water, I am so disconcerted that I can neither make certain of setting my feet on the bottom, nor can I swim and so support myself on the surface. I shall nevertheless make an effort and follow anew the same path as that on which I yesterday entered, i.e. I shall proceed by setting aside all that in which the least doubt could be supposed to exist, just as if I had discovered that it was absolutely false; and I shall ever follow in this road until I have met with something which is certain, or at least, if I can do nothing else, until I have learned for certain that there is nothing in the world that is certain. Archimedes, in order that he might draw the terrestrial globe out of its place, and transport it elsewhere, demanded only that one point should be fixed and immoveable; in the same way I shall have the right to conceive high hopes if I am happy enough to discover one thing only which is certain and indubitable.

I suppose, then, that all the things that I see are false; I persuade myself that nothing has ever existed of all that my fallacious memory represents to me. I consider that I possess no senses; I imagine that body, figure, extension, movement and place are but the fictions of my mind. What, then, can be esteemed as true? Perhaps nothing at all, unless that there is nothing in the world that is certain.

But how can I know there is not something different from those things that I have just considered, of which one cannot have the slightest doubt? Is there not some God, or some other being by whatever name we call it, who puts these reflections into my mind? That is not necessary, for is it not possible that I am capable of producing them myself? I myself, am I not at least something? But I have already denied that I had senses and body. Yet I hesitate, for what follows from that? Am I so dependent on body and senses that I cannot exist without these? But I was persuaded that there was nothing in all the world, that there was no heaven, no earth, that there were no minds, nor any bodies: was I not then likewise persuaded that I did not exist? Not at all; of a surety I myself did exist since I persuaded myself of something [or merely because I thought of something]. But there is some deceiver or other, very powerful and very cunning, who ever employs his ingenuity in deceiving me. Then without doubt I exist also if he deceives me, and let him deceive me as much as he will, he can never cause me to be nothing so long as I think that I am something. So that after having reflected well and carefully examined all things, we must come to the definite conclusion that this proposition: I am, I exist, is necessarily true each time that I pronounce it, or that I mentally conceive it.

But I do not yet know clearly enough what I am, I who am certain that I am; and hence I must be careful to see that I do not imprudently take some other object in place of myself, and thus that I do not go astray in respect of this knowledge that I hold to be the most certain and most evident of all that I have formerly learned. That is why I shall now consider anew what I believed myself to be before I embarked upon these last reflections; and of my former opinions I shall withdraw all that might even in a small degree be invalidated by the reasons which I have just brought forward, in order that there may be nothing at all left beyond what is absolutely certain and indubitable.

What then did I formerly believe myself to be? Undoubtedly I believed myself to be a man. But what is a man? Shall I say a reasonable animal? Certainly not; for then I should have to inquire what an animal is, and what is reasonable; and thus from a single question I should insensibly fall into an infinitude of others more difficult; and I should not wish to waste the little time and leisure remaining to me in trying to unravel subtleties like these. But I shall rather stop here to consider the thoughts which of themselves spring up in my mind, and which were not inspired by anything beyond my own nature alone when I applied myself to the consideration of my being. In the first place, then, I considered myself as having a face, hands, arms, and all that system of members composed of bones and flesh as seen in a corpse which I designated by the name of body. In addition to this I considered that I was nourished, that I walked, that I felt, and that I thought, and I referred all these actions to the soul: but I did not stop to consider what the soul was, or if I did stop, I imagined that it was something extremely rare and subtle like a wind, a flame, or an ether, which was spread throughout my grosser parts. As to body I had no manner of doubt about its nature, but thought I had a very clear knowledge of it; and if I had desired to explain it according to the notions that I had then formed of it, I should have described it thus: By the body I understand all that which can be defined by a certain figure: something which can be confined in a certain place, and which can fill a given space in such a way that every other body will be excluded from it; which can be perceived either by touch, or by sight, or by hearing, or by taste, or by smell: which can be moved

in many ways not, in truth, by itself, but by something which is
foreign to it, by which it is touched [and from which it receives im-
pressions]: for to have the power of self-movement, as also of feeling or of thinking, I did not consider to appertain to the nature of
body: on the contrary, I was rather astonished to find that faculties
similar to them existed in some bodies.

But what am I, now that I suppose that there is a certain genius
which is extremely powerful, and, if I may say so, malicious, who
employs all his powers in deceiving me? Can I affirm that I possess
the least of all those things which I have just said pertain to the
nature of body? I pause to consider, I resolve all these things in
my mind, and find none of which I can say that it pertains to me.
It would be tedious to stop to enumerate them. Let us pass to the
attributes of soul and see if there is any one which is in me? What
of nutrition or walking [the first mentioned]? But if it is so that
I have no body it is also true that I can neither walk nor take
nourishment. Another attribute is sensation. But one cannot feel
without body, and besides I have thought I perceived many things
during sleep that I recognised in my waking moments as not having been experienced at all. What of thinking? I find here that
thought is an attribute that belongs to me; it alone cannot be
separated from me. I am, I exist, that is certain. But how often?
Just when I think; for it might possibly be the case if I ceased entirely to think, that I should likewise cease altogether to exist. I
do not now admit anything which is not necessarily true: to speak
accurately I am not more than a thing which thinks, that is to say
a mind or a soul, or an understanding, or a reason, which are terms
whose significance was formerly unknown to me. I am, however,
a real thing and really exist; but what thing? I have answered: a
thing which thinks.

And what more? I shall exercise my imagination [in order to
see if I am not something more]. I am not a collection of members
which we call the human body: I am not a subtle air distributed
through these members, I am not a wind, a fire, a vapour, a breath,
nor anything at all which I can imagine or conceive; because I
have assumed that all these were nothing. Without changing that
supposition I find that I only leave myself certain of the fact that
I am somewhat. But perhaps it is true that these same things which
I supposed were non-existent because they are unknown to me, are
really not different from the self which I know. I am not sure about
this, I shall not dispute about it now; I can only give judgment
on things that are known to me. I know that I exist, and I inquire
what I am, I whom I know to exist. But it is very certain that the
knowledge of my existence taken in its precise significance does

not depend on things whose existence is not yet known to me; consequently it does not depend on those which I can feign in imagination. And indeed the very term *feign* in imagination proves to me my error, for I really do this if I image myself a something, since to imagine is nothing else than to contemplate the figure or image of a corporeal thing. But I already know for certain that I am, and that it may be that all these images, and, speaking generally, all things that relate to the nature of body are nothing but dreams [and chimeras]. For this reason I see clearly that I have as little reason to say, "I shall stimulate my imagination in order to know more distinctly what I am," than if I were to say, "I am now awake, and I perceive somewhat that is real and true: but because I do not yet perceive it distinctly enough, I shall go to sleep of express purpose, so that my dreams may represent the perception with greatest truth and evidence." And, thus, I know for certain that nothing of all that I can understand by means of my imagination belongs to this knowledge which I have of myself, and that it is necessary to recall the mind from this mode of thought with the utmost diligence in order that it may be able to know its own nature with perfect distinctness.

But what then am I? A thing which thinks. What is a thing which thinks? It is a thing which doubts, understands, [conceives], affirms, denies, wills, refuses, which also imagines and feels.

Certainly it is no small matter if all these things pertain to my nature. But why should they not so pertain? Am I not that being who now doubts nearly everything, who nevertheless understands certain things, who affirms that one only is true, who denies all the others, who desires to know more, is averse from being deceived, who imagines many things, sometimes indeed despite his will, and who perceives many likewise, as by the intervention of the bodily organs? Is there nothing in all this which is as true as it is certain that I exist, even though I should always sleep and though he who has given me being employed all his ingenuity in deceiving me? Is there likewise any one of these attributes which can be distinguished from my thought, or which might be said to be separated from myself? For it is so evident of itself that it is I who doubts, who understands, and who desires, that there is no reason here to add anything to explain it. And I have certainly the power of imagining likewise; for although it may happen (as I formerly supposed) that none of the things which I imagine are true, nevertheless this power of imagining does not cease to be really in use, and it forms part of my thought. Finally, I am the same who feels, that is to say, who perceives certain things, as by the organs of sense, since in truth I see light, I hear noise, I feel heat. But it will be said that these phenomena are false and that I am dreaming. Let it be so; still it is at least quite certain that it seems to me that I see light, that I hear noise and that I feel heat. That cannot be false; properly speaking it is what is in me called feeling; and used in this precise sense that is no other thing than thinking.

From this time I begin to know what I am with a little more clearness and distinction than before; but nevertheless it still seems to me, and I cannot prevent myself from thinking, that corporeal things, whose images are framed by thought, which are tested by the senses, are much more distinctly known than that obscure part of me which does not come under the imagination. Although really it is very strange to say that I know and understand more distinctly these things whose existence seems to me dubious, which are unknown to me, and which do not belong to me, than others of the truth of which I am convinced, which are known to me and which pertain to my real nature, in a word, than myself. But I see clearly how the case stands: my mind loves to wander, and cannot yet suffer itself to be retained within the just limits of truth. Very good, let us once more give it the freest rein, so that, when afterwards we seize the proper occasion for pulling up, it may the more easily be regulated and controlled.

Let us begin by considering the commonest matters, those which we believe to be the most distinctly comprehended, to wit, the bodies which we touch and see; not indeed bodies in general, for these general ideas are usually a little more confused, but let us consider one body in particular. Let us take for example, this piece of wax: it has been taken quite freshly from the hive, and it has not yet lost the sweetness of the honey which it contains; it still retains somewhat of the odour of the flowers from which it has been culled; its colour, its figure, its size are apparent; it is hard, cold, easily handled, and if you strike it with the finger, it will emit a sound. Finally all the things which are requisite to cause us distinctly to recognise a body, are met within it. But notice that while I speak and approach the fire what remained of the taste is exhaled, the smell evaporates, the colour alters, the figure is destroyed, the size increases, it becomes liquid, it heats, scarcely can one handle it, and when one strikes it, no sound is emitted. Does the same wax remain after this change? We must confess that it remains; none would judge otherwise. What then did I know so distinctly in this piece of wax? It could certainly be nothing of all that the senses brought to my notice, since all these things which fall under taste, smell, sight, touch, and hearing, are found to be changed, and yet the same wax remains.

Perhaps it was what I now think, viz. that this wax was not that sweetness of honey, nor that agreeable scent of flowers, nor that particular whiteness, nor that figure, nor that sound, but simply a body which a little before appeared to me as perceptible under these forms, and which is now perceptible under others. But what, precisely, is it that I imagine when I form such conceptions? Let us attentively consider this, and, abstracting from all that does not belong to the wax, let us see what remains. Certainly nothing remains excepting a certain extended thing which is flexible and movable. But what is the meaning of flexible and movable? Is it not that I imagine that this piece of wax being round is capable of becoming square and of passing from a square to a triangular figure? No, certainly it is not that, since I imagine it admits of an infinitude of similar changes, and I nevertheless do not know how to compass the infinitude by my imagination, and consequently this conception which I have of the wax is not brought about by the faculty of imagination. What now is this extension? Is it not also unknown? For it becomes greater when the wax is melted, greater when it is boiled, and greater still when the heat increases; and I should not conceive [clearly] according to truth what wax is, if I did not think that even this piece that we are considering is capable of receiving more variations in extension than I have ever imagined. We must then grant that I could not even understand through the imagination what this piece of wax is, and that it is my mind alone which perceives it. I say this piece of wax in particular, for as to wax in general it is yet clearer. But what is this piece of wax which cannot be understood excepting by the [understanding or] mind? It is certainly the same that I see, touch, imagine, and finally it is the same which I have always believed it to be from the beginning. But what must particularly be observed is that its perception is neither an act of vision, nor of touch, nor of imagination, and has never been such although it may have appeared formerly to be so, but only an intuition of the mind, which may be imperfect and confused as it was formerly, or clear and distinct as it is at present, according as my attention is more or less directed to the elements which are found in it, and of which it is composed.

Yet in the meantime I am greatly astonished when I consider [the great feebleness of mind] and its proneness to fall [insensibly] into error; for although without giving expression to my thoughts I consider all this in my own mind, words often impede me and I am almost deceived by the terms of ordinary language. For we say that we see the same wax, if it is present, and not that we simply judge that it is the same from its having the same colour and figure. From this I should conclude that I knew the wax by means

of vision and not simply by the intuition of the mind; unless by
chance I remember that, when looking from a window and saying
I see men who pass in the street, I really do not see them, but
infer that what I see is men, just as I say that I see wax. And yet
what do I see from the window but hats and coats which may
cover automatic machines? Yet I judge these to be men. And
similarly solely by the faculty of judgment which rests in my mind,
I comprehend that which I believed I saw with my eyes.

A man who makes it his aim to raise his knowledge above the
common should be ashamed to derive the occasion for doubting
from the forms of speech invented by the vulgar; I prefer to pass
on and consider whether I had a more evident and perfect conception of what the wax was when I first perceived it, and when I
believed I knew it by means of the external senses or at least by
the common sense as it is called, that is to say by the imaginative
faculty, or whether my present conception is clearer now that I
have most carefully examined what it is, and in what way it can be
known. It would certainly be absurd to doubt as to this. For what
was there in this first perception which was distinct? What was
there which might not as well have been perceived by any of the
animals? But when I distinguish the wax from its external forms,
and when, just as if I had taken from it its vestments, I consider it
quite naked, it is certain that although some error may still be
found in my judgment, I can nevertheless not perceive it thus without a human mind.

But finally what shall I say of this mind, that is, of myself, for
up to this point I do not admit in myself anything but mind?
What then, I who seem to perceive this piece of wax distinctly, do
I not know myself, not only with much more truth and certainty,
but also with much more distinctness and clearness? For if I judge
that the wax is or exists from the fact that I see it, it certainly
follows much more clearly that I am or that I exist myself from
the fact that I see it. For it may be that what I see is not really
wax, it may also be that I do not possess eyes with which to see
anything; but it cannot be that when I see, or (for I no longer
take account of the distinction) when I think I see, that I myself
who think am nought. So if I judge that the wax exists from the
fact that I touch it, the same thing will follow, to wit, that I am;
and if I judge that my imagination, or some other cause, whatever
it is, persuades me that the wax exists, I shall still conclude the
same. And what I have here remarked of wax may be applied to all
other things which are external to me [and which are met with outside of me]. And further, if the [notion or] perception of wax has
seemed to me clearer and more distinct, not only after the sight or

the touch, but also after many other causes have rendered it quite manifest to me, with how much more [evidence] and distinctness must it be said that I now know myself, since all the reasons which contribute to the knowledge of wax, or any other body whatever, are yet better proofs of the nature of my mind! And there are so many other things in the mind itself which may contribute to the elucidation of its nature, that those which depend on body such as these just mentioned, hardly merit being taken into account.

But finally here I am, having insensibly reverted to the point I desired, for, since it is now manifest to me that even bodies are not properly speaking known by the senses or by the faculty of imagination, but by the understanding only, and since they are not known from the fact that they are seen or touched, but only because they are understood, I see clearly that there is nothing which is easier for me to know than my mind. But because it is difficult to rid oneself so promptly of an opinion to which one was accustomed for so long, it will be well that I should halt a little at this point, so that by the length of my meditation I may more deeply imprint on my memory this new knowledge.

4

ARE THINGS DIFFERENT FROM IDEAS? *

by

GEORGE BERKELEY

(1685–1753)

Hylas. I am glad to find there was nothing in the accounts I heard of you.

Philonous. Pray, what were those?

Hyl. You were represented in last night's conversation, as one who

* [The greater part of the first dialogue in *Three Dialogues between Hylas and Philonous* (1713).]

maintained the most extravagant opinion that ever entered into the mind of man, to wit, that there is no such thing as *material substance* in the world.

Phil. That there is no such thing as what Philosophers call *material substance,* I am seriously persuaded: but, if I were made to see anything absurd or sceptical in this, I should then have the same reason to renounce this that I imagine I have now to reject the contrary opinion.

Hyl. What! can anything be more fantastical, more repugnant to common sense, or a more manifest piece of Scepticism, than to believe there is no such thing as *matter?*

Phil. Softly, good *Hylas.* What if it should prove, that you, who hold there is, are, by virtue of that opinion, a greater sceptic, and maintain more paradoxes and repugnances to common sense, than I who believe no such thing?

Hyl. You may as soon persuade me, the part is greater than the whole, as that, in order to avoid absurdity and Scepticism, I should ever be obliged to give up my opinion in this point.

Phil. Well then, are you content to admit that opinion for true, which, upon examination, shall appear most agreeable to common sense, and remote from Scepticism?

Hyl. With all my heart. Since you are for raising disputes about the plainest things in nature, I am content for once to hear what you have to say.

Phil. Pray, *Hylas,* what do you mean by a *sceptic?*

Hyl. I mean what all men mean, one that doubts of everything.

Phil. He then who entertains no doubt concerning some particular point, with regard to that point cannot be thought a sceptic.

Hyl. I agree with you.

Phil. Whether doth doubting consist in embracing the affirmative or negative side of a question?

Hyl. In neither; for whoever understands English cannot but know that *doubting* signifies a suspense between both.

Phil. He then that denieth any point, can no more be said to doubt of it, than he who affirmeth it with the same degree of assurance.

Hyl. True.

Phil. And, consequently, for such his denial is no more to be esteemed a sceptic than the other.

Hyl. I acknowledge it.

Phil. How cometh it to pass then, *Hylas,* that you pronounce me a *sceptic,* because I deny what you affirm, to wit, the existence of Matter? Since, for aught you can tell, I am as peremptory in my denial, as you in your affirmation.

Hyl. Hold, *Philonous,* I have been a little out in my definition; but every false step a man makes in discourse is not to be insisted on. I said indeed that a *sceptic* was one who doubted of everything; but I should have added, or who denies the reality and truth of things.

Phil. What things? Do you mean the principles and theorems of sciences? But these you know are universal intellectual notions, and consequently independent of Matter; the denial therefore of this doth not imply the denying them.

Hyl. I grant it. But are there no other things? What think you of distrusting the senses, of denying the real existence of sensible things, or pretending to know nothing of them. Is not this sufficient to denominate a man a *sceptic?*

Phil. Shall we therefore examine which of us it is that denies the reality of sensible things, or professes the greatest ignorance of them; since, if I take you rightly, he is to be esteemed the greatest *sceptic?*

Hyl. That is what I desire.

Phil. What mean you by Sensible Things?

Hyl. Those things which are perceived by the senses. Can you imagine that I mean anything else?

Phil. Pardon me, *Hylas,* if I am desirous clearly to apprehend your notions, since this may much shorten our inquiry. Suffer me then to ask you this farther question. Are those things only perceived by the senses which are perceived immediately? Or, may those things properly be said to be *sensible* which are perceived mediately, or not without the intervention of others?

Hyl. I do not sufficiently understand you.

Phil. In reading a book, what I immediately perceive are the letters, but mediately, or by means of these, are suggested to my mind the notions of God, virtue, truth, &c. Now, that the letters are truly sensible things, or perceived by sense, there is no doubt: but I would know whether you take the things suggested by them to be so too.

Hyl. No, certainly; it were absurd to think *God* or *virtue* sensible things, though they may be signified and suggested to the mind by sensible marks, with which they have an arbitrary connexion.

Phil. It seems then, that by *sensible things* you mean those only which can be perceived *immediately* by sense?

Hyl. Right.

Phil. Doth it not follow from this, that though I see one part of the sky red, and another blue, and that my reason doth thence evidently conclude there must be some cause of that diversity of colours, yet that cause cannot be said to be a sensible thing, or perceived by the sense of seeing?

Hyl. It doth.

Phil. In like manner, though I hear variety of sounds, yet I cannot be said to hear the causes of those sounds?

Hyl. You cannot.

Phil. And when by my touch I perceive a thing to be hot and heavy, I cannot say, with any truth or propriety, that I feel the cause of its heat or weight?

Hyl. To prevent any more questions of this kind, I tell you once for all, that by *sensible things* I mean those only which are perceived by sense, and that in truth the senses perceive nothing which they do not perceive immediately: for they make no inferences. The deducing therefore of causes or occasions from effects and appearances, which alone are perceived by sense, entirely relates to reason.

Phil. This point then is agreed between us—that *sensible things are those only which are immediately perceived by sense.* You will farther inform me, whether we immediately perceive by sight anything beside light, and colours, and figures; or by hearing, anything but sounds; by the palate, anything beside tastes; by the smell, beside odours; or by the touch, more than tangible qualities.

Hyl. We do not.

Phil. It seems, therefore, that if you take away all sensible qualities, there remains nothing sensible?

Hyl. I grant it.

Phil. Sensible things therefore are nothing else but so many sensible qualities, or combinations of sensible qualities?

Hyl. Nothing else.

Phil. Heat is then a sensible thing?

Hyl. Certainly.

Phil. Doth the reality of sensible things consist in being perceived? or, is it something distinct from their being perceived, and that bears no relation to the mind?

Hyl. To *exist* is one thing, and to be *perceived* is another.

Phil. I speak with regard to sensible things only: and of these I ask, whether by their real existence you mean a subsistence exterior to the mind, and distinct from their being perceived?

Hyl. I mean a real absolute being, distinct from, and without any relation to their being perceived.

Phil. Heat therefore, if it be allowed a real being, must exist without the mind?

Hyl. It must.

Phil. Tell me, *Hylas,* is this real existence equally compatible to all degrees of heat, which we perceive; or is there any reason why we should attribute it to some, and deny it to others? and if there be, pray let me know that reason.

Hyl. Whatever degree of heat we perceive by sense, we may be sure the same exists in the object that occasions it.

Phil. What! the greatest as well as the least?

Hyl. I tell you, the reason is plainly the same in respect of both: they are both perceived by sense; nay, the greater degree of heat is more sensibly perceived; and consequently, if there is any difference, we are more certain of its real existence than we can be of the reality of a lesser degree.

Phil. But is not the most vehement and intense degree of heat a very great pain?

Hyl. No one can deny it.

Phil. And is any unperceiving thing capable of pain or pleasure?

Hyl. No certainly.

Phil. Is your material substance a senseless being, or a being endowed with sense and perception?

Hyl. It is senseless without doubt.

Phil. It cannot therefore be the subject of pain?

Hyl. By no means.

Phil. Nor consequently of the greatest heat perceived by sense, since you acknowledge this to be no small pain?

Hyl. I grant it.

Phil. What shall we say then of your external object; is it a material Substance, or no?

Hyl. It is a material substance with the sensible qualities inhering in it.

Phil. How then can a great heat exist in it, since you own it cannot in a material substance? I desire you would clear this point.

Hyl. Hold, *Philonous,* I fear I was out in yielding intense heat to be a pain. It should seem rather, that pain is something distinct from heat, and the consequence or effect of it.

Phil. Upon putting your hand near the fire, do you perceive one simple uniform sensation, or two distinct sensations?

Hyl. But one simple sensation.

Phil. Is not the heat immediately perceived?

Hyl. It is.

Phil. And the pain?

Hyl. True.

Phil. Seeing therefore they are both immediately perceived at the same time, and the fire affects you only with one simple, or uncompounded idea, it follows that this same simple idea is both the intense heat immediately perceived, and the pain; and, consequently, that the intense heat immediately perceived, is nothing distinct from a particular sort of pain.

Hyl. It seems so.

Phil. Again, try in your thoughts, *Hylas,* if you can conceive a vehement sensation to be without pain or pleasure.

Hyl. I cannot.

Phil. Or can you frame to yourself an idea of sensible pain or pleasure, in general, abstracted from every particular idea of heat, cold, tastes, smells? &c.

Hyl. I do not find that I can.

Phil. Doth it not therefore follow, that sensible pain is nothing distinct from those sensations or ideas,—in an intense degree?

Hyl. It is undeniable; and, to speak the truth, I begin to suspect a very great heat cannot exist but in a mind perceiving it.

Phil. What! are you then in that *sceptical* state of suspense, between affirming and denying?

Hyl. I think I may be positive in the point. A very violent and painful heat cannot exist without the mind.

Phil. It hath not therefore, according to you, any real being?

Hyl. I own it.

Phil. Is it therefore certain, that there is no body in nature really hot?

Hyl. I have not denied there is any real heat in bodies. I only say, there is no such thing as an intense real heat.

Phil. But, did you not say before that all degrees of heat were equally real; or, if there was any difference, that the greater were more undoubtedly real than the lesser?

Hyl. True: but it was because I did not then consider the ground there is for distinguishing between them, which I now plainly see. And it is this:—because intense heat is nothing else but a particular kind of painful sensation; and pain cannot exist but in a perceiving being; it follows that no intense heat can really exist in an unperceiving corporeal substance. But this is no reason why we should deny heat in an inferior degree to exist in such a substance.

Phil. But how shall we be able to discern those degrees of heat which exist only in the mind from those which exist without it?

Hyl. That is no difficult matter. You know the least pain cannot exist unperceived; whatever, therefore, degree of heat is a pain exists only in the mind. But, as for all other degrees of heat, nothing obliges us to think the same of them.

Phil. I think you granted before that no unperceiving being was capable of pleasure, any more than of pain.

Hyl. I did.

Phil. And is not warmth, or a more gentle degree of heat than what causes uneasiness, a pleasure?

Hyl. What then?

Phil. Consequently, it cannot exist without the mind in an unperceiving substance, or body.

Hyl. So it seems.

Phil. Since, therefore, as well those degrees of heat that are not painful, as those that are, can exist only in a thinking substance; may we not conclude that external bodies are absolutely incapable of any degree of heat whatsoever?

Hyl. On second thoughts, I do not think it is so evident that warmth is a pleasure, as that a great degree of heat is a pain.

Phil. I do not pretend that warmth is as great a pleasure as heat is a pain. But, if you grant it to be even a small pleasure, it serves to make good my conclusion.

Hyl. I could rather call it an *indolence.* It seems to be nothing more than a privation of both pain and pleasure. And that such a quality or state as this may agree to an unthinking substance, I hope you will not deny.

Phil. If you are resolved to maintain that warmth, or a gentle degree of heat, is no pleasure, I know not how to convince you otherwise, than by appealing to your own sense. But what think you of cold?

Hyl. The same that I do of heat. An intense degree of cold is a pain; for to feel a very great cold, is to perceive a great uneasiness: it cannot therefore exist without the mind; but a lesser degree of cold may, as well as a lesser degree of heat.

Phil. Those bodies, therefore, upon whose application to our own, we perceive a moderate degree of heat, must be concluded to have a moderate degree of heat or warmth in them; and those, upon whose application we feel a like degree of cold, must be thought to have cold in them.

Hyl. They must.

Phil. Can any doctrine be true that necessarily leads a man into an absurdity?

Hyl. Without doubt it cannot.

Phil. Is it not an absurdity to think that the same thing should be at the same time both cold and warm?

Hyl. It is.

Phil. Suppose now one of your hands hot, and the other cold, and that they are both at once put into the same vessel of water, in an intermediate state; will not the water seem cold to one hand, and warm to the other?

Hyl. It will.

Phil. Ought we not therefore, by our principles, to conclude it is really both cold and warm at the same time, that is, according to your own concession, to believe an absurdity?

Hyl. I confess it seems so.

Phil. Consequently, the principles themselves are false, since you have granted that no true principle leads to an absurdity.

Hyl. But, after all, can anything be more absurd than to say, *there is no heat in the fire?*

Phil. To make the point still clearer; tell me whether, in two cases exactly alike, we ought not to make the same judgment?

Hyl. We ought.

Phil. When a pin pricks your finger, doth it not rend and divide the fibres of your flesh?

Hyl. It doth.

Phil. And when a coal burns your finger, doth it any more?

Hyl. It doth not.

Phil. Since, therefore, you neither judge the sensation itself occasioned by the pin, nor anything like it to be in the pin; you should not, conformably to what you have now granted, judge the sensation occasioned by the fire, or anything like it, to be in the fire.

Hyl. Well, since it must be so, I am content to yield this point, and acknowledge that heat and cold are only sensations existing in our minds. But there still remain qualities enough to secure the reality of external things.

Phil. But what will you say, *Hylas,* if it shall appear that the case is the same with regard to all other sensible qualities, and that they can no more be supposed to exist without the mind, than heat and cold?

Hyl. Then indeed you will have done something to the purpose; but that is what I despair of seeing proved.

Phil. Let us examine them in order. What think you of *tastes—* do they exist without the mind, or no?

Hyl. Can any man in his senses doubt whether sugar is sweet, or wormwood bitter?

Phil. Inform me, *Hylas.* Is a sweet taste a particular kind of pleasure or pleasant sensation, or is it not?

Hyl. It is.

Phil. And is not bitterness some kind of uneasiness or pain?

Hyl. I grant it.

Phil. If therefore sugar and wormwood are unthinking corporeal substances existing without the mind, how can sweetness and bitterness, that is, pleasure and pain, agree to them?

Hyl. Hold, *Philonous,* I now see what it was deluded me all this time. You asked whether heat and cold, sweetness and bitterness, were not particular sorts of pleasure and pain; to which I answered simply, that they were. Whereas I should have thus distinguished: —those qualities, as perceived by us, are pleasures or pains; but not as existing in the external objects. We must not therefore conclude absolutely, that there is no heat in the fire, or sweetness in the sugar, but only that heat or sweetness, as perceived by us, are not in the fire or sugar. What say you to this?

Phil. I say it is nothing to the purpose. Our discourse proceeded altogether concerning sensible things, which you defined to be, *the things we immediately perceive by our senses*. Whatever other qualities, therefore, you speak of, as distinct from these, I know nothing of them, neither do they at all belong to the point in dispute. You may, indeed, pretend to have discovered certain qualities which you do not perceive, and assert those insensible qualities exist in fire and sugar. But what use can be made of this to your present purpose, I am at a loss to conceive. Tell me then once more, do you acknowledge that heat and cold, sweetness and bitterness (meaning those qualities which are perceived by the senses), do not exist without the mind?

Hyl. I see it is to no purpose to hold out, so I give up the cause as to those mentioned qualities. Though I profess it sounds oddly, to say that sugar is not sweet.

Phil. But, for your farther satisfaction, take this along with you: that which at other times seems sweet, shall, to a distempered palate, appear bitter. And, nothing can be plainer than that divers persons perceive different tastes in the same food; since that which one man delights in, another abhors. And how could this be, if the taste was something really inherent in the food?

Hyl. I acknowledge I know not how. . . .

Phil. And I hope you will make no difficulty to acknowledge the same of *colours*.

Hyl. Pardon me: the case of colours is very different. Can anything be plainer than that we see them on the objects?

Phil. The objects you speak of are, I suppose, corporeal Substances existing without the mind?

Hyl. They are.

Phil. And have true and real colours inhering in them?

Hyl. Each visible object hath that colour which we see in it.

Phil. How! is there anything visible but what we perceive by sight?

Hyl. There is not.

Phil. And, do we perceive anything by sense which we do not perceive immediately?

Hyl. How often must I be obliged to repeat the same thing? I tell you, we do not.

Phil. Have patience, good *Hylas*; and tell me once more, whether there is anything immediately perceived by the senses, except sensible qualities. I know you asserted there was not; but I would now be informed, whether you still persist in the same opinion.

Hyl. I do.

Phil. Pray, is your corporeal substance either a sensible quality, or made up of sensible qualities?

Hyl. What a question that is! who ever thought it was?

Phil. My reason for asking was, because in saying, *each visible object hath that colour which we see in it,* you make visible objects to be corporeal substances; which implies either that corporeal substances are sensible qualities, or else that there is something beside sensible qualities perceived by sight: but, as this point was formerly agreed between us, and is still maintained by you, it is a clear consequence, that your corporeal substance is nothing distinct from sensible qualities.

Hyl. You may draw as many absurd consequences as you please, and endeavour to perplex the plainest things; but you shall never persuade me out of my senses. I clearly understand my own meaning.

Phil. I wish you would make me understand it too. But, since you are unwilling to have your notion of corporeal substance examined, I shall urge that point no farther. Only be pleased to let me know, whether the same colours which we see exist in external bodies, or some other.

Hyl. The very same.

Phil. What! are then the beautiful red and purple we see on yonder clouds really in them? Or do you imagine they have in themselves any other form than that of a dark mist or vapour?

Hyl. I must own, *Philonous,* those colours are not really in the clouds as they seem to be at this distance. They are only apparent colours.

Phil. Apparent call you them? how shall we distinguish these apparent colours from real?

Hyl. Very easily. Those are to be thought apparent which, appearing only at a distance, vanish upon a nearer approach.

Phil. And those, I suppose, are to be thought real which are discovered by the most near and exact survey.

Hyl. Right.

Phil. Is the nearest and exactest survey made by the help of a microscope, or by the naked eye?

Hyl. By a microscope, doubtless.

Phil. But a microscope often discovers colours in an object different from those perceived by the unassisted sight. And, in case we had microscopes magnifying to any assigned degree, it is certain that no object whatsoever, viewed through them, would appear in the same colour which it exhibits to the naked eye.

Hyl. And what will you conclude from all this? You cannot argue that there are really and naturally no colours on objects: because by artificial managements they may be altered, or made to vanish.

Phil. I think it may evidently be concluded from your own concessions, that all the colours we see with our naked eyes are only apparent as those on the clouds, since they vanish upon a more close and accurate inspection which is afforded us by a microscope. Then, as to what you say by way of prevention: I ask you whether the real and natural state of an object is better discovered by a very sharp and piercing sight, or by one which is less sharp?

Hyl. By the former without doubt.

Phil. Is it not plain from *Dioptrics* that microscopes make the sight more penetrating, and represent objects as they would appear to the eye in case it were naturally endowed with a most exquisite sharpness?

Hyl. It is.

Phil. Consequently the microscopical representation is to be thought that which best sets forth the real nature of the thing, or what it is in itself. The colours, therefore, by it perceived are more genuine and real than those perceived otherwise.

Hyl. I confess there is something in what you say.

Phil. Besides, it is not only possible but manifest, that there actually are animals whose eyes are by nature framed to perceive those things which by reason of their minuteness escape our sight. What think you of those inconceivably small animals perceived by glasses? must we suppose they are all stark blind? Or, in case they see, can it be imagined their sight hath not the same use in preserving their bodies from injuries, which appears in that of all other animals? And if it hath, is it not evident they must see particles less than their own bodies, which will present them with a far different view in each object from that which strikes our senses? Even our own eyes do not always represent objects to us after the same manner. In the *jaundice* every one knows that all things seem yellow. Is it not therefore highly probable those animals in whose eyes we discern a very different texture from that of ours. and whose bodies abound with different humours, do not see the same colours in every object that we do? From all which, should it not seem to follow that all colours are equally apparent, and that none of those which we perceive are really inherent in any outward object?

Hyl. It should.

Phil. The point will be past all doubt, if you consider that, in case colours were real properties or affections inherent in external bodies, they could admit of no alteration without some change wrought in the very bodies themselves: but, is it not evident from what hath been said that, upon the use of microscopes, upon a change happening in the humours of the eye, or a variation of distance, without any manner of real alteration in the thing itself, the colours of any object are either changed, or totally disappear? Nay, all other circumstances remaining the same, change but the situation of some objects, and they shall present different colours to the eye. The same thing happens upon viewing an object in various degrees of light. And what is more known than that the same bodies appear differently coloured by candlelight from what they do in the open day? Add to these the experiment of a prism which, separating the heterogeneous rays of light, alters the colour of any object, and will cause the whitest to appear of a deep blue or red to the naked eye. And now tell me whether you are still of opinion that every body hath its true real colour inhering in it; and, if you think it hath, I would fain know farther from you, what certain distance and position of the object, what peculiar texture and formation of the eye, what degree or kind of light is necessary for ascertaining that true colour, and distinguishing it from apparent ones.

Hyl. I own myself entirely satisfied, that they are all equally apparent, and that there is no such thing as colour really inhering in external bodies. . . . Light and colours, as immediately perceived by us, I grant cannot exist without the mind. But, in themselves they are only the motions and configurations of certain insensible particles of matter.

Phil. Colours, then, in the vulgar sense, or taken for the immediate objects of sight, cannot agree to any but a perceiving substance.

Hyl. That is what I say.

Phil. Well then, since you give up the point as to those sensible qualities which are alone thought colours by all mankind beside, you may hold what you please with regard to those invisible ones of the philosophers. It is not my business to dispute about them; only I would advise you to bethink yourself, whether, considering the inquiry we are upon, it be prudent for you to affirm—*the red and blue which we see are not real colours, but certain unknown motions and figures, which no man ever did or can see, are truly so.* Are not these shocking notions, and are not they subject to as many ridiculous inferences, as those you were obliged to renounce before? . . .

Hyl. I frankly own, *Philonous*, that it is in vain to stand out any longer. Colours, sounds, tastes, in a word all those termed *secondary qualities,* have certainly no existence without the mind. But, by this acknowledgment I must not be supposed to derogate anything from the reality of Matter or external objects; seeing it is no more than several philosophers maintain, who nevertheless are the farthest imaginable from denying Matter. For the clearer understanding of this, you must know sensible qualities are by philosophers divided into *primary* and *secondary.* The former are

Extension, Figure, Solidity, Gravity, Motion, and Rest. And these they hold exist really in bodies. The latter are those above enumerated; or, briefly, all sensible qualities beside the Primary, which they assert are only so many sensations or ideas existing nowhere but in the mind. But all this, I doubt not, you are apprised of. For my part, I have been a long time sensible there was such an opinion current among philosophers, but was never thoroughly convinced of its truth until now.

Phil. You are still then of opinion that *extension* and *figures* are inherent in external unthinking substances?

Hyl. I am.

Phil. But what if the same arguments which are brought against Secondary Qualities will hold good against these also?

Hyl. Why then I shall be obliged to think, they too exist only in the mind.

Phil. Is it your opinion the very figure and extension which you perceive by sense exist in the outward object or material substance?

Hyl. It is.

Phil. Have all other animals as good grounds to think the same of the figure and extension which they see and feel?

Hyl. Without doubt, if they have any thought at all.

Phil. Answer me, *Hylas.* Think you the senses were bestowed upon all animals for their preservation and well-being in life? or were they given to men alone for this end?

Hyl. I make no question but they have the same use in all other animals.

Phil. If so, is it not necessary they should be enabled by them to perceive their own limbs, and those bodies which are capable of harming them?

Hyl. Certainly.

Phil. A mite therefore must be supposed to see his own foot, and things equal or even less than it, as bodies of some considerable dimension; though at the same time they appear to you scarce discernible, or at best as so many visible points?

Hyl. I cannot deny it.

Phil. And to creatures less than the mite they will seem yet larger?

Hyl. They will.

Phil. Insomuch that what you can hardly discern will to another extremely minute animal appear as some huge mountain?

Hyl. All this I grant.

Phil. Can one and the same thing be at the same time in itself of different dimensions?

Hyl. That were absurd to imagine.

Phil. But, from what you have laid down it follows that both the extension by you perceived, and that perceived by the mite itself, as likewise all those perceived by lesser animals, are each of them the true extension of the mite's foot; that is to say, by your own principles you are led into an absurdity.

Hyl. There seems to be some difficulty in the point.

Phil. Again, have you not acknowledged that no real inherent property of any object can be changed without some change in the thing itself?

Hyl. I have.

Phil. But, as we approach to or recede from an object, the visible extension varies, being at one distance ten or a hundred times greater than at another. Doth it not therefore follow from hence likewise that it is not really inherent in the object?

Hyl. I own I am at a loss what to think.

Phil. Your judgment will soon be determined, if you will venture to think as freely concerning this quality as you have done concerning the rest. Was it not admitted as a good argument, that neither heat nor cold was in the water, because it seemed warm to one hand and cold to the other?

Hyl. It was.

Phil. Is it not the very same reasoning to conclude there is no extension or figure in an object, because to one eye it shall seem little, smooth, and round, when at the same time it appears to the other, great, uneven, and angular?

Hyl. The very same. But does this latter fact ever happen?

Phil. You may at any time make the experiment, by looking with one eye bare, and with the other through a microscope.

Hyl. I know not how to maintain it, and yet I am loath to give up *extension*, I see so many odd consequences following upon such a concession.

Phil. Odd, say you? After the concessions already made, I hope you will stick at nothing for its oddness.

Hyl. I give up the point for the present, reserving still a right to retract my opinion, in case I shall hereafter discover any false step in my progress to it.

Phil. That is a right you cannot be denied. Figures and extension being despatched, we proceed next to *motion*. Can a real motion in any external body be at the same time both very swift and very slow?

Hyl. It cannot.

Phil. Is not the motion of a body swift in a reciprocal proportion to the time it takes up in describing any given space? Thus a body that describes a mile in an hour moves three times faster than it would in case it described only a mile in three hours.

Hyl. I agree with you.

Phil. And is not time measured by the succession of ideas in our minds?

Hyl. It is.

Phil. And is it not possible ideas should succeed one another twice as fast in your mind as they do in mine, or in that of some spirit of another kind?

Hyl. I own it.

Phil. Consequently, the same body may to another seem to perform its motion over any space in half the time that it doth to you. And the same reasoning will hold as to any other proportion: that is to say, according to your principles (since the motions perceived are both really in the object) it is possible one and the same body shall be really moved the same way at once, both very swift and very slow. How is this consistent either with common sense, or with what you just now granted?

Hyl. I have nothing to say to it.

Phil. Then as for *solidity;* either you do not mean any sensible quality by that word, and so it is beside our inquiry: or if you do, it must be either hardness or resistance. But both the one and the other are plainly relative to our senses: it being evident that what seems hard to one animal may appear soft to another, who hath greater force and firmness of limbs. Nor is it less plain that the resistance I feel is not in the body.

Hyl. I own the very sensation of resistance, which is all you immediately perceive, is not in the *body,* but the cause of that sensation is.

Phil. But the causes of our sensations are not things immediately perceived, and therefore not sensible. This point I thought had been already determined.

Hyl. I own it was; but you will pardon me if I seem a little embarrassed: I know not how to quit my old notions.

Phil. To help you out, do but consider that if *extension* be once acknowledged to have no existence without the mind, the same must necessarily be granted of motion, solidity, and gravity—since they all evidently suppose extension. It is therefore superfluous to inquire particularly concerning each of them. In denying extension, you have denied them all to have any real existence. . . .

Hyl. It is just come into my head, *Philonous,* that I have somewhere heard of a distinction between absolute and sensible extension. Now, though it be acknowledged that *great* and *small,* consisting merely in the relation which other extended beings have to the parts of our own bodies, do not really inhere in the Substances themselves; yet nothing obliges us to hold the same with regard to *absolute extension*, which is something abstracted from *great* and *small*, from this or that particular magnitude or figure. So likewise as to motion; *swift* and *slow* are altogether relative to the succession of ideas in our own minds. But, it doth not follow, because those modifications of motion exist not without the mind, that therefore absolute motion abstracted from them doth not.

Phil. Pray what is it that distinguishes one motion, or one part of extension, from another? Is it not something sensible, as some degree of swiftness or slowness, some certain magnitude or figure peculiar to each?

Hyl. I think so.

Phil. These qualities, therefore, stripped of all sensible properties, are without all specific and numerical differences, as the schools call them.

Hyl. They are.

Phil. That is to say, they are extension in general, and motion in general.

Hyl. Let it be so.

Phil. But it is a universally received maxim that *Everything which exists is particular*. How then can motion in general, or extension in general, exist in any corporeal Substance?

Hyl. I will take time to solve your difficulty.

Phil. But I think the point may be speedily decided. Without doubt you can tell whether you are able to frame this or that idea. Now I am content to put our dispute on this issue. If you can frame in your thoughts a distinct abstract idea of motion or extension; divested of all those sensible modes, as swift and slow, great and small, round and square, and the like, which are acknowledged to exist only in the mind, I will then yield the point you contend for. But, if you cannot, it will be unreasonable on your side to insist any longer upon what you have no notion of.

Hyl. To confess ingenuously, I cannot.

Phil. Can you even separate the ideas of extension and motion from the ideas of all those qualities which they who make the distinction term *secondary?*

Hyl. What! is it not an easy matter to consider extension and motion by themselves, abstracted from all other sensible qualities? Pray how do the mathematicians treat of them?

Phil. I acknowledge, *Hylas*, it is not difficult to form general propositions and reasonings about those qualities, without mentioning any other; and, in this sense, to consider or treat of them abstractedly. But, how doth it follow that, because I can pronounce the word *motion* by itself, I can form the idea of it in my mind exclusive of body? Or, because theorems may be made of extension and figures, without any mention of *great* or *small,* or any other sensible mode or quality, that therefore it is possible such an abstract idea of extension, without any particular size or figure, or sensible quality, should be distinctly formed, and apprehended by the mind? Mathematicians treat of quantity, without regarding what other sensible qualities it is attended with, as being altogether indifferent to their demonstrations. But, when laying aside the words, they contemplate the bare ideas, I believe you will find, they are not the pure abstracted ideas of extension. . . . but, for your farther satisfaction, try if you can frame the idea of any figure, abstracted from all particularities of size, or even from other sensible qualities.

Hyl. Let me think a little——I do not find that I can.

Phil. And can you think it possible that should really exist in nature which implies a repugnancy in its conception?

Hyl. By no means.

Phil. Since therefore it is impossible even for the mind to disunite the ideas of extension and motion from all other sensible qualities, doth it not follow, that where the one exist there necessarily the other exist likewise?

Hyl. It should seem so.

Phil. Consequently, the very same arguments which you admitted as conclusive against the Secondary Qualities are, without any farther application of force, against the Primary too. Besides, if you will trust your senses, is it not plain all sensible qualities coexist, or to them appear as being in the same place? Do they ever represent a motion, or figure, as being divested of all other visible and tangible qualities?

Hyl. You need say no more on this head. I am free to own, if there be no secret error or oversight in our proceedings hitherto, that all sensible qualities are alike to be denied existence without the mind. But, my fear is that I have been too liberal in my former concessions, or overlooked some fallacy or other. In short, I did not take time to think.

Phil. For that matter, *Hylas,* you may take what time you please in reviewing the progress of our inquiry. You are at liberty to recover any slips you might have made, or offer whatever you have omitted which makes for your first opinion.

Hyl. One great oversight I take to be this—that I did not sufficiently distinguish the *object* from the *sensation.* Now, though this latter may not exist without the mind, yet it will not thence follow that the former cannot.

Phil. What object do you mean? The object of the senses?

Hyl. The same.

Phil. It is then immediately perceived?

Hyl. Right.

Phil. Make me to understand the difference between what is immediately perceived, and a sensation.

Hyl. The sensation I take to be an act of the mind perceiving; besides which, there is something perceived; and this I call the *object*. For example, there is red and yellow on that tulip. But then the act of perceiving those colours is in me only, and not in the tulip.

Phil. What tulip do you speak of? Is it that which you see?

Hyl. The same.

Phil. And what do you see beside colour, figure, and extension?

Hyl. Nothing.

Phil. What you would say then is that the red and yellow are co-existent with the extension; is it not?

Hyl. That is not all; I would say they have a real existence without the mind, in some unthinking substance.

Phil. That the colours are really in the tulip which I see is manifest. Neither can it be denied that this tulip may exist independent of your mind or mine; but, that any immediate object of the senses —that is, any idea, or combination of ideas—should exist in an unthinking substance, or exterior to all minds, is in itself an evident contradiction. Nor can I imagine how this follows from what you said just now, to wit, that the red and yellow were on the tulip *you saw,* since you do not pretend to *see* that unthinking substance.

Hyl. You have an artful way, *Philonous,* of diverting our inquiry from the subject.

Phil. I see you have no mind to be pressed that way. To return then to your distinction between *sensation* and *object;* if I take you right, you distinguish in every perception two things, the one an action of the mind, the other not.

Hyl. True.

Phil. And this action cannot exist in, or belong to, any unthinking thing; but, whatever beside is implied in a perception may?

Hyl. That is my meaning.

Phil. So that if there was a perception without any act of the mind, it were possible such a perception should exist in an unthinking substance?

Hyl. I grant it. But it is impossible there should be such a perception.

Phil. When is the mind said to be active?

Hyl. When it produces, puts an end to, or changes, anything.

Phil. Can the mind produce, discontinue, or change anything, but by an act of the will?

Hyl. It cannot.

Phil. The mind therefore is to be accounted *active* in its perceptions so far forth as *volition* is included in them?

Hyl. It is.

Phil. In plucking this flower I am active; because I do it by the motion of my hand, which was consequent upon my volition; so likewise in applying it to my nose. But is either of these smelling?

Hyl. No.

Phil. I act too in drawing the air through my nose; because my breathing so rather than otherwise is the effect of my volition. But neither can this be called *smelling:* for, if it were, I should smell every time I breathed in that manner?

Hyl. True.

Phil. Smelling then is somewhat consequent to all this?

Hyl. It is.

Phil. But I do not find my will concerned any farther. Whatever more there is—as that I perceive such a particular smell, or any smell at all—this is independent of my will, and therein I am altogether passive. Do you find it otherwise with you, *Hylas?*

Hyl. No, the very same.

Phil. Then, as to seeing, is it not in your power to open your eyes, or keep them shut; to turn them this or that way?

Hyl. Without doubt.

Phil. But, doth it in like manner depend on your will that in look-ing on this flower you perceive *white* rather than any other colour? Or, directing your open eyes towards yonder part of the heaven, can you avoid seeing the sun? Or is light or darkness the effect of your volition?

Hyl. No certainly.

Phil. You are then in these respects altogether passive?

Hyl. I am.

Phil. Tell me now, whether *seeing* consists in perceiving light and colours, or in opening and turning the eyes?

Hyl. Without doubt, in the former.

Phil. Since therefore you are in the very perception of light and colours altogether passive, what is become of that action you were speaking of as an ingredient in every sensation? And, doth it not follow from your own concessions, that the perception of light and colours, including no action in it, may exist in an unperceiving substance? And is not this a plain contradiction?

Hyl. I know not what to think of it.

Phil. Besides, since you distinguish the *active* and *passive* in every perception, you must do it in that of pain. But how is it possible that pain, be it as little active as you please, should exist in an unperceiving substance? In short, do but consider the point, and then confess ingenuously, whether light and colours, tastes, sounds, &c., are not all equally passions or sensations in the soul. You may indeed call them *external objects,* and give them in words what subsistence you please. But, examine your own thoughts, and then tell me whether it be not as I say?

Hyl. I acknowledge, *Philonous,* that, upon a fair observation of what passes in my mind, I can discover nothing else but that I am a thinking being, affected with variety of sensations; neither is it possible to conceive how a sensation should exist in an unperceiving substance. . . . But still I fear there is some fallacy or other. Pray what think you of this? It is just come into my head that the ground of all our mistake lies in your treating of each quality by itself. Now, I grant that each quality cannot singly subsist without the mind. Colour cannot without extension, neither can figure without some other sensible quality. But, as the several qualities united or blended together form entire sensible things, nothing hinders why such things may not be supposed to exist without the mind.

Phil. Either, *Hylas,* you are jesting, or have a very bad memory. Though indeed we went through all the qualities by name one after another; yet my arguments, or rather your concessions, nowhere tended to prove that the Secondary Qualities did not subsist each alone by itself; but, that they were not *at all* without the mind. Indeed, in treating of figure and motion we concluded they could not exist without the mind, because it was impossible even in thought to separate them from all secondary qualities, so as to conceive them existing by themselves. But then this was not the only argument made use of upon that occasion. But (to pass by all that hath been hitherto said, and reckon it for nothing, if you will have it so) I am content to put the whole upon this issue. If you can conceive it possible for any mixture or combination of qualities, or any sensible object whatever, to exist without the mind, then I will grant it actually to be so.

Hyl. If it comes to that the point will soon be decided. What more easy than to conceive a tree or house existing by itself, independent of, and unperceived by, any mind whatsoever? I do at this present time conceive them existing after that manner.

Phil. How say you, *Hylas,* can you see a thing which is at the same time unseen?

Hyl. No, that were a contradiction.

Phil. Is it not as great a contradiction to talk of *conceiving* a thing which is *unconceived?*

Hyl. It is.

Phil. The tree or house therefore which you think of is conceived by you?

Hyl. How should it be otherwise?

Phil. And what is conceived is surely in the mind?

Hyl. Without question, that which is conceived is in the mind.

Phil. How then came you to say, you conceived a house or tree existing independent and out of all minds whatsoever?

Hyl. That was I own an oversight; but stay, let me consider what led me into it.—It is a pleasant mistake enough. As I was thinking of a tree in a solitary place where no one was present to see it, methought that was to conceive a tree as existing unperceived or unthought of—not considering that I myself conceived it all the while. But now I plainly see that all I can do is to frame ideas in my own mind. I may indeed conceive in my own thoughts the idea of a a tree, or a house, or a mountain, but that is all. And this is far from proving that I can conceive them *existing out of the minds of all Spirits.*

Phil. You acknowledge then that you cannot possibly conceive how any one corporeal sensible thing should exist otherwise than in a mind?

Hyl. I do.

Phil. And yet you will earnestly contend for the truth of that which you cannot so much as conceive? . . .

Hyl. To speak the truth, *Philonous,* I think there are two kinds of objects:—the one perceived immediately, which are likewise called *ideas;* the other are real things or external objects, perceived by the mediation of ideas, which are their images and representations. Now, I own ideas do not exist without the mind; but the latter sort of objects do. I am sorry I did not think of this distinction sooner; it would probably have cut short your discourse.

Phil. Are those external objects perceived by sense, or by some other faculty?

Hyl. They are perceived by sense.

Phil. How! is there anything perceived by sense which is not immediately perceived?

Hyl. Yes, *Philonous,* in some sort there is. For example, when I look on a picture or statue of Julius Cæsar, I may be said after a manner to perceive him (though not immediately) by my senses.

Phil. It seems then you will have our ideas, which alone are immediately perceived, to be pictures of external things: and that these also are perceived by sense, inasmuch as they have a conformity or resemblance to our ideas?

Hyl. That is my meaning.

Phil. And, in the same way that Julius Cæsar, in himself invisible, is nevertheless perceived by sight; real things, in themselves imperceptible, are perceived by sense.

Hyl. In the very same.

Phil. Tell me, *Hylas,* when you behold the picture of Julius Cæsar, do you see with your eyes any more than some colours and figures, with a certain symmetry and composition of the whole?

Hyl. Nothing else.

Phil. And would not a man who had never known anything of Julius Cæsar see as much?

Hyl. He would.

Phil. Consequently he hath his sight, and the use of it, in as perfect a degree as you?

Hyl. I agree with you.

Phil. Whence comes it then that your thoughts are directed to the Roman emperor, and his are not? This cannot proceed from the sensations or ideas of sense by you then perceived; since you acknowledge you have no advantage over him in that respect. It should seem therefore to proceed from reason and memory: should it not?

Hyl. It should.

Phil. Consequently, it will not follow from that instance that anything is perceived by sense which is not immediately perceived. Though I grant we may, in one acceptation, be said to perceive sensible things mediately by sense—that is, when, from a frequently perceived connexion, the immediate perception of ideas by one sense suggests to the mind others, perhaps belonging to another sense, which are wont to be connected with them. For instance, when I hear a coach drive along the streets, immediately I perceive only the sound; but, from the experience I have had that such a sound is connected with a coach, I am said to hear the coach. It is nevertheless evident that, in truth and strictness, nothing can be *heard* but *sound;* and the coach is not then properly perceived by sense, but suggested from experience. So likewise when we are said to see a red-hot bar of iron; the solidity and heat of the iron are not the objects of sight, but suggested to the imagination by the colour and figure which are properly perceived by that sense. In short, those things alone are actually and strictly perceived by any sense, which would have been perceived in case that same sense had then been first conferred on us. As for other things, it is plain they are only suggested to the mind by experience, grounded on former perceptions. But, to return to your comparison of Cæsar's picture, it is plain, if you keep to that, you must hold the real things or archetypes of our ideas are not perceived by sense, but by some internal faculty of the soul, as reason or memory. I would therefore fain know what arguments you can draw from reason for the existence of what you call *real things* or *material objects*. Or, whether you remember to have seen them formerly as they are in themselves; or, if you have heard or read of any one that did.

Hyl. I see, *Philonous,* you are disposed to raillery; but that will never convince me.

Phil. My aim is only to learn from you the way to come at the knowledge of *material beings.* Whatever we perceive is perceived immediately or mediately: by sense; or by reason and reflection. But, as you have excluded sense, pray shew me what reason you have to believe their existence; or what *medium* you can possibly make use of to prove it, either to mine or your own understanding.

Hyl. To deal ingenuously, *Philonous,* now I consider the point, I do not find I can give you any good reason for it. But, thus much seems pretty plain, that it is at least possible such things may really exist. And, as long as there is no absurdity in supposing them, I am resolved to believe as I did, till you bring good reasons to the contrary.

Phil. What! is it come to this, that you only believe the existence of material objects, and that your belief is founded barely on the possibility of its being true? Then you will have me bring reasons against it: though another would think it reasonable the proof should lie on him who holds the affirmative. And, after all, this very point which you are now resolved to maintain, without any reason, is in effect what you have more than once during this discourse seen good reason to give up. But, to pass over all this; if I understand you rightly, you say our ideas do not exist without the mind; but that they are copies, images, or representations, of certain originals that do?

Hyl. You take me right.

Phil. They are then like external things?

Hyl. They are.

Phil. Have those things a stable and permanent nature, independent of our senses; or are they in a perpetual change, upon our

producing any motions in our bodies, suspending, exerting, or altering, our faculties or organs of sense?

Hyl. Real things, it is plain, have a fixed and real nature, which
remains the same notwithstanding any change in our senses, or in the
posture and motion of our bodies; which indeed may affect the ideas
in our minds, but it were absurd to think they had the same effect
on things existing without the mind.

Phil. How then is it possible that things perpetually fleeting and
variable as our ideas should be copies or images of anything fixed
and constant? Or, in other words, since all sensible qualities, as size,
figure, colour, &c., that is, our ideas, are continually changing upon
every alteration in the distance, medium, or instruments of sensation; how can any determinate material objects be properly represented or painted forth by several distinct things, each of which is
so different from and unlike the rest? Or, if you say it resembles
some one only of our ideas, how shall we be able to distinguish
the true copy from all the false ones?

Hyl. I profess, *Philonous,* I am at a loss. I know not what to say
to this.

Phil. But neither is this all. Which are material objects in themselves—perceptible or imperceptible?

Hyl. Properly and immediately nothing can be perceived but ideas.
All material things, therefore, are in themselves insensible, and to
be perceived only by our ideas.

Phil. Ideas then are sensible, and their archetypes or originals insensible?

Hyl. Right.

Phil. But how can that which is sensible be like that which is insensible? Can a real thing, in itself *invisible,* be like a *colour;* or a
real thing, which is not *audible,* be like a *sound?* In a word, can
anything be like a sensation or idea, but another sensation or idea?

Hyl. I must own, I think not.

Phil. Is it possible there should be any doubt on the point? Do you
not perfectly know your own ideas?

Hyl. I know them perfectly; since what I do not perceive or
know can be no part of my idea.

Phil. Consider, therefore, and examine them, and then tell me
if there be anything in them which can exist without the mind? or
if you can conceive anything like them existing without the mind?

Hyl. Upon inquiry, I find it is impossible for me to conceive or
understand how anything but an idea can be like an idea. And it is
most evident that *no idea can exist without the mind.*

Phil. You are therefore, by our principles, forced to deny the reality of sensible things; since you made it to consist in an absolute existence exterior to the mind. That is to say, you are a downright sceptic. So I have gained my point, which was to shew your principles led to Scepticism.

Hyl. For the present I am, if not entirely convinced, at least silenced.

5

METHODS OF BECOMING CONVINCED *

by

CHARLES SANDERS PEIRCE

(1839–1914)

Few persons care to study logic, because everybody conceives himself to be proficient enough in the art of reasoning already. But I observe that this satisfaction is limited to one's own ratiocination, and does not extend to that of other men.

We come to the full possession of our power of drawing inferences, the last of all our faculties; for it is not so much a natural gift as a long and difficult art. The history of its practice would make a grand subject for a book. The medieval schoolmen, following the Romans, made logic the earliest of a boy's studies after grammar, as being

* [The greater part of the article "The Fixation of Belief," originally printed in *Popular Science Monthly* (1877)]

very easy. So it was as they understood it. Its fundamental principle, according to them, was, that all knowledge rests either on authority or reason; but that whatever is deduced by reason depends ultimately on a premiss derived from authority. Accordingly, as soon as a boy was perfect in the syllogistic procedure, his intellectual kit of tools was held to be complete.

To Roger Bacon, that remarkable mind who in the middle of the thirteenth century was almost a scientific man, the schoolmen's conception of reasoning appeared only an obstacle to truth. He saw that experience alone teaches anything—a proposition which to us seems easy to understand, because a distinct conception of experience has been handed down to us from former generations; which to him likewise seemed perfectly clear, because its difficulties had not yet unfolded themselves. Of all kinds of experience, the best, he thought, was interior illumination, which teaches many things about Nature which the external senses could never discover, such as the transubstantiation of bread.

Four centuries later, the more celebrated Bacon, in the first book of his *Novum Organum,* gave his clear account of experience as something which must be open to verification and reëxamination. But, superior as Lord Bacon's conception is to earlier notions, a modern reader who is not in awe of his grandiloquence is chiefly struck by the inadequacy of his view of scientific procedure. That we have only to make some crude experiments, to draw up briefs of the results in certain blank forms, to go through these by rule, checking off everything disproved and setting down the alternatives, and that thus in a few years physical science would be finished up —what an idea! "He wrote on science like a Lord Chancellor," indeed, as Harvey, a genuine man of science, said.

The early scientists, Copernicus, Tycho Brahe, Kepler, Galileo, Harvey, and Gilbert, had methods more like those of their modern brethren. Kepler undertook to draw a curve through the places of Mars, and to state the times occupied by the planet in describing the different parts of that curve; but perhaps his greatest service to science was in impressing on men's minds that this was the thing to be done if they wished to improve astronomy; that they were not to content themselves with inquiring whether one system of epicycles was better than another but that they were to sit down to the figures and find out what the curve, in truth, was. . . .

In the same way, every work of science great enough to be well remembered for a few generations affords some exemplification of the defective state of the art of reasoning of the time when it was written; and each chief step in science has been a lesson in logic. It was so when Lavoisier and his contemporaries took up the study of Chemistry. The old chemist's maxim had been, "Lege, lege, lege, labora, ora, et relege." Lavoisier's method was not to read and pray, but to dream that some long and complicated chemical process would have a certain effect, to put it into practice with dull patience, after its inevitable failure, to dream that with some modification it would have another result, and to end by publishing the last dream as a fact: his way was to carry his mind into his laboratory, and literally to make of his alembics and cucurbits instruments of thought, giving a new conception of reasoning as something which was to be done with one's eyes open, in manipulating real things instead of words and fancies. . . .

The object of reasoning is to find out, from the consideration of what we already know, something else which we do not know. Consequently, reasoning is good if it be such as to give a true conclusion from true premisses, and not otherwise. Thus, the question of validity is purely one of fact and not of thinking. A being the facts stated in the premisses and B being that concluded, the question is, whether these facts are really so related that if A were B would generally be. If so, the inference is valid; if not, not. It is not in the least the question whether, when the premisses are accepted by the mind, we feel an impulse to accept the conclusion also. It is true that we do generally reason correctly by nature. But that is an accident; the true conclusion would remain true if we had no impulse to accept it; and the false one would remain false, though we could not resist the tendency to believe in it.

We are, doubtless, in the main logical animals, but we are not perfectly so. Most of us, for example, are naturally more sanguine and hopeful than logic would justify. We seem to be so constituted that in the absence of any facts to go upon we are happy and self-satisfied; so that the effect of experience is continually to contract our hopes and aspirations. Yet a lifetime of the application of this corrective does not usually eradicate our sanguine disposition. Where hope is unchecked by any experience, it is likely that our optimism is extravagant. Logicality in regard to practical matters (if this be understood, not in the old sense, but as consisting in a wise union of security with fruitfulness of reasoning) is the most useful quality an animal can possess, and might, therefore, result from the action of natural selection; but outside of these it is probably of more advantage to the animal to have his mind filled with pleasing and encouraging visions, independently of their truth; and thus, upon unpractical subjects, natural selection might occasion a fallacious tendency of thought.

That which determines us, from given premisses, to draw one inference rather than another, is some habit of mind, whether it be constitutional or acquired. The habit is good or otherwise, according as it produces true conclusions from true premises or not; and an inference is regarded as valid or not, without reference to the truth or falsity of its conclusion specially, but according as the habit which determines it is such as to produce true conclusions in general or not. The particular habit of mind which governs this or that inference may be formulated in a proposition whose truth depends on the validity of the inferences which the habit determines; and such a formula is called a *guiding principle* of inference. Suppose, for example, that we observe that a rotating disk of copper quickly comes to rest when placed between the poles of a magnet, and we infer that this will happen with every disk of copper. The guiding principle is, that what is true of one piece of copper is true of another. Such a guiding principle with regard to copper would be much safer than with regard to many other substances—brass, for example.

A book might be written to signalize all the most important of these guiding principles of reasoning. It would probably be, we must confess, of no service to a person whose thought is directed wholly to practical subjects, and whose activity moves along thor- oughly-beaten paths. The problems that present themselves to such a mind are matters of routine which he has learned once for all to handle in learning his business. But let a man venture into an un- familiar field, or where his results are not continually checked by experience, and all history shows that the most masculine intellect will ofttimes lose his orientation and waste his efforts in directions which bring him no nearer to his goal, or even carry him entirely astray. He is like a ship in the open sea, with no one on board who understands the rules of navigation. And in such a case some gen- eral study of the guiding principles of reasoning would be sure to be found useful.

The subject could hardly be treated, however, without being first limited; since almost any fact may serve as a guiding principle. But it so happens that there exists a division among facts, such that in one class are all those which are absolutely essential as guiding principles, while in the others are all which have any other interest as objects of research. This division is between those which are necessarily taken for granted in asking why a certain conclusion is thought to follow from certain premises, and those which are not implied in such a question. A moment's thought will show that a variety of facts are already assumed when the logical question is first asked. It is implied, for instance, that there are such states of mind as doubt and belief—that a passage from one to the other is pos- sible, the object of thought remaining the same, and that this transition is subject to some rules by which all minds are alike bound. As these are facts which we must already know before we can have any clear conception of reasoning at all, it cannot be supposed to be any longer of much interest to inquire into their truth or falsity. On the other hand, it is easy to believe that those rules of reasoning which are deduced from the very idea of the process are the ones which are the most essential; and, indeed, that so long as it conforms to these it will, at least, not lead to false conclusions from true premises. In point of fact, the importance of what may be deduced from the assumptions involved in the logical question turns out to be greater than might be supposed, and this for reasons which it is difficult to exhibit at the outset. The only one which I shall here mention is, that conceptions which are really products of logical reflection, without being readily seen to be so, mingle with our ordinary thoughts, and are frequently the causes of great confusion. This is the case, for example, with the conception of quality. A quality, as such, is never an object of observation. We can see that a thing is blue or green, but the quality of being blue and the quality of being green are not things which we see; they are products of logical reflections. The truth is, that common-sense, or thought as it first emerges above the level of the narrowly practical, is deeply imbued with that bad logical quality to which the epithet *metaphysical* is commonly applied; and nothing can clear it up but a severe course of logic.

We generally know when we wish to ask a question and when we wish to pronounce a judgment, for there is a dissimilarity between the sensation of doubting and that of believing.

But this is not all which distinguishes doubt from belief. There is a practical difference. Our beliefs guide our desires and shape our actions. The Assassins, or followers of the Old Man of the Mountain, used to rush into death at his least command, because they believed that obedience to him would insure everlasting felicity. Had they doubted this, they would not have acted as they did. So it is with every belief, according to its degree. The feeling of believing is a more or less sure indication of there being established in our nature some habit which will determine our actions. Doubt never has such an effect.

Nor must we overlook a third point of difference. Doubt is an uneasy and dissatisfied state from which we struggle to free ourselves and pass into the state of belief; while the latter is a calm and satisfactory state which we do not wish to avoid, or to change to a belief in anything else. On the contrary, we cling tenaciously, not merely to believing, but to believing just what we do believe.

Thus, both doubt and belief have positive effects upon us, though very different ones. Belief does not make us act at once, but puts us into such a condition that we shall behave in some certain way, when the occasion arises. Doubt has not the least such active effect, but stimulates us to inquiry until it is destroyed. This reminds us of the irritation of a nerve and the reflex action produced thereby; while for the analogue of belief, in the nervous system, we must look to what are called nervous associations—for example, to that habit of the nerves in consequence of which the smell of a peach will make the mouth water.

The irritation of doubt causes a struggle to attain a state of belief. I shall term this struggle *Inquiry*, though it must be admitted that this is sometimes not a very apt designation.

The irritation of doubt is the only immediate motive for the struggle to attain belief. It is certainly best for us that our beliefs should be such as may truly guide our actions so as to satisfy our desires; and this reflection will make us reject every belief which does not seem to have been so formed as to insure this result. But it will only do so by creating a doubt in the place of that belief. With the doubt, therefore, the struggle begins, and with the cessation of doubt it ends. Hence, the sole object of inquiry is the settlement of opinion. We may fancy that this is not enough for us, and that we seek, not merely an opinion, but a true opinion. But put this fancy to the test, and it proves groundless; for as soon as a firm belief is reached we are entirely satisfied, whether the belief be true or false. And it is clear that nothing out of the sphere of our knowledge can be our object, for nothing which does not affect the mind can be the motive for mental effort. The most that can be maintained is, that we seek for a belief that we shall *think* to be true. But we think each one of our beliefs to be true, and, indeed, it is mere tautology to say so.

That the settlement of opinion is the sole end of inquiry is a very important proposition. It sweeps away, at once, various vague and erroneous conceptions of proof. A few of these may be noticed here.

1. Some philosophers have imagined that to start an inquiry it was only necessary to utter a question whether orally or by setting it down upon paper, and have even recommended us to begin our studies with questioning everything! But the mere putting of a proposition into the interrogative form does not stimulate the mind to any struggle after belief. There must be a real and living doubt, and without this all discussion is idle.

2. It is a very common idea that a demonstration must rest on some ultimate and absolutely indubitable propositions. These, according to one school, are first principles of a general nature; according to another, are first sensations. But, in point of fact, an inquiry,

to have that completely satisfactory result called demonstration, has only to start with propositions perfectly free from all actual doubt. If the premisses are not in fact doubted at all, they cannot be more satisfactory than they are.

3. Some people seem to love to argue a point after all the world is fully convinced of it. But no further advance can be made. When doubt ceases, mental action on the subject comes to an end; and, if it did go on, it would be without a purpose.

If the settlement of opinion is the sole object of inquiry, and if belief is of the nature of a habit, why should we not attain the desired end, by taking as answer to a question any we may fancy, and constantly reiterating it to ourselves, dwelling on all which may conduce to that belief, and learning to turn with contempt and hatred from anything that might disturb it? This simple and direct method is really pursued by many men. I remember once being entreated not to read a certain newspaper lest it might change my opinion upon free-trade. "Lest I might be entrapped by its fallacies and misstatements," was the form of expression. "You are not," my friend said, "a special student of political economy. You might, therefore, easily be deceived by fallacious arguments upon the subject. You might, then, if you read this paper, be led to believe in protection. But you admit that free-trade is the true doctrine; and you do not wish to believe what is not true." I have often known this system to be deliberately adopted. Still oftener, the instinctive dislike of an undecided state of mind, exaggerated into a vague dread of doubt, makes men cling spasmodically to the views they already take. The man feels that, if he only holds to his belief without wavering, it will be entirely satisfactory. Nor can it be denied that a steady and immovable faith yields great peace of mind. It may, indeed, give rise to inconveniences, as if a man should resolutely continue to believe that fire would not burn him, or that he would be eternally damned if he received his *ingesta* otherwise than through a stomach-pump. But then the man who adopts this method will not allow that its inconveniences are greater than its advantages. He will say, "I hold steadfastly to the truth, and the truth is always wholesome." And in many cases it may very well be that the pleasure he derives from his calm faith overbalances any inconveniences resulting from its deceptive character. Thus, if it be true that death is annihilation, then the man who believes that he will certainly go straight to heaven when he dies, provided he has fulfilled certain simple observances in this life, has a cheap pleasure which will not be followed by the least disappointment. A similar consideration seems to have weight with many persons in religious topics, for we frequently hear it said, "Oh, I could not believe so-and-so, because I should be wretched if I did."

When an ostrich buries its head in the sand as danger approaches, it very likely takes the happiest course. It hides the danger, and then calmly says there is no danger; and, if it feels perfectly sure there is none, why should it raise its head to see? A man may go through life, systematically keeping out of view all that might cause a change in his opinions, and if he only succeeds—basing his method, as he does, on two fundamental psychological laws—I do not see what can be said against his doing so. It would be an egotistical impertinence to object that his procedure is irrational, for that only amounts to saying that his method of settling belief is not ours. He does not propose to himself to be rational, and, indeed, will often talk with scorn of man's weak and illusive reason. So let him think as he pleases.

But this method of fixing belief, which may be called the method of tenacity, will be unable to hold its ground in practice. The social impulse is against it. The man who adopts it will find that other men think differently from him, and it will be apt to occur to him, in some saner moment, that their opinions are quite as good as his own, and this will shake his confidence in his belief. This conception, that another man's thought or sentiment may be equivalent to one's own, is a distinctly new step, and a highly important one. It arises from an impulse too strong in man to be suppressed, without danger of destroying the human species. Unless we make ourselves hermits, we shall necessarily influence each other's opinions; so that the problem becomes how to fix belief, not in the individual merely, but in the community.

Let the will of the state act, then, instead of that of the individual. Let an institution be created which shall have for its object to keep correct doctrines before the attention of the people, to reiterate them perpetually, and to teach them to the young; having at the same time power to prevent contrary doctrines from being taught, advocated, or expressed. Let all possible causes of a change of mind be removed from men's apprehensions. Let them be kept ignorant, lest they should learn of some reason to think otherwise than they do. Let their passions be enlisted, so that they may regard private and unusual opinions with hatred and horror. Then, let all men who reject the established belief be terrified into silence. Let the people turn out and tar-and-feather such men, or let inquisitions be made into the manner of thinking of suspected persons, and when they are found guilty of forbidden beliefs, let them be subjected to some signal punishment. When complete agreement could not otherwise be reached, a general massacre of all who have not thought in a certain way has proved a very effective means of settling opinion in a country. If the power to do this be wanting, let a list of opinions be drawn up, to which no man of the least independence of thought can assent, and let the faithful be required to accept all these propositions, in order to segregate them as radically as possible from the influence of the rest of the world.

This method has, from the earliest times, been one of the chief means of upholding correct theological and political doctrines, and of preserving their universal or catholic character. In Rome, especially, it has been practised from the days of Numa Pompilius to those of Pius Nonus. This is the most perfect example in history; but wherever there is a priesthood—and no religion has been without one—this method has been more or less made use of. Wherever there is an aristocracy, or a guild, or any association of a class of men whose interests depend, or are supposed to depend, on certain propositions, there will be inevitably found some traces of this natural product of social feeling. Cruelties always accompany this system; and when it is consistently carried out, they become atrocities of the most horrible kind in the eyes of any rational man. Nor should this occasion surprise, for the officer of a society does not feel justified in surrendering the interests of that society for the sake of mercy, as he might his own private interests. It is natural, therefore, that sympathy and fellowship should thus produce a most ruthless power.

In judging this method of fixing belief, which may be called the method of authority, we must, in the first place, allow its immeasurable mental and moral superiority to the method of tenacity. Its success is proportionately greater; and, in fact, it has over and over again worked the most majestic results. The mere structures of stone which it has caused to be put together—in Siam, for example, in Egypt, and in Europe—have many of them a sublimity hardly more than rivalled by the greatest works of Nature. And, except the geological epochs, there are no periods of time so vast as those which are measured by some of these organized faiths. If we scrutinize the matter closely, we shall find that there has not been one of their creeds which has remained always the same; yet the change is so slow as to be imperceptible during one person's life, so that individual belief remains sensibly fixed. For the mass of mankind, then, there is perhaps no better method than this. If it is their highest impulse to be intellectual slaves, then slaves they ought to remain.

But no institution can undertake to regulate opinions upon every subject. Only the most important ones can be attended to, and on the rest men's minds must be left to the action of natural causes. This imperfection will be no source of weakness so long as men are in such a state of culture that one opinion does not influence another

—that is, so long as they cannot put two and two together. But in the most priest-ridden states some individuals will be found who are raised above that condition. These men possess a wider sort of social feeling; they see that men in other countries and in other ages have held to very different doctrines from those which they themselves have been brought up to believe; and they cannot help seeing that it is the mere accident of their having been taught as they have, and of their having been surrounded with the manners and associations they have, that has caused them to believe as they do and not far differently. Nor can their candour resist the reflection that there is no reason to rate their own views at a higher value than those of other nations and other centuries; thus giving rise to doubts in their minds.

They will further perceive that such doubts as these must exist in their minds with reference to every belief which seems to be determined by the caprice either of themselves or of those who originated the popular opinions. The willful adherence to a belief, and the arbitrary forcing of it upon others, must, therefore, both be given up. A different new method of settling opinions must be adopted, that shall not only produce an impulse to believe, but shall also decide what proposition it is which is to be believed. Let the action of natural preferences be unimpeded, then, and under their influence let men, conversing together and regarding matters in different lights, gradually develop beliefs in harmony with natural causes. This method resembles that by which conceptions of art have been brought to maturity. The most perfect example of it is to be found in the history of metaphysical philosophy. Systems of this sort have not usually rested upon any observed facts, at least not in any great degree. They have been chiefly adopted because their fundamental propositions seemed "agreeable to reason." This is an apt expression; it does not mean that which agrees with experience, but that which we find ourselves inclined to believe. Plato, for example, finds it agreeable to reason that the distances of the celestial spheres from one another should be proportional to the different lengths of strings which produce harmonious chords. Many philosophers have been led to their main conclusions by considerations like this; but this is the lowest and least developed form which the method takes, for it is clear that another man might find Kepler's theory, that the celestial spheres are proportional to the inscribed and circumscribed spheres of the different regular solids, more agreeable to *his* reason. But the shock of opinions will soon lead men to rest on preferences of a far more universal nature. Take, for example, the doctrine that man only acts selfishly—that is, from the consideration that acting in one way will afford him more pleasure than acting in another. This rests on no fact in the world, but it has had a wide acceptance as being the only reasonable theory.

This method is far more intellectual and respectable from the point of view of reason than either of the others which we have noticed. Indeed, as long as no better method can be applied, it ought to be followed, since it is then the expression of instinct which must be the ultimate cause of belief in all cases. But its failure has been the most manifest. It makes of inquiry something similar to the development of taste; but taste, unfortunately, is always more or less a matter of fashion, and accordingly metaphysicians have never come to any fixed agreement, but the pendulum has swung backward and forward between a more material and a more spiritual philosophy, from the earliest times to the latest. And so from this, which has been called the *a priori* method, we are driven, in Lord Bacon's phrase, to a true induction. We have examined into this *a priori* method as something which promised to deliver our opinions from their accidental and capricious element. But development, while it is a process which eliminates the effect of some casual circumstances, only magnifies that of others. This method, therefore, does not differ in a very essential way from that of authority. The government may not have lifted its finger to influence my convictions; I may have been left outwardly quite free to choose, we will say, between monogamy and polygamy, and, appealing to my conscience only, I may have concluded that the latter practice is in itself licentious. But when I come to see that the chief obstacle to the spread of Christianity among a people of as high culture as the Hindoos has been a conviction of the immorality of our way of treating women, I cannot help seeing that, though governments do not interfere, sentiments in their development will be very greatly determined by accidental causes. Now, there are some people, among whom I must suppose that my reader is to be found, who, when they see that any belief of theirs is determined by any circumstance extraneous to the facts, will from that moment not merely admit in words that that belief is doubtful, but will experience a real doubt of it, so that it ceases in some degree at least to be a belief.

To satisfy our doubts, therefore, it is necessary that a method should be found by which our beliefs may be determined by nothing human, but by some external permanency—by something upon which our thinking has no effect. Some mystics imagine that they have such a method in a private inspiration from on high. But that is only a form of the method of tenacity, in which the conception of truth as something public is not yet developed. Our external permanency would not be external, in our sense, if it was restricted in its influence to one individual. It must be something which affects, or might affect, every man. And, though these affections are necessarily as various as are individual conditions, yet the method must be such that the ultimate conclusion of every man shall be the same. Such is the method of science. Its fundamental hypothesis, restated in more familiar language, is this: There are Real things, whose characters are entirely independent of our opinions about them; those Reals affect our senses according to regular laws, and, though our sensations are as different as are our relations to the objects, yet, by taking advantage of the laws of perception, we can ascertain by reasoning how things really and truly are; and any man, if he have sufficient experience and he reason enough about it, will be led to the one True conclusion, The new conception here involved is that of Reality. It may be asked how I know that there are any Reals. If this hypothesis is the sole support of my method of inquiry, my method of inquiry must not be used to support my hypothesis. The reply is this: 1. If investigation cannot be regarded as proving that there are Real things, it at least does not lead to a contrary conclusion; but the method and the conception on which it is based remain ever in harmony. No doubts of the method, therefore, necessarily arise from its practice, as is the case with all the others. 2. The feeling which gives rise to any method of fixing belief is a dissatisfaction at two repugnant propositions. But here already is a vague concession that there is some *one* thing which a proposition should represent. Nobody, therefore, can really doubt that there are Reals, for, if he did, doubt would not be a source of dissatisfaction. The hypothesis, therefore, is one which every mind admits. So that the social impulse does not cause men to doubt it. 3. Everybody uses the scientific method about a great many things, and only ceases to use it when he does not know how to apply it. 4. Experience of the method has not led us to doubt it, but, on the contrary, scientific investigation has had the most wonderful triumphs in the way of settling opinion. These afford the explanation of my not doubting the method or the hypothesis which it supposes; and not having any doubt, nor believing that anybody else whom I could influence has, it would be the merest babble for me to say more about it. If there be anybody with a living doubt upon the subject, let him consider it. . . .

This is the only one of the four methods which presents any distinction of a right and a wrong way. If I adopt the method of tenacity, and shut myself out from all influences, whatever I think necessary to doing this, is necessary according to that method. So with the method of authority: the state may try to put down heresy by means which, from a scientific point of view, seem very ill-calculated to accomplish its purposes; but the only test *on that method* is what the state thinks; so that it cannot pursue the method wrongly. So with the *a priori* method. The very essence of it is to think as one is inclined to think. . . . But with the scientific method the case is different. I may start with known and observed facts to proceed to the unknown; and yet the rules which I follow in doing so may not be such as investigation would approve. The test of whether I am truly following the method is not an immediate appeal to my feelings and purposes, but, on the contrary, itself involves the application of the method. Hence it is that bad reasoning as well as good reasoning is possible; and this fact is the foundation of the practical side of logic.

It is not to be supposed that the first three methods of settling opinion present no advantage whatever over the scientific method. On the contrary, each has some peculiar convenience of its own. The *a priori* method is distinguished for its comfortable conclusions. It is the nature of the process to adopt whatever belief we are inclined to, and there are certain flatteries to the vanity of man which we all believe by nature, until we are awakened from our pleasing dream by rough facts. The method of authority will always govern the mass of mankind; and those who wield the various forms of organized force in the state will never be convinced that dangerous reasoning ought not to be suppressed in some way. If liberty of speech is to be untrammelled from the grosser forms of constraint, then uniformity of opinion will be secured by a moral terrorism to which the respectability of society will give its thorough approval. Following the method of authority is the path of peace. Certain nonconformities are permitted; certain others (considered unsafe) are forbidden. These are different in different countries and in different ages; but, wherever you are, let it be known that you seriously hold a tabooed belief, and you may be perfectly sure of being treated with a cruelty less brutal but more refined than hunting you like a wolf. Thus, the greatest intellectual benefactors of mankind have never dared, and dare not now, to utter the whole of their thought; and thus a shade of *prima facie* doubt is cast upon every proposition which is considered essential to the security of society. Singularly enough, the persecution does not all come from without; but a man torments himself and is oftentimes most distressed at finding himself believing propositions which he has been brought up to regard with aversion. The peaceful and sympathetic man will, therefore, find it hard to resist the temptation to submit his opinions to authority. But most of all I admire the method of tenacity for its strength, simplicity, and directness. Men who pursue it are distinguished for their decision of character, which becomes very easy with such a mental rule. They do not waste time in trying to make up their minds what they want, but, fastening like lightning upon whatever alternative comes first, they hold it to the end, whatever happens, without an instant's irresolution. This is one of the splendid qualities which generally accompany brilliant, unlasting success. It is impossible not to envy the man who can dismiss reason, although we know how it must turn out at last.

Such are the advantages which the other methods of settling opinion have over scientific investigation. A man should consider well of them; and then he should consider that, after all, he wishes his opinions to coincide with the fact, and that there is no reason why the results of those three first methods should do so. To bring about this effect is the prerogative of the method of science. Upon such considerations he has to make his choice—a choice which is far more than the adoption of any intellectual opinion, which is one of the ruling decisions of his life, to which, when once made, he is bound to adhere. The force of habit will sometimes cause a man to hold on to old beliefs, after he is in a condition to see that they have no sound basis. But reflection upon the state of the case will overcome these habits, and he ought to allow reflection its full weight. People sometimes shrink from doing this, having an idea that beliefs are wholesome which they cannot help feeling rest on nothing. But let such persons suppose an analogous though different case from their own. Let them ask themselves what they would say to a reformed Mussulman who should hesitate to give up his old notions in regard to the relations of the sexes; or to a reformed Catholic who should still shrink from reading the Bible. Would they not say that these persons ought to consider the matter fully, and clearly understand the new doctrine, and then ought to embrace it, in its entirety? But, above all, let it be considered that what is more wholesome than any particular belief is integrity of belief, and that to avoid looking into the support of any belief from a fear that it may turn out rotten is quite as immoral as it is disadvantageous. The person who confesses that there is such a thing as truth, which is distinguished from falsehood simply by this, that if acted on it should, on full consideration, carry us to the point we aim at and not astray, and then, though convinced of this, dares not know the truth and seeks to avoid it, is in a sorry state of mind indeed.

Yes, the other methods do have their merits: a clear logical conscience does cost something—just as any virtue, just as all that we cherish, costs us dear. But we should not desire it to be otherwise. The genius of a man's logical method should be loved and reverenced as his bride, whom he has chosen from all the world. He need not contemn the others; on the contrary, he may honour them deeply, and in doing so he only honours her the more. But she is the one that he has chosen, and he knows that he was right in making that choice. And having made it, he will work and fight for her, and will not complain that there are blows to take, hoping that there may be as many and as hard to give, and will strive to be the worthy knight and champion of her from the blaze of whose splendours he draws his inspiration and his courage.

6

BELIEVING: WITH AND WITHOUT EVIDENCE *

by

JOHN HENRY (CARDINAL) NEWMAN

(1801–1890)

[Certain writers] wish to maintain that there are degrees of assent, and that, as the reasons for a proposition are strong or weak, so is the assent. It follows from this that absolute assent has no legitimate exercise, except as ratifying acts of intuition or demonstration. What is thus brought home to us is to be accepted unconditionally; but reasonings in concrete matters are never more than probabilities, and the probability in each conclusion which we draw is the measure of our assent to that conclusion. Thus assent becomes a sort of necessary shadow, following upon inference, which is the substance; and is never without some alloy of doubt, because inference in the concrete never reaches more than probability. . . . Assent cannot rise higher than its source; inference in such matters is at best conditional, therefore assent is conditional also.

Abstract argument is always dangerous, and this instance is no exception to the rule; I prefer to go by facts. The theory to which I have referred cannot be carried out in practice. It may be rightly said to prove too much; for it debars us from unconditional assent in cases in which the common voice of mankind, its advocates included, would protest against the prohibition. There are many truths in concrete matters, which no one can demonstrate, yet every one unconditionally accepts; and though of course there are in-

* [From Chs. 6 and 7 of *An Essay in Aid of a Grammar of Assent* (1870).]

numerable propositions to which it would be absurd to give an absolute assent, still the absurdity lies in the circumstances of each particular case, as it is taken by itself, not in their common violation of the pretentious axiom that probable reasoning can never lead to certitude.

Locke's remarks on the subject are an illustration of what I have been saying. This celebrated writer, after the manner of his school, speaks freely of degrees of assent, and considers that the strength of assent given to each proposition varies with the strength of the inference on which the assent follows; yet he is obliged to make exceptions to his general principle,—exceptions, unintelligible on his abstract doctrine, but demanded by the logic of facts. The practice of mankind is too strong for the antecedent theorem, to which he is desirous to subject it.

First he says, in his chapter "On Probability," "Most of the propositions we think, reason, discourse, nay, act upon, are such as we cannot have undoubted knowledge of their truth; yet some of them *border so near* upon certainty that *we make no doubt at all* about them, but *assent* to them, *as firmly,* and act according to that assent as resolutely, *as if they were infallibly demonstrated,* and that our knowledge of them was perfect and certain." Here he allows that inferences, which are only "near upon certainty," are so near, that we legitimately accept them with "no doubt at all," and "assent to them as firmly as if they were infallibly demonstrated." That is, he affirms and sanctions the very paradox to which I am committed myself.

Again; he says, in his chapter on "The Degrees of Assent," that "when any particular thing, consonant to the constant observation of ourselves and others in the like case, comes attested by the concurrent reports of all that mention it, we receive it as easily, and build as firmly upon it, as if it were certain knowledge, and we reason and act thereupon, *with as little doubt as if it were perfect demonstration.*" And he repeats, "These *probabilities* rise so near to certainty, that they *govern our thoughts as absolutely,* and influence all our actions as fully, as *the most evident demonstration;* and in what concerns us, we make little or no difference between them and certain knowledge. *Our belief thus grounded, rises to assurance.*" Here again, "probabilities" may be so strong as to "govern our thoughts as absolutely" as sheer demonstration, so strong that belief, grounded on them, "rises to assurance," that is, certitude.

I have so high a respect both for the character and the ability of Locke, for his manly simplicity of mind and his outspoken candour, and there is so much in his remarks upon reasoning and proof in which I fully concur, that I feel no pleasure in considering him in the light of an opponent to views which I myself have ever cherished as true, with an obstinate devotion; and I would willingly think that in the passage which follows in his chapter on "Enthusiasm," he is aiming at superstitious extravagances which I should repudiate myself as much as he can do; but, if so, his words go beyond the occasion, and contradict what I have quoted from him above.

"He that would seriously set upon the search of truth, ought, in the first place, to prepare his mind with a love of it. For he that loves it not will not take much pains to get it, nor be much concerned when he misses it. There is nobody, in the commonwealth of learning, who does not profess himself a lover of truth,—and there is not a rational creature, that would not take it amiss, to be thought otherwise of. And yet, for all this, one may truly say, there are very few lovers of truth, for truth-sake, even amongst those who persuade themselves that they are so. How a man may know, whether he be so, in earnest, is worth inquiry; and I think, there is this one unerring mark of it, viz. *the not entertaining any proposition with greater assurance than the proofs it is built on will warrant*. Whoever goes beyond this measure of assent, it is plain, receives not truth in the love of it, loves not truth for truth-sake, but for some other by-end. For the evidence that any proposition is true (*except such as are self-evident*) lying only in the proofs a man has of it, whatsoever degrees of assent he affords it *beyond the degrees of that* evidence, it is plain *all that surplusage of assurance* is owing to some other affection, and not to the love of truth; it being as *impossible* that the love of truth should carry *any assent above the evidence* there is to one that it is true, as that the love of truth should be assent to any proposition for the sake of that evidence which it has not that it is true; which is in effect to love it as a truth, because it is possible or probable that it may not be true."

Here he says that it is not only illogical, but immoral to "carry our *assent above* the *evidence* that a proposition is true," to have "a surplusage of *assurance beyond* the degrees of that evidence." And he excepts from this rule only self-evident propositions. How then is it not inconsistent with right reason, with the love of truth for its own sake, to allow, in his words quoted above, certain strong "probabilities" to "govern our thoughts as absolutely as the most evident demonstration"? how is there no "surplusage of assurance beyond the degrees of evidence" when in the case of those strong probabilities, we permit "our belief, thus grounded, to rise to assurance," as he pronounces we are rational in doing? Of course he had in view one set of instances, when he implied that demonstration was the condition of absolute assent, and another set when he said that it was no such condition; but he surely cannot be acquitted of slovenly thinking in thus treating a cardinal subject. A philosopher should so anticipate the application, and guard the enunciation of his principles, as to secure them against the risk of their being made to change places with each other, to defend what he is eager to denounce, and to condemn what he finds it necessary to sanction. However, whatever is to be thought of his *a priori* method and his logical consistency, his *animus*, I fear, must be understood as hostile to the doctrine which I am going to maintain. He takes a view of the human mind, in relation to inference and assent, which to me seems theoretical and unreal. Reasonings and convictions which I deem natural and legitimate, he apparently would call irrational, enthusiastic, perverse, and immoral; and that, as I think, because he consults his own ideal of what ought to be, instead of interrogating human nature, as an existing thing, as it is found in the world. Instead of going by the testimony of psychological facts, and thereby determining our constitutive faculties and our proper condition, and being content with the mind as God has made it, he would form men as he thinks they ought to be formed, into something better and higher, and calls them irrational and immoral, if (so to speak) they take to the water, instead of remaining under the narrow wings of his own arbitrary theory.

1. Now the first question which this theory leads me to consider is, whether there is such an act of the mind as assent at all. If there is, it is plain it ought to show itself unequivocally as such, as distinct from other acts. For if a professed act can only be viewed as the necessary and immediate repetition of another act, if assent is a sort of reproduction and double of an act of inference, if when inference determines that a proposition is somewhat, or not a little, or a good deal, or very like truth, assent as its natural and normal counterpart says that it *is* somewhat, or not a little, or a good deal, or very like truth, then I do not see what we mean by saying, or why we say at all, that there is any such act. It is simply superfluous, in a psychological point of view, and a curiosity of subtle minds, and the sooner it is got out of the way the better. When I assent, I am supposed, it seems, to do precisely what I do when I infer, or rather not quite so much, but something which is included in inferring; for, while the disposition of my mind towards a given proposition is identical in assent and in inference, I merely drop the thought of the premisses when I assent, though not of their influence on the proposition inferred. This then, it seems, is what nature prescribes, and this the conscientious use of our faculties, so to assent as to do nothing else than infer. Then, I say, if this be really the state of the case, if assent in no real way differs from inference, it is one and the same thing with it. It is another name for inference, and to speak of it at all does but mislead. Nor can it fairly be argued that an act of consciousness, though distinct from an act of knowledge, is after all only its repetition. On the contrary, it is a reflex act with its own

object, viz. the act of knowledge itself. As well might it be said that the hearing of the notes of my voice is a repetition of the act of singing·—it supplies no parallel then to the anomaly I am combating.

I lay it down, then, as a principle that either assent is intrinsically distinct from inference, or the sooner we get rid of the word in philosophy the better. . . . The first step then towards deciding the point, will be to inquire what the experience of human life, as it is daily brought before us, teaches us of the relation to each other of inference and assent.

(1.) First, we know from experience that assents may endure without the presence of the inferential acts upon which they were given. It is plain, that, as life goes on, we are not only inwardly formed and changed by the accession of habits, but we are also enriched by a great multitude of beliefs and opinions, and that, on a variety of subjects. These beliefs and opinions, held, as some of them are, almost as first principles, are assents, and they constitute, as it were, the clothing and furniture of the mind. . . . Sometimes we are fully conscious of them; sometimes they are implicit, or only now and then come directly before our reflective faculty. Still they are assents; and, when we first admitted them, we had some kind of reason, slight or strong, recognized or not, for doing so. However, whatever those reasons were, even if we ever realized them, we have long forgotten them. Whether it was the authority of others, or our own observation, or our reading, or our reflections, which became the warrant of our assent, any how we received the matters in question into our minds as true, and gave them a place there. We assented to them, and we still assent, though we have forgotten what the warrant was. At present they are self-sustained in our minds, and have been so for long years; they are in no sense conclusions; they imply no process of thought. Here then is a case in which assent stands out as distinct from inference.

(2.) Again; sometimes assent fails, while the reasons for it and the inferential act, which is the recognition of those reasons, are still present, and in force. Our reasons may seem to us as strong as ever, yet they do not secure our assent. Our beliefs, founded on them, were and are not; we cannot perhaps tell when they went; we may have thought that we still held them, till something happened to call our attention to the state of our minds, and then we found that our assent had become an assertion. Sometimes, of course, a cause may be found why they went; there may have been some vague feeling that a fault lay at the ultimate basis, or the underlying conditions, of our reasonings; or some misgiving that the subject-matter of them was beyond the reach of the human mind; or a consciousness that we had gained a broader view of things in general than when we first gave our assent; or that there were strong objections to our first convictions, which we had never taken into account. But this is not always so; sometimes our mind changes so quickly, so unaccountably, so disproportionately to any tangible arguments to which the change can be referred, and with such abiding recognition of the force of the old arguments, as to suggest the suspicion that moral causes, arising out of our condition, age, company, occupations, fortunes, are at the bottom. However, what once was assent is gone; yet the perception of the old arguments remains, showing that inference is one thing, and assent another.

(3.) And as assent sometimes dies out without tangible reasons, sufficient to account for its failure. so sometimes, in spite of strong and convincing arguments, it is never given. We sometimes find men loud in their admiration of truths which they never profess. As, by the law of our mental constitution, obedience is quite distinct from faith, and men may believe without practising, so is assent also independent of our acts of inference. Again, prejudice hinders assent to the most incontrovertible proofs. Again, it not unfrequently happens, that while the keenness of the ratiocinative faculty enables a man to see the ultimate result of a complicated problem in a moment, it takes years for him to embrace it as a truth, and to recognize it as an item in the circle of his knowledge. Yet he does at last so accept it, and then we say that he assents.

(4.) Again; very numerous are the cases, in which good arguments, and really good as far as they go, and confessed by us to be good, nevertheless are not strong enough to incline our minds ever so little to the conclusion at which they point. But why is it that we do not assent a little, in proportion to those arguments? On the contrary, we throw the full *onus probandi* [burden of proof] on the side of the conclusion, and we refuse to assent to it at all, until we can assent to it altogether. The proof is capable of growth; but the assent either exists or does not exist.

(5.) I have already alluded to the influence of moral motives in hindering assent to conclusions which are logically unimpeachable. According to the couplet,

"A man convinced against his will
Is of the same opinion still."

assent then is not the same as inference.

(6.) Strange as it may seem, this contrast between inference and assent is exemplified even in the province of mathematics. Argument is not always able to command our assent, even though it be demonstrative. Sometimes of course it forces its way, that is, when the steps of the reasoning are few, and admit of being viewed by the mind altogether. Certainly, one cannot conceive a man having before him the series of conditions and truths on which it depends that the three angles of a triangle are together equal to two right angles, and yet not assenting to that proposition. Were all propositions as plain, though assent would not in consequence be the same act as inference, yet it would certainly follow immediately upon it. I allow then as much as this, that, when an argument is in itself and by itself conclusive of a truth, it has by a law of our nature the same command over our assent, or rather the truth which it has reached has the same command, as our senses have. Certainly our intellectual nature is under laws, and the correlative of ascertained truth is unreserved assent.

But I am not speaking of short and lucid demonstrations; but of long and intricate mathematical investigations; and in that case, though every step may be indisputable, it still requires a specially sustained attention and an effort of memory to have in the mind all at once all the steps of the proof, with their bearings on each other, and the antecedents which they severally involve; and these conditions of the inference may interfere with the promptness of our assent.

Hence it is that party spirit or national feeling or religious prepossessions have before now had power to retard the reception of truths of a mathematical character; which never could have been, if demonstrations were *ipso facto* [by that very fact] assents. Nor indeed would any mathematician, even in questions of pure science, assent to his own conclusions, on new and difficult ground, and in the case of abstruse calculations, however often he went over his work, till he had the corroboration of other judgments besides his own. He would have carefully revised his inference, and would assent to the probability of his accuracy in inferring, but still he would abstain from an immediate assent to the truth of his conclusion. Yet the corroboration of others cannot add to his perception of the proof; he would still perceive the proof, even though he failed in gaining their corroboration. And yet again he might arbitrarily make it his rule, never to assent to his conclusions without such corroboration, or at least before the lapse of a sufficient interval. Here again inference is distinct from assent. . . .

Locke's theory of the duty of assenting more or less according to degrees of evidence, is invalidated by the testimony of high and low, young and old, ancient and modern, as continually given in their ordinary sayings and doings. Indeed . . . he does not strictly maintain it himself; yet, though he feels the claims of nature and fact to be too strong for him in certain cases, he gives no reason why he should violate his theory in these, and yet not in many more.

Now let us review some of those assents, which men give on evidence short of intuition and demonstration, yet which are as unconditional as if they had that evidence.

First of all, starting from intuition, of course we all believe, without any doubt, that we exist; that we have an individuality and identity all our own; that we think, feel, and act, in the home of our own minds; that we have a present sense of good and evil, of a right and a wrong, of a true and a false, of a beautiful and a hideous, however we analyze our ideas of them. We have an absolute vision before us of what happened yesterday or last year, so as to be able without any chance of mistake to give evidence upon it in a court of justice, let the consequences be ever so serious. We are sure that of many things we are ignorant, that of many things we are in doubt, and that of many things we are not in doubt.

Nor is the assent which we give to facts limited to the range of self-consciousness. We are sure beyond all hazard of a mistake, that our own self is not the only being existing; that there is an external world; that it is a system with parts and a whole, a universe carried on by laws; and that the future is affected by the past. We accept and hold with an unqualified assent, that the earth, considered as a phenomenon, is a globe; that all its regions see the sun by turns; that there are vast tracts on it of land and water; that there are really existing cities on definite sites, which go by the names of London, Paris, Florence, and Madrid. We are sure that Paris or London, unless swallowed up by an earthquake or burned to the ground, is to-day just what it was yesterday, when we left it.

We laugh to scorn the idea that we had no parents, though we have no memory of our birth; that we shall never die, though we can have no experience of the future; that we are able to live without food, though we have never tried; that a world of men did not live before our time, or that that world has had no history; that there has been no rise and fall of states, no great men, no wars, no revolutions, no art, no science, no literature, no religion.

We should be either shocked or amused at the report of our intimate friend being false to us; and we are able sometimes, without any hesitation, to accuse certain parties of hostility and injustice to us. We may have a deep consciousness, which we never can lose, that we on our part have been cruel to others, and that they have felt us to be so, or that we have been, and have been felt to be, ungenerous to those who love us. We may have an overpowering sense of our moral weakness, of the precariousness of our life, health, wealth, position, and good fortune. We may have a clear view of the weak points of our physical constitution, of what food or medicine is good for us, and what does us harm. We may be able to master, at least in part, the course of our past history; its turning-points, our hits, and our great mistakes. We may have a sense of the presence of a Supreme Being, which never has been dimmed by even a passing shadow, which has inhabited us ever since we can recollect any thing, and which we cannot imagine our losing. We may be able, for others have been able, so to realize the precepts and truths of Christianity, as deliberately to surrender our life, rather than transgress the one or to deny the other.

On all these truths we have an immediate and an unhesitating hold, nor do we think ourselves guilty of not loving truth for truth's sake, because we cannot reach them through a series of intuitive propositions. Assent on reasonings not demonstrative is too widely recognized an act to be irrational, unless man's nature is irrational, too familiar to the prudent and clear-minded to be an infirmity or an extravagance. None of us can think or act without the acceptance of truths, not intuitive, not demonstrated, yet sovereign. If our nature has any constitution, any laws, one of them is this absolute reception of propositions as true, which lie outside the narrow range of conclusions to which logic, formal or virtual, is tethered; nor has any philosophical theory the power to force on us a rule which will not work for a day.

When, then, philosophers lay down principles, on which it follows that our assent, except when given to objects of intuition or demonstration, is conditional, that the assent given to propositions by well-ordered minds necessarily varies with the proof producible for them, and that it does not and cannot remain one and the same while the proof is strengthened or weakened,—are they not to be considered as confusing together two things very distinct from each other, a mental act or state and a scientific rule, an interior assent and a set of logical formulas? When they speak of degrees of assent, surely they have no intention at all of defining the position of the mind itself relative to the adoption of a given conclusion, but they mean to determine the relation of that conclusion towards its premisses. They are contemplating how representative symbols work, not how the intellect is affected towards the thing which those symbols represent. In real truth they as little mean to assert the principle of measuring our assents by our logic, as they would fancy they could record the refreshment which we receive from the open air by the readings of the graduated scale of a thermometer. There is a connexion doubtless between a logical conclusion and an assent, as there is between the variation of the mercury and our sensations; but the mercury is not the cause of life and health, nor is verbal argumentation the principle of inward belief. If we feel hot or chilly, no one will convince us to the contrary by insisting that the glass is at 60°. It is the mind that reasons and assents, not a diagram on paper. I may have difficulty in the management of a proof, while I remain unshaken in my adherence to the conclusion. Supposing a boy cannot make his answer to some arithmetical or alegebraical question tally with the book, need he at once distrust the book? Does his trust in it fall down a certain number of degrees, according to the force of his difficulty? On the contrary, he keeps to the principle, implicit but present to his mind, with which he took up the book, that the book is more likely to be right than he is; and this mere preponderance of probability is sufficient to make him faithful to his belief in its correctness, till its incorrectness is actually proved.

My own opinion is, that the class of writers of whom I have been speaking, have themselves as little misgiving about the truths which they pretend to weigh out and measure as their unsophisticated neighbours; but they think it a duty to remind us, that since the full etiquette of logical requirements has not been satisfied, we must believe those truths at our peril. They warn us, that a result which can never come to pass, in matter of fact, is nevertheless in theory a possible supposition. They do not, for instance, intend for a moment to imply that there is even the shadow of a doubt that Great Britain is an island, but they think we ought to know, if we do not know, that there is no proof of the fact, in mode and figure, equal to the proof of a proposition of Euclid; and that in consequence they and we are all bound to suspend our judgment about such a fact, though it be in an infinitesimal degree, lest we should seem not to love truth for truth's sake. Having made their protest, they subside without scruple into that same absolute assurance of only partially-proved truths, which is natural to the illogical imagination of the multitude. . . .

A great many of our assents are merely expressions of our personal likings, tastes, principles, motives, and opinions, as dictated by nature, or resulting from habit; in other words, they are acts and manifestations of self: now what is more rare than self-knowledge? In proportion then to our ignorance of self, is our unconsciousness of those innumerable acts of assent, which we are incessantly making. And so again in what may be almost called the mechanical operation of our minds, in our continual acts of apprehension and inference, speculation and resolve, propositions pass before us and receive our assent without our consciousness. Hence it is that we are so apt to confuse together acts of assent and acts of inference. Indeed, I may fairly say, that those assents which we give with a direct knowledge of what we are doing, are few compared with the multitude of like acts which pass through our minds in long succession without our observing them.

That mode of assent which includes this unconscious exercise, I may call simple assent . . . but now I am going to speak of such assents as must be made consciously and deliberately, and which I shall call complex or reflex assents. And I begin by recalling what

I have already stated about the relation in which Assent and Inference stand to each other,—inference, which holds propositions
conditionally, and assent, which unconditionally accepts them; the
relation is this:—

Acts of inference are both the antecedents of assent before assenting, and its usual concomitants after assenting. For instance, I hold
absolutely that the country which we call India exists, upon trustworthy testimony; and next, I may continue to believe it on the same
testimony. In like manner, I have ever believed that Great Britain
is an island, for certain sufficient reasons; and on the same reasons
I may persist in the belief. But it may happen that I forget my
reasons for what I believe to be so absolutely true; or I may never
have asked myself about them, or formally marshalled them in order,
and have been accustomed to assent without a recognition of my
assent or of its grounds, and then perhaps something occurs which
leads to my reviewing and completing those grounds, analyzing and
arranging them, yet without on that account implying of necessity
any suspense, ever so slight, of assent, to the proposition that India
is in a certain part of the earth, and that Great Britain is an island.
With no suspense of assent at all; any more than the boy in my
former illustration had any doubt about the answer set down in his
arithmetic-book, when he began working out the question; any more
than he would be doubting his eyes and his common sense, that
the two sides of a triangle are together greater than the third, because he drew out the geometrical proof of it. He does but repeat,
after his formal demonstration, that assent which he made before it,
or assents to his previous assenting. This is what I call a reflex
or complex assent.

I say, there is no necessary incompatibility between thus assenting
and yet proving,—for the conclusiveness of a proposition is not
synonymous with its truth. A proposition may be true, yet not admit of being concluded;—it may be a conclusion and yet not a
truth. To contemplate it under one aspect, is not to contemplate it
under another; and the two aspects may be consistent, from the
very fact that they are two. Therefore to set about concluding a
proposition is not *ipso facto* to doubt its truth; we may aim at inferring a proposition, while all the time we assent to it. We have to
do this as a common occurrence, when we take on ourselves to convince another on any point in which he differs from us. We do not
deny our faith, because we become controversialists; and in like
manner we may employ ourselves in proving what we believe to be
true, simply in order to ascertain the producible evidence in its
favour, and in order to fulfill what is due to ourselves and to the
claims and responsibilities of our education and social position.

I have been speaking of investigation, not of inquiry; it is quite true that inquiry is inconsistent with assent, but inquiry is something more than the mere exercise of inference. He who inquires has not found; he is in doubt where the truth lies, and wishes his present profession either proved or disproved. We cannot without absurdity call ourselves at once believers and inquirers also. Thus it is sometimes spoken of as a hardship that a Catholic is not allowed to inquire into the truth of his creed;—of course he cannot, if he would retain the name of believer. He cannot be both inside and outside of the Church at once. It is merely common sense to tell him that, if he is seeking, he has not found. If seeking includes doubting, and doubting excludes believing, then the Catholic who sets about inquiring, thereby declares that he is not a Catholic. He has already lost faith. And this is his best defence to himself for inquiring, viz. that he is no longer a Catholic, and wishes to become one. They who would forbid him to inquire, would in that case be shutting the stable-door after the steed is stolen. What can he do better than inquire, if he is in doubt? how else can he become a Catholic again? Not to inquire is in his case to be satisfied with disbelief.

However, in thus speaking, I am viewing the matter in the abstract, and without allowing for the manifold inconsistencies of individuals, as they are found in the world, who attempt to unite incompatibilities; who do not doubt, but who act as if they did; who, though they believe, are weak in faith, and put themselves in the way of losing it by unnecessarily listening to objections. Moreover, there are minds, undoubtedly, with whom at all times to question a truth is to make it questionable, and to investigate is to inquire; and again, there may be beliefs so sacred or so delicate, that, if I may use the metaphor, they will not wash without shrinking and losing colour. I grant all this; but here I am discussing broad principles, not individual cases; and these principles are, that inquiry implies doubt, and that investigation does not imply it, and that those who assent to a doctrine or fact may without inconsistency investigate its credibility, though they literally cannot inquire about its truth.

Next, I consider that, in the case of educated minds, investigations into the argumentative proof of the things to which they have given their assent, is an obligation, or rather a necessity. Such a trial of their intellects is a law of their nature, like the growth of childhood into manhood, and analogous to the moral ordeal which is the instrument of their spiritual life. The lessons of right and wrong, which are taught them at school, are to be carried out into action amid the good and evil of the world; and the intellectual assents, in which they have in like manner been instructed from the first, have also to be tested, realized, and developed by the exercise of their mature judgment.

Certainly, such processes of investigation, whether in religious subjects or secular, often issue in the reversal of the assents which they
were originally intended to confirm; as the boy who works out an
arithmetical problem from his book may end in detecting, or thinking he detects, a false print in the answer. But the question before
us is whether acts of assent and of inference are compatible; and
my vague consciousness of the possibility of a reversal of my belief
by the course of my researches, as little interferes with the honesty
and firmness of that belief while those researches proceed, as the
recognition of the possibility of my train's oversetting is an evidence
of an intention on my part of undergoing so great a calamity. My
mind is not moved by a scientific computation of chances, nor can
any law of averages affect my particular case. To incur a risk is not
to expect reverse; and if my opinions are true, I have a right to
think that they will bear examining. Nor, on the other hand, does
belief, viewed in its idea, imply a positive resolution in the party
believing never to abandon that belief. What belief, as such, does
imply is, not an intention never to change, but the utter absence of
all thought, or expectation, or fear of changing. A spontaneous resolution never to change is inconsistent with the idea of belief; for the
very force and absoluteness of the act of assent precludes any such
resolution. We do not commonly determine not to do what we cannot fancy ourselves ever doing. We should readily indeed make such
a formal promise if we were called upon to do so; for, since we
have the truth, and truth cannot change, how can we possibly change
in our belief, except indeed through our own weakness or fickleness?
We have no intention whatever of being weak or fickle; so our
promise is but the natural guarantee of our sincerity. It is possible
then, without disloyalty to our convictions, to examine their grounds,
even though they are to fail under the examination, for we have no
suspicion of this failure.

And such examination, as I have said, does but fulfil a law of
our nature. Our first assents, right or wrong, are often little more
than prejudices. The reasonings, which precede and accompany
them, though sufficient for their purpose, do not rise up to the
importance and energy of the assents themselves. As time goes on,
by degrees and without set purpose, by reflection and experience, we
begin to confirm or to correct the notions and the images to which
those assents are given. At times it is a necessity formally to undertake a survey and revision of this or that class of them, of those
which relate to religion, or to social duty, or to politics, or to the
conduct of life. Sometimes this review begins in doubt as to the
matters which we propose to consider, that is, in a suspension of the
assents hitherto familiar to us; sometimes those assents are too
strong to allow of being lost on the first stirring of the inquisitive

intellect, and if, as time goes on, they give way, our change of mind, be it for good or for evil, is owing to the accumulating force of the arguments, sound or unsound, which bear down upon the propositions which we have hitherto received. Objections, indeed, as such, have no direct force to weaken assent; but, when they multiply, they tell against the implicit reasonings or the formal inferences which are its warrant, and suspend its acts and gradually undermine its habit. Then the assent goes; but whether slowly or suddenly, noticeably or imperceptibly, is a matter of circumstance or accident. However, whether the original assent is continued or not, the new assent differs from the old in this, that it has the strength of explicitness and deliberation, that it is not a mere prejudice, and its strength the strength of prejudice. It is an assent, not only to a given proposition, but to the claim of that proposition on our assent as true; it is an assent to an assent, or what is commonly called a conviction. . . . Let the proposition to which the assent is given be as absolutely true as the reflex act pronounces it to be, that is, objectively true as well as subjectively, then the assent may be called a *perception*, the conviction a *certitude*, the proposition or truth a *certainty*, or thing known, or a matter of *knowledge*, and to assent to it is to *know*. . . .

In proceeding to compare together simple assent and complex, that is, assent and certitude, I begin by observing, that popularly no distinction is made between the two; or rather, that in religious teaching that is called certitude to which I have given the name of assent. I have no difficulty in adopting such a use of the words, though the course of my investigation has led me to another. Perhaps religious assent may be called, to use a theological term, "material certitude;" and the first point of comparison which I shall make between the two states of mind, will serve to set me right with the common way of speaking.

1. It certainly follows then, from the distinctions which I have made, that great numbers of men must be considered to pass through life with neither doubt nor, on the other hand, certitude (as I have used the words) on the most important propositions which can occupy their minds, but with only a simple assent, that is, an assent which they barely recognize, or bring home to their consciousness or reflect upon, as being assent. Such an assent is all that religious Protestants commonly have to show, who believe nevertheless with their whole hearts the contents of Holy Scripture. Such too is the state of mind of multitudes of good Catholics, perhaps the majority, who live and die in a simple, full, firm belief in all that the Church teaches, because she teaches it,—in the belief of the irreversible truth of whatever she defines and declares,—but who, as being far removed from Protestant and other dissentients, and having but lit-

tle intellectual training, have never had the temptation to doubt, and never the opportunity to be certain. There were whole nations in the middle ages thus steeped in the Catholic Faith, who never used its doctrines as matter for argument or research, or changed the original belief of their childhood into the more scientific convictions of philosophy. As there is a condition of mind which is characterized by invincible ignorance, so there is another which may be said to be possessed of invincible knowledge; and it would be paradoxical in me to deny to such a mental state the highest quality of religious faith,—I mean certitude.

I allow this, and therefore I will call simple assent *material* certitude; or, to use a still more apposite term for it, *interpretative* certitude. I call it interpretative, signifying thereby that, though the assent in the individuals contemplated is not a reflex act, still the question only has to be started about the truth of the objects of their assent, in order to elicit from them an act of faith in response which will fulfil the conditions of certitude, as I have drawn them out. As to the argumentative process necessary for such an act, it is valid and sufficient, if it be carried out seriously, and proportionate to their several capacities. "The Catholic Religion is true, because its objects, as present to my mind, control and influence my conduct as nothing else does;" or "because it has about it an odour of truth and sanctity *sui generis*, as perceptible to my moral nature as flowers to my sense, such as can only come from heaven;" or "because it has never been to me any thing but peace, joy, consolation, and strength, all through my troubled life." And if the particular argument used in some instances needs strengthening, then let it be observed, that the keenness of the real apprehension with which the assent is made, though it cannot be the legitimate basis of the assent, may still legitimately act, and strongly act, in confirmation. Such, I say, would be the promptitude and effectiveness of the reasoning, and the facility of the change from assent to certitude proper, in the case of the multitudes in question, did the occasion for reflection occur; but it does not occur; and accordingly, most genuine and thorough as is the assent, it can only be called virtual, material, or interpretative certitude, if I have above explained certitude rightly.

Of course these remarks hold good in secular subjects as well as religious:—I believe, for instance, that I am living in an island, that Julius Cæsar once invaded it, that it has been conquered by successive races, that it has had great political and social changes, and that at this time it has colonies, establishments, and imperial dominion all over the earth. All this I am accustomed to take for granted without a thought; but, were the need to arise, I should not find much difficulty in drawing out from my own mental resources reasons sufficient to justify me in these beliefs.

7

THE FOUR IDOLS *
by
FRANCIS BACON
(1561–1626)

i

Man, being the servant and interpreter of Nature, can do and understand so much and so much only as he has observed in fact or in thought of the course of nature: beyond this he neither knows anything nor can do anything.

ii

Neither the naked hand nor the understanding left to itself can effect much. It is by instruments and helps that the work is done, which are as much wanted for the understanding as for the hand. And as the instruments of the hand either give motion or guide it, so the instruments of the mind supply either suggestions for the understanding or cautions.

iii

Human knowledge and human power meet in one; for where the cause is not known the effect cannot be produced. Nature to be commanded must be obeyed; and that which in contemplation is as the cause is in operation as the rule.

xxxviii

The idols and false notions which are now in possession of the human understanding, and have taken deep root therein, not only so beset men's minds that truth can hardly find entrance, but even after entrance obtained, they will again in the very instauration of the sciences meet and trouble us, unless men being forewarned of the danger fortify themselves as far as may be against their assaults.

* [From *Novum Organum* (1620), Spedding, Ellis, and Heath edition (1861).]

xxxix

There are four classes of Idols which beset men's minds. To these for distinction's sake I have assigned names,—calling the first class *Idols of the Tribe;* the second, *Idols of the Cave;* the third, *Idols of the Market-place;* the fourth, *Idols of the Theatre.*

xl

The formation of ideas and axioms by true induction is no doubt the proper remedy to be applied for the keeping off and clearing away of idols. To point them out, however, is of great use; for the doctrine of Idols is to the Interpretation of Nature what the doctrine of the refutation of Sophisms is to common Logic.

xli

The Idols of the Tribe have their foundation in human nature itself, and in the tribe or race of men. For it is a false assertion that the sense of man is the measure of things. On the contrary, all perceptions as well of the sense as of the mind are according to the measure of the individual and not according to the measure of the universe. And the human understanding is like a false mirror, which, receiving rays irregularly, distorts and discolours the nature of things by mingling its own nature with it.

xlii

The Idols of the Cave are the idols of the individual man. For everyone (besides the errors common to human nature in general) has a cave or den of his own, which refracts and discolours the light of nature; owing either to his own proper and peculiar nature; or to his education and conversation with others; or to the reading of books, and the authority of those whom he esteems and admires; or to the differences of impressions, accordingly as they take place in a mind preoccupied and predisposed or in a mind indifferent and settled; or the like. So that the spirit of man (according as it is meted out to different individuals) is in fact a thing variable and full of perturbation, and governed as it were by chance. Whence it was well observed by Heraclitus that men look for sciences in their own lesser worlds, and not in the greater or common world.

xliii

There are also Idols formed by the intercourse and association of men with each other, which I call Idols of the Market-place, on account of the commerce and consort of men there. For it is by discourse that men associate; and words are imposed according to the apprehension of the vulgar. And therefore the ill and unfit choice of words wonderfully obstructs the understanding. Nor do the definitions or explanations wherewith in some things learned men are wont to guard and defend themselves, by any means set the matter right. But words plainly force and over-rule the understanding, and throw all into confusion, and lead men away into numberless empty controversies and idle fancies.

xliv

Lastly, there are Idols which have immigrated into men's minds from the various dogmas of philosophies, and also from wrong laws of demonstration. These I call Idols of the Theatre; because in my judgment all the received systems are but so many stage-plays, representing worlds of their own creation after an unreal and scenic fashion. Nor is it only of the systems now in vogue, or only of the ancient sects and philosophies, that I speak: for many more plays of the same kind may yet be composed and in like artificial manner set forth; seeing that errors the most widely different have nevertheless causes for the most part alike. Neither again do I mean this only of entire systems, but also of many principles and axioms in science, which by tradition, credulity, and negligence have come to be received.

But of these several kinds of Idols I must speak more largely and exactly, that the understanding may be duly cautioned.

xlv

The human understanding is of its own nature prone to suppose the existence of more order and regularity in the world than it finds. And though there be many things in nature which are singular and unmatched, yet it devises for them parallels and conjugates and relatives which do not exist. Hence the fiction that all celestial bodies move in perfect circles; spirals and dragons being (except in name) utterly rejected. Hence too the element of Fire with its orb is brought in, to make up the square with the other three which the sense perceives. Hence also the ratio of density of the so-called elements is arbitrarily fixed at ten to one. And so on of other dreams. And these fancies affect not dogmas only, but simple notions also.

xlvi

The human understanding when it has once adopted an opinion (either as being the received opinion or as being agreeable to itself) draws all things else to support and agree with it. And though there be a greater number and weight of instances to be found on the other side, yet these it either neglects and despises, or else by some distinction sets aside and rejects; in order that by this great and pernicious predetermination the authority of its former conclusions may remain inviolate. And therefore it was a good answer that was made by one who when they showed him hanging in a temple a picture of those who had paid their vows as having escaped shipwreck, and would have him say whether he did not now acknowledge the power of the gods,—"Aye," asked he again, "but where are they painted that were drowned after their vows?" And such is the way of all superstition, whether in astrology, dreams, omens, divine judgments, or the like; wherein men, having a delight in such vanities, mark the events where they are fulfilled, but where they fail, though this happen much oftener, neglect and pass them by. But with far more subtlety does this mischief insinuate itself into philosophy and the sciences; in which the first conclusion colours and brings into conformity with itself all that come after, though far sounder and better. Besides, independently of that delight and vanity which I have described, it is the peculiar and perpetual error of the human intellect to be more moved and excited by affirmatives than by negatives; whereas it ought properly to hold itself indifferently disposed towards both alike. Indeed in the establishment of any true axiom, the negative instance is the more forcible of the two.

xlvii

The human understanding is moved by those things most which strike and enter the mind simultaneously and suddenly, and so fill the imagination; and then it feigns and supposes all other things to be somehow, though it cannot see how, similar to those few things by which it is surrounded. But for that going to and fro to remote and heterogeneous instances, by which axioms are tried as in the fire, the intellect is altogether slow and unfit, unless it be forced thereto by severe laws and overruling authority.

xlviii

The human understanding is unquiet; it cannot stop or rest, and still presses onward, but in vain. Therefore it is that we cannot conceive of any end or limit to the world, but always as of necessity it occurs to us that there is something beyond. Neither again can it be conceived how eternity has flowed down to the present day: for that distinction which is commonly received of infinity in time past and in time to come can by no means hold; for it would thence follow that one infinity is greater than another, and that infinity is wasting away and tending to become finite.

The like subtlety arises touching the infinite divisibility of lines, from the same inability of thought to stop. But this inability interferes more mischievously in the discovery of causes: for although the most general principles in nature ought to be held merely positive, as they are discovered, and cannot with truth be referred to a cause; nevertheless the human understanding being unable to rest still seeks something prior in the order of nature. And then it is that in struggling towards that which is further off it falls back upon that which is more nigh at hand; namely, on final causes [or aims]: which have relation clearly to the nature of man rather than to the nature of the universe; and from this source have strangely defiled philosophy. But he is no less an unskilled and shallow philosopher who seeks causes of that which is most general, than he who in things subordinate and subaltern omits to do so.

xlix

The human understanding is no dry light, but receives an infusion from the will and affections [or emotions]; whence proceed sciences which may be called "sciences as one would." For what a man had rather were true he more readily believes. Therefore he rejects difficult things from impatience of research; sober things, because they narrow hope; the deeper things of nature, from superstition; the light of experience, from arrogance and pride, lest his mind should seem to be occupied with things mean and transitory; things not commonly believed, out of deference to the opinion of the vulgar. Numberless in short are the ways, and sometimes imperceptible, in which the affections colour and infect the understanding.

l

But by far the greatest hindrance and aberration of the human understanding proceeds from the dullness, incompetency, and deceptions of the senses; in that things which strike the sense outweigh things which do not immediately strike it, though they be more important. Hence it is that speculation commonly ceases where sight ceases; insomuch that of things invisible there is little or no observation. Hence all the working of the spirits inclosed in tangible bodies lies hid and unobserved of men. So also all the more subtle changes of form in the parts of coarser substances (which they commonly call alteration, though it is in truth local motion through exceedingly small spaces) is in like manner unobserved. And yet unless these two things just mentioned be searched out and brought to light, nothing great can be achieved in nature, as far as the production of works is concerned. So again the essential nature of our common air, and of all bodies less dense than air (which are very many), is almost unknown. For the sense by itself is a thing infirm and erring; neither can instruments for enlarging or sharpening the senses do much; but all the truer kind of interpretation of nature is effected by instances and experiments fit and apposite; wherein the sense decides touching the experiment only, and the experiment touching the point in nature and the thing itself.

li

The human understanding is of its own nature prone to abstractions and gives a substance and reality to things which are fleeting. But to resolve nature into abstractions is less to our purpose than to dissect her into parts; as did the school of Democritus, which went further into nature than the rest. Matter rather than forms should be the object of our attention, its configurations and changes of configuration, and simple action, and law of action or motion; for forms are figments of the human mind, unless you will call those laws of action forms.

lii

Such then are the idols which I call *Idols of the Tribe;* and which take their rise either from the homogeneity of the substance of the human spirit, or from its preoccupation, or from its narrowness, or from its restless motion, or from an infusion of the affections, or from the incompetency of the senses, or from the mode of impression.

liii

The *Idols of the Cave* take their rise in the peculiar constitution, mental or bodily, of each individual; and also in education, habit, and accident. Of this kind there is a great number and variety; but I will instance those the pointing out of which contains the most important caution, and which have most effect in disturbing the clearness of the understanding.

liv

Men become attached to certain particular sciences and speculations, either because they fancy themselves the authors and inventors thereof, or because they have bestowed the greatest pains upon them and become most habituated to them. But men of this kind, if they betake themselves to philosophy and contemplations of a general character, distort and colour them in obedience to their former fancies; a thing especially to be noticed in Aristotle, who made his natural philosophy a mere bond-servant to his logic, thereby rendering it contentious and well nigh useless. The race of chemists again out of a few experiments of the furnace have built up a fantastic philosophy, framed with reference to a few things; and Gilbert also, after he had employed himself most laboriously in the study and observation of the loadstone, proceeded at once to construct an entire system in accordance with his favourite subject.

lv

There is one principal and as it were radical distinction between different minds, in respect of philosophy and the sciences; which is this: that some minds are stronger and apter to mark the differences of things, others to mark their resemblances. The steady and acute mind can fix its contemplations and dwell and fasten on the subtlest distinctions; the lofty and discursive mind recognizes and puts together the finest and most general resemblances. Both kinds however, easily err in excess, by catching the one at gradations the other at shadows.

lvi

There are found some minds given to an extreme admiration of antiquity, others to an extreme love and appetite for novelty; but few so duly tempered that they can hold the mean, neither carping at what has been well laid down by the ancients, nor despising what is well introduced by the moderns. This however turns to the great injury of the sciences and philosophy: since these affectations of antiquity and novelty are the humours of partisans rather than judgments; and truth is to be sought for not in the felicity of any age, which is an unstable thing, but in the light of nature and experience, which is eternal. These factions therefore must be abjured, and care must be taken that the intellect be not hurried by them into assent.

lvii

Contemplations of nature and of bodies in their simple form break up and distract the understanding, while contemplations of nature and bodies in their composition and configuration overpower and dissolve the understanding: a distinction well seen in the school of Leucippus and Democritus as compared with the other philosophies. For that school is so busied with the particles that it hardly attends to the structure; while the others are so lost in admiration of the structure that they do not penetrate to the simplicity of nature. These kinds of contemplation should therefore be alternated and taken by turns; that so the understanding may be rendered at once penetrating and comprehensive, and the inconveniences above mentioned, with the idols which proceed from them, may be avoided.

lviii

Let such then be our provision and contemplative prudence for keeping off and dislodging the Idols of the Cave, which grow for the most part either out of the predominance of a favourite subject, or out of an excessive tendency to compare or to distinguish, or out of partiality for particular ages, or out of the largeness or minuteness of the objects contemplated. And generally let every student of nature take this as a rule,—that whatever his mind seizes and dwells upon with peculiar satisfaction is to be held in suspicion, and that so much the more care is to be taken in dealing with such questions to keep the understanding even and clear.

lix

But the *Idols of the Market-place* are the most troublesome of all: idols which have crept into the understanding through the alliances of words and names. For men believe that their reason governs words; but it is also true that words react on the understanding; and this it is that has rendered philosophy and the sciences sophistical and inactive. Now words, being commonly framed and applied according to the capacity of the vulgar, follow those lines of division which are most obvious to the vulgar understanding. And whenever an understanding of greater acuteness or a more diligent observation would alter those lines to suit the true divisions of nature, words stand in the way and resist the change. Whence it comes to pass that the high and formal discussions of learned men end oftentimes in disputes about words and names; with which (according to the use and wisdom of the mathematicians) it would be more prudent to begin, and so by means of definitions reduce them to order. Yet even definitions cannot cure this evil in dealing with natural and material things; since the definitions themselves consist of words, and those words beget others: so that it is necessary to recur to individual instances, and those in due series and order. . . .

lx

The Idols imposed by words on the understanding are of two kinds. They are either names of things which do not exist (for as there are things left unnamed through lack of observation, so likewise are there names which result from fantastic suppositions and to which nothing in reality corresponds), or they are names of things which exist, but yet confused and ill-defined, and hastily and irregularly derived from realities. Of the former kind are Fortune, the Prime Mover, Planetary Orbits, Element of Fire, and like fictions which owe their origin to false and idle theories. And this class of idols is more easily expelled, because to get rid of them it is only necessary that all theories should be steadily rejected and dismissed as obsolete.

But the other class, which springs out of a faulty and unskillful abstraction, is intricate and deeply rooted. Let us take for example such a word as *humid,* and see how far the several things which the word is used to signify agree with each other; and we shall find the word *humid* to be nothing else than a mark loosely and confusedly applied to denote a variety of actions which will not bear to be reduced to any constant meaning. For it both signifies that which easily spreads itself round any other body; and that which in itself is indeterminate and cannot solidise; and that which readily yields in every direction; and that which easily divides and scatters itself; and that which easily unites and collects itself; and that which readily flows and is put in motion; and that which readily clings to another body and wets it; and that which is easily reduced to a liquid, or being solid easily melts. Accordingly when you come to apply the word,—if you take it in one sense, flame is humid; if in another, air is not humid; if in another, fine dust is humid; if in another, glass is humid. So that it is easy to see that the notion is taken by abstraction only from water and common and ordinary liquids, without any due verification.

There are however in words certain degrees of distortion and error. One of the least faulty kinds is that of names of substances, especially of lowest species and well-deduced (for the notion of *chalk* and of *mud* is good, of *earth* bad); a more faulty kind is that of actions, as *to generate, to corrupt, to alter;* the most faulty is of qualities (except such as are the immediate objects of the sense) as *heavy, light, rare, dense,* and the like. Yet in all these cases some notions are of necessity a little better than others, in proportion to the greater variety of subjects that fall within the range of the human sense.

lxi

But the *Idols of the Theatre* are not innate, nor do they steal into the understanding secretly, but are plainly impressed and received into the mind from the play-books of philosophical systems and the perverted rules of demonstration. To attempt refutations in this case would be merely inconsistent with what I have already said: for since we agree neither upon principles nor upon demonstrations there is no place for argument. And this is so far well, inasmuch as it leaves the honour of the ancients untouched. For they are no wise disparaged—the question between them and me being only as to the way. For as the saying is, the lame man who keeps the right road outstrips the runner who takes a wrong one. Nay it is obvious that when a man runs the wrong way, the more active and swift he is the further he will go astray.

But the course I propose for the discovery of sciences is such as leaves but little to the acuteness and strength of wits, but places all wits and understandings nearly on a level. For as in the drawing of a straight line or a perfect circle, much depends on the steadiness and practice of the hand, if it be done by aim of hand only, but if with the aid of rule or compass, little or nothing; so is it exactly with my plan. But though particular confutations would be of no avail, yet touching the sects and general divisions of such systems I must say something; something also touching the external signs which show that they are unsound; and finally something touching the causes of such great infelicity and of such lasting and general agreement in error; that so the access to truth may be made less difficult, and the human understanding may the more willingly submit to its purgation and dismiss its idols.

lxii

Idols of the Theatre, or of Systems, are many, and there can be and perhaps will be yet many more. For were it not that now for many ages men's minds have been busied with religion and theology; and were it not that civil governments, especially mon archies, have been averse to such novelties, even in matters specu-lative; so that men labour therein to the peril and harming of their fortunes,—not only unrewarded, but exposed also to con- tempt and envy: doubtless there would have arisen many other philosophical sects like to those which in great variety flourished once among the Greeks. For as on the phenomena of the heavens many hypotheses may be constructed, so likewise (and more also) many various dogmas may be set up and established on the phenomena of philosophy. And in the plays of this philosophical theatre you may observe the same thing which is found in the theatre of the poets, that stories invented for the stage are more compact and elegant, and more as one would wish them to be, than true stories out of history.

In general however there is taken for the material of philosophy either a great deal out of a few things, or a very little out of many things; so that on both sides philosophy is based on too narrow a foundation of experiment and natural history, and decides on the authority of too few cases. For the Rational School of philosophers snatches from experience a variety of common instances, neither duly ascertained nor diligently examined and weighed, and leaves all the rest to meditation and agitation of wit.

There is also another class of philosophers, who having bestowed much diligent and careful labour on a few experiments, have thence made bold to educe and construct systems; wresting all other facts in a strange fashion to conformity therewith.

And there is yet a third class, consisting of those who out of faith and veneration mix their philosophy with theology and traditions; among whom the vanity of some has gone so far aside as to seek the origin of sciences among spirits and genii. So that this parent stock of errors—this false philosophy—is of three kinds; the Sophistical, the Empirical, and the Superstitious.

8

THE USES OF LANGUAGE *

by

BERTRAND RUSSELL
(1872–1970)

Language, like other things of mysterious importance, such as breath, blood, sex, and lightning, has been viewed superstitiously ever since men were capable of recording their thoughts. Savages fear to disclose their true name to an enemy, lest he should work evil magic by means of it. Origen assures us that pagan sorcerers could achieve more by using the sacred name Jehovah than by means of the names Zeus, Osiris, or Brahma. Familiarity makes us blind to the linguistic emphasis in the Commandment: "Thou shalt not take the *name* of the Lord in vain." The habit of viewing language superstitiously is not yet extinct. "In the beginning was the Word", says our version of St. John's Gospel, and in reading some logical positivists I am tempted to think that their view is represented by this mistranslated text.

* [Except for a few lines, the whole of Chapter I of Part II in *Human Knowledge: Its Scope and Limits.* Copyright 1948 by Bertrand Russell. Reprinted by permission of Simon and Schuster, Inc.]

Philosophers, being bookish and theoretical folk, have been interested in language chiefly as a means of making statements and conveying information, but this is only one of its purposes, and perhaps not the most primitive. What is the purpose of language to a sergeant-major? On the one hand there is the language of words of command, designed to cause identical simultaneous bodily movements in a number of hearers; on the other hand there is bad language, designed to cause humility in those in whom the expected bodily movements have not been caused. In neither case are words used, except incidentally, to state facts or convey information.

Language can be used to express emotions, or to influence the behaviour of others. Each of these functions can be performed, though with less adequacy, by pre-linguistic methods. Animals emit shrieks of pain, and infants, before they can speak, can express rage, discomfort, desire, delight, and a whole gamut of feelings, by cries and gurgles of different kinds. A sheep dog emits imperatives to his flock by means hardly distinguishable from those that the shepherd employs towards him. Between such noises and speech no sharp line can be drawn. When the dentist hurts you, you may emit an involuntary groan; this does not count as speech. But if he says "let me know if I hurt you", and you then make the very same sound, it has become speech, and moreover speech of the sort intended to convey information. This example illustrates the fact that, in the matter of language as in other respects, there is a continuous gradation from animal behaviour to that of the most precise man of science, and from pre-linguistic noises to the polished diction of the lexicographer.

A sound expressive of emotion I shall call an "interjection". Imperatives and interjections can already be distinguished in the noises emitted by animals. When a hen clucks at her brood of chickens, she is uttering imperatives, but when she squawks in terror she is expressing emotion. But as appears from your groan at the dentist's, an interjection may convey information, and the outside observer cannot tell whether or not it is intended to do so. Gregarious animals emit distinctive noises when they find food, and other members of the herd are attracted when they hear these noises, but we cannot know whether the noises merely express pleasure or are also intended to state "food here".

Whenever an animal is so constructed that a certain kind of circumstance causes a certain kind of emotion, and a certain kind of emotion causes a certain kind of noise, the noise conveys to a suitable observer two pieces of information, first, that the animal has a certain kind of feeling, and second, that a certain kind of circumstance is present. The sound that the animal emits is public, and the circumstance may be public—e.g. the presence of a shoal of fish if the animal is a sea-gull. The animal's cry may act directly on the other members of its species, and *we* shall then say that they "understand" its cry. But this is to suppose a "mental" intermediary between the hearing of the cry and the bodily reaction to the sound, and there is no real reason to suppose any such intermediary except when the response is delayed. Much of the importance of language is connected with delayed responses, but I will not yet deal with this topic.

Language has two primary purposes, expression and communication. In its most primitive forms it differs little from some other forms of behaviour. A man may express sorrow by sighing, or by saying "alas!" or "woe is me!" He may communicate by pointing or by saying "look". Expression and communication are not necessarily separated; if you say "look" because you see a ghost, you may say it in a tone that expresses horror. This applies not only to elementary forms of language; in poetry, and especially in songs, emotion and information are conveyed by the same means. Music may be considered as a form of language in which emotion is divorced from information, while the telephone book gives information without emotion. But in ordinary speech both elements are usually present.

Communication does not consist only of giving information; commands and questions must be included. Sometimes the two are scarcely separable: if you are walking with a child, and you say "there's a puddle there", the command "don't step in it" is implicit. Giving information may be due solely to the fact that the information interests you, or may be designed to influence behaviour. If you have just seen a street accident, you will wish to tell your friends about it because your mind is full of it; but if you tell a child that six times seven is forty-two you do so merely in the hope of influencing his (verbal) behaviour.

Language has two interconnected merits: first, that it is social, and second that it supplies public expression for "thoughts" which would otherwise remain private. Without language, or some pre-linguistic analogue, our knowledge of the environment is confined to what our own senses have shown us, together with such inferences as our congenital constitution may prompt; but by the help of speech we are able to know what others can relate, and to relate what is no longer sensibly present but only remembered. When we see or hear something which a companion is not seeing or hearing, we can often make him aware of it by the one word "look" or "listen", or even by gestures. But if half an hour ago we saw a fox, it is not possible to make another person aware of this fact without language. This depends upon the fact that the word "fox" applies equally to a fox seen or a fox remembered, so that our memories, which in themselves are private, are represented to others by uttered sounds, which are public. Without language, only that part of our life which consists of public sensations would be communicable, and that only to those so situated as to be able to share the sensations in question.

It will be seen that the utility of language depends upon the distinction between public and private experiences, which is important in considering the empirical basis of physics. This distinction, in turn, depends partly on physiology, partly on the persistence of sound-waves and light quanta, which makes possible the two forms of language, speech and writing. Thus language depends upon physics, and could not exist without the approximately separable causal chains which . . . make physical knowledge possible, and since the publicity of sensible objects is only approximate, language applying to them, considered socially, must have a certain lack of precision. I need hardly say that I am *not* asserting that the existence of language requires a *knowledge* of physics. What I am saying is that language would be impossible if the physical world did not in fact have certain characteristics, and that the *theory* of language is at certain points dependent upon a knowledge of the physical world. Language is a means of externalizing and publicizing our own experiences. A dog cannot relate his autobiography; however eloquently he may bark, he cannot tell you that his parents were honest though poor. A man can do this, and he does it by correlating "thoughts" with public sensations.

Language serves not only to express thoughts, but to make possible thoughts which could not exist without it. It is sometimes maintained that there can be no thought without language, but to this view I cannot assent: I hold that there can be thought, and even true and false belief, without language. But however that may be, it cannot be denied that all fairly elaborate thoughts require words. I can know, in a sense, that I have five fingers, without knowing the word "five", but I cannot know that the population of London is about eight millions unless I have acquired the language of arithmetic, nor can I have any thought at all closely corresponding to what is asserted in the sentence: "the ratio of the circumference of a circle to the diameter is approximately $3·14159$". Language, once evolved, acquires a kind of autonomy: we can know, especially in mathematics, that a sentence asserts something true, although what it asserts is too complex to be apprehended even by the best minds. Let us consider for a moment what happens psychologically in such cases.

In mathematics, we start from rather simple sentences which we believe ourselves capable of understanding, and proceed, by rules of inference which we also believe ourselves to understand, to build up more and more complicated symbolic statements, which, if our initial assumptions are true, must be true whatever they may mean. As a rule it is unnecessary to know what they "mean", if their "meaning" is taken to be a thought which might occur in the mind of a superhuman mathematical genius. But there is another kind of "meaning", which gives occasion for pragmatism and instrumentalism. According to those who adopt this view of "meaning", what a complicated mathematical sentence does is to give a rule for practical procedure in certain kinds of cases. Take, for instance, the above statement about the ratio of the circumference of a circle to the diameter. Suppose you are a brewer, and you desire hoops of a given diameter for your beer barrels, then the sentence gives you a rule by which you can find out how much material you will need. This rule may consist of a fresh sentence for each decimal point, and there is therefore no need ever to grasp its significance as a whole. The autonomy of language enables you to forego this tedious process of interpretation except at crucial moments.

There are two other uses of language that are of great importance; it enables us to conduct our transactions with the outer world by means of symbols that have (1) a certain degree of permanence in time, (2) a considerable degree of discreteness in space. Each of these merits is more marked in writing than in speech, but is by no means wholly absent in speech. Suppose you have a friend called Mr. Jones. As a physical object his boundaries are somewhat vague, both because he is continually losing and acquiring electrons, and because an electron, being a distribution of energy, does not cease abruptly at a certain distance from its centre. The surface of Mr. Jones, therefore, has a certain ghostly impalpable quality, which you do not like to associate with your solid-seeming friend. It is not necessary to go into the niceties of theoretical physics in order to show that Mr. Jones is sadly indeterminate. When he is cutting his toe nails, there is a finite time, though a short one, during which it is doubtful whether the parings are still part of him or not. When he eats a mutton chop, at what moment does it become part of him? When he breathes out carbon dioxide, is the carbon part of him until it passes his nostrils? Even if we answer in the affirmative, there is a finite time during which it is questionable whether certain molecules have or have not passed beyond his nostrils. In these and other ways, it is doubtful what is part of Mr. Jones and what is not. So much for spatial vagueness.

There is the same problem as regards time. To the question "what are you looking at?" you may answer "Mr. Jones", although at one time you see him full-face, at another in profile, and at another from behind, and although at one time he may be running a race and at another time dozing in an arm-chair. There is another question, namely "what are you thinking of?" to which you may also answer "Mr. Jones", though what is actually in your mind may be very different on different occasions: it may be Mr. Jones as a baby, or Mr. Jones being cross because his breakfast is late, or Mr. Jones receiving the news that he is to be knighted. What you are experiencing is very different on these various occasions, but for many practical purposes it is convenient to regard them as all having a common object, which we suppose to be the meaning of the name "Mr. Jones". This name, especially when printed, though it cannot wholly escape the indefiniteness and transience of all physical objects, has much less of both than Mr. Jones has. Two instances of the printed words "Mr. Jones" are much more alike than (for instance) the spectacle of Mr. Jones running and the memory of Mr. Jones as a baby. And each instance, if printed, changes much more slowly than Mr. Jones does: it does not eat or breathe or cut its toe nails. The name, accordingly, makes it much easier than it would otherwise be to think of Mr. Jones as a single quasi-permanent entity, which, though untrue, is convenient in daily life.

Language, as appears from the above discussion of Mr. Jones, though a useful and even indispensable tool, is a dangerous one, since it begins by suggesting a definiteness, discreteness, and quasi-permanence in objects which physics seems to show that they do not possess. The philosopher, therefore, is faced with the difficult task of using language to undo the false beliefs that it suggests. Some philosophers, who shrink from the problems and uncertainties and complications involved in such a task, prefer to treat language as autonomous, and try to forget that it is intended to have a relation to fact and to facilitate dealings with the environment. Up to a point, such a treatment has great advantages: logic and mathematics would not have prospered as they have done if logicians and mathematicians had continually remembered that symbols should mean something. "Art for art's sake" is a maxim which has a legitimate sphere in logic as in painting (though in neither case does it give the whole truth). It may be that singing began as an incident in courtship, and that its biological purpose was to promote sexual intercourse; but this fact (if it be a fact) will not help a composer to produce good music. Language is useful when you wish to order a meal in a restaurant, but this fact, similarly, is of no importance to the pure mathematician.

The philosopher, however, must pursue truth even at the expense of beauty, and in studying language he must not let himself be seduced by the siren songs of mathematics. Language, in its beginnings, is pedestrian and practical, using rough and ready approximations which have at first no beauty and only a very limited degree of truth.

9

NATURE *

by

JOHN STUART MILL

(1806–1873)

According to the Platonic method which is still the best type of such investigations, the first thing to be done with so vague a term is to ascertain precisely what it means. It is also a rule of the same method, that the meaning of an abstraction is best sought for in the concrete—of an universal in the particular. Adopting this course with the word Nature, the first question must be, what is meant by the "nature" of a particular object? as of fire, of water, or of some individual plant or animal? Evidently the *ensemble* or aggregate of its powers or properties: the modes in which it acts on other things (counting among those things the senses of the observer) and the modes in which other things act upon it; to which, in the case of a sentient being, must be added, its own capacities of feeling, or being conscious. The Nature of the thing means all this; means its entire capacity of exhibiting phenomena. And since the phenomena which a thing exhibits, however much they vary in different circumstances, are always the same in the same circumstances, they admit of being described in general forms of words, which are called the *laws* of the thing's nature. Thus it is a law of the nature of water that under the mean pressure of the atmosphere at the level of the sea, it boils at 212° Fahrenheit.

As the nature of any given thing is the aggregate of its powers

* [The greater part of the first essay in *Three Essays on Religion* (1874).]

and properties, so Nature in the abstract is the aggregate of the powers and properties of all things. Nature means the sum of all phenomena, together with the causes which produce them; including not only all that happens, but all that is capable of happening; the unused capabilities of causes being as much a part of the idea of Nature, as those which take effect. Since all phenomena which have been sufficiently examined are found to take place with regularity, each having certain fixed conditions, positive and negative, on the occurrence of which it invariably happens; mankind have been able to ascertain, either by direct observation or by reasoning processes grounded on it, the conditions of the occurrence of many phenomena; and the progress of science mainly consists in ascertaining those conditions. When discovered they can be expressed in general propositions, which are called laws of the particular phenomenon, and also, more generally, Laws of Nature. Thus, the truth that all material objects tend towards one another with a force directly as their masses and inversely as the square of their distance, is a law of Nature. The proposition that air and food are necessary to animal life, if it be as we have good reason to believe, true without exception, is also a law of nature, though the phenomenon of which it is the law is special, and not, like gravitation, universal.

Nature, then, in this its simplest acceptation, is a collective name for all facts, actual and possible: or (to speak more accurately) a name for the mode, partly known to us and partly unknown, in which all things take place. For the word suggests, not so much the multitudinous detail of the phenomena, as the conception which might be formed of their manner of existence as a mental whole, by a mind possessing a complete knowledge of them: to which conception it is the aim of science to raise itself, by successive steps of generalization from experience.

Such, then, is a correct definition of the word Nature. But this definition corresponds only to one of the senses of that ambiguous term. It is evidently inapplicable to some of the modes in which the word is familarly employed. For example, it entirely conflicts with the common form of speech by which Nature is opposed to Art, and natural to artificial. For in the sense of the word Nature which has just been defined, and which is the true scientific sense, Art is as much Nature as anything else; and everything which is artificial is natural—Art has no independent powers of its own: Art is but the employment of the powers of Nature for an end. Phenomena produced by human agency, no less than those which as far as we are concerned are spontaneous, depend on the properties of the elementary forces, or of the elementary substances and their compounds. The united powers of the whole human race could not create a new property of matter in general, or of any one of its species. We can only take advantage for our purposes of the properties which we find. A ship floats by the same laws of specific gravity and equilibrium, as a tree uprooted by the wind and blown into the water. The corn which men raise for food, grows and produces its grain by the same laws of vegetation by which the wild rose and the mountain strawberry bring forth their flowers and fruit. A house stands and holds together by the natural properties, the weight and cohesion of the materials which compose it: a steam engine works by the natural expansive force of steam, exerting a pressure upon one part of a system of arrangements, which pressure, by the mechanical properties of the lever, is transferred from that to another part where it raises the weight or removes the obstacle brought into connexion with it. In these and all other artificial operations the office of man is, as has often been remarked, a very limited one; it consists in moving things into certain places. We move objects, and by doing this, bring some things into contact which were separate, or separate others which were in contact: and by this simple change of place, natural forces previously dormant are called into action, and produce the desired effect. Even the volition which designs, the intelligence which contrives, and the muscular force which executes these movements, are themselves powers of Nature.

It thus appears that we must recognize at least two principal meanings in the word Nature. In one sense, it means all the powers existing in either the outer or the inner world and everything which takes place by means of those powers. In another sense, it means, not everything which happens, but only what takes place without the agency, or without the voluntary and intentional agency, of man. This distinction is far from exhausting the ambiguities of the word; but it is the key to most of those on which important consequences depend.

Such, then, being the two principal senses of the word Nature; in which of these is it taken, or is it taken in either, when the word and its derivatives are used to convey ideas of commendation, approval, and even moral obligation?

It has conveyed such ideas in all ages. *Naturam sequi* [follow nature] was the fundamental principle of morals in many of the most admired schools of philosophy. Among the ancients, especially in the declining period of ancient intellect and thought, it was the test to which all ethical doctrines were brought. The Stoics and the Epicureans, however irreconcilable in the rest of their systems, agreed in holding themselves bound to prove that their respective maxims of conduct were the dictates of nature. Under their influence the Roman jurists, when attempting to systematize jurisprudence, placed in the front of their exposition a certain *Jus Naturale* [natural law], "quod natura," as Justinian declares in the Institutes, "omnia animalia docuit" ["what nature has taught all animals"]: and as the modern systematic writers not only on law but on moral philosophy, have generally taken the Roman jurists for their models, treatises on the so-called Law of Nature have abounded; and references to this Law as a supreme rule and ultimate standard have pervaded literature. The writers on International Law have done more than any others to give currency to this style of ethical speculation; inasmuch as having no positive law to write about, and yet being anxious to invest the most approved opinions respecting international morality with as much as they could of the authority of law, they endeavoured to find such an authority in Nature's imaginary code. The Christian theology during the period of its greatest ascendancy, opposed some, though not a complete, hindrance to the modes of thought which erected Nature into the criterion of morals, inasmuch as, according to the creed of most denominations of Christians (though assuredly not of Christ) man is by nature wicked. But this very doctrine, by the reaction which it provoked, has made the deistical moralists almost unanimous in proclaiming the divinity of Nature, and setting up its fancied dictates as an authoritative rule of action. . . . Though perhaps no one could now be found who like the institutional writers of former times, adopts the so-called Law of Nature as the foundation of ethics, and endeavours consistently to reason from it, the word and its cognates must still be counted among those which carry great weight in moral argumentation. That any mode of thinking, feeling, or acting, is "according to nature" is usually accepted as a strong argument for its goodness. If it can be said with any plausibility that "nature enjoins" anything, the propriety of obeying the injunction is by most people considered to be made out: and conversely, the imputation of being contrary to nature, is thought to bar the door against any pretension on the part of the thing so designated, to be tolerated or excused; and the word unnatural has not ceased to be one of the most vituperative epithets in the language. Those who deal in these expressions, may avoid making themselves responsible for any fundamental theorem respecting the standard of moral obligation, but they do not the less imply such a theorem, and one which must be the same in substance with that on which the more logical thinkers of a more laborious age grounded their systematic treatises on Natural Law.

Is it necessary to recognize in these forms of speech, another distinct meaning of the word Nature? Or can they be connected, by any rational bond of union, with either of the two meanings already treated of? At first it may seem that we have no option but to admit another ambiguity in the term. All inquiries are either into what is, or into what ought to be: science and history belonging to the first division, art, morals and politics to the second. But the two senses of the word Nature first pointed out, agree in referring only to what is. In the first meaning, Nature is a collective name for everything which is. In the second, it is a name for everything which is of itself, without voluntary human intervention. But the employment of the word Nature as a term of ethics seems to disclose a third meaning, in which Nature does not stand for what is, but for what ought to be; or for the rule or standard of what ought to be. A little consideration, however, will show that this is not a case of ambiguity; there is not here a third sense of the word. Those who set up Nature as a standard of action do not intend a merely verbal proposition; they do not mean that the standard, whatever it be, should be *called* Nature; they think they are giving some information as to what the standard of action really is. Those who say that we ought to act according to Nature do not mean the mere identical proposition that we ought to do what we ought to do. They think that the word Nature affords some external criterion of what we should do; and if they lay down as a rule for what ought to be, a word which in its proper signification denotes what is, they do so because they have a notion, either clearly or confusedly, that what is, constitutes the rule and standard of what ought to be.

The examination of this notion, is the object of the present Essay. It is proposed to inquire into the truth of the doctrines which make Nature a test of right and wrong, good and evil, or which in any mode or degree attach merit or approval to following, imitating, or obeying Nature. To this inquiry the foregoing discussion respecting the meaning of terms, was an indispensable introduction. Language is as it were the atmosphere of philosophical investigation, which must be made transparent before anything can be seen through it in the true figure and position. In the present case it is necessary to guard against a further ambiguity, which though abundantly obvious, has sometimes misled even sagacious minds, and of which it is well to take distinct note before proceeding further. No word is more commonly associated with the word Nature, than Law; and this last word has distinctly two meanings, in one of which it denotes some definite portion of what is, in the other, of what ought to be. We speak of the law of gravitation, the three laws of motion, the law of definite proportions in chemical combination, the vital laws of organized beings. All these are portions of what is. We also speak of the criminal law, the civil law, the law of honour, the law of veracity, the law of justice; all of which are portions of what ought to be, or of somebody's suppositions, feelings, or commands respecting what ought to be. The first kind of laws, such as the laws of motion, and of gravitation, are neither more nor less than the observed uniformities in the occurrence of phenomena: partly uniformities of antecedence and sequence, partly of concomitance. These are what, in science, and even in ordinary parlance, are meant by laws of nature. Laws in the other sense are the laws of the land, the law of nations, or moral laws; among which, as already noticed, is dragged in, by jurists and publicists, something which they think proper to call the Law of Nature. Of the liability of these two meanings of the word to be confounded there can be no better example than the first chapter of Montesquieu; where he remarks, that the material world has its laws, the inferior animals have their laws, and man has his laws; and calls attention to the much greater strictness with which the first two sets of laws are observed, than the last; as if it were an inconsistency, and a paradox, that things always are what they are, but men not always what they ought to be. A similar confusion of ideas pervades the writings of Mr. George Combe, from whence it has overflowed into a large region of popular literature, and we are now continually reading injunctions to obey the physical laws of the universe, as being obligatory in the same sense and manner as the moral. The conception which the ethical use of the word Nature implies, of a close relation if not absolute identity between what is and what ought to be, certainly derives part of its hold on the mind from the custom of designating what is, by the expression "laws of nature," while the same word Law is also used, and even more familiarly and emphatically, to express what ought to be.

When it is asserted, or implied, that Nature, or the laws of Nature, should be conformed to, is the Nature which is meant, Nature in the first sense of the term, meaning all which is—the powers and properties of all things? But in this signification, there is no need of a recommendation to act according to nature, since it is what nobody can possibly help doing, and equally whether he acts well or ill. There is no mode of acting which is not conformable to Nature in this sense of the term, and all modes of acting are so in exactly the same degree. Every action is the exertion of some natural power, and its effects of all sorts are so many phenomena of nature, produced by the powers and properties of some of the objects of nature, in exact obedience to some law or laws of nature. When I voluntarily use my organs to take in food, the act, and its consequences, take place according to laws of nature: if instead of food I swallow poison, the case is exactly the same. To bid people conform to the laws of nature when they have no power but what the laws of nature give them—

when it is a physical impossibility for them to do the smallest thing otherwise than through some law of nature, is an absurdity. The thing they need to be told is, what particular law of nature they should make use of in a particular case. When, for example, a person is crossing a river by a narrow bridge to which there is no parapet, he will do well to regulate his proceedings by the laws of equilibrium in moving bodies, instead of conforming only to the law of gravitation, and falling into the river.

Yet, idle as it is to exhort people to do what they cannot avoid doing, and absurd as it is to prescribe as a rule of right conduct what agrees exactly as well with wrong; nevertheless a rational rule of conduct *may* be constructed out of the relation which it ought to bear to the laws of nature in this widest acceptation of the term. Man necessarily obeys the laws of nature, or in other words the properties of things, but he does not necessarily *guide* himself by them. Though all conduct is in conformity to laws of nature, all conduct is not grounded on knowledge of them, and intelligently directed to the attainment of purposes by means of them. Though we cannot emancipate ourselves from the laws of nature as a whole, we can escape from any particular law of nature, if we are able to withdraw ourselves from the circumstances in which it acts. Though we can do nothing except through laws of nature, we can use one law to counteract another. According to Bacon's maxim, we can obey nature in such a manner as to command it. Every alteration of circumstances alters more or less the laws of nature under which we act; and by every choice which we make either of ends or of means, we place ourselves to a greater or less extent under one set of laws of nature instead of another. If, therefore, the useless precept to follow nature were changed into a precept to study nature; to know and take heed of the properties of the things we have to deal with, so far as these properties are capable of forwarding or obstructing any given purpose; we should have arrived at the first principle of all intelligent action, or rather at the definition of intelligent action itself. And a confused notion of this true principle, is, I doubt not, in the minds of many of those who set up the unmeaning doctrine which superficially resembles it. They perceive that the essential difference between wise and foolish conduct consists in attending, or not attending, to the particular laws of nature on which some important result depends. And they think, that a person who attends to a law of nature in order to shape his conduct by it, may be said to obey it, while a person who practically disregards it, and acts as if no such law existed, may be said to disobey it: the circumstance being overlooked, that what is thus called disobedience to a law of nature is obedience to some other or perhaps to the very law itself.

For example, a person who goes into a powder magazine either not knowing, or carelessly omitting to think of, the explosive force of gunpowder, is likely to do some act which will cause him to be blown to atoms in obedience to the very law which he has disregarded.

But however much of its authority the "Naturam sequi" doctrine may owe to its being confounded with the rational precept "Naturam observare" ["observe" nature], its favourers and promoters unquestionably intend much more by it than that precept. To acquire knowledge of the properties of things, and make use of the knowledge for guidance, is a rule of prudence, for the adaptation of means to ends; for giving effect to our wishes and intentions whatever they may be. But the maxim of obedience to Nature, or conformity to Nature, is held up not as a simply prudential but as an ethical maxim; and by those who talk of *jus naturæ*, even as a law, fit to be administered by tribunals and enforced by sanctions. Right action, must mean something more and other than merely intelligent action: yet no precept beyond this last, can be connected with the word Nature in the wider and more philosophical of its acceptations. We must try it therefore in the other sense, that in which Nature stands distinguished from Art, and denotes, not the whole course of the phenomena which come under our observation, but only their spontaneous course.

Let us then consider whether we can attach any meaning to the supposed practical maxim of following Nature, in this second sense of the word, in which Nature stands for that which takes place without human intervention. In Nature as thus understood, is the spontaneous course of things when left to themselves, the rule to be followed in endeavouring to adapt things to our use? But it is evident at once that the maxim, taken in this sense, is not merely, as it is in the other sense, superfluous and unmeaning, but palpably absurd and self-contradictory. For while human action cannot help conforming to Nature in the one meaning of the term, the very aim and object of action is to alter and improve Nature in the other meaning. If the natural course of things were perfectly right and satisfactory, to act at all would be a gratuitous meddling, which as it could not make things better, must make them worse. Or if action at all could be justified, it would only be when in direct obedience to instincts, since these might perhaps be accounted part of the spontaneous order of Nature; but to do anything with forethought and purpose, would be a violation of that perfect order. If the artificial is not better than the natural, to what end are all the arts of life? To dig, to plough, to build, to wear clothes, are direct infringements of the injunction to follow nature.

Accordingly it would be said by everyone, even of those most under the influence of the feelings which prompt the injunction, that to apply it to such cases as those just spoken of, would be to push it too far. Everybody professes to approve and admire many great triumphs of Art over Nature: the junction by bridges of shores which Nature had made separate, the draining of Nature's marshes, the excavation of her wells, the dragging to light of what she has buried at immense depths in the earth; the turning away of her thunderbolts by lightning rods, of her inundations by embankments, of her ocean by breakwaters. But to commend these and similar feats, is to acknowledge that the ways of Nature are to be conquered, not obeyed: that her powers are often towards man in the position of enemies, from whom he must wrest, by force and ingenuity, what little he can for his own use, and deserves to be applauded when that little is rather more than might be expected from his physical weakness in comparison to those gigantic powers. All praise of Civilization, or Art, or Contrivance, is so much dispraise of Nature; an admission of imperfection, which it is man's business, and merit, to be always endeavouring to correct or mitigate.

The consciousness that whatever man does to improve his condition is in so much a censure and a thwarting of the spontaneous order of Nature, has in all ages caused new and unprecedented attempts at improvement to be generally at first under a shade of religious suspicion; as being in any case uncomplimentary, and very probably offensive to the powerful beings (or, when polytheism gave place to monotheism, to the all-powerful Being) supposed to govern the various phenomena of the universe, and of whose will the course of nature was conceived to be the expression. Any attempt to mould natural phenomena to the convenience of mankind might easily appear an interference with the government of those superior beings: and though life could not have been maintained, much less made pleasant, without perpetual interferences of the kind, each new one was doubtless made with fear and trembling, until experience had shown that it could be ventured on without drawing down the vengeance of the Gods. The sagacity of priests showed them a way to reconcile the impunity of particular infringements with the maintenance of the general dread of encroaching on the divine administration. This was effected by representing each of the principal human inventions as the gift and favour of some God. The old religions also afforded many resources for consulting the Gods, and obtaining their express permission for what would otherwise have appeared a breach of their prerogative. When oracles had ceased, any religon which recognized a revelation afforded expedients for the same purpose. The Catholic religion had the resource of an infallible Church, authorized to declare what exertions of human spontaneity were permitted or forbidden; and in default of this, the case was always open to argument from the Bible whether any particular practice had expressly or by implication been sanctioned. The notion remained that this liberty to control Nature was conceded to man only by special indulgence, and as far as required by his necessities; and there was always a tendency, though a diminishing one, to regard any attempt to exercise power over nature, beyond a certain degree, and a certain admitted range, as an impious effort to usurp divine power, and dare more than was permitted to man. The lines of Horace in which the familiar arts of shipbuilding and navigation are reprobated as *vetitum nefas* [a forbidden sin], indicate even in that sceptical age a still unexhausted vein of the old sentiment. The intensity of the corresponding feeling in the middle ages is not a precise parallel, on account of the superstition about dealing with evil spirits with which it was complicated: but the imputation of prying into the secrets of the Almighty long remained a powerful weapon of attack against unpopular inquirers into nature; and the charge of presumptuously attempting to defeat the designs of Providence, still retains enough of its original force to be thrown in as a make-weight along with other objections when there is a desire to find fault with any new exertion of human forethought and contrivance. No one, indeed, asserts it to be the intention of the Creator that the spontaneous order of the creation should not be altered, or even that it should not be altered in any new way. But there still exists a vague notion that though it is very proper to control this or the other natural phenomenon, the general scheme of nature is a model for us to imitate: that with more or less liberty in details, we should on the whole be guided by the spirit and general conception of nature's own ways: that they are God's work, and as such perfect; that man cannot rival their unapproachable excellence, and can best show his skill and piety by attempting, in however imperfect a way, to reproduce their likeness; and that if not the whole, yet some particular parts of the spontaneous order of nature, selected according to the speaker's predilections, are in a peculiar sense, manifestations of the Creator's will; a sort of finger posts pointing out the direction which things in general, and therefore our voluntary actions, are intended to take. Feelings of this sort, though repressed on ordinary occasions by the contrary current of life, are ready to break out whenever custom is silent, and the native promptings of the mind have nothing opposed to them but reason: and appeals are continually made to them by rhetoricians, with the effect, if not of convincing opponents, at least of making those who already hold the opinion which the rhetorician desires to recommend, better satisfied with it. For in the present day it probably seldom happens that any one is persuaded to approve any course of action because it appears to him to bear an analogy to the divine government of the world, though the argument tells on him with great force, and is felt by him to be a great support, in behalf of anything which he is already inclined to approve.

If this notion of imitating the ways of Providence as manifested in Nature, is seldom expressed plainly and downrightly as a maxim of general application, it also is seldom directly contradicted. Those who find it on their path, prefer to turn the obstacle rather than to attack it, being often themselves not free from the feeling, and in any case afraid of incurring the charge of impiety by saying anything which might be held to disparage the works of the Creator's power. They therefore, for the most part, rather endeavour to show, that they have as much right to the religious argument as their opponents, and that if the course they recommend seems to conflict with some part of the ways of Providence, there is some other part with which it agrees better than what is contended for on the other side. In this mode of dealing with the great *a priori* fallacies, the progress of improvement clears away particular errors while the causes of errors are still left standing, and very little weakened by each conflict: yet by a long series of such partial victories precedents are accumulated, to which an appeal may be made against these powerful prepossessions, and which afford a growing hope that the misplaced feeling, after having so often learnt to recede, may some day be compelled to an unconditional surrender. For however offensive the proposition may appear to many religious persons, they should be willing to look in the face the undeniable fact, that the order of nature, in so far as unmodified by man, is such as no being, whose attributes are justice and benevolence, would have made, with the intention that his rational creatures should follow it as an example. If made wholly by such a Being, and not partly by beings of very different qualities, it could only be as a designedly imperfect work, which man, in his limited sphere, is to exercise justice and benevolence in amending. The best persons have always held it to be the essence of religion, that the paramount duty of man upon earth is to amend himself: but all except monkish quietists have annexed to this in their inmost minds (though seldom willing to enunciate the obligation with the same clearness) the additional religious duty of amending the world, and not solely the human part of it but the material; the order of physical nature.

In considering this subject it is necessary to divest ourselves of certain preconceptions which may justly be called natural prejudices, being grounded on feelings which, in themselves natural and inevitable, intrude into matters with which they ought to have no concern. One of these feelings is the astonishment, rising into awe, which is inspired (even independently of all religious sentiment) by any of the greater natural phenomena. A hurricane; a mountain precipice; the desert; the ocean, either agitated or at rest; the solar system, and the great cosmic forces which hold it together; the boundless firmament, and to an educated mind any single star; excite feelings which make all human enterprises and powers appear so insignificant, that to a mind thus occupied it seems insufferable presumption in so puny a creature as man to look critically on things so far above him, or dare to measure himself against the grandeur of the universe. But a little interrogation of our own consciousness will suffice to convince us, that what makes these phenomena so impressive is simply their vastness. The enormous extension in space and time, or the enormous power they exemplify, constitutes their sublimity; a feeling in all cases, more allied to terror than to any moral emotion. And though the vast scale of these phenomena may well excite wonder, and sets at defiance all idea of rivalry, the feeling it inspires is of a totally different character from admiration of excellence. Those in whom awe produces admiration may be æsthetically developed, but they are morally uncultivated. It is one of the endowments of the imaginative part of our mental nature that conceptions of greatness and power, vividly realized, produce a feeling which though in its higher degrees closely bordering on pain, we prefer to most of what are accounted pleasures. But we are quite equally capable of experiencing this feeling towards maleficent power; and we never experience it so strongly towards most of the powers of the universe, as when we have most present to our consciousness a vivid sense of their capacity of inflicting evil. Because these natural powers have what we cannot imitate, enormous might, and overawe us by that one attribute, it would be a great error to infer that their other attributes are such as we ought to emulate, or that we should be justified in using our small powers after the example which Nature sets us with her vast forces.

For, how stands the fact? That next to the greatness of these cosmic forces, the quality which most forcibly strikes every one who does not avert his eyes from it, is their perfect and absolute recklessness. They go straight to their end, without regarding what or whom they crush on the road. Optimists, in their attempts to prove that "whatever is, is right," are obliged to maintain, not that Nature ever turns one step from her path to avoid trampling us into destruction, but that it would be very unreasonable in us to expect that she should. Pope's "Shall gravitation cease when you go by?" may be a just rebuke to any one who should be so silly as to expect common human morality from nature. But if the question were between two men, instead of between a man and a natural phenomenon, that triumphant apostrophe would be thought a rare piece of impudence. A man who should persist in hurling stones or firing cannon when another man "goes by," and having killed him should urge a similar plea in exculpation, would very deservedly be found guilty of murder.

In sober truth, nearly all the things which men are hanged or imprisoned for doing to one another, are nature's every day performances. Killing, the most criminal act recognized by human laws, Nature does once to every being that lives; and in a large proportion of cases, after protracted tortures such as only the greatest monsters whom we read of ever purposely inflicted on their living fellow-creatures. If, by an arbitrary reservation, we refuse to account anything murder but what abridges a certain term supposed to be allotted to human life, nature also does this to all but a small percentage of lives, and does it in all the modes, violent or insidious, in which the worst human beings take the lives of one another. Nature impales men, breaks them as if on the wheel, casts them to be devoured by wild beasts, burns them to death, crushes them with stones like the first Christian martyr, starves them with hunger, freezes them with cold, poisons them by the quick or slow venom of her exhalations, and has hundreds of other hideous deaths in reserve, such as the ingenious cruelty of a Nabis or a Domitian never surpassed. All this, Nature does with the most supercilious disregard both of mercy and of justice, emptying her shafts upon the best and noblest indifferently with the meanest and worst; upon those who are engaged in the highest and worthiest enterprises, and often as the direct consequence of the noblest acts; and it might almost be imagined as a punishment for them. . . . Even the love of "order" which is thought to be a following of the ways of Nature, is in fact a contradiction of them. All which people are accustomed to deprecate as "disorder" and its consequences, is precisely a counterpart of Nature's ways. Anarchy and the Reign of Terror are overmatched in injustice, ruin, and death, by a hurricane and a pestilence.

But, it is said, all these things are for wise and good ends. On this I must first remark that whether they are so or not, is altogether beside the point. Supposing it true that contrary to appearances these horrors when perpetrated by Nature, promote good ends, still as no one believes that good ends would be promoted by our following the example, the course of Nature cannot be a proper model for us to imitate. Either it is right that we should kill because nature kills; torture because nature tortures; ruin and devastate because nature does the like; or we ought not to consider at all what nature does, but what it is good to do. If there is such a thing as a *reductio ad absurdum,* this surely amounts to one. If it is a sufficient reason for doing one thing, that nature does it, why not another thing? If not all things, why anything? The physical government of the world being full of the things which when done by men are deemed the greatest enormities, it cannot be religious or moral in us to guide our actions by the analogy of the course of nature. This proposition remains true, whatever occult quality of producing good may reside in those facts of nature which to our perceptions are most noxious, and which no one considers it other than a crime to produce artificially.

But, in reality, no one consistently believes in any such occult quality. The phrases which ascribe perfection to the course of nature can only be considered as the exaggerations of poetic or devotional feeling, not intended to stand the test of a sober examination. No one, either religious or irreligious, believes that the hurtful agencies of nature, considered as a whole, promote good purposes, in any other way than by inciting human rational creatures to rise up and struggle against them. If we believed that those agencies were appointed by a benevolent Providence as the means of accomplishing wise purposes which could not be compassed if they did not exist, then everything done by mankind which tends to chain up these natural agencies or to restrict their mischievous operation, from draining a pestilential marsh down to curing the toothache, or putting up an umbrella, ought to be accounted impious; which assuredly nobody does account them, notwithstanding an undercurrent of sentiment setting in that direction which is occasionally perceptible. On the contrary, the improvements on which the civilized part of mankind most pride themselves, consist in more successfully warding off those natural calamities which if we really believed what most people profess to believe, we should cherish as medicines provided for our earthly state by infinite wisdom. Inasmuch too as each generation greatly surpasses its predecessors in the amount of natural evil which it succeeds in averting, our condition, if the theory were true, ought by this time to have become a terrible manifestation of some tremendous calamity, against which the physical evils we have learnt to overmaster, had previously operated as a preservative. Any one, however, who acted as if he supposed this to be the case, would be more likely, I think, to be confined as a lunatic, than reverenced as a saint.

It is undoubtedly a very common fact that good comes out of evil, and when it does occur, it is far too agreeable not to find people eager to dilate on it. But in the first place, it is quite as often true of human crimes, as of natural calamities. The fire of London, which is believed to have had so salutary an effect on the healthiness of the city, would have produced that effect just as much if it had been really the work of the "furor papisticus" ["popish madness"] so long commemorated on the Monument. The deaths of those whom tyrants or persecutors have made martyrs in any noble cause, have done a service to mankind which would not have been obtained if they had died by accident or disease. Yet whatever incidental and unexpected benefits may result from crimes, they are crimes nevertheless. In the second place, if good frequently comes out of evil, the converse fact, evil coming out of good, is equally common. Every event public or private, which, regretted on its occurrence, was declared providential at a later period on account of some unforeseen good consequence, might be matched by some other event, deemed fortunate at the time, but which proved calamitous or fatal to those whom it appeared to benefit. Such conflicts between the beginning and the end, or between the event and the expectation, are not only as frequent, but as often held up to notice, in the painful cases as in the agreeable; but there is not the same inclination to generalize on them; or at all events they are not regarded by the moderns (though they were by the ancients) as similarly an indication of the divine purposes: men satisfy themselves with moralizing on the imperfect nature of our foresight, the uncertainty of events, and the vanity of human expectations. The simple fact is, human interests are so complicated, and the effects of any incident whatever so multitudinous, that if it touches mankind at all, its influence on them is, in the great majority of cases, both good and bad. If the greater number of personal misfortunes have their good side, hardly any good fortune ever befel any one which did not give either to the same or to some other person, something to regret: and unhappily there are many misfortunes so overwhelming that their favourable side, if it exist, is entirely overshadowed and made insignificant; while the corresponding statement can seldom be made concerning blessings. The effects too of every cause depend so much on the circumstances which accidentally accompany it, that many cases are sure to occur in which even the total result is markedly opposed to the predominant tendency: and thus not only evil has its good and good its evil side, but good often produces an overbalance of evil and evil an overbalance of good. This, however, is by no means the general tendency of either phenomenon. On the contrary, both good and evil naturally tend to fructify, each in its own kind, good producing good, and evil, evil. It is one of Nature's general rules, and part of her habitual injustice, that "to him that hath shall be given, but from him that hath not, shall be taken even that which he hath." The ordinary and predominant tendency of good is towards more good. Health, strength, wealth, knowledge, virtue, are not only good in themselves but facilitate and promote the acquisition of good, both of the same and of other kinds. The person who can learn easily, is he who already knows much: it is the strong and not the sickly person who can do everything which most conduces to health; those who find it easy to gain money are not the poor but the rich; while health, strength, knowledge, talents, are all means of acquiring riches, and riches are often an indispensable means of acquiring these. Again, *e converso* [and conversely], whatever may be said of evil turning into good, the general tendency of evil is towards further evil. Bodily illness renders the body more susceptible of disease; it produces incapacity of exertion, sometimes debility of mind, and often the loss of means of subsistence. All severe pain, either bodily or mental, tends to increase the susceptibilities of pain for ever after. Poverty is the parent of a thousand mental and moral evils. What is still worse, to be injured or oppressed, when habitual, lowers the whole tone of the character. One bad action leads to others, both in the agent himself, in the bystanders, and in the sufferers. All bad qualities are strengthened by habit, and all vices and follies tend to spread. Intellectual defects generate moral, and moral, intellectual; and every intellectual or moral defect generates others, and so on without end.

That much applauded class of authors, the writers on natural theology, have, I venture to think, entirely lost their way, and missed the sole line of argument which could have made their speculations acceptable to any one who can perceive when two propositions contradict one another. They have exhausted the resources of sophistry to make it appear that all the suffering in the world exists to prevent greater—that misery exists, for fear lest there should be misery: a thesis which if ever so well maintained, could only avail to explain and justify the works of limited beings, compelled to labour under conditions independent of their own will; but can have no application to a Creator assumed to be omnipotent, who, if he bends to a supposed necessity, himself makes the necessity which he bends to. If the maker of the world *can* all that he will, he wills misery, and there is no escape from the conclusion. The more consistent of those who have deemed themselves qualified to "vindicate the ways of God to man" have endeavoured to avoid the alternative by hardening their hearts, and denying that misery is an evil. The goodness of God, they say, does not consist in willing the happiness of his creatures, but their virtue; and the universe, if not a happy, is a just, universe. But waiving the objections to this scheme of ethics, it does not at all get rid of the difficulty. If the Creator of mankind willed that they should all be virtuous, his designs are as completely baffled as if he had willed that they should all be happy: and the order of nature is constructed with even less regard to the requirements of justice than to those of benevolence. If the law of all creation were justice and the Creator omnipotent, then in whatever amount suffering and happiness might be dispensed to the world, each person's share of them would be exactly proportioned to that person's good or evil deeds; no human being would have a worse lot than another, without worse deserts; accident or favouritism would have no part in such a world, but every human life would be the playing out of a drama constructed like a perfect moral tale. No one is able to blind himself to the fact that the world we live in is totally different from this; insomuch that the necessity of re-dressing the balance has been deemed one of the strongest argu-ments for another life after death, which amounts to an admission that the order of things in this life is often an example of injustice, not justice. If it be said that God does not take sufficient account of pleasure and pain to make them the reward or punishment of the good or the wicked, but that virtue is itself the greatest good and vice the greatest evil, then these at least ought to be dispensed to all according to what they have done to deserve them; instead of which, every kind of moral depravity is entailed upon multitudes by the fatality of their birth; through the fault of their parents, of society, or of uncontrollable circumstances, certainly through no fault of their own. Not even on the most distorted and contracted theory of good which ever was framed by religious or philosophical fanaticism, can the government of Nature be made to resemble the work of a being at once good and omnipotent. . . .

But even though unable to believe that Nature, as a whole, is a realization of the designs of perfect wisdom and benevolence, men do not willingly renounce the idea that some part of Nature, at least, must be intended as an exemplar, or type; that on some portion or other of the Creator's works, the image of the moral qualities which they are accustomed to ascribe to him, must be impressed; that if not all which is, yet something which is, must not only be a faultless model of what ought to be, but must be intended to be our guide and standard in rectifying the rest. It does not suffice them to believe, that what tends to good is to be imitated and perfected, and what tends to evil is to be corrected: they are anxious for some more definite indication of the Creator's de-signs; and being persuaded that this must somewhere be met with in his works, undertake the dangerous responsibility of picking and choosing among them in quest of it. A choice which except so far as directed by the general maxim that he intends all the good and none of the evil, must of necessity be perfectly arbitrary; and if it leads to any conclusions other than such as can be deduced from that maxim, must be, exactly in that proportion, pernicious.

It has never been settled by any accredited doctrine, what particular departments of the order of nature shall be reputed to be designed for our moral instruction and guidance; and accordingly each person's individual predilections, or momentary convenience, have decided to what parts of the divine government the practical conclusions that he was desirous of establishing, should be recommended to approval as being analogous. One such recommendation must be as fallacious as another, for it is impossible to decide that certain of the Creator's works are more truly expressions of his character than the rest; and the only selection which does not lead to immoral results, is the selection of those which most conduce to the general good, in other words, of those which point to an end which if the entire scheme is the expression of a single omnipotent and consistent will, is evidently not the end intended by it.

There is however one particular element in the construction of the world, which to minds on the look-out for special indication of the Creator's will, has appeared, not without plausibility, peculiarly fitted to afford them; viz. the active impulses of human and other animated beings. One can imagine such persons arguing that when the Author of Nature only made circumstances, he may not have meant to indicate the manner in which his rational creatures were to adjust themselves to those circumstances; but that when he implanted positive stimuli in the creatures themselves, stirring them up to a particular kind of action, it is impossible to doubt that he intended that sort of action to be practised by them. This reasoning, followed out consistently, would lead to the conclusion that the Deity intended, and approves, whatever human beings do; since all that they do being the consequence of some of the impulses with which their Creator must have endowed them, all must equally be considered as done in obedience to his will. As this practical conclusion was shrunk from, it was necessary to draw a distinction, and to pronounce that not the whole, but only parts of the active nature of mankind point to a special intention of the Creator in respect to their conduct. These parts it seemed natural to suppose, must be those in which the Creator's hand is manifested rather than the man's own: and hence the frequent antithesis between man as God made him, and man as he has made himself. Since what is done with deliberation seems more the man's own act, and he is held more completely responsible for it than for what he does from sudden impulse, the considerate part of human conduct is apt to be set down as man's share in the business, and the inconsiderate as God's.

The result is the vein of sentiment so common in the modern world (though unknown to the philosophic ancients) which exalts instinct at the expense of reason; an aberration rendered still more mischievous by the opinion commonly held in conjunction with it, that every, or almost every, feeling or impulse which acts promptly without waiting to ask questions, is an instinct. Thus almost every variety of unreflecting and uncalculating impulse receives a kind of consecration, except those which, though unreflecting at the moment, owe their origin to previous habits of reflection: these, being evidently not instinctive, do not meet with the favour accorded to the rest; so that all unreflecting impulses are invested with authority over reason, except the only ones which are most probably right. I do not mean, of course, that this mode of judgment is even pretended to be consistently carried out: life could not go on if it were not admitted that impulses must be controlled, and that reason ought to govern our actions. The pretension is not to drive Reason from the helm but rather to bind her by articles to steer only in a particular way. Instinct is not to govern, but reason is to practise some vague and unassignable amount of deference to Instinct. Though the impression in favour of instinct as being a peculiar manifestation of the divine purposes, has not been cast into the form of a consistent general theory, it remains a standing prejudice, capable of being stirred up into hostility to reason in any case in which the dictate of the rational faculty has not acquired the authority of prescription.

I shall not here enter into the difficult psychological question, what are, or are not instincts: the subject would require a volume to itself. Without touching upon any disputed theoretical points, it is possible to judge how little worthy is the instinctive part of human nature to be held up as its chief excellence—as the part in which the hand of infinite goodness and wisdom is peculiarly visible. Allowing everything to be an instinct which anybody has ever asserted to be one, it remains true that nearly every respectable attribute of humanity is the result not of instinct, but of a victory over instinct; and that there is hardly anything valuable in the natural man except capacities—a whole world of possibilities, all of them dependent upon eminently artificial discipline for being realized.

It is only in a highly artificialized condition of human nature that the notion grew up, or, I believe, ever could have grown up, that goodness was natural: because only after a long course of artificial education did good sentiments become so habitual, and so predominant over bad, as to arise unprompted when occasion called for them. In the times when mankind were nearer to their natural state, cultivated observers regarded the natural man as a sort of wild animal, distinguished chiefly by being craftier than the other beasts of the field; and all worth of character was deemed the result of a sort of taming; a phrase often applied by the ancient philosophers to the appropriate discipline of human beings. The truth is that there is hardly a single point of excellence belonging to human character, which is not decidedly repugnant to the untutored feelings of human nature.

If there be a virtue which more than any other we expect to find, and really do find, in an uncivilized state, it is the virtue of courage. Yet this is from first to last a victory achieved over one of the most powerful emotions of human nature. If there is any one feeling or attribute more natural than all others to human beings, it is fear; and no greater proof can be given of the power of artificial discipline than the conquest which it has at all times and places shown itself capable of achieving over so mighty and so universal a sentiment. The widest difference no doubt exists between one human being and another in the facility or difficulty with which they acquire this virtue. There is hardly any department of human excellence in which difference of original temperament goes so far. But it may fairly be questioned if any human being is naturally courageous. Many are naturally pugnacious, or irascible, or enthusiastic, and these passions when strongly excited may render them insensible to fear. But take away the conflicting emotion, and fear reasserts its dominion: consistent courage is always the effect of cultivation. The courage which is occasionally though by no means generally found among tribes of savages, is as much the result of education as that of the Spartans or Romans. In all such tribes there is a most emphatic direction of the public sentiment into every channel of expression through which honour can be paid to courage and cowardice held up to contempt and derision. It will perhaps be said, that as the expression of a sentiment implies the sentiment itself, the training of the young to courage presupposes an originally courageous people. It presupposes only what all good customs presuppose —that there must have been individuals better than the rest, who set the customs going. Some individuals, who like other people had fears to conquer, must have had strength of mind and will to conquer them for themselves. These would obtain the influence belonging to heroes, for that which is at once astonishing and obviously useful never fails to be admired: and partly through this admiration, partly through the fear they themselves excite, they would obtain the power of legislators, and could establish whatever customs they pleased.

Let us next consider a quality which forms the most visible, and one of the most radical of the moral distinctions between human beings and most of the lower animals; that of which the absence, more than of anything else, renders men bestial; the quality of cleanliness. Can anything be more entirely artificial? Children, and the lower classes of most countries, seem to be actually fond of dirt: the vast majority of the human race are indifferent to it: whole nations of otherwise civilized and cultivated human beings tolerate it in some of its worst forms, and only a very small minority are consistently offended by it. Indeed the universal law of the subject appears to be, that uncleanliness offends only those to whom it is unfamiliar, so that those who have lived in so artificial a state as to be unused to it in any form, are the sole persons whom it disgusts in all forms. Of all virtues this is the most evidently not instinctive, but a triumph over instinct. Assuredly neither cleanliness nor the love of cleanliness is natural to man, but only the capacity of acquiring a love of cleanliness.

Our examples have thus far been taken from the personal, or as they are called by Bentham, the self regarding virtues, because these, if any, might be supposed to be congenial even to the uncultivated mind. Of the social virtues it is almost superfluous to speak; so completely is it the verdict of all experience that selfishness is natural. By this I do not in any wise mean to deny that sympathy is natural also; I believe on the contrary that on that important fact rests the possibility of any cultivation of goodness and nobleness, and the hope of their ultimate entire ascendancy. But sympathetic characters, left uncultivated, and given up to their sympathetic instincts, are as selfish as others. The difference is in the *kind* of selfishness: theirs is not solitary but sympathetic selfishness; *l' egoïsme à deux, à trois,* or *à quatre* [selfishness extending to two, three, or four]; and they may be very amiable and delightful to those with whom they sympathize, and grossly unjust and unfeeling to the rest of the world. Indeed the finer nervous organizations which are most capable of and most require sympathy, have, from their fineness, so much stronger impulses of all sorts, that they often furnish the most striking examples of selfishness, though of a less repulsive kind than that of colder natures. Whether there ever was a person in whom, apart from all teaching of instructors, friends or books, and from all intentional self-modelling according to an ideal, natural benevolence was a more powerful attribute than selfishness in any of its forms, may remain undecided. That such cases are extremely rare, every one must admit, and this is enough for the argument. . . .

This brief survey is amply sufficient to prove that the duty of man is the same in respect to his own nature as in respect to the nature of all other things, namely not to follow but to amend it. Some people however who do not attempt to deny that instinct ought to be subordinate to reason, pay deference to nature so far as to maintain that every natural inclination must have some sphere of action granted to it, some opening left for its gratification. All natural wishes, they say, must have been implanted for a purpose: and this argument is carried so far, that we often hear it maintained that every wish, which it is supposed to be natural to entertain, must have a corresponding provision in the order of the universe for its gratification: insomuch (for instance) that the desire of an indefinite prolongation of existence, is believed by many to be in itself a sufficient proof of the reality of a future life.

I conceive that there is a radical absurdity in all these attempts to discover, in detail, what are the designs of Providence, in order when they are discovered to help Providence in bringing them about. Those who argue, from particular indications, that Providence intends this or that, either believe that the Creator can do all that he will or that he cannot. If the first supposition is adopted—if Providence is omnipotent, Providence intends whatever happens, and the fact of its happening proves that Providence intended it. If so, everything which a human being can do, is predestined by Providence and is a fulfillment of its designs. But if as is the more religious theory, Providence intends not all which happens, but only what is good, then indeed man has it in his power, by his voluntary actions, to aid the intentions of Providence; but he can only learn those intentions by considering what tends to promote the general good, and not what man has a natural inclination to; for, limited as, on this showing, the divine power must be, by inscrutable but insurmountable obstacles, who knows that man *could* have been created without desires which never are to be, and even which never ought to be, fulfilled? The inclinations with which man has been endowed, as well as any of the other contrivances which we observe in Nature, may be the expression not of the divine will, but of the fetters which impede its free action; and to take hints from these for the guidance of our own conduct may be falling into a trap laid by the enemy. The assumption that everything which infinite goodness can desire, actually comes to pass in this universe, or at least that we must never say or suppose that it does not, is worthy only of those whose slavish fears make them offer the homage of lies to a Being who, they profess to think, is incapable of being deceived and holds all falsehood in abomination.

With regard to this particular hypothesis, that all natural impulses, all propensities sufficiently universal and sufficiently spontaneous to be capable of passing for instincts, must exist for good ends, and ought to be only regulated, not repressed; this is of course true of the majority of them, for the species could not have continued to exist unless most of its inclinations had been directed to things needful or useful for its preservation. But unless the instincts can be reduced to a very small number indeed, it must be allowed that we have also bad instincts which it should be the aim of education not simply to regulate but to extirpate, or rather (what can be done even to an instinct) to starve them by disuse. Those who are inclined to multiply the number of instincts, usually include among them one which they call destructiveness: an instinct to destroy for destruction's sake. I can conceive no good reason for preserving this, no more than another propensity which if not an instinct is very like one, what has been called the instinct of domination; a delight in exercising despotism, in holding other beings in subjection to our will. The man who takes pleasure in the mere exertion of authority, apart from the purpose for which it is to be employed, is the last person in whose hands one would willingly entrust it. . . .

But even if it were true that every one of the elementary impulses of human nature has its good side, and may by a sufficient amount of artificial training be made more useful than hurtful; how little would this amount to, when it must in any case be admitted that without such training all of them, even those which are necessary to our preservation, would fill the world with misery, making human life an exaggerated likeness of the odious scene of violence and tyranny which is exhibited by the rest of the animal kingdom, except in so far as tamed and disciplined by man. There, indeed, those who flatter themselves with the notion of reading the purposes of the Creator in his works, ought in consistency to have seen grounds for inferences from which they have shrunk. If there are any marks at all of special design in creation, one of the things most evidently designed is that a large proportion of all animals should pass their existence in tormenting and devouring other animals. They have been lavishly fitted out with the instruments necessary for that purpose; their strongest instincts impel them to it, and many of them seem to have been constructed incapable of supporting themselves by any other food. If a tenth part of the pains which have been expended in finding benevolent adaptations in all nature had been employed in collecting evidence to blacken the character of the Creator, what scope for comment would not have been found in the entire existence of the lower animals, divided, with scarcely an exception, into devourers and devoured, and a prey to a thousand ills from which they are denied the faculties necessary for protecting themselves! If we are not obliged to believe the animal creation to be the work of a demon, it is because we need not sup-

pose it to have been made by a Being of infinite power. But if
imitation of the Creator's will as revealed in nature, were applied
as a rule of action in this case, the most atrocious enormities of the
worst men would be more than justified by the apparent intention of
Providence that throughout all animated nature the strong should
prey upon the weak.

The preceding observations are far from having exhausted the
almost infinite variety of modes and occasions in which the idea of
conformity to nature is introduced as an element into the ethical
appreciation of actions and dispositions. The same favourable pre-
judgment follows the word nature through the numerous acceptations, in which it is employed as a distinctive term for certain parts
of the constitution of humanity as contrasted with other parts. We
have hitherto confined ourselves to one of these acceptations, in
which it stands as a general designation for those parts of our
mental and moral constitution which are supposed to be innate,
in contradistinction to those which are acquired; as when nature
is contrasted with education; or when a savage state, without laws,
arts, or knowledge, is called a state of nature; or when the question
is asked whether benevolence, or the moral sentiment, is natural or
acquired; or whether some persons are poets or orators by nature
and others not. But in another and a more lax sense, any manifestations by human beings are often termed natural, when it is merely
intended to say that they are not studied or designedly assumed in
the particular case; as when a person is said to move or speak with
natural grace; or when it is said that a person's natural manner or
character is so and so; meaning that it is so when he does not attempt to control or disguise it. In a still looser acceptation, a person
is said to be naturally, that which he was until some special cause
had acted upon him, or which it is supposed he would be if some
such cause were withdrawn. Thus a person is said to be naturally
dull, but to have made himself intelligent by study and perse-
verance; to be naturally cheerful, but soured by misfortune; naturally ambitious, but kept down by want of opportunity. Finally,
the word natural, applied to feelings or conduct, often seems to
mean no more than that they are such as are ordinarily found in
human beings; as when it is said that a person acted, on some particular occasion, as it was natural to do; or that to be affected in a
particular way by some sight, or sound, or thought, or incident in
life, is perfectly natural.

In all these senses of the term, the quality called natural is very
often confessedly a worse quality than the one contrasted with it;
but whenever its being so is not too obvious to be questioned, the
idea seems to be entertained that by describing it as natural, some-

thing has been said amounting to a considerable presumption in its favour. For my part I can perceive only one sense in which nature, or naturalness, in a human being, are really terms of praise; and then the praise is only negative: namely when used to denote the absence of affectation. Affectation may be defined, the effort to appear what one is not, when the motive or the occasion is not such as either to excuse the attempt, or to stamp it with the more odious name of hypocrisy. . . .

Sometimes also, in cases where the term affectation would be inappropriate, since the conduct or demeanour spoken of is really praiseworthy, people say in disparagement of the person concerned, that such conduct or demeanour is not natural to him; and make uncomplimentary comparisons between him and some other person, to whom it is natural: meaning that what in the one seemed excellent was the effect of temporary excitement, or of a great victory over himself, while in the other it is the result to be expected from the habitual character. This mode of speech is not open to censure, since nature is here simply a term for the person's ordinary disposition, and if he is praised it is not for being natural, but for being naturally good.

Conformity to nature, has no connection whatever with right and wrong. The idea can never be fitly introduced into ethical discussions at all, except, occasionally and partially, into the question of degrees of culpability. To illustrate this point, let us consider the phrase by which the greatest intensity of condemnatory feeling is conveyed in connection with the idea of nature—the word unnatural. That a thing is unnatural, in any precise meaning which can be attached to the word, is no argument for its being blamable; since the most criminal actions are to a being like man, not more unnatural than most of the virtues. The acquisition of virtue has in all ages been accounted a work of labour and difficulty, while the *descensus Averni* [descent to hell] on the contrary is of proverbial facility: and it assuredly requires in most persons a greater conquest over a greater number of natural inclinations to become eminently virtuous than transcendently vicious. But if an action, or an inclination, has been decided on other grounds to be blamable, it may be a circumstance in aggravation that it is unnatural, that is, repugnant to some strong feeling usually found in human beings; since the bad propensity, whatever it be, has afforded evidence of being both strong and deeply rooted, by having overcome that repugnance. This presumption of course fails if the individual never had the repugnance: and the argument, therefore, is not fit to be urged unless the feeling which is violated by the act, is not only justifiable and reasonable, but is one which it is blamable to be without.

The corresponding plea in extenuation of a culpable act because it was natural, or because it was prompted by a natural feeling, never, I think, ought to be admitted. There is hardly a bad action ever perpetrated which is not perfectly natural, and the motives to which are not perfectly natural feelings. In the eye of reason, therefore, this is no excuse, but it is quite "natural" that it should be so in the eyes of the multitude; because the meaning of the expression is, that they have a fellow feeling with the offender. When they say that something which they cannot help admitting to be blamable, is nevertheless natural, they mean that they can imagine the possibility of their being themselves tempted to commit it. Most people have a considerable amount of indulgence towards all acts of which they feel a possible source within themselves, reserving their rigour for those which, though perhaps really less bad, they cannot in any way understand how it is possible to commit. If an action convinces them (which it often does on very inadequate grounds) that the person who does it must be a being totally unlike themselves, they are seldom particular in examining the precise degree of blame due to it, or even if blame is properly due to it at all. They measure the degree of guilt by the strength of their antipathy; and hence differences of opinion, and even differences of taste, have been objects of as intense moral abhorrence as the most atrocious crimes.

It will be useful to sum up in a few words the leading conclusions of this Essay.

The word Nature has two principal meanings: it either denotes the entire system of things, with the aggregate of all their properties, or it denotes things as they would be, apart from human intervention.

In the first of these senses, the doctrine that man ought to follow nature is unmeaning; since man has no power to do anything else than follow nature; all his actions are done through, and in obedience to, some one or many of nature's physical or mental laws.

In the other sense of the term, the doctrine that man ought to follow nature, or in other words, ought to make the spontaneous course of things the model of his voluntary actions, is equally irrational and immoral.

Irrational, because all human action whatever, consists in altering, and all useful action in improving, the spontaneous course of nature:

Immoral, because the course of natural phenomena being replete with everything which when committed by human beings is most worthy of abhorrence, any one who endeavoured in his actions to imitate the natural course of things would be universally seen and acknowledged to be the wickedest of men.

The scheme of Nature regarded in its whole extent, cannot have had, for its sole or even principal object, the good of human or other sentient beings. What good it brings to them, is mostly the result of their own exertions. Whatsoever, in nature, gives indication of beneficent design, proves this beneficence to be armed only with limited power; and the duty of man is to co-operate with the beneficent powers, not by imitating but by perpetually striving to amend the course of nature—and bringing that part of it over which we can exercise control, more nearly into conformity with a high standard of justice and goodness.

10

TWO CONCEPTS: "CAUSE" AND "CHANCE" *

by

ARISTOTLE

(B.C. 384–322)

I

. . . One only knows a thing when one knows why it is, its reason. . . .

In the first place, one calls cause that which composes a thing, and that from which it arises. Thus one can say in this sense that bronze is the cause of the statue, and silver is the cause of the phial; and one applies this way of speaking to all things of the same kind. (*Material cause.*) In a second sense, the cause is the form and the model of things; it is the essential character of the thing and its kind. Thus in music, the cause of the octave is the ratio 2:1, and, in a more general way, it is number; and with number, it is the part which enters into its definition. (*Formal cause.*) In a third sense, the cause is the source from which movement or rest comes. Thus he who, in a certain case, has given advice to act is the cause of the acts which are accomplished; the father is the cause of the child; and generally speaking that which acts is the cause of that

* [Chs. 3–6 in Bk. II of the *Physics*. Part I is a translation by Henry M. Magid in *Landmarks for Beginners in Philosophy*, copyright by the editors, Irwin Edman and Herbert W. Schneider; Reynal and Hitchcock, 1941. Part II is from *Aristotle: From Natural Science, Psychology, Nicomachean Ethics*, translated by Philip Wheelwright, copyright by The Odyssey Press, 1935. By kind permission of the editors and publishers concerned.]

which is done; that which produces a change is the cause of the change produced. (*Efficient cause.*) Fourthly, cause signifies the end and the goal of a thing. Thus health is the cause of walking. If we ask, "Why is he walking?" the answer is, "In order to be well," and when we say this, we believe that we have the cause of the walking. This meaning applies to all the intermediaries who contribute to the attainment of the final end, after the first mover has started the movement. For example, dieting and purgation, or drugs and the instruments of the surgeon can be regarded as means to health; and the only difference is that some are acts and others are instruments. (*Final cause.*)

These are briefly the meanings of the word cause. In accordance with this diversity of senses, a single thing can have several causes at the same time, and not simply. Thus, for the statue, one can assign to it as causes both the art of the sculptor who has made it and the bronze of which it is made, and not in any other sense than as a statue. The two causes are not to be understood in the same sense; they differ in that one is the material and the other is the source of the movement. It is also because of this that there can be said to be things that are reciprocally the causes of each other. Thus exercise is the cause of health, and health is the cause of exercise; but not in the same sense, for, in the first case, health is the end, while in the second health is the source of the movement. Moreover, a single thing is at times the cause of opposite results; for, the same thing which is the cause of a given effect when it is present, can be the cause of an opposite effect when it is absent. For example, the absence of the pilot can be considered the cause of the loss of the ship, because the presence of the same pilot could have guaranteed its safety.

All the causes mentioned can be reduced to these four very obvious kinds. The letters of the alphabet are the cause of the syllables; the material is the cause of the things which art produces; fire and the other elements are the causes of the bodies which they compose; the parts are the cause of the whole, and the propositions are the causes of the conclusions which are drawn from them. Each of these is a cause since it is that out of which the other thing comes. Of these, the causes are either the subject of the thing, as parts relative to the whole; or the essential character of the thing, as the whole and the synthesis and the form; or the source of change or rest, as the germ, the physician, the giver of advice, and in general that which has effects; and finally, in the fourth place, the end and the good of other things; the attainment of the best is that for the sake of which the thing exists, and it would make no difference whether one said the real or the apparent good.

II

"Luck" and "pure spontaneous chance" are sometimes included in the list of causal determinants, and many things are said to come about "as luck would have it" or "by chance." In what sense may luck and chance be included among the types of determinant just enumerated? Further, is luck the same thing as pure chance or something different? And exactly what is each of them?

Some people question even their existence. Nothing, they declare, happens fortuitously; whatever we ascribe to luck or pure chance has been somehow determined. Take, for instance, the case of a man who goes to market and "as luck would have it" meets someone whom he wanted but did not expect to meet: his going to market, they say, was responsible for this. So they argue that of any other occurrence ascribed to luck there is always some more positive explanation to be found. Luck [they say] cannot have been the cause, for it would be paradoxical to regard luck as something real. Further, they consider it noteworthy that none of the ancient philosophers mentioned luck when discussing the causes of becoming and perishing—an indication, apparently, that they disbelieved in the possibility of fortuitous occurrences.

Yet it is odd that while people theoretically accept the venerable argument which assumes that every chance happening and stroke of luck can be attributed to some cause or other, they nevertheless continue to speak of some things as matters of luck, others not. The earlier philosophers ought to have taken some account of this popular distinction, but among their various principles—love and strife, mind, fire, etc.—luck finds no place. The omission is equally surprising whether we suppose them to have disbelieved in luck or to have believed in but disregarded it; for at any rate they were not above employing the idea in their explanations. Empedocles, for example, remarks that air is sifted up into the sky not uniformly but "as it may chance"; or, in the words of his *Cosmogony*, "Now it 'happened' to run this way, now that." And the parts of animals, he declares, came to be what they are purely by chance.

Some go so far as to attribute the heavens and all the worlds to "chance happenings," declaring that the vortex—i.e., the motion which separated and arranged the entire universe in its present order —arose "of itself." We may well be surprised at this assertion that while the existence and generation of animals and plants must be attributed not to chance but to nature or mind or something of the sort (what issues from a particular sperm or seed is obviously not a matter of chance, since from one kind of seed there comes forth an olive, from another a man), yet the heavens and the divinest of visible things have come into existence spontaneously and have no such causes as animals and plants have. Even if this were true, it would be something to give us pause, and ought to have elicited some comment. For apart from the generally paradoxical nature of such a theory it is rather odd that people should accept it when they can find no evidence of spontaneous occurrences among celestial phenomena but plenty of such evidence among the things in which they deny the presence of chance. The evidence is just the opposite of what should have been expected if their theory were true.

There are other people who, while accepting luck as a cause of things, regard it as something divinely mysterious, inscrutable to human intelligence.

Accordingly we must investigate the nature of luck and chance, and see whether they are the same as each other or different, and how they fit into our classification of causes.

To begin with, when we see certain things occurring in a certain way either uniformly or "as a general rule," we obviously would not ascribe them to mere luck. A stroke of luck is not something that comes to pass either by uniform necessity or as a general rule. But as there is also a third sort of event which is found to occur, which everyone speaks of as being a matter of luck, and which we all know is meant when the word "lucky" is used, it is plain that such a thing as luck and "pure spontaneous chance" must exist.

Some events "serve a purpose," others do not. Of the former class, some are in accordance with the intention of the purposer, others not; but both are in the class of things that serve a purpose. Evidently, then, even among occurrences that are not the predictable (i.e., neither the constant nor normal) results of anyone's actual intention, there are some which may be spoken of as serving a purpose. What serves a purpose may have originated either in thought or in nature: in either case when its occurrence is accidental we call it a matter of luck. Just as everything has both an essential nature and a number of incidental attributes, so when anything is considered as a causal determinant it may have similarly a twofold aspect. When a man builds a house, for instance, his faculty of house-building is the essential determinant of the house, while the fact that he is blond or cultured is only incidental to that result. The essential determinant can be calculated, but the incidentally related factors are incalculable, for any number of them may inhere in one subject.

As already explained, then, we attribute to chance or luck whatever happens [accidentally] in such a way as to serve a purpose. (The specific difference between chance and luck will be explained later; for the present it is enough to emphasize that both of them refer to actions that happen to serve a purpose.) As an illustration, suppose that we wish to solicit a man for a contribution of money. Had we known where he was we should have gone there and accosted him. But if with some other end in view we go to a place which it is not our invariable nor even our usual practice to visit, then, since the end effected (getting the money) is not a spontaneous process of nature, but is the type of thing that results from conscious choice and reflection, we describe the meeting as a stroke of luck. It would not be a matter of luck, however, if we were to visit the place for the express purpose of seeking our man, or if we regularly went there when taking up subscriptions. Luck, then, is evidently an incidental aspect of causation in the sphere of actions that involve purposive choice and reflection. Hence, since choice implies "intelligent reflection," we may conclude that luck and intelligent reflection both refer to the same sphere of things and activities. . . .

According as the result of a fortuitous action is good or bad we speak of good and bad luck. In more serious matters we use the terms "good fortune" and "misfortune;" and when we escape by a hair's breadth some great evil or just miss some great good we consider ourselves fortunate or unfortunate accordingly—the margin having been so slight that we can reflect upon the good or ill in question as if it were actually present. Moreover, as all luck is unstable (for nothing invariable or normal could be attributed to luck), we are right in regarding good fortune as also unstable.

Both luck and spontaneous chance, then, as has been said, are incidental to a causal situation, and are attributed to the type of occurrence which is neither constant nor normal and which might have been aimed at for its own sake.

The difference between luck and chance is that "chance" is the more inclusive term. Every case of luck is a case of chance, but not all cases of chance are cases of luck.

Luck, together with lucky or unlucky occurrences, is spoken of only in connection with agents that are capable of enjoying good [or ill] fortune and of performing moral actions. It follows, then, that luck always has some reference to conduct—a conclusion which is further enforced by the popular belief that "good fortune" is the same, or practically the same, as "happiness"; and that happiness, as it involves "well-doing," is a kind of "moral action." Hence only what is capable of moral conduct can perform actions that are lucky or the reverse. Luck does not pertain to the activities of a lifeless thing, a beast, or a child, for these exercise no "deliberate choice." If we call them lucky or unlucky we are speaking figuratively—as when Protarchus speaks of altar stones as fortunate because they are treated with reverence while their fellows are trampled underfoot.

All such objects are affected by luck only in so far as a moral agent may deal with them in a manner that is lucky or unlucky [to himself].

"Pure spontaneous chance," on the other hand, is found both among the lower animals and in many lifeless things. We say of a horse, for example, that it went "by chance" to a place of safety, meaning that it was not for the sake of safety that it went there [but owing to some external cause]. Again, we say of a tripod that it fell onto its feet "by chance," because although it could then be used to sit on, it did not fall for the sake of that.

[The distinction, then, may be summarized as follows.] We attribute to "chance" all those events which are such as ordinarily admit of a telic explanation [i.e., which come about for the sake of something], but which happen on this occasion to have been produced without any reference to the actual result. The word "luck," on the other hand, is restricted to that special type of chance events which (1) are possible objects of choice, and (2) affect persons capable of exercising choice. . . . The difference between chance and luck becomes clearest when applied to the productions of nature: when she produces a monster we attribute it to chance but we do not call nature unlucky. Even this, however, is not quite the same type of situation as that of the horse who chances to escape; for the horse's escape was due to an external cause, while the causes of nature's miscarriages are private to herself.

Thus we have explained the meaning of, and distinction between, chance and luck. Both, it may be added, belong to the order of "efficient determinants" [efficient causes] or "sources of movement"; for the determinants to which they are incidental are either natural forces or intelligent agents—the particular kinds of which are too numerous to mention.

Inasmuch as the results of chance and luck, while of a sort that nature or a conscious intelligence might well have intended, have in fact emerged as a purely incidental result of some causal process, and as no effect can be incidental without some prior and authentic cause for it to be incidental to, it is clear that incidental causation presupposes a causal relation that is authentic and direct. Chance and luck, then, presuppose intelligence and nature as causal agents. Hence, however true it may be that the heavens are due to spontaneous chance, intelligence and nature must be the prior causes, not only of many other things, but of this universe itself.

11

MIRACLES *

by

DAVID HUME

(1711–1776)

There is, in Dr. Tillotson's writings, an argument against the *real presence* † which is as concise, and elegant, and strong as any argument can possibly be supposed against a doctrine, so little worthy of a serious refutation. It is acknowledged on all hands, says that learned prelate, that the authority, either of the scripture or of tradition, is founded merely in the testimony of the apostles, who were eye-witnesses to those miracles of our Saviour, by which he proved his divine mission. Our evidence, then, for the truth of the *Christian* religion is less than the evidence for the truth of our senses; because, even in the first authors of our religion, it was no greater; and it is evident it must diminish in passing from them to their disciples; nor can any one rest such confidence in their testimony, as in the immediate object of his senses. But a weaker evidence can never destroy a stronger; and therefore, were the doctrine of the real presence ever so clearly revealed in scripture, it were directly contrary to the rules of just reasoning to give our assent to it. It contradicts sense, though both the scripture and tradition, on which it is supposed to be built, carry not such evidence with them as sense; when they are considered merely as external evidences, and are not brought home to every one's breast, by the immediate operation of the Holy Spirit.

Nothing is so convenient as a decisive argument of this kind, which must at least *silence* the most arrogant bigotry and superstition, and free us from their impertinent solicitations. I flatter myself, that I have discovered an argument of a like nature, which, if just, will, with the wise and learned, be an everlasting check to all

* [The whole of Ch. 10 in *An Enquiry Concerning Human Understanding* (1748).]

† [The doctrine that the body and blood of Christ are "really present" in the bread and wine during communion.]

kinds of superstitious delusion, and consequently, will be useful as long as the world endures. For so long, I presume, will the accounts of miracles and prodigies be found in all history, sacred and profane.

Though experience be our only guide in reasoning concerning matters of fact; it must be acknowledged, that this guide is not altogether infallible, but in some cases is apt to lead us into errors. One, who in our climate, should expect better weather in any week of June than in one of December, would reason justly, and conformably to experience; but it is certain, that he may happen, in the event, to find himself mistaken. However, we may observe, that, in such a case, he would have no cause to complain of experience; because it commonly informs us beforehand of the uncertainty, by that contrariety of events, which we may learn from a diligent observation. All effects follow not with like certainty from their supposed causes. Some events are found, in all countries and all ages, to have been constantly conjoined together: Others are found to have been more variable, and sometimes to disappoint our expectations; so that, in our reasonings concerning matter of fact, there are all imaginable degrees of assurance, from the highest certainty to the lowest species of moral evidence.

A wise man, therefore, proportions his belief to the evidence. In such conclusions as are founded on an infallible experience, he expects the event with the last degree of assurance, and regards his past experience as a full *proof* of the future existence of that event. In other cases, he proceeds with more caution: He weighs the opposite experiments: He considers which side is supported by the greater number of experiments: to that side he inclines, with doubt and hesitation; and when at last he fixes his judgement, the evidence exceeds not what we properly call *probability*. All probability, then, supposes an opposition of experiments and observations, where the one side is found to overbalance the other, and to produce a degree of evidence, proportioned to the superiority. A hundred instances or experiments on one side, and fifty on another, afford a doubtful expectation of any event; though a hundred uniform experiments, with only one that is contradictory, reasonably begets a pretty strong degree of assurance. In all cases, we must balance the opposite experiments, where they are opposite, and deduct the smaller number from the greater, in order to know the exact force of the superior evidence.

To apply these principles to a particular instance; we may observe, that there is no species of reasoning more common, more useful, and even necessary to human life, than that which is derived from the testimony of men, and the reports of eye-witnesses and spectators. This species of reasoning, perhaps, one may deny to be founded on the relation of cause and effect. I shall not dispute about a word. It will be sufficient to observe that our assurance in any argument of this kind is derived from no other principle than our observation of the veracity of human testimony, and of the usual conformity of facts to the reports of witnesses. It being a general maxim, that no objects have any discoverable connexion together, and that all the inferences, which we can draw from one to another, are founded merely on our experience of their constant and regular conjunction; it is evident, that we ought not to make an exception to this maxim in favour of human testimony, whose connexion with any event seems, in itself, as little necessary as any other. Were not the memory tenacious to a certain degree; had not men commonly an inclination to truth and a principle of probity, were they not sensible to shame, when detected in a falsehood: Were not these, I say, discovered by *experience* to be qualities, inherent in human nature, we should never repose the least confidence in human testimony. A man delirious, or noted for falsehood and villany, has no manner of authority with us.

And as the evidence, derived from witnesses and human testimony, is founded on past experience, so it varies with the experience, and is regarded either as *proof* or a *probability,* according as the conjunction between any particular kind of report and any kind of object has been found to be constant or variable. There are a number of circumstances to be taken into consideration in all judgements of this kind; and the ultimate standard, by which we determine all disputes, that may arise concerning them, is always derived from experience and observation. Where this experience is not entirely uniform on any side, it is attended with an unavoidable contrariety in our judgements, and with the same opposition and mutual destruction of argument as in every other kind of evidence. We frequently hesitate concerning the reports of others. We balance the opposite circumstances, which cause any doubt or uncertainty; and when we discover a superiority on one side, we incline to it; but still with a diminution of assurance, in proportion to the force of its antagonist.

This contrariety of evidence, in the present case, may be derived from several different causes; from the opposition of contrary testimony; from the character or number of the witnesses; from the manner of their delivering their testimony; or from the union of all these circumstances. We entertain a suspicion concerning any matter of fact, when the witnesses contradict each other; when they are but few, or of a doubtful character; when they have an interest in what they affirm; when they deliver their testimony with hesitation, or on the contrary, with too violent asseverations. There are many other particulars of the same kind, which may diminish or destroy the force of any argument, derived from human testimony.

Suppose, for instance, that the fact, which the testimony endeavours to establish, partakes of the extraordinary and the marvellous; in that case, the evidence, resulting from the testimony, admits of a diminution, greater or less, in proportion as the fact is more or less unusual. The reason why we place any credit in witnesses and historians, is not derived from any *connexion*, which we perceive *a priori*, between testimony and reality, but because we are accustomed to find a conformity between them. But when the fact attested is such a one as has seldom fallen under our observation, here is a contest of two opposite experiences; of which the one destroys the other, as far as its force goes, and the superior can only operate on the mind by the force, which remains. The very same principle of experience, which gives us a certain degree of assurance in the testimony of witnesses, gives us also, in this case, another degree of assurance against the fact, which they endeavour to establish; from which contradiction there necessarily arises a counterpoize, and mutual destruction of belief and authority.

I should not believe such a story were it told me by Cato, was a proverbial saying in Rome, even during the lifetime of that philosophical patriot. The incredibility of a fact, it was allowed, might invalidate so great an authority.

The Indian prince, who refused to believe the first relations concerning the effects of frost, reasoned justly; and it naturally required very strong testimony to engage his assent to facts, that arose from a state of nature, with which he was unacquainted, and which bore so little analogy to those events, of which he had had constant and uniform experience. Though they were not contrary to his experience, they were not conformable to it.

But in order to encrease the probability against the testimony of witnesses, let us suppose, that the fact, which they affirm, instead of being only marvellous, is really miraculous; and suppose also, that the testimony considered apart and in itself, amounts to an entire proof; in that case, there is proof against proof, of which the strongest must prevail, but still with a diminution of its force, in proportion to that of its antagonist.

A miracle is a violation of the laws of nature; and as a firm and unalterable experience has established these laws, the proof against a miracle, from the very nature of the fact, is as entire as any argument from experience can possibly be imagined. Why is it more than probable, that all men must die; that lead cannot, of itself, remain suspended in the air; that fire consumes wood, and is extinguished by water; unless it be, that these events are found agreeable to the laws of nature, and there is required a violation of these laws, or in other words, a miracle to prevent them? Nothing is esteemed a miracle, if it ever happen in the common course of nature. It is no miracle that a man, seemingly in good health, should die on a sudden: because such a kind of death, though more unusual than any other, has yet been frequently observed to happen. But it is a miracle, that a dead man should come to life; because that has never been observed in any age or country. There must, therefore, be a uniform experience against every miraculous event, otherwise the event would not merit that appellation. And as a uniform experience amounts to a proof, there is here a direct and full *proof*, from the nature of the fact, against the existence of any miracle; nor can such a proof be destroyed, or the miracle rendered credible, but by an opposite proof, which is superior.

The plain consequence is (and it is a general maxim worthy of our attention), "That no testimony is sufficient to establish a miracle, unless the testimony be of such a kind, that its falsehood would be more miraculous, than the fact, which it endeavours to establish; and even in that case there is a mutual destruction of arguments, and the superior only gives us an assurance suitable to that degree of force, which remains, after deducting the inferior." When anyone tells me, that he saw a dead man restored to life, I immediately consider with myself, whether it be more probable, that this person should either deceive or be deceived, or that the fact, which he relates, should really have happened. I weigh the one miracle against the other; and according to the superiority, which I discover, I pronounce my decision, and always reject the greater miracle. If the falsehood of his testimony would be more miraculous, than the event which he relates; then, and not till then, can he pretend to command my belief or opinion.

In the foregoing reasoning we have supposed, that the testimony, upon which a miracle is founded, may possibly amount to an entire proof, and that the falsehood of that testimony would be a real prodigy: But it is easy to shew, that we have been a great deal too liberal in our concession, and that there never was a miraculous event established on so full an evidence.

For *first*, there is not to be found, in all history, any miracle attested by a sufficient number of men, of such unquestioned good-sense, education, and learning, as to secure us against all delusion in themselves; of such undoubted integrity, as to place them beyond all suspicion of any design to deceive others; of such credit and reputation in the eyes of mankind, as to have a great deal to lose in case of their being detected in any falsehood; and at the same time, attesting facts performed in such a public manner and in so celebrated a part of the world, as to render the detection unavoidable: All which circumstances are requisite to give us a full assurance in the testimony of men.

Secondly. We may observe in human nature a principle which, if strictly examined, will be found to diminish extremely the assurance, which we might, from human testimony, have, in any kind of prodigy. The maxim, by which we commonly conduct ourselves in our reasonings, is, that the objects, of which we have no experience, resemble those, of which we have; that what we have found to be most usual is always most probable; and that where there is an opposition of arguments, we ought to give the preference to such as are founded on the greatest number of past observations. But though, in proceeding by this rule, we readily reject any fact which is unusual and incredible in an ordinary degree; yet in advancing farther, the mind observes not always the same rule; but when anything is affirmed utterly absurd and miraculous, it rather the more readily admits of such a fact, upon account of that very circumstance, which ought to destroy all its authority. The passion of *surprise* and *wonder,* arising from miracles, being an agreeable emotion, gives a sensible tendency towards the belief of those events, from which it is derived. And this goes so far, that even those who cannot enjoy this pleasure immediately, nor can believe those miraculous events, of which they are informed, yet love to partake of the satisfaction at second-hand or by rebound, and place a pride and delight in exciting the admiration of others.

With what greediness are the miraculous accounts of travellers received, their descriptions of sea and land monsters, their relations of wonderful adventures, strange men, and uncouth manners? But if the spirit of religion join itself to the love of wonder, there is an end of common sense; and human testimony, in these circumstances, loses all pretensions to authority. A religionist may be an enthusiast, and imagine he sees what has no reality: he may know his narrative to be false, and yet persevere in it, with the best intentions in the world, for the sake of promoting so holy a cause: or even where this delusion has not place, vanity, excited by so strong a temptation, operates on him more powerfully than on the rest of mankind in any other circumstances; and self-interest with equal force. His auditors may not have, and commonly have not, sufficient judgement to canvass his evidence: what judgement they have, they renounce by principle, in these sublime and mysterious subjects: or if they were ever so willing to employ it, passion and a heated imagination disturb the regularity of its operations. Their credulity increases his impudence: and his impudence overpowers their credulity.

Eloquence, when at its highest pitch, leaves little room for reason or reflection; but addressing itself entirely to the fancy or the affections, captivates the willing hearers, and subdues their understanding. Happily, this pitch it seldom attains. But what a Tully or a Demosthenes could scarcely effect over a Roman or Athenian audience, every *Capuchin,* every itinerant or stationary teacher can perform over the generality of mankind, and in a higher degree, by touching such gross and vulgar passions.

The many instances of forged miracles, and prophecies, and supernatural events, which, in all ages, have either been detected by contrary evidence, or which detect themselves by their absurdity, prove sufficiently the strong propensity of mankind to the extraordinary and the marvellous, and ought reasonably to beget a suspicion against all relations of this kind. This is our natural way of thinking, even with regard to the most common and most credible events. For instance: There is no kind of report which rises so easily, and spreads so quickly, especially in country places and provincial towns, as those concerning marriages; insomuch that two young persons of equal condition never see each other twice, but the whole neighbourhood immediately join them together. The pleasure of telling a piece of news so interesting, of propagating it, and of being the first reporters of it, spreads the intelligence. And this is so well known, that no man of sense gives attention to these reports, till he find them confirmed by some greater evidence. Do not the same passions, and others still stronger, incline the generality of mankind to believe and report, with the greatest vehemence and assurance, all religious miracles?

Thirdly. It forms a strong presumption against all supernatural and miraculous relations, that they are observed chiefly to abound among ignorant and barbarous nations; or if a civilized people has ever given admission to any of them, that people will be found to have received them from ignorant and barbarous ancestors, who transmitted them with that inviolable sanction and authority, which always attend received opinions. When we peruse the first histories of all nations, we are apt to imagine ourselves transported into some new world; where the whole frame of nature is disjointed, and every element performs its operations in a different manner, from what it does at present. Battles, revolutions, pestilence, famine and death, are never the effect of those natural causes, which we experience. Prodigies, omens, oracles, judgements, quite obscure the few natural events, that are intermingled with them. But as the former grow thinner every page, in proportion as we advance nearer the enlightened ages, we soon learn, that there is nothing mysterious or supernatural in the case, but that all proceeds from the usual propensity of mankind towards the marvellous, and that, though this inclination may at intervals receive a check from sense and learning, it can never be thoroughly extirpated from human nature.

It is strange, a judicious reader is apt to say, upon the perusal of these wonderful historians, *that such prodigious events never happen in our days.* But it is nothing strange, I hope, that men should lie in all ages. You must surely have seen instances enough of that frailty. You have yourself heard many such marvellous relations started, which, being treated with scorn by all the wise and judicious, have at last been abandoned even by the vulgar. Be assured, that those renowned lies, which have spread and flourished to such a monstrous height, arose from like beginnings; but being sown in a more proper soil, shot up at last into prodigies almost equal to those which they relate.

It was a wise policy in that false prophet, Alexander, who though now forgotten, was once so famous, to lay the first scene of his impostures in Paphlagonia, where, as Lucian tells us, the people were extremely ignorant and stupid, and ready to swallow even the grossest delusion. People at a distance, who are weak enough to think the matter at all worth enquiry, have no opportunity of receiving better information. The stories come magnified to them by a hundred circumstances. Fools are industrious in propagating the imposture; while the wise and learned are contented, in general, to deride its absurdity, without informing themselves of the particular facts, by which it may be distinctly refuted. And thus the impostor above mentioned was enabled to proceed, from his ignorant Paphlagonians, to the enlisting of votaries, even among the Grecian philosophers, and men of the most eminent rank and distinction in Rome: nay, could engage the attention of that sage emperor Marcus Aurelius; so far as to make him trust the success of a military expedition to his delusive prophecies.

The advantages are so great, of starting an imposture among an

ignorant people, that, even though the delusion should be too gross
to impose on the generality of them (*which, though seldom, is sometimes the case*) it has a much better chance for succeeding in remote
countries, than if the first scene had been laid in a city renowned for
arts and knowledge. The most ignorant and barbarous of these bar-
barians carry the report abroad. None of their countrymen have a
large correspondence, or sufficient credit and authority to contradict
and beat down the delusion. Men's inclination to the marvellous has
full opportunity to display itself. And thus a story, which is universally exploded in the place where it was first started, shall pass
for certain at a thousand miles distance. But had Alexander fixed
his residence at Athens, the philosophers of that renowned mart of
learning had immediately spread, throughout the whole Roman empire, their sense of the matter; which, being supported by so great
authority, and displayed by all the force of reason and eloquence, had
entirely opened the eyes of mankind. It is true; Lucian, passing by
chance through Paphlagonia, had an opportunity of performing this
good office. But, though much to be wished, it does not always happen, that every Alexander meets with a Lucian, ready to expose and
detect his impostures.

I may add as a *fourth* reason, which diminishes the authority of
prodigies, that there is no testimony for any, even those which have
not been expressly detected, that is not opposed by an infinite number of witnesses; so that not only the miracle destroys the credit of
testimony, but the testimony destroys itself. To make this the better
understood, let us consider, that, in matters of religion, whatever
is different is contrary; and that it is impossible the religions of
ancient Rome, of Turkey, of Siam, and of China should, all of them,
be established on any solid foundation. Every miracle, therefore,
pretended to have been wrought in any of these religions (and all of
them abound in miracles), as its direct scope is to establish the particular system to which it is attributed; so has it the same force,
though more indirectly, to overthrow every other system. In destroying a rival system, it likewise destroys the credit of those miracles,
on which that system was established; so that all the prodigies of
different religions are to be regarded as contrary facts, and the evidences of these prodigies, whether weak or strong, as opposite to
each other. According to this method of reasoning, when we believe any miracle of Mahomet or his successors, we have for our
warrant the testimony of a few barbarous Arabians: And on the
other hand, we are to regard the authority of Titus Livius, Plutarch,
Tacitus, and, in short, of all the authors and witnesses, Grecian,

Chinese, and Roman Catholic, who have related any miracle in their particular religion; I say, we are to regard their testimony in the same light as if they had mentioned that Mahometan miracle, and had in express terms contradicted it, with the same certainty as they have for the miracle they relate. This argument may appear over subtile and refined; but is not in reality different from the reasoning of a judge, who supposes, that the credit of two witnesses, maintaining a crime against any one, is destroyed by the testimony of two others, who affirm him to have been two hundred leagues distant, at the same instant when the crime is said to have been committed.

One of the best attested miracles in all profane history, is that which Tacitus reports of Vespasian, who cured a blind man in Alexandria, by means of his spittle, and a lame man by the mere touch of his foot; in obedience to a vision of the god Serapis, who had enjoined them to have recourse to the Emperor, for these miraculous cures. The story may be seen in that fine historian; where every circumstance seems to add weight to the testimony, and might be displayed at large with all the force of argument and eloquence, if any one were now concerned to enforce the evidence of that exploded and idolatrous superstition. The gravity, solidity, age, and probity of so great an emperor, who, through the whole course of his life, conversed in a familiar manner with his friends and courtiers, and never affected those extraordinary airs of divinity assumed by Alexander and Demetrius. The historian, a contemporary writer, noted for candour and veracity, and withal, the greatest and most penetrating genius, perhaps, of all antiquity; and so free from any tendency to credulity, that he even lies under the contrary imputation, of atheism and profaneness: The persons, from whose authority he related the miracle, of established character for judgement and veracity, as we may well presume; eye-witnesses of the fact, and confirming their testimony, after the Flavian family was despoiled of the empire, and could no longer give any reward, as the price of a lie. *Utrumque, qui interfuere, nunc quoque memorant, postquam nullum mendacio pretium* [People who were present relate even now both cures, though there is no longer any value in lying (Tacitus)]. To which if we add the public nature of the facts, as related, it will appear, that no evidence can well be supposed stronger for so gross and so palpable a falsehood.

There is also a memorable story related by Cardinal de Retz, which may well deserve our consideration. When that intriguing politician fled into Spain, to avoid the persecution of his enemies, he passed through Saragossa, the capital of Arragon, where he was shewn, in the cathedral, a man, who had served seven years as a doorkeeper, and was well known to every body in town, that had ever paid his devotions at that church. He had been seen, for so long a time, wanting a leg; but recovered that limb by the rubbing of holy oil upon the stump; and the cardinal assures us that he saw him with two legs. This miracle was vouched by all the canons of the church; and the whole company in town were appealed to for a confirmation of the fact; whom the cardinal found, by their zealous devotion, to be thorough believers of the miracle. Here the relater was also cotemporary to the supposed prodigy, of an incredulous and libertine character, as well as of great genius; the miracle of so *singular* a nature as could scarcely admit of a counterfeit, and the witnesses very numerous, and all of them, in a manner, spectators of the fact, to which they gave their testimony. And what adds mightily to the force of the evidence, and may double our surprise on this occasion, is, that the cardinal himself, who relates the story, seems not to give any credit to it, and consequently cannot be suspected of any concurrence in the holy fraud. He considered justly, that it was not requisite, in order to reject a fact of this nature, to be able accurately to disprove the testimony, and to trace its falsehood, through all the circumstances of knavery and credulity which produced it. He knew, that, as this was commonly altogether impossible at any small distance of time and place; so was it extremely difficult, even where one was immediately present, by reason of the bigotry, ignorance, cunning, and roguery of a great part of mankind. He therefore concluded, like a just reasoner, that such an evidence carried falsehood upon the very face of it, and that a miracle, supported by any human testimony, was more properly a subject of derision than of argument.

There surely never was a greater number of miracles ascribed to one person, than those, which were lately said to have been wrought in France upon the tomb of Abbé Paris, the famous Jansenist, with whose sanctity the people were so long deluded. The curing of the sick, giving hearing to the deaf, and sight to the blind, were every where talked of as the usual effects of that holy sepulchre. But what is more extraordinary; many of the miracles were immediately proved upon the spot, before judges of unquestioned integrity, attested by witnesses of credit and distinction, in a learned age, and on the most eminent theatre that is now in the world. Nor is this all: a relation of them was published and dispersed everywhere; nor were the *Jesuits*, though a learned body, supported by the civil magistrate, and determined enemies to those opinions, in whose favour the miracles were said to have been wrought, ever able distinctly to refute or detect them. Where shall we find such a number of circumstances, agreeing to the corroboration of one fact? And what have we to oppose to such a cloud of witnesses, but the absolute impossibility or miraculous nature of the events, which they relate? And this surely, in the eyes of all reasonable people, will alone be regarded as a sufficient refutation.

Is the consequence just, because some human testimony has the utmost force and authority in some cases, when it relates the battle of Philippi or Pharsalia for instance; that therefore all kinds of testimony must, in all cases, have equal force and authority? Suppose that the Cæsarean and Pompeian factions had, each of them, claimed the victory in these battles, and that the historians of each party had uniformly ascribed the advantage to their own side; how could mankind, at this distance, have been able to determine between them? The contrariety is equally strong between the miracles related by Herodotus or Plutarch, and those delivered by Mariana, Bede, or any monkish historian.

The wise lend a very academic faith to every report which favours the passion of the reporter; whether it magnifies his country, his family, or himself, or in any other way strikes in with his natural inclinations and propensities. But what greater temptation than to appear a missionary, a prophet, an ambassador from heaven? Who would not encounter many dangers and difficulties, in order to attain so sublime a character? Or if, by the help of vanity and a heated imagination, a man has first made a convert of himself, and entered seriously into the delusion; who ever scruples to make use of pious frauds, in support of so holy and meritorious a cause?

The smallest spark may here kindle into the greatest flame; because the materials are always prepared for it. The *avidum genus auricularum,* the gazing populace, receive greedily, without examination, whatever soothes superstition, and promotes wonder.

How many stories of this nature have, in all ages, been detected and exploded in their infancy? How many more have been celebrated for a time, and have afterwards sunk into neglect and oblivion? Where such reports, therefore, fly about, the solution of the phenomenon is obvious; and we judge in conformity to regular experience and observation, when we account for it by the known and natural principles of credulity and delusion. And shall we, rather than have a recourse to so natural a solution, allow of a miraculous violation of the most established laws of nature?

I need not mention the difficulty of detecting a falsehood in any private or even public history, at the place, where it is said to happen; much more when the scene is removed to ever so small a distance. Even a court of judicature, with all the authority, accuracy, and judgement, which they can employ, find themselves often at a loss to distinguish between truth and falsehood in the most recent actions. But the matter never comes to any issue, if trusted to the common method of altercations and debate and flying rumours; especially when men's passions have taken part on either side.

In the infancy of new religions, the wise and learned commonly esteem the matter too inconsiderable to deserve their attention or regard. And when afterwards they would willingly detect the cheat, in order to undeceive the deluded multitude, the season is now past, and the records and witnesses, which might clear up the matter, have perished beyond recovery.

No means of detection remain, but those which must be drawn from the very testimony itself of the reporters: and these, though always sufficient with the judicious and knowing, are commonly too fine to fall under the comprehension of the vulgar.

Upon the whole, then, it appears, that no testimony for any kind of miracle has ever amounted to a probability, much less to a proof; and that, even supposing it amounted to a proof, it would be opposed by another proof; derived from the very nature of the fact, which it would endeavour to establish. It is experience only, which gives authority to human testimony; and it is the same experience, which assures us of the laws of nature. When, therefore, these two kinds of experience are contrary, we have nothing to do but subtract the one from the other, and embrace an opinion, either on one side or the other, with that assurance which arises from the remainder. But according to the principle here explained, this subtraction, with regard to all popular religions, amounts to an entire annihilation; and therefore we may establish it as a maxim, that no human testimony can have such force as to prove a miracle, and make it a just foundation for any such system of religion.

I beg the limitations here made may be remarked, when I say, that a miracle can never be proved, so as to be the foundation of a system of religion. For I own, that otherwise, there may possibly be miracles, or violations of the usual course of nature, of such a kind as to admit of proof from human testimony; though, perhaps, it will be impossible to find any such in all the records of history. Thus, suppose, all authors, in all languages, agree, that, from the first of January 1600, there was a total darkness over the whole earth for eight days: suppose that the tradition of this extraordinary event is still strong and lively among the people: that all travellers, who return from foreign countries, bring us accounts of the same tradition, without the least variation or contradiction: it is evident, that our present philosophers, instead of doubting the fact, ought to receive it as certain, and ought to search for the causes whence it might be derived. The decay, corruption, and dissolution of nature, is an event rendered probable by so many analogies, that any phenomenon, which seems to have a tendency towards that catastrophe, comes within the reach of human testimony, if that testimony be very extensive and uniform.

But suppose, that all the historians who treat of England, should agree, that, on the first of January 1600, Queen Elizabeth died; that both before and after her death she was seen by her physicians and the whole court, as is usual with persons of her rank; that her successor was acknowledged and proclaimed by the parliament; and that, after being interred a month, she again appeared, resumed the throne, and governed England for three years: I must confess that I should be surprised at the concurrence of so many odd circumstances, but should not have the least inclination to believe so miraculous an event. I should not doubt of her pretended death, and of those other public circumstances that followed it: I should only assert it to have been pretended, and that it neither was, nor possibly could be real. You would in vain object to me the difficulty, and almost impossibility of deceiving the world in an affair of such consequence; the wisdom and solid judgement of that renowned queen; with the little or no advantage which she could reap from so poor an artifice: All this might astonish me; but I would still reply, that the knavery and folly of men are such common phenomena, that I should rather believe the most extraordinary events to arise from their concurrence, than admit of so signal a violation of the laws of nature.

But should this miracle be ascribed to any new system of religion; men, in all ages, have been so much imposed on by ridiculous stories of that kind, that this very circumstance would be a full proof of a cheat, and sufficient, with all men of sense, not only to make them reject the fact, but even reject it without farther examination. Though the Being to whom the miracle is ascribed, be, in this case, Almighty, it does not, upon that account, become a whit more probable; since it is impossible for us to know the attributes or actions of such a Being, otherwise than from the experience which we have of his productions, in the usual course of nature. This still reduces us to past observation, and obliges us to compare the instances of the violation of truth in the testimony of men, with those of the violation of the laws of nature by miracles, in order to judge which of them is most likely and probable. As the violations of truth are more common in the testimony concerning religious miracles, than in that concerning any other matter of fact; this must diminish very much the authority of the former testimony, and make us form a general resolution, never to lend any attention to it, with whatever specious pretence it may be covered.

Lord Bacon seems to have embraced the same principles of reasoning. "We ought," says he, "to make a collection or particular history of all monsters and prodigious births or productions, and in a word of every thing new, rare, and extraordinary in nature. But this must be done with the most severe scrutiny, lest we depart from truth.

Above all, every relation must be considered as suspicious, which depends in any degree upon religion, as the prodigies of Livy: And no less so, every thing that is to be found in the writers of natural magic or alchimy, or such authors, who seem, all of them, to have an unconquerable appetite for falsehood and fable."

I am the better pleased with the method of reasoning here delivered, as I think it may serve to confound those dangerous friends or disguised enemies to the *Christian Religion,* who have undertaken to defend it by the principles of human reason. Our most holy religion is founded on *Faith,* not on reason; and it is a sure method of exposing it to put it to such a trial as it is, by no means, fitted to endure. To make this more evident, let us examine those miracles, related in scripture; and not to lose ourselves in too wide a field, let us confine ourselves to such as we find in the *Pentateuch,* which we shall examine, according to the principles of these pretended Christians, not as the word or testimony of God himself, but as the production of a mere human writer and historian. Here then we are first to consider a book, presented to us by a barbarous and ignorant people, written in an age when they were still more barbarous, and in all probability long after the facts which it relates, corroborated by no concurring testimony, and resembling those fabulous accounts, which every nation gives of its origin. Upon reading this book, we find it full of prodigies and miracles. It gives an account of a state of the world and of human nature entirely different from the present: Of our fall from that state: Of the age of man, extended to near a thousand years: Of the destruction of the world by a deluge: Of the arbitrary choice of one people, as the favourites of heaven; and that people the countrymen of the author: Of their deliverance from bondage by prodigies the most astonishing imaginable: I desire any one to lay his hand upon his heart, and after a serious consideration declare, whether he thinks that the falsehood of such a book, supported by such a testimony, would be more extraordinary and miraculous than all the miracles it relates; which is, however, necessary to make it be received, according to the measures of probability above established.

What we have said of miracles may be applied, without any variation, to prophecies; and indeed, all prophecies are real miracles, and as such only, can be admitted as proofs of any revelation. If it did not exceed the capacity of human nature to foretell future events, it would be absurd to employ any prophecy as an argument for a divine mission or authority from heaven. So that, upon the whole, we may conclude, that the *Christian Religion* not only was at first attended with miracles, but even at this day cannot be believed by any reasonable person without one. Mere reason is insufficient to convince us of its veracity: And whoever is moved by *Faith* to assent to it, is conscious of a continued miracle in his own person, which subverts all the principles of his understanding, and gives him a determination to believe what is most contrary to custom and experience.

12

ON THE EXISTENCE OF GOD *

by

ST. ANSELM

(1033–1109)

. . . I do not seek to understand that I may believe, but I believe in order to understand. For this also I believe,—that unless I believed, I should not understand.

And so, Lord, do thou, who dost give understanding to faith, give me, so far as thou knowest it to be profitable, to understand that thou art as we believe; and that thou art that which we believe. And, indeed, we believe that thou art a being than which nothing greater can be conceived. Or is there no such nature, since the fool hath said in his heart, there is no God? (Psalms xiv. 1). But, at any rate, this very fool, when he hears of this being of which I speak— a being than which nothing greater can be conceived—understands what he hears, and what he understands is in his understanding; although he does not understand it to exist.

For, it is one thing for an object to be in the understanding, and another to understand that the object exists. When a painter first conceives of what he will afterwards perform, he has it in his understanding, but he does not yet understand it to be, because he has not yet performed it. But after he has made the painting, he both has it in his understanding, and he understands that it exists, because he has made it.

* [From the *Proslogium*, translated by Sidney Norton Deane, Open Court Publishing Co., 1903.]

Hence, even the fool is convinced that something exists in the understanding, at least, than which nothing greater can be conceived. For, when he hears of this, he understands it. And whatever is understood, exists in the understanding. And assuredly that, than which nothing greater can be conceived, cannot exist in the understanding alone. For, suppose it exists in the understanding alone: then it can be conceived to exist in reality; which is greater.

Therefore, if that, than which nothing greater can be conceived, exists in the understanding alone, the very being, than which nothing greater can be conceived, is one, than which a greater can be conceived. But obviously this is impossible. Hence, there is no doubt that there exists a being, than which nothing greater can be conceived, and it exists both in the understanding and in reality.

And it assuredly exists so truly, that it cannot be conceived not to exist. For, it is possible to conceive of a being which cannot be conceived not to exist; and this is greater than one which can be conceived not to exist. Hence, if that, than which nothing greater can be conceived, can be conceived not to exist, it is not that, than which nothing greater can be conceived. But this is an irreconcilable contradiction. There is, then, so truly a being than which nothing greater can be conceived to exist, that it cannot even be conceived not to exist; and this being thou art, O Lord, our God.

So truly, therefore, dost thou exist, O Lord, my God, that thou canst not be conceived not to exist; and rightly. For, if a mind could conceive of a being better than thee, the creature would rise above the Creator; and this is most absurd. And, indeed, whatever else there is, except thee alone, can be conceived not to exist. To thee alone, therefore, it belongs to exist more truly than all other beings, and hence in a higher degree than all others. For, whatever else exists does not exist so truly, and hence in a less degree it belongs to it to exist. Why, then, has the fool said in his heart, there is no God, since it is so evident, to a rational mind, that thou dost exist in the highest degree of all? Why, except that he is dull and a fool?

1 that be exists
2 " " necessarily exists

13

IMAGINING *

by

JEAN-PAUL SARTRE
(b. 1905)

1. Perception and Imagination

When I form the image of Peter, it is Peter who is the object of my actual consciousness. As long as this consciousness remains unaltered, I can give a description of the object as it appears to me in imagination, but not of the image as such. To specify the properties of the image as an image, I must resort to a new act of consciousness: I must *reflect*. Thus the image as image can be described only by a higher-order act of consciousness in which attention is diverted from the object and directed to the way in which the object is given. . . .

To perceive, to conceive, to imagine: these are the three modes of consciousness by which the same object can be given.

When I am perceiving, I am *observing* objects. The object, although it enters entirely into my perception, is never given from one side at a time. Take the example of a cube: I cannot know that it is a cube until I have apprehended its six sides, but of these I can see only three at a time, never more. I must therefore apprehend them successively. And when I make the transition, for example, from sides ABC to sides BCD, there always remains a possibility that side A has disappeared during my change of position. The existence of the cube therefore remains doubtful. Note too that when I see three sides of the cube at the same time, these three sides never present them-

* [From pages 3, 9–11, 13, 23–24, 26–27, 34, 40, 169–171, 177–179, 199, 200, 210–212 of *The Psychology of Imagination* by Jean-Paul Sartre, copyright Philosophical Library, Inc., 1948. Reprinted by permission of the publisher. The selection here used is from that edited and re-translated by Robert Denoon Cumming in his anthology *The Philosophy of Jean-Paul Sartre* (New York, Random House, 1965).]

selves to me as squares: their angles become obtuse, and starting from these appearances I must reconstruct their character as square. This has all been said a hundred times: it is characteristic of perception that the object appears only in a series of profiles, of aspects. The cube is certainly present to me, I can touch it, see it; but I always see it only in a certain way which solicits and excludes at one and the same time an infinite number of other points of view. We must *learn* about objects—i.e., multiply possible points of view toward them. The object itself is the synthesis of all these appearances. . . .

When, in contrast, I conceive of a cube, I think of its six sides and its eight angles all at once. I think that its angles are right angles, its sides square. I am at the center of my idea, I grasp all of it immediately. . . . There is no learning process, no apprenticeship to serve. This is beyond doubt the clearest difference between thought and perception. This is why we can never perceive a thought nor think a perception. The two phenomena are radically distinct. . . .

What about the image? Is it apprenticeship or knowledge? Note first that it seems to fall on the side of perception. In both cases the object is given by profiles, by aspects, by what the Germans designate by the apt term *Abschattungen*. Only we don't have to tour around it: the cube when imagined is given immediately as what it is. When I say, "The object that I perceive is a cube," I am making an hypothesis which the further progress of my perceptions may force me to reject. When I say, "The object which I am at this moment imagining is a cube," my judgment is conclusive. It is absolutely certain that the object I am imagining is a cube.

This is not all. Consider this piece of paper on the table. The longer I look at it, the more it discloses its particular features. Each new orientation of my attention, of my analysis, discloses a new detail: the upper edge of the sheet is slightly warped; the end of the third line is dotted. But no matter how long I may contemplate an image, I shall never find anything in it but what I have put there. This is of central importance for distinguishing between an image and a perception. In the world of perception nothing can appear without entertaining an infinite number of relations with other things. Rather it is this infinite number of relationships—as well as the infinite number of relationships between the elements of this thing—which constitute the essence of a thing. There is accordingly something *overflowing* about the world of "things." There is always, at each moment, infinitely *more* than we can see; to exhaust the abundance of my actual perception, would require infinite time. This way of "overflowing" constitutes the very nature of objects. When we say, "No object can exist without having definite individuality," we must be understood to mean "without having an infinite number of specific relationships with an infinite number of other objects."

Now the image, in contrast, suffers from a sort of essential poverty. The different elements of an image have no relationship with the rest of the world, while among themselves they have but two or three relationships—either those that I have been able to ascertain, or those it is important for me at the moment to retain. It must not be said that other relationships exist covertly, that they wait for a bright light to be focused on them. They do not exist at all. Two colors, for example, which would clash in reality, can exist together in an image without any sort of relationship between them. . . .

The image presents its object all in one piece. No risk, no expectation; instead a certainty. My perception can deceive me, but not my image. Our attitude toward the object of the image could be called "quasi-observation." Our attitude is indeed that of observation, but it is an observation from which nothing is learned. If I imagine the page of a book, I am adopting the attitude of a reader, I *look* at the printed pages. But I am not reading. And in fact I am not even looking, since I already *know* what is written there.

2. Mental and Material Images

I wish to recall the face of my friend Peter. I make an effort and I produce a certain imaginative consciousness of Peter. The object is very imperfectly rendered: certain details are lacking, others are doubtful, the whole is rather vague. There is a certain feeling of sympathy and pleasantness which I wanted to revive when confronted by this face, but which has not been recovered. I do not give up, I get up and take a photograph from a drawer. It is a fine photograph of Peter, I retrieve all the details of his face, even some which had eluded me. But the photograph lacks life: it is a perfect rendering of the external traits of his face, but it does not give his expression. Fortunately I own a carefully drawn caricature. Here the relations between the different features of his face are deliberately distorted, the nose is much too long, the cheekbones are too prominent, etc. Nevertheless, something which was missing in the photograph—vitality, expression—is clearly evident in this drawing. I have found Peter again.

Mental representation, photograph, caricature: these three very different realities appeared in our example as three stages of the same process, three moments of a single act. From the beginning to the end, the intention remains the same: to represent [*rendre présent*] the face of Peter, who is not there. But it is only the subjective representation that psychology terms an image. Is this legitimate?

Consider our example again. We have used three procedures to recall the face of Peter. In all three we found an "intention" and this intention envisages the same object. This object is neither the representation, nor the photograph, nor the caricature: it is my friend Peter. Furthermore, in the three cases, I envisaged the object in the same way: I want to make the face of Peter appear as a perception, I want to "make him present" to myself. And since I cannot make this perception emerge directly, I have recourse to a certain material which acts as an *analogue,* as an equivalent for the perception.

In the first two cases, at least, the material can be perceived for its own sake, though it is not its own nature that it should function as the material for the image. The photo, taken by itself, is a *thing:* I can try to ascertain its exposure time by its color, the chemical used to tone it and fix it, etc. The caricature is a *thing,* I can take pleasure in investigating its lines and colors, without reflecting that they have the function of representing something. . . .

It is obvious that the mental image must also have a material, and a material which derives its meaning solely from the intention that animates it. To recognize this, all I need do is compare my initial empty intention with my mental image of Peter, which is something that emerged and arrived to fill my intention. The three cases are thus strictly parallel. They are three situations with the same form, but with material that varies. . . .

We can conclude that the act of imagining envisages an absent or non-existent object in its corporality, through a physical or psychical content, which is given not for its own sake, but only as an analogical representative of the object envisaged. The species of this genus depend on the material, since the informing intention remains the same. We shall therefore distinguish between images whose material is derived from the world of things (engravings, photos, caricatures, actors' impersonations, etc.) and those whose material is derived from the mental world (consciousness of movements, feelings, etc.). There are intermediary types which present us with syntheses of external elements and of psychical elements, as when we see a face in a flame, in the arabesques of a tapestry, or in the case of hypnagogic images, which are constructed . . . on the basis of entoptic lights.

The mental image cannot be investigated by itself. There is not a world of images and a world of objects. Every object, whether it is presented by an outward or an inner perception, can function either as a present reality or as an image, depending on what center of reference has been chosen. The two worlds, real and imaginary, are composed of the same objects: only the grouping and the interpretation of these objects vary.

3. From the Sign to the Image

On the stage of the music hall, Franconay is doing some impersonations. I recognize the person she is imitating; it is Maurice Chevalier. I appraise the imitation: "That really is Maurice Chevalier," or "It doesn't come off." What is going on in my consciousness?

Only, some will say, an association by resemblance, followed by a comparison: the imitation has produced in my consciousness an image of Maurice Chevalier; I then compare the two. This view is unacceptable. We have completely succumbed to the illusion of immanence. William James' objection, moreover, carries its full weight here: what is this resemblance which goes in search of images in the unconscious—this resemblance which precedes the consciousness we have of it?

We might attempt to retain this view by introducing several corrections. We might discard the resemblance and resort instead to contiguity. The name "Maurice Chevalier" calls forth in us an image by contiguity. Will the explanation hold for the numerous instances where the impersonator suggests without supplying the name? There are a large number of signs comparable to a name: Franconay, without naming Chevalier, might suddenly put on a straw hat. Posters, newspapers, caricatures, have gradually built up a whole arsenal of signs. They need only be borrowed. . . .

The difference between the consciousness of an impersonation and the consciousness of a portrait derives from the materials. The material of the portrait itself solicits the spectator to carry out the synthesis, inasmuch as the painter endowed it with a perfect resemblance to its model. The material of the impersonation is a human body. It is rigid, and resists the imitation. The impersonator is small, plump, and dark-haired; a woman who is imitating a man. The result is that the imitation can only be approximate. The object which Franconay produces by means of her body is a weak form which can always be interpreted in two distinct ways: I am always free to see Maurice Chevalier as an image or a small woman making faces. Hence the essential role of signs in clarifying and guiding consciousness.

Consciousness is first oriented toward the general situation: it is disposed to interpret everything as an imitation. But it remains empty; it is only a question (Whom is she going to imitate?), only an oriented anticipation. From the outset it is oriented, through the imitator, toward an indeterminate person, conceived as the object X of the imitation. Consciousness undertakes a double assignment: to determine the object X in accordance with the signs provided by the imitator; and to realize the object as an image through the person who is imitating it.

The impersonator appears. She is wearing a straw hat; she is sticking out her lower lip, she is keeping her head forward. I stop perceiving, I *read*—*i.e.*, I carry through a synthesis involving these signs. The straw hat is at first a simple sign, just as the cap and the foulard of a real singer are signs that he is about to sing an apache song. In other words, I do not at first perceive Chevalier's hat *through* the straw hat; I recognize that the hat of the impersonator *refers* to Chevalier, just as the cap refers to the *"milieu apache."* To decipher the signs is to produce the concept "Chevalier." At the same time I am making the judgment, "She is imitating Chevalier." With this judgment the structure of my consciousness is transformed. Now its theme is Chevalier. In virtue of its crucial intention, my consciousness is imaginative, my knowledge is realized in the intuitive material furnished me.

This intuitive material is very poor; the imitation reproduces only a few elements—relationships, which are only minimally intuitive: the rakish angle of the straw hat and the angle formed by the neck and chin. In addition, certain of these relationships are deliberately altered: the angle of the straw hat is exaggerated, since this is the principal sign which must strike us first and around which all the others are ordered. A portrait is a faithful rendering of its model in all its complexity, and imposes on us, as life does, an effort of simplification, if we would abstract characteristic traits; but an imitation presents characteristic traits as such from the very outset. A portrait is in some respect, at least in appearance, something natural. An imitation is already a model that has been thought through and reduced to formulae, to schemata. Into these conventional formulae, consciousness wants an imaginative intuition to flow. But these arid schemata—so arid, so abstract that they could be read a moment ago as signs—are engulfed in a mass of details which seem to get in the way of this intuition. How is Maurice Chevalier to be discovered in these plump painted cheeks, this dark hair, this female body, these female clothes?

We should recall here a famous passage from [Bergson's] *Matter and Memory:*

> *A priori* . . . it does seem that the sharp distinction between individual objects is a luxury of perception. . . . It does seem that we set out neither from the perception of the individual, nor from the conception of the genus, but from some intermediate form of knowledge —from a confused sense of a striking quality or resemblance.

That dark hair we do not see as dark; that body we do not perceive as a female body, we do not see its prominent curves. Nevertheless, since it is a matter of descending to the level of intuition, we employ the sensory content with respect to its most general traits. The hair, the body are perceived as vague masses, as filled spaces. They have sensory opacity; beyond this they are but a *setting*. For the first time in our description of imaginative consciousnesses, we see appear—and at the heart of perception—a fundamental indeterminacy. . . . These qualities which are so vague and which are perceived only with respect to their general traits, have no value in themselves: they are integrated into the imaginative synthesis. They represent the indeterminate body, the indeterminate hair of Maurice Chevalier.

These elements are not sufficient. Positive specifications must be realized. It is not a matter of constituting, with the body of the impersonator Franconay, a perfect *analogue* of the body of Chevalier. All I have available are a few elements which were functioning just now as signs. Since I do not have a complete equivalent of the person imitated, I have to realize in the intuition a certain *expressive nature*, the essence, as it were, of Chevalier presented to intuition.

First I must lend life to these arid schemata. But we have to be careful: if I perceive them for their own sake, if I notice the edges of the lips, the color of the straw of the hat, the consciousness of the image vanishes. I must carry through the movement of perception in reverse, starting out with knowledge and determining the intuition as a function of this knowledge. That lip was just now a sign; I make an image of it. But it is an image only to the extent to which it was a sign. I see it only as a "large protruding lip." Here we meet again an essential characteristic of the mental image—the phenomenon of quasi-observation. What I perceive is what I know; I cannot learn anything from the object, and the intuition is only knowledge which has been weighed down and degraded. At the same time, these differentiated features are joined together by vaguely intuited zones: the cheeks, the ears, the neck of the impersonator function as an indeterminate connective tissue. Here too, it is knowledge which is primary: what is perceived corresponds to the vague knowledge that Maurice Chevalier has cheeks, ears, a neck. The details fade away, and what cannot disappear resists the imaginative synthesis.

But these different intuitive elements are insufficient to realize the expressive nature. Here a new factor emerges—feeling.

Two principles are to be recognized:

1   Any perception is accompanied by an affective reaction.
2   Any feeling is a feeling of something, that is, it envisages its object in a certain fashion and projects upon it a certain quality. To have sympathy for Peter is to be conscious of Peter as sympathetic.

Now the role of feeling in the consciousness of imitation can be understood. When I see Maurice Chevalier, this perception involves a certain affective reaction. I project on the physiognomy of Maurice Chevalier a certain indefinable quality which might be called his meaning [*sens*]. In the consciousness of imitation, the knowledge intended, on the basis of the signs and the commencement of the intuitive realization, awakens this affective reaction, which becomes incorporated into the intentional synthesis. Correlatively, the affective meaning of the face of Chevalier begins to appear on the face of Franconay. It is this affective meaning which realizes the synthetic union of the various signs, animating their rigid aridity and giving them a certain life and density. It is this affective meaning which endows the isolated elements of the imitation with an indefinable meaning and the unity of an object and which functions as the real intuitive material of the consciousness of the imitation. Finally, it is this object as an image which we contemplate on the body of the impersonator: the signs reunited by an affective meaning—*i.e.*, the *expressive nature*. This is the first occasion, but not the last, that we see feeling take the place of the strictly intuitive elements of perception in order to realize the object as an image.

The imaginative synthesis is accompanied by a vigorous consciousness of spontaneity—we might even say, of freedom. This is because, in the last analysis, only a definite act of will can keep consciousness from sliding from the level of the image to that of perception. Even so, this sliding usually occurs at one moment or another. It often happens that the synthesis is not completely carried out: the face and body of the impersonator do not lose all of their individuality; but the expressive something "Maurice Chevalier" nevertheless appears on this face, on this female body. A hybrid state develops, which is neither entirely perceptive nor entirely imaginative, and which would be well worth describing for its own sake. This unstable and transitory state is obviously what is most entertaining for the spectator in an impersonation.

4. Thought and Imagination

Always ready to bog down in the materiality of an image, thought escapes by flowing into another image, and from it to still another. But in most cases this distrust, which is like a memory of reflection, does not appear. In these cases the laws of development that are native to the image are often confused with the laws of the essence under consideration. . . . The dangers of this substitution are illustrated by the following example: "I wanted to convince myself of the idea that every oppressed individual or group derives from its oppression the strength needed to shake off its oppressors. But I had the definite impression that such a theory was arbitrary and I felt a certain uneasiness. I made a new effort of thought: now there emerged the image of a compressed spring. At the same time I felt in my muscles the latent force of the spring. It would expand the more violently, the more it had been compressed. For a moment I felt with complete evidence the necessity of the idea which I could not convince myself of before."

We see what is involved. The oppressed *is* the spring. *On* the compressed spring can already be observed as evident the force with which it will expand; but a compressed force clearly represents potential energy, and this potential energy is that of the oppressed, since the oppressed *is* the spring. Here we see clearly the contamination between the laws of the image and those of the essence represented. This idea of potential energy which increases in proportion to the force exercised, it is the spring which *presents* it; it can be apprehended on the spring. Change the term of comparison and substitute for the spring an organism, for example, and you will have an entirely opposed intuition—something which could be expressed by saying, "Oppression demeans and degrades those who suffer it." But the image of the spring, left to itself and envisaged purely and simply as the image of a spring, would not be sufficient to carry conviction. No doubt the spring accumulates force. But never enough to throw off the weight, since the force accumulated in the spring is always less than that compressing the spring. The conclusion that then would be drawn from the image would be that the oppressed gains in strength and value from the very fact of its oppression, but it will never succeed in throwing off its yoke. In fact . . . more is involved. The image is falsified by the meaning: the energy which accumulates in the compressed spring, is not felt as stored up purely passively, but as a living force which will increase with the passage of *time*. Here the image of the spring is no longer a simple image of a spring. It is also something indefinable: an image of a living spring. Here there is no doubt a contradiction, but there is . . . no image without inherent contradiction. It is in and by this very contradiction that the impression of evidence is constituted. Thus the image carries within itself a power to convince which is spurious and which comes from the ambiguity of its nature.

5. Feeling and Imagination

The object as an image is something unreal [*irréel*]. It is no doubt present, but at the same time it is out of reach. I cannot touch it, change its place; or rather I can indeed do so, but on condition that

I do it unreally, by not using my own hands but phantom hands which administer unreal blows to this face. To act upon these unreal objects, I must double myself, make myself *unreal*. But then none of these objects require me to act, to do anything. They are neither heavy, nor demanding, nor compelling: they are purely passive, they wait. The feeble life that we breathe into them comes from us, from our own spontaneity. If we turn away from them, they vanish into nothing. . . .

This passive object, kept artificially alive, but about to vanish at any moment, cannot fulfill our desires. But it is not entirely pointless: to constitute an unreal object is a way of deceiving for a moment our desires, if only to aggravate them later, somewhat like the effect of sea water on thirst. If I desire to see a friend I make him appear unreally. This is a way of playing at satisfying my desire. But the satisfaction is only play-acting, for in fact my friend is not really there. What is more, it is the desire which constitutes the object for the most part. To the extent that it projects the unreal object before it, the desire specifies itself as desire. At first it is only Peter that I desire to see. But my desire becomes desire for that smile, for that look. It thus becomes limited and aggravated at the same time, and the unreal object—at any rate so far as its affective aspect is concerned—is precisely the limitation and the aggravation of this desire. It is but a mirage; in the imaginative act desire feeds on itself. To be more exact, the object as an image is a *specific lack;* it is hollow. . . .

In organizing itself with knowledge into an imaginative form, desire becomes precise and concentrated. Enlightened by this knowledge, the desire projects outside itself its object. It thereby becomes conscious of itself. The act by which a feeling becomes conscious of its exact nature, limits and defines itself—this act is one and the same as the act by which it presents itself with a transcendent object. . . . It is impossible for the image to link itself to desire from the outside; for this would involve a desire which is natively anonymous and entirely indifferent to the object on which it will finally fix itself. Instead the affective state, *being consciousness*, cannot exist without a transcendent correlative.

When feeling is oriented toward something real, actually perceived, the thing, like a reflector, returns the light it has received from it. As a result of this continual interaction, the feeling is continually enriched at the same time as the object soaks up affective qualities.†
The feeling thus obtains its own particular depth and richness. The affective state follows the progress of attention, it develops with each

† Such as gracious, troubling, congenial, light, heavy, refined, disturbing, horrible, repulsive, etc.

new discovery of perception, it assimilates all the features of the object; as a result its development is unpredictable, since it is subordinate to the development of its real correlative, even while it remains spontaneous. At each moment perception overflows it and sustains it, and its density and depth come from its being confused with the perceived object: each affective quality is so deeply incorporated in the object that it is impossible to distinguish between what is felt and what is perceived.

In the constitution of the unreal object knowledge plays the role of perception; it is with it that the feeling is incorporated. Thus the unreal object emerges. . . . Feeling then behaves in the face of the unreal as in the face of the real. It seeks to fuse with it, to adapt itself to its contours, to feed on it. Only this unreal, so well specified and defined, is empty; or rather it is the simple reflection of the feeling.

To prefer to the real the imaginary is not only to prefer to a mediocre present a richness, a beauty, a splendor which are imaginary, *in spite of* the fact that they are unreal. It is also to adopt feelings and behavior which are imaginary *because* they are imaginary. It is not this or that image alone that is chosen, but the imaginary state with all its implications, it is not just an escape from features of reality (poverty, frustrated love, failure of our undertakings, etc.) that is sought, but from the form itself of reality, its character of *presence*, the responsiveness it demands of us, the subordination of our actions to their object, the inexhaustibility of our perceptions, their independence, the very way our feelings have of developing. This artificial, congealed, formalized life in slow motion, which is for most of us but a makeshift, is exactly what a schizophrenic desires. The morbid dreamer who imagines he is a king, would not adjust himself to a real throne, nor even to a tyranny where all his desires would be granted. A desire is in fact never literally granted because of the abyss which separates the real from the imaginary. The object which I desired, can indeed be given to me, but only on another level of existence to which I must adapt myself. Here it is now in front of me. If I did not have to act at once, I would hesitate for a long time, surprised, not able to recognize this reality so full and rich in consequences. I would ask myself: "Is it really *this* I wanted?" The morbid dreamer will not hesitate; it is not *this* which he wanted. More than any other consideration is the fact that the present requires an adaptation which he is no longer able to muster; a sort of indeterminacy on the part of our feelings is needed, a real plasticity, for the real is always new, always *unpredictable*. I wanted Anny to come; but the Anny I desired was only the correlative of my desires. Here she is, but she overflows my desire on all sides; I must begin my apprenticeship all over again. In contrast the feelings of the morbid dreamer are solemn and congealed; they keep recurring with the same forms and the same labels. He has taken his time in constructing them; nothing has been left to chance; they will not tolerate the slightest deviation. The traits of the unreal objects corresponding to their feelings have been correlatively fixed for ever. Thus the dreamer can choose from the storeroom of accessories the feelings he wishes to put on and the objects that go with these feelings, as an actor chooses his costumes. Today it is ambition, tomorrow sexual love. Only objects as images with their "essential poverty" can submissively minister to his feeling, without ever taking it by surprise, deceiving it, or guiding it. Only unreal objects can vanish into nothingness when the caprice of the dreamer is over, since they are only its reflection; only unreal objects have no other consequences than those he wants to draw from them. It is therefore a mistake to look upon the world of the schizophrenic as a torrent of images with a richness and a glitter which compensate for the monotony of reality. His world is poor and meticulous, where the same scenes keep on tirelessly recurring to the slightest detail, accompanied by the same ceremonial, where everything is regulated in advance, foreseen—where above all, nothing can escape, resist, or surprise. In short, if the schizophrenic imagines so many amorous scenes, it is not just because his real love has been frustrated, it is rather because he is no longer capable of love.

14

CONSCIOUSNESS *

by

GILBERT RYLE
(b. 1900)

Before starting to discuss the philosophers' concept or concepts of consciousness, it is advisable to consider some ways in which the words 'conscious' and 'consciousness' are used, when uncommitted to special theories, in ordinary life.

(a) People often speak in this way; they say, 'I was conscious that the furniture had been rearranged', or, 'I was conscious that he was less friendly than usual'. In such contexts the word 'conscious' is used instead of words like 'found out', 'realised' and 'discovered'

* [From Chapter VI in *The Concept of Mind* (1949). Reprinted by permission of the author, Gilbert Ryle, and the publishers, Hutchinson and Co., Ltd.]

to indicate a certain noteworthy nebulousness and consequent inarticulateness of the apprehension. The furniture looked different somehow, but the observer could not say what the differences were; or the man's attitude was unaccommodating in a number of ways, but the speaker could not enumerate or specify them. Though there are philosophically interesting problems about vagueness as well as about the inexpressibility of the very nebulous, this use of 'conscious' does not entail the existence of any special faculties, methods, or channels of apprehension. What we are consicous of, in this sense, may be a physical fact, or a fact about someone else's state of mind.

(b) People often use 'conscious' and 'self-conscious' in describing the embarrassment exhibited by persons, especially youthful persons, who are anxious about the opinions held by others of their qualities of character or intellect. Shyness and affectation are ways in which self-consciousness, in this sense, is commonly exhibited.

(c) 'Self-conscious' is sometimes used in a more general sense to indicate that someone has reached the stage of paying heed to his own qualities of character or intellect, irrespective of whether or not he is embarrassed about other people's estimations of them. When a boy begins to notice that he is fonder of arithmetic, or less homesick, than are most of his acquaintances he is beginning to be self-conscious, in this enlarged sense.

Self-consciousness, in this enlarged sense is, of course, of primary importance for the conduct of life, and the concept of it is therefore of importance for Ethics; but its ingenuous use entails no special doctrines about how a person makes and checks his estimates of his own qualities of character and intellect, or how he compares them with those of his acquaintances.

The Freudian idioms of the 'Unconscious' and the 'Subconscious' are closely connected with this use of 'conscious'; for at least part of what is meant by describing jealousy, phobias or erotic impulses as 'unconscious' is that the victim of them not only does not recognise their strength, or even existence, in himself, but in a certain way *will* not recognise them. He shirks a part of the task of appreciating what sort of a person he is, or else he systematically biases his appreciations. The epistemological question how a person makes his estimates or mis-estimates of his own dispositions is not, or need not be, begged by the Freudian account of the aetiology, diagnosis, prognosis and cure of the tendencies to shirk and bias such estimates.

(d) Quite different from the foregoing uses of 'conscious', 'self-conscious' and 'unconscious', is the use in which a numbed or anaesthetised person is said to have lost consciousness from his feet up to his knees. In this use 'conscious' means 'sensitive' or 'sentient' and 'unconscious' means anaesthetised or insensitive. We say that a person has lost consciousness when he had ceased to be sensitive to any slaps, noises, pricks or smells.

(e) Different from, though closely connected with this last use, there is the sense in which a person can be said to be unconscious of a sensation, when he pays no heed to it. A walker engaged in a heated dispute may be unconscious, in this sense, of the sensations in his blistered heel, and the reader of these words was, when he began this sentence, probably unconscious of the muscular and skin sensations in the back of his neck, or in his left knee. A person may also be unconscious or unaware that he is frowning, beating time to the music, or muttering.

'Conscious' in this sense means 'heeding'; and it makes sense to say that a sensation is hardly noticed even when the sensation is moderately acute, namely when the victim's attention is fixed very strongly on something else. Conversely, a person may pay sharp heed to very faint sensations; when, for instance, he is scared of appendicitis, he will be acutely conscious, in this sense, of stomachic twinges which are not at all acute. In this sense, too, a person may be keenly conscious, hardly conscious, or quite unconscious, of feelings like twinges of anxiety, or qualms of doubt.

The fact that a person takes heed of his organic sensations and feelings does not entail that he is exempt from error about them. He can make mistakes about their causes and he can make mistakes about their locations. Furthermore, he can make mistakes about whether they are real or fancied, as hypochondriacs do. 'Heeding' does not denote a peculiar conduit of cognitive certainties.

Philosophers, chiefly since Descartes, have in their theories of knowledge and conduct operated with a concept of consciousness which has relatively little affinity with any of the concepts described above. Working with the notion of the mind as a second theatre, the episodes enacted in which enjoy the supposed status of 'the mental' and correspondingly lack the supposed status of 'the physical', thinkers of many sorts have laid it down as the cardinal positive property of these episodes that, when they occur, they occur consciously. The states and operations of a mind are states and operations of which it is necessarily aware, in some sense of 'aware', and this awareness is incapable of being delusive. The things that a mind does or experiences are self-intimating, and this is supposed to be a feature which characterises these acts and feelings not just sometimes but always. It is part of the definition of their being mental that their occurrence entails that they are self-intimating. If I think, hope, remember, will, regret, hear a noise, or feel a pain, I must, *ipso facto* [by that very fact], know that I do so. Even if I dream that I see a dragon, I must be apprised of my dragon-seeing, though, it is often conceded, I may not know that I am dreaming.

It is naturally difficult, if one denies the existence of the second theatre, to elucidate what is meant by describing the episodes which are supposed to take place in it as self-intimating. But some points are clear enough. It is not supposed that when I am wondering, say, what is the answer to a puzzle and am *ipso facto* consciously doing so, that I am synchronously performing two acts of attention, one to the puzzle and the other to my wondering about it. Nor, to generalise this point, is it supposed that my act of wondering and its self-intimation to me are two distinct acts or processes indissolubly welded together. Rather, to relapse perforce into simile, it is supposed that mental processes are phosphorescent, like tropical sea-water, which makes itself visible by the light which it itself emits. Or, to use another simile, mental processes are 'overheard' by the mind whose processes they are, somewhat as a speaker overhears the words he is himself uttering.

When the epistemologists' concept of consciousness first became popular, it seems to have been in part a transformed application of the Protestant notion of conscience. The Protestants had to hold that a man could know the moral state of his soul and the wishes of God without the aid of confessors and scholars; they spoke therefore of the God-given 'light' of private conscience. When Galileo's and Descartes' representations of the mechanical world seemed to require that minds should be salved from mechanism by being represented as constituting a duplicate world, the need was felt to explain how the contents of this ghostly world could be ascertained, again without the help of schooling, but also without the help of sense perception. The metaphor of 'light' seemed peculiarly appropriate, since Galilean science dealt so largely with the optically discovered world. 'Consciousness' was imported to play in the mental world the part played by light in the mechanical world. In this metaphorical sense, the contents of the mental world were thought of as being self-luminous or refulgent.

This model was employed again by Locke when he described the deliberate observational scrutiny which a mind can from time to time turn upon its current states and processes. He called this supposed inner perception 'reflexion' (our 'introspection') borrowing the word 'reflexion' from the familiar optical phenomenon of the reflections of faces in mirrors. The mind can 'see' or 'look at' its own operations in the 'light' given off by themselves. The myth of consciousness is a piece of para-optics.

These similes of 'over-hearing', 'phosphorescence' or 'self-luminousness' suggest another distinction which needs to be made. It is certainly true that when I do, feel or witness something, I usually could and frequently do pay swift retrospective heed to what I have just done, felt or witnessed. I keep, much of the time, some sort of log or score of what occupies me, in such a way that, if asked what I had just been hearing or picturing or saying, I could usually give a correct answer. Of course, I cannot always be actually harking back to the immediate past; or else, within a few seconds of being called in the morning, I should be recalling that I had just been recalling that I had just been recalling . . . hearing the knock on the door; one event would generate an endless series of recollections of recollections . . . of it, leaving no room for me to pay heed to any subsequent happening. There is, however, a proper sense in which I can be said generally to know what has just been engaging my notice or half-notice, namely that I generally could give a memory report of it, if there was occasion to do so. This does not exclude the possibility that I might sometimes give a misreport, for even short-term reminiscence is not exempt from carelessness or bias.

The point of mentioning this fact that we generally could, if required, report what had just been engaging our notice is that consciousness, as the prevalent view describes it, differs from this log-keeping in one or two important respects. First, according to the theory, mental processes are conscious, not in the sense that we do or could report on them *post mortem,* but in the sense that their intimations of their own occurrences are properties of those occurrences and so are not posterior to them. The supposed deliverances of consciousness, if verbally expressible at all, would be. expressed in the present, not in the past tense. Next, it is supposed that in being conscious of my present mental states and acts I know what I am experiencing and doing in a non-dispositional sense of 'know'; that is to say, it is not merely the case that I could, if occasion demanded, tell myself or you what I am experiencing and doing, but that I am actively cognisant of it. Though a double act of attention does not occur, yet when I discover that my watch has stopped, I am synchronously discovering that I am discovering that my watch has stopped; a truth about myself is flashed or shone upon me at the same moment as a truth about my watch is ascertained by me.

I shall argue that consciousness, as so described, is a myth and shall probably therefore be construed as arguing that mental processes are, in some mortifying sense, unconscious, perhaps in the sort of way in which I often cannot tell of my own habitual and reflex movements. To safeguard against this misinterpretation I say quite summarily first, that we do usually know what we are about, but that no phosphorescence-story is required to explain how we are apprised of it; second, that knowing what we are about does not entail an incessant actual monitoring or scrutiny of our doings and feelings, but only the propensity *inter alia* to avow them, when we are in the mood to do so; and, third, that the fact that we generally know what we are about does not entail our coming across any happenings of ghostly status.

The radical objection to the theory that minds must know what they are about, because mental happenings are by definition conscious, or metaphorically self-luminous, is that there are no such happenings; there are no occurrences taking place in a second-status world, since there is no such status and no such world and consequently no need for special modes of acquainting ourselves with the denizens of such a world. But there are also other objections which do not depend for their acceptance upon the rejection of the dogma of the ghost in the machine.

First, and this is not intended to be more than a persuasive argument, no one who is uncommitted to a philosophical theory ever tries to vindicate any of his assertions of fact by saying that he found it out 'from consciousness', or 'as a direct deliverance of consciousness', or 'from immediate awareness'. He will back up some of his assertions of fact by saying that he himself sees, hears, feels, smells or tastes so and so; he will back up other such statements somewhat more tentatively, by saying that he remembers seeing, hearing, feeling, smelling or tasting it. But if asked whether he really knows, believes, infers, fears, remembers or smells something, he never replies 'Oh yes, certainly I do, for I am conscious and even vividly conscious of doing so'. Yet just such a reply should, according to the doctrine, be his final appeal.

Next, it is supposed that my being conscious of my mental states and operations either is my knowing them, or is the necessary and sufficient ground for my doing so. But to say this is to abuse the logic and even the grammar of the verb 'to know'. It is nonsense to speak of knowing, or not knowing, this clap of thunder or that twinge of pain, this coloured surface or that act of drawing a conclusion or seeing a joke; these are accusatives of the wrong types to follow the verb 'to know'. To know and to be ignorant are to know and not to know that something is the case, for example that that rumble is a clap of thunder or that that coloured surface is a cheese-rind. And this is just the point where the metaphor of light is unhelpful. Good illumination helps us to see cheese-rinds, but we could not say 'the light was too bad for me to know the cheese-rind', since knowing is not the same sort of thing as looking at, and what is known is not the same sort of thing as what is illuminated. True, we can say 'owing to the darkness I could not recognise what I saw for a cheese-rind', but again recognising what I see is not another optical performance. We do not ask for one torch to help us to see and another to help us to recognise what we see. So even if there were some analogy between a thing's being illuminated and a mental process's being conscious, it would not follow that the owner of the process would recognise that process for what it was. It might conceivably explain how mental processes were discernible but it could not possibly explain how we ascertain truths and avoid or correct mistakes about them.

Next, there is no contradiction in asserting that someone might fail to recognise his frame of mind for what it is; indeed, it is notorious that people constantly do so. They mistakenly suppose themselves to know things which are actually false; they deceive themselves about their own motives; they are surprised to notice the clock stopping ticking, without their having, as they think, been aware that it had been ticking; they do not know that they are dreaming, when they are dreaming, and sometimes they are not sure that they are not dreaming, when they are awake; and they deny, in good faith, that they are irritated or excited, when they are flustered in one or other of those ways. If consciousness was what it is described as being, it would be logically impossible for such failures and mistakes in recognition to take place.

Finally, even though the self-intimation supposed to be inherent in any mental state or process is not described as requiring a separate act of attention, or as constituting a separate cognitive operation, still what I am conscious of in a process of inferring, say, is different from what the inferring is an apprehension of. My consciousness is of a process of inferring, but my inferring is, perhaps, of a geometrical conclusion from geometrical premisses. The verbal expression of my inference might be, 'because this is an equilateral triangle, therefore each angle is 60 degrees', but the verbal expression of what I am conscious of might be 'Here I am deducing such and such from so and so'. But, if so, then it would seem to make sense to ask whether, according to the doctrine, I am not also conscious of being conscious of inferring, that is, in a position to say 'Here I am spotting the fact that here I am deducing such and such from so and so'. And then there would be no stopping-place; there would have to be an infinite number of onion-skins of consciousness embedding any mental state or process whatsoever. If this conclusion is rejected, then it will have to be allowed that some elements in mental processes are not themselves things we can be conscious of, namely those elements which constitute the supposed outermost self-intimations of mental processes; and then 'conscious' could no longer be retained as part of the definition of 'mental'.

The argument, then, that mental events are authentic, because the deliverances of consciousness are direct and unimpeachable testimony to their existence, must be rejected.

15

ON THE BEAUTIFUL *
by
PLATO
(B.C. 427–347)

Socrates. Hippias, the fine and the wise! what a long time it is since last you touched at Athens!

Hippias. It is because I have not had leisure, Socrates. For the Eleans, you are to know, whenever they have any public affairs to negotiate with any of the neighbouring cities, constantly apply to me, and appoint me their ambassador for that purpose, in preference to all others: because they consider me as a person the ablest to form a right judgement of what is argued and alleged by every one of the cities, and to make a proper report of it to them. My embassies, therefore, have been frequent to many of those powers; but oftenest, and upon points the most in number, as well as of the highest importance, have I gone to Sparta to treat with the Lacedaemonians. This is the reason, then, in answer to your question, why so seldom I visit these parts.

Soc. This it is, Hippias, to be a man truly wise and perfectly accomplished. For, being thus qualified, you have, in your private capacity, great presents made you by the young men of the age; and are able to make them ample amends by the greater advantages which they derive from you: then, in your public character, you are able to do service to your country, as a man ought who would raise himself above contempt, and acquire reputation among the multitude. . . . I conceive the reason why, in all probability, the Spartans are delighted with you: it is because you know such a multitude of things, and are of the same use to them that old women are to chil-

---

* [The greater part of the dialogue *Hippias Major*, in the 18th century translation by Floyer Sydenham. (Some minor verbal changes in the translation have been made by the editors.)]

dren, to entertain them with the recital of pretty fables and old stories.

Hip. And by Zeus, Socrates, upon a manly subject too, that of beauty in manners. For, discoursing there lately of a complete rule of manners becoming a young man, I gained much applause. And I take this opportunity to inform you, that I have a dissertation upon this subject extremely beautiful, finely framed in every respect, but particularly admirable for the choice of words. The occasion, or way of introducing my discourse, is this:—After the taking of Troy, Neoptolemus is supposed to ask advice of Nestor, and to inquire of him, what course of life a young man ought to follow in order to acquire renown and glory. Upon this Nestor speaks, and lays down a great many excellent precepts concerning the beauty of manners and a well-regulated life. This dissertation I exhibited at Sparta; and three days hence am to exhibit the same here at Athens, in the school of Phidostratus, together with several other pieces of mine worth the hearing. I do it at the request of Eudicus, the son of Apemantus. You will not fail, I hope, being present at it yourself, and bringing others with you to be of the audience, such as are capable judges of performances of this kind.

Soc. We shall do so, Hippias; if so it please God. But at present answer me a short question relating to your dissertation. For you have happily reminded me. You must know, my friend, that a certain person puzzled me lately in a conversation we had together—after I had been inveighing against some things for their baseness and deformity, and praising some other things for their excellence and beauty—by attacking me with these questions in a very insolent manner.—"Whence came you, Socrates, said he, to know what things are beautiful, and what are otherwise? For can you tell me, now, what the beautiful is?" I, through the meanness of my knowledge, found myself at a loss, and had nothing to answer him with any propriety. So, quitting his company, I grew angry with myself, reproached myself, and threatened that, as soon as ever I could meet with any one of you wise men, I would hear what he had to say upon the subject, and learn and study it thoroughly; and, that done, would return to my questioner, and battle the point with him over again. Now, therefore, as I said, you are come happily for me. Give me ample information then accordingly concerning the nature of the beautiful itself: and endeavour to be as accurate as possible in your answers to what I shall ask you; that I may not be confuted a second time, and deservedly again laughed at. For you understand the question, no doubt, perfectly well. To you such a piece of knowledge can be but a little one, amongst the multitude of those which you are master of.

Hip. Little enough, by Zeus, Socrates; and scarcely of any value at all.

Soc. The more easily then shall I learn it; and not be confuted or puzzled any more upon that point by any man.

Hip. Not by any man. For otherwise would my skill be mean, and nothing beyond vulgar attainment.

Soc. It will be a brave thing, by Hera, Hippias, to get the better of the man, as you promise me we shall. But shall I be any obstacle to the victory if I imitate his manner, and, after you have answered some question of mine, make objections to your answer; for the sake only of more thorough information from you? for I have a tolerable share of experience in the practice of making objections. If it be no difference therefore to you, I should be glad to have the part of an objector allowed me, in order to be made a better master of the subject.

Hip. Take the part of an objector, then: for, as I said just now, it is no very knotty point, that which you inquire about. I could teach you to answer questions much more difficult than this, in such a manner that none should ever be able to refute you.

Soc. O rare! what good news you tell me! But come, since you bid me yourself, I will put myself in the place of my antagonist, try to be what he is, to the best of my power, and in his person begin to question you. Now, if he were of the audience, when you exhibited that dissertation which you talk of, concerning the beauty of manners, after he had heard it through, and you had done speaking, this point rather than any other would be uppermost in his mind to question you upon, this relating to the beautiful: for he has a certain habit of so doing; and thus would he introduce it.—"Elean stranger! I would ask you, whether it is not by having honesty that honest men are honest?" Answer now, Hippias, as if he proposed the question.

Hip. I shall answer—It is by their having honesty.

Soc. Is not this some certain thing then, this honesty?

Hip. Clearly so.

Soc. And is it not likewise by their having wisdom that wise men are wise? and by having good in them that all good things are good?

Hip. Without dispute.

Soc. And are not these some certain real things? for they are not surely non-entities, by whose intimate presence with other things those things are what they are.

Hip. Undoubtedly, real things.

Soc. I ask you then, whether all things which are beautiful are not in like manner beautiful by their having beauty?

Hip. They are, by their having beauty.

Soc. Some certain real thing, this beauty.

Hip. A real thing. But what is to come of all this?

Soc. Tell me now, friend stranger, will he say, what this thing is, this beauty, or the beautiful.

Hip. Does not the proposer of this question desire to have it told him, what is beautiful?

Soc. I think not, Hippias: but to have it told him what the beautiful is.

Hip. How does this differ from that?

Soc. Do you think there is no difference between them?

Hip. There is not any.

Soc. You certainly know better. Observe, my good friend, what the question is. For he asks you, not what is beautiful, but what is the beautiful.

Hip. I apprehend you, honest friend. And to that question, What is the beautiful? I shall give an answer, such a one as can never be confuted. For be assured, Socrates, if the truth must be told, a beautiful maiden is the thing beautiful.

Soc. An excellent answer, by the dog, Hippias; and such a one as cannot fail of being applauded. Shall I then, in answering thus, have answered the question asked me? and that so well as not to be refuted?

Hip. How should you be refuted, Socrates, in avowing that which is the opinion of all the world; and the truth of which all who hear you will attest?

Soc. Be it so then, by all means. But now, Hippias, let me alone to resume the question, with your answer to it, by myself. The man will interrogate me after this manner: "Answer me, Socrates, and tell me, if there be any such thing as the beautiful itself, to whose presence is owing the beauty of all those things which you call beautiful?" Then shall I answer him thus: "A beautiful maiden is that beautiful, to whose presence these other things owe their beauty."

Hip. Well. And do you imagine, after this, that he will ever think of refuting you? or attempt to prove your answer concerning the thing beautiful not a just answer? or, if he should attempt it, that he would not be ridiculous?

Soc. That he will attempt it, friend, I am well assured: but whether in so doing he will be ridiculous, will appear in the attempt itself. However, I'll tell you what he will say.

Hip. Tell me then.

Soc. "How pleasant you are, Socrates!" he will say. "Is not a beautiful mare then a thing beautiful? commended as such even by the divine oracle." What shall we answer, Hippias? Shall we not acknowledge, that a mare is beautiful likewise? meaning a beautiful mare. For, indeed, how should we dare deny that a beautiful thing is beautiful?

Hip. True, Socrates. And no doubt the God rightly gave that commendation: for with us, too, there are mares exceedingly beautiful.

Soc. "Very well now," will he say: "but what, is not a beautiful lyre too a thing beautiful?" Shall we allow it, Hippias?

Hip. Certainly.

Soc. After this he will say (for with tolerable certainty I can guess he will, from my knowledge of his character), "But what think you of a beautiful soup-pan, you simpleton you? Is not that a thing beautiful then?"

Hip. Who is this man, Socrates? I warrant, some unmannerly and ill-bred fellow, to dare to mention things so mean and contemptible, upon a subject so noble and so respectable.

Soc. Such is the man, Hippias; not nice and delicate; but a mean shabby fellow, without consideration or regard for aught except this in every inquiry—What is true? The man, however, must have an answer; and in order to it, I thus premise: If the pan be made by a good workman, smooth and round, and well-baked, like some of our handsome soup-pans with two handles, those which hold six coas, exceedingly beautiful in truth; if he mean such a pan as these are, the pan must be confessed beautiful. For how, indeed, could we deny that to be beautiful which has real beauty?

Hip. By no means, Socrates.

Soc. "Is not a beautiful soup-pan, then," he will say, "a thing beautiful? Answer."

Hip. Well then, Socrates, My opinion of the case is this: Even this vessel, if well and handsomely made, is a beautiful thing likewise. But nothing of this kind deserves to be mentioned as beautiful, when we are speaking of a mare, and a maiden, or any other thing thus admirable for its beauty.

Soc. So; now I apprehend you, Hippias. When the man asks such a question as that, we are thus, it seems, to answer him: "Honest man! Are you ignorant how it was well said by Heraclitus, 'that the most beautiful ape, in comparison with the human kind, is a creature far from beautiful?' Just so, the most beautiful soup-pan is a thing far from beautiful in comparison with the maiden kind; as it is said by Hippias the wise." Is it not thus, Hippias, that we must answer?

Hip. By all means, Socrates: your answer is perfectly right.

Soc. Mind me now: for upon this, I am well assured, he will say to me thus: "But suppose, Socrates, the maiden kind were to be set in comparison with the Goddess kind; would not the same accident befall the maidens in that case, which happened to the soup-pans compared with them? Would not the fairest maiden appear far from beautiful? Does not Heraclitus further teach this very doctrine, which you yourself must needs infer to be true, that the wisest of men, compared with a God, will appear an ape in wisdom and beauty and every other excellence?" Shall we own, Hippias, the fairest maiden far from beautiful, in comparison with a Goddess?

Hip. Who, Socrates, would presume to call this in question?

Soc. No sooner then shall I have agreed with him in this, than he will laugh at me, and say, "Do you remember, Socrates, what question you were asked?" "I do," I shall tell him, "it was this: What kind of thing is the beautiful itself?" "When the question then," he will say, "concerned the beautiful itself, your answer was concerning that which happens to be far from beautiful, according to your own confession, as beautiful as it is." "So it seems," shall I say? Or what other reply, my friend, do you advise me to make him?

Hip. I think, for my part, you must reply in those very words. For, when he says that the human kind compared with the divine is far from beautiful, without doubt he will have the truth on his side.

Soc. "But were I to have asked you at first this question," will he say, 'What is beautiful, and at the same time far from beautiful?' and you were to have answered me in the manner you did; would not you in that case have answered rightly? And does the beautiful then itself, by which every other thing is ornamented, and looks beautiful, whenever this form of beauty supervenes and invests it, imparting thus the virtue of its presence,—does this still appear to you to be a maiden, or a mare, or a lyre?"

Hip. Truly, Socrates, if this be the question which he asks, it is the easiest thing imaginable to answer it; and to tell him what that beautiful thing is, by which other things are ornamented; and which, by supervening and investing them, makes them look beautiful. So that he must be a very simple fellow, and entirely a stranger to things elegant and fine. For, if you only answer him thus, "that the beautiful, which he inquires after, is nothing else than gold," he will have no more to say, nor attempt ever to refute such an answer. Because none of us can be insensible that, wherever gold be applied or superinduced, let the thing have looked ever so vile and sordid before, yet then it will look beautiful, when it is invested or ornamented with gold.

Soc. You have no experience of the man, Hippias, how unyielding he is, and how hard in admitting any assertion.

Hip. What signifies that, Socrates? He must of necessity admit what is rightly asserted; or, in not admitting it, expose himself to ridicule.

Soc. And yet will he be so far from admitting this answer, my friend, that he will treat me with open derision, and say to me, "You that are so puffed up with the opinion of your own skill and knowledge, do you think Phidias was a bad workman?" And I believe I shall answer, that he was far from being so.

Hip. You will answer rightly, Socrates.

Soc. Rightly, without dispute. But he, when I have agreed with him that Phidias was a good workman, will say, "Do you imagine, then, that Phidias was ignorant of that which you call the beautiful?" —"To what purpose do you ask this?" I shall say.—"Because Athena's eyes," will he reply, "Phidias made not of gold, nor yet the rest of her face; nor the feet, nor the hands neither: though she would have looked handsomest, it seems, had she been a golden Goddess: but he made these all of ivory. It is evident that he committed this error through ignorance; not knowing that gold it was which beautified all things, wherever it was applied." When he talks after this manner, what answer shall we make him, Hippias?

Hip. There is no difficulty at all in the matter. We shall answer, "Phidias was in the right; for things made of ivory are also, as I presume, beautiful."

Soc. "What was the reason, then," will he say, "why Phidias made not the pupil of the eyes out of ivory, but out of stone rather? choosing for that purpose such stone as (in colour) most resembled ivory. Is a beautiful stone then a thing beautiful too?" Shall we admit it so to be, Hippias?

Hip. We will; in a place where the stone is becoming.

Soc. But, where it is unbecoming, shall I allow it to be unhandsome, or not?

Hip. Allow it; where the stone becomes not the place.

Soc. "Well now; and is it not the same with ivory and gold, you wise man you?" will he say. "Do not these, where they are becoming, make things appear handsome; but far otherwise where they are unbecoming?" Shall we deny this, or acknowledge the man to be in the right?

Hip. We must acknowledge this, that whatever is becoming to any thing makes it appear handsome.

Soc. Upon this, he will say thus: "When that fine soup-pan, then, which we have been speaking of, is set upon the stove full of excellent soup, whether is a golden spoon the most becoming and proper for it, or a sycamore spoon?"

Hip. Herakles! what a strange sort of man, Socrates, is he whom you are talking of! Will you not tell me who he is?

Soc. Should I tell you his name, you would not know him.

Hip. But I know already that he is some ignorant silly fellow.

Soc. He is a very troublesome questioner indeed, Hippias. But, however, what shall we answer? Which of the two spoons shall we say is most becoming and proper for the soup and for the pan? Is it not clearly the sycamore spoon? For this gives a better scent and flavour to the soup; and at the same time, my friend, it would not break the pan, and spill the soup, and put out the fire, and, when the guests were come prepared for feasting, rob them of an excellent dish. But all these mischiefs would be done by that golden spoon. We must, I think, therefore, answer, that the sycamore spoon is more becoming and proper in this case than the golden spoon: unless you say otherwise.

Hip. Well, Socrates; more becoming and proper be it then: but, for my part, I would not hold discourse with a fellow who asked such sort of questions.

Soc. Right, my dear friend. For it would not be becoming or proper for you to be bespattered with such vile dirty words, so finely dressed as you are from top to toe, and so illustrious for wisdom through all Greece. But for me—it is nothing to dirty myself against the man. Give me my lesson, therefore, what I am to say; and answer in my name. For the man now will say thus: "If the syca-more spoon then be more becoming and proper than the golden one, must it not be handsomer?"

Hip. Yes. Since the proper and becoming, Socrates, you have granted to be handsomer than the improper and unbecoming.

Soc. What, Hippias; and shall we grant him too, that the sycamore spoon has more beauty in it than the golden spoon?

Hip. Shall I tell you, Socrates, what you shall say the beautiful is, so as to prevent him from all further cavilling and disputing?

Soc. By all means: but not before you tell me whether of the two spoons we have been talking of is the most beautiful, as well as the most proper and becoming.

Hip. Well then; if it pleases you, answer him, "It is that made of the sycamore tree."

Soc. Now say what you were just going to say. For this answer, in which I pronounce gold to be the beautiful, will be refuted; and gold will be demonstrated, I find, not to be at all more beautiful than sycamore wood. But what, say you, is the beautiful now?

Hip. I will tell you. For when you ask me, "What is the beautiful?" you would have me, I perceive, give you for answer something which shall never, in any place, or to any person, appear otherwise than beautiful.

Soc. By all means, Hippias. And now you apprehend me perfectly well. But observe what I say: Be assured, that if any man shall be able to controvert our new answer, I shall vow never more to praise any thing for its beauty. Now in the name of the Gods proceed, and tell it me without delay.

Hip. I say then, that always, and to every person, and in every place it will appear the most beautiful, lovely, and desirable thing in the world, to be rich, healthy, honoured by his country, to arrive at a good old age, to give his parents an honourable burial, and at length to have the last offices performed for himself honourably and magnificently by his own issue.

Soc. O brave! O rare! How admirable, how great, and how worthy of yourself, Hippias, is the speech you have now spoken! By Hera, I receive with much pleasure that hearty willingness of yours to give me all the assistance in your power. But we reach not the point yet. For now will the man laugh at us more than ever, you may be assured.

Hip. An ill-timed laugh, Socrates. For in laughing, when he has nothing to object, he will in reality laugh only at himself; and be the ridicule of all who happen to be present.

Soc. Perhaps so. But perhaps, also, as soon as I have thus answered, I shall be in danger, if I prophesy aright, of something besides the being laught at.

Hip. What besides?

Soc. That, if he happens to have a cane in his hand, unless I run away and escape him, he will aim some very serious strokes at me.

Hip. How say you? What, is the man some master of yours then? for, otherwise, would he not be punished for the injury done you? Or, is there no justice in your city? but the citizens are permitted to assault and beat one another injuriously.

Soc. By no means are they permitted to do any such thing.

Hip. Will he not, therefore, be condemned to punishment, as having beaten you injuriously?

Soc. I should think he would not, Hippias; not having beaten me injuriously if I had made him such an answer; but very deservedly, as it seems to me.

Hip. It seems so then to me, Socrates; if you are of that opinion yourself.

Soc. Shall I tell you, why, in my own opinion, I should have deserved a beating, if I had so answered?—Will you condemn me too without trying the cause? or will you hear what I have to say?

Hip. It would be a hard case indeed, Socrates, should I deny you a hearing. But what have you to say then?

Soc. I will tell you; but in the same way as I talked with you just now, assuming his character, whilst you personate me. I shall do this, to avoid treating you in your own person with such language as he will use in reprimanding me, with harsh and out-of-the-way terms. For I assure you that he will say thus:—"Tell me, Socrates; think you not that you deserve a beating, for having sung that pompous strain, so foreign to the design of the music; spoiling thus the harmony, and wandering wide of the point proposed to you?"— "How so?" I shall ask him.—"How?" he will reply: "can you not remember that I asked you concerning the beautiful itself, that which makes every thing beautiful, wherever it comes and imparts the virtue of its presence; whether it communicates it to stone or wood, to man or God, to actions and manners, or to any part of science. Beauty itself, man, I ask you what it is: and I can no more beat into your head what I say, than if you were a stone lying by my side, nay a mill-stone too, without ears or brains." Now, Hippias, would not you be angry with me, if I, frightened with this reprimand, should say to him thus:—"Why, Hippias said, this was the beautiful; and I asked him, just as you ask me, what was beautiful to all persons, and at all times."—What say you? will you not be angry if I tell him thus?

Hip. That which I described, Socrates, is beautiful, I am very positive, in the eyes of all men.

Soc. "And always will it be so?" he will say: "for the beautiful itself must be always beautiful."

Hip. To be sure.

Soc. "And always was it so in former times?" he will say.

Hip. It always was so.

Soc. "What? and to Achilles too," he will say, "did the Elean stranger affirm it was a beautiful and desirable thing to survive his progenitors? and that it was the same to his grandfather Æacus, and the rest of those who were the progeny of the Gods? nay, that it was so even to the Gods themselves?"

Hip. What a fellow is this! Away with him! Such questions as these are profane, and improper to be asked.

Soc. But is it not much more profane for any man, when these questions are asked him, to answer in the affirmative, and to maintain such propositions?

Hip. Perhaps it is.

Soc. "Perhaps then you are this man," will he say, "who affirm it to be a thing always, and to every person, beautiful and desirable, to be buried by his descendants, and to bury his parents. Was not Herakles one of these very persons? and those whom we just now mentioned, are not they also to be included in the number?"

Hip. But I did not affirm it was so to the Gods.

Soc. Nor to the heroes, I presume.

Hip. Not to such as were children of the Gods.

Soc. But to such only as were not so.

Hip. Right.

Soc. Amongst the number of heroes then, it seems, according to your account, to Tantalus, and Dardanus, and Zethus, it would have been a sad thing, a horrible profanation of deity, to suppose it, and a fatal blow to their own honour; but to Pelops, and others born of men like him, it was a glorious thing, beautiful and desirable.

Hip. So I think it to be.

Soc. "You think this then to be true, the contrary of which you maintained just now," will he say, "that to survive their ancestors, and to be buried by their descendants, is, in some cases, and to some persons, a dishonourable and a horrible thing: nay more, it seems not possible that such a thing should be, or ever become, beautiful and desirable to all. So that this which you now hold to be the beautiful, happens to be in the same case with those your former favourites, the maiden and the gold; sometimes it is beautiful, and sometimes otherwise: but a circumstance still more ridiculous attends this: it is beautiful only to some persons, whilst to others it is quite the contrary. And not yet," will he say, "not all this day long, are you able, Socrates, to answer the question which you were asked,—What the beautiful is." In terms such as these will he reproach me justly, should I answer him as you directed me. Much after the manner, Hippias, which I have now represented to you, proceed the conversations usually held between the man and me. But now and then, as if in pity to my ignorance and want of learning, he proposes to me himself some particular matter of inquiry; and asks me whether I think such or such a thing to be the beautiful; or whatever else be the general subject of the question which he has been pleased to put to me, or upon which the conversation happens at that time to turn.

Hip. How mean you, Socrates?

Soc. I will explain my meaning to you by an instance in the present subject.—"Friend Socrates," says he, "let us have done with disputing in this way: give me no more answers of this sort; for they are very silly, and easily confuted. But consider now, whether the beautiful be something of this kind; such as in our dispute just now we touched upon, when we said that gold, where it was proper and becoming, was beautiful; but otherwise, where it was improper and unbecoming: and that the beauty of all other things depended on the same principle; that is, they were beautiful only where they were becoming. Now this very thing, the proper and becoming, essential

propriety and decorum itself, see whether this may not happen to
be the beautiful." Now, for my part, I am used to give my assent,
in such matters, to every thing proposed to me. For I find in myself
nothing to object. But what think you of it? are you of opinion
that the becoming is the beautiful?

Hip. Entirely am I, Socrates, of that opinion.

Soc. Let us consider it, however; for fear we should be guilty of
some mistake in this point.

Hip. I agree we ought so to do.

Soc. Observe then. That which we call the becoming, is it not
either something whose presence, wherever it comes, gives all things
a beautiful appearance; or something which gives them the reality
of beauty; or something which bestows both, and causes them not
only to appear beautiful, but really so to be?

Hip. I think it must be one or other of these.

Soc. Whether of these then is the becoming? Is it that which only
gives a beautiful appearance? as a man whose body is of a de-
formed make, when he has put on clothes or shoes which fit him,
looks handsomer than he really is. Now, if the becoming causes every
thing to look handsomer than it really is, the becoming must then
be a kind of fraud or imposition with regard to beauty, and cannot be that which we are in search of, Hippias. For we were inquiring what that was by which all beautiful things are beautiful.
As, if we were asked what that was, by which all great things are
great, we should answer, "it was by surpassing other things of the
same kind." For thus it is, that all things are great: and though they
may not all appear great to us, yet, in as much as they surpass
others, great of necessity they must be. So is it, we say, with the
beautiful; it must be something by which things are beautiful,
whether they appear to be so or not. Now this cannot be the becoming: for the becoming causes things to appear more beautiful
than they really are, according to your account of it; concealing the
truth of things, and not suffering this ever to appear. But that which
causes them to be really beautiful, as I just now said, whether they
appear to be so or not, this it is our business to find out, and declare
the nature of it: for this it is which is the subject of our search, if
we are searching for the beautiful.

Hip. But the becoming, Socrates, causes things both to be, and to
appear beautiful, by virtue of its presence.

Soc. If so, then it is impossible for things really beautiful to appear otherwise; inasmuch as there is present with them the cause of
beautiful appearance.

Hip. Admit it impossible.

Soc. Shall we admit this then, Hippias, that all laws, and rules of

action, manners, or behaviour, truly beautiful, are beautiful in common estimation, and appear so always to all men? Or shall we not
rather say quite the reverse, that men are ignorant of their beauty,
and that above all things these are the subjects of controversy and
contention, not only private but public, not only between man and
man, but between different communities and civil states?

Hip. Thus indeed rather, Socrates, that in those points men are
ignorant of the beautiful.

Soc. But this would not be the case if those beautiful things had
the appearance of beauty, added to the reality: and this appearance
would they have, if the becoming were the beautiful, and caused
things, as you say it does, both to be and to appear beautiful, be-
stowing on them real and apparent beauty at the same time. Hence
it follows, that if the becoming should be that by which things are
made truly beautiful, then the becoming must be the beautiful which
we are in search of, not that by which things are only made beautiful in appearance. But if the becoming should be that by which
things are made beautiful only in appearance, it cannot be the
beautiful which we are in search of; for this bestows the reality of
beauty. Nor is it in the power of the same thing to cause the appearance and the reality, both, not only in the case of beauty, but neither
in any other instance whatever. Let us choose now, whether of these
two we shall take for the becoming, that which causes the appearance
of beauty, or that which causes the reality.

Hip. The becoming, Socrates, I take it, must be that which causes
the appearance.

Soc. Fie upon it, Hippias! Our discovery of the beautiful is fled
away, and hath escaped us. For the becoming has turned out to be
a thing different from the beautiful.

Hip. So it seems; and very unaccountably too.

Soc. But however, my friend, we must not give it up for lost. I
have still some hope left, that the nature of the beautiful may come
forth into light, and show itself.

Hip. With great clearness, Socrates, beyond doubt: for it is by
no means difficult to find. I am positive that, if I were to go aside for
a little while, and consider by myself, I should describe it to you
with an accuracy beyond that of any thing ever so accurate.

Soc. Ah! talk not, Hippias, in so high a tone. You see what
trouble it has given us already; and I fear lest it should grow angry
with us, and run away still further than before. But I talk idly:
for you, I presume, will easily find it out, when you come to be
alone. Yet, in the name of the Gods, I conjure you, make the discovery while I am with you: and, if it be agreeable to you, admit
me, as you did before, your companion in the search. If we find it

together, it will be best of all: and, if we miss it in this way of joint inquiry, I shall be contented, I hope, with my disappointment, and you will depart and find better success without any difficulty. Besides, if we now find it, I shall not, you know, be troublesome afterwards, teasing you to tell me what was the event of that inquiry by yourself, and what was the great discovery which you had made. Now therefore consider, if you think this to be the beautiful. I say then, that it is. But pray observe, and give me all your attention, for fear I should say any thing foolish, or foreign to the purpose. Let this then be in our account the beautiful, that which is useful. I was induced to think it might be so by these considerations. Beautiful, we say, are eyes; not those which look as if they had not the faculty of sight; but such as appear to have that faculty strong, and to be useful for the purpose of seeing. Do we not?

Hip. We do.

Soc. And the whole body also, do we not call it beautiful with a view to its utility; one for the race, another for wrestling? So further, through all the animal kind, as a beautiful horse, cock, and quail: in the same manner all sorts of domestic utensils, and all the conveniencies for carriage abroad, be they land vehicles, or ships and barges for the sea; instruments of music likewise, with the tools and instruments subservient to the other arts: to these you may please to add moral rules and laws. Every thing almost of any of these kinds we call beautiful upon the same account; respecting the end for which it was born, or framed, or instituted. In whatever way it be useful, to whatever purpose, and upon whatever occasion; agreeably to these circumstances we pronounce it beautiful. But that which is in every respect useless, we declare totally void of beauty. Are not you of this opinion, Hippias?

Hip. I am.

Soc. We are right, therefore, now in saying, that above all things the useful proves to be the beautiful.

Hip. Most certainly right, Socrates.

Soc. Now that which is able to operate or effect any thing, is it not useful so far as it has power, and is able? But that which is powerless and unable, is it not useless?

Hip. Without doubt.

Soc. Power then is beautiful, and want of power is the contrary.

Hip. Quite right. And many things there are, Socrates, which evince the truth of this conclusion: but particularly it holds good in politics. For the having ability in public affairs, and power in the state of which we are members, is of all things the most beautiful: and want of such power, with a total defect of any such ability, has of all things the meanest aspect.

Soc. You say well. In the name of the Gods then, Hippias, does it not follow from all this, that skill and knowledge are of all things the most beautiful, and want of them the contrary?

Hip. Ay, what think you of this, Socrates?

Soc. Softly, my dear friend: for I am under some fears about the rectitude of our present conclusions.

Hip. What are you afraid of, Socrates? For the business of our inquiry is now in a fair way, and goes on as we could wish.

Soc. I would it were so. But let you and I consider together upon this point. Could any man execute a work, of which he has neither knowledge nor any other kind of abilities for the performance?

Hip. By no means. For how should a man do that, for the doing of which he has no abilities?

Soc. Those people then who do wrong, and who err in the execution of any thing, without erroneous or wrong intention, would they ever have done or executed things wrong, had they not been able to do or execute them in that manner?

Hip. Clearly they would not.

Soc. But the able are able through their abilities: for it is not inability which any way enables them.

Hip. Certainly not.

Soc. And all who do any thing are able to do what they do.

Hip. True.

Soc. And all men do many more wrong things than right; and commit errors from their infancy, without intending to do wrong, or to err.

Hip. The fact is so.

Soc. Well then: those abilities, and those means or instruments, which help and are useful in the doing or executing any thing wrong, whether shall we say they are beautiful? or are they not rather far from being so?

Hip. Far from it, in my opinion, Socrates.

Soc. The able and useful, therefore, Hippias, in our opinion, it seems, no longer is the beautiful.

Hip. Still it is so, Socrates, if it has power to do what is right, or is useful to a good purpose.

Soc. That account is then rejected, that the able and useful simply and absolutely is the beautiful. But the thought, Hippias, which our mind laboured with, and wanted to express, was this, that the useful and able for the producing of any good, that is the beautiful.

Hip. This indeed seems to be the case.

Soc. But the thing thus described is the profitable. Is it not?

Hip. It is.

Soc. From hence then is derived the beauty of bodies, the beauty of moral precepts, of knowledge and wisdom, and of all those things just now enumerated; they are beautiful, because profitable.

Hip. Evidently so.

Soc. The profitable, therefore, Hippias, should seem to be our beautiful.

Hip. Beyond all doubt, Socrates.

Soc. But the profitable is that which effects or produces good.

Hip. True.

Soc. And the producer is no other thing than the cause. Is it?

Hip. Nothing else.

Soc. The cause of good, therefore, is the beautiful.

Hip. Right.

Soc. Now the cause, Hippias, is a thing different from that which it causes. For the cause can by no means be the cause of itself. Consider it thus: Did not the cause appear to be the producer?

Hip. Clearly.

Soc. And by the producer no other thing is effected than that which is produced or generated; but this is not the producer itself.

Hip. You are in the right.

Soc. Is not that then which is produced or generated one thing, and the producer a thing different?

Hip. It is.

Soc. The cause, therefore, is not the cause of itself; but of that which is generated or produced by it.

Hip. Without doubt.

Soc. If the beautiful be then the cause of good, good itself must be produced or generated by the beautiful. And for this reason, it should seem, we cultivate and study prudence, and every other fair virtue, because their production and their issue are well worth our study and our care, as being good itself. Thus are we likely to find from our inquiries, that the beautiful, as it stands related to good, has the nature of a kind of father.

Hip. The very case, Socrates. You are perfectly right in what you say.

Soc. Am I not right also in this, that neither is the father the son, nor is the son the father?

Hip. Right in that also.

Soc. Nor is the cause the production, nor the production, on the other hand, the cause.

Hip. Very right.

Soc. By Zeus then, my friend, neither is the beautiful good, nor is the good beautiful. Do you think it is possible it should be so? Is it consistent with what we have said, and are agreed in?

Hip. By Zeus. I think not.

Soc. Would this opinion please us then, and should we choose to abide by it, that the beautiful is not good, nor the good beautiful?

Hip. By Zeus, no; it would not please me at all.

Soc. Well said, by Zeus, Hippias: and me it pleases the least of any of those descriptions or accounts which we have hitherto given of the beautiful.

Hip. So I perceive.

Soc. That definition of it, therefore, which we thought just now the most excellent of all, that the profitable, the useful and able to produce some good or other, was that beautiful, is in danger of losing all its credit with us; and of appearing, if possible, more ridiculous than our former accounts of it, where we reckoned the maiden to be the beautiful, or any other particular whose defect we have before discovered.

Hip. It seems so, indeed.

Soc. And for my own part, Hippias, I see no way where to turn myself any more, but am absolutely at a loss. Have you any thing to say?

Hip. Not at present. But, as I said just now, after a little considering I am certain I shall find it out.

Soc. But I fear, so extreme is my desire of knowing it, that I shall not be able to wait your time. Besides, I have just met with, as I imagine, a fair kind of opening to the discovery. For consider that which gives us delight and joy (I speak not of all kinds of pleasure, but of that only which arises in us through the hearing and the sight), whether we should not call this the beautiful. And how, indeed, could we dispute it? Seeing that it is the beautiful of our own species, Hippias, with the sight of whom we are so delighted: that we take pleasure in viewing all beautiful works of the loom or needle; and whatever is well painted, carved, or moulded. It is the same with the hearing: for well-measured sounds and all musical harmony, the beauties of prosaic composition also, with pretty fables and well-framed stories, have the like effect upon us, to be agreeable, to be delightful, and to charm. Were we to give, therefore, that petulant and saucy fellow this answer—"Noble sir, the beautiful is that which gives us pleasure through the hearing, and through the sight," do you think we should not restrain his insolence?

Hip. For my part, Socrates, I think the nature of the beautiful now truly well explained.

Soc. But what shall we say of the beauty of manners, and of laws, Hippias? Shall we say it gives us pleasure through the hearing, or through the sight? or is it to be ranked under some other kind?

Hip. Perhaps the man may not think of this.

Soc. By the Dog, Hippias, but that man would, of whom I stand in awe the most of all men; and before whom I should be most ashamed if I trifled, and pretended to utter something of great importance, when in reality I talked idly, and spoke nothing to the purpose.

Hip. Who is he?

Soc. Socrates, the son of Sophroniscus; who would no more suffer me to throw out such random speeches, or so readily decide on points which I had not thoroughly sifted, than he would allow me to talk of things which I am ignorant of, as if I knew them.

Hip. Why, really, I must own, that to me myself, since you have started the observation, the beauty of laws seems referable to another kind.

Soc. Softly, Hippias. For, though we have fallen into fresh difficulties, equal to our former ones, about the nature of the beautiful, we are in a fair way, I think, of extricating ourselves out of them.

Hip. How so, Socrates?

Soc. I will tell you how the matter appears to me: whether or no there be any thing material in what I say, you will consider. The beauty then of laws and of manners, I imagine, may possibly be found not altogether abstracted from that kind of sensation which arises in the soul through the senses of hearing and of sight. But let us abide awhile by this definition, that "what gives us pleasure through these senses is the beautiful," without bringing the beauty of laws the least into question. Suppose then, that either the man of whom I am speaking, or any other, should interrogate us after this manner: "For what reason, Hippias and Socrates, have you separated from the pleasant in general that species of it in which you say consists the beautiful; denying the character of beautiful to those species of pleasure which belong to the other senses, to the pleasures of taste, the joys of Aphrodite, and all others of the same class? Do you refuse them the character of pleasant also, and maintain that no pleasure neither is to be found in these sensations, or in any thing beside seeing and hearing?" Now, Hippias, what shall we say to this?

Hip. By all means, Socrates, we must allow pleasure to be found also in these sensations; a pleasure very exquisite.

Soc. "Since these sensations then afford pleasure," will he say, "no less than those others, why do you deprive them of the name of beautiful, and rob them of their proper share of beauty?" "Because there is no one who would not laugh at us," we shall answer, "were we to call eating a beautiful thing, instead of a pleasant; or the smelling sweet odours, were we to say, not that it was pleasant, but that it was beautiful. Above all, in amorous enjoyments, all the world would contend, there was the highest degree of the sweet and pleasant; but that whoever was engaged in them should take care not to be seen, the act of love being far from agreeable to the sight, or beautiful." Now, Hippias, when we have thus answered, he may reply, perhaps, in this manner:—"I apprehend perfectly well the reason why you have always been ashamed to call these pleasures beautiful; it is because they seem not so to men. But the question which I asked you was not, What seemed beautiful to the multitude; but, What was so in reality." Then shall we answer, I presume, only by repeating our last hypothesis, that "we ourselves give the name of beautiful to that part only of the pleasant which ariseth in us by means of our sight and hearing." But have you any thing to say which may be of service to our argument? Shall we answer aught besides, Hippias?

Hip. To what he has said, Socrates, it is unnecessary to make any further answer.

Soc. "Very well now," will he say. "If the pleasant then, arising through the sight and hearing, be the beautiful, whatever portion of the pleasant happens not to be this, it is clear it cannot be the beautiful." Shall we admit this?

Hip. Certainly.

Soc. "Is that portion of the pleasant then," he will say, "which arises through the sight, the same with that which arises through the sight and hearing? Or is that which arises through the hearing, the same with that which arises through the hearing and the sight?" "That which ariseth in us through either of those senses alone, and not through the other," we shall answer, "is by no means the same with that which arises through them both. For this seems to be the import of your question. But our meaning was, that each of these species of the pleasant was, by itself separately, the beautiful; and that they were also, both of them together, the same beautiful." Should we not answer so?

Hip. By all means.

Soc. "Does any species of the pleasant then," he will say, "differ from any other, whatever it be, so far as it is pleasant? Observe; I ask you not if one pleasure is greater or less than another, or whether it is more or less a pleasure: but whether there is any difference between the pleasures in this respect, that one of them is pleasure, the other not pleasure." In our opinion there is no difference between them, of this kind. Is there any?

Hip. I agree with you, there is not any.

Soc. "For some other reason, therefore," he will say it is, "than because they are pleasures, that you have selected these species of pleasure from the rest, and given them the preference. You have discerned that there is something or other in them by which they

differ from the rest; with a view to which difference you distinguish
them by the epithet of beautiful. Now the pleasure which ariseth in
us through the sense of seeing, deriveth not its beauty from any
thing peculiarly belonging to that sense. For, if this were the cause
of its being beautiful, that other pleasure which arises through the
hearing never would be beautiful, as not partaking of that which is
peculiar to the sense of seeing." "You are in the right," shall we say?

Hip. We will.

Soc. "So neither, on the other hand, does the pleasure produced
in us through the sense of hearing derive its beauty from any circumstance which peculiarly attends the hearing. For, in that case, the
pleasure produced through seeing would not be beautiful, as not
partaking of that which is peculiar to the sense of hearing." Shall
we allow, Hippias, that the man is in the right when he says this?

Hip. Allow it.

Soc. "But both these pleasures now are beautiful, you say." For
so we say: do we not?

Hip. We do.

Soc. "There is something in them, therefore, the same in both, to
which they owe their beauty, a beauty common to them both. There
is something, I say, which they have belonging to them both in
common, and also in particular to each. For otherwise they would
not, both and each of them, be beautiful." Answer now, as if you
were speaking to him.

Hip. I answer then, that, in my opinion, you give a true account
of the matter.

Soc. Should there be any circumstance, therefore, attending on
both these pleasures of the sight and hearing taken together; yet if
the same circumstance attend not on each taken separately; or
should any attend on each separately, yet not on both together; they
cannot derive their beauty from this circumstance.

Hip. How is it possible, Socrates, that any circumstance whatever,
which attends on neither of them, should ever attend on both?

Soc. Do you think this impossible?

Hip. I must be quite ignorant, I own, in things of this sort; as I
am quite unused to such kind of disputes.

Soc. You jest, Hippias. But I am in danger, perhaps, of fancying
that I see something, so circumstanced, as you aver to be impossible.

Hip. You are in no danger of any such fancy, Socrates; but are
pleased to look asquint purposely: that is all.

Soc. Many things, I assure you, of that kind appear to me very
evident. But I give no credit to them; because they are not evident
to you, who have raised a larger fortune than any man living, by
the profession of philosophy; and because they appear only to me,

who have never in that way earned a farthing. I have some suspicion, however, that possibly you are not in earnest with me, but design to impose upon me: so many things of that kind do I perceive so plainly.

Hip. No one will know better than yourself, Socrates, whether I am in earnest with you or not, if you will but begin and tell me, what those things are which you perceive so plainly. You will soon see that you talk idly. For you will never find a circumstance attending us both together, which attends separately neither you nor me.

Soc. How say you, Hippias? But perhaps you have reason on your side, and I may not apprehend it. Let me, therefore, explain to you my meaning more distinctly. To me then it appears, that some circumstance of being, which attends not my individual person, nor yours, something which belongs neither to me, nor to you, may yet possibly belong to both of us, and attend both our persons taken together: and, on the other hand, that certain circumstances of being, not attending us both taken together, may attend each of our separate and single persons.

Hip. You tell me of prodigies still greater, I think, now, Socrates, than those which you told me of just before. For consider: if both of us are honest, man, must not each of us be honest? or, supposing each of us dishonest, must we not both be so? If both are sound and well, is not each also? Or, should each of us now be tired of any thing, or come off ill in some combat between us, or be amazed and confounded, or be affected any other way, would not both of us be in the same plight? To go further: in case that we had, both of us, images of ourselves made of gold, or silver, or ivory; or that both of us, if you will give me leave to say it, were generous, or wise, or honourable; did both of us happen to be old or young; or to be possessed of any other human quality; or to be in any condition whatever incident to human life; must not each of us be, of absolute necessity, that very same kind of man, and in those very same circumstances?

Soc. Beyond all doubt.

Hip. But you, Socrates, with your companions and fellow disputants, consider not things universally, or in the whole. Thus you take the beautiful and chop it into pieces: and every thing in nature, which happens to be the subject of your discourse, you serve in the same manner, splitting and dividing it. Hence you are unacquainted with the greatness of things, with bodies of infinite magnitude, through the natural continuity of being. And now so much are you a stranger to the vastness of this view of the universe, as to imagine that any thing, whether being or circumstance of being, can possibly belong to both those pleasures which we are speaking of, taken together, yet not belong to each of them; or, on the other hand, may belong to each, without belonging to both. So void of thought and consideration, so simple, and so narrow-minded are you and your companions.

Soc. Such is the lot of our condition, Hippias. It is not what a man will, says the common proverb, but what he can. However, you are always kind in assisting us with your instructions. For but just now, before you had taught me better, how simple my mind was, and how narrow my way of thinking, I shall give you still a plainer proof, by telling you what were my thoughts upon the present subject:—if you will give me leave.

Hip. You will tell them to one who knows them already, Socrates. For I am well acquainted with the different ways of thinking, and know the minds of all who philosophize. Notwithstanding, if it will give pleasure to yourself, you may tell me.

Soc. To me, I confess, it will. You must know then, my friend, that I was so foolish, till I had received from you better information, as to imagine of myself and you, that each of us was one person; and that this, which each of us was, both of us were not, as not being one, but two persons.—Such a simpleton was I!—But from you have I now learnt, that if both of us are two persons, each of us also by necessity is two; and that, if each of us be but one, it follows by the same necessity, that both of us are no more. For, by reason of the continuity of being, according to Hippias, it is impossible it should be otherwise; each of us being of necessity whatever both of us are, and both whatever each. And now, persuaded by you to believe these things, here I sit me down and rest contented. But first inform me, Hippias, whether we are one person, you and I together; or whether you are two persons, and I two persons.

Hip. What mean you, Socrates?

Soc. The very thing which I say. For I am afraid of entering with you into a further discussion of the subject, because you fall into a passion with me, whenever you say any thing which you take to be important. To venture for once, however; tell me—Is not each of us one? and is not the being one a circumstance attendant upon our being?

Hip. Without doubt.

Soc. If each of us then be one, each of us must be also odd. Or think you that one is not an odd number?

Hip. I think it is.

Soc. Are we odd both together then, notwithstanding that we are two?

Hip. That is absurd, Socrates.

Soc. But both together, we are even. Is it not so?

Hip. Certainly.

Soc. Now, because both of us together we are even, does it follow from thence that each of us singly too is even?

Hip. Certainly not.

Soc. There is not, therefore, such an absolute necessity, as you said just now there was, that, whatever both of us were, each should be the same; and that, whatever each of us was, the same must we be both.

Hip. Not in such cases as these, I acknowledge; but still it holds true in such as I enumerated before.

Soc. That suffices, Hippias. I am contented with this acknowledgment, that it appears to be so in some cases, but in others otherwise. For, if you remember from whence the present dispute arose, I said, that the pleasures of sight and hearing could not derive their beauty from any circumstance which attended on each, yet not on both; neither from any which attended on both, yet not on each: but that the beauty of them was derived from something which they had belonging to both of them in common, and in particular to each. And this I said, because you had admitted the beauty of them both together, and of each separately. From which I drew this consequence, that they were indebted for their beauty to some being, whose presence still followed and attended on them both; and not to such as fell short of either. And I continue still in the same mind. But answer me, as if we were now beginning this last inquiry afresh. Pleasure through the sight and pleasure through the hearing, then, being supposed beautiful, both of them and each; tell me, does not the cause of their beauty follow and attend on both of them taken together, and upon each also considered separate?

Hip. Without doubt.

Soc. Is it then because they are pleasures, both and each of them, that they are beautiful? Or, if this were the cause, would not the pleasures of the other senses be beautiful, as well as these? For it appeared that they were pleasures as well as these:—if you remember.

Hip. I remember it well.

Soc. But because these pleasures arise in us through sight and hearing, this we assigned for the cause of their being beautiful.

Hip. It was so determined.

Soc. Observe now, whether I am right or not: for, as well as I can remember, we agreed that the pleasant was the beautiful; not the pleasant in general, but those species of it only which are produced through sight and hearing.

Hip. It is true.

Soc. Does not this circumstance then attend on both these pleasures taken together? and is it not wanting to each of them alone? For by no means is either of them alone, as was said before, produced through both those senses. Both of them are indeed through both, but not so is each. Is this true?

Hip. It is.

Soc. They are not beautiful, therefore, either of them, from any circumstance which attends on either by itself. For we cannot argue from either to both; nor, from what each is separately, infer what they both are jointly. So that we may assert the joint beauty of both these pleasures, according to our present hypothesis of the beautiful: but this hypothesis will not support us in asserting any beauty separate in either. Or how say we? Is it not of necessity so?

Hip. So it appears.

Soc. Say we then that both are beautiful, but deny that each is so?

Hip. What reason is there to the contrary?

Soc. This reason, my friend, as it seems to me; because we had supposed certain circumstances attendant upon things with this condition, that, if they appertained to any two things, both together, they appertained at the same time to each; and, if they appertained to each, that they appertained also to both. Of this kind are all such circumstances and attendants of things as were enumerated by you. Are they not?

Hip. They are.

Soc. But such circumstances or appendages of being, as those related by me, are otherwise: and of this kind are the being each, and the being both. Have not I stated the case rightly?

Hip. You have.

Soc. Under which kind then, Hippias, do you rank the beautiful? Do you rank it among those mentioned by yourself? as when you inferred that if I was well and hearty, and you well and hearty, then both of us were well and hearty: or, if I was honest and you honest, then both of us were honest: or, if we both were so, it followed that so was each of us. Does the same kind of inference hold true in this case? If I am beautiful, and you are beautiful, then both of us are beautiful; and if both of us, then each. Or is there no reason why it should not here be as it is in numbers? two of which, taken together, may be even; though each separately is perhaps odd, perhaps even: or, as it is in magnitudes; where two of them, though each is incommensurable with some third, yet both together may perhaps be commensurable with it, perhaps incommensurable. A thousand such other things there are, which I perceived, as I said, with great clearness. Now, to whether of these two orders of being do you refer the beautiful? Does the proper rank of it appear as evident to you as it does to me? For to me it appears highly absurd, to suppose both of us beautiful, yet each of us not so; or each of us beautiful, yet not so both; no less absurd, than it is to suppose the same kind of difference between the natures of both and each in any of the cases put by you. Do you agree with me then in ranking the beautiful among these, or do you refer it to the opposite class of things?

Hip. I entirely agree with you, Socrates.

Soc. You do well, Hippias: because we shall thus be freed from any further inquiry upon this article. For, if the beautiful be in that class of things where we agree to place it, the pleasant then, which arises in us through sight and hearing, can no longer be supposed the beautiful. Because that which comes through both those senses jointly, may make the pleasures which arise from thence beautiful indeed both taken together; but cannot make either of them so, considered as separate from the other. But that the beautiful should have such an effect, or communicate itself in this manner, is absurd to suppose; as you and I have agreed, Hippias.

Hip. We agreed it was so, I own.

Soc. It is impossible, therefore, that the pleasant, arising in us through sight and hearing, should be the beautiful; because from this hypothesis an absurdity would follow.

Hip. You have reason on your side.

Soc. "Begin again then, and tell me," will he say, "for you have missed it now, what is that beautiful, the associate of both these pleasures, for the sake of which you give them the preference to all others, by honouring them with the name of beautiful?" It appears to me, Hippias, necessary for us to answer thus; that "these are of all pleasures the most innocent and good, as well both of them taken together, as each taken singly." Or can you tell me of any circumstance beside, in which they differ from other pleasures?

Hip. I know of none beside: for they are indeed the best of all.

Soc. "This then," he will say, "do you now maintain to be the beautiful, pleasure profitable?"—"It is so in my opinion," I shall answer.—What answer would you make?

Hip. The same.

Soc. "Well then," will he say: "the profitable, you know, is that which is the cause of good. And the cause, as we agreed lately, is a thing different from the effect. Our reasoning, therefore, has brought us round to the same point again: for thus neither would the good be beautiful, nor would the beautiful be good; each of these being, upon this hypothesis, different from the other." "Most evidently so;" is the answer we must make, Hippias, if we are of sound mind.

For the sacredness of truth will never suffer us to oppose the man who has truth with him on his side.

Hip. But now, Socrates, what think you all these matters are which we have been disputing about? They are the shreds and tatters of an argument, cut and torn, as I said before, into a thousand pieces. But the thing which is beautiful, as well as highly valuable, is this: to be able to exhibit a fine speech, in a becoming and handsome manner, before the council, or court of justice, or any other assembly or person in authority, to whom the speech is addressed; such a speech as hath the power of persuasion; and having ended to depart, not with mean and insignificant trophies of victory, but with a prize the noblest, the preservation of ourselves, our fortunes, and our friends. This you ought to be ambitious of, and bid adieu to such petty and paltry disputes; or you will appear as if you had quite lost your senses, playing with straws and trifles, as you have been now doing.

Soc. O friend Hippias! you are happy that you know what course of life it is best for a man to follow, and have followed it, according to your own account, so successfully yourself. But I seem fated to be under the power of a dæmoniacal nature, who keeps me wandering continually in search of truth, and still at a loss where to find it. And whenever I lay my difficulties and perplexities before you wise men, I meet with no other answer from you than contumely and reproach. For you all tell me the same thing which you tell me now, "That I busy myself about silly, minute, and insignificant matters." On the other hand, when, upon giving credit to what you all tell me, I say, as you do, "That to be able to exhibit a fine speech in a court of justice, or any other assembly, and to go through it in a proper and handsome manner, is the finest thing in the world; and that no employment is so beautiful, or so well becomes a man;" I then meet with censure and obloquy from some who are here present, but especially from that man who is always reproving me. For he is my nearest of kin, and lives with me in the same house. So, whenever I return home, and am entered in, as soon as he hears me talking in this strain, he asks me if I am not ashamed to pronounce, with so much confidence, what professions and employments are fine, or beautiful, or becoming; when I have plainly shown myself so ignorant with regard to things beautiful, as not to know wherein the nature of beauty consists. "And how can you judge," says he, "who has spoken a beautiful or fine speech, or done anything else in a handsome manner, and who not, ignorant as you are what the beautiful and handsome is? Such then being the disposition of your mind, is it possible that you can think life more eligible to you than death?" Thus have I had the ill fortune, as I told you, to suffer obloquy and reproach from you, to suffer obloquy also and reproach from him. But, perhaps, it is necessary to endure all this. If I have received benefit or improvement from it, there is no harm done. And I seem to myself, Hippias, improved and benefited by the conversation of you both. For the meaning of the proverb, "Things of beauty are things of difficulty," if I am not mistaken in myself, I know.

16

THE PROCESS OF SCIENTIFIC THINKING *

by

JOHN DEWEY

(1859–1952)

ILLUSTRATIONS OF REFLECTIVE ACTIVITY

Practical needs in connection with existing conditions, natural and social, evoke and direct thought. We begin [in the following illustrations taken from students' papers] with an instance of that sort. . . . Curiosity is a strong drive from within, and accordingly our second example is drawn from that field. Finally, a mind that is already exercised in scientific subjects will have inquiry aroused by intellectual problems, and our third instance is of that type.

A Case of Practical Deliberation. The other day, when I was down town on 16th Street, a clock caught my eye. I saw that the hands pointed to 12:20. This suggested that I had an engagement at 124th Street, at one o'clock. I reasoned that as it had taken me an hour to come down on a surface car, I should probably be twenty minutes late if I returned the same way. I might save twenty minutes by a subway express. But was there a station near? If not, I might lose more than twenty minutes in looking for one. Then I thought of the elevated, and I saw there was such a line within two blocks. But where was the station? If it were several blocks above or below the street I was on, I should lose time instead of gaining it. My mind went back to the subway express as quicker than the elevated; furthermore, I remembered that it went nearer than the elevated

* [From Chs. 6, 7, and 11 of *How We Think*, revised edition (1933). By kind permission of the author and the publishers, D. C. Heath and Co.]

to the part of 124th Street I wished to reach, so that time would be saved at the end of the journey. I concluded in favor of the subway, and reached my destination by one o'clock.

A Case of Reflection upon an Observation. Projecting nearly horizontally from the upper deck of the ferryboat on which I daily cross the river is a long white pole, bearing a gilded ball at its tip. It suggested a flagpole when I first saw it; its color, shape, and gilded ball agreed with this idea, and these reasons seemed to justify me in this belief. But soon difficulties presented themselves. The pole was nearly horizontal, an unusual position for a flagpole; in the next place, there was no pulley, ring, or cord by which to attach a flag; finally, there were elsewhere two vertical staffs from which flags were occasionally flown. It seemed probable that the pole was not there for flag-flying.

I then tried to imagine all possible purposes of such a pole, and to consider for which of these it was best suited: (*a*) Possibly it was an ornament. But as all the ferryboats and even the tugboats carried poles, this hypothesis was rejected. (*b*) Possibly it was the terminal of a wireless telegraph. But the same considerations made this improbable. Besides, the more natural place for such a terminal would be the highest part of the boat, on top of the pilot house. (*c*) Its purpose might be to point out the direction in which the boat is moving.

In support of this conclusion, I discovered that the pole was lower than the pilot house, so that the steersman could easily see it. Moreover, the tip was enough higher than the base, so that, from the pilot's position, it must appear to project far out in front of the boat. Moreover, the pilot being near the front of the boat, he would need some such guide as to its direction. Tugboats would also need poles for such a purpose. This hypothesis was so much more probable than the others that I accepted it. I formed the conclusion that the pole was set up for the purpose of showing the pilot the direction in which the boat pointed, to enable him to steer correctly.

A Case of Reflection Involving Experiment. In washing tumblers in hot soapsuds and placing them mouth downward on a plate, I noticed that bubbles appeared on the outside of the mouth of the tumblers and then went inside. Why? The presence of bubbles suggests air, which I note must come from inside the tumbler. I see that the soapy water on the plate prevents escape of the air save as it may be caught in bubbles. But why should air leave the tumbler? There was no substance entering to force it out. It must have expanded. It expands by increase of heat or by increase of pressure, or by both. Could the air have become heated after the tumbler was taken from the hot suds? Clearly not the air that was already entangled in the water. If heated air was the cause, cold air must have entered in transferring the tumblers from the suds to the plate. I test to see whether this supposition is true by taking several more tumblers out. Some I shake so as to make sure of entrapping cold air in them. Some I take out, holding them mouth downward in order to prevent cold air from entering. Bubbles appear on the outside of every one of the former and on none of the latter. I must be right in my inference. Air from the outside must have been expanded by the heat of the tumbler, which explains the appearance of the bubbles on the outside.

But why do they then go inside? Cold contracts. The tumbler cooled and also the air inside it. Tension was removed, and hence bubbles appeared inside. To be sure of this, I test by placing a cap of ice on the tumbler while the bubbles are still forming outside. They soon reverse.

These Three Cases Form a Series. These three cases have been purposely selected so as to form a series from the more rudimentary to more complicated cases of reflection. The first illustrates the kind of thinking done by everyone during the day's business, in which neither the data nor the ways of dealing with them lie outside the limits of everyday experience. The last furnishes a case in which neither problem nor mode of solution would have occurred except to one with some prior scientific training. The second case forms a natural transition; its materials lie well within the bounds of everyday, unspecialized experience; but the problem, instead of being directly involved in the person's business, arises indirectly in connection with what he happened to be doing and appeals to a somewhat theoretic and impartial interest.

In the next chapter we shall give an analytic account of what the three instances exhibit in common. In what immediately follows we shall set forth, first, how they all illustrate the nature of that operation of *inference* which is the heart of all intelligent action, and second, how the aim and outcome of thinking in all cases is the transformation of a *dubious* and perplexing situation into a *settled,* or determinate, one.

Inference to the Unknown

No Thought without Inference. In every case of reflective activity, a person finds himself confronted with a given, present situation from which he has to arrive at, or conclude to, something else that is not present. This process of arriving at an idea of what is absent on the basis of what is at hand is *inference.* What is present *carries* or *bears* the mind over to the idea and ultimately the acceptance of something else. From the consideration of established facts of location and time of day, the person in the first case cited made an inference as to the best way to travel in order to keep an appointment, which is a future and, at first, uncertain event. From observed and remembered facts, the second person inferred the probable use of a long pole. From the presence under certain conditions of bubbles and from a knowledge of securely established physical facts and principles, the third person inferred the explanation or cause of a particular event, previously unknown; namely, the movement of water in the form of bubbles from the outside to the inside of a tumbler.

Inference Involves a Leap. Every inference, just because it goes beyond ascertained and known facts, which are given either by observation or by recollection of prior knowledge, involves a *jump from the known into the unknown*. It involves a leap beyond what is given and already established. . . . the inference occurs via or through the suggestion that is aroused by what is seen and remembered. Now, while the suggestion pops into the mind, just *what* suggestion occurs depends first upon the experience of the person. This in turn is dependent upon the general state of culture of the time; suggestions, for example, that occur readily now could not possibly spring up in the mind of a savage. Second, suggestions depend upon the person's own preferences, desires, interests, or even his immediate state of passion. The inevitableness of suggestion, the lively force with which it springs before the mind, the natural tendency to accept it if it is plausible or not obviously contradicted by facts, indicate the necessity of controlling the suggestion which is made the basis of an inference that is to be believed.

Proving Is Testing. This control of inference prior to, and on behalf of, belief constitutes *proof*. To prove a thing means primarily to *test* it. The guest bidden to the wedding feast excused himself because he had to *prove* his oxen. Exceptions are said to prove a rule; *i.e.*, they furnish instances so extreme that they try in the severest fashion its applicability; if the rule will stand such a test, there is no good reason for further doubting it. Not until a thing has been tried—'tried out,' in colloquial language—do we know its true worth. Till then it may be pretense, a bluff. But the thing that has come out victorious in a test or trial of strength carries its credentials with it; it is approved, because it has been proved. Its value is clearly evinced, shown; *i.e.*, demonstrated. So it is with inferences. The mere fact that inference in general is an invaluable function does not guarantee, nor does it even help out, the correctness of any particular inference. Any inference may go astray; as we have seen, there are standing influences ever ready to instigate it to go wrong. *What is important is that every inference be a tested* *inference; or* (since often this is not possible) *that we discriminate between beliefs that rest upon tested evidence and those that do not, and be accordingly on our guard as to the kind and degree of assent or belief that is justified.*

Two Kinds of Testing. All three instances manifest the presence of testing operations that transform what would otherwise have been loose thinking into reflective activity. Examination reveals that the testing is of two kinds. Suggested inferences are tested in *thought* to see whether different elements in the suggestion are coherent with one another. They are also tested, after one has been adopted, by *action* to see whether the consequences that are anticipated in *thought* occur in *fact*. A good example of this second kind of proving is found in the first case cited, where reasoning had led to the conclusion that the use of the subway would bring the person to the place of his appointment in time. He tried or tested the idea by acting upon it, and the result confirmed the idea by bringing what was inferred actually to pass.

In the second case, the test by action could occur only as the person *imagined* himself in the place of the pilot who was using the pole to steer by. The test of coherence or consistency is markedly in evidence. Suggestions of flagpole, ornament, wireless, were rejected because, as soon as they were reflected upon, it was seen that they did not fit into some elements of the observed facts; they were dropped because they failed to agree with these elements. The idea that the pole was used to show the direction of movement of the boat, on the contrary, was found to agree with a number of important elements, such as (*a*) the need of the pilot, (*b*) the height of the pole, (*c*) the relative locations of its base and tip.

In the third instance, both kinds of testing are employed. After the conclusion was reached, it was acted upon by a further experiment, undertaken not only in imagination but also in fact. A cap of ice was placed upon the tumbler, and the bubbles behaved as they should behave if the inference was the correct one. Hence it was borne out, corroborated, verified. Other testing acts occurred in the process by using different ways of taking tumblers out of the water. The testing of consistency in thought occurred by reflecting upon the nature of expansion in its relation to heat and by considering whether the observed phenomena agreed with the facts that would have to follow from this principle. Obviously the use of both methods of proving a proposed inference is better than one alone. The two methods do not differ, however, in kind. Testing in thought for consistency involves acting in *imagination*. The other mode carries the imagined act out overtly. True inference is defined first as involving a leap to a suggested conclusion, and second as *trying* the suggestion to determine its agreement with the requirements of the situation. The original pattern of reflective action is set by cases in which the need for doing something is urgent, and where the results of what is done test the value of thought. As intellectual curiosity develops, connection with overt action becomes indirect and incidental. Yet it persists even if only in imagination.

THINKING MOVES FROM A DOUBTFUL TO A SETTLED SITUATION

It Arises from a Directly Experienced Situation. Examination of the instances will show that in each case thinking arises out of a directly experienced situation. Persons do not just think at large, nor do ideas arise out of nothing. In one case a student is busy in a certain part of a city and is reminded of an engagement at another place. In the second case a person is engaged in riding on a ferry-boat and begins to wonder about something in the construction of the boat. In the third case a student with prior scientific training is busy washing dishes. In each case the nature of the situation as it is actually experienced arouses inquiry and calls out reflection.

There is nothing in this fact peculiar to these special instances. Go through your own experience and you will not find a case where thinking started up out of nothing. Sometimes the train of thoughts will have taken you so far away from the starting point that you will have difficulty in getting back to that prior something out of which the thinking arose, but follow the thread far enough and you will find some situation that is directly experienced, something undergone, done, enjoyed, or suffered, and not just thought of. Reflection is occasioned by the character of this primary situation. It does not merely *grow out* of it, but it *refers back* to it. Its aim and outcome are decided by the situation out of which it arose.

Probably the most frequent cause of failure in school to secure genuine thinking from students is the failure to insure the existence of an experienced situation of such a nature as to call out thinking in the way in which these out-of-school situations do. A teacher was troubled by the failure of pupils, when dealing with arithmetical problems in multiplication involving decimals, to place the decimal point correctly. The numerical figures would be correct, but the values all wrong. One student might, for example, say $320.16; another, $32.016; and a third, $3201.60. This result showed that, while the pupils could manipulate figures correctly, they did not *think*. For if they had used thought, they would not vary so arbitrarily in grasping the values involved. Accordingly he sent the pupils to a lumberyard to purchase boards for use in the manual-training shop, having arranged with the dealer to let *them* figure the cost of their purchases. The same numerical operations were involved as in the textbook problems. No mistakes at all were made in placing the decimal. The situation itself induced them to think and controlled their grasp of the values involved. The contrast between the textbook problem and the requirements of the actual purchase in the lumberyard provides an excellent example of the necessity of a situation in order to induce and direct thought.

It Moves toward a Settled Situation. Examination of the three cases also shows that each situation is in some fashion uncertain, perplexed, troublesome, if only in offering to the mind an unresolved difficulty, an unsettled question. It shows in each case that the function of reflection is to bring about a new situation in which the difficulty is resolved, the confusion cleared away, the trouble smoothed out, the question it puts answered. Any particular process of thinking naturally comes to its close when the situation before the mind is settled, decided, orderly, clear, for then there is nothing to call out reflection until a new bothersome or doubtful situation arises.

The function of reflective thought is, therefore, to transform a situation in which there is experienced obscurity, doubt, conflict, disturbance of some sort, into a situation that is clear, coherent, settled, harmonious.

The *stated* conclusion, the conclusion that is set forth in a proposition, is not the *final* conclusion but is the key to its formation. For example, the first person reached the conclusion "the best way to 124th Street is the subway train." But that conclusion was only the *key* to reaching the ultimate conclusion; namely, the keeping of an engagement. Thinking was the means of developing the original, perplexed situation into an eventual, satisfactory one. You can readily make similar analyses in the case of the other two illustrations. One great difficulty with the 'logical,' the exclusively formal type . . . is that it begins and ends with mere propositions instead of bringing before the imagination the two actual life-situations to which the propositions refer; the one, which contains the doubt or difficulty, and the other, which is the final desired outcome and which was brought about by means of reflection.

There is no better way to decide whether genuine inference has taken place than to ask whether it terminated in the substitution of a clear, orderly, and satisfactory situation for a perplexed, confused, and discordant one. Partial and ineffectual thinking ends in conclusions that are formally correct but that make no difference in what is personally and immediately experienced. Vital inference always leaves one who thinks with a world that is experienced as different in some respect, for some object in it has gained in clarity and orderly arrangement. Genuine thinking winds up, in short, with an appreciation of new values.

FACTS AND IDEAS

When a situation arises containing a difficulty or perplexity, the person who finds himself in it may take one of a number of courses. He may dodge it, dropping the activity that brought it about, turning to something else. He may indulge in a flight of fancy, imagining himself powerful or wealthy, or in some other way in possession of the means that would enable him to deal with the difficulty. Or, finally, he may face the situation. In this case, he begins to reflect.

Reflection Includes Observation. The moment he begins to reflect, he begins of necessity to observe in order to take stock of conditions. Some of these observations are made by direct use of the senses; others by recollecting observations previously made either by himself or by others. The person who had the engagement to keep, notes with his eyes his present location, recalls the place where he should arrive at one o'clock, and brings back to mind the means of transportation with which he is acquainted and their respective locations. In this way he gets as clear and distinct a recognition as possible of the nature of the situation with which he has to deal. Some of the conditions are obstacles and others are aids, resources. No matter whether these conditions come to him by direct perception or by memory, they form the 'facts of the case.' They are the things that are *there*, that have to be reckoned with. Like all facts, they are stubborn. They cannot be got out of the way by magic just because they are disagreeable. It is no use to *wish* they did not exist or were different. They must be taken for just what they are. Hence observation and recollection must be used to the full so as not to glide over or to mistake important features. Until the habit of thinking is well formed, facing the situation to discover the facts requires an effort. For the mind tends to dislike what is unpleasant and so to sheer off from an adequate notice of that which is especially annoying.

Reflection Includes Suggestions. Along with noting the conditions that constitute the facts to be dealt with, suggestions arise of possible courses of action. Thus the person of our illustration thinks of surface cars, elevated trains, and the subway. These alternative suggestions compete with one another. By comparison he judges which alternative is best, which one is the more likely to give a satisfactory solution. The comparison takes place indirectly. The moment one thinks of a possible solution and holds it in suspense, he turns back to the facts. He has now a point of view that leads him to new observations and recollections and to a reconsideration of observations already made in order to test the worth of the suggested way out. Unless he uses the suggestion so as to guide to new observations instead of exercising suspended judgment, he accepts it as soon as it presents itself. Then he falls short of truly reflective thought. The newly noted facts may (and in any complex situation surely will) cause new suggestions to spring up. These become clews to further investigation of conditions. The results of this survey test and correct the proposed inference or suggest a new one. This continuous interaction of the facts disclosed by observation and of the suggested proposals of solution and the suggested methods of dealing with conditions goes on till some suggested solution meets all the conditions of the case and does not run counter to any discoverable feature of it.

Data and Ideas Are Correlative and Indispensable Factors in Reflection. A technical term for the observed facts is *data*. The data form the material that has to be interpreted, accounted for, explained; or, in the case of deliberation as to what to do or how to do it, to be managed and utilized. The suggested solutions for the difficulties disclosed by observation form *ideas*. Data (facts) and ideas (suggestions, possible solutions) thus form the two indispensable and correlative factors of all reflective activity. The two factors are carried on by means respectively of *observation* (in which for convenience is included memory of prior observations of similar cases) and *inference*. The latter runs beyond what is actually noted, beyond what is found, upon careful examination, to be actually present. It relates, therefore, to what is *possible*, rather than to what is actual. It proceeds by anticipation, supposition, conjecture, imagination. All foresight, prediction, planning, as well as theorizing and speculation, are characterized by excursion from the actual into the possible. Hence (as we have already seen) what is inferred demands a double test: first, the process of forming the idea or supposed solution is checked by constant cross reference to the conditions observed to be actually present; secondly, the idea *after* it is formed is tested by *acting* upon it, overtly if possible, otherwise in imagination. The consequences of this action confirm, modify, or refute the idea.

We shall illustrate what has been said by a simple case. Suppose you are walking where there is no regular path. As long as everything goes smoothly, you do not have to think about your walking; your already formed habit takes care of it. Suddenly you find a ditch in your way. You think you will jump it (supposition, plan); but to make sure, you survey it with your eyes (observation), and you find that it is pretty wide and that the bank on the other side is slippery (facts, data). You then wonder if the ditch may not be narrower somewhere else (idea), and you look up and down the stream (observation) to see how matters stand (test of idea by observation). You do not find any good place and so are thrown back upon forming a new plan. As you are casting about, you discover a log (fact again). You ask yourself whether you could not haul that to the ditch and get it across the ditch to use as a bridge (idea again). You judge that idea is worth trying, and so you get the log and manage to put it in place and walk across (test and confirmation by overt action).

If the situation were more complicated, thinking would of course be more elaborate. You can imagine a case in which making a raft, constructing a pontoon bridge, or making a dugout would be the ideas that would finally come to mind and have to be checked by reference to conditions of action (facts). Simple or complicated, relating to what to do in a practical predicament or what to infer in a scientific or philosophic problem, there will always be the two sides: the conditions to be accounted for, dealt with, and the ideas that are plans for dealing with them or are suppositions for interpreting and explaining the phenomena.

In predicting an eclipse, for example, a multitude of observed facts regarding position and movements of earth, sun, and moon, comes in on one side, while on the other side the ideas employed to predict and explain involve extensive mathematical calculations. In a philosophic problem, the facts or data may be remote and not susceptible of direct observation by the senses. But still there will be data, perhaps of science, or of morals, art, or the conclusions of past thinkers, that supply the subject matter to be dealt with and by which theories are checked. On the other side, there are the speculations that come to mind and that lead to search for additional subject matter which will both develop the proposed theories as ideas and test their value. Mere facts or data are dead, as far as mind is concerned, unless they are used to suggest and test some idea, some way out of a difficulty. Ideas, on the other hand, are *mere* ideas, idle speculations, fantasies, dreams, unless they are used to guide new observations of, and reflections upon, actual situations, past, present, or future. Finally, they must be brought to some sort of check by actual given material or else remain ideas. Many ideas are of great value as material of poetry, fiction, or the drama, but not as the stuff of knowledge. However, ideas may be of intellectual use to a penetrating mind even when they do not find any immediate reference to actuality, provided they stay in the mind for use when new facts come to light.

The Essential Functions of Reflective Activity

We now have before us the material for the analysis of a complete act of reflective activity. In the preceding chapter we saw that the two limits of every unit of thinking are a perplexed, troubled, or confused situation at the beginning and a cleared-up, unified, resolved situation at the close. The first of these situations may be called *pre*-reflective. It sets the problem to be solved; out of it grows the question that reflection has to answer. In the final situation the doubt has been dispelled; the situation is *post*-reflective; there results a direct experience of mastery, satisfaction, enjoyment. Here, then, are the limits within which reflection falls.

Five Phases, or Aspects, of Reflective Thought. In between, as states of thinking, are (1) *suggestions*, in which the mind leaps forward to a possible solution; (2) an intellectualization of the difficulty or perplexity that has been *felt* (directly experienced) into a *problem* to be solved, a question for which the answer must be sought; (3) the use of one suggestion after another as a leading idea, or *hypothesis*, to initiate and guide observation and other operations in collection of factual material; (4) the mental elaboration of the idea or supposition as an idea or supposition (*reasoning*, in the sense in which reasoning is a part, not the whole, of inference); and (5) testing the hypothesis by overt or imaginative action.

We shall now take up the five phases, or functions, one by one.

The First Phase, Suggestion. The most 'natural' thing for anyone to do is to go ahead; that is to say, to *act* overtly. The disturbed and perplexed situation arrests such direct activity temporarily. The tendency to continue *acting* nevertheless persists. It is diverted and takes the form of an idea or a suggestion. The *idea* of what to do when we find ourselves 'in a hole' is a substitute for direct action. It is a vicarious, anticipatory way of acting, a kind of dramatic rehearsal. Were there only one suggestion popping up, we should undoubtedly adopt it at once. But where there are two or more, they collide with one another, maintain the state of suspense, and produce further inquiry. The first suggestion in the instance recently cited was to jump the ditch, but the perception of conditions inhibited that suggestion and led to the occurrence of other ideas.

Some inhibition of *direct* action is necessary to the condition of hesitation and delay that is essential to thinking. Thought is, as it were, conduct turned in upon itself and examining its purpose and its conditions, its resources, aids, and difficulties and obstacles.

The Second Phase, Intellectualization. We have already noted that it is artificial, so far as thinking is concerned, to start with a ready-made problem, a problem made out of whole cloth or arising out of a vacuum. In reality such a 'problem' is simply an assigned *task*. There is not at first a situation *and* a problem, much less just a problem and no situation. There is a troubled, perplexed, trying situation, where the difficulty is, as it were, spread throughout the entire situation, infecting it as a whole. If we knew just what the difficulty was and where it lay, the job of reflection would be much easier than it is. As the saying truly goes, a question well put is half answered. In fact, we know what the problem *exactly* is simultaneously with finding a way out and getting it resolved. Problem and solution stand out *completely* at the same time. Up to that point, our grasp of the problem has been more or less vague and tentative.

A blocked suggestion leads us to reinspect the conditions that confront us. Then our uneasiness, the shock of disturbed activity, gets stated in some degree on the basis of observed conditions, of objects. The width of the ditch, the slipperiness of the banks, not the mere presence of a ditch, is the trouble. The difficulty is getting located and defined; it is becoming a true problem, something intellectual, not just an annoyance at being held up in what we are doing. The person who is suddenly blocked and troubled in what he is doing by the thought of an engagement to keep at a time that is near and a place that is distant has the suggestion of getting there at once. But in order to carry this suggestion into effect, he has to find means of transportation. In order to find them he has to note his present position and its distance from the station, the present time, and the interval at his disposal. Thus the perplexity is more precisely located: just so much ground to cover, so much time to do it in.

The word 'problem' often seems too elaborate and dignified to denote what happens in minor cases of reflection. But in every case where reflective activity ensues, there is a process of *intellectualizing* what at first is merely an *emotional* quality of the whole situation. This conversion is effected by noting more definitely the conditions that constitute the trouble and cause the stoppage of action.

The Third Phase, the Guiding Idea, Hypothesis. The first suggestion occurs spontaneously; it comes to mind automatically; it *springs* up; it "pops," as we have said, "into the mind"; it flashes upon us. There is no direct control of its occurrence; the idea just comes or it does not come; that is all that can be said. There is nothing *intellectual* about its occurrence. The intellectual element consists in *what we do with it,* how we use it, *after* its sudden occurrence as an idea. A controlled use of it is made possible by the state of affairs just described. In the degree in which we define the difficulty (which is effected by stating it in terms of objects), we get a better idea of the kind of solution that is needed. The facts or data set the problem before us, and insight into the problem corrects, modifies, expands the suggestion that originally occurred. In this fashion the suggestion becomes a definite supposition or, stated more technically, a *hypothesis*.

Take the case of a physician examining a patient or a mechanic inspecting a piece of complicated machinery that does not behave properly. There is something wrong, so much is sure. But how to remedy it cannot be told until it is known *what* is wrong. An untrained person is likely to make a wild guess—the suggestion—and then proceed to act upon it in a random way, hoping that by good luck the right thing will be hit upon. So some medicine that appears to have worked before or that a neighbor has recommended is tried. Or the person fusses, monkeys, with the machine, poking here and hammering there on the chance of making the right move. The trained person proceeds in a very different fashion. He *observes* with unusual care, using the methods, the techniques, that the experience of physicians and expert mechanics in general, those familiar with the structure of the organism or the machine, have shown to be helpful in detecting trouble.

The idea of the solution is thus controlled by the diagnosis that has been made. But if the case is at all complicated, the physician or mechanic does not foreclose further thought by assuming that the suggested method of remedy is certainly right. He proceeds to act upon it tentatively rather than decisively. That is, he treats it as a guiding idea, a working hypothesis, and is led by it to make more observations, to collect more facts, so as to see if the *new* material is what the hypothesis calls for. He reasons that *if* the disease is typhoid, *then* certain phenomena will be found; and he looks particularly to see if *just* these conditions are present. Thus both the first and second operations are brought under control; the sense of the problem becomes more adequate and refined and the suggestion ceases to be a *mere* possibility, becoming a *tested* and, if possible, a *measured* probability.

The Fourth Phase, Reasoning (in the Narrower Sense). Observations pertain to what exists in nature. They constitute the facts, and these facts both regulate the formation of suggestions, ideas, hypotheses, and test their probable value as indications of solutions. The ideas, on the other hand, occur, as we say, in our heads, in our minds. They not only occur there, but are capable, as well, of great development there. Given a fertile suggestion occurring in an experienced, well-informed mind, that mind is capable of elaborating it until there results an idea that is quite different from the one with which the mind started

For example, the idea of heat in the third instance in the earlier chapter was linked up with what the person already knew about heat—in his case, its expansive force—and this in turn with the contractive tendency of cold, so that the idea of expansion could be used as an explanatory idea, though the mere idea of heat would not have been of any avail. Heat was quite directly suggested by the observed conditions; water was felt to be hot. But only a mind with some prior information about heat would have reasoned that heat meant expansion, and then used the idea of expansion as a working hypothesis. In more complex cases, there are long trains of reasoning in which one idea leads up to another idea known by previous test to be related to it. The stretch of links brought to light by reasoning depends, of course, upon the store of knowledge that the mind is already in possession of. And this depends not only upon the prior experience and special education of the individual who is carrying on the inquiry, but also upon the state of culture and science of the age and place. Reasoning helps extend knowledge, while at the same time it depends upon what is already known and upon the facilities that exist for communicating knowledge and making it a public, open resource.

A physician to-day can develop, by reasoning from his knowledge, the implications of the disease that symptoms suggest to him as probable in a way that would have been impossible even a generation ago; just as, on the other hand, he can carry his observation of symptoms much farther because of improvement in clinical instruments and the technique of their use.

Reasoning has the same effect upon a suggested solution that more intimate and extensive observation has upon the original trouble. Acceptance of a suggestion in its first form is prevented by looking into it more thoroughly. Conjectures that seem plausible at first sight are often found unfit or even absurd when their full consequences are traced out. Even when reasoning out the bearings of a supposition does not lead to its rejection, it develops the idea into a form in which it is more apposite to the problem. Only when, for example, the conjecture that a pole was an index pole had been thought out in its implications could its particular applicability to the case in hand be judged. Suggestions at first seemingly remote and wild are frequently so transformed by being elaborated into what follows from them as to become apt and fruitful. The development of an idea through reasoning helps supply intervening or intermediate terms which link together into a consistent whole elements that at first seemingly conflict with each other, some leading the mind to one inference and others to an opposed one.

Mathematics as Typical Reasoning. Mathematics affords the typical example of how far can be carried the operation of relating ideas to one another, without having to depend upon the observations of the senses. In geometry we start with a few simple conceptions, line, angle, parallel, surfaces formed by lines meeting, etc., and a few principles defining equalities. Knowing something about the equality of angles made by parallel lines when they intersect a straight line, and knowing, by definition, that a perpendicular to a straight line forms two right angles, by means of a combination of these ideas we readily determine that the sum of the interior angles of a triangle is equal to two right angles. By continuing to trace the implications of theorems already demonstrated, the whole subject of plane figures is finally elaborated. The manipulation of algebraic symbols so as to establish a series of equations and other mathematical functions affords an even more striking example of what can be accomplished by developing the relation of ideas to one another.

When the hypothesis indicated by a series of scientific observations and experiments can be stated in mathematical form, that idea can be transformed to almost any extent, until it assumes a form in which a problem can be dealt with most expeditiously and effectively. Much of the accomplishment of physical science depends upon an intervening mathematical elaboration of ideas. It is not the mere presence of measurements in quantitative form that yields scientific knowledge, but that particular kind of mathematical statement which can be developed by reasoning into other and more fruitful forms—a consideration which is fatal to the claim to scientific standing of many educational measurements merely because they have a quantitative form.

The Fifth Phase, Testing the Hypothesis by Action. The concluding phase is some kind of testing by overt action to give *experimental corroboration,* or *verification,* of the conjectural idea. Reasoning shows that *if* the *idea* be adopted, certain consequences follow. So far the conclusion is hypothetical or conditional. If when we look we find present all the conditions demanded by the theory, and if we find the characteristic traits called for by rival alternatives to be lacking, the tendency to believe, to accept, is almost irresistible. Sometimes direct observation furnishes corroboration, as in the case of the pole on the boat. In other cases, as in that of the bubbles, experiment is required; that is, *conditions are deliberately arranged in accord with the requirements of an idea or hypothesis to see whether the results theoretically indicated by the idea actually occur.* If it is found that the experimental results agree with the theoretical, or rationally deduced, results, and if there is reason to believe that *only* the conditions in question would yield such results, the confirmation is so strong as to induce a conclusion—at least until contrary facts shall indicate the advisability of its revision.

Of course, verification does not always follow. Sometimes consequences show failure to confirm instead of corroboration. The idea in question is refuted by the court of final appeal. But a great advantage of possession of the habit of reflective activity is that failure is not *mere* failure. It is instructive. The person who really thinks learns quite as much from his failures as from his successes. For a failure indicates to the person whose thinking has been involved in it, and who has not come to it by mere blind chance, what further observations should be made. It suggests to him what modifications should be introduced in the hypothesis upon which he has been operating. It either brings to light a new problem or helps to define and clarify the problem on which he has been engaged. Nothing shows the trained thinker better than the use he makes of his errors and mistakes. What merely annoys and discourages a person not accustomed to thinking, or what starts him out on a new course of aimless attack by mere cut-and-try methods, is a stimulus and a guide to the trained inquirer.

The Sequence of the Five Phases Is Not Fixed. The five phases, terminals, or functions of thought, that we have noted do not follow one another in a set order. On the contrary, each step in genuine thinking does something to perfect the formation of a suggestion and promote its change into a leading idea or directive hypothesis. It does something to promote the location and definition of the problem. Each improvement in the idea leads to new observations that yield new facts or data and help the mind judge more accurately the relevancy of facts already at hand. The elaboration of the hypothesis does not wait until the problem has been defined and adequate hypothesis has been arrived at; it may come in at any intermediate time. And as we have just seen, any particular overt test need not be final; it may be introductory to new observations and new suggestions, according to what happens in consequence of it.

There is, however, an important difference between test by overt action in practical deliberations and in scientific investigations. In the former the practical commitment involved in overt action is much more serious than in the latter. An astronomer or a chemist performs overt actions, but they are for the sake of knowledge; they serve to test and develop his conceptions and theories. In practical matters, the main result desired lies outside of knowledge. One of the great values of thinking, accordingly, is that it defers the commitment to action that is irretrievable, that, once made, cannot be revoked. Even in moral and other practical matters, therefore, a thoughtful person treats his overt deeds as experimental so far as possible; that is to say, while he cannot call them back and must stand their consequences, he gives alert attention to what they teach him about his conduct as well as to the non-intellectual consequences. He makes a problem out of consequences of conduct, looking into the causes from which they probably resulted, especially the causes that lie in his own habits and desires. . . .

METHOD AS DELIBERATE TESTING OF FACTS AND IDEAS

The Need for Systematized Method. Method of a systematic sort is required in order to safeguard the operations by which we move from one to the other, from facts to ideas, and back again from ideas to the facts that will test them. Without adequate method a person grabs, as it were, at the first facts that offer themselves; he does not examine them to see whether they are truly facts or whether, even though they be real facts, they are relevant to the inference that needs to be made. On the other side, we are given to jumping at the first solution that occurs to us, accepting it as a conclusion without examination and test. We are given also to generalizing an idea far beyond support by evidence. We extend it to new cases without careful study to see whether these cases may not be so different as not to justify the generalization. Method is particularly needed in complex cases and cases of generalization, in order to safeguard us from falling into these errors.

We shall first give an illustration of the way in which the discovery of relevant facts on which to base, and by which to support and test, an inferred solution goes on in company with the formation and use of ideas to interpret the facts.

A man who has left his room in order finds it upon his return in a state of confusion, articles being scattered at random. Automatically, the notion comes to his mind that burglary would account for the disorder. He has not seen the burglars; their presence is not a fact of observation; it is a thought, an idea. The state of the room is a *fact*, certain, speaking for itself; the presence of burglars is a possibility that may explain the facts. Moreover, the man has no special burglar in mind. The state of his room is perceived and is particular, definite—exactly as it is; a burglar is inferred. But no particular individual is thought of; merely some indefinite, unspecified, member of a class.

The original fact, the room as it is first observed, does not by any means *prove* the fact of burglary. The latter conjecture may be correct, but evidence to justify accepting it positively is lacking. The total 'fact' as given contains both too much and too little; too much, because there are many features in it that are irrelevant to inference, that are therefore *logically* superfluous. Too little, because the considerations that are crucial—that, if they were ascertained, would be decisive—do not appear on the surface. Thoughtful search for the *kind* of facts that are clews is therefore necessitated. If the illustration were followed out beyond the judgment as to whether there had been a burglary to the question of who the criminal was and how he was to be discovered and the crime brought home to him, the need for extensive and careful examination of the fact side of the case would be even clearer.

Observation Valuable When Guided by Hypotheses. This search needs guidance. If it is conducted purely at random a multitude of facts will be turned up, but they will be so unrelated that their very number will add to the difficulty of the case. It is quite possible for thinking to be swamped by the mere multiplicity and diversity of facts. The real problem is: What facts are *evidence* in this case? The search for evidential facts is best conducted when some suggested *possible* meaning is used as a guide in exploring facts, especially in instituting a hunt for some fact that would point conclusively to one explanation and exclude all others. So the person entertains various hypotheses. Besides burglary, there is the possibility that some member of the family had an urgent need to find some article and, being in a hurry, had not taken the time to put things in order again. There are children also in the family, and they are not above mischief on occasion. Each of these conjectured possibilities is developed to some extent. *If* it were a burglar, or an adult in a hurry, or mischief on the part of children, *then* certain features characteristic of each particular cause would be present. *If* it were a case of burglary, *then* articles of value would be missing. Guided by this idea, the person looks again, not any longer at the scene as a whole, but analytically, with reference to this one item. He finds jewelry gone; he finds that some silver articles have been twisted and bent, and left behind as merely plated ware. These data are incompatible with any hypothesis except burglary. Looking further, he finds data that are most naturally interpreted to mean that a window has been tampered with—a fact consistent only with the action of a burglar. Under any ordinary circumstances these data would give adequate evidence of the visit of a burglar; if the conditions were very unusual, there would be nothing but to continue thinking of further possibilities and looking for further facts as data by which to test them. The instance is taken from ordinary life. Scientific method represents the same sort of thing carried on with greater elaborateness, by means especially of instruments and apparatus devised for the purpose and of mathematical calculations.

THE IMPORTANCE OF METHOD IN JUDGING DATA

. . . From what has been said it is clear that the formation of the idea or hypothesis that is employed to interpret data and to unify them into a coherent situation is indirect. Fundamentally, suggestions just occur or do not occur, depending, as we have seen, on the state of culture and knowledge at the time; upon the discernment and experience and native genius of the individual; upon his recent activities; to some extent upon chance; for many of the most pregnant inventions and discoveries have come about almost accidentally, although these happy accidents never happen except to persons especially prepared by interest and prior thought. But while the original happening of a suggestion, whether it be brilliant or stupid, is not *directly* controlled, the acceptance and use of the suggestion is capable of control, given a person of a thoughtful habit of mind.

The primary method of control is that indicated in the illustration. The person who is confronted with the situation that has to be thought through returns upon, revises, extends, analyzes, and makes more precise and definite the facts of the case. He strives to convert them into just those data which will test the suggestions that occur to mind. This testing will take place, as in the burglary incident, by finding upon examination traits that are *incompatible* with some suggested possibility and consistent with some other. They are just what *should* be there in fact *if* that particular hypothesis is correct. The ideal of course is discovery of traits that could be present *only* upon a particular hypothesis. This type of evidence can rarely be found in fact, but it is approximated by the methods of control of observation and collection of data that have been found to work well in scientific inquiry.

The Interrelations of Observation and Thought. It will be noted, then, that observation is not an operation that is opposed to thought or that is even independent of it. On the contrary, *thoughtful* observing is at least one half of thinking, the other half being the entertaining and elaboration of multiple hypotheses. Features that are glaringly conspicuous often need to be ignored; hidden traits need to be brought to light; obscure characteristics to be emphasized and cleared up.

Consider, for example, how a physician makes his diagnosis, his interpretation. If he is scientifically trained, he suspends—postpones —reaching a conclusion in order that he may not be led by superficial occurrences into a snap judgment. There are some facts that are given in an obvious way to his observation. But what is obvious may be, *when regarded as an evidential sign,* most misleading; the evidential facts, the real data, may show themselves only after a prolonged search involving artificial apparatus and a technique that expresses the methods found useful by a whole body of experts.

Conspicuous phenomena may forcibly suggest typhoid, but the physician avoids a conclusion or even any strong preference for this or that conclusion until he has both greatly *enlarged* the scope of his data and also rendered them more *minute*. He not only questions the patient as to his feelings and as to his acts prior to the disease, but by various manipulations with his hands (and with instruments made for the purpose) brings to light a large number of facts of which the patient is quite unaware. The state of temperature, respiration, and heart action is accurately noted, and their fluctuations from time to time are exactly recorded. Until this examination has worked *out* toward a wider collection and *in* toward a minuter scrutiny of details, inference is deferred. . . .

Experimental Variation of Conditions . . . The object of experimentation is the *construction, by regular steps taken on the basis of a plan thought out in advance, of a typical, crucial case,* a case formed with express reference to throwing light on the difficulty in question. All methods on the fact side rest, as already stated, upon regulation of the conditions of observation and memory; experiment is simply the most adequate regulation of these conditions that is possible. We try to make the observation such that every factor entering into it, together with the mode and the amount of its operation, may be open to recognition. Making observations open, overt, precise, constitutes experiment.

Three Advantages of Experiment. Such observations have many and obvious advantages over observations—no matter how extensive —with respect to which we simply wait for an event to happen or an object to present itself. Experiment overcomes defects due to (*a*) the *rarity,* (*b*) the *subtlety* and minuteness (or the violence), and (*c*) the rigid *fixity* of facts as we ordinarily experience them. The following quotations from Jevons's *Elementary Lessons in Logic* bring out all these points:

> We might have to wait years or centuries to meet accidentally with facts which we can readily produce at any moment in a laboratory; and it is probable that most of the chemical substances now known and many excessively useful products would never have been discovered at all by waiting till nature presented them spontaneously to our observation.

This quotation refers to the infrequency, or rarity, of certain facts of nature, even very important ones. The passage then goes on to speak of the minuteness of many phenomena that makes them escape ordinary experience:

Electricity doubtless operates in every particle of matter, perhaps at every moment of time; and even the ancients could not but notice its action in the loadstone, in lightning, in the Aurora Borealis, or in a piece of rubbed amber. But in lightning electricity was too intense and dangerous; in the other cases it was too feeble to be properly understood. The science of electricity and magnetism could only advance by getting regular supplies of electricity from the common electric machine or the galvanic battery and by making powerful electromagnets. Most, if not all, the effects which electricity produces must go on in nature, but altogether too obscurely for observation.

Jevons then deals with the fact that, under ordinary conditions of experience, phenomena that can be understood only by seeing them under varying conditions are presented in a fixed and uniform way.

Thus carbonic acid is only met in the form of a gas, proceeding from the combustion of carbon; but when exposed to extreme pressure and cold, it is condensed into a liquid, and may even be converted into a snowlike solid substance. Many other gases have in like manner been liquefied or solidified, and there is reason to believe that every substance is capable of taking all three forms of solid, liquid, and gas, if only the conditions of temperature and pressure can be sufficiently varied. Mere observation of nature would have led us, on the contrary, to suppose that nearly all substances were fixed in one condition only, and could not be converted from solid into liquid and from liquid into gas.

Many volumes would be required to describe in detail all the methods that investigators have developed in various subjects for analyzing and restating the facts of ordinary experience so that we may escape from capricious and routine suggestions and may get the facts in such a form and in such a light (or context) that exact and far-reaching explanations may be suggested in place of vague and limited ones. But these various devices of inductive inquiry all have one goal in view: the indirect regulation of the function of suggestions, or formation of ideas. . . .

17

FREE WILL, MAN, AND HISTORY *
by
JOHN STUART MILL
(1806–1873)

I

OF LIBERTY AND NECESSITY.

§ 1. The question, whether the law of causality applies in the same strict sense to human actions as to other phenomena, is the celebrated controversy concerning the freedom of the will; which, from at least as far back as the time of Pelagius, has divided both the philosophical and religious world. The affirmative opinion is commonly called the doctrine of Necessity, as asserting human volitions and actions to be necessary and inevitable. The negative maintains that the will is not determined, like other phenomena, by antecedents, but determines itself; that our volitions are not, properly speaking, the effects of causes, or at least have no causes which they uniformly and implicitly obey.

. . . The former of these opinions is that which I consider the true one; but the misleading terms in which it is often expressed, and the indistinct manner in which it is usually apprehended, have both obstructed its reception, and perverted its influence when received. The metaphysical theory of free-will, as held by philosophers (for the practical feeling of it, common in a greater or less degree to all mankind, is in no way inconsistent with the contrary theory), was invented because the supposed alternative of admitting human actions to be *necessary* was deemed inconsistent with every one's instinctive consciousness, as well as humiliating to the pride and even degrading to the moral nature of man. Nor do I deny that the doctrine, as sometimes held, is open to these imputations; for the misapprehension in which I shall be able to show that they originate, unfortunately is not confined to the opponents of the doctrine, but is participated in by many, perhaps we might say by most, of its supporters.

* [Virtually all of Chs. 2, 3, and 11 in Bk. VI of *A System of Logic* (1843).]

§ 2. Correctly conceived, the doctrine called Philosophical Necessity is simply this: that, given the motives which are present to an individual's mind, and given likewise the character and disposition of the individual, the manner in which he will act might be unerringly inferred; that if we knew the person thoroughly, and knew all the inducements which are acting upon him, we could foretell his conduct with as much certainty as we can predict any physical event. This proposition I take to be a mere interpretation of universal experience, a statement in words of what every one is internally convinced of. No one who believed that he knew thoroughly the circumstances of any case, and the characters of the different persons concerned, would hesitate to foretell how all of them would act. Whatever degree of doubt he may in fact feel, arises from the uncertainty whether he really knows the circumstances, or the character of some one or other of the persons, with the degree of accuracy required; but by no means from thinking that if he did know these things, there could be any uncertainty what the conduct would be. Nor does this full assurance conflict in the smallest degree with what is called our feeling of freedom. We do not feel ourselves the less free, because those to whom we are intimately known are well assured how we shall will to act in a particular case. We often, on the contrary, regard the doubt what our conduct will be, as a mark of ignorance of our character, and sometimes even resent it as an imputation. The religious metaphysicians who have asserted the freedom of the will, have always maintained it to be consistent with divine foreknowledge of our actions: and if with divine, then with any other foreknowledge. We may be free, and yet another may have reason to be perfectly certain what use we shall make of our freedom. It is not, therefore, the doctrine that our volitions and actions are invariable consequents of our antecedent states of mind, that is either contradicted by our consciousness, or felt to be degrading.

But the doctrine of causation, when considered as obtaining between our volitions and their antecedents, is almost universally conceived as involving more than this. Many do not believe, and very few practically feel, that there is nothing in causation but invariable, certain, and unconditional sequence. There are few to whom mere constancy of succession appears a sufficiently stringent bond of union for so peculiar a relation as that of cause and effect. Even if the reason repudiates, the imagination retains, the feeling of some more intimate connection, of some peculiar tie, or mysterious constraint exercised by the antecedent over the consequent. Now this it is which, considered as applying to the human will, conflicts with our consciousness, and revolts our feelings. We are certain that, in the case of our volitions, there is not this mysterious constraint. We know that we are not compelled, as by a magical spell, to obey any particular motive. We feel, that if we wished to prove that we have the power of resisting the motive, we could do so (that wish being, it needs scarcely be observed, a *new antecedent*); and it would be humiliating to our pride, and (what is of more importance) paralyzing to our desire of excellence, if we thought otherwise. But neither is any such mysterious compulsion now supposed, by the best philosophical authorities, to be exercised by any other cause over its effect. Those who think that causes draw their effects after them by a mystical tie, are right in believing that the relation between volitions and their antecedents is of another nature. But they should go farther, and admit that this is also true of all other effects and their antecedents. If such a tie is considered to be involved in the word Necessity, the doctrine is not true of human actions; but neither is it then true of inanimate objects. It would be more correct to say that matter is not bound by necessity, than that mind is so.

That the free-will metaphysicians, being mostly of the school which rejects Hume's and Brown's analysis of Cause and Effect, should miss their way for want of the light which that analysis affords, can not surprise us. The wonder is, that the necessitarians, who usually admit that philosophical theory, should in practice equally lose sight of it. The very same misconception of the doctrine called Philosophical Necessity, which prevents the opposite party from recognizing its truth, I believe to exist more or less obscurely in the minds of most necessitarians, however they may in words disavow it. I am much mistaken if they habitually feel that the necessity which they recognize in actions is but uniformity of order, and capability of being predicted. They have a feeling as if there were at bottom a stronger tie between the volitions and their causes; as if, when they asserted that the will is governed by the balance of motives, they meant something more cogent than if they had only said, that whoever knew the motives, and our habitual susceptibilities to them, could predict how we should will to act. They commit, in opposition to their own scientific system, the very same mistake which their adversaries commit in obedience to theirs; and in consequence do really in some instances suffer those depressing consequences which their opponents erroneously impute to the doctrine itself.

§ 3. I am inclined to think that this error is almost wholly an effect of the associations with a word, and that it would be prevented, by forbearing to employ, for the expression of the simple fact of causation, so extremely inappropriate a term as Necessity. That word, in its other acceptations, involves much more than mere uniformity of sequence: it implies irresistibleness. Applied to the will, it only means that the given cause will be followed by the effect, subject to all possibilities of counteraction by other causes; but in common use it stands for the operation of those causes exclusively which are supposed too powerful to be counteracted at all. When we say that all human actions take place of necessity, we only mean that they will certainly happen if nothing prevents; when we say that dying of want, to those who can not get food, is a necessity, we mean that it will certainly happen whatever may be done to prevent it. The application of the same term to the agencies on which human actions depend, as is used to express those agencies of nature which are really uncontrollable, can not fail, when habitual, to create a feeling of uncontrollableness in the former also. This, however, is a mere illusion. There are physical sequences which we call necessary, as death for want of food or air; there are others which, though as much cases of causation as the former, are not said to be necessary, as death from poison, which an antidote, or the use of the stomach-pump, will sometimes avert. It is apt to be forgotten by people's feelings, even if remembered by their understandings, that human actions are in this last predicament: they are never (except in some cases of mania) ruled by any one motive with such absolute sway that there is no room for the influence of any other. The causes, therefore, on which action depends, are never uncontrollable; and any given effect is only necessary provided that the causes tending to produce it are not controlled. That whatever happens, could not have happened otherwise, unless something had taken place which was capable of preventing it, no one surely needs hesitate to admit. But to call this by the name Necessity is to use the term in a sense so different from its primitive and familiar meaning, from that which it bears in the common occasions of life, as to amount almost to a play upon words. The associations derived from the ordinary sense of the term will adhere to it in spite of all we can do; and though the doctrine of Necessity, as stated by most who hold it, is very remote from fatalism, it is probable that most necessitarians are fatalists, more or less, in their feelings.

A fatalist believes, or half believes (for nobody is a consistent fatalist), not only that whatever is about to happen will be the infallible result of the causes which produce it (which is the true necessitarian doctrine), but moreover that there is no use in struggling against it; that it will happen, however we may strive to prevent it. Now, a necessitarian, believing that our actions follow from our characters, and that our characters follow from our organization, our education, and our circumstances, is apt to be, with more or less of consciousness on his part, a fatalist as to his own actions, and to believe that his nature is such, or that his education and circumstances have so moulded his character, that nothing can now prevent him from feeling and acting in a particular way, or at least that no effort of his own can hinder it. In the words of the sect which in our own day has most perseveringly inculcated and most perversely misunderstood this great doctrine, his character is formed *for* him, and not *by* him; therefore his wishing that it had been formed differently is of no use; he has no power to alter it. But this is a grand error. He has, to a certain extent, a power to alter his character. Its being, in the ultimate resort, formed for him, is not inconsistent with its being, in part, formed *by* him as one of the intermediate agents. His character is formed by his circumstances (including among these his particular organization); but his own desire to mould it in a particular way, is one of those circumstances, and by no means one of the least influential. We can not, indeed, directly will to be different from what we are. But neither did those who are supposed to have formed our characters directly will that we should be what we are. Their will had no direct power except over their own actions. They made us what they did make us, by willing, not the end, but the requisite means; and we, when our habits are not too inveterate, can, by similarly willing the requisite means, make ourselves different. If they could place us under the influence of certain circumstances, we, in like manner, can place ourselves under the influence of other circumstances. We are exactly as capable of making our own character, *if we will*, as others are of making it for us.

Yes (answers the Owenite), but these words, "if we will," surrender the whole point: since the will to alter our own character is given us, not by any efforts of ours, but by circumstances which we can not help, it comes to us either from external causes, or not at all. Most true: if the Owenite stops here, he is in a position from which nothing can expel him. Our character is formed by us as well as for us; but the wish which induces us to attempt to form it is formed for us; and how? Not, in general, by our organization, nor wholly by our education, but by our experience; experience of the painful consequences of the character we previously had; or by some strong feeling of admiration or aspiration, accidentally aroused. But to think that we have no power of altering our character, and to think that we shall not use our power unless we desire to use it, are very different things, and have a very different effect on the mind. A person who does not wish to alter his character, can not be the person who is supposed to feel discouraged or paralyzed by thinking himself unable to do it. The depressing effect of the fatalist doctrine can only be felt where there *is* a wish to do what that doctrine represents as impossible. It is of no consequence what we think forms our character, when we have no desire of our own about forming it; but it is of great consequence that we should not be prevented from forming such a desire by thinking the attainment impracticable, and that if we have the desire, we should know that the work is not so irrevocably done as to be incapable of being altered.

And indeed, if we examine closely, we shall find that this feeling, of our being able to modify our own character *if we wish,* is itself the feeling of moral freedom which we are conscious of. A person feels morally free who feels that his habits or his temptations are not his masters, but he theirs; who, even in yielding to them, knows that he could resist; that were he desirous of altogether throwing them off, there would not be required for that purpose a stronger desire than he knows himself to be capable of feeling. It is of course necessary, to render our consciousness of freedom complete, that we should have succeeded in making our character all we have hitherto attempted to make it; for if we have wished and not attained, we have, to that extent, not power over our own character; we are not free. Or at least, we must feel that our wish, if not strong enough to alter our character, is strong enough to conquer our character when the two are brought into conflict in any particular case of conduct. And hence it is said with truth, that none but a person of confirmed virtue is completely free.

The application of so improper a term as Necessity to the doctrine of cause and effect in the matter of human character, seems to me one of the most signal instances in philosophy of the abuse of terms, and its practical consequences one of the most striking examples of the power of language over our associations. The subject will never be generally understood until that objectionable term is dropped. The free-will doctrine, by keeping in view precisely that portion of the truth which the word Necessity puts out of sight, namely the power of the mind to co-operate in the formation of its own character, has given to its adherents a practical feeling much nearer to the truth than has generally (I believe) existed in the minds of necessitarians. The latter may have had a stronger sense of the importance of what human beings can do to shape the characters of one another; but the free-will doctrine has, I believe, fostered in its supporters a much stronger spirit of self-culture.

§ 4. There is still one fact which requires to be noticed (in addition to the existence of a power of self-formation) before the doctrine of the causation of human actions can be freed from the confusion and misapprehensions which surround it in many minds.

When the will is said to be determined by motives, a motive does not mean always, or solely, the anticipation of a pleasure or of a pain. I shall not here inquire whether it be true that, in the commencement, all our voluntary actions are mere means consciously employed to obtain some pleasure or avoid some pain. It is at least certain that we gradually, through the influence of association, come to desire the means without thinking of the end; the action itself becomes an object of desire, and is performed without reference to any motive beyond itself. Thus far, it may still be objected that, the action having through association become pleasurable, we are, as much as before, moved to act by the anticipation of a pleasure, namely, the pleasure of the action itself. But granting this, the matter does not end here. As we proceed in the formation of habits, and become accustomed to will a particular act or a particular course of conduct because it is pleasurable, we at last continue to will it without any reference to its being pleasurable. Although, from some change in us or in our circumstances, we have ceased to find any pleasure in the action, or perhaps to anticipate any pleasure as the consequence of it, we still continue to desire the action, and consequently to do it. In this manner it is that habits of hurtful excess continue to be practiced although they have ceased to be pleasurable; and in this manner also it is that the habit of willing to persevere in the course which he has chosen, does not desert the moral hero, even when the reward, however real, which he doubtless receives from the consciousness of well-doing, is any thing but an equivalent for the sufferings he undergoes, or the wishes which he may have to renounce.

A habit of willing is commonly called a purpose; and among the causes of our volitions, and of the actions which flow from them, must be reckoned not only likings and aversions, but also purposes. It is only when our purposes have become independent of the feelings of pain or pleasure from which they originally took their rise, that we are said to have a confirmed character. "A character," says Novalis, "is a completely fashioned will:" and the will, once so fashioned, may be steady and constant, when the passive susceptibilities of pleasure and pain are greatly weakened or materially changed. . . .

II

THAT THERE IS, OR MAY BE, A SCIENCE OF HUMAN NATURE.

§ 1. It is a common notion, or at least it is implied in many common modes of speech, that the thoughts, feelings, and actions of sentient beings are not a subject of science, in the same strict sense in which this is true of the objects of outward nature. This notion seems to involve some confusion of ideas, which it is necessary to begin by clearing up.

Any facts are fitted, in themselves, to be a subject of science which follow one another according to constant laws, although those laws may not have been discovered, nor even be discoverable by our existing resources. Take, for instance, the most familiar class of meteorological phenomena, those of rain and sunshine. Scientific inquiry has not yet succeeded in ascertaining the order of antecedence and consequence among these phenomena, so as to be able, at least in our regions of the earth, to predict them with certainty, or even with any high degree of probability. Yet no one doubts that the phenomena depend on laws, and that these must be derivative laws resulting from known ultimate laws, those of heat, electricity, vaporization, and elastic fluids. Nor can it be doubted that if we were acquainted with all the antecedent circumstances, we could, even from those more general laws, predict (saving difficulties of calculation) the state of the weather at any future time. Meteorology, therefore, not only has in itself every natural requisite for being, but actually is, a science; though, from the difficulty of observing the facts on which the phenomena depend (a difficulty inherent in the peculiar nature of those phenomena), the science is extremely imperfect; and were it perfect, might probably be of little avail in practice, since the data requisite for applying its principles to particular instances would rarely be procurable.

A case may be conceived, of an intermediate character, between the perfection of science and this its extreme imperfection. It may happen that the greater causes, those on which the principal part of the phenomena depends, are within the reach of observation and measurement; so that if no other causes intervened, a complete explanation could be given not only of the phenomena in general, but of all the variations and modifications which it admits of. But inasmuch as other, perhaps many other causes, separately insignificant in their effects, co-operate or conflict in many or in all cases with those greater causes, the effect, accordingly, presents more or less of aberration from what would be produced by the greater causes alone. Now if these minor causes are not so constantly accessible, or not accessible at all, to accurate observation, the principal mass of the effect may still, as before, be accounted for, and even predicted; but there will be variations and modifications which we shall not be competent to explain thoroughly, and our predictions will not be fulfilled accurately, but only approximately.

It is thus, for example, with the theory of the tides. No one doubts that Tidology (as Dr. Whewell proposes to call it) is really a science. As much of the phenomena as depends on the attraction of the sun and moon is completely understood, and may, in any, even unknown, part of the earth's surface, be foretold with certainty; and the far greater part of the phenomena depends on those causes. But circumstances of a local or casual nature, such as the configuration of the bottom of the ocean, the degree of confinement from shores, the direction of the wind, etc., influence, in many or in all places, the height and time of the tide; and a portion of these circumstances being either not accurately knowable, not precisely measurable, or not capable of being certainly foreseen, the tide in known places commonly varies from the calculated result of general principles by some difference that we can not explain, and in unknown ones may vary from it by a difference that we are not able to foresee or conjecture. Nevertheless, not only is it certain that these variations depend on causes, and follow their causes by laws of unerring uniformity; not only, therefore, is tidology a science, like meteorology, but it is, what hitherto at least meteorology is not, a science largely available in practice. General laws may be laid down respecting the tides, predictions may be founded on those laws, and the result will in the main, though often not with complete accuracy, correspond to the predictions.

And this is what is or ought to be meant by those who speak of sciences which are not *exact* sciences. Astronomy was once a science, without being an exact science. It could not become exact until not only the general course of the planetary motions, but the perturbations also, were accounted for, and referred to their causes. It has become an exact science, because its phenomena have been brought under laws comprehending the whole of the causes by which the phenomena are influenced, whether in a great or only in a trifling degree, whether in all or only in some cases, and assigning to each of those causes the share of effect which really belongs to it. But in the theory of the tides the only laws as yet accurately ascertained are those of the causes which affect the phenomenon in all cases, and in a considerable degree; while others which affect it in some cases only, or, if in all, only in a slight degree, have not been sufficiently ascertained and studied to enable us to lay down their laws; still less to deduce the completed law of the phenomenon, by compounding the effects of the greater with those of the minor causes. Tidology, therefore, is not yet an exact science; not from any inherent incapacity of being so, but from the difficulty of ascertaining with complete precision the real derivative uniformities. By combining, however, the exact laws of the greater causes, and of such of the minor ones as are sufficiently known, with such empirical laws or

such approximate generalizations respecting the miscellaneous variations as can be obtained by specific observation, we can lay down
general propositions which will be true in the main, and on which,
with allowance for the degree of their probable inaccuracy, we may
safely ground our expectations and our conduct.

§ 2. The science of human nature is of this description. It falls
far short of the standard of exactness now realized in Astronomy;
but there is no reason that it should not be as much a science as
Tidology is, or as Astronomy was when its calculations had only
mastered the main phenomena, but not the perturbations.

The phenomena with which this science is conversant being the
thoughts, feelings, and actions of human beings, it would have
attained the ideal perfection of a science if it enabled us to foretell how an individual would think, feel, or act throughout life,
with the same certainty with which astronomy enables us to predict
the places and the occultations of the heavenly bodies. It need
scarcely be stated that nothing approaching to this can be done.
The actions of individuals could not be predicted with scientific accuracy, were it only because we can not foresee the whole of the
circumstances in which those individuals will be placed. But
further, even in any given combination of (present) circumstances,
no assertion, which is both precise and universally true, can be
made respecting the manner in which human beings will think,
feel, or act. This is not, however, because every person's modes of
thinking, feeling, and acting do not depend on causes; nor can we
doubt that if, in the case of any individual, our data could be
complete, we even now know enough of the ultimate laws by which
mental phenomena are determined, to enable us in many cases to
predict, with tolerable certainty, what, in the greater number of
supposable combinations of circumstances, his conduct or sentiments would be. But the impressions and actions of human beings
are not solely the result of their present circumstances, but the
joint result of those circumstances and of the characters of the individuals; and the agencies which determine human character are
so numerous and diversified (nothing which has happened to the
person throughout life being without its portion of influence), that
in the aggregate they are never in any two cases exactly similar.
Hence, even if our science of human nature were theoretically
perfect, that is, if we could calculate any character as we can
calculate the orbit of any planet, *from given data;* still, as the data
are never all given, nor ever precisely alike in different cases, we
could neither make positive predictions, nor lay down universal
propositions.

Inasmuch, however, as many of those effects which it is of most importance to render amenable to human foresight and control are determined, like the tides, in an incomparably greater degree by general causes, than by all partial causes taken together; depending in the main on those circumstances and qualities which are common to all mankind, or at least to large bodies of them, and only in a small degree on the idiosyncrasies of organization or the peculiar history of individuals; it is evidently possible with regard to all such effects, to make predictions which will *almost* always be verified, and general propositions which are almost always true. And whenever it is sufficient to know how the great majority of the human race, or of some nation or class of persons, will think, feel, and act, these propositions are equivalent to universal ones. For the purposes of political and social science this *is* sufficient. As we [elsewhere] remarked, an approximate generalization is, in social inquiries, for most practical purposes equivalent to an exact one; that which is only probable when asserted of individual human beings indiscriminately selected, being certain when affirmed of the character and collective conduct of masses.

It is no disparagement, therefore, to the science of Human Nature, that those of its general propositions which descend sufficiently into detail to serve as a foundation for predicting phenomena in the concrete, are for the most part only approximately true. But in order to give a genuinely scientific character to the study, it is indispensable that these approximate generalizations, which in themselves would amount only to the lowest kind of empirical laws, should be connected deductively with the laws of nature from which they result; should be resolved into the properties of the causes on which the phenomena depend. In other words, the science of Human Nature may be said to exist in proportion as the approximate truths, which compose a practical knowledge of mankind, can be exhibited as corollaries from the universal laws of human nature on which they rest; whereby the proper limits of those approximate truths would be shown, and we should be enabled to deduce others for any new state of circumstances, in anticipation of specific experience. . . .

III

. . . OF THE SCIENCE OF HISTORY.

§ 1. . . . Among the impediments to the general acknowledgment, by thoughtful minds, of the subjection of historical facts to scientific laws, the most fundamental continues to be that which is grounded on the doctrine of Free Will, or, in other words, on the denial that the law of invariable Causation holds true of human volitions; for if it does not, the course of history, being the result of human volitions, can not be a subject of scientific laws, since the volitions on which it depends can neither be foreseen, nor reduced to any canon of regularity even after they have occurred. I have discussed this question, as far as seemed suitable to the occasion, in a former chapter; and I only think it necessary to repeat, that the doctrine of the Causation of human actions, improperly called the doctrine of Necessity, affirms no mysterious *nexus,* or overruling fatality: it asserts only that men's actions are the joint result of the general laws and circumstances of human nature, and of their own particular characters; those characters again being the consequence of the natural and artificial circumstances that constituted their education, among which circumstances must be reckoned their own conscious efforts. Any one who is willing to take (if the expression may be permitted) the trouble of thinking himself into the doctrine as thus stated, will find it, I believe, not only a faithful interpretation of the universal experience of human conduct, but a correct representation of the mode in which he himself, in every particular case, spontaneously interprets his own experience of that conduct.

But if this principle is true of individual man, it must be true of collective man. If it is the law of human life, the law must be realized in history. The experience of human affairs when looked at *en masse,* must be in accordance with it if true, or repugnant to it if false. The support which this *a posteriori* verification affords to the law, is the part of the case which has been most clearly and triumphantly brought out by Mr. Buckle.

The facts of statistics, since they have been made a subject of careful recordation and study, have yielded conclusions, some of which have been very startling to persons not accustomed to regard moral actions as subject to uniform laws. The very events which in their own nature appear most capricious and uncertain, and which in any individual case no attainable degree of knowledge would enable us to foresee, occur, when considerable numbers are taken into the account, with a degree of regularity approaching to mathematical. What act is there which all would consider as more completely dependent on individual character, and on the exercise of individual free will, than that of slaying a fellow-creature? Yet in any large country, the number of murders, in proportion to the population, varies (it has been found) very little from one year to another, and in its variations never deviates widely from a certain average. What is still more remarkable, there is a similar approach to constancy in the proportion of these murders annually committed with every particular kind of instrument. There is a like approximation to identity, as between one year and another, in the comparative number of legitimate and of illegitimate births. The same thing is found true of suicides, accidents, and all other social phenomena of which the registration is sufficiently perfect; one of the most curiously illustrative examples being the fact, ascertained by the registers of the London and Paris post-offices, that the number of letters posted which the writers have forgotten to direct, is nearly the same, in proportion to the whole number of letters posted, in one year as in another. "Year after year," says Mr. Buckle, "the same proportion of letter-writers forget this simple act; so that for each successive period we can actually foretell the number of persons whose memory will fail them in regard to this trifling, and as it might appear, accidental occurrence."

This singular degree of regularity *en masse*, combined with the extreme of irregularity in the cases composing the mass, is a felicitous verification *a posteriori* of the law of causation in its application to human conduct. Assuming the truth of that law, every human action, every murder, for instance, is the concurrent result of two sets of causes. On the one part, the general circumstances of the country and its inhabitants; the moral, educational, economical, and other influences operating on the whole people, and constituting what we term the state of civilization. On the other part, the great variety of influences special to the individual: his temperament, and other peculiarities of organization, his parentage, habitual associates, temptations, and so forth. If we now take the whole of the instances which occur within a sufficiently large field to exhaust all the combinations of these special influences, or, in other words, to eliminate chance; and if all these instances have occurred within such narrow limits of time, that no material change can have taken place in the general influences constituting the state of civilization of the country; we may be certain, that if human actions are governed by invariable laws, the aggregate result will be something like a constant quantity. The number of murders committed within that space and time, being the effect partly of general causes which have not varied, and partly of partial causes the whole round of whose variations has been included, will be, practically speaking, invariable.

Literally and mathematically invariable it is not, and could not be expected to be: because the period of a year is too short to include *all* the possible combinations of partial causes, while it is, at the same time, sufficiently long to make it probable that in some years at least, of every series, there will have been introduced new influences of a more or less general character; such as a more vigorous or a more relaxed police; some temporary excitement from political or religious causes; or some incident generally notorious, of a nature to act morbidly on the imagination. That in spite of these unavoidable imperfections in the data, there should be so very trifling a margin of variation in the annual results, is a brilliant confirmation of the general theory.

§ 2. The same considerations which thus strikingly corroborate the evidence of the doctrine, that historical facts are the invariable effects of causes, tend equally to clear that doctrine from various misapprehensions, the existence of which has been put in evidence by the recent discussions. Some persons, for instance, seemingly imagine the doctrine to imply, not merely that the total number of murders committed in a given space and time is entirely the effect of the general circumstances of society, but that every particular murder is so too—that the individual murderer is, so to speak, a mere instrument in the hands of general causes; that he himself has no option, or, if he has, and chose to exercise it, some one else would be necessitated to take his place; that if any one of the actual murderers had abstained from the crime, some person who would otherwise have remained innocent, would have committed an extra murder to make up the average. Such a corollary would certainly convict any theory which necessarily led to it of absurdity. It is obvious, however, that each particular murder depends, not on the general state of society only, but on that combined with causes special to the case, which are generally much more powerful; and if these special causes, which have greater influence than the general ones in causing every particular murder, have no influence on the number of murders in a given period, it is because the field of observation is so extensive as to include all possible combinations of the special causes—all varieties of individual character and individual temptation compatible with the general state of society. The collective experiment, as it may be termed, exactly separates the effect of the general from that of the special causes, and shows the net result of the former; but it declares nothing at all respecting the amount of influence of the special causes, be it greater or smaller, since the scale of the experiment extends to the number of cases within which the effects of the special causes balance one another, and disappear in that of the general causes.

I will not pretend that all the defenders of the theory have always kept their language free from this same confusion, and have shown no tendency to exalt the influence of general causes at the expense of special. I am of opinion, on the contrary, that they have done so in a very great degree, and by so doing have encumbered their theory with difficulties, and laid it open to objections, which do not necessarily affect it. Some, for example (among whom is Mr. Buckle himself), have inferred, or allowed it to be supposed that they inferred, from the regularity in the recurrence of events which depend on moral qualities, that the moral qualities of mankind are little capable of being improved, or are of little importance in the general progress of society, compared with intellectual or economic causes. But to draw this inference is to forget that the statistical tables, from which the invariable averages are deduced, were compiled from facts occurring within narrow geographical limits and in a small number of successive years; that is, from a field the whole of which was under the operation of the same general causes, and during too short a time to allow of much change therein. All moral causes but those common to the country generally, have been eliminated by the great number of instances taken; and those which are common to the whole country have not varied considerably, in the short space of time comprised in the observations. If we admit the supposition that they have varied; if we compare one age with another, or one country with another, or even one part of a country with another, differing in position and character as to the moral elements, the crimes committed within a year give no longer the same, but a widely different numerical aggregate. And this can not but be the case: for, inasmuch as every single crime committed by an individual mainly depends on his moral qualities, the crimes committed by the entire population of the country must depend in an equal degree on their collective moral qualities. To render this element inoperative upon the large scale, it would be necessary to suppose that the general moral average of mankind does not vary from country to country or from age to age; which is not true, and, even if it were true, could not possibly be proved by any existing statistics. I do not on this account the less agree in the opinion of Mr. Buckle, that the intellectual element in mankind, including in that expression the nature of their beliefs, the amount of their knowledge, and the development of their intelligence, is the predominant circumstance in determining their progress. But I am of this opinion, not because I regard their moral or economical condition either as less powerful or less variable agencies, but because these are in a great degree the consequences of the intellectual condition, and are, in all cases, limited by it. . . . The intellectual changes are the most conspicuous agents in history, not from their superior force, considered in themselves, but because practically they work with the united power belonging to all three.

§ 3. There is another distinction often neglected in the discussion of this subject, which it is extremely important to observe. The theory of the subjection of social progress to invariable laws, is often held in conjunction with the doctrine, that social progress can not be materially influenced by the exertions of individual persons, or by the acts of governments. But though these opinions are often held by the same persons, they are two very different opinions, and the confusion between them is the eternally recurring error of confounding Causation with Fatalism. Because whatever happens will be the effect of causes, human volitions among the rest, it does not follow that volitions, even those of peculiar individuals, are not of great efficacy as causes. If any one in a storm at sea, because about the same number of persons in every year perish by shipwreck, should conclude that it was useless for him to attempt to save his own life, we should call him a Fatalist; and should remind him that the efforts of shipwrecked persons to save their lives are so far from being immaterial, that the average amount of those efforts is one of the causes on which the ascertained annual number of deaths by shipwreck depend. However universal the laws of social development may be, they can not be more universal or more rigorous than those of the physical agencies of nature; yet human will can convert these into instruments of its designs, and the extent to which it does so makes the chief difference between savages and the most highly civilized people. Human and social facts, from their more complicated nature, are not less, but more, modifiable than mechanical and chemical facts; human agency, therefore, has still greater power over them. And accordingly, those who maintain that the evolution of society depends exclusively, or almost exclusively, on general causes, always include among these the collective knowledge and intellectual development of the race. But if of the race, why not also of some powerful monarch or thinker, or of the ruling portion of some political society, acting through its government? Though the varieties of character among ordinary individuals neutralize one another on any large scale, exceptional individuals in important positions do not in any given age neutralize one another; there was not another Themistocles, or Luther, or Julius Cæsar, of equal powers and contrary dispositions, who exactly balanced the given Themistocles, Luther, and Cæsar, and prevented them from having any permanent effect. Moreover, for aught that appears, the volitions of exceptional persons, or the opinions and purposes of the individuals who at some particular time compose a government, may be indispensable links in the chain of causation by which even the general causes produce their effects; and I believe this to be the only tenable form of the theory.

Lord Macaulay, in a celebrated passage of one of his early essays (let me add that it was one which he did not himself choose to reprint), gives expression to the doctrine of the absolute inoperative-ness of great men, more unqualified, I should think, than has been given to it by any writer of equal abilities. He compares them to persons who merely stand on a loftier height, and thence receive the sun's rays a little earlier, than the rest of the human race. "The sun illuminates the hills while it is still below the horizon, and truth is discovered by the highest minds a little before it becomes manifest to the multitude. This is the extent of their superiority. They are the first to catch and reflect a light which, without their assistance, must in a short time be visible to those who lie far beneath them." If this metaphor is to be carried out, it follows that if there had been no Newton, the world would not only have had the Newtonian system, but would have had it equally soon; as the sun would have risen just as early to spectators in the plain if there had been no mountain at hand to catch still earlier rays. And so it would be, if truths, like the sun, rose by their own proper motion, without human effort; but not otherwise. I believe that if Newton had not lived, the world must have waited for the Newtonian philosophy until there had been another Newton, or his equivalent. No ordinary man, and no succession of ordinary men, could have achieved it. I will not go the length of saying that what Newton did in a single life, might not have been done in successive steps by some of those who followed him, each singly inferior to him in genius. But even the least of those steps required a man of great intellectual superiority. Eminent men do not merely see the coming light from the hill-top, they mount on the hill-top and evoke it; and if no one had ever ascended thither, the light, in many cases, might never have risen upon the plain at all. Philosophy and religion are abundantly amenable to general causes; yet few will doubt that, had there been no Socrates, no Plato, and no Aristotle, there would have been no philosophy for the next two thousand years, nor in all probability then; and that if there had been no Christ, and no St. Paul, there would have been no Christianity.

The point in which, above all, the influence of remarkable individuals is decisive, is in determining the celerity of the movement. In most states of society it is the existence of great men which decides even whether there shall be any progress. It is conceivable that Greece, or that Christian Europe, might have been progressive in certain periods of their history through general causes only: but if there had been no Mohammed, would Arabia have produced Avicenna or Averroes, or Caliphs of Bagdad or of Cordova? In determining, however, in what manner and order the progress of mankind shall take place if it take place at all, much less depends on the character of individuals. There is a sort of necessity established in this respect by the general laws of human nature—by the constitution of the human mind. Certain truths can not be discovered, nor inventions made, unless certain others have been made first; certain social improvements, from the nature of the case, can only follow, and not precede, others. The order of human progress, therefore, may to a certain extent have definite laws assigned to it: while as to its celerity, or even as to its taking place at all, no generalization, extending to the human species generally, can possibly be made; but only some very precarious approximate generalizations, confined to the small portion of mankind in whom there has been any thing like consecutive progress within the historical period, and deduced from their special position, or collected from their particular history. Even looking to the *manner* of progress, the order of succession of social states, there is need of great flexibility in our generalizations. The limits of variation in the possible development of social, as of animal life, are a subject of which little is yet understood, and are one of the great problems in social science. It is, at all events, a fact, that different portions of mankind, under the influence of different circumstances, have developed themselves in a more or less different manner and into different forms; and among these determining circumstances, the individual character of their great speculative thinkers or practical organizers may well have been one. Who can tell how profoundly the whole subsequent history of China may have been influenced by the individuality of Confucius? and of Sparta (and hence of Greece and the world) by that of Lycurgus?

Concerning the nature and extent of what a great man under favorable circumstances can do for mankind, as well as of what a government can do for a nation, many different opinions are possible; and every shade of opinion on these points is consistent with the fullest recognition that there are invariable laws of historical phenomena. Of course the degree of influence which has to be assigned to these more special agencies, makes a great difference in the precision which can be given to the general laws, and in the confidence with which predictions can be grounded on them. Whatever depends on the peculiarities of individuals, combined with the accident of the positions they hold, is necessarily incapable of being foreseen. Undoubtedly these casual combinations might be eliminated like any others, by taking a sufficiently large cycle: the peculiarities of a great historical character make their influence felt in history sometimes for several thousand years, but it is highly probable that they will make no difference at all at the end of fifty millions. Since, however, we can not obtain an average of the vast length of time necessary to exhaust all the possible combinations of great men and circumstances, as much of the law of evolution of human affairs as depends upon this average, is and remains inaccessible to us; and within the next thousand years, which are of considerably more importance to us than the whole remainder of the fifty millions, the favorable and unfavorable combinations which will occur will be to us purely accidental. We can not foresee the advent of great men. Those who introduce new speculative thoughts or great practical conceptions into the world, can not have their epoch fixed beforehand. What science can do, is this. It can trace through past history the general causes which had brought mankind into that preliminary state which, when the right sort of great man appeared, rendered them accessible to his influence. If this state continues, experience renders it tolerably certain that in a longer or shorter period the great man will be produced; provided that the general circumstances of the country and people are (which very often they are not) compatible with his existence; of which point also, science can in some measure judge. It is in this manner that the results of progress, except as to the celerity of their production, can be, to a certain extent, reduced to regularity and law. And the belief that they can be so, is equally consistent with assigning very great, or very little efficacy, to the influence of exceptional men, or of the acts of governments. And the same may be said of all other accidents and disturbing causes.

§ 4. It would nevertheless be a great error to assign only a trifling importance to the agency of eminent individuals, or of governments. It must not be concluded that the influence of either is small, because they can not bestow what the general circumstances of society, and the course of its previous history, have not prepared it to receive. Neither thinkers nor governments effect all that they intend, but in compensation they often produce important results which they did not in the least foresee. Great men, and great actions, are seldom wasted; they send forth a thousand unseen influences, more effective than those which are seen; and though nine out of every ten things done, with a good purpose, by those who are in advance of their age, produce no material effect, the tenth thing produces effects twenty times as great as any one would have dreamed of predicting from it. Even the men who for want of sufficiently favorable circumstances left no impress at all upon their own age, have often been of the greatest value to posterity. Who could appear to have lived more entirely in vain than some of the early heretics? They were burned or massacred, their writings extirpated, their memory anathematized, and their very names and existence left for seven or eight centuries in the obscurity of musty manuscripts—their history to be gathered, perhaps, only from the sentences by which they were condemned. Yet the memory of these men—men who resisted certain pretensions or certain dogmas of the Church in the very age in which the unanimous assent of Christendom was afterward claimed as having been given to them, and asserted as the ground of their authority—broke the chain of tradition, established a series of precedents for resistance, inspired later Reformers with the courage, and armed them with the weapons, which they needed when mankind were better prepared to follow their impulse. To this example from men, let us add another from governments. The comparatively enlightened rule of which Spain had the benefit during a considerable part of the eighteenth century, did not correct the fundamental defects of the Spanish people; and in consequence, though it did great temporary good, so much of that good perished with it, that it may plausibly be affirmed to have had no permanent effect. The case has been cited as a proof how little governments can do in opposition to the causes which have determined the general character of the nation. It does show how much there is which they can not do; but not that they can do nothing. Compare what Spain was at the beginning of that half-century of liberal government, with what she had become at its close. That period fairly let in the light of European thought upon the more educated classes; and it never afterward ceased to go on spreading. Previous to that time the change was in an inverse direction; culture, light, intellectual and even material activity, were becoming extinguished. Was it nothing to arrest this downward and convert it into an upward course? How much that Charles the Third and Aranda could not do, has been the ultimate consequence of what they did! To that half-century Spain owes that she has got rid of the Inquisition, that she has got rid of the monks, that she now has parliaments and (save in exceptional intervals) a free press, and the feelings of freedom and citizenship, and is acquiring railroads and all the other constituents of material and economical progress. In the Spain which preceded that era, there was not a single element at work which could have led to these results in any length of time, if the country had continued to be governed as it was by the last princes of the Austrian dynasty, or if the Bourbon rulers had been from the first what, both in Spain and in Naples, they afterward became.

And if a government can do much, even when it seems to have done little, in causing positive improvement, still greater are the issues dependent on it in the way of warding off evils, both internal and external, which else would stop improvement altogether. A good or a bad counselor, in a single city at a particular crisis, has affected the whole subsequent fate of the world. It is as certain as any contingent judgment respecting historical events can be, that if there had been no Themistocles there would have been no victory of Salamis; and had there not, where would have been all our civilization? How different, again, would have been the issue if Epaminondas, or Timoleon, or even Iphicrates, instead of Chares and Lysicles, had commanded at Chæroneia. As is well said in the second of two Essays on the Study of History, in my judgment the soundest and most philosophical productions which the recent controversies on this subject have called forth, historical science authorizes not absolute, but only conditional predictions. General causes count for much, but individuals also "produce great changes in history, and color its whole complexion long after their death. . . . No one can doubt that the Roman republic would have subsided into a military despotism if Julius Cæsar had never lived" (thus much was rendered practically certain by general causes); "but is it at all clear that in that case Gaul would ever have formed a province of the empire? Might not Varus have lost his three legions on the banks of the Rhone? and might not that river have become the frontier instead of the Rhine? This might well have happened if Cæsar and Crassus had changed provinces; and it is surely impossible to say that in such an event the venue (as lawyers say) of European civilization might not have been changed. The Norman Conquest in the same way was as much the act of a single man, as the writing of a newspaper article; and knowing as we do the history of that man and his family, we can retrospectively predict with all but infallible certainty, that no other person" (no other in that age, I presume, is meant) "could have accomplished the enterprise. If it had not been accomplished, is there any ground to suppose that either our history or our national character would have been what they are?"

As is most truly remarked by the same writer, the whole stream of Grecian history, as cleared up by Mr. Grote, is one series of examples how often events on which the whole destiny of subsequent civilization turned, were dependent on the personal character for good or evil of some one individual. It must be said, however, that Greece furnishes the most extreme example of this nature to be found in history, and is a very exaggerated specimen of the general tendency. It has happened only that once, and will probably never happen again, that the fortunes of mankind depended upon keeping a certain order of things in existence in a single town, or a country scarcely larger than Yorkshire; capable of being ruined or saved by a hundred causes, of very slight magnitude in comparison with the general tendencies of human affairs. Neither ordinary accidents, nor the characters of individuals, can ever again be so vitally important as they then were. The longer our species lasts, and the more civilized it becomes, the more, as Comte remarks, does the influence of past generations over the present, and of mankind *en masse* over every individual in it, predominate over other forces; and though the course of affairs never ceases to be susceptible of alteration both by accidents and by personal qualities, the increasing preponderance of the collective agency of the species over all minor causes, is constantly bringing the general evolution of the race into something which deviates less from a certain and preappointed track. Historical science, therefore, is always becoming more possible; not solely because it is better studied, but because, in every generation, it becomes better adapted for study.

PART TWO

Emphasis on

THE DEVELOPMENT
OF PHILOSOPHIC PERSPECTIVE

18

THE STATE *

by

ARISTOTLE

(B.C. 384–322)

. . . As the State was formed to make life possible, so it exists to make life good. Consequently if it be allowed that the simple associations, i.e. the household and the village, have a natural existence, so has the State in all cases; for in the State they attain complete development, and Nature implies complete development, as the nature of anything, e.g., of a man, a house or a horse, may be defined to be its condition when the process of production is complete. Or the naturalness of the State may be proved in another way: the object proposed or the complete development of a thing is its highest Good; but independence which is first attained in the State is a complete development or the highest Good and is therefore natural.

Thus we see that the State is a natural institution, that Man is naturally a political animal and that one who is not a citizen of any State, if the cause of his isolation be natural and not accidental, is either a superhuman being or low in the scale of civilization, as he stands alone like a "blot" on the backgammon board. The "clanless, lawless, hearthless" man so bitterly described by Homer is a case in point; for he is naturally a citizen of no state and a lover of war. Also that Man is a political animal in a higher sense than a bee or any other gregarious creature is evident from the fact that Nature, as we are fond of asserting, creates nothing without a purpose and Man is the only animal endowed with speech. Now mere sounds serve to indicate sensations of pain and pleasure and are therefore assigned to other animals as well as to Man; for their nature does not advance beyond the point of perceiving pain and

* [From Bk. I, Ch. 2 and Bk. III, Chs. 9, 11 in J. E. C. Welldon's translation (1883) of the *Politics*.]

245

pleasure and signifying these perceptions to one another. The object of speech on the other hand is to indicate advantage and disadvantage and therefore also justice and injustice. For it is a special characteristic which distinguishes Man from all other animals that he alone enjoys perception of good and evil, justice and injustice and the like. But these are the principles of that association which constitutes a household or a State.

Again, in the order of Nature the State is prior to the household or the individual. For the whole must needs be prior to its part. For instance, if you take away the body which is the whole, there will not remain any such thing as a foot or a hand, unless we use the same word in a different sense as when we speak of a stone hand as a hand. For a hand separated from the body will be a disabled hand; whereas it is the function or faculty of a thing which makes it what it is, and therefore when things lose their function or faculty it is not correct to call them the same things but rather homonymous, i.e. different things having the same name.

We see then that the State is a natural institution, and also that it is prior to the individual. For if the individual as a separate unit is not independent, he must be a part and must bear the same relation to the State as other parts to their wholes; and one who is incapable of association with others or is independent and has no need of such association is no member of a State, in other words he is either a brute or a God. Now the impulse to political association is innate in all men. Nevertheless the author of the first combination whoever he was was a great benefactor of human kind. For man, as in his condition of complete development, i.e. in the State, he is the noblest of all animals, so apart from law and justice he is the vilest of all. For injustice is always most formidable when it is armed; and Nature has endowed Man with arms which are intended to subserve the purposes of prudence and virtue but are capable of being wholly turned to contrary ends. Hence if Man be devoid of virtue, no animal is so unscrupulous or savage, none so sensual, none so gluttonous. Just action on the other hand is bound up with the existence of a State; for the administration of justice is an ordinance of the political association and the administration of justice is nothing else than the decision of what is just. . . .

. . . Oligarchs and Democrats agree in this, that they both adhere to a certain principle of justice; but they do not advance beyond a certain point or put forward a full statement of justice in the proper sense of the word. Thus the one party, i.e. the Democrats, hold that justice is equality; and so it is, but not for all the world but only for equals. The others, i.e. the Oligarchs, hold that inequality is just, as indeed it is, but not for all the world but only for unequals. Both put out of sight one side of the relation, viz. the persons who are to enjoy the equality or inequality, and consequently form a wrong judgment. The reason is that they are judging of matters which affect themselves, and we are all sorry judges when our personal interests are at stake. And thus whereas justice is a relative term and, as has been already stated in the Ethics, implies that the ratio of distribution is constant in respect of the things distributed and the persons who receive them, the two parties, while they are of one mind about the equality of the thing, differ as to what constitutes equality in the recipients, principally for the reason just alleged, viz. that they are bad judges where their own interests are concerned, but secondly also because the fact that each maintains a certain principle of justice up to a certain point is one which itself leads them to suppose that they are maintaining a principle of justice in the absolute sense. For the Oligarchs, if they are superior in a particular point, viz. in money, assume themselves to be superior altogether; while the Democrats, if they are equal in a particular point, viz. in personal liberty, assume themselves to be equal altogether. But they omit the point of capital importance. If a multitude of possessions was the sole object of their association or union, then their share in the State is proportionate to their share in the property, and in this case there would seem to be no resisting the argument of the oligarchical party that, where there is, e.g., a capital of one hundred minae, the contributor of a single mina ought not in justice to enjoy the same share either of the principal or of the profits accruing as a person who has given the remaining ninety-nine. But the truth is that the object of their association is to live well—not merely to live; otherwise slaves and the lower animals might form a State, whereas this is in fact impossible, as they are incapable of happiness or of a life regulated by a definite moral purpose, i.e. of the conditions necessary to a State. Nor is the object military alliance and security against injury from any quarter. Nor again is the end proposed barter and intercommunion; for, if it were, the Tyrrhenians and Carthaginians and all such nations as are connected by commercial treaties might be regarded as citizens of a single State. Among them there certainly exist contracts in regard to Customs, covenants against mutual injury and formal articles of alliance. But there are no magistracies common to all the contracting parties instituted to secure these objects, but different magistracies exist in each of the States; nor do the members of the one feel any concern about the right character of members of the other or about the means of preserving all who come under the treaties from being unjust and harbouring any kind of wickedness or indeed about any point whatever, except the prevention of mutually injurious actions. Virtue and vice on the other hand are matters of earnest consideration to all whose hearts are set upon good and orderly government. And from this fact it is evident that a State which is not merely nominally but in the true sense of the word a State should devote its attention to virtue. To neglect virtue is to convert the political association into an alliance differing in nothing except in the local contiguity of its members from the alliances formed between distant States, to convert the law into a mere covenant, or, as the sophist Lycophron said, a mere surety for the mutual respect of rights, without any qualification for producing goodness or justice in the citizens. But it is clear that this is the true view of the State, *i.e. that it promotes the virtue of its citizens*. For if one were to combine different localities in one, so that e.g. the walls of Megara and Corinth were contiguous, yet the result would not be a single State. Nor again does the practice of intermarriage necessarily imply a single State, although intermarriage is one of the forms of association which are especially characteristic of States. So too if we suppose the case of certain persons living separately, although not so far apart as to prevent association, but under laws prohibitive of mutual injury in the exchange of goods, if we suppose e.g. A to be a carpenter, B a husbandman, C a cobbler, D something else, and the total to amount to ten thousand, but their association to be absolutely confined to such things as barter and military alliance, here again there would certainly not be a State. What then is the reason? It is assuredly not the absence of local contiguity in the association. For suppose the members were actually to form a union upon such terms of association as we have described, suppose at the same time that each individual were to use his own household as a separate State, and their intercourse were limited as under the conditions of a defensive alliance to rendering mutual assistance against aggression, still the conception of a State in the strict view would not even then be realized, if their manner of social dealings after the union were to be precisely the same as when they lived apart.

It is clear then that the State is not merely a local association or an association existing to prevent mutual injury and to promote commercial exchange. So far is this from being the case that, although these are indispensable conditions, if a State is to exist, yet all these conditions do not necessarily imply a State. A State on the contrary is first realized when there is an association of households and families in well living with a view to a complete and independent existence. (This will not be the case, however, unless the members inhabit one and the same locality and have the practice of intermarriage.) It is for this reason that there were established in the different States matrimonial connexions, clanships, common sacrifices and such amusements as promote a common life. But all this is the work of friendship, for the choice of a common life implies no more than friendship. And thus while the end of a State is living well, these are only means to the end. A State on the contrary is the association of families and villages in a complete and independent existence or in other words, according to our definition, in a life of felicity and nobleness. We must assume then that the object of the political association is not merely a common life but noble action. And from this it follows that they who contribute most to the association, as so conceived, possess a larger interest in the State than they who are equal or superior in personal liberty or birth but inferior in political virtue, or than they who have the superiority in wealth but the inferiority in virtue.

. . . The theory that supreme power should be vested in the masses rather than in a few persons, although they are the best, is one which would seem to be refuted by the remarks we have made; and indeed there is a certain difficulty involved in it, although there is probably also a certain degree of truth. For it is possible that the Many, of whom each individual is not a virtuous man, are still collectively superior to the few best persons, i.e. superior not as individuals but as a body, as picnics are superior to feasts supplied at the expense of a single person. For as the total number is large, it is possible that each has a fractional share of virtue and prudence and that, as the multitude collectively may be compared to an individual with many feet, hands and senses, so the same is true of their character and intelligence. It is thus that the Many are better judges than the Few even of musical and poetical compositions; for some judge one part, some another, and all of them collectively the whole. But the point in which virtuous men are superior to any ordinary persons is the same in which handsome people, it is said, are superior to those who are not handsome and the representations of art to the realities, viz. that the features which in real life are distributed among a number of objects are in the works of art collected into one; for, if we take each feature by itself, the eye of one living person and another part of another are more beautiful than those in the painting. Whether the superiority of the Many to the few virtuous persons is possible, whatever be the character of the commons or the masses, is uncertain, or perhaps in some cases it is plainly impossible. For the same line of argument would be equally applicable to the lower animals. It would be absurd however to pretend that a number of the lower animals are superior to a few men; yet there are human beings who may be described as not appreciably superior to the lower animals. At the same time there do exist masses of people in whose case our theory is open to no objection.

These considerations then supply us with an answer to the question which was raised before, viz. what ought to be the supreme authority in the State, as well as to one closely connected with it, viz. what should be the limits set to the authority of the free citizens or the masses, i.e. of all who are not wealthy and do not enjoy any especial reputation for virtue? There is a certain danger in their eligibility to the highest offices of State, a danger that injustice on the one hand will lead them into crime, and folly on the other hand into error; whereas their exclusion in theory and practice from all office is a condition of things which may well inspire alarm, as there never exists a large body of persons excluded from all honours or of poor, but the State of which they are members is sure to have a large number of enemies within its pale. It remains then that they should participate in deliberative and judicial functions. It is in accordance with this view that various law-givers, and Solon among the number, empower the commons to elect officers of State and to hold them responsible, but deny them all individual tenure of office. For in their collective capacity they possess an adequate perceptive power and by admixture with their superiors subserve the interests of the State, in the same way as adulterated food if mixed with unadulterated makes the whole more nutritious than the small amount of unadulterated food would have been, although individually each has but an imperfect faculty of judgment.

There are however difficulties incident to this system of polity; first, that the faculty of judging, e.g. who has adopted a right course of medical treatment, would seem to belong exclusively to the person who is also capable of treating the patient medically and restoring him from his actual malady to health, in other words to the physician. The same is true of any other art empirical or scientific. It may be argued then that, as a physician should be responsible to physicians, so should any other class of persons be responsible to their peers. The answer is that the word "physician" may mean either the ordinary medical practitioner or the scientific student of medicine, or, thirdly, one who has just mastered the principles of the art; there is hardly any art in which we do not find persons answering to these three classes, and the right of judgment is assigned as much to those who have merely mastered the principles as to those who possess a scientific knowledge of the subject. And secondly the same appears to be the case in regard to the election of officers. The right exercise of the elective power, it may be urged, as well as of the power of scrutiny is the function exclusively of those who are masters of the science. Thus a geometrician or a pilot ought to be elected solely by persons who understand geometry or navigation. Even granted that there are some occupations and arts in which certain non-professional persons have a vote in the election, they certainly do not exercise a greater influence than the experts. According to this theory then it is inadvisable to entrust the masses with final authority either in electing officers of State or in holding them responsible. It is probable however that there is some mistake in this mode of argu-ment, partly—unless the character of the masses is absolutely slavish —for the reason already alleged, that, although individually they are worse judges than the experts, yet in their collective capacity they are better or at least as good, and partly because there are some subjects in which the artist himself is not the sole or best judge, viz. all subjects in which the results produced are criticized equally well by persons who are not masters of the art. Thus it is not the builder alone whose function it is to criticize the merits of a house; the person who uses it, i.e. the householder, is actually a better judge, and similarly a pilot is a better judge of a helm than a carpenter or one of the company of a dinner than the cook.

This difficulty we may perhaps regard as being thus satisfactorily settled. There is another however closely connected with it. Is it not an absurdity, it is often said, to invest the lower orders with supreme authority in matters of higher moment than the respectable classes? Yet there are no more momentous duties than those of elect-ing officers of State and holding them responsible, and it is just these which in some polities, as has been already remarked, are conferred upon the commons. For the Public Assembly is supreme in all such matters, although the members of the Assembly, the Council and the Law-courts need not be persons of large property or of suitable age, whereas a higher property qualification is required for lords of the treasury, generals and the highest officers of State. Yet this difficulty admits of a similar solution. It may reasonably be argued that the existing state of things is right. For it is not the individual juror or the individual member of the Council or Assembly who exercises official power but the whole Court or Council or body of commons, of which the individuals specified are but fractions. It is as a mere fraction of the whole and so deriving all importance from the whole that I conceive of the individual member of the Council, Assembly or Law-court. Hence it is right that the masses should control greater interests than the Few, as there are many members of the commons, the Council or the Law-court, and the actual col-lective property of them all exceeds the property of those who hold high offices of State as individuals or in limited bodies.

With this discussion of these points we must be content. But the

initial difficulty we mentioned as to the supreme authority in the
State brings out nothing so clearly as that it is the laws, if rightly
enacted, which should be supreme, and that the officers of State,
whether one or many, should have supreme authority only in those
matters upon which it is wholly impossible for the laws to pronounce
exactly because of the difficulty of providing in a general statement
for all cases. What should be the character of the laws if rightly
enacted has not yet been ascertained; on the contrary our old difficulty still remains. This only is indisputable, that the laws enacted
are necessarily relative to the polity in which they exist.

19

HUMAN NATURE AND POLITICAL POWER *

by

THOMAS HOBBES

(1588–1679)

I

. . . We are to consider, that the felicity of this life, consisteth not
in the repose of a mind satisfied. For there is no such *finis ultimus,*
utmost aim, nor *summum bonum,* greatest good, as is spoken of in
the books of the old moral philosophers. Nor can a man any more
live, whose desires are at an end, than he, whose senses and imagination are at a stand. Felicity is a continual progress of the desire,
from one object to another; the attaining of the former, being still
but the way to the latter. The cause whereof is, that the object of
man's desire, is not to enjoy once only, and for one instant of time;
but to assure for ever, the way of his future desire. And therefore
the voluntary actions, and inclinations of all men, tend, not only
to the procuring, but also to the assuring of a contented life; and
differ only in the way: which ariseth partly from the diversity of
passions, in divers men; and partly from the difference of the knowledge, or opinion each one has of the causes, which produce the effect
desired.

* [From Chs. 11, 13–15, 17, and 18 of *Leviathan* (1651), Molesworth edition
(1839).]

So that in the first place, I put for a general inclination of all mankind, a perpetual and restless desire of power after power, that ceaseth only in death. And the cause of this, is not always that a man hopes for a more intensive delight, than he has already attained to; or that he cannot be content with a moderate power: but because he cannot assure the power and means to live well, which he hath present, without the acquisition of more. And from hence it is, that kings, whose power is greatest, turn their endeavours to the assuring it at home by laws, or abroad by wars: and when that is done, there succeedeth a new desire; in some, of fame from new conquest; in others, of ease and sensual pleasure; in others, of admiration, or being flattered for excellence in some art, or other ability of the mind.

Competition of riches, honour, command, or other power, inclineth to contention, enmity, and war: because the way of one competitor, to the attaining of his desire, is to kill, subdue, supplant, or repel the other. Particularly, competition of praise, inclineth to a reverence of antiquity. For men contend with the living, not with the dead; to these ascribing more than due, that they may obscure the glory of the other.

Desire of ease, and sensual delight, disposeth men to obey a common power: because by such desires, a man doth abandon the protection that might be hoped for from his own industry, and labour. Fear of death, and wounds, disposeth to the same; and for the same reason. On the contrary, needy men, and hardy, not contented with their present condition; as also, all men that are ambitious of military command, are inclined to continue the causes of war; and to stir up trouble and sedition: for there is no honour military but by war; nor any such hope to mend an ill game, as by causing a new shuffle.

Desire of knowledge, and arts of peace, inclineth men to obey a common power: for such desire, containeth a desire of leisure; and consequently protection from some other power than their own.

Desire of praise, disposeth to laudable actions, such as please them whose judgment they value; for of those men whom we contemn, we contemn also the praises. Desire of fame after death does the same. And though after death, there be no sense of the praise given us on earth, as being joys, that are either swallowed up in the unspeakable joys of Heaven, or extinguished in the extreme torments of hell: yet is not such fame vain; because men have a present delight therein from the foresight of it, and of the benefit that may redound thereby to their posterity: which though they now see not, yet they imagine; and anything that is pleasure to the sense, the same also is pleasure in the imagination.

To have received from one, to whom we think ourselves equal, greater benefits than there is hope to requite, disposeth to counterfeit love; but really secret hatred; and puts a man into the estate of a desperate debtor, that in declining the sight of his creditor, tacitly wishes him there, where he might never see him more. For benefits oblige, and obligation is thraldom; and unrequitable obligation perpetual thraldom; which is to one's equal, hateful. But to have received benefits from one, whom we acknowledge for superior, inclines to love; because the obligation is no new depression: and cheerful acceptation, which men call *gratitude,* is such an honour done to the obliger, as is taken generally for retribution. Also to receive benefits, though from an equal, or inferior, as long as there is hope of requital, disposeth to love: for in the intention of the receiver, the obligation is of aid and service mutual; from whence proceedeth an emulation of who shall exceed in benefiting; the most noble and profitable contention possible; wherein the victor is pleased with his victory, and the other revenged by confessing it.

To have done more hurt to a man, than he can, or is willing to expiate, inclineth the doer to hate the sufferer. For he must expect revenge, or forgiveness; both which are hateful.

Fear of oppression, disposeth a man to anticipate, or to seek aid by society: for there is no other way by which a man can secure his life and liberty.

Men that distrust their own subtlety, are, in tumult and sedition, better disposed for victory, than they that suppose themselves wise, or crafty. For these love to consult, the other, fearing to be circumvented, to strike first. And in sedition, men being always in the precincts of battle, to hold together, and use all advantages of force, is a better stratagem, than any that can proceed from subtlety of wit.

Vain-glorious men, such as without being conscious to themselves of great sufficiency, delight in supposing themselves gallant men, are inclined only to ostentation; but not to attempt: because when danger or difficulty appears, they look for nothing but to have their insufficiency discovered.

Vain-glorious men, such as estimate their sufficiency by the flattery of other men, or the fortune of some precedent action, without assured ground of hope from the true knowledge of themselves, are inclined to rash engaging; and in the approach of danger, or difficulty, to retire if they can: because not seeing the way of safety, they will rather hazard their honour, which may be salved with an excuse; than their lives, for which no salve is sufficient.

Men that have a strong opinion of their own wisdom in matter of government, are disposed to ambition. Because without public employment in council or magistracy, the honour of their wisdom is lost. And therefore eloquent speakers are inclined to ambition; for eloquence seemeth wisdom, both to themselves and others.

Pusillanimity disposeth men to irresolution, and consequently to lose the occasions, and fittest opportunities of action. For after men have been in deliberation till the time of action approach, if it be not then manifest what is best to be done, it is a sign, the difference of motives, the one way and the other, are not great: therefore not to resolve then, is to lose the occasion by weighing of trifles; which is pusillanimity.

Frugality, though in poor men a virtue, maketh a man unapt to achieve such actions, as require the strength of many men at once: for it weakeneth their endeavour, which is to be nourished and kept in vigour by reward.

Eloquence, with flattery, disposeth men to confide in them that have it; because the former is seeming wisdom, the latter seeming kindness. Add to them military reputation, and it disposeth men to adhere, and subject themselves to those men that have them. The two former having given them caution against danger from him; the latter gives them caution against danger from others.

Want of science, that is, ignorance of causes, disposeth, or rather constraineth a man to rely on the advice, and authority of others. For all men whom the truth concerns, if they rely not on their own, must rely on the opinion of some other, whom they think wiser than themselves, and see not why he should deceive them.

Ignorance of the signification of words, which is want of understanding, disposeth men to take on trust, not only the truth they know not; but also the errors: and which is more, the nonsense of them they trust: for neither error nor nonsense, can without a perfect understanding of words, be detected.

From the same it proceedeth, that men give different names, to one and the same thing, from the difference of their own passions: as they that approve a private opinion, call it opinion; but they that mislike it, heresy: and yet heresy signifies no more than private opinion; but has only a greater tincture of choler.

From the same also it proceedeth, that men cannot distinguish, without study and great understanding, between one action of many men, and many actions of one multitude; as for example, between one action of all the senators of Rome in killing Cataline, and the many actions of a number of senators in killing Cæsar; and therefore are disposed to take for the action of the people, that which is a multitude of actions done by a multitude of men, led perhaps by the persuasion of one.

Ignorance of the causes, and original constitution of right, equity,

law, and justice, disposeth a man to make custom and example the
rule of his actions; in such manner, as to think that unjust which it
hath been the custom to punish; and that just, of the impunity and
approbation whereof they can produce an example, or, as the lawyers which only use this false measure of justice barbarously call it,
a precedent; like little children, that have no other rule of good and
evil manners, but the correction they receive from their parents and
masters; save that children are constant to their rule, whereas, men
are not so; because grown old, and stubborn, they appeal from
custom to reason, and from reason to custom, as it serves their turn;
receding from custom when their interest requires it, and setting
themselves against reason, as oft as reason is against them: which
is the cause, that the doctrine of right and wrong, is perpetually
disputed, both by the pen and the sword: whereas the doctrine of
lines, and figures, is not so; because men care not, in that subject,
what be truth, as a thing that crosses no man's ambition, profit or
lust. For I doubt not, but if it had been a thing contrary to any
man's right of dominion, or to the interest of men that have dominion, *that the three angles of a triangle, should be equal to two
angles of a square;* that doctrine should have been, if not disputed,
yet by the burning of all books of geometry, suppressed, as far as
he whom it concerned was able.

Ignorance of remote causes, disposeth men to attribute all events,
to the causes immediate, and instrumental: for these are all the causes
they perceive. And hence it comes to pass, that in all places, men
that are grieved with payments to the public, discharge their anger
upon the publicans, that is to say, farmers, collectors, and other
officers of the public revenue; and adhere to such as find fault with
the public government; and thereby, when they have engaged themselves beyond hope of justification, fall also upon the supreme authority, for fear of punishment, or shame of receiving pardon.

Ignorance of natural causes, disposeth a man to credulity, so as
to believe many times impossibilities: for such know nothing to
the contrary, but that they may be true; being unable to detect the
impossibility. And credulity, because men like to be hearkened unto
in company, disposeth them to lying: so that ignorance itself without
malice, is able to make a man both to believe lies, and tell them;
and sometimes also to invent them.

Anxiety for the future time, disposeth men to inquire into the
causes of things: because the knowledge of them, maketh men the
better able to order the present to their best advantage.

Curiosity, or love of the knowledge of causes, draws a man from
the consideration of the effect, to seek the cause; and again, the cause
of that cause; till of necessity he must come to this thought at last,

that there is some cause, whereof there is no former cause, but is eternal; which is it men call God. So that it is impossible to make any profound inquiry into natural causes, without being inclined thereby to believe there is one God eternal; though they cannot have any idea of him in their mind, answerable to his nature. For as a man that is born blind, hearing men talk of warming themselves by the fire, and being brought to warm himself by the same, may easily conceive, and assure himself, there is somewhat there, which men call *fire*, and is the cause of the heat he feels; but cannot imagine what it is like; nor have an idea of it in his mind, such as they have that see it: so also by the visible things in this world, and their admirable order, a man may conceive there is a cause of them, which men call God; and yet not have an idea, or image of him in his mind.

And they that make little, or no inquiry into the natural causes of things, yet from the fear that proceeds from the ignorance itself, of what it is that hath the power to do them much good or harm, are inclined to suppose, and feign unto themselves, several kinds of powers invisible; and to stand in awe of their own imaginations; and in time of distress to invoke them; as also in the time of an expected good success, to give them thanks; making the creatures of their own fancy, their gods. By which means it hath come to pass, that from the innumerable variety of fancy, men have created in the world innumerable sorts of gods. And this fear of things invisible, is the natural seed of that, which every one in himself calleth religion; and in them that worship, or fear that power otherwise than they do, superstition.

And this seed of religion, having been observed by many; some of those that have observed it, have been inclined thereby to nourish, dress, and form it into laws; and to add to it of their own invention, any opinion of the causes of future events, by which they thought they should be best able to govern others, and make unto themselves the greatest use of their powers.

II

Nature hath made men so equal, in the faculties of the body, and mind; as that though there be found one man sometimes manifestly stronger in body, or of quicker mind than another; yet when all is reckoned together, the difference between man, and man, is not so considerable, as that one man can thereupon claim to himself any benefit, to which another may not pretend, as well as he. For as to the strength of body, the weakest has strength enough to kill the strongest, either by secret machination, or by confederacy with others, that are in the same danger with himself.

And as to the faculties of the mind, setting aside the arts grounded upon words, and especially that skill of proceeding upon general, and infallible rules, called science; which very few have, and but in few things; as being not a native faculty, born with us; nor attained, as prudence, while we look after somewhat else, I find yet a greater equality amongst men, than that of strength. For prudence, is but experience; which equal time, equally bestows on all men, in those things they equally apply themselves unto. That which may perhaps make such equality incredible, is but a vain conceit of one's own wisdom, which almost all men think they have in a greater degree, than the vulgar; that is, than all men but themselves, and a few others, whom by fame, or for concurring with themselves, they approve. For such is the nature of men, that howsoever they may acknowledge many others to be more witty, or more eloquent, or more learned; yet they will hardly believe there be many so wise as themselves; for they see their own wit at hand, and other men's at a distance. But this proveth rather that men are in that point equal, than unequal. For there is not ordinarily a greater sign of the equal distribution of any thing, than that every man is contented with his share.

From this equality of ability, ariseth equality of hope in the attaining of our ends. And therefore if any two men desire the same thing, which nevertheless they cannot both enjoy, they become enemies; and in the way to their end, which is principally their own conservation, and sometimes their delectation only, endeavour to destroy, or subdue one another. And from hence it comes to pass, that where an invader hath no more to fear, than another man's single power; if one plant, sow, build, or possess a convenient seat, others may probably be expected to come prepared with forces united, to dispossess, and deprive him, not only of the fruit of his labour, but also of his life, or liberty. And the invader again is in the like danger of another.

And from this diffidence of one another, there is no way for any man to secure himself, so reasonable, as anticipation; that is, by force, or wiles, to master the persons of all men he can, so long, till he see no other power great enough to endanger him: and this is no more than his own conservation requireth, and is generally allowed. Also because there be some, that taking pleasure in contemplating their own power in the acts of conquest, which they pursue farther than their security requires; if others, that otherwise would be glad to be at ease within modest bounds, should not by invasion increase their power, they would not be able, long time, by standing only on their defence, to subsist. And by consequence, such augmentation of dominion over men being necessary to a man's conservation, it ought to be allowed him.

Again, men have no pleasure, but on the contrary a great deal of grief, in keeping company, where there is no power able to over-awe them all. For every man looketh that his companion should value him, at the same rate he sets upon himself: and upon all signs of contempt, or undervaluing, naturally endeavours, as far as he dares, (which amongst them that have no common power to keep them in quiet, is far enough to make them destroy each other), to extort a greater value from his contemners, by damage; and from others, by the example.

So that in the nature of man, we find three principal causes of quarrel. First, competition; second, diffidence; thirdly, glory.

The first, maketh men invade for gain; the second, for safety; and the third, for reputation. The first use violence, to make them-selves masters of other men's persons, wives, children, and cattle; the second, to defend them; the third, for trifles, as a word, a smile, a different opinion, and any other sign of undervalue, either direct in their persons, or by reflection in their kindred, their friends, their nation, their profession, or their name.

Hereby it is manifest, that during the time men live without a common power to keep them all in awe, they are in that condition which is called war; and such a war, as is of every man, against every man. For WAR, consisteth not in battle only, or the act of fighting; but in a tract of time, wherein the will to contend by battle is sufficiently known: and therefore the notion of *time*, is to be con-sidered in the nature of war; as it is in the nature of weather. For as the nature of foul weather, lieth not in a shower or two of rain; but in an inclination thereto of many days together: so the nature of war, consisteth not in actual fighting; but in the known dis-position thereto, during all the time there is no assurance to the contrary. All other time is PEACE.

Whatsoever therefore is consequent to a time of war, where every man is enemy to every man; the same is consequent to the time, wherein men live without other security, than what their own strength, and their own invention shall furnish them withal. In such condition, there is no place for industry; because the fruit thereof is uncertain: and consequently no culture of the earth; no navigation, nor use of the commodities that may be imported by sea; no com-modious building; no instruments of moving, and removing, such things as require much force; no knowledge of the face of the earth; no account of time; no arts; no letters; no society; and which is worst of all, continual fear, and danger of violent death; and the life of man, solitary, poor, nasty, brutish, and short.

It may seem strange to some man, that has not well weighed these things; that nature should thus dissociate, and render men apt to invade, and destroy one another: and he may therefore, not trusting to this inference, made from the passions, desire perhaps to have the same confirmed by experience. Let him therefore consider with himself, when taking a journey, he arms himself, and seeks to go well accompanied; when going to sleep, he locks his doors; when even in his house he locks his chests; and this when he knows there be laws, and public officers, armed, to revenge all injuries shall be done him; what opinion he has of his fellow-subjects, when he rides armed; of his fellow citizens, when he locks his doors; and of his children, and servants, when he locks his chests. Does he not there as much accuse mankind by his actions, as I do by my words? But neither of us accuse man's nature in it. The desires, and other passions of man, are in themselves no sin. No more are the actions, that proceed from those passions, till they know a law that forbids them: which till laws be made they cannot know: nor can any law be made, till they have agreed upon the person that shall make it.

It may peradventure be thought, there was never such a time, nor condition of war as this; and I believe it was never generally so, over all the world: but there are many places, where they live so now. For the savage people in many places of America, except the government of small families, the concord whereof dependeth on natural lust, have no government at all; and live at this day in that brutish manner, as I said before. Howsoever, it may be perceived what manner of life there would be, where there were no common power to fear, by the manner of life, which men that have formerly lived under a peaceful government, use to degenerate into, in a civil war.

But though there had never been any time, wherein particular men were in a condition of war one against another; yet in all times, kings, and persons of sovereign authority, because of their independency, are in continual jealousies, and in the state and posture of gladiators; having their weapons pointing, and their eyes fixed on one another; that is, their forts, garrisons, and guns upon the frontiers of their kingdoms; and continual spies upon their neighbours; which is a posture of war. But because they uphold thereby, the industry of their subjects; there does not follow from it, that misery, which accompanies the liberty of particular men.

To this war of every man, against every man, this also is consequent; that nothing can be unjust. The notions of right and wrong, justice and injustice have there no place. Where there is no common power, there is no law: where no law, no injustice. Force, and fraud, are in war the two cardinal virtues. Justice, and injustice are none of the faculties neither of the body, nor mind. If they were, they might be in a man that were alone in the world, as well as his senses, and passions. They are qualities, that relate to men in society, not in solitude. It is consequent also to the same condition, that there be no propriety, no dominion, no *mine* and *thine* distinct; but only that to be every man's, that he can get; and for so long, as he can keep it. And thus much for the ill condition, which man by mere nature is actually placed in; though with a possibility to come out of it, consisting partly in the passions, partly in his reason.

The passions that incline men to peace, are fear of death; desire of such things as are necessary to commodious living; and a hope by their industry to obtain them. And reason suggesteth convenient articles of peace, upon which men may be drawn to agreement. These articles, are they, which otherwise are called the Laws of Nature. . . .

The RIGHT OF NATURE, which writers commonly call *jus naturale*, is the liberty each man hath, to use his own power, as he will himself, for the preservation of his own nature; that is to say, of his own life; and consequently, of doing anything, which in his own judgment, and reason, he shall conceive to be the aptest means thereunto.

By LIBERTY, is understood, according to the proper signification of the word, the absence of external impediments: which impediments, may oft take away part of a man's power to do what he would; but cannot hinder him from using the power left him, according as his judgment, and reason shall dictate to him.

A LAW OF NATURE, *lex naturalis*, is a precept or general rule, found out by reason, by which a man is forbidden to do that, which is destructive of his life, or taketh away the means of preserving the same; and to omit that, by which he thinketh it may be best preserved. For though they that speak of this subject, use to confound *jus*, and *lex*, *right* and *law*: yet they ought to be distinguished; because RIGHT, consisteth in liberty to do, or to forbear; whereas LAW, determineth, and bindeth to one of them: so that law, and right, differ as much, as obligation, and liberty; which in one and the same matter are inconsistent.

And because the condition of man, as hath been declared in the precedent chapter, is a condition of war of every one against every one; in which case every one is governed by his own reason; and there is nothing he can make use of, that may not be a help unto him, in preserving his life against his enemies; it followeth, that in such a condition, every man has a right to every thing; even to one another's body. And therefore, as long as this natural right of every man to every thing endureth, there can be no security to any man, how strong or wise soever he be, of living out the time, which nature ordinarily alloweth men to live. And consequently it is a precept, or general rule of reason, *that every man, ought to endeavour peace, as far as he has hope of obtaining it; and when he cannot obtain it, that he may seek, and use, all helps, and advantages of war.* The first branch of which rule, containeth the first, and fundamental law of nature; which is, *to seek peace, and follow it.* The second, the sum of the right of nature; which is, *by all means we can, to defend ourselves.*

From this fundamental law of nature, by which men are commanded to endeavour peace, is derived this second law; *that a man be willing, when others are so too, as far forth, as for peace, and defence of himself he shall think it necessary, to lay down this right to all things; and be contented with so much liberty against other men, as he would allow other men against himself.* For as long as every man holdeth this right, of doing any thing he liketh; so long are all men in the condition of war. But if other men will not lay down their right, as well as he; then there is no reason for anyone, to divest himself of his: for that were to expose himself to prey, which no man is bound to, rather than to dispose himself to peace. This is that law of the Gospel; *whatsoever you require that others should do to you, that do ye to them. . . .*

If a covenant be made, wherein neither of the parties perform presently, but trust one another; in the condition of mere nature, which is a condition of war of every man against every man, upon any reasonable suspicion, it is void: but if there be a common power set over them both, with right and force sufficient to compel performance, it is not void. For he that performeth first, has no assurance the other will perform after; because the bonds of words are too weak to bridle men's ambition, avarice, anger, and other passions, without the fear of some coercive power; which in the condition of mere nature, where all men are equal, and judges of the justness of their own fears, cannot possibly be supposed. . . .

The force of words, being . . . too weak to hold men to the performance of their covenants; there are in man's nature, but two imaginable helps to strengthen it. And those are either a fear of the consequence of breaking their word; or a glory, or pride in appearing not to need to break it. This latter is a generosity too rarely found to be presumed on, especially in the pursuers of wealth, command, or sensual pleasure; which are the greatest part of mankind. The passion to be reckoned upon, is fear; whereof there be two very general objects: one, the power of spirits invisible; the other, the power of those men they shall therein offend. Of these two, though the former be the greater power, yet the fear of the latter is commonly the greater fear. The fear of the former is in every man, his own religion: which hath place in the nature of man before civil society. The latter hath not so; at least not place enough, to keep men to their promises; because in the condition of mere nature, the inequality of power is not discerned, but by the event of battle. So that before the time of civil society, or in the interruption thereof by war, there is nothing can strengthen a covenant of peace agreed on, against the temptations of avarice, ambition, lust, or other strong desire, but the fear of that invisible power, which they every one worship as God; and fear as a revenger of their perfidy. . . .

From that law of nature, by which we are obliged to transfer to another, such rights, as being retained, hinder the peace of mankind, there followeth a third; which is this, *that men perform their covenants made:* without which, covenants are in vain, and but empty words; and the right of all men to all things remaining, we are still in the condition of war.

And in this law of nature, consisteth the fountain and original of JUSTICE. For where no covenant hath preceded, there hath no right been transferred, and every man has right to every thing; and consequently, no action can be unjust. But when a covenant is made, then to break it is *unjust:* and the definition of INJUSTICE, is no other than *the not performance of covenant.* And whatsoever is not unjust, is *just.*

But because covenants of mutual trust, where there is a fear of not performance on either part, as hath been said in the former chapter, are invalid; though the original of justice be the making of covenants; yet injustice actually there can be none, till the cause of such fear be taken away; which while men are in the natural condition of war, cannot be done. Therefore before the names of just, and unjust can have place, there must be some coercive power, to compel men equally to the performance of their covenants, by the terror of some punishment, greater than the benefit they expect by the breach of their covenant; and to make good that propriety, which by mutual contract men acquire, in recompense of the universal right they abandon: and such power there is none before the erection of a commonwealth. And this is also to be gathered out of the ordinary definition of justice in the Schools: for they say, that *justice is the constant will of giving to every man his own.* And therefore where there is no *own,* that is no propriety, there is no injustice; and where there is no coercive power erected, that is, where there is no commonwealth, there is no propriety; all men having right to all things: therefore where there is no commonwealth, there nothing is unjust. So that the nature of justice, consisteth in keeping of valid covenants: but the validity of covenants begins not but with the constitution of a civil power, sufficient to compel men to keep them: and then it is also that propriety begins. . . .

. . . No man giveth, but with intention of good to himself; because gift is voluntary; and of all voluntary acts, the object is to every man his own good; of which if men see they shall be frustrated, there will be no beginning of benevolence, or trust; nor consequently of mutual help; nor of reconciliation of one man to another; and therefore they are to remain still in the condition of *war;* which is contrary to the first and fundamental law of nature, which commandeth men to *seek peace.* . . .

. . . Moral philosophy is nothing else but the science of what is *good,* and *evil,* in the conversation, and society of mankind. *Good,* and *evil,* are names that signify our appetites, and aversions; which in different tempers, customs, and doctrines of men, are different: and divers men, differ not only in their judgment, on the senses of what is pleasant, and unpleasant to the taste, smell, hearing, touch, and sight; but also of what is conformable, or disagreeable to reason, in the actions of common life. Nay, the same man, in divers times, differs from himself; and one time praiseth, that is, calleth good, what another time he dispraiseth, and calleth evil: from whence arise disputes, controversies, and at last war. And therefore so long as a man is in the condition of mere nature, which is a condition of war, his private appetite is the measure of good, and evil: and consequently all men agree on this, that peace is good, and therefore also the way, or means of peace, which, as I have shewed before, are *justice, gratitude, modesty, equity, mercy,* and the rest of the laws of nature, are good; that is to say, *moral virtues;* and their contrary *vices,* evil. . . .

III

The final cause, end, or design of men, who naturally love liberty, and dominion over others, in the introduction of that restraint upon themselves, in which we see them live in commonwealths, is the foresight of their own preservation, and of a more contented life thereby; that is to say, of getting themselves out from that miserable condition of war, which is necessarily consequent, as hath been shown [above] to the natural passions of men, when there is no visible power to keep them in awe, and tie them by fear of punishment to the performance of their covenants, and observation of those laws of nature set down [above].

For the laws of nature, as *justice, equity, modesty, mercy,* and, in sum, *doing to others, as we would be done to,* of themselves, without the terror of some power, to cause them to be observed, are contrary to our natural passions, that carry us to partiality, pride, revenge, and the like. And covenants, without the sword, are but words, and of no strength to secure a man at all. Therefore notwithstanding the laws of nature, which every one hath then kept, when he has the will to keep them, when he can do it safely, if there be no power erected, or not great enough for our security; every man will, and may lawfully rely on his own strength and art, for caution against all other men. And in all places, where men have lived by small families, to rob and spoil one another, has been a trade, and so far from being reputed against the law of nature, that the greater spoils they gained, the greater was their honour; and men observed no other laws therein, but the laws of honour; that is, to abstain from cruelty, leaving to men their lives, and instruments of husbandry. And as small families did then; so now do cities and kingdoms which are but greater families, for their own security, enlarge their dominions, upon all pretences of danger, and fear of invasion, or assistance that may be given to invaders, and endeavour as much as they can, to subdue, or weaken their neighbours, by open force, and secret arts, for want of other caution, justly; and are remembered for it in after ages with honour.

Nor is it the joining together of a small number of men, that gives them this security; because in small numbers, small additions on the one side or the other, make the advantage of strength so great, as is sufficient to carry the victory; and therefore gives encouragement to an invasion. The multitude sufficient to confide in for our security, is not determined by any certain number, but by comparison with the enemy we fear; and is then sufficient, when the odds of the enemy is not of so visible and conspicuous moment, to determine the event of war, as to move him to attempt.

And be there never so great a multitude; yet if their actions be directed according to their particular judgments, and particular appetites, they can expect thereby no defence, nor protection, neither against a common enemy, nor against the injuries of one another. For being distracted in opinions concerning the best use and application of their strength, they do not help but hinder one another; and reduce their strength by mutual opposition to nothing: whereby they are easily, not only subdued by a very few that agree together; but also when there is no common enemy, they make war upon each other, for their particular interests. For if we could suppose a great multitude of men to consent in the observation of justice, and other laws of nature, without a common power to keep them all in awe; we might as well suppose all mankind to do the same; and then there neither would be, nor need to be any civil government, or commonwealth at all; because there would be peace without subjection.

Nor is it enough for the security, which men desire should last all the time of their life, that they be governed, and directed by one judgment, for a limited time; as in one battle, or one war. For though they obtain a victory by their unanimous endeavour against a foreign enemy; yet afterwards, when either they have no common enemy, or he that by one part is held for an enemy, is by another part held for a friend, they must needs by the difference of their interests dissolve, and fall again into a war amongst themselves.

It is true, that certain living creatures, as bees, and ants, live sociably one with another, which are therefore by Aristotle numbered amongst political creatures; and yet have no other direction, than their particular judgments and appetites; nor speech, whereby one of them can signify to another, what he thinks expedient for the common benefit: and therefore some man may perhaps desire to know, why mankind cannot do the same. To which I answer,

First, that men are continually in competition for honour and dignity, which these creatures are not; and consequently amongst men there ariseth on that ground, envy and hatred, and finally war; but amongst these not so.

Secondly, that amongst these creatures, the common good differeth not from the private; and being by nature inclined to their private, they procure thereby the common benefit. But man, whose joy consisteth in comparing himself with other men, can relish nothing but what is eminent.

Thirdly, that these creatures, having not, as man, the use of reason, do not see, nor think they see any fault, in the administration of their common business; whereas amongst men, there are very many, that think themselves wiser, and able to govern the public, better than the rest; and these strive to reform and innovate, one this way, another that way; and thereby bring it into distraction and civil war.

Fourthly, that these creatures, though they have some use of voice, in making known to one another their desires, and other affections; yet they want that art of words, by which some men can represent to others, that which is good, in the likeness of evil; and evil, in the likeness of good; and augment, or diminish the apparent greatness of good and evil; discontenting men, and troubling their peace at their pleasure.

Fifthly, irrational creatures cannot distinguish between *injury*, and *damage;* and therefore as long as they be at ease, they are not offended with their fellows: whereas man is then most troublesome, when he is most at ease: for then it is that he loves to shew his wisdom, and control the actions of them that govern the commonwealth.

Lastly, the agreement of these creatures is natural; that of men, is by covenant only, which is artificial: and therefore it is no wonder if there be somewhat else required, besides covenant, to make their agreement constant and lasting; which is a common power, to keep them in awe, and to direct their actions to the common benefit. The only way to erect such a common power, as may be able to defend them from the invasion of foreigners, and the injuries of one another, and thereby to secure them in such sort, as that by their own industry, and by the fruits of the earth, they may nourish themselves and live contentedly; is, to confer all their power and strength upon one man, or upon one assembly of men, that may reduce all their wills, by plurality of voices, unto one will: which is as much as to say, to appoint one man, or assembly of men, to bear their person; and every one to own, and acknowledge himself to be author of whatsoever he that so beareth their person, shall act, or cause to be acted, in those things which concern the common peace and safety; and therein to submit their wills, every one to his will, and their judgments, to his judgment. This is more than consent, or concord; it is a real unity of them all, in one and the same person, made by covenant of every man with every man, in such manner, as if every man should say to every man, *I authorize and give up my right of governing myself, to this man, or to this assembly of men, on this condition, that thou give up thy right to him, and authorize all his actions in like manner.* This done, the multitude so united in one person, is called a COMMONWEALTH, in Latin CIVITAS. This is the generation of that great LEVIATHAN, or rather, to speak more reverently, of that *mortal god,* to which we owe under the *immortal God,* our peace and defence. For by this authority, given him by every particular man in the commonwealth, he hath the use of so much power and strength conferred on him, that by terror thereof, he is enabled to perform the wills of them all, to peace at home, and mutual aid against their enemies abroad. And in him consisteth the essence of the commonwealth; which, to define it, is *one person, of whose acts a great multitude, by mutual covenants one with another, have made themselves every one the author, to the end he may use the strength and means of them all, as he shall think expedient, for their peace and common defence.*

And he that carrieth this person, is called SOVEREIGN, and said to have *sovereign power;* and every one besides, his SUBJECT.

The attaining to this sovereign power, is by two ways. One, by natural force; as when a man maketh his children, to submit themselves, and their children, to his government, as being able to destroy them if they refuse; or by war subdueth his enemies to his will, giving them their lives on that condition. The other, is when men agree amongst themselves, to submit to some man, or assembly of men, voluntarily, on confidence to be protected by him against all others. This latter, may be called a political commonwealth, or commonwealth by *institution;* and the former, a commonwealth by *acquisition.* And first, I shall speak of a commonwealth by institution.

A *commonwealth* is said to be *instituted,* when a *multitude* of men do agree, and *covenant, every one, with every one,* that to whatsoever *man,* or *assembly of men,* shall be given by the major part, the *right* to *present* the person of them all, that is to say, to be their *representative;* every one, as well he that *voted for it,* as he that *voted against it,* shall *authorize* all the actions and judgments, of that man, or assembly of men, in the same manner, as if they were his own, to the end, to live peaceably amongst themselves, and be protected against other men.

From this institution of a commonwealth are derived all the *rights,* and *faculties* of him, or them, on whom sovereign power is conferred by the consent of the people assembled.

First, because they covenant, it is to be understood, they are not obliged by former covenant to anything repugnant hereunto. And consequently they that have already instituted a commonwealth, being thereby bound by covenant, to own the actions, and judgments of one, cannot lawfully make a new covenant, amongst themselves, to be obedient to any other, in any thing whatsoever, without his permission. And therefore, they that are subject to a monarch, cannot without his leave cast off monarchy, and return to the confusion of a disunited multitude; nor transfer their person from him that beareth it, to another man, or other assembly of men: for they are bound, every man to every man, to own, and be reputed author of all, that he that already is their sovereign, shall do, and judge fit to be done: so that any one man dissenting, all the rest should break their covenant made to that man, which is injustice: and they have also every man given the sovereignty to him that beareth their person; and therefore if they depose him, they take from him that which is his own, and so again it is injustice. Besides, if he that attempteth to depose his sovereign, be killed, or punished by him for such attempt, he is author of his own punishment, as being by the institution, author of all his sovereign shall do: and because it is injustice for a man to do anything, for which he may be punished by his own authority, he is also upon that title, unjust. And whereas some men have pretended for their disobedience to their sovereign, a new covenant, made, not with men, but with God; this also is unjust: for there is no covenant with God, but by mediation of somebody that representeth God's person; which none doth but God's lieutenant, who hath the sovereignty under God. But this pretence of covenant with God, is so evident a lie, even in the pretenders' own consciences, that it is not only an act of an unjust, but also of a vile and unmanly disposition.

Secondly, because the right of bearing the person of them all, is given to him they make sovereign, by covenant only of one to another, and not of him to any of them; there can happen no breach of covenant on the part of the sovereign; and consequently none of his subjects, by any pretence of forfeiture, can be freed from his subjection. That he which is made sovereign maketh no covenant with his subjects beforehand, is manifest; because either he must make it with the whole multitude, as one party to the covenant; or he must make a several covenant with every man. With the whole, as one party, it is impossible; because as yet they are not one person: and if he make so many several covenants as there be men, those covenants after he hath the sovereignty are void; because what act soever can be pretended by any one of them for breach thereof, is the act both of himself, and of all the rest, because done in the person, and by the right of every one of them in particular. Besides, if any one, or more of them, pretend a breach of the covenant made by the sovereign at his institution; and others, or one other of his subjects, or himself alone, pretend there was no such breach, there is in this case, no judge to decide the controversy; it returns therefore to the sword again; and every man recovereth the right of protecting himself by his own strength, contrary to the design they had in the institution. It is therefore in vain to grant sovereignty by way of precedent covenant. The opinion that any monarch receiveth his power by covenant, that is to say, on condition, proceedeth from want of understanding this easy truth, that covenants being but words and breath, have no force to oblige, contain, constrain, or protect any man, but what it has from the public sword; that is, from the untied hands of that man, or assembly of men that hath the sovereignty, and whose actions are avouched by them all, and performed by the strength of them all, in him united. But when an assembly of men is made sovereign; then no man imagineth any such covenant to have passed in the institution; for no man is so dull as to say, for example, the people of Rome made a covenant with the Romans, to hold the sovereignty on such or such conditions; which not performed, the Romans might lawfully depose the Roman people. That men see not the reason to be alike in a monarchy, and in a popular government, proceedeth from the ambition of some, that are kinder to the government of an assembly, whereof they may hope to participate, than of monarchy, which they despair to enjoy.

20

EVOLUTION AND ETHICS *
by
THOMAS HENRY HUXLEY
(1825–1895)

There is a delightful child's story, known by the title of "Jack and the Bean-stalk," with which my contemporaries who are present will be familiar. But so many of our grave and reverend juniors have been brought up on severer intellectual diet, and, perhaps, have become acquainted with fairyland only through primers of comparative mythology, that it may be needful to give an outline of the tale. It is a legend of a bean-plant, which grows and grows until it reaches the high heavens and there spreads out into a vast canopy of foliage. The hero, being moved to climb the stalk, discovers that the leafy expanse supports a world composed of the same elements as that below, but yet strangely new; and his adventures there, on which I may not dwell, must have completely changed his views of the nature of things; though the story, not having been composed by, or for, philosophers, has nothing to say about views.

My present enterprise has a certain analogy to that of the daring adventurer. I beg you to accompany me in an attempt to reach a world which, to many, is probably strange, by the help of a bean. It is, as you know, a simple, inert-looking thing. Yet, if planted under proper conditions, of which sufficient warmth is one of the most important, it manifests active powers of a very remarkable kind. A small green seedling emerges, rises to the surface of the soil, rapidly increases in size and, at the same time, undergoes a series of metamorphoses which do not excite our wonder as much as those which meet us in legendary history, merely because they are to be seen every day and all day long.

By insensible steps, the plant builds itself up into a large and various fabric of root, stem, leaves, flowers, and fruit, every one moulded within and without in accordance with an extremely complex but, at the same time, minutely defined pattern. In each of

* [The greater part of the lecture of 1893, published by the Macmillan Company.]

these complicated structures, as in their smallest constituents, there is an immanent energy which, in harmony with that resident in all the others, incessantly works towards the maintenance of the whole and the efficient performance of the part which it has to play in the economy of nature. But no sooner has the edifice, reared with such exact elaboration, attained completeness, than it begins to crumble. By degrees, the plant withers and disappears from view, leaving behind more or fewer apparently inert and simple bodies, just like the bean from which it sprang; and, like it, endowed with the potentiality of giving rise to a similar cycle of manifestations.

Neither the poetic nor the scientific imagination is put to much strain in the search after analogies with this process of going forth and, as it were, returning to the starting-point. It may be likened to the ascent and descent of a slung stone, or the course of an arrow along its trajectory. Or we may say that the living energy takes first an upward and then a downward road. Or it may seem preferable to compare the expansion of the germ into the full-grown plant, to the unfolding of a fan, or to the rolling forth and widening of a stream; and thus to arrive at the conception of "development," or "evolution." Here, as elsewhere, names are "noise and smoke"; the important point is to have a clear and adequate conception of the fact signified by a name. And, in this case, the fact is the Sisyphæan process, in the course of which, the living and growing plant passes from the relative simplicity and latent potentiality of the seed to the full epiphany of a highly differentiated type, thence to fall back to simplicity and potentiality.

The value of a strong intellectual grasp of the nature of this process lies in the circumstance that what is true of the bean is true of living things in general. From very low forms up to the highest— in the animal no less than in the vegetable kingdom—the process of life presents the same appearance of cyclical evolution. Nay, we have but to cast our eyes over the rest of the world and cyclical change presents itself on all sides. It meets us in the water that flows to the sea and returns to the springs; in the heavenly bodies that wax and wane, go and return to their places; in the inexorable sequence of the ages of man's life; in that successive rise, apogee, and fall of dynasties and of states which is the most prominent topic of civil history.

As no man fording a swift stream can dip his foot twice into the same water, so no man can, with exactness, affirm of anything in the sensible world that it is. As he utters the words, nay, as he thinks them, the predicate ceases to be applicable; the present has become the past; the "is" should be "was." And the more we learn of the nature of things, the more evident is it that what we call rest is only unperceived activity; that seeming peace is silent but strenuous battle. In every part, at every moment, the state of the cosmos is the expression of a transitory adjustment of contending forces; a scene of strife, in which all the combatants fall in turn. What is true of each part, is true of the whole. Natural knowledge tends more and more to the conclusion that "all the choir of heaven and furniture of the earth" are the transitory forms of parcels of cosmic substance wending along the road of evolution, from nebulous potentiality, through endless growths of sun and planet and satellite; through all varieties of matter; through infinite diversities of life and thought; possibly, through modes of being of which we neither have a conception, nor are competent to form any, back to the indefinable latency from which they arose. Thus the most obvious attribute of the cosmos is its impermanence. It assumes the aspect not so much of a permanent entity as of a changeful process in which naught endures save the flow of energy and the rational order which pervades it.

We have climbed our bean-stalk and have reached a wonderland in which the common and the familiar become things new and strange. In the exploration of the cosmic process thus typified, the highest intelligence of man finds inexhaustible employment; giants are subdued to our service; and the spiritual affections of the contemplative philosopher are engaged by beauties worthy of eternal constancy.

But there is another aspect of the cosmic process, so perfect as a mechanism, so beautiful as a work of art. Where the cosmopoietic energy works through sentient beings, there arises, among its other manifestations, that which we call pain or suffering. This baleful product of evolution increases in quantity and in intensity, with advancing grades of animal organization, until it attains its highest level in man. Further, the consummation is not reached in man, the mere animal; nor in man, the whole or half savage; but only in man, the member of an organized polity. And it is a necessary consequence of his attempt to live in this way; that is, under those conditions which are essential to the full development of his noblest powers.

Man, the animal, in fact, has worked his way to the headship of the sentient world, and has become the superb animal which he is, in virtue of his success in the struggle for existence. The conditions having been of a certain order, man's organization has adjusted itself to them better than that of his competitors in the cosmic strife. In the case of mankind, the self-assertion, the unscrupulous seizing upon all that can be grasped, the tenacious holding of all that can be kept, which constitute the essence of the struggle for existence, have answered. For his successful progress, throughout the savage state, man has been largely indebted to those qualities which he shares with the ape and the tiger; his exceptional physical organization; his cunning, his sociability, his curiosity, and his imitativeness; his ruthless and ferocious destructiveness when his anger is roused by opposition.

But, in proportion as men have passed from anarchy to social organization, and in proportion as civilization has grown in worth, these deeply ingrained serviceable qualities have become defects. After the manner of successful persons, civilized man would gladly kick down the ladder by which he has climbed. He would be only too pleased to see "the ape and tiger die." But they decline to suit his convenience; and the unwelcome intrusion of these boon companions of his hot youth into the ranged existence of civil life adds pains and griefs, innumerable and immeasurably great, to those which the cosmic process necessarily brings on the mere animal. In fact, civilized man brands all these ape and tiger promptings with the name of sins; he punishes many of the acts which flow from them as crimes; and, in extreme cases, he does his best to put an end to the survival of the fittest of former days by axe and rope.

I have said that civilized man has reached this point; the assertion is perhaps too broad and general; I had better put it that ethical man has attained thereto. The science of ethics professes to furnish us with a reasoned rule of life; to tell us what is right action and why it is so. Whatever differences of opinion may exist among experts there is a general consensus that the ape and tiger methods of the struggle for existence are not reconcilable with sound ethical principles.

The hero of our story descended the bean-stalk, and came back to the common world, where fare and work were alike hard; where ugly competitors were much commoner than beautiful princesses; and where the everlasting battle with self was much less sure to be crowned with victory than a turn-to with a giant. We have done the like. Thousands upon thousands of our fellows, thousands of years ago, have preceded us in finding themselves face to face with the same dread problem of evil. They also have seen that the cosmic process is evolution; that it is full of wonder, full of beauty, and, at the same time, full of pain. They have sought to discover the bearing of these great facts on ethics; to find out whether there is, or is not, a sanction for morality in the ways of the cosmos.

Theories of the universe, in which the conception of evolution plays a leading part, were extant at least six centuries before our era. Certain knowledge of them, in the fifth century, reaches us from localities as distant as the valley of the Ganges and the Asiatic coasts of the Ægean. To the early philosophers of Hindostan, no less than to those of Ionia, the salient and characteristic feature of the phenomenal world was its changefulness; the unresting flow of all things, through birth to visible being and thence to not being, in which they could discern no sign of a beginning and for which they saw no prospect of an ending. It was no less plain to some of these antique forerunners of modern philosophy that suffering is the badge of all the tribe of sentient things; that it is no accidental accompaniment, but an essential constituent of the cosmic process. The energetic Greek might find fierce joys in a world in which "strife is father and king"; but the old Aryan spirit was subdued to quietism in the Indian sage; the mist of suffering which spread over humanity hid everything else from his view; to him life was one with suffering and suffering with life.

In Hindostan, as in Ionia, a period of relatively high and tolerably stable civilization had succeeded long ages of semi-barbarism and struggle. Out of wealth and security had come leisure and refinement, and, close at their heels, had followed the malady of thought. To the struggle for bare existence, which never ends, though it may be alleviated and partially disguised for a fortunate few, succeeded the struggle to make existence intelligible and to bring the order of things into harmony with the moral sense of man, which also never ends, but, for the thinking few, becomes keener with every increase of knowledge and with every step towards the realization of a worthy ideal of life.

Two thousand five hundred years ago, the value of civilization was as apparent as it is now; then, as now, it was obvious that only in the garden of an orderly polity can the finest fruits humanity is capable of bearing be produced. But it had also become evident that the blessings of culture were not unmixed. The garden was apt to turn into a hothouse. The stimulation of the senses, the pampering of the emotions, endlessly multiplied the sources of pleasure. The constant widening of the intellectual field indefinitely extended the range of that especially human faculty of looking before and after, which adds to the fleeting present those old and new worlds of the past and the future, wherein men dwell the more the higher their culture. But that very sharpening of the sense and that subtle refinement of emotion, which brought such a wealth of pleasures, were fatally attended by a proportional enlargement of the capacity for suffering; and the divine faculty of imagination, while it created new heavens and new earths, provided them with the corresponding hells of futile regret for the past and morbid anxiety for the future. Finally, the inevitable penalty of over-stimulation, exhaustion, opened the gates of civilization to its great enemy, ennui; the stale and flat weariness when man delights not, nor woman neither; when all things are vanity and vexation; and life seems not worth living except to escape the bore of dying.

Even purely intellectual progress brings about its revenges. Problems settled in a rough and ready way by rude men, absorbed in action, demand renewed attention and show themselves to be still unread riddles when men have time to think. The beneficent demon, doubt, whose name is Legion and who dwells amongst the tombs of old faiths, enters into mankind and thenceforth refuses to be cast out. Sacred customs, venerable dooms of ancestral wisdom, hallowed by tradition and professing to hold good for all time, are put to the question. Cultured reflection asks for their credentials; judges them by its own standards; finally, gathers those of which it approves into ethical systems, in which the reasoning is rarely much more than a decent pretext for the adoption of foregone conclusions.

One of the oldest and most important elements in such systems is the conception of justice. Society is impossible unless those who are associated agree to observe certain rules of conduct towards one another; its stability depends on the steadiness with which they abide by that agreement; and, so far as they waver, that mutual trust which is the bond of society is weakened or destroyed. Wolves could not hunt in packs except for the real, though unexpressed, understanding that they should not attack one another during the chase. The most rudimentary polity is a pack of men living under the like tacit, or expressed, understanding; and having made the very important advance upon wolf society, that they agree to use the force of the whole body against individuals who violate it and in favour of those who observe it. This observance of a common understanding, with the consequent distribution of punishments and rewards according to accepted rules, received the name of justice, while the contrary was called injustice. Early ethics did not take much note of the animus of the violator of the rules. But civilization could not advance far, without the establishment of a capital distinction between the case of involuntary and that of wilful misdeed; between a merely wrong action and a guilty one. And, with increasing refinement of moral appreciation, the problem of desert, which arises out of this distinction, acquired more and more theoretical and practical importance. If life must be given for life, yet it was recognized that the unintentional slayer did not altogether deserve death; and, by a sort of compromise between the public and the private conception of justice, a sanctuary was provided in which he might take refuge from the avenger of blood.

The idea of justice thus underwent a gradual sublimation from punishment and reward according to acts, to punishment and reward according to desert; or, in other words, according to motive. Righteousness, that is, action from right motive, not only became synonymous with justice, but the positive constituent of innocence and the very heart of goodness.

Now when the ancient sage, whether Indian or Greek, who had attained to this conception of goodness, looked the world, and especially human life, in the face, he found it as hard as we do to bring the course of evolution into harmony with even the elementary requirements of the ethical ideal of the just and the good.

If there is one thing plainer than another, it is that neither the pleasures nor the pains of life, in the merely animal world, are distributed according to desert; for it is admittedly impossible for the lower orders of sentient beings to deserve either the one or the other. If there is a generalization from the facts of human life which has the assent of thoughtful men in every age and country, it is that the violator of ethical rules constantly escapes the punishment which he deserves; that the wicked flourishes like a green bay tree, while the righteous begs his bread; that the sins of the fathers are visited upon the children; that, in the realm of nature, ignorance is punished just as severely as wilful wrong; and that thousands upon thousands of innocent beings suffer for the crime, or the unintentional trespass of one.

Greek and Semite and Indian are agreed upon this subject. The book of Job is at one with the "Works and Days" and the Buddhist Sutras; the Psalmist and the Preacher of Israel, with the Tragic Poets of Greece. What is a more common motive of the ancient tragedy in fact, than the unfathomable injustice of the nature of things; what is more deeply felt to be true than its presentation of the destruction of the blameless by the work of his own hands, or by the fatal operation of the sins of others? Surely Œdipus was pure of heart; it was the natural sequence of events—the cosmic process— which drove him, in all innocence, to slay his father and become the husband of his mother, to the desolation of his people and his own headlong ruin. Or to step, for a moment, beyond the chronological limits I have set myself, what constitutes the sempiternal attraction of Hamlet but the appeal to deepest experience of that history of a no less blameless dreamer, dragged, in spite of himself, into a world out of joint; involved in a tangle of crime and misery, created by one of the prime agents of the cosmic process as it works in and through man?

Thus, brought before the tribunal of ethics, the cosmos might well seem to stand condemned. The conscience of man revolted against the moral indifference of nature, and the microscopic atom should have found the illimitable macrocosm guilty. But few, or none, ventured to record that verdict.

In the great Semitic trial of this issue, Job takes refuge in silence and submission; the Indian and the Greek, less wise perhaps, attempt to reconcile the irreconcilable and plead for the defendant. To this end, the Greeks invented Theodicies; while the Indians devised what, in its ultimate form, must rather be termed a Cosmodicy. For, although Buddhism recognizes gods many and lords many, they are products of the cosmic process; and transitory, however long enduring, manifestations of its eternal activity. In the doctrine of transmigration, whatever its origin, Brahminical and Buddhist speculation found, ready to hand, the means of constructing a plausible vindication of the ways of the cosmos to man. If this world is full of pain and sorrow; if grief and' evil fall, like the rain, upon both the just and the unjust; it is because, like the rain, they are links in the endless chain of natural causation by which past, present, and future are indissolubly connected; and there is no more injustice in the one case than in the other. Every sentient being is reaping as it has sown; if not in this life, then in one or other of the infinite series of antecedent existences of which it is the latest term. The present distribution of good and evil is, therefore, the algebraical sum of accumulated positive and negative deserts; or, rather, it depends on the floating balance of the account. For it was not thought necessary that a complete settlement should ever take place. Arrears might stand over as a sort of "hanging gale"; a period of celestial happiness just earned might be succeeded by ages of torment in a hideous nether world, the balance still overdue for some remote ancestral error.

Whether the cosmic process looks any more moral than at first, after such a vindication, may perhaps be questioned. Yet this plea of justification is not less plausible than others; and none but very hasty thinkers will reject it on the ground of inherent absurdity. Like the doctrine of evolution itself, that of transmigration has its roots in the world of reality; and it may claim such support as the great argument from analogy is capable of supplying.

Everyday experience familiarizes us with the facts which are grouped under the name of heredity. Every one of us bears upon him obvious marks of his parentage, perhaps of remoter relationships. More particularly, the sum of tendencies to act in a certain way, which we call "character," is often to be traced through a long series of progenitors and collaterals. So we may justly say that this "character"—this moral and intellectual essence of a man—does veritably pass over from one fleshly tabernacle to another, and does really transmigrate from generation to generation. In the new-born infant, the character of the stock lies latent, and the Ego is little more than a bundle of potentialities. But, very early, these become actualities; from childhood to age they manifest themselves in dulness or brightness, weakness or strength, viciousness or uprightness; and with each feature modified by confluence with another character, if by nothing else, the character passes on to its incarnation in new bodies.

The Indian philosophers called character, as thus defined, "karma." It is this karma which passed from life to life and linked them in the chain of transmigrations; and they held that it is modified in each life, not merely by confluence of parentage, but by its own acts. They were, in fact, strong believers in the theory, so much disputed just at present, of the hereditary transmission of acquired characters. That the manifestation of the tendencies of a character may be greatly facilitated, or impeded, by conditions, of which self-discipline, or the absence of it, are among the most important, is indubitable; but that the character itself is modified in this way is by no means so certain; it is not so sure that the transmitted character of an evil liver is worse, or that of a righteous man better, than that which he received. Indian philosophy, however, did not admit of any doubt on this subject; the belief in the influence of conditions, notably of self-discipline, on the karma was not merely a necessary postulate of its theory of retribution, but it presented the only way of escape from the endless round of transmigrations.

The earlier forms of Indian philosophy agreed with those prevalent in our own times, in supposing the existence of a permanent reality, or "substance," beneath the shifting series of phenomena, whether of matter or of mind. The substance of the cosmos was "Brahma," that of the individual man "Atman"; and the latter was separated from the former only, if I may so speak, by its phenomenal envelope, by the casing of sensations, thoughts and desires, pleasures and pains, which make up the illusive phantasmagoria of life. This the ignorant take for reality; their "Atman" therefore remains eternally imprisoned in delusions, bound by the fetters of desire and scourged by the whip of misery. But the man who has attained enlightenment sees that the apparent reality is mere illusion, or, as was said a couple of thousand years later, that there is nothing good nor bad but thinking makes it so. If the cosmos is just "and of our pleasant vices makes instruments to scourge us," it would seem that the only way to escape from our heritage of evil is to destroy that fountain of desire whence our vices flow; to refuse any longer to be the instruments of the evolutionary process, and withdraw from the struggle for existence. If the karma is modifiable by self-discipline, if its coarser desires, one after another, can be extinguished, the ultimate fundamental desire of self-assertion, or the desire to be, may also be destroyed. Then the bubble of illusion will burst, and the freed individual "Atman" will lose itself in the universal "Brahma."

Such seems to have been the pre-Buddhistic conception of salvation, and of the way to be followed by those who would attain thereto. No more thorough mortification of the flesh has ever been attempted than that achieved by the Indian ascetic anchorite; no later monachism has so nearly succeeded in reducing the human mind to that condition of impassive quasi-somnambulism, which, but for its acknowledged holiness, might run the risk of being confounded with idiocy.

And this salvation, it will be observed, was to be attained through knowledge, and by action based on that knowledge; just as the experimenter, who would obtain a certain physical or chemical result, must have a knowledge of the natural laws involved and the persistent disciplined will adequate to carry out all the various operations required. The supernatural, in our sense of the term, was entirely excluded. There was no external power which could affect the sequence of cause and effect which gives rise to karma; none but the will of the subject of the karma which could put an end to it.

Only one rule of conduct could be based upon the remarkable theory of which I have endeavoured to give a reasoned outline. It was folly to continue to exist when an overplus of pain was certain; and the probabilities in favour of the increase of misery with the prolongation of existence, were so overwhelming. Slaying the body only made matters worse; there was nothing for it but to slay the soul by the voluntary arrest of all its activities. Property, social ties, family affections, common companionship, must be abandoned; the most natural appetites, even that for food, must be suppressed, or at least minimized; until all that remained of a man was the impassive, extenuated, mendicant monk, self-hypnotised into cataleptic trances, which the deluded mystic took for foretastes of the final union with Brahma.

The founder of Buddhism accepted the chief postulates demanded by his predecessors. But he was not satisfied with the practical annihilation involved in merging the individual existence in the unconditioned—the Atman in Brahma. It would seem that the admission of the existence of any substance whatever—even of the tenuity of that which has neither quality nor energy and of which no predicate whatever can be asserted—appeared to him to be a danger and a snare. Though reduced to a hypostatized negation, Brahma was not to be trusted; so long as entity was there, it might conceivably resume the weary round of evolution, with all its train of immeasurable miseries. Gautama got rid of even that shade of a shadow of permanent existence by a metaphysical *tour de force* of great interest to the student of philosophy. . . .

Accepting the prevalent Brahminical doctrine that the whole cosmos, celestial, terrestrial, and infernal, with its population of gods and other celestial beings, of sentient animals, of Mara and his devils, is incessantly shifting through recurring cycles of production and destruction, in each of which every human being has his transmigratory representative, Gautama proceeded to eliminate substance altogether; and to reduce the cosmos to a mere flow of sensations, emotions, volitions, and thoughts, devoid of any substratum. As, on the surface of a stream of water, we see ripples and whirlpools, which last for a while and then vanish with the causes that gave rise to them, so what seem individual existences are mere temporary associations of phenomena circling round a centre, "like a dog tied to a post." In the whole universe there is nothing permanent, no eternal substance either of mind or of matter. Personality is a metaphysical fancy; and in very truth, not only we, but all things, in the worlds without end of the cosmic phantasmagoria, are such stuff as dreams are made of.

What then becomes of karma? Karma remains untouched. As the peculiar form of energy we call magnetism may be transmitted from a loadstone to a piece of steel, from the steel to a piece of nickel, as it may be strengthened or weakened by the conditions to which it is subjected while resident in each piece, so it seems to have been conceived that karma might be transmitted from one phenomenal association to another by a sort of induction. However this may be, Gautama doubtless had a better guarantee for the abolition of transmigration, when no wrack of substance, either of Atman or of Brahma, was left behind; when, in short, a man had but to dream that he willed not to dream, to put an end to all dreaming.

This end of life's dream is Nirvana. What Nirvana is the learned do not agree. But, since the best original authorities tell us there is neither desire nor activity, nor any possibility of phenomenal reappearance for the sage who has entered Nirvana, it may be safely said of this acme of Buddhistic philosophy—"the rest is silence."

Thus there is no very great practical disagreement between Gautama and his predecessors with respect to the end of action; but it is otherwise as regards the means to that end. With just insight into human nature, Gautama declared extreme ascetic practices to be useless and indeed harmful. The appetites and the passions are not to be abolished by mere mortification of the body; they must, in addition, be attacked on their own ground and conquered by steady cultivation of the mental habits which oppose them; by universal benevolence; by the return of good for evil; by humility; by abstinence from evil thought; in short, by total renunciation of that self-assertion which is the essence of the cosmic process.

Doubtless, it is to these ethical qualities that Buddhism owes its marvellous success. A system which knows no God in the western sense; which denies a soul to man; which counts the belief in immortality a blunder and the hope of it a sin; which refuses any efficacy to prayer and sacrifice; which bids men look to nothing but their own efforts for salvation; which, in its original purity, knew nothing of vows of obedience, abhorred intolerance, and never sought the aid of the secular arm; yet spread over a considerable moiety of the Old World with marvellous rapidity, and is still, with whatever base admixture of foreign superstitions, the dominant creed of a large fraction of mankind.

Let us now set our faces westwards. . . . The attempt of the Stoics to blind themselves to the reality of evil, as a necessary concomitant of the cosmic process, had less success than that of the Indian philosophers to exclude the reality of good from their purview. Unfortunately, it is much easier to shut one's eyes to good than to evil. Pain and sorrow knock at our doors more loudly than pleasure and happiness; and the prints of their heavy footsteps are less easily effaced. Before the grim realities of practical life the pleasant fictions of optimism vanished. If this were the best of all possible worlds, it nevertheless proved itself a very inconvenient habitation for the ideal sage.

The stoical summary of the whole duty of man, "Live according to nature," would seem to imply that the cosmic process is an exemplar for human conduct. Ethics would thus become applied Natural History. In fact, a confused employment of the maxim, in this sense, has done immeasurable mischief in later times. It has furnished an axiomatic foundation for the philosophy of philosophasters and for the moralizing of sentimentalists. But the Stoics were, at bottom, not merely noble, but sane, men; and if we look closely into what they really meant by this ill-used phrase, it will be found to present no justification for the mischievous conclusions that have been deduced from it.

In the language of the Stoa, "Nature" was a word of many meanings. There was the "Nature" of the cosmos and the "Nature" of man. In the latter, the animal "nature," which man shares with a moiety of the living part of the cosmos, was distinguished from a higher "nature." Even in this higher nature there were grades of rank. The logical faculty is an instrument which may be turned to account for any purpose. The passions and the emotions are so closely tied to the lower nature that they may be considered to be pathological, rather than normal, phenomena. The one supreme, hegemonic, faculty, which constitutes the essential "nature" of man, is most nearly represented by that which, in the language of a later philosophy, has been called the pure reason. It is this "nature" which holds up the ideal of the supreme good and demands absolute submission of the will to its behests. It is this which commands all men to love one another, to return good for evil, to regard one another as fellow-citizens of one great state. Indeed, seeing that the progress towards perfection of a civilized state, or polity, depends on the obedience of its members to these commands, the Stoics sometimes termed the pure reason the "political" nature. Unfortunately, the sense of the adjective has undergone so much modification, that the application of it to that which commands the sacrifice of self to the common good would now sound almost grotesque.

But what part is played by the theory of evolution in this view of ethics? So far as I can discern, the ethical system of the Stoics . . . might have been just what it was if they had held any other theory; whether that of special creation, on the one side, or that of the eternal existence of the present order, on the other. To the Stoic, the cosmos had no importance for the conscience, except in so far as he chose to think it a pedagogue to virtue. The pertinacious optimism of our philosophers hid from them the actual state of the case. It prevented them from seeing that cosmic nature is no school of virtue, but the headquarters of the enemy of ethical nature. The logic of facts was necessary to convince them that the cosmos works through the lower nature of man, not for righteousness, but against it. And it finally drove them to confess that the existence of their ideal "wise man" was incompatible with the nature of things; that even a passable approximation to that ideal was to be attained only at the cost of renunciation of the world and mortification, not merely of the flesh, but of all human affections. The state of perfection was that "apatheia" in which desire, though it may still be felt, is powerless to move the will, reduced to the sole function of executing the commands of pure reason. Even this residuum of activity was to be regarded as a temporary loan, as an efflux of the divine world-pervading spirit, chafing at its imprisonment in the flesh, until such time as death enabled it to return to its source in the all-pervading logos.

I find it difficult to discover any very great difference between Apatheia and Nirvana, except that stoical speculation agrees with pre-Buddhistic philosophy, rather than with the teachings of Gautama, in so far as it postulates a permanent substance equivalent to "Brahma" and "Atman"; and that, in stoical practice, the adoption of the life of the mendicant cynic was held to be more a counsel of perfection than an indispensable condition of the higher life.

Thus the extremes touch. Greek thought and Indian thought set out from ground common to both, diverge widely, develop under very different physical and moral conditions, and finally converge to practically the same end.

The Vedas and the Homeric epos set before us a world of rich and vigorous life, full of joyous fighting men

> That ever with a frolic welcome took
> The thunder and the sunshine . . . .

and who were ready to brave the very Gods themselves when their blood was up. A few centuries pass away, and under the influence of civilization the descendants of these men are "sicklied o'er with the pale cast of thought"—frank pessimists, or, at best, make-believe optimists. The courage of the warlike stock may be as hardly tried as before, perhaps more hardly, but the enemy is self. The hero has become a monk. The man of action is replaced by the quietist, whose highest aspiration is to be the passive instrument of the divine Reason. By the Tiber, as by the Ganges, ethical man admits that the cosmos is too strong for him; and, destroying every bond which ties him to it by ascetic discipline, he seeks salvation in absolute renunciation.

Modern thought is making a fresh start from the base whence Indian and Greek philosophy set out; and, the human mind being very much what it was six-and-twenty centuries ago, there is no ground for wonder if it presents indications of a tendency to move along the old lines to the same results.

We are more than sufficiently familiar with modern pessimism, at least as a speculation; for I cannot call to mind that any of its present votaries have sealed their faith by assuming the rags and the bowl of the mendicant Bhikku, or the cloak and the wallet of the Cynic. The obstacles placed in the way of sturdy vagrancy by an unphilosophical police have, perhaps, proved too formidable for philosophical consistency. We also know modern speculative optimism, with its perfectibility of the species, reign of peace, and lion and lamb transformation scenes; but one does not hear so much of it as one did forty years ago; indeed, I imagine it is to be met with more commonly at the tables of the healthy and wealthy, than in the congregations of the wise. The majority of us, I apprehend, profess neither pessimism nor optimism. We hold that the world is neither so good, nor so bad, as it conceivably might be; and, as most of us have reason, now and again, to discover that it can be. Those who have failed to experience the joys that make life worth living are, probably, in as small a minority as those who have never known the griefs that rob existence of its savour and turn its richest fruits into mere dust and ashes.

Further, I think I do not err in assuming that, however diverse their views on philosophical and religious matters, most men are agreed that the proportion of good and evil in life may be very sensibly affected by human action. I never heard anybody doubt that the evil may be thus increased, or diminished; and it would seem to follow that good must be similarly susceptible of addition or subtraction. Finally, to my knowledge, nobody professes to doubt that, so far forth as we possess a power of bettering things, it is our paramount duty to use it and to train all our intellect and energy to this supreme service of our kind.

Hence the pressing interest of the question, to what extent modern progress in natural knowledge, and, more especially, the general outcome of that progress in the doctrine of evolution, is competent to help us in the great work of helping one another?

The propounders of what are called the "ethics of evolution," when the "evolution of ethics" would usually better express the object of their speculations, adduce a number of more or less interesting facts and more or less sound arguments in favour of the origin of the moral sentiments, in the same way as other natural phenomena, by a process of evolution. I have little doubt, for my own part, that they are on the right track; but as the immoral sentiments have no less been evolved, there is, so far, as much natural sanction for the one as the other. The thief and the murderer follow nature just as much as the philanthropist. Cosmic evolution may teach us how the good and the evil tendencies of man may have come about; but, in itself, it is incompetent to furnish any better reason why what we call good is preferable to what we call evil than we had before. Some day, I doubt not, we shall arrive at an understanding of the evolution of the æsthetic faculty; but all the understanding in the world will neither increase nor diminish the force of the intuition that this is beautiful and that is ugly.

There is another fallacy which appears to me to pervade the so-called "ethics of evolution." It is the notion that because, on the whole, animals and plants have advanced in perfection of organization by means of the struggle for existence and the consequent "survival of the fittest"; therefore men in society, men as ethical beings, must look to the same process to help them towards perfection. I suspect that this fallacy has arisen out of the unfortunate ambiguity of the phrase "survival of the fittest." "Fittest" has a connotation of "best"; and about "best" there hangs a moral flavour. In cosmic nature, however, what is "fittest" depends upon the conditions. Long since, I ventured to point out that if our hemisphere were to cool again, the survival of the fittest might bring about, in the vegetable kingdom, a population of more and more stunted and humbler and humbler organisms, until the "fittest" that survived might be nothing but lichens, diatoms, and such microscopic organisms as those which give red snow its colour; while, if it became hotter, the pleasant valleys of the Thames and Isis might be uninhabitable by any animated beings save those that flourish in a tropical jungle. They, as the fittest, the best adapted to the changed conditions, would survive.

Men in society are undoubtedly subject to the cosmic process. As among other animals, multiplication goes on without cessation, and involves severe competition for the means of support. The struggle for existence tends to eliminate those less fitted to adapt themselves to the circumstances of their existence. The strongest, the most self-assertive, tend to tread down the weaker. But the influence of the cosmic process on the evolution of society is the greater the more rudimentary its civilization. Social progress means a checking of the cosmic process at every step and the substitution for it of another, which may be called the ethical process; the end of which is not the survival of those who may happen to be the fittest, in respect of the whole of the conditions which obtain, but of those who are ethically the best.

As I have already urged, the practice of that which is ethically best—what we call goodness or virtue—involves a course of conduct which, in all respects, is opposed to that which leads to success in the cosmic struggle for existence. In place of ruthless self-assertion it demands self-restraint; in place of thrusting aside, or treading down, all competitors, it requires that the individual shall not merely respect, but shall help his fellows; its influence is directed, not so much to the survival of the fittest, as to the fitting of as many as possible to survive. It repudiates the gladiatorial theory of existence. It demands that each man who enters into the enjoyment of the advantages of a polity shall be mindful of his debt to those who have laboriously constructed it; and shall take heed that no act of his weakens the fabric in which he has been permitted to live. Laws and moral precepts are directed to the end of curbing the cosmic process and reminding the individual of his duty to the community, to the protection and influence of which he owes, if not existence itself, at least the life of something better than a brutal savage.

It is from neglect of these plain considerations that the fanatical individualism of our time attempts to apply the analogy of cosmic nature to society. Once more we have a misapplication of the stoical injunction to follow nature; the duties of the individual to the state are forgotten, and his tendencies to self-assertion are dignified by the name of rights. It is seriously debated whether the members of a community are justified in using their combined strength to constrain one of their number to contribute his share to the maintenance of it; or even to prevent him from doing his best to destroy it. The struggle for existence which has done such admirable work in cosmic nature, must, it appears, be equally beneficent in the ethical sphere. Yet if that which I have insisted upon is true; if the cosmic process has no sort of relation to moral ends; if the imitation of it by man is inconsistent with the first principles of ethics; what becomes of this surprising theory?

Let us understand, once for all, that the ethical progress of society depends, not on imitating the cosmic process, still less in running away from it, but in combating it. It may seem an audacious proposal thus to pit the microcosm against the macrocosm and to set man to subdue nature to his higher ends; but I venture to think that the great intellectual difference between the ancient times with which we have been occupied and our day, lies in the solid foundation we have acquired for the hope that such an enterprise may meet with a certain measure of success.

The history of civilization details the steps by which men have succeeded in building up an artificial world within the cosmos. Fragile reed as he may be, man, as Pascal says, is a thinking reed: there lies within him a fund of energy operating intelligently and so far akin to that which pervades the universe, that it is competent to influence and modify the cosmic process. In virtue of his intelligence, the dwarf bends the Titan to his will. In every family, in every polity that has been established, the cosmic process in man has been restrained and otherwise modified by law and custom; in surrounding nature, it has been similarly influenced by the art of the shepherd, the agriculturist, the artisan. As civilization has advanced, so has the extent of this interference increased; until the organized and highly developed sciences and arts of the present day have endowed man with a command over the course of non-human nature greater than that once attributed to the magicians. The most impressive, I might say startling, of these changes have been brought about in the course of the last two centuries; while a right comprehension of the process of life and of the means of influencing its manifestations is only just dawning upon us. We do not yet see our way beyond generalities; and we are befogged by the obtrusion of false analogies and crude anticipations. But Astronomy, Physics,

Chemistry, have all had to pass through similar phases, before they reached the stage at which their influence became an important factor in human affairs. Physiology, Psychology, Ethics, Political Science, must submit to the same ordeal. Yet it seems to me irrational to doubt that, at no distant period, they will work as great a revolution in the sphere of practice.

The theory of evolution encourages no millennial anticipations. If, for millions of years, our globe has taken the upward road, yet, some time, the summit will be reached and the downward route will be commenced. The most daring imagination will hardly venture upon the suggestion that the power and the intelligence of man can ever arrest the procession of the great year.

Moreover, the cosmic nature born with us and, to a large extent, necessary for our maintenance, is the outcome of millions of years of severe training, and it would be folly to imagine that a few centuries will suffice to subdue its masterfulness to purely ethical ends. Ethical nature may count upon having to reckon with a tenacious and powerful enemy as long as the world lasts. But, on the other hand, I see no limit to the extent to which intelligence and will, guided by sound principles of investigation, and organized in common effort, may modify the conditions of existence, for a period longer than that now covered by history. And much may be done to change the nature of man himself. The intelligence which has converted the brother of the wolf into the faithful guardian of the flock ought to be able to do something towards curbing the instincts of savagery in civilized men.

But if we may permit ourselves a larger hope of abatement of the essential evil of the world than was possible to those who, in the infancy of exact knowledge, faced the problem of existence more than a score of centuries ago, I deem it an essential condition of the realization of that hope that we should cast aside the notion that the escape from pain and sorrow is the proper object of life.

We have long since emerged from the heroic childhood of our race, when good and evil could be met with the same "frolic welcome"; the attempts to escape from evil, whether Indian or Greek, have ended in flight from the battle-field; it remains to us to throw aside the youthful over-confidence and the no less youthful discouragement of nonage. We are grown men, and must play the man

strong in will
To strive, to seek, to find, and not to yield,

cherishing the good that falls in our way, and bearing the evil, in and around us, with stout hearts set on diminishing it. So far, we all may strive in one faith towards one hope:

It may be that the gulfs will wash us down,
It may be we shall touch the Happy Isles,

. . . . but something ere the end,
Some work of noble note may yet be done.

21

DEMOCRACY *

by

JOHN DEWEY

(1859–1952)

Democracy is much broader than a special political form, a method of conducting government, of making laws and carrying on governmental administration by means of popular suffrage and elected officers. It is that, of course. But it is something broader and deeper than that. The political and governmental phase of democracy is a means, the best means so far found, for realizing ends that lie in the wide domain of human relationships and the development of human personality. It is, as we often say, though perhaps without appreciating all that is involved in the saying, a way of life, social and individual. The key-note of democracy as a way of life may be expressed, it seems to me, as the necessity for the participation of every mature human being in formation of the values that regulate the living of men together: which is necessary from the standpoint of both the general social welfare and the full development of human beings as individuals.

Universal suffrage, recurring elections, responsibility of those who are in political power to the voters, and the other factors of democratic government are means that have been found expedient for realizing democracy as the truly human way of living. They are not a final end and a final value. They are to be judged on the basis of their contribution to the end. It is a form of idolatry to erect means into the end which they serve. Democratic political forms are simply the best means that human wit has devised up to a special time in history. But they rest back upon the idea that no man or

* [The greater part of an address published in the magazine *School and Society*, 1937.]

limited set of men is wise enough or good enough to rule others without their consent; the positive meaning of this statement is that all those who are affected by social institutions must have a share in producing and managing them. The two facts that each one is influenced in what he does and enjoys and in what he becomes by the institutions under which he lives, and that therefore he shall have, in a democracy, a voice in shaping them, are the passive and active sides of the same fact.

The development of political democracy came about through substitution of the method of mutual consultation and voluntary agreement for the method of subordination of the many to the few enforced from above. Social arrangements which involve fixed subordination are maintained by coercion. The coercion need not be physical. There have existed, for short periods, benevolent despotisms. But coercion of some sort there has been; perhaps economic, certainly psychological and moral. The very fact of exclusion from participation is a subtle form of suppression. It gives individuals no opportunity to reflect and decide upon what is good for them. Others who are supposed to be wiser and who in any case have more power decide the question for them and also decide the methods and means by which subjects may arrive at the enjoyment of what is good for them. This form of coercion and suppression is more subtle and more effective than is overt intimidation and restraint. When it is habitual and embodied in social institutions, it seems the normal and natural state of affairs. The mass usually become unaware that they have a claim to a development of their own powers. Their experience is so restricted that they are not conscious of restriction. It is part of the democratic conception that they as individuals are not the only sufferers, but that the whole social body is deprived of the potential resources that should be at its service. The individuals of the submerged mass may not be very wise. But there is one thing they are wiser about than anybody else can be, and that is where the shoe pinches, the troubles they suffer from.

The foundation of democracy is faith in the capacities of human nature; faith in human intelligence and in the power of pooled and cooperative experience. It is not belief that these things are complete but that if given a show they will grow and be able to generate progressively the knowledge and wisdom needed to guide collective action. Every autocratic and authoritarian scheme of social action rests on a belief that the needed intelligence is confined to a superior few, who because of inherent natural gifts are endowed with the ability and the right to control the conduct of others; laying down principles and rules and directing the ways in which they are carried out. It would be foolish to deny that much can be said for this point of view. It is that which controlled human relations in social groups for much the greater part of human history. The democratic faith has emerged very, very recently in the history of mankind. Even where democracies now exist, men's minds and feelings are still permeated with ideas about leadership imposed from above, ideas that developed in the long early history of mankind. After democratic political institutions were nominally established, beliefs and ways of looking at life and of acting that originated when men and women were externally controlled and subjected to arbitrary power, persisted in the family, the church, business and the school, and experience shows that as long as they persist there, political democracy is not secure.

Belief in equality is an element of the democratic credo. It is not, however, belief in equality of natural endowments. Those who proclaimed the idea of equality did not suppose they were enunciating a psychological doctrine, but a legal and political one. All individuals are entitled to equality of treatment by law and in its administration. Each one is affected equally in quality if not in quantity by the institutions under which he lives and has an equal right to express his judgment, although the weight of his judgment may not be equal in amount when it enters into the pooled result to that of others. In short, each one is equally an individual and entitled to equal opportunity of development of his own capacities, be they large or small in range. Moreover, each has needs of his own, as significant to him as those of others are to them. The very fact of natural and psychological inequality is all the more reason for establishment by law of equality of opportunity, since otherwise the former becomes a means of oppression of the less gifted.

While what we call intelligence be distributed in unequal amounts, it is the democratic faith that it is sufficiently general so that each individual has something to contribute, whose value can be assessed only as enters into the final pooled intelligence constituted by the contributions of all. Every authoritarian scheme, on the contrary, assumes that its value may be assessed by some *prior* principle, if not of family and birth or race and color or possession of material wealth, then by the position and rank a person occupies in the existing social scheme. The democratic faith in equality is the faith that each individual shall have the chance and opportunity to contribute whatever he is capable of contributing and that the value of his contribution be decided by its place and function in the organized total of similar contributions, not on the basis of prior status of any kind whatever.

I have emphasized in what precedes the importance of the effective release of intelligence in connection with personal experience in the democratic way of living. I have done so purposely because democracy is so often and so naturally associated in our minds with freedom of *action*, forgetting the importance of freed intelligence which is necessary to direct and to warrant freedom of action. Unless freedom of individual action has intelligence and informed conviction back of it, its manifestation is almost sure to result in confusion and disorder. The democratic idea of freedom is not the right of each individual to *do* as he pleases, even if it be qualified by adding "provided he does not interfere with the same freedom on the part of others." While the idea is not always, not often enough, expressed in words, the basic freedom is that of freedom of *mind* and of whatever degree of freedom of action and experience is necessary to produce freedom of intelligence. The modes of freedom guaranteed in the Bill of Rights are all of this nature: Freedom of belief and conscience, of expression of opinion, of assembly for discussion and conference, of the press as an organ of communication. They are guaranteed because without them individuals are not free to develop and society is deprived of what they might contribute. . . .

There is some kind of government, of control, wherever affairs that concern a number of persons who act together are engaged in. It is a superficial view that holds government is located in Washington and Albany. There is government in the family, in business, in the church, in every social group. There are regulations, due to custom if not to enactment, that settle how individuals in a group act in connection with one another.

It is a disputed question of theory and practice just how far a democratic political government should go in control of the conditions of action within special groups. At the present time, for example, there are those who think the federal and state governments leave too much freedom of independent action to industrial and financial groups, and there are others who think the government is going altogether too far at the present time. I do not need to discuss this phase of the problem, much less to try to settle it. But it must be pointed out that if the methods of regulation and administration in vogue in the conduct of secondary social groups are non-democratic, whether directly or indirectly or both, there is bound to be an unfavorable reaction back into the habits of feeling, thought and action of citizenship in the broadest sense of that word. The way in which any organized social interest is controlled necessarily plays an important part in forming the dispositions and tastes, the attitudes, interests, purposes and desires, of those engaged in carrying on the activities of the group. For illustration, I do not need to do more than point to the moral, emotional and intellectual effect upon both employers and laborers of the existing industrial system. Just what the effects specifically are is a matter about which we know very little. But I suppose that every one who reflects upon the subject admits that it is impossible that the ways in which activities are carried on for the greater part of the waking hours of the day; and the way in which the share of individuals is involved in the management of affairs in such a matter as gaining a livelihood and attaining material and social security, can not but be a highly important factor in shaping personal dispositions; in short, forming character and intelligence.

In the broad and final sense all institutions are educational in the sense that they operate to form the attitudes, dispositions, abilities and disabilities that constitute a concrete personality. The principle applies with special force to the school. For it is the main business of the family and the school to influence directly the formation and growth of attitudes and dispositions, emotional, intellectual and moral. Whether this educative process is carried on in a predominantly democratic or non-democratic way becomes, therefore, a question of transcendent importance not only for education itself but for its final effect upon all the interests and activities of a society that is committed to the democratic way of life. . . .

There are certain corollaries which clarify the meaning of the issue. Absence of participation tends to produce lack of interest and concern on the part of those shut out. The result is a corresponding lack of effective responsibility. Automatically and unconsciously, if not consciously, the feeling develops, "This is none of our affair; it is the business of those at the top; let that particular set of Georges do what needs to be done." The countries in which autocratic government prevails are just those in which there is least public spirit and the greatest indifference to matters of general as distinct from personal concern. Can we expect a different kind of psychology to actuate teachers? Where there is little power, there is correspondingly little sense of positive responsibility. It is enough to do what one is told to do sufficiently well to escape flagrant unfavorable notice. About larger matters, a spirit of passivity is engendered. In some cases, indifference passes into evasion of duties when not directly under the eye of a supervisor; in other cases, a carping, rebellious spirit is engendered. . . .

It still is also true that incapacity to assume the responsibilities involved in having a voice in shaping policies is bred and increased by conditions in which that responsibility is denied. I suppose there has never been an autocrat, big or little, who did not justify his conduct on the ground of the unfitness of his subjects to take part in government. . . . What the argument for democracy implies is that the best way to produce initiative and constructive power is to exercise it. Power, as well as interest, comes by use and practice.

Moreover, the argument from incapacity proves too much. If it is
so great as to be a permanent bar, then teachers can not be expected
to have the intelligence and skill that are necessary to execute the
directions given them. The delicate and difficult task of developing
character and good judgment in the young needs every stimulus
and inspiration possible. It is impossible that the work should not
be better done when teachers have that understanding of what they
are doing that comes from having shared in forming its guiding
ideas. . . .

The fundamental beliefs and practices of democracy are now
challenged as they never have been before. In some nations they are
more than challenged. They are ruthlessly and systematically destroyed. Everywhere there are waves of criticism and doubt as to
whether democracy can meet pressing problems of order and security.
The causes for the destruction of political democracy in countries
where it was nominally established are complex. But of one thing
I think we may be sure. Wherever it has fallen it was too exclusively
political in nature. It had not become part of the bone and blood of
the people in daily conduct of its life. Democratic forms were limited
to Parliament, elections and combats between parties. What is happening proves conclusively, I think, that unless democratic habits of
thought and action are part of the fiber of a people, political democracy is insecure. It can not stand in isolation. It must be buttressed
by the presence of democratic methods in all social relationships.
The relations that exist in educational institutions are second only
in importance in this respect to those which exist in industry and
business, perhaps not even to them.

22

THE CONCEPT OF LAW *

by

ROSCOE POUND

(1870–1964)

As ideas of what law is for are so largely implicit in ideas of what
law is, a brief survey of ideas of the nature of law from this stand-

* [The greater part of Ch. 2 of *An Introduction to the Philosophy of Law*
(1922). By kind permission of Yale University Press.]

point will be useful. No less than twelve conceptions of what law is may be distinguished.

First, we may put the idea of a divinely ordained rule or set of rules for human action, as for example, the Mosaic law, or Hammurapi's code, handed him ready-made by the sun god, or Manu, dictated to the sages by Manu's son Bhrigu in Manu's presence and by his direction.

Second, there is an idea of law as a tradition of the old customs which have proved acceptable to the gods and hence point the way in which man may walk with safety. For primitive man, surrounded by what seem vengeful and capricious powers of nature, is in continual fear of giving offence to these powers and thus bringing down their wrath upon himself and his fellows. The general security requires that men do only those things and do them only in the way which long custom has shown at least not displeasing to the gods. Law is the traditional or recorded body of precepts in which that custom is preserved and expressed. Whenever we find a body of primitive law possessed as a class tradition by a political oligarchy it is likely to be thought of in this way just as a body of like tradition in the custody of a priesthood is certain to be thought of as divinely revealed.

A third and closely related idea conceives of law as the recorded wisdom of the wise men of old who had learned the safe course or the divinely approved course for human conduct. When a traditional custom of decision and custom of action has been reduced to writing in a primitive code it is likely to be thought of in this way, and Demosthenes in the fourth century B.C. could describe the law of Athens in these terms.

Fourth, law may be conceived as a philosophically discovered system of principles which express the nature of things, to which, therefore, man ought to conform his conduct. Such was the idea of the Roman jurisconsult, grafted, it is true, on the second and third ideas and on a political theory of law as the command of the Roman people, but reconciled with them by conceiving of tradition and recorded wisdom and command of the people as mere declarations or reflections of the philosophically ascertained principles, to be measured and shaped and interpreted and eked out thereby. In the hands of philosophers the foregoing conception often takes another form so that, fifth, law is looked upon as a body of ascertainments and declarations of an eternal and immutable moral code.

Sixth, there is an idea of law as a body of agreements of men in politically organized society as to their relations with each other. This is a democratic version of the identification of law with rules of law and hence with the enactments and decrees of the city-state which is discussed in the Platonic *Minos*. Not unnaturally Demosthenes suggests it to an Athenian jury. Very likely in such a theory a philosophical idea would support the political idea and the inherent moral obligation of a promise would be invoked to show why men should keep the agreements made in their popular assemblies.

Seventh, law has been thought of as a reflection of the divine reason governing the universe; a reflection of that part which determines the "ought" addressed by that reason to human beings as moral entities, in distinction from the "must" which it addresses to the rest of creation. Such was the conception of Thomas Aquinas, which had great currency down to the seventeenth century and has had much influence ever since.

Eighth, law has been conceived as a body of commands of the sovereign authority in a politically organized society as to how men should conduct themselves therein, resting ultimately on whatever basis was held to be behind the authority of that sovereign. So thought the Roman jurists of the Republic and of the classical period with respect to positive law. And as the emperor had the sovereignty of the Roman people devolved upon him, the Institutes of Justinian could lay down that the will of the emperor had the force of a law. Such a mode of thought was congenial to the lawyers who were active in support of royal authority in the centralizing French monarchy of the sixteenth and seventeenth centuries and through them passed into public law. It seemed to fit the circumstance of parliamentary supremacy in England after 1688, and became the orthodox English juristic theory. Also it could be made to fit a political theory of popular sovereignty in which the people were thought of as succeeding to the sovereignty of parliament at the American Revolution or of the French king at the French Revolution.

A ninth idea of law takes it to be a system of precepts discovered by human experience whereby the individual human will may realize the most complete freedom possible consistently with the like freedom of will of others. This idea, held in one form or another by the historical school, divided the allegiance of jurists with the theory of law as command of the sovereign during almost the whole of the past century. It assumed that the human experience by which legal principles were discovered was determined in some inevitable way. It was not a matter of conscious human endeavor. The process was determined by the unfolding of an idea of right and justice or an idea of liberty which was realizing itself in human administration of justice, or by the operation of biological or psychological laws or of race characters, whose necessary result was the system of law of the time and people in question.

Again, tenth, men have thought of law as a system of principles, discovered philosophically and developed in detail by juristic writing and judicial decision, whereby the external life of man is measured by reason, or in another phase, whereby the will of the individual in action is harmonized with those of his fellow men. This mode of thought appeared in the nineteenth century after the natural-law † theory in the form in which it had prevailed for two centuries had been abandoned and philosophy was called upon to provide a critique for systematic arrangement and development of details.

Eleventh, law has been thought of as a body or system of rules imposed on men in society by the dominant class for the time being in furtherance, conscious or unconscious, of its own interest. This economic interpretation of law takes many forms. In an idealistic form it thinks of the inevitable unfolding of an economic idea. In a mechanical sociological form it thinks of class struggle or a struggle for existence in terms of economics, and of law as the result of the operation of forces or laws involved in or determining such struggles. In a positivist-analytical form it thinks of law as the command of the sovereign, but of that command as determined in its economic content by the will of the dominant social class, determined in turn by its own interest. All of these forms belong to transition from the stability of the maturity of law to a new period of growth. When the idea of the self-sufficiency of law gives way and men seek to relate jurisprudence to the other social sciences, the relation to economics challenges attention at once. Moreover in a time of copious legislation the enacted rule is easily taken as the type of legal precept and an attempt to frame a theory of legislative lawmaking is taken to give an account of all law.

Finally, twelfth, there is an idea of law as made up of the dictates of economic or social laws with respect to the conduct of men in society, discovered by observation, expressed in precepts worked out through human experience of what would work and what not in the administration of justice. This type of theory likewise belongs to the end of the nineteenth century, when men had begun to look for physical or biological bases, discoverable by observation, in place of metaphysical bases, discoverable by philosophical reflection. Another form finds some ultimate social fact by observation and develops the logical implications of that fact much after the manner of the metaphysical jurist. This again results from the tendency in recent years to unify the social sciences and consequent attention to sociological theories. . . .

What common elements may we find in the foregoing twelve pictures of what law is? For one thing, each shows us a picture of some ultimate basis, beyond reach of the individual human will, that stands fast in the whirl of change of which life is made up. This steadfast

† [See pp. 109–110 above.]

ultimate basis may be thought of as the divine pleasure or will or reason, revealed immediately or mediately through a divinely ordained immutable moral code. It may be put in the form of some ultimate metaphysical datum which is so given us that we may rest in it forever. It may be portrayed as certain ultimate laws which inexorably determine the phenomena of human conduct. Or it may be described in terms of some authoritative will for the time and place, to which the wills of others are subjected, that will deriving its authority ultimately and absolutely in some one of the preceding forms, so that what it does is by and large in no wise a matter of chance. This fixed and stable starting point is usually the feature upon which the chief emphasis is placed. Next we shall find in all theories of the nature of law a picture of a determinate and mechanically absolute mode of proceeding from the fixed and absolute starting point. The details may come from this starting point through divine revelation or a settled authoritative tradition or record, or an inevitable and infallible philosophical or logical method, or an authoritative political machinery, or a scientific system of observation, or historically verifiable ideas which are logically demonstrable to be implications of the fundamental metaphysically given datum. Third, we shall see in these theories a picture of a system of ordering human conduct and adjusting human relations resting upon the ultimate basis and derived therefrom by the absolute process. In other words, they all picture, not merely an ordering of human conduct and adjustment of human relations, which we have actually given, but something more which we should like to have, namely, a doing of these things in a fixed, absolutely predetermined way, excluding all merely individual feelings or desires of those by whom the ordering and adjustment are carried out. Thus in these subconscious picturings of the end of law it seems to be conceived as existing to satisfy a paramount social want of general security. . . .

If we turn to the ideas which have obtained in conscious thinking about the end of law, we may recognize three which have held the ground successively in legal history and a fourth which is beginning to assert itself. The first and simplest idea is that law exists in order to keep the peace in a given society; to keep the peace at all events and at any price. This is the conception of what may be called the stage of primitive law. It puts satisfaction of the social want of general security, stated in its lowest terms, as the purpose of the legal order. So far as the law goes, other individual or social wants are ignored or are sacrificed to this one. . . . In a society organized on the basis of kinship, in which the greater number of social wants were taken care of by the kin-organizations, there are two sources of friction: the clash of kin-interests, leading to controversies of one kindred with another, and the kinless man, for whom no kin-organization is responsible, who also has no kin-organization to stand behind him in asserting his claims. Peace between kindreds and peace between clansmen and the growing mass of non-gentile population is the unsatisfied social want to which politically organized society must address itself. The system of organized kindreds gradually breaks down. Groups of kinsmen cease to be the fundamental social units. Kin-organization is replaced by political organization as the primary agency of social control. The legal unit comes to be the free citizen or the free man. In this transition regulation of self-redress and prevention of private war among those who have no strong clan-organizations to control them or respond for them are demanded by the general security. The means of satisfying these social wants are found in a legal order conceived solely in terms of keeping the peace.

Greek philosophers came to conceive of the general security in broader terms and to think of the end of the legal order as preservation of the social *status quo*. They came to think of maintaining the general security mediately through the security of social institutions. They thought of law as a device to keep each man in his appointed groove in society and thus prevent friction with his fellows. The virtue on which they insisted was *sophrosyne* [self-control], knowing the limits which nature fixes for human conduct and keeping within them. The vice which they denounced was *hybris* [pride], wilful bond-breaking—wilful transgression of the socially appointed bounds. This mode of thinking follows the substitution of the city-state political organization of society for the kin-organization. The organized kindreds were still powerful. An aristocracy of the kin-organized and kin-conscious, on the one hand, and a mass of those who had lost or severed their ties of kinship, or had come from without, on the other hand, were in continual struggle for social and political mastery. . . . The chief social want, which no other social institution could satisfy, was the security of social institutions generally. In the form of maintenance of the social *status quo* this became the Greek and thence the Roman and medieval conception of the end of law.

Transition from the idea of law as a device to keep the peace to the idea of law as a device to maintain the social *status quo* may be seen in the proposition of Heraclitus, that men should fight for their laws as for the walls of their city. In Plato the idea of maintaining the social order through the law is fully developed. The actual social order was by no means what it should be. Men were to be reclassified and everyone assigned to the class for which he was best fitted. But when the classification and the assignment had been made the law was to keep him there. It was not a device to set him free that he might find his own level by free competition with his fellows and free experiment with his natural powers. It was a device to prevent such disturbances of the social order by holding each individual to his appointed place. . . . Aristotle puts the same idea in another way, asserting that justice is a condition in which each keeps within his appointed sphere; that we first take account of relations of inequality, treating individuals according to their worth, and then secondarily of relations of equality in the classes into which their worth requires them to be assigned. When St. Paul exhorted wives to obey their husbands, and servants to obey their masters, and thus everyone to exert himself to do his duty in the class where the social order had put him, he expressed this Greek conception of the end of law.

Roman lawyers made the Greek philosophical conception into a juristic theory. For the famous three precepts to which the law is reduced in Justinian's Institutes come to this: Everyone is to live honorably; he is to "preserve moral worth in his own person" by conforming to the conventions of the social order. Everyone is to respect the personality of others; he is not to interfere with those interests and powers of action, conceded to others by the social order, which make up their legal personality. Everyone is to render to everyone else his own; he is to respect the acquired rights of others. The social system has defined certain things as belonging to each individual. Justice is defined in the Institutes as the set and constant purpose of giving him these things. It consists in rendering them to him and in not interfering with his having and using them within the defined limits. This is a legal development of the Greek idea of harmoniously maintaining the social *status quo*. . . .

In the Middle Ages the primitive idea of law as designed only to keep the peace came back with Germanic law. But the study of Roman law presently taught the Roman version of the Greek conception and the legal order was thought of once more as an orderly maintenance of the social *status quo*. This conception answered to the needs of medieval society, in which men had found relief from anarchy and violence in relations of service and protection and a social organization which classified men in terms of such relations and required them to be held to their functions as so determined. Where the Greeks thought of a stationary society corrected from time to time with reference to its nature or ideal, the Middle Ages thought of a stationary society resting upon authority and determined by custom or tradition. To each, law was a system of precepts existing to maintain this stationary society as it was.

In the feudal social order reciprocal duties involved in relations established by tradition and taken to rest on authority were the sig-

nificant legal institutions. With the gradual disintegration of this order and the growing importance of the individual in a society engaged
in discovery, colonization and trade, to secure the claims of individuals to assert themselves freely in the new fields of human activity
which were opening on every side became a more pressing social
want than to maintain the social institutions by which the system of
reciprocal duties was enforced and the relations involving those duties
were preserved. Men did not so much desire that others perform for
them the duties owing in some relation, as that others keep hands off
while they achieved what they might for themselves in a world that
continually afforded new opportunities to the active and the daring.
The demand was no longer that men be kept in their appointed
grooves. Friction and waste were apprehended, not from men getting
out of these grooves, but from attempts to hold them there by means
devised to meet the needs of a different social order whereby they
were made to chafe under arbitrary restraint and their powers were
not utilized in the discovery and exploitation of the resources of nature, to which human powers were to be devoted in the succeeding
centuries. Accordingly the end of law comes to be conceived as a making possible of the maximum of individual free self-assertion.

Transition to the newer way of thinking may be seen in the Spanish
jurist-theologians of the sixteenth century. Their juristic theory was
one of natural limits of activity in the relations of individuals with
each other, that is, of limits to human action which expressed the
rational ideal of man as a moral creature and were imposed upon men
by reason. This theory differs significantly from the idea of antiquity,
although it goes by the old name. The Greeks thought of a system of
limiting men's activities in order that each might be kept in the place
for which he was best fitted by nature—the place in which he might
realize an ideal form of his capacities—and thus to preserve the social
order as it stands or as it shall stand after a rearrangement. The six-
teenth-century jurists of the Counter-Reformation held that men's
activities were naturally limited, and hence that positive law might
and should limit them in the interest of other men's activities, because
all men have freedom of will and ability to direct themselves to conscious ends. Where Aristotle thought of inequalities arising from the
different worth of individual men and their different capacities for the
things which the social order called for, these jurists thought of a
natural (i.e., ideal) equality, involved in the like freedom of will and
the like power of conscious employment of one's faculties inherent in
all men. Hence law did not exist to maintain the social *status quo*
with all its arbitrary restraints on the will and on employment of
individual powers; it existed rather to maintain the natural equality

which often was threatened or impaired by the traditional restrictions, on individual activity. Since this natural equality was conceived positively as an ideal equality in opportunity to do things, it could easily pass into a conception of free individual self-assertion as the thing sought, and of the legal order as existing to make possible the maximum thereof in a world abounding in undiscovered resources, undeveloped lands and unharnessed natural forces. The latter idea took form in the seventeenth century and prevailed for two centuries thereafter, culminating in the juristic thought of the last generation.

Law as a securing of natural equality became law as a securing of natural rights. The nature of man was expressed by certain qualities possessed by him as a moral, rational creature. The limitations on human activity, of which the Spanish jurist-theologians had written, got their warrant from the inherent moral qualities of men which made it right for them to have certain things and do certain things. These were their natural rights and the law existed simply to protect and give effect to these rights. There was to be no restraint for any other purpose. Except as they were to be compelled to respect the rights of others, which the natural man or ideal man would do without compulsion as a matter of reason, men were to be left free. In the nineteenth century this mode of thought takes a metaphysical turn. The ultimate thing for juristic purposes is the individual consciousness. The social problem is to reconcile conflicting free wills of conscious individuals independently asserting their wills in the varying activities of life. The natural equality becomes an equality in freedom of will. Kant rationalized the law in these terms as a system of principles or universal rules, to be applied to human action, whereby the free will of the actor may co-exist along with the free will of everyone else. Hegel rationalized the law in these terms as a system of principles wherein and whereby the idea of liberty was realizing in human experience. Bentham rationalized it as a body of rules, laid down and enforced by the state's authority, whereby the maximum of happiness, conceived in terms of free self-assertion, was secured to each individual. Its end was to make possible the maximum of free individual action consistent with general free individual action. Spencer rationalized it as a body of rules, formulating the "government of the living by the dead," whereby men sought to promote the liberty of each limited only by the like liberty of all. In any of these ways of putting it, the end of law is to secure the greatest possible general individual self-assertion; to let men do freely everything they may consistently with a like free doing of everything they may by their fellow men. This is indeed a philosophy of law for discoverers and colonizers and pioneers and traders and entrepreneurs and captains of industry. Until the world became crowded, it served well to eliminate friction and to promote the widest discovery and utilization of the natural resources of human existence.

Looking back at the history of this conception, which has governed theories of the end of law for more than two hundred years, we may note that it has been put to three uses. It has been used as a means of clearing away the restraints upon free economic activity which accumulated during the Middle Ages as incidents of the system of relational duties and as expressions of the idea of holding men to their place in a static social order. This negative side played an important part in the English legislative reform movement in the last century. The English utilitarians insisted upon removal of all restrictions upon individual free action beyond those necessary for securing like freedom on the part of others. This, they said, was the end of legislation. Again it has been used as a constructive idea, as in the seventeenth and eighteenth centuries, when a commercial law which gave effect to what men did as they willed it, which looked at intention and not at form, which interpreted the general security in terms of the security of transactions and sougnt to effectuate the will of individuals to bring about legal results, was developed out of Roman law and the custom of merchants through juristic theories of natural law. Finally it was used as a stabilizing idea, as in the latter part of the nineteenth century, when men proved that law was an evil, even if a necessary evil, that there should be as little law made as possible, since all law involved restraint upon free exertion of the will, and hence that jurist and legislator should be content to leave things legal as they are and allow the individual "to work out in freedom his own happiness or misery" on that basis.

When this last stage in the development of the idea of law as existing to promote or permit the maximum of free individual self-assertion had been reached, the juristic possibilities of the conception had been exhausted. There were no more continents to discover. Natural resources had been discovered and exploited and the need was for conservation of what remained available. The forces of nature had been harnessed to human use. Industrial development had reached large proportions, and organization and division of labor in our economic order had gone so far that anyone who would could no longer go forth freely and do anything which a restless imagination and daring ambition suggested to him as a means of gain. Although lawyers went on repeating the old formula, the law began to move in another direction. The freedom of the owner of property to do upon it whatever he liked, so he did not overstep his limits or endanger the public health or safety, began to be restricted. Nay, the law began to make men act affirmatively upon their property in fashions which it dictated, where the general health was endangered by non-action. The power to make contracts began to be limited where industrial conditions made abstract freedom of contract defeat rather than advance full individual human life. The power of the owner to dispose freely of his property began to be limited in order to safeguard the security of the social institutions of marriage and the family. . . . Freedom of engaging in lawful callings came to be restricted, and an elaborate process of education and examination to be imposed upon those who would engage in them, lest there be injury to the public health, safety or morals. A regime in which anyone might freely set up a corporation to engage in a public service, or freely compete in such service, was superseded by one of legal exemption of existing public utilities from destructive competition. In a crowded world, whose resources had been exploited, a system of promoting the maximum of individual self-assertion had come to produce more friction than it relieved and to further rather than to eliminate waste.

At the end of the last and the beginning of the present century, a new way of thinking grew up. Jurists began to think in terms of human wants or desires rather than of human wills. They began to think that what they had to do was not simply to equalize or harmonize wills, but, if not to equalize, at least to harmonize the satisfaction of wants. They began to weigh or balance and reconcile claims or wants or desires, as formerly they had balanced or reconciled wills. They began to think of the end of law not as a maximum of self-assertion, but as a maximum satisfaction of wants. Hence for a time they thought of the problem of ethics, of jurisprudence, and of politics as chiefly one of valuing; as a problem of finding criteria of the relative value of interests. In jurisprudence and politics they saw that we must add practical problems of the possibility of making interests effective through governmental action, judicial or administrative. But the first question was one of the wants to be recognized—of the interests to be recognized and secured. Having inventoried the wants or claims or interests which are asserting and for which legal security is sought, we were to value them, select those to be recognized, determine the limits within which they were to be given effect in view of other recognized interests, and ascertain how far we might give them effect by law in view of the inherent limitations upon effective legal action. This mode of thinking may be seen, concealed under different terminologies, in more than one type of jurist in the last three decades.

Three elements contributed to shift the basis of theories as to the end of law from wills to wants, from a reconciling or harmonizing of wills to a reconciling or harmonizing of wants. The most important part was played by psychology which undermined the foundation of the metaphysical will-philosophy of law. Through the movement for unification of the social sciences, economics also played an important part, especially indirectly through the attempts at economic interpretation by legal history, reinforcing psychology by showing the extent to which law had been shaped by the pressure of economic wants. Also the differentiation of society, involved in industrial organization, was no mean factor, when classes came to exist in which claims to a minimum human existence, under the standards of the given civilization, became more pressing than claims to self-assertion. Attention was turned from the nature of law to its purpose, and a functional attitude, a tendency to measure legal rules and doctrines and institutions by the extent to which they further or achieve the ends for which law exists, began to replace the older method of judging law by criteria drawn from itself. In this respect the thought of the present is more like that of the seventeenth and eighteenth centuries than that of the nineteenth century. . . .

In its earlier form social-utilitarianism, in common with all nineteenth-century philosophies of law, was too absolute. Its teleological theory was to show us what actually and necessarily took place in lawmaking rather than what we were seeking to bring about. Its service to the philosophy of law was in compelling us to give over the ambiguous term "right" and to distinguish between the claims or wants or demands, existing independently of law, the legally recognized or delimited claims or wants or demands, and the legal institutions, which broadly go by the name of legal rights, whereby the claims when recognized and delimited are secured. Also it first made clear how much the task of the lawmaker is one of compromise. To the law-of-nature school, lawmaking was but an absolute development of absolute principles. A complete logical development of the content implicit in each natural right would give a body of law adequate to every time and place. It is true an idea of compromise did lurk behind the theory of the metaphysical jurists in the nineteenth century. But they sought an absolute harmonizing rather than a working compromise for the time and place. Conflicting individual wills were to be reconciled absolutely by a formula which had ultimate and universal authority. When we think of law as existing to secure social interests, so far as they may be secured through an ordering of men and of human relations through the machinery of organized political society, it becomes apparent that we may reach a practicable system of compromises of conflicting human desires here and now, by means of a mental picture of giving effect to as much as we can, without believing that we have a perfect solution for all time and for every place. . . .

Social utilitarianism has stood in need of correction both from psychology and from sociology. It must be recognized that lawmaking and adjudication are not in fact determined precisely by a weighing of interests. In practice the pressure of wants, demands, desires, will warp the actual compromises made by the legal system this way or that. In order to maintain the general security we endeavor in every way to minimize this warping. But one needs only to look below the surface of the law anywhere at any time to see it going on, even if covered up by mechanical devices to make the process appear an absolute one and the result a predetermined one. We may not expect that the compromises made and enforced by the legal order will always and infallibly give effect to any picture we may make of the nature or ends of the process of making and enforcing them. Yet there will be less of this subconscious warping if we have a clear picture before us of what we are seeking to do and to what end, and if we build in the image thereof so far as we consciously build and shape the law.

Difficulties arise chiefly in connection with criteria of value. If we say that interests are to be catalogued or inventoried, that they are then to be valued, that those which are found to be of requisite value are to be recognized legally and given effect within limits determined by the valuation, so far as inherent difficulties in effective legal securing of interests will permit, the question arises at once, How shall we do this work of valuing? Philosophers have devoted much ingenuity to the discovery of some method of getting at the intrinsic importance of various interests, so that an absolute formula may be reached in accordance wherewith it may be assured that the weightier interests intrinsically shall prevail. But I am skeptical as to the possibility of an absolute judgment. We are confronted at this point by a fundamental question of social and political philosophy. I do not believe the jurist has to do more than recognize the problem and perceive that it is presented to him as one of securing all social interest so far as he may, of maintaining a balance or harmony among them that is compatible with the securing of all of them. The last century preferred the general security. The present century has shown many signs of preferring the individual moral and social life. I doubt whether such preferences can maintain themselves.

Social utilitarians would say, weigh the several interests in terms of the end of law. But have we any given to us absolutely? Is the end of law anything less than to do whatever may be achieved thereby to satisfy human desires? . . . I do not mean that the law should interfere as of course in every human relation and in every situation where some one chances to think a social want may be satisfied thereby. Experience has shown abundantly how futile legal machinery may be in its attempts to secure certain kinds of interests. What I do say is, that if in any field of human conduct or in any human relation the law, with such machinery as it has, may satisfy a social want without a disproportionate sacrifice of other claims, there is no eternal limitation inherent in the nature of things, there are no bounds imposed at creation, to stand in the way of its doing so.

Let us apply some of the other theories which are now current. The Neo-Hegelians say: Try the claims in terms of civilization, in terms of the development of human powers to the most of which they are capable—the most complete human mastery of nature, both human nature and external nature. The Neo-Kantians say: Try them in terms of a community of free-willing men as the social ideal. Duguit says: Try them in terms of social interdependence and social function. Do they promote or do they impede social interdependence through similarity of interest and division of labor? In these formulas do we really get away from the problem of a balance compatible with maintaining all the interests, with responding to all the wants and claims, which are involved in civilized social existence?

For the purpose of understanding the law of today I am content with a picture of satisfying as much of the whole body of human wants as we may with the least sacrifice. I am content to think of law as a social institution to satisfy social wants—the claims and demands involved in the existence of civilized society—by giving effect to as much as we may with the least sacrifice, so far as such wants may be satisfied or such claims given effect by an ordering of human conduct through politically organized society. For present purposes I am content to see in legal history the record of a continually wider recognizing and satisfying of human wants or claims or desires through social control; a more embracing and more effective securing of social interests; a continually more complete and effective elimination of waste and precluding of friction in human enjoyment of the goods of existence—in short, a continually more efficacious social engineering.

23

MATERIALISM *

by

HUGH ELLIOT

(1881–1930)

The main purpose of the present work is to defend the doctrine of materialism. . . . The outlines of this system are not new; the main features of it, indeed, have been admittedly associated with scientific progress for centuries past. An age of science is necessarily an age of materialism; ours is a scientific age, and it may be said with truth that we are all materialists now. The main principles which I shall endeavour to emphasize are three.

1. The uniformity of law. In early times events appeared to be entirely hazardous and unaccountable, and they still seem so, if we confine attention purely to the passing moment. But as science advances, there is disclosed a uniformity in the procedure of Nature. When the conditions at any one moment are precisely identical with those which prevailed at some previous moment, the results flowing from them will also be identical. It is found, for instance, that a body of given mass attracts some other body of given mass at a given distance with a force of a certain strength. It is found that when the masses, distances, and other conditions are precisely repeated, the attraction between the bodies is always exactly the same. It is found, further, that when the distance between the bodies is increased the force of their attraction is diminished in a fixed proportion, and this again is found to hold true at all distances at which they may be placed. The force of their attraction again varies in a different but still constant proportion to their masses. And hence results the law of gravitation, by which the force of attraction can be precisely estimated from a knowledge of the masses and distances between any two bodies whatever. A uniformity is established which remains absolute within the experience of Man, and to an equivalent extent the haphazard appearance of events is found to be only an appearance. Innumerable other laws of a similar character are gradually discovered, establishing a sort of nexus between every

* [From Chs. 5 and 6 of *Modern Science and Materialism* (1919). By special arrangement with Longmans, Green and Co.]

kind of event. If oxygen and hydrogen in the proportion by weight of eight to one are mixed together, and an electric spark is passed through them, water is formed; and on every occasion where precisely the same conditions are realized precisely the same result ensues. This truth is the basis of the experimental method. If from similar conditions it were possible that dissimilar results should follow on various occasions, then experiments would be useless for advancing knowledge.

This uniformity of sequence confers the power of prophesy; and the more we learn about the nexus of natural phenomena, the greater becomes our power of prophesying future events. Such prophesies are made and fulfilled at the present day in all departments of knowledge where the data or conditions are sufficiently few and simple to be dealt with by calculation, as, for instance, in many astronomical problems. They are made even when the data are numerous and complicated, though with much less accuracy. We can foretell at what minute on what day an eclipse of the Sun will begin to take place. We can equally foretell that a rise in the bank-rate will, under normal conditions, cause an influx of gold; but precisely how much gold we cannot tell. With a larger knowledge of the conditions, we could arrive at a closer approximation to the amount of the influx. With an absolute knowledge of all the conditions at work, we could prophesy the exact number of ounces of gold that any specified rise of bank-rate would divert into this country. Such a knowledge, of course, is for ever impossible, since the factors concerned are innumerable and severally minute; to apply mathematical analysis to them, even if they could all be collected, would infinitely transcend our powers. Nevertheless, we shall be led to adopt the proposition of Laplace, to the effect that if we knew the precise disposition at any moment of all the matter and energy existing in the Universe, and the direction of motion of every moving particle, and if we were armed with a mathematics of infinite power, we should be able to prophesy the exact disposition of all the matter and energy in the Universe at any future time. Any being who possessed such powers, and who, a myriad ages ago, had acquired absolute knowledge at some moment of the nebula from which the solar system arose, would have been able to prophesy that at this present moment there would exist a being identical with myself who would be writing the words that are now flowing from my pen; he would have been able to prophesy that a little later other beings, identical with my readers, would be perusing those words, and he would be aware of what emotions would be excited within them by the perusal. In other words, the uniformity of Nature and the paramountcy of law are universal and without exception.

2. The denial of teleology. Scientific materialism warmly denies that there exists any such thing as purpose in the Universe, or that events have any ulterior motive or goal to which they are striving. It asserts that all events are due to the interaction of matter and motion acting by blind necessity in accordance with those invariable sequences to which we have given the name of laws. This is an important bond of connection between the materialism of the ancient Greeks and that of modern science. Among all peoples not highly cultivated there reigns a passionate conviction, not only that the Universe as a whole is working out some pre-determined purpose, but that every individual part of it subserves some special need in the fulfilment of this purpose. Needless to say, the purpose has always been regarded as associated with human welfare. The Universe, down to its smallest parts, is regarded by primitive superstition as existing for the special benefit of man. To such extreme lengths has this view been carried that even Bernardin de Saint-Pierre, who only died last century, argued that the reason why melons are ribbed is that they may be eaten more easily by families.

The reason for this early teleology is obvious. We all of us survey the Universe from the standpoint of our own centrality. Subjectively we all do stand actually at the centre of the Universe. Our entire experience of the Universe is an experience of it as it affects ourselves; for if it does not affect ourselves, we know of it only indirectly, and in primitive stages we do not know of it at all. As our education endows us with a wider outlook and a wider knowledge, we come to see that the objective Universe is very different from our own private subjective Universe. At first we discover that we as individuals are not the centre of the Universe, as appears to uncorrected experience, but that we are merely one individual among many others of equal status constituting a nation or society. We then perhaps regard our own society as the centre of the Universe, as many primitive peoples do, such, for instance, as the ancient Romans and the modern Chinese. Or we may regard our own sex as the purposed product of the Universe, as in many Mohammedan peoples, who hold that women have not souls like men, and that they exist purely for the benefit or use of men, in the same way that cattle exist in order to be eaten, or that melons are ribbed to indicate the proper amount of one portion.

With still further cultivation, the entire human species becomes regarded as the centre and object of all events in the Universe. This is the stage now reached by the masses in modern civilizations. Just as the existence of one particular individual has not the world-wide or cosmic importance that that individual is apt to suppose; just as the existence of a particular tribe or society is not of the profound historic import that that tribe or society very commonly imagines; so too the human species as a whole is far from being, as it too often believes, the sole object for which the Universe was created, with all things in it, great and small. The human species is, indeed, a mere incident in the universal redistribution of matter and motion; its existence has not the smallest cosmic significance. Our species is biologically very modern. Neither in numbers nor in antiquity can it compare with infinitely numerous species of other animals inhabiting the Earth. The Earth itself is one of the smaller planets, revolving round a minor star. The entire solar system, of which the Earth is so insignificant a portion, is itself a system of contemptible minuteness, set among other luminaries and other systems which surpass it many times in magnitude, in brightness. and in every other ascertainable quality that we are accustomed to admire. . . . Most men have as yet not shaken off the habit, which all men necessarily start from, that they themselves, or their family, nation or kind, are in fact, as in appearance, the very centre of the cosmos.

3. The denial of any form of existence other than those envisaged by physics and chemistry, that is to say, other than existences that have some kind of palpable material characteristics and quality. It is here that modern materialism begins to part company with ancient materialism, and it is here that I expect the main criticisms of opponents to be directed. The modern doctrine stands in direct opposition to a belief in any of those existences that are vaguely classed as "spiritual." To this category belong not only ghosts, gods, souls, *et hoc genus omne* [and everything of the kind], for these have long been rejected from the beliefs of most advanced thinkers. The time has now come to include also in the condemned list that further imaginary entity which we call "mind," "consciousness," etc., together with its various sub-species of intellect, will, feeling, etc., in so far as they are supposed to be independent or different from material existences or processes. . . .

The proposition which I here desire to advance is that every event occurring in the Universe, including those events known as mental processes, and all kinds of human action or conduct, are expressible purely in terms of matter and motion. If we assume in the primeval nebula of the solar system no other elementary factors beyond those of matter and energy or motion, we can theoretically, as above remarked, deduce the existing Universe, including mind, consciousness, etc., without the introduction of any new factor whatsoever. The existing Universe and all other things and events therein may be theoretically expressed in terms of matter and energy, undergoing continuous redistribution in accordance with the ordinary laws of physics and chemistry. If all manifestations within our experience can be thus expressed, as has for long been believed by men of science, what need is there for the introduction of any new entity of spiritual character, called mind? It has no part to play; it is impotent in causation. According to Huxley's theory it accompanies certain physical processes as a shadow, without any power, or any reason, or any use. The world, as Huxley and the great majority of physiologists affirm, would be just the same without it. Now there is an ancient logical precept which retains a large validity: *entia non sunt multiplicanda praeter necessitatem* [no more entities should be posited than are necessary]. It is sometimes referred to as William of Occam's razor, which cuts off and rejects from our theories all factors or entities which are superfluous in guiding us to an explanation. "Mind" as a separate entity is just such a superfluity. I will not deny—indeed I cordially affirm—that it is a direct datum of experience; but there is no direct datum of experience to the effect that it is anything different from certain cerebral processes. . . . The ancient materialists believed to a certain extent in an unseen world; they believed even in the existence of souls. They asserted their materialism only by the theory that these entities were material in character. Democritus conceived the soul as consisting of smooth, round, material particles. The scientific materialist of today does not believe in any separate existence of this kind whatever. He regards what is called soul or mind as *identical* with certain physical processes passing in a material brain, processes of which the ancient Greeks knew nothing, and, indeed, which are still entirely unknown to all who have not acquired some smattering of physiology. . . .

The materialism which I shall advocate, therefore, is centred round three salient points: the uniformity of law, the exclusion of purpose, and the assertion of monism; that is to say, that there exists no kind of spiritual substance or entity of a different nature from that of which matter is composed.

The first of these propositions, otherwise called the Law of Universal Causation, affirms that nothing happens without a cause, and that the same causes under the same conditions always produce the same effects. In order to gain a true comprehension of this law, we have to define what we mean by "cause" and "effect," and what is the nature of the nexus between them. The conception of the Universe from which we start is that of a great system of matter and motion undergoing redistribution according to fixed sequences, which in the terminology of science are called laws. The matter is constantly undergoing transformation from one of its forms into another, and the energy is redistributed and transformed in a corresponding manner. From this primary conception alone, we are able to derive a precise definition of what is meant by cause, a problem which is almost insuperable from any other standpoint. Mill defined one event as being the cause of another when the first event is found invariably in experience to be followed by the second. In cause and effect he saw nothing further than an invariable sequence. His view was at once demolished when he was asked whether he considered that day was the cause of night, for this also is a sequence invariable in our experience. But if we apply analysis, the difficulty vanishes. If we regard an event as a momentary phase in the redistribution of matter and motion, then the cause of the event is found in the immediately preceding state of distribution of that same matter and motion. Let us ask, for instance, what is the cause of the sudden appearance of a new fixed star in the heavens. Supposing that there were previously two extinct suns moving rapidly towards each other and coming into collision, we should be making a statement of events which would be recognized as a possibly true "cause." The second event, or "effect," is represented exclusively in terms of matter and motion by the idea of two coalesced and volatilized bodies giving rise to vast quantities of heat and light. And the cause is given merely by stating the previous distribution of that matter and energy which is concerned in the production of the event. The *matter* concerned in the event consisted of two solid bodies at a rapidly diminishing distance from one another. The *energy* consisted of half the product of their momentum and velocity. By the collision the matter contained in the solid bodies underwent that redistribution involved in passing into a gaseous state, with the decomposition of many of its molecules, that is to say, with a rearrangement or redistribution of its atoms. The energy of motion previously contained in the solid bodies underwent at the same time a transformation into heat and light. The sudden light, therefore, is explained, or derives its cause, merely by furnishing a statement of the previous distribution of the matter and energy concerned in its production.

Let me now take a slightly more complex instance, that, namely, of a specific bacillus as the cause of tuberculosis. What is the cause of tuberculosis? The disease is characterized by lesions of a specific type, which may occur in very various parts of the body. The effect, therefore, or the tuberculous condition, may be analyzed into a particular arrangement of matter and energy. The arrangement, indeed, is very similar to that which prevails in, and constitutes, a healthy organism; but here and there the matter and energy are somewhat differently located, so as to constitute what is called a tuberculous organism.

Before infection, the matter and energy of the organism were normally distributed. At the moment of infection there is an addition of a minute quantity of other matter and energy specifically distributed into a number of little bodies, which are called bacilli; and their matter and energy, combined with the matter and energy of a healthy organism, undergo further redistribution, resulting ultimately in that new arrangement which is characteristic of the disease. All this works by inevitable laws, just those same laws which control the unceasing redistribution of matter and motion in every part of the Universe. The cause of any phenomenon is found when we have described the antecedent state of distribution of the matter and energy which are combined to constitute that phenomenon.

It happens, however, that in practical life we are commonly interested only in one element out of the numerous constituent parts that go to make up a phenomenon. From the objective point of view this element is very often extremely insignificant, yet we confine the appellation of cause to it alone. In the example above cited, the objective or absolute cause of a tubercular lung is furnished only by an account of the origin or previous state of distribution of the matter and energy constituting the lung, as well as of that constituting the bacilli. But we are in the habit of taking the lung for granted, and referring to the bacilli as the cause of the disease. . . .

The notion of cause has, therefore, both an objective and a subjective element. Objectively, the cause of any phenomenon is the preceding state of distribution of the matter and energy concerned in that phenomenon. From this point of view, it is plain that the efficient cause † of the existing state of the Universe at any one moment is its state at the moment immediately preceding. Subjectively, we are interested, however, only in the evolution of some part of the component matter and energy, and we are in the habit of conferring the name of cause only on that particular factor in the evolution that happens to interest us, while designating the other factors conditions.

The above definition of cause at once clears up the problem of the difference between "how" and "why." Many men of science, following Mach and Karl Pearson, have affirmed that science can never explain more than "how" events occur: it can never touch the problem of "why" they occur. On this second point humanity must always rest ignorant. They have thus set up a deep and fundamental distinction between "how" and "why" which a very moderate amount of analysis suffices altogether to dispel. I must ask the reader

† [See pp. 133–134, and footnote p. 333.]

once more to visualize the Universe as consisting of a fixed sum of matter and energy undergoing redistribution. Consider some momentary and circumscribed phase of that evolution, which in ordinary language is called an event, and let us see how we should answer the two questions "how" and "why" this event comes about. Clearly we describe "how" it comes about, when we render a complete statement of the immediately preceding history of all the matter and energy engaged in it. "How" corresponds to the purely objective definition of cause given above. Now let us ask "why" the event occurs. The answer is given by naming the immediately preceding history, not of all the matter and motion engaged, but of that part of it *in which we happen to be interested*. "Why" corresponds to that final definition of cause, offered above, in which both objective and subjective elements are included. In fact, "why" is simply a limited "how"; it covers less ground; it demands the history, not of the whole of the matter and energy engaged in the event, but only of a particular section of it which happens to arouse special interest.

It follows from the above that, whereas to the question "how" an event takes place there can be but one complete answer, to the question "why" it takes place there may be many answers, and all equally true. . . .

Suppose the question asked is, "Why is the moon full tonight?" a great variety of true answers may be offered, when we are ignorant of the questioner's special interest in the matter. The moon is full because it is placed on the opposite side of the Earth from the Sun; because it has a surface which reflects light; because a month has elapsed since the last full moon; because it is a little out of the direct straight line with the Sun and Earth; because the Sun is shining upon that half of its surface turned toward the Earth; because the rays of light can traverse space, etc., etc. Our answer to a child would be different from our answer to an astronomer; for the former would be interested in different features of the process from the latter. But in order to furnish a comprehensive answer to the question *how* or by what process the full moon occurs, all these factors one after another would have to be enumerated. The "why" of phenomena is no more than a special case of the "how"; and all questions "why" certain phenomena occur are answered, if at all, only by relating how they occur; nor can they be answered in any other way; nor has the interrogative "why" any other significance that is conceivable to mankind. In explaining why some phenomenon occurs, we merely have to exercise an eclectic discrimination in deciding which of the numerous factors concerned in the process is most likely to satisfy the curiosity of the inquirer. And all those factors, under analysis, may be resolved into a graphical or historical account of the changes undergone from moment to moment by the matter and energy engaged in the production of the phenomenon. . . .

And this leads me to the second problem which I have here to deal with, the problem of teleology. I have hitherto endeavoured to represent the notion of cause and effect in purely materialistic terms, to the exclusion of all metaphysical transcendentalism; to state the relation of cause and effect in terms of the redistribution of matter and motion. I now have to perform the same task for the conception of purpose, and more particularly of human purpose, in order to show how purposiveness may be translated into purely materialistic and mechanical terms; that is to say, how it, too, may be expressed as a phase of the normal process of redistribution of matter and motion under fixed and invariable laws.

At the outset of this inquiry, we have to notice that the word purpose is involved in the same vagueness of significance that attends almost all words used in popular speech. In general a word in popular use has to be defined and limited to some precise meaning before it is fit for employment in a philosophical discussion. In the present case the word is commonly employed in at least two meanings, which differ greatly from each other; and this duality of meaning leads to a duality in the derivative conceptions of "teleology," "finalism," "end," etc., which has not infrequently given rise to confusion and error. The two significations may be roughly grouped as intelligent purposiveness and unintelligent purposiveness, and the reduction of each of these to mechanistic terms involves two different lines of analysis. I shall deal first with unintelligent purposiveness.

In this case, the word is usually applied to a certain kind of organic reactions that bear an obvious relation to the requirements of the reacting organism. An *Amœba* in the water throws out pseudopodia at random in all directions. When one of these pseudopodia comes into contact with some substance suitable for food, the protoplasm streams round and encloses the particle, which is thus incorporated in the body of the *Amœba* and there digested. The reaction is purposive in the sense that a somewhat complicated series of movements is carried out, which leads to the preservation of the active organism.

In just the same way, when we ascend the animal scale, the sea-anemone spreads its tentacles at large under the surface of the water. On contact with any substance suitable for food the tentacles contract around the substance and draw it into the interior of the sea-anemone. This action is similarly purposive in that it procures the continued existence of the animal. In all animals the common movements and reactions are predominantly of this purposive type. If an object suddenly appears close to our eyes, we involuntarily close them for an instant, and this reaction is obviously purposive, as directed towards the protection of the eyes.

All these instinctive actions are purposive in character, yet equally, without doubt, they are all of the nature of reflex action, working blindly and inevitably to their conclusion. On contact with the tentacle of a sea-anemone, the stimulus thus applied to that tentacle sets up by entirely mechanical procedure organic processes which necessarily result in the observed contractions. Similarly, in the case of the human being, the sudden appearance of a near object causes an impulse to be conveyed down the optic nerve, which immediately and mechanically propagates its effect to the efferent nerves which lead to the muscles that close the eyelids. The same kind of reaction is characteristic of the functions in plants. The turning of flowers towards the light, and all the processes of absorption, transpiration, etc., are, on the one hand, subservient to the life and prosperity of the plant, while, on the other hand, they are blind mechanical reactions to stimuli.

Seeing that a single action may thus be at the same time both purposive and mechanical, it is plain that there can be no antithesis between the two; but that the difference between purpose and blind mechanism arises simply from our point of view, and not from any difference of objective character. Purposive reactions are not different from mechanical reactions, but they *are* mechanical reactions of a certain kind. Not all mechanical reactions are purposive, but all purposive reactions are mechanical; and it remains to determine *what* mechanical actions may be correctly described as purposive, and what are simply blind and meaningless.

The distinction is entirely one of convention. I have represented all events in the light of a redistribution of matter and energy under fixed mechanical laws. Certain particular phases in this redistribution, certain particular collocations of the evolving matter and energy, happen to possess for us a very special interest, and we watch with peculiar attention the material developments and antecedents which give rise to those particular collocations that concern us. Of such collocations, the most enthralling is the maintenance of that moving equilibrium which we call the life of an organism. This equilibrium is due to a succession of stimuli from without, met by "adapted" reactions on the part of the organism; and it is to that particular item of the universal mechanism called an adapted organic reaction, that we apply the name of purpose.

The material origin of all purposive reactions would be adequately explained by the theory of Natural Selection. We must suppose that, at the origin of life, the primeval little speck of organic matter would respond in any haphazard kind of way to the stimuli affecting it from without. These organisms or pre-organisms would in every case give a blind response, due to the chemical or material constitution of their protoplasm. By the ordinary laws of chance, the vast majority of these reactions would not be such as to promote the continuance of life, and in many cases would be such as immediately to destroy life. But again, by the ordinary laws of chance, it would happen in some cases that the response to external stimuli would be such as in some way or other to favour the continuance of life. Pre-organisms, the chemical constitution of whose protoplasm was of this type, would flourish and be perpetuated, while all other types of incipient life would be extinguished. The reactions of the surviving pre-organisms are what we should call "purposive." In this sense, therefore, we mean by purpose those reactions of organic matter which happen to promote the continued existence of that organic matter. By the mechanical process of Natural Selection, all varieties of organic matter that respond unpurposively—that is, whose responses do not happen to promote their continued existence—perish, with the result that either the whole or the larger part of every animal's activities are purposive in character. At first, therefore, Natural Selection is the great teleological agent. The net result of this analysis is that purpose is a name given to certain material phenomena which fulfil some arbitrarily chosen condition, and withheld from all other material phenomena which do not fulfil that condition. The condition usually taken in simple cases is the maintenance of life, and among the factors in this maintenance of life are commonly selected those which involve organic activity. All such organic activity is then said to be purposive.

The point specially to be noticed is that purpose is purely arbitrary and subjective; it corresponds to nothing in outer nature, nor are purposive acts in any way objectively different from random acts. By selecting a new set of conditions to be satisfied, or a new standard, it is possible to represent any kind of mechanical event as being purposive. Supposing, for instance, that the condition to be fulfilled was that the planets of our solar system should revolve round the Sun in the orbits that they actually do; supposing that we had a great personal interest in their doing so, and anxiously watched all material developments in the primeval nebula which appeared to lead to such a consummation; supposing that we can transfer ourselves to this cosmic point of view, we might then rightly affirm that gravitation is purposive, just as we now affirm that Natural Selection is purposive. The one leads to the moving equilibrium of the solar system, the other leads to the moving equilibrium of a living organism. Extinguish gravitation, so that the planets move at hazard, and the solar system will not survive. Extinguish Natural Selection, so that organisms react at hazard, and those organisms will not survive. The parallel is complete. . . . If we do not call the cosmic manifestations purposive, but do call vital manifestations purposive, it is because we are intensely interested in the latter, and but slightly interested in the former. The continuance of life, the satisfaction of needs, etc., are conditions that appear to us so important as to demand a special name for the most prominent group of factors concerned in them; whereas the continuance of the solar system, and the unfailing adherence of the planets to their present orbits, is not a subject of such overweening importance, or of such unceasing allusion in common life, as to require the establishment of a special name. A purposive movement, therefore, is an ordinary case of the redistribution of matter and energy. The name is used in those cases where the matter and energy are knotted up into that structure which we call a living organism, and is applied to such activities of the organism as conduce to its own continued existence.

I now come to the second class of activities to which the name of purpose is applied, that is to say, cases of activity which bear reference to an end consciously and intelligently foreseen, such as the acts inspired by the conscious will in human beings. These activities are commonly regarded as being in a higher degree teleological than the unintelligent reactions hitherto considered; and in many uses of the word "purpose," reference is intended exclusively to these intelligent anticipations of future events, and to the activities carried out in consequence of such anticipations. In this sense purpose is allied to will, and purposive actions are more or less synonymous with voluntary actions. The question before us, therefore, is whether the will can be comprised in the materialistic scheme which governs all other natural phenomena, or whether it is something outside and independent, knowing no laws, and therefore not amenable to scientific discussion. And this question, again, is nothing more than the problem of free-will and determinism; of vitalism and mechanism; of spiritualism and materialism; according to the standpoint from which we approach it.

. . . There is no qualitative difference between the simpler reflex action and the highest or most complicated reactions that the developed nervous system is capable of evincing. In the lowest animals, the nervous system is adapted simply for conveying impulses from the outer surface to some nerve-centre, whence proceeds a new impulse along another nerve back to the periphery, causing a contraction or some other movement. The whole procedure is purely mechanical. Now the most developed known nervous system arises by evolution in gradual stages from this most elementary form, and the mode of development consists in the compounding of reflex action. From the simple reflex-arc arise multitudinous other reflex-arcs, integrated together into one great nervous system. Instead of one nerve running from periphery to centre, many nerves run; a corresponding multiplication occurs in the outgoing nerves. The centre likewise increases beyond recognition in elaboration and complexity. It is broken up into a number of constituent parts, themselves connected by bundles of nerve-fibres, and higher centres grow up, which receive impulses from the lower centres, and send back others. But the simple reflex-arc remains the unit of functional activity and of structural form. However infinite the complication of the developed system, it is still based on the simple reflex-arc, and, indeed, consists of innumerable reflex-arcs compounded together in every variety. The reflex-arc is mechanical in function; hence the developed nervous system is mechanical in function. Nowhere is there any break in development, at which we might suppose that a new and non-mechanical factor makes its appearance.

The relation between the highly compounded nervous system of a man to the elementary reflex-arc corresponds to the relation between the intelligent purposiveness now under discussion and the unintelligent purposiveness analyzed above. We now have to consider which of the reactions of the nervous system are to be called purposive, and which are to be looked upon as merely random.

One of the most striking features of the developed nervous system as compared with the primitive system is that a stimulus does not give immediate rise to an action. In the elementary animal, stimulus is promptly followed by contraction. In the highly developed animal, the stimulus may simply take effect on the nervous system without causing any external response. The nervous system, however, is to some degree affected by the stimulus, so that at future times different actions will arise from it from those that would have arisen if no such stimulus had ever been experienced. So, too, the nervous system may initiate an action without any immediately preceding external stimulus. Instead of the primitive arrangement by which a stimulus elicits a simple and immediate response, a stimulus may now impinge upon the nervous system and leave its effects stored up there. It buries itself, and is lost in the complex maze of nervous tissue; in so doing it causes some modification of that tissue, which will thereafter affect the responses to stimuli upon it. The sequence of stimulus and response is obscured. In a highly developed nervous system, the stimuli incessantly entering no longer bear any immediate relation with the responses incessantly given out. The brain provides a great storehouse and clearing-ground for nervous impulses, so that the impressions entering and the impulses departing from it lose a great part of their immediate connection. The incoming currents spend themselves in effecting some rearrangement of the matter and energy belonging to the brain. Outgoing currents are similarly due in very many cases to rearrangements occurring in the brain, the product of a number of elements internal and external, rather than to any individual external stimulus. To this is due what appears to an outside observer as the initiating power of the brain, and all those kind of activities known to psychologists as choice, will, etc.

We are now in a position to appreciate the true meaning of those acts which are described as intelligently purposive. Being deliberate and reasoned activities, they are as far as possible removed from the simple type of reflex action in which response follows immediately on external stimulus. They belong to the category in which the immediate stimulus is in the brain itself, and is to be regarded as consisting of rearrangements of the matter and energy contained in the nervous substance of the brain. The brain during consciousness can never be still, and its unceasing activities supply the stimulus, not only for purposive, but for all actions of an intellectual character. Now this permanent cerebral activity can be divided into a number of different types, known psychologically by such names as memory, imagination, reason, etc. Although nervous physiology has not yet advanced far enough to enable us to say what are the different kinds of material processes in the brain corresponding to these psychical processes, yet there is no doubt that the psychical distinction is based upon some actual distinction in the corresponding activities occurring in the brain. Among these cerebral processes is that which is known psychologically as a desire for some external object or event, a visualization of some external phenomenon as an end or purpose to be attained. This desire may then act upon efferent nerves and give rise to the activities which we know as purposive. The essence of a purposive action, and the standard by which it is distinguished from other kinds of actions, is that the "end" to which the action leads was previously represented in the brain of the agent, and composes the stimulus of action. The compound stimulus arises, as I have said, from the composition of large numbers of elementary stimuli previously received. It consists psychologically of a faint representation of the sensation which would be vividly presented by the realization of some outward occurrence. And when this faint representation actually functions as a stimulus which innervates the muscles whose contraction brings about the external occurrence represented, we have what is called an action of intelligent purpose. Hereafter the analysis is identical with that employed in the description of unintelligent purpose. The only difference is that the stimulus which in the latter case consisted of a simple external contact, is replaced by a complex cerebral pattern, based upon, and produced by, a large number of these stimuli acquired at various former periods, and of course determined by the structure of the brain. It may be asked by what process it happens that a faint psychical (or cerebral) representation of some desired sensation can give rise to just that complicated series of muscular activities needed for the actual realization of this sensation. The answer is the same as in the case of unintelligent purpose, when we inquired how the stimulus provided by contact of a food-particle set up just the right contractions for absorbing that particle into the substance of the organism. The answer suggested was *Natural Selection*. In all cases where the complex cerebral stimulus causes a muscular activity that does not happen to meet the end in view, the organism is extinguished. Only that small minority survive in which the correct muscular activity is brought about.

24

FAITH AND REASON *

by

ST. THOMAS AQUINAS

(1225?–1274)

In What Way It Is Possible to Make Known the Divine Truth. Since . . . not every truth is to be made known in the same way, *and it is the part of an educated man to seek for conviction in each subject, only so far as the nature of the subject allows,* as the Philosopher [i.e. Aristotle] most rightly observes as quoted by Boethius, it is necessary to show first of all in what way it is possible to make known the aforesaid truth.

* [From Bk. I, Chs. 3–13 of the *Summa Contra Gentiles* and Pt. I, Question 2 of the *Summa Theologica*. Translated by the English Dominican Fathers (1912–1924). By kind permission of Benziger Brothers, New York, and Burns, Oates, and Washbourne, London.]

Now in those things which we hold about God there is truth in two ways. For certain things that are true about God wholly surpass the capability of human reason, for instance that God is three and one: while there are certain things to which even natural reason can attain, for instance that God is, that God is one, and others like these, which even the philosophers proved demonstratively of God, being guided by the light of natural reason.

That certain divine truths wholly surpass the capability of human reason, is most clearly evident. For since the principle of all the knowledge which the reason acquires about a thing, is the understanding of that thing's essence, because according to the Philosopher's teaching the principle of a demonstration is *what a thing is,* it follows that our knowledge about a thing will be in proportion to our understanding of its essence. Wherefore, if the human intellect comprehends the essence of a particular thing, for instance a stone or a triangle, no truth about that thing will surpass the capability of human reason. But this does not happen to us in relation to God, because the human intellect is incapable by its natural power of attaining to the comprehension of His essence: since our intellect's knowledge, according to the mode of the present life, originates from the senses: so that things which are not objects of sense cannot be comprehended by the human intellect, except in so far as knowledge of them is gathered from sensibles. Now sensibles cannot lead our intellect to see in them what God is, because they are effects unequal to the power of their cause. And yet our intellect is led by sensibles to the divine knowledge so as to know about God that He is, and other such truths, which need to be ascribed to the first principle. Accordingly some divine truths are attainable by human reason, while others altogether surpass the power of human reason.

Again. The same is easy to see from the degrees of intellects. For if one of two men perceives a thing with his intellect with greater subtlety, the one whose intellect is of a higher degree understands many things which the other is altogether unable to grasp; as instanced in a yokel who is utterly incapable of grasping the subtleties of philosophy. Now the angelic intellect surpasses the human intellect more than the intellect of the cleverest philosopher surpasses that of the most uncultured. For an angel knows God through a more excellent effect than does man, for as much as the angel's essence, through which he is led to know God by natural knowledge, is more excellent than sensible things, even than the soul itself, by which the human intellect mounts to the knowledge of God. And the divine intellect surpasses the angelic intellect much more than the angelic surpasses the human. For the divine intellect by its capacity equals the divine essence, wherefore God perfectly understands of Himself what He is, and He knows all things that can be understood about Him: whereas the angel knows not what God is by his natural knowledge, because the angel's essence, by which he is led to the knowledge of God, is an effect unequal to the power of its cause. Consequently an angel is unable by his natural knowledge to grasp all that God understands about Himself: nor again is human reason capable of grasping all that an angel understands by his natural power. Accordingly just as a man would show himself to be a most insane fool if he declared the assertions of a philosopher to be false because he was unable to understand them, so, and much more, a man would be exceedingly foolish, were he to suspect of falsehood the things revealed by God through the ministry of His angels, because they cannot be the object of reason's investigations.

Furthermore. The same is made abundantly clear by the deficiency which every day we experience in our knowledge of things. For we are ignorant of many of the properties of sensible things, and in many cases we are unable to discover the nature of those properties which we perceive by our senses. Much less therefore is human reason capable of investigating all the truths about that most sublime essence.

With this the saying of the Philosopher is in accord where he says that *our intellect in relation to those primary things which are most evident in nature is like the eye of a bat in relation to the sun.*

To this truth Holy Writ also bears witness. For it is written: *Peradventure thou wilt comprehend the steps of God and wilt find out the Almighty perfectly?* and: *Behold God is great, exceeding our knowledge,* and: *We know in part.*

Therefore all that is said about God, though it cannot be investigated by reason, must not be forthwith rejected as false, as the Manicheans and many unbelievers have thought.

That the Truth about Divine Things Which Is Attainable by Reason Is Fittingly Proposed to Man as An Object of Belief. While then the truth of the intelligible things of God is twofold, one to which the inquiry of reason can attain, the other which surpasses the whole range of human reason, both are fittingly proposed by God to man as an object of belief. We must first show this with regard to that truth which is attainable by the inquiry of reason, lest it appears to some, that since it can be attained by reason, it was useless to make it an object of faith by supernatural inspiration. Now three disadvantages would result if this truth were left solely to the inquiry of reason. One is that few men would have knowledge of God: because very many are hindered from gathering the fruit of diligent inquiry, which is the discovery of truth, for three reasons. Some indeed on account of an indisposition of temperament, by reason of which many are naturally indisposed to knowledge; so that no efforts of theirs would enable them to reach to the attainment of the highest degree of human knowledge, which consists in knowing God. Some are hindered by the needs of household affairs. For there must needs be among men some that devote themselves to the conduct of temporal affairs, who would be unable to devote so much time to the leisure of contemplative research as to reach the summit of human inquiry, namely the knowledge of God. And some are hindered by laziness. For in order to acquire the knowlledge of God in those things which reason is able to investigate, it is necessary to have a previous knowledge of many things: since almost the entire consideration of philosophy is directed to the knowledge of God: for which reason metaphysics, which is about divine things, is the last of the parts of philosophy to be studied. Wherefore it is not possible to arrive at the inquiry about the aforesaid truth except after a most laborious study: and few are willing to take upon themselves this labour for the love of a knowledge, the natural desire for which has nevertheless been instilled into the mind of man by God.

The second disadvantage is that those who would arrive at the discovery of the aforesaid truth would scarcely succeed in doing so after a long time. First, because this truth is so profound, that it is only after long practice that the human intellect is enabled to grasp it by means of reason. Secondly, because many things are required beforehand, as stated above. Thirdly, because at the time of youth, the mind, when tossed about by the various movements of the passions, is not fit for the knowledge of so sublime a truth, whereas *calm gives prudence and knowledge,* as stated in [Aristotle]. Hence mankind would remain in the deepest darkness of ignorance, if the path of reason were the only available way to the knowledge of God: because the knowledge of God which especially makes men perfect and good, would be acquired only by the few, and by these only after a long time.

The third disadvantage is that much falsehood is mingled with the investigations of human reason, on account of the weakness of our intellect in forming its judgments, and by reason of the admixture of phantasms. Consequently many would remain in doubt about those things even which are most truly demonstrated, through ignoring the force of the demonstration: especially when they perceive that different things are taught by the various men who are called wise. Moreover among the many demonstrated truths, there is sometimes a mixture of falsehood that is not demonstrated, but assumed for some probable or sophistical reason which at times is mistaken for a demonstration. Therefore it was necessary that definite certainty and pure truth about divine things should be offered to man by the way of faith.

Accordingly the divine clemency has made this salutary commandment, that even some things which reason is able to investigate must be held by faith: so that all may share in the knowledge of God easily, and without doubt or error.

Hence it is written: That *henceforward you walk not as also the Gentiles walk in the vanity of their mind, having their understanding darkened,* and: *All thy children shall be taught of the Lord.*

That Those Things Which Cannot Be Investigated by Reason Are Fittingly Proposed to Man as An Object of Faith. It may appear to some that those things which cannot be investigated by reason ought not to be proposed to man as an object of faith: because divine wisdom provides for each thing according to the mode of its nature. We must therefore prove that it is necessary also for those things which surpass reason to be proposed by God to man as an object of faith.

For no man tends to do a thing by his desire and endeavour unless it be previously known to him. Wherefore since man is directed by divine providence to a higher good than human frailty can attain in the present life, as we shall show in the sequel, it was necessary for his mind to be bidden to something higher than those things to which our reason can reach in the present life, so that he might learn to aspire, and by his endeavours to tend to something surpassing the whole state of the present life. And this is especially competent to the Christian religion, which alone promises goods spiritual and eternal: for which reason it proposes many things surpassing the thought of man: whereas the old law which contained promises of temporal things, proposed few things that are above human inquiry. It was with this motive that the philosophers, in order to wean men from sensible pleasures to virtue, took care to show that there are other goods of greater account than those which appeal to the senses, the taste of which things affords much greater delight to those who devote themselves to active or contemplative virtues.

Again it is necessary for this truth to be proposed to man as an object of faith in order that he may have truer knowledge of God. For then alone do we know God truly, when we believe that He is far above all that man can possibly think of God, because the divine essence surpasses man's natural knowledge, as stated above. Hence by the fact that certain things about God are proposed to man, which surpass his reason, he is strengthened in his opinion that God is far above what he is able to think.

There results also another advantage from this, namely, the checking of presumption which is the mother of error. For some there are who presume so far on their wits that they think themselves capable of measuring the whole nature of things by their intellect, in that they esteem all things true which they see, and false which they see not. Accordingly, in order that man's mind might be freed from this presumption, and seek the truth humbly, it was necessary that certain things far surpassing his intellect should be proposed to man by God.

Yet another advantage is made apparent by the words of the Philosopher. For when a certain Simonides maintained that man should neglect the knowledge of God, and apply his mind to human affairs, and declared that *a man ought to relish human things, and a mortal, mortal things:* the Philosopher contradicted him, saying that *a man ought to devote himself to immortal and divine things as much as he can.* Hence he says that though it is but little that we perceive of higher substances, yet that little is more loved and desired than all the knowledge we have of lower substances. He says also that when questions about the heavenly bodies can be answered by a short and probable solution, it happens that the hearer is very much rejoiced. All this shows that however imperfect the knowledge of the highest things may be, it bestows very great perfection on the soul: and consequently, although human reason is unable to grasp fully things that are above reason, it nevertheless acquires much perfection, if at least it hold things, in any way whatever, by faith.

Wherefore it is written: *Many things are shown to thee above the understanding of men,* and: *The things . . . that are of God no man knoweth, but the Spirit of God: but to us God hath revealed them by His Spirit.*

That It Is Not a Mark of Levity to Assent to the Things That Are of Faith, Although They Are above Reason. Now those who believe this truth, of *which reason affords a proof,* believe not lightly, as though *following foolish fables.* For divine Wisdom Himself, Who knows all things most fully, deigned to reveal to man *the secrets of God's wisdom:* and by suitable arguments proves His presence, and the truth of His doctrine and inspiration, by performing works surpassing the capability of the whole of nature, namely, the wondrous healing of the sick, the raising of the dead to life, a marvellous control over the heavenly bodies, and what excites yet more wonder, the inspiration of human minds, so that unlettered

and simple persons are filled with the Holy Ghost, and in one instant
are endowed with the most sublime wisdom and eloquence. And
after considering these arguments, convinced by the strength of the
proof, and not by the force of arms, nor by the promise of delights,
but—and this is the greatest marvel of all—amidst the tyranny of
persecutions, a countless crowd of not only simple but also of the
wisest men, embraced the Christian faith, which inculcates things
surpassing all human understanding, curbs the pleasures of the flesh,
and teaches contempt of all worldly things. That the minds of mortal
beings should assent to such things, is both the greatest of miracles,
and the evident work of divine inspiration, seeing that they despise
visible things and desire only those that are invisible. And that this
happened not suddenly nor by chance, but by the disposition of
God, is shown by the fact that God foretold that He would do so by
the manifold oracles of the prophets, whose books we hold in
veneration as bearing witness to our faith. This particular kind
of proof is alluded to in the words of [the Apostle Paul]: *Which,*
namely the salvation of mankind, *having begun to be declared by
the Lord, was confirmed with us by them that heard Him, God
also bearing witness by signs and wonders, and divers . . . distribu-
tions of the Holy Ghost.*

Now such a wondrous conversion of the world to the Christian
faith is a most indubitable proof that such signs did take place, so
that there is no need to repeat them, seeing that there is evidence
of them in their result. For it would be the most wondrous sign of all
if without any wondrous signs the world were persuaded by simple
and lowly men to believe things so arduous, to accomplish things so
difficult, and to hope for things so sublime. Although God ceases not
even in our time to work miracles through His saints in confirmation
of the faith. . . .

**That the Truth of Reason Is Not in Opposition to the
Truth of the Christian Faith.** Now though the aforesaid truth
of the Christian faith surpasses the ability of human reason, nevertheless those things which are naturally instilled in human reason
cannot be opposed to this truth. For it is clear that those things
which are implanted in reason by nature, are most true, so much so
that it is impossible to think them to be false. Nor is it lawful to
deem false that which is held by faith, since it is so evidently confirmed by God. Seeing then that the false alone is opposed to the
true, as evidently appears if we examine their definitions, it is impossible for the aforesaid truth of faith to be contrary to those
principles which reason knows naturally.

Again. The same thing which the disciple's mind receives from its teacher is contained in the knowledge of the teacher, unless he teach insincerely, which it were wicked to say of God. Now the knowledge of naturally known principles is instilled into us by God, since God Himself is the author of our nature. Therefore the divine Wisdom also contains these principles. Consequently whatever is contrary to these principles, is contrary to the divine Wisdom; wherefore it cannot be from God. Therefore those things which are received by faith from divine revelation cannot be contrary to our natural knowledge.

Moreover. Our intellect is stayed by contrary arguments, so that it cannot advance to the knowledge of truth. Wherefore if conflicting knowledges were instilled into us by God, our intellect would thereby be hindered from knowing the truth. And this cannot be ascribed to God.

Furthermore. Things that are natural are unchangeable so long as nature remains. Now contrary opinions cannot be together in the same subject. Therefore God does not instill into man any opinion or belief contrary to natural knowledge.

Hence the Apostle says: *The word is nigh thee even in thy heart and in thy mouth. This is the word of faith which we preach.* Yet because it surpasses reason some look upon it as though it were contrary thereto; which is impossible.

This is confirmed also by the authority of Augustine who says: *That which truth shall make known can nowise be in opposition to the holy books whether of the Old or of the New Testament.*

From this we may evidently conclude that whatever arguments are alleged against the teachings of faith, they do not rightly proceed from the first self-evident principles instilled by nature. Wherefore they lack the force of demonstration, and are either probable or sophistical arguments, and consequently it is possible to solve them.

In What Relation Human Reason Stands to the Truth of Faith. It would also seem well to observe that sensible things from which human reason derives the source of its knowledge, retain a certain trace of likeness to God, but so imperfect that it proves altogether inadequate to manifest the substance itself of God. For effects resemble their causes according to their own mode, since like action proceeds from like agent; and yet the effect does not always reach to a perfect likeness to the agent. Accordingly human reason is adapted to the knowledge of the truth of faith, which can be known in the highest degree only by those who see the divine substance, in so far as it is able to put together certain probable arguments in support thereof, which nevertheless are insufficient to enable us to understand the aforesaid truth as though it were demonstrated to us or understood by us in itself. And yet however weak these arguments may be, it is useful for the human mind to be practised therein, so long as it does not pride itself on having comprehended or demonstrated; since although our view of the sublimest things is limited and weak, it is most pleasant to be able to catch but a glimpse of them, as appears from what has been said.

The authority of Hilary is in agreement with this statement: for he says while speaking of this same truth: *Begin by believing these things, advance and persevere; and though I know thou wilt not arrive, I shall rejoice at thy advance. For he who devoutly follows in pursuit of the infinite, though he never come up with it, will always advance by setting forth. Yet pry not into that secret, and meddle not in the mystery of the birth of the infinite, nor presume to grasp that which is the summit of understanding: but understand that there are things thou canst not grasp.*

Of the Order and Mode of Procedure in This Work. Accordingly, from what we have been saying it is evident that the intention of the wise man must be directed to the twofold truth of divine things and to the refutation of contrary errors: and that the research of reason is able to reach to one of these, while the other surpasses every effort of reason. And I speak of a twofold truth of divine things, not on the part of God Himself Who is Truth one and simple, but on the part of our knowledge, the relation of which to the knowledge of divine things varies.

Wherefore in order to deduce the first kind of truth we must proceed by demonstrative arguments whereby we can convince our adversaries. But since such arguments are not available in support of the second kind of truth, our intention must be not to convince our opponent by our arguments, but to solve the arguments which he brings against the truth, because, as shown above, natural reason cannot be opposed to the truth of faith. In a special way may the opponent of this kind of truth be convinced by the authority of Scripture confirmed by God with miracles: since we believe not what is above human reason save because God has revealed it. In support, however, of this kind of truth, certain probable arguments must be adduced for the practice and help of the faithful, but not for the conviction of our opponents, because the very insufficiency of these arguments would rather confirm them in their error, if they thought that we assented to the truth of faith on account of such weak reasonings.

With the intention then of proceeding in the manner laid down, we shall first of all endeavour to declare that truth which is the object of faith's confession and of reason's researches, by adducing arguments both demonstrative and probable. . . .

Of the Opinion of Those Who Aver That It Cannot Be Demonstrated That There Is a God, Since This is Self-Evident. Possibly it will seem to some that it is useless to endeavour to show that there is a God: they say that it is self-evident that God is, so that it is impossible to think the contrary, and thus it cannot be demonstrated that there is a God. The reasons for this view are as follow.

(1) Those things are said to be self-evident which are known as soon as the terms are known: thus as soon as it is known what is a whole, and what is a part, it is known that the whole is greater than its part. Now such is the statement *God is*. For by this word *God* we understand a thing a greater than which cannot be thought of: this is what a man conceives in his mind when he hears and understands this word *God:* so that God must already be at least in his mind. Nor can he be in the mind alone, for that which is both in the mind and in reality is greater than that which is in the mind only. And the very signification of the word shows that nothing is greater than God. Wherefore it follows that it is self-evident that God is, since it is made clear from the very signification of the word.

(2) It is possible to think that there is a thing which cannot be thought not to exist: and such a thing is evidently greater than that which can be thought not to exist. Therefore if God can be thought not to exist, it follows that something can be thought greater than God: and this is contrary to the signification of the term. Therefore it remains that it is self-evident that God is.

(3) Those propositions are most evident in which the selfsame thing is predicated of itself, for instance: *Man is man;* or wherein the predicate is included in the definition of the subject, for instance: *Man is an animal.* Now . . . in God alone do we find that His being is His essence, as though the same were the answer to the question, *What is He?* as to the question, *Is He?* Accordingly when we say, *God is,* the predicate is either identified with the subject, or at least is included in the definition of the subject. And thus it will be self-evident that God is.

(4) Things that are known naturally are self-evident, for it is not by a process of research that they become evident. Now it is naturally known that God is, since man's desire tends naturally to God as his last end. . . . Therefore it is self-evident that God is.

(5) That whereby all things are known must needs be self-evident. Now such is God. For just as the light of the sun is the principle of all visual perception, so the divine light is the principle of all intellectual knowledge, because it is therein that first and foremost intellectual light is to be found. Therefore it must needs be self-evident that God is.

On account of these and like arguments some are of opinion that it is so self-evident that God is, that it is impossible for the mind to think the contrary.

Refutation of the Foregoing Opinion and Solution of the Aforesaid Arguments. The foregoing opinion arose from their being accustomed from the beginning to hear and call upon the name of God. Now custom, especially if it date from our childhood, acquires the force of nature, the result being that the mind holds those things with which it was imbued from childhood as firmly as though they were self-evident. It is also a result of failing to distinguish between what is self-evident simply, and that which is self-evident to us. For it is simply self-evident that God is, because the selfsame thing which God is, is His existence. But since we are unable to conceive mentally the selfsame thing which is God, that thing remains unknown in regard to us. Thus it is self-evident simply that every whole is greater than its part, but to one who fails to conceive mentally the meaning of a whole, it must needs be unknown. Hence it is that those things which are most evident of all are to the intellect what the sun is to the eye of an owl, as stated in [Aristotle].

Nor does it follow, as the first argument alleged, that as soon as the meaning of the word *God* is understood, it is known that God is. First, because it is not known to all, even to those who grant that there is a God, that God is that thing than which no greater can be thought of, since many of the ancients asserted that this world is God. Nor can any such conclusion be gathered from the significations which Damascene assigns to this word *God*. Secondly because, granted that everyone understands this word *God* to signify something than which a greater cannot be thought of, it does not follow that something than which a greater cannot be thought of exists in reality. For we must needs allege a thing in the same way as we allege the signification of its name. Now from the fact that we conceive mentally that which the word *God* is intended to convey, it does not follow that God is otherwise than in the mind. Wherefore neither will it follow that the thing than which a greater cannot be thought of is otherwise than in the mind. And thence it does not follow that there exists in reality something than which a greater cannot be thought of. Hence this is no argument against those who assert that there is no God, since whatever be granted to exist, whether in reality or in the mind, there is nothing to prevent a person from thinking of something greater, unless he grants that there is in reality something than which a greater cannot be thought of.

Again it does not follow, as the second argument pretended, that if it is possible to think that God is not, it is possible to think of something greater than God. For that it be possible to think that He is not, is not on account of the imperfection of His being or the uncertainty thereof, since in itself His being is supremely manifest, but is the result of the weakness of our mind which is able to see Him, not in Himself but in His effects, so that it is led by reasoning to know that He is.

Wherefore the third argument also is solved. For just as it is self-evident to us that a whole is greater than its part, so is it most evident to those who see the very essence of God that God exists, since His essence is His existence. But because we are unable to see His essence, we come to know His existence not in Himself out in His effects.

The solution to the fourth argument is also clear. For man knows God naturally in the same way as he desires Him naturally. Now man desires Him naturally in so far as he naturally desires happiness, which is a likeness of the divine goodness. Hence it does not follow that God considered in Himself is naturally known to man, but that His likeness is. Wherefore man must needs come by reasoning to know God in the likenesses to Him which he discovers in God's effects.

It is also easy to reply to the fifth argument. For God is that in which all things are known, not so that other things be unknown except He be known, as happens in self-evident principles, but because all knowledge is caused in us by His outpouring.

Arguments in Proof of God's Existence. . . . The first way is as follows. Whatever is in motion is moved by another: and it is clear to the sense that something, the sun for instance, is in motion. Therefore it is set in motion by something else moving it. Now that which moves it is itself either moved or not. If it be not moved, then the point is proved that we must needs postulate an immovable mover: and this we call God. If, however, it be moved, it is moved by another mover. Either, therefore, we must proceed to infinity, or we must come to an immovable mover. But it is not possible to proceed to infinity. Therefore it is necessary to postulate an immovable mover.

This argument contains two propositions that need to be proved: namely that *whatever is in motion is moved by another,* and that *it is not possible to proceed to infinity in movers and things moved.* . . .

The second way is from the nature of the efficient cause.† In the world of sense we find there is an order of efficient causes. There is no case known (neither is it, indeed, possible) in which a thing is found to be the efficient cause of itself; for so it would be prior to itself, which is impossible. Now in efficient causes it is not possible to go on to infinity, because in all efficient causes following in order, the first is the cause of the intermediate cause, and the intermediate is the cause of the ultimate cause, whether the intermediate cause be several, or one only. Now to take away the cause is to take away the effect. Therefore, if there be no first cause among efficient causes, there will be no ultimate, nor any intermediate cause. But, if in efficient causes it is possible to go on to infinity, there will be no first efficient cause, neither will there be an ultimate effect, nor any intermediate efficient causes; all of which is plainly false. Therefore it is necessary to admit a first efficient cause to which every one gives the name of God.

The third way is taken from possibility and necessity, and runs thus. We find in nature things that are possible to be and not to be, since they are found to be generated, and to corrupt, and consequently they are possible to be and not to be. But it is impossible for these always to exist, for that which is possible not to be at some time is not. Therefore, if everything is possible not to be, then at one time there could have been nothing in existence. Now if this were true, even now there would be nothing in existence, because that which does not exist only begins to exist by something already existing. Therefore, if at one time nothing was in existence, it would have been impossible for anything to have begun to exist; and thus even now nothing would be in existence—which is absurd. Therefore, not all beings are merely possible, but there must exist something, the existence of which is necessary. But every necessary thing either has its necessity caused by another, or not. Now it is impossible to go on to infinity in necessary things which have their necessity caused by another, as has been already proved in regard to efficient causes. Therefore, we cannot but postulate the existence of some being having of itself its own necessity and not receiving it from another, but rather causing in others their necessity. This all men speak of as God.

† [The term "cause" is used in more than one sense. For example, the "cause" of a man's going to Mexico is a political convention that is to be held there. But in another sense the "cause" of his going is the set of physical forces in his body and in the train that actually transport him. When philosophers wish to limit the use of the term to the latter sense; in other words, to indicate that which physically produces the effect and usually precedes it in time, they employ the expression "efficient cause." See pp. 133–134 above.]

The fourth way is taken from the gradation to be found in things.
Among beings there are some more and some less good, true, noble,
and the like. But "more" and "less" are predicated of different
things, according as they resemble in their different ways something
which is the maximum, as a thing is said to be hotter according as
it more nearly resembles that which is hottest; so that there is something which is truest, something best, something noblest, and, consequently, something which is uttermost being; for those things that
are greatest in truth are greatest in being, as it is written in [Aris-
totle]. Now the maximum in any genus is the cause of all in that
genus; as fire, which is the maximum of heat, is the cause of all
hot things. Therefore there must also be something which is to all
beings the cause of their being, goodness, and every other perfection;
and this we call God.

The fifth way is taken from the governance of the world. We see
that things which lack intelligence, such as natural bodies, act for an
end, and this is evident from their acting always, or nearly always,
in the same way, so as to obtain the best result. Hence it is plain
that not fortuitously, but designedly, do they achieve their end.
Now whatever lacks intelligence cannot move towards an end, unless it be directed by some being endowed with knowledge and intelligence; as the arrow is shot to its mark by the archer. Therefore
some intelligent being exists by whom all natural things are directed
to their end; and this being we call God.

25

BEING, FACT, AND EXISTENCE *

by

GEORGE EDWARD MOORE
(1873–1958)

What do we commonly mean by the five phrases 'is real', 'exists',
'is a fact', 'is', and 'is true'? What property or properties do those

* [The greater part of Ch. XVI in *Some Main Problems of Philosophy*
(1953). Reprinted by permission of George Allen and Unwin, Ltd.]

phrases commonly stand for?. . . It seems as if purely imaginary things, even though they be absolutely self-contradictory like a round square, must still have some kind of *being*—must still *be* in a sense—simply because we can think and talk about them. It seems quite clear that, in a sense, there *is* not and cannot be such a thing as a round square: but, if there is not, how can I possibly think and talk about it? And I certainly can think and talk about it. I am doing so now. And not only can I make and believe propositions about it: I can make *true* propositions about it. I know that a round square, if there were such a thing, would be both round and not round: it is a fact that this is so. And now in saying that there is no such thing as a round square, I seem to imply that there *is* such a thing. It seems as if there must *be* such a thing, merely in order that it may have the property of *not* being. It seems, therefore, as if to say of anything whatever that we can mention that it absolutely *is not*, were to contradict ourselves: as if absolutely everything we can mention must *be,* must have some kind of being.

But, if we consider the analogous case of false beliefs, it seems to me to become quite clear that we can think of things which nevertheless are *not:* have no being at all. For instance, one of my friends might be believing of me now, *that I am not in London.* This is a belief which certainly might quite easily be now occurring. And yet there certainly is no such thing as my *not* being now in London. I *am* in London; and that settles the matter. As we have seen, it may be held that, *if* any friend of mine is believing this now, then there *is,* in a sense, such a thing as my *not* being now in London; it may be held that there *must* be such a thing as the object of my friend's belief—the *proposition* which he believes—and that the words 'that I am not now in London' are a name for this proposition, which undoubtedly *is.* And I don't mean now to dispute this view, though as I said, I don't think it is true. Let us grant that it *is* true. Even if it is true, it remains a fact that *one* thing, which those words *would* stand for, if his belief were true, certainly *is not.* It remains true that in *one* sense of the words there *is* no such thing as my not being now in London. In other words, even though we take the view that, where a belief is true, there are in the Universe two different things having the same name, and that, where it is false, then there is only one of those two things—even though we take this view, yet it remains a fact that, if the belief is false, there certainly is, in a sense, no such thing as my not being now in London; and that this very thing which certainly *is not,* is the very thing that we are now conceiving or imagining, even if, in order to do so, we have also at the same time to think of something else, having the same name, which certainly is. We must, therefore, I think, admit that we can, in a sense, think of things, which absolutely have no being. We must *talk* as if we did. And when we so talk and *say* that we do, we certainly do mean *something* which is a fact, by so talking. When, for instance, my friend believes that I am *not* in London, whereas in fact I am, he *is* believing that I am not in London: there is no doubt of that. That is to say this whole expression 'he believes that I am not in London' does express, or is the name for, a fact. But the solution of the difficulty seems to me to be this, namely that this whole expression does *not* merely express, as it seems to, a relation between my friend on the one hand and a fact of which the name is 'that I am not in London' on the other. It does *seem* to do this; and that is where the difficulty comes in. It does seem as if the words 'that I am not in London' *must* be a name for something to which my·friend is related, something which certainly *has being*. But we must admit, I think, that these words may not really be a name for anything at all. Taken by themselves they are not a name for anything at all, although the whole expression 'he believes that I am not in London' are a name for something. This fact that single words and phrases which we use will constantly seem to be names for something, when in fact they are not names for anything at all, is what seems to me to create the whole difficulty. Owing to it, we must, in talking of this subject, constantly seem to be contradicting ourselves. And I don't thing it is possible wholly to avoid this appearance of contradiction. In merely saying 'There is no such thing as a chimaera' you must seem to contradict yourself, because you seem to imply that 'a chimaera' is a name for something, whereas at the same time the very thing which you assert about this something is that it *is not:* that there is no such thing. The point to remember is that though we *must* use such expressions, and that though the whole expressions *are* names for facts, which certainly *are,* these facts cannot be analysed into a subject 'a chimaera' on the one hand, and something which is asserted of that subject on the other hand.

The question how such facts *are* to be analysed is of course another question, which presents great difficulties; and I don't pretend to be able to answer it. But what, I think, is clear is that they *can't* be analysed in the way proposed. In short we mustn't suppose that there *is* such a thing as a chimaera, merely because we can do something which we call thinking of it and making propositions about it. We aren't in fact really even mentioning a chimaera when we talk of one; we are using a word which isn't, by itself, a name for anything whatever.

I am going to say, then, in spite of the contradiction which such language seems to imply, that certain things which we can think of and talk about really have *no* being, in any sense at all. I think it is quite plain that wherever we entertain a false belief—whenever we make a mistake—there really is, in a sense, no such thing as *what* we believe in; and though such language does *seem* to contradict itself, I don't think we can express the facts at all except by the use of language which does seem to contradict itself; and if you understand what the language means, the apparent contradiction doesn't matter. And the first and most fundamental property which I wish to call attention to, as sometimes denoted by some of our five phrases, is just this one which *does* belong to *what* we believe in, whenever our belief is true, and which does *not* belong to *what* we believe in, whenever our belief is false. I propose to confine the name *being* to this property; and I think you can all see what the property in question is. If, for instance, you are believing now that I, while I look at this paper, am directly perceiving a whitish patch of colour, and, if your belief is true then there *is* such a thing as *my being now directly perceiving* a whitish patch of colour. And I think you can all understand in what sense there is such a thing. As a matter of fact, there really *is*. I *am* now directly perceiving a patch of whitish colour. But even if there weren't, you could all understand what would be meant by supposing that there *is*. This property, then, which does so plainly belong to this event (or whatever you like to call it) is the one I am going to call 'being'; and this seems to me to be the most fundamental property that can be denoted by any of our five phrases.

Another way of pointing out what this property is which I mean by 'being', and a way which does, I think, serve to make it clearer in some respects, is to say that to have being is equivalent to belonging *to the Universe,* being a constituent of the Universe, being *in* the Universe. We may say that whatever has being *is* a constituent of the Universe; and that *only* what has being can be a constituent of the Universe: to say of anything that there *is no such thing,* that it simply *is not,* is to say of it that it is not one among the constituents of the Universe, that it has no place in the Universe at all. This distinction between belonging to the Universe and not belonging to it does, I think, seem clearer in some respects than the mere distinction between being and not-being. Only, if we use this way of explaining what we mean we must recognise that the explanation is, in certain respects, inaccurate, and liable to be misunderstood. In the first place, if we say that 'to be' is equivalent to being a constituent of the Universe, this, taken strictly, would imply that it is *only* things which are constituents of the Universe which have being at all, and hence that the Universe, itself, as a whole, has no being—that there *is* no such thing. But this is perhaps absurd. It is natural to think that the Universe as a whole has being in exactly the same sense in which its constituents have it. So that, to speak quite strictly, we should perhaps have to say that the only things which have being are (1) the whole Universe itself and (2) all its constituents. For this reason alone it is not quite accurate to say that to 'be' is equivalent to 'being a constituent of the Universe'; since the Universe itself may form an exception to this rule: the Universe as a whole is certainly not a mere constituent of itself, and yet it seems as if it had being.

In the second place, if we use this conception of 'belonging to the Universe' to explain what we mean by 'being', we may be tempted to suppose that to say that a thing 'is' or 'has being' is not merely *equivalent* to but strictly the *same thing* as to say that it belongs to the Universe. And this, I think, would be also a mistake. If this were so, we should not be able to think that a thing had being, without first thinking of the Universe as a whole, and thinking that the thing in question belonged to it. But this is certainly not the case. People can think that certain things *are* and others *are not,* before they have even formed the conception of the Universe as a whole; and even when we have formed it, we certainly don't have it before our minds every time that we think that one thing *is* and another *is not.* The conception of 'being' is certainly, therefore not the *same* as that of belonging to the Universe, even though the two may be *equivalent* to the extent I pointed out. The truth is that though the conception of belonging to the Universe does seem in some ways clearer than that of being, yet the former can really only be defined by reference to the latter; not *vice versa.* If we want to say what we mean by the Universe, we can only do so by reference to the conception of 'being'—by saying, for instance, that by the Universe is meant the sum of all things which *are,* or in some such way as this. In other words, the conception of the Universe presupposes the conception of 'being', and can only be defined by reference to it; so that we cannot really define the latter by reference to the former.

And this brings me to the last respect, in which the proposal to explain 'being' by saying that it is equivalent to 'belonging to the Universe', is inaccurate and may be misleading. Suppose it really is the case, as we commonly do suppose, that besides the things which *are now* there are some things which *have been* in the past, and are *no longer* now; and others which will be in the future, but *are not yet.* It seems quite plain that, of these three classes of things, it is only those which are now that actually have, in one sense of the word, the property of 'being': of those which were, but are no longer, it is only true that they *did* have it, *not* that they have it now; and similarly of those which will be, but are not yet, it is only true that they *will* possess it, *not* that they do possess it. Of course, as we have seen, there are some philosophers who seem to think that there is nothing whatever which either has been, or is now, or will be: that everything which *has* being at all, *has* it in some timeless sense—that is to say, has *not* got it *now*, but nevertheless *has* got it; and that nothing whatever either *has* had it in the past, or will have it in the future: that in short there has been no past, is no present and will be no future. One of the things we are trying to discover is whether [anyone] really does think this or not. And I don't mean now to assume that these philosophers, if any do think this, are wrong. What I want to point out is that, *supposing* they are wrong—supposing some things *have been,* which are no longer, and others *will be,* which are not yet, there does arise a difficulty as to what we are to mean by the Universe. The difficulty is this: Are we going to say or are we not, that all the things which *have been* and *will be* do belong to the Universe—are constituents of it—just as much as those which are now? I think many people would say 'Yes': that the past and future *do* belong to the Universe just as much as the present does. And I think this is certainly *one* common sense in which we use the expression 'the Universe': we do use it to include the past and future as well as the present. But if we are going to say this, then, you see, we must admit that, for still another reason 'belonging to the Universe' is *not* strictly equivalent to 'being'. For we must admit that many things, which *do* belong to the Universe, nevertheless, in a sense, *have* not got the property we mean by 'being', but only have *had* it, or *will* have it. We should have to say that to 'belong to the Universe' means, *not* to *have* now the property we call 'being', but *either* to have had it, *or* to have it now, *or* to be about to have it; and we might have further to add a fourth alternative: namely to *have* it, in some timeless sense—to *have* it in a sense which is *not* equivalent to having it now. For, as we have seen, some philosophers believe that the only sense in which anything can *be* at all is some timeless sense; and even those philosophers who believe that there has been a past, is a present, and will be a future, do many of them believe that there is *besides* a timeless sense of the word 'is'; and that beside the things which have been, are now, and will be, there are many other things also belonging to the Universe, which *are* and yet are not *now*. In other words they believe that 'being' is a property which not only *did* belong to many things, does belong to many *now,* and *will* belong to many in the future, but that it also belongs in some timeless sense to many things, to which it does *not* belong *now*. I am not at all sure, whether these philosophers are right or not. For my part, I cannot think of any instance of a thing, with regard to which it seems quite certain that it *is,* and yet also that it is not *now*. But we must I think admit that the alternative is a possible one: that the very same property called 'being' which *did* belong and *will* belong to things, to which it does *not* belong now, may also *belong* in some timeless sense to things to which it does not belong now. And hence we must admit that the phrase 'So and so *belongs* to the Universe' may mean either of four different things: it may mean *either* 'So and so *has* been', *or* 'So and so *is* now', *or* 'So and so will be', *or* 'So and so *is*, but *not* now'. For this reason I think that to explain what we mean by 'being' by saying that it is equivalent to 'belonging to the Universe' or being a constituent of it, may possibly lead to misunderstanding. If we are going to mean by 'being' a property which did and will belong to some things to which it doesn't belong *now*, then we must say that *in a sense* these things *do* not belong to the Universe, but only did or will belong to it; while in *another sense* they *do* belong to it, in spite of the fact that they *have* not got the property we mean by 'being', but only did have it or will have it. And these two senses of the phrase 'belonging to the Universe' are, I think, liable to be confused with one another. Each is also liable to be identified with the property which we mean by 'being': so that we get two different senses of the word 'being', which are liable to be confused with one another. But, apart from this possible misunderstanding, and the two others which I mentioned before, I think it does really serve to make clearer what I mean by 'being', if I say that it is equivalent to being a constituent of the Universe—if I say that in asking what things *are* and what things *are not*, we are merely asking what things really are or are not constituents of the Universe.

So much, then, to explain what I mean by the first and most fundamental property denoted by our five phrases—the one which I propose to call 'being'.

And secondly I want to consider the phrase 'is a fact', in that use of it, in which we say: It is a fact that bears exist; It is a fact that I am now talking; It is a fact that twice two are four. Obviously we do mean something immensely important by this phrase too. It is a phrase which we constantly use to express things which we particularly want to insist on. The question is: '*What* do we mean by it? Do we use it to express the very same property to which I have given the name "being" or a different one? And, if different, different in what respect?' There certainly is some difference between our *use* of this phrase, and our use of the word 'being', for, whereas it is quite natural to say 'It is a fact that bears exist', 'It is a fact that twice two are four', it is not quite natural to say 'That bears exist' *is;* or 'That twice two are four' *is;* and conversely, while it is quite natural to say that bears are constituents of the Universe, or that the number 2 is a constituent of the Universe, it is not quite natural to say that the

fact that bears exist or the fact that twice two are four is a constituent of the Universe. But nevertheless I am inclined to think that
this difference of usage does not really indicate any difference in the
nature of the predicates or properties meant by the two phrases. So
far as I can see, when we say of one thing that it is a fact, and of
another that it has being or is a constituent of the Universe, the
property which we mean to assert of the two things is exactly the
same in both cases. The reason for the difference of usage is, I think,
only that we instinctively tend to use the one phrase, when we wish
to attribute the property in question to certain *kinds* of things, and
the other when we wish to attribute it to *other kinds* of things. In
short, the difference of usage expresses not a difference of *predicate,*
but a difference in the character of the *subjects* to which it is applied.
And the difference of character which leads us to make this distinction, really is, I think, one of the most fundamental differences that
there is among the constituents of the Universe. We may divide all
the constituents of the Universe—all things which are, into two
classes, putting in one class those which we can only express by a
clause beginning with 'that' or by the corresponding verbal noun,
and in the other all the rest. Thus we have, in the first class, such
things as 'the fact that lions exist' or (to express it by a verbal noun)
'the existence of lions', 'the fact that twice two are four', 'the fact
that I am now talking', and absolutely all the immense number of
facts which we thus express by phrases beginning with 'that'.

In short, this class of constituents of the Universe consists of the
sort of entities which *correspond* (in the sense I explained) to true
beliefs. Each true belief corresponds to one such entity; and it is
only to entities of this sort that true beliefs do correspond. And this
first class of entities—the class of entities which correspond to true
beliefs, certainly constitutes I think, one of the largest and most
important classes of things in the Universe. The precise respect in
which they differ from all other constituents of the Universe is, I
think, very difficult to define. So far as I can see, you can only point
out the character which distinguishes them, by pointing out, as I
have just done, that they are the class of entities which we name by
calling them 'The fact that so and so', or that they are the kind of
entities which correspond to true beliefs. But the difference between
them and all other kinds of entities is, I think, easy to *see,* even if it is
not easy to define. Surely everybody can see that the fact that a lion
does exist is quite a different sort of entity from the lion himself? or
the fact that twice two are four quite a different sort of entity from
the number 2 itself? Of course, to say that things of this sort form a
class by themselves is to say that they do, in fact, possess some
common property which is not shared by other things. And hence

we might say that when we use the phrase 'It is a fact that so and so', we are *not* merely attributing 'being' to the thing in question, but are *also,* as well, ascribing to it this other peculiar property, which is *not* shared by *all* the things which have being. If this were so, there would be a real difference between the property meant by 'being a fact' and the property meant by merely 'being'. But as I said, I don't think we commonly do mean to *attribute* this property when we say 'It is a fact that so and so', but only the property of being. We do instinctively use the phrase 'it is a fact' instead of 'it *is*', when we are talking of things which *have,* in fact, got this property as well as that of being: but I don't think that what we mean to say of them is that they have it. However, the question whether this is so or not, is a question of comparatively little importance. The important thing is to recognise what the property is, which makes us apply this phrase 'It is a fact that' to some things, whereas we can't apply it equally naturally to others. And I am going now, for the purposes of this discussion to restrict the name 'facts' to those constituents of the Universe and those only which have this property. Thus we shall say that the existence of lions is a fact, but that lions themselves are not facts; we shall say it is a fact that twice two are four, but that the number two itself is not a fact. And if we understand the word 'facts' in this sense it is important to notice that 'facts' are neither more nor less than what are often called 'truths'. I pointed out before that a phrase of the form 'It is *true* that so and so' can absolutely *always* be used as equivalent to the corresponding phrase of the form 'It is a *fact* that so and so'. And similarly anything which is a fact, in this sense, can always equally naturally be called 'a truth'. Instead of talking of the fact that $2 + 2 = 4$ we can equally well talk of the truth that $2 + 2 = 4$; instead of talking of the fact that lions exist, we can equally well talk of the truth that lions exist: and so on, in absolutely every case. And it is important to notice this because this property which belongs to a 'truth', and which makes it a truth, is an utterly different one from that which . . . belongs to *'true' beliefs*, and in virtue of which we call them 'true'. To say of a truth that it is a truth is merely to say of it that it is a fact in the sense we are considering; whereas to say of an act of belief that it is 'true' is, as we saw, to say only that it *corresponds* to a fact. No one, in fact, would think of calling a true act of belief a truth: it is quite unnatural to use such language. And yet, I think, it is very common to find the two things confused. It has, for instance, been very commonly supposed that truths are entirely dependent on the mind; that there could be no truths in the Universe if there were no minds in it. And, so far as I can see, the chief reason why this has been supposed, is because it has been supposed that the word 'true' stands for a property which can belong only to acts of belief, and that nothing can be a 'truth' unless it has *this* property. It is, of course, quite obvious that there could be no true beliefs in the Universe, if there were no minds in it: no act of belief could be true, unless there *were* acts of belief; and there could be no acts of belief if there were no minds, because an act of belief is an act of consciousness. It is therefore, quite obvious that the existence of *true acts of belief* is entirely dependent on the existence of mind. But the moment we realise that by a 'truth' is meant *not* a true act of belief, but merely a fact—something which corresponds to a true belief, when there are true beliefs, but which may *be* equally even when no one is believing in it, there ceases to be any reason to suppose that there could be no truths in the Universe, if there were no minds in it. It is the very reverse of obvious that there could be no facts in the Universe, if there were no minds in it. And as soon as we realise that 'a truth' is merely another name for a fact, and is something utterly different from a true act of belief, it becomes quite plainly possible that there *could* be truths in the Universe, even if there were no minds in it. For this reason it is, I think, important to notice that 'a truth' is merely another name for a fact, although the word 'true', as applied to *acts of belief*, means something quite different—does *not* mean that the act of belief in question is a truth. And it is also I think, worth while to notice a connection between the phrase 'It is a fact that' and the word 'real'. To say 'It is a fact that lions exist' is obviously merely equivalent to saying 'Lions *really* do exist'. That is to say we use the word 'real', in this adverbial form, merely to express the same idea which we also express by 'It is a fact that'. Of course, though it is natural to say 'Lions *really* do exist', it is not at all natural to say 'It is *real* that lions do exist': nothing could be more unnatural. And this shows that there is some difference in the usage of the phrases 'is real' and 'is a fact'. But at the same time this use of the adverb 'really' does, I think, point to a connection between the two.

I am going, then, to use the name 'facts' simply and solely as a name for that kind of constituents of the Universe which correspond to true beliefs—for the kind of things which we express by phrases beginning with 'that'. But, of course, I don't mean to say that this is the *only* sense in which the word 'facts' is commonly used. Philosophers, at all events, certainly sometimes use it in a wider sense: they will say for instance not merely that the existence of lions is a fact, but that a lion itself is a fact, or they will say that this whitish patch of colour—which I am now directly perceiving—this sensedatum itself—is a fact. And I don't mean to say that this wider usage is wrong: I only want to make it quite plain that I am not going to adopt it for the purposes of the present discussion. And what I think is still more important is to point out that in ordinary life, we very often use the word 'fact' in a *narrower* sense than that in which I am using it: we apply it only to *some* among the class of things which I am calling facts. The usage I am thinking of is that in which *facts* are often opposed to theories, or in which it is said that questions ought to be settled by an appeal to *the facts*. In *my* sense of the word a theory *may* be a fact, in spite of its being a mere theory; it will be a fact *if*, when anybody believes in it, his belief is true. And, so far as I can see, the chief distinction between this narrow usage of the word 'fact' and my usage of it, is that in the common usage the word is confined to those kind of facts, which we do or can absolutely *know* to be facts. It is held, that is to say, that among the many *facts*, in my sense of the word, which there are in the Universe, there are certain kinds which we can, under certain circumstances, absolutely *know* to be facts, whereas there are other kinds, which we can never (in the present state of knowledge) absolutely *know* to be facts. Thus it might be said that where a man believes in a thing, and his belief is true, yet what he believes is *not* a fact, unless it is something which some man now is capable of absolutely knowing. Whereas in my sense of the word, whenever a man believes in a thing, and his belief is true, what he believes in *is* a fact, even if nobody living could absolutely know it to be so. And, of course, my sense of the word is one of the senses in which the word is commonly used; everybody does constantly use language which implies that, when a belief is true, then what is believed in is, in a sense, a fact, whether anybody can know it to be so or not. But there certainly is also, I think, a narrower sense of the word, in which it is confined to things which are held (rightly or wrongly) to be capable of being absolutely known; and I want to make it clear that I am *not* confining it to this narrow sense.

I have, then, so far, tried to give definite meanings to two of our five phrases—the phrase 'is' or 'has being', and the phrase 'is a fact'. But the phrase I want most to consider is the phrase 'exists'. This also is certainly a phrase of the utmost importance. Nothing can well be more important than to know whether certain kinds of things do exist, or will probably exist in the future, or not: there is nothing which we are more constantly anxious to know. And the question we have to raise is: What exactly is 'existence'? What is the property which we denote by the word? Is 'to exist' simply the same thing as to be or to be a constituent of the Universe, or is it not? And, if not, how do they differ? And, as regards this question, I used to hold very strongly, what many other people are also inclined to hold, that the words 'being' and 'existence' do stand for two entirely different properties; and that though everything which exists must also 'be', yet many things which 'are' nevertheless do emphatically *not* exist. I did, in fact, actually hold this view when I began these lectures; and I have based the whole scheme of the lectures upon the distinction, having said that I would deal first with the question what sort of things exist, and then separately, as a quite distinct matter, with the question what sort of things *are,* but don't exist. But nevertheless I am inclined to think that I was wrong, and that there is no such distinction between 'being' and 'existence' as I thought there was. There is, of course, a distinction of usage, but I am inclined to think that this distinction is only of the same kind as that which I tried to explain as holding between 'being' and 'being a fact'. That is to say, when we say of a thing that it exists, we don't, I think, mean to attribute to it any property different from that of 'being'; all that we mean to say of it is simply that it *is* or is a constituent of the Universe. And the distinction of usage only comes in, because we instinctively tend to use the word 'existence' only when we mean to attribute this property to certain kinds of things and not when we mean to attribute it to *other* kinds which also, in fact, have it, and are constituents of the Universe just as much as the former. But as I said in the other case, I do not think the question whether this is so or not is really of much importance. In merely saying that there is a class of things, to which we tend to confine the word 'existence', we are, of course, saying that these things have some common property, which is *not* shared by other constituents of the Universe. And, of course, you may say, if you like (though I don't think it is strictly true) that when we say of anything that it exists we mean to say of it two things at once namely (1) that it *is*, or is a constituent of the Universe and (2) that it has this peculiar property, which does *not* belong to all the constituents of the Universe. The important thing is to recognise as clearly as possible *that* there is such a property, and *what* it is: that there is a class of things in the Universe, of which we tend to say exclusively that they exist, and how this class of things differs from other kinds of things, which do quite equally belong to the Universe, and are constituents of it, though we should not say of them that they 'exist'.

And I think the best way of doing this is to point out what are the classes of things in the Universe, of which we *cannot* quite naturally say that they 'exist'. And so far as I can see we can divide these into two classes. The first is simply the class of things which I have just called 'facts'. It is in the highest degree unnatural to say of these that they exist. No one, for instance, would think of saying that the fact that lions exist, *itself* exists; or that the fact that $2 + 2 = 4$ exists. We do, therefore, I think, certainly tend to apply the word 'existence' *only to* constituents of the Universe, *other* than facts.

But there is, it seems to me, also another class of things, which really are constituents of the Universe, in the case of which it is also unnatural, though not, perhaps, quite so unnatural, to say that they 'exist'. The class of things I mean is the class of things which Locke and Berkeley and Hume called 'general ideas' or 'abstract ideas', and which have been often called by that name by other English philosophers. This is, I think, their most familiar name.

And in order to explain quite clearly what the distinction is which seems to me to justify a distinction between 'being' and 'existing', I think it is absolutely essential to discuss the nature of 'general' or 'abstract' ideas. And this is, I think, a subject which is eminently worth discussing for its own sake too. I have hitherto said nothing at all about it. But questions as to the nature of general ideas have, in fact, played an immensely large part in philosophy. There are some philosophers who say that there are no such things at all: that general ideas are pure fictions like chimaeras or griffins. Berkeley and Hume, for instance, said this. But a majority of philosophers would, I think, say that there are such things; and *if* there are, then, I think there is no doubt that they are one of the most important kinds of things in the Universe. *If* there are any at all, there are tremendous numbers of them, and we are all constantly thinking and talking of them. But the question *what* they are, if there are such things, seems to me to be one of the most perplexing questions in philosophy. Many philosophers are constantly talking about them; but so far as I know there is no perfectly clear account of what a general idea is, and as to exactly how it differs from other constituents of the Universe. I want, therefore, to do the best I can to shew that there *are* general ideas, and what properties they have which distinguish them from other things. But, as I say, the subject seems to me to be fearfully confusing: for one thing, there seem to be so many different kinds of general ideas and it is very difficult to see what they have in common. I don't suppose, therefore, that I can make the subject really clear, but I want to do the best I can.

The first point that it is necessary to be quite clear about is that the name 'general idea' or 'abstract idea', like the name 'idea' generally, is dangerously ambiguous: it may stand for two entirely different things. I have already had occasion to insist several times on this ambiguity in the word 'idea'; but it seems to be a point which some people find it very difficult to grasp. Let us take an example. Everybody would agree that the number two, or any other number, is an abstract idea if anything is. But when I, or anybody else, *think* of the number two, two entirely different things are involved, *both* of which may be called an 'idea'. There is in the first place my mental act, the act which consists in thinking of or being conscious of or apprehending the number two; and this mental act itself may be called 'an idea'. And if we use the word in this sense, then ideas are things which can be only in the mind: they are another name for acts of consciousness. The mental act which I perform in thinking of the number 2 is, in this sense, 'an idea'; it is an idea of *mine,* and belongs exclusively to me. But obviously the number two *itself* does *not* belong exclusively to me; it is not an idea of *mine* in this sense. So that we have to recognise as something quite distinct from my mental act the thing *thought* of—the number two itself—the *object* of my act of apprehension—*what* I apprehend: and this also is often called an 'idea'. And obviously if we use the word 'idea' in this sense, then an 'idea' is a thing which can quite well *be,* without being in any mind. There may be two things, and they may really be two, even when nobody is thinking of them, or of the fact that they are two. I want, therefore, to make it quite plain that when I talk of 'general ideas' I mean, *not* acts of apprehension, but the things apprehended: *not* my act of apprehending the number two, but the number two itself, which is *what* I apprehend. With regard to the act of apprehension, the mental act, I don't wish to suggest for a moment that it doesn't exist. I think myself that *it does,* though some people would doubt this. It is only with regard to the object apprehended, that I wish to suggest that it doesn't 'exist'. The object apprehended, then, *not* the act of apprehension is what we are going to discuss; and in order to avoid confusion between the two, I think I had perhaps better not use the name 'general idea' or 'abstract idea' at all. I will use instead another name which is often used for these kind of objects, though it is not so familiar: I will call them 'universals'. What, then, I want to do is to point out what kind of things 'universals' are and that there are such things—that they are not pure fictions, like chimaeras and griffins.

And I will begin with an instance, which is not perhaps in some respects as simple as could be taken, but which I want to take, because it brings out one point which will presently be of importance. When I look at my two hands so, I directly perceive two sets of sense-data, two patches of flesh colour, of the sort of shape you all know very well, which are at a certain distance from one another. The distance, as you see, is not great, so we will say they are *near* one another. And for the sake of convenience, I will talk of these two flesh-coloured patches as *my hands,* though, as we have seen, there is reason to suppose these flesh-coloured patches are not, in fact, my hands, or any part of them. When, therefore, I talk of my *hands* you will please understand that I am talking *solely* of these two flesh-coloured patches, which I directly perceive. I don't want to assume that I have any hands at all, in the ordinary sense of the word. I want to talk solely of things which indubitably *are*; and so I want to talk only of these sense-data which I am directly perceiving, and for the sake of convenience I will call them 'my hands'. Well, then, it is a *fact*, in my sense of the word, that this hand—this flesh-coloured patch—is at this moment at a certain distance from (a distance which we will call 'near') this other hand—this other flesh-coloured patch. It is a fact that this right hand is now near this left hand. But this fact seems plainly capable of being analysed into the following constituents. When I say that it can be analysed into them, I don't mean to say that it *is* nothing more than the sum of its constituents: I think plainly it is *not*—it is not merely identical with the sum of its constituents: I only mean to say that the constituents in question *are* parts or constituents of it—that they are contained in it. The constituents I mean are these. This right hand—this sense-datum— is one of them—and the other is *what* we assert of this sense-datum, the property which we attribute to it—namely the property *of being near the left hand*. The fact is *that* the right hand is *near* the left: and we can analyse this into (1) the right hand itself—that is one thing which enters into the constitution of the fact: and (2) what is asserted of this right hand—namely the property of being now near the left. Well, this second constituent—the property of being near this left hand—is a *universal*, and one of the most indubitable instances of a universal. You see why it should be called a 'universal'. It is so called, because it is a property which can be (and is) *common* to this hand and to other things. Other things can in fact also share the property of being near this hand: other things do: this white patch which I see in looking at the paper, is also *near* this hand, and so is the coloured patch which I see in looking at the desk. All these three things have the common property of being near this hand. They are all *near* it in exactly the same sense, though, of course, each of them *also* has relations to it which the others have not got. And this property of being *near* this patch of colour, in the sense in which it is *common* both to the sense-datum of my right hand and the sense-datum of the desk and the sense-datum of the paper, really is what is commonly called a 'general' or 'abstract' idea. The relation which I mean by 'being *near*' is certainly not *identical* either with the space which I see between this hand and that, or between the hand and the desk, or between the hand and the paper. All these spaces are different. But what I mean by being 'near' is something which is absolutely identical in all three cases. We have, therefore, in this property of *being near this sense-datum*, a real instance of a 'universal' or abstract idea. And why I have begun with this instance, is because, in this case, the universal seems to me obviously to consist in the having of a relation to something which is *not* a universal. This coloured patch which I actually see, is obviously not a universal or abstract idea; nothing could be more of a *particular*. But yet the universal consists in the having of a relation—the relation of nearness—just to *this* coloured patch: the property of *being near this coloured patch* really is a property which is and may be shared in common by several different things.

We have, then, one type of universal which consists in the having of one identical relation to something which is *not* a universal. But, if we consider the following facts, we get an instance of another new sort of universal. This left hand of mine is not the only left hand in the Universe: there are ever so many other left hands, and there may even be other sense-data similar to this which I am now directly perceiving. But, in the same sense in which these things here are near my left hand, other things may be near the left hands of other people. So that there is such a property as that of *being near some left hand or other*. This, you see, is a property which these things here share with all the things that are near anybody else's left hand. All of them are near *some left hand or other*. This property also, therefore, is a universal, and it is plainly of a different type from the first one which we took. This property does not consist in the having of a specific relation to some *one* thing which is *not* a universal; but in the having of a specific relation to *some one or other* of a group of things which are not universals. And universals of this type are universals which we are constantly thinking about and talking about. Many of the very commonest words we use are names for them. For instance when we say of a man that he is a father, what we mean is that he has the relation of fatherhood to *some* human being *or other*: this is the property which is shared in common by all fathers, and obviously a great many of the commonest words are names for universals of this sort: universals which consist in the having of a certain relation to *some one or other* of a group of things which are *not* universals.

We have got, therefore, examples of two different types of universals: (1) the universal which consists in being near this hand of mine; and (2) the universal which consists in being near some left hand or other. And it might be thought that there can be no doubt at all that there *are* such things as these two universals. There certainly is, it would seem, such a thing as the property of being near *this* hand, and also such a thing as the property of being near *some hand or other*. But, in order to see why there has been doubt about the matter, we have to consider another quite different type of universal, which is involved as a constituent in both of these. Both

of those properties [have,] as a constituent, a *relation*—the relation
which I have called 'being *near*'. And most people would say that
this relation is itself a 'universal': it certainly is a 'general idea'.
Indeed, if this relation were *not* a universal, in at least one sense of
the word, neither of these two properties could be so either.

26

ART AND EXISTENCE *

by

ARTHUR SCHOPENHAUER

(1788–1860)

Not merely philosophy but also the fine arts work at bottom towards the solution of the problem of existence. For in every mind
that once gives itself up to the purely objective contemplation of
nature a desire has been excited, however concealed and unconscious
it may be, to comprehend the true nature of things, of life and existence. For this alone has interest for the intellect as such, *i.e.*, for
the pure subject of knowledge which has become free from the aims
of the will; as for the subject which knows as a mere individual the
aims of the will alone have interest. On this account the result of the
purely objective apprehension of things is an expression more of the
nature of life and existence, more an answer to the question, "What
is life?" Every genuine and successful work of art answers this
question in its own way with perfect correctness. But all the arts
speak only the naïve and childish language of perception, not the
abstract and serious language of *reflection;* their answer is therefore
a fleeting image: not permanent and general knowledge. Thus for
perception every work of art answers that question, every painting,

* [From Bk. III, Supplement, Ch. 34, and Bk. III, Sec 52 of *The World as
Will and Idea* (1819). Translated from the German by R. B. Haldane and
J. Kemp (1883–1886).]

every statue, every poem, every scene upon the stage: music also answers it; and indeed more profoundly than all the rest, for in its language, which is understood with absolute directness, but which is yet untranslatable into that of the reason, the inner nature of all life and existence expresses itself. Thus all the other arts hold up to the questioner a perceptible image, and say, "Look here, this is life." Their answer, however correct it may be, will yet always afford merely a temporary, not a complete and final, satisfaction. For they always give merely a fragment, an example instead of the rule, not the whole, which can only be given in the universality of the *conception*. For this, therefore, thus for reflection and in the abstract, to give an answer which just on that account shall be permanent and suffice for always, is the task of philosophy. However, we see here upon what the relationship of philosophy to the fine arts rests, and can conclude from that to what extent the capacity of both, although in its direction and in secondary matters very different, is yet in its root the same.

Every work of art accordingly really aims at showing us life and things as they are in truth, but cannot be directly discerned by every one through the mist of objective and subjective contingencies. Art takes away this mist.

The works of the poets, sculptors, and representative artists in general contain an unacknowledged treasure of profound wisdom; just because out of them the wisdom of the nature of things itself speaks, whose utterances they merely interpret by illustrations and purer repetitions. On this account, however, every one who reads the poem or looks at the picture must certainly contribute out of his own means to bring that wisdom to light; accordingly he comprehends only so much of it as his capacity and culture admit of; as in the deep sea each sailor only lets down the lead as far as the length of the line will allow. Before a picture, as before a prince, every one must stand, waiting to see whether and what it will speak to him; and, as in the case of a prince, so here he must not himself address it, for then he would only hear himself. It follows from all this that in the works of the representative arts all truth is certainly contained, yet only *virtualiter* or *implicite;* philosophy, on the other hand, endeavours to supply the same truth *actualiter* and *explicite,* and therefore, in this sense, is related to art as wine to grapes. What it promises to supply would be, as it were, an already realised and clear gain, a firm and abiding possession; while that which proceeds from the achievements and works of art is one which has constantly to be reproduced anew. Therefore, however, it makes demands, not only upon those who produce its works, but also upon those who are to enjoy them which are discouraging and hard to comply with. Therefore its public remains small, while that of art is large.

The co-operation of the beholder, which is referred to above, as demanded for the enjoyment of a work of art, depends partly upon the fact that every work of art can only produce its effect through the medium of the fancy; therefore it must excite this, and can never allow it to be left out of the play and remain inactive. This is a condition of the aesthetic effect, and therefore a fundamental law of all fine arts. But it follows from this that, through the work of art, everything must not be directly given to the senses, but rather only so much as is demanded to lead the fancy on to the right path; something, and indeed the ultimate thing, must always be left over for the fancy to do. Even the author must always leave something over for the reader to think; for Voltaire has very rightly said, *"Le secret d'être ennuyeux, c'est de tout dire"* [The surest way to be a bore is to leave nothing unsaid]. But besides this, in art the best of all is too spiritual to be given directly to the senses; it must be born in the imagination of the beholder, although begotten by the work of art. It depends upon this that the sketches of great masters often effect more than their finished pictures; although another advantage certainly contributes to this, namely, that they are completed offhand in the moment of conception; while the perfected painting is only produced through continued effort, by means of skilful deliberation and persistent intention, for the inspiration cannot last till it is completed. From the fundamental aesthetical law we are speaking of, it is further to be explained why wax figures never produce an aesthetic effect, and therefore are not properly works of fine art, although it is just in them that the imitation of nature is able to reach its highest grade. For they leave nothing for the imagination to do. Sculpture gives merely the form without the colour; painting gives the colour, but the mere appearance of the form; thus both appeal to the imagination of the beholder. The wax figure, on the other hand, gives all, form and colour at once; whence arises the appearance of reality, and the imagination is left out of account. Poetry, on the contrary, appeals indeed to the imagination alone, which it sets in action by means of mere words.

An arbitrary playing with the means of art without a proper knowledge of the end is, in every art, the fundamental characteristic of the dabbler. Such a man shows himself in the pillars that support nothing, aimless volutes, juttings and projections of bad architecture, in the meaningless runs and figures, together with the aimless noise of bad music, in the jingling of the rhymes of senseless poetry. . . .

. . . A work of art which has proceeded from mere distinct conceptions is always ungenuine. If now, in considering a work of plastic art, or in reading a poem, or in hearing a piece of music (which aims at describing something definite), we see, through all the rich materials of art, the distinct, limited, cold, dry conception shine out, and at last come to the front, the conception which was the kernel of this work, the whole notion of which consequently consisted in the distinct thinking of it, and accordingly is absolutely exhausted by its communication, we feel disgusted and indignant, for we see ourselves deceived and cheated out of our interest and attention. We are only perfectly satisfied by the impression of a work of art when it leaves something which, with all our thinking about it, we cannot bring down to the distinctness of conception. The mark of that hybrid origin from mere conceptions is that the author of a work of art could, before he set about it, give in distinct words what he intended to present; for then it would have been possible to attain his whole end through these words. Therefore it is an undertaking as unworthy as it is absurd if, as has often been tried at the present day, one seeks to reduce a poem of Shakspeare's or Goethe's to the abstract truth which it was its aim to communicate. Certainly the artist ought to think in the arranging of his work; but only that thought which was *perceived* before it was thought has afterwards, in its communication, the power of animating or rousing, and thereby becomes imperishable. We shall not refrain from observing here that certainly the work which is done at a stroke, like the sketches of painters already referred to, the work which is completed in the inspiration of its first conception, and as it were unconsciously dashed off, like the melody which comes entirely without reflection, and quite as if by inspiration, and finally, also the lyrical poem proper, the mere song, in which the deeply felt mood of the present, and the impression of the surroundings, as if involuntarily, pours itself forth in words, whose metre and rhyme come about of their own accord—that all these, I say, have the great advantage of being purely the work of the ecstasy of the moment, the inspiration, the free movement of genius, without any admixture of intention and reflection; hence they are through and through delightful and enjoyable, without shell and kernel, and their effect is much more inevitable than that of the greatest works of art, of slower and more deliberate selection has had an important part; understanding, technical skill, and routine must here fill up the gaps which the conception and inspiration of genius has left, and must mix with these all kinds of necessary supplementary work as cement of the only really genuinely brilliant parts. This explains why all such works, only excepting the perfect masterpieces of the very greatest masters (as, for example, "Hamlet," "Faust," the opera of "Don Juan"), inevitably contain an admixture of something insipid and wearisome, which in some measure hinders the enjoyment of them. Proofs of this are the "Messiah," "*Gerusalemme liberata*," even "Paradise Lost" and the "Æneid"; and Horace already makes the bold remark, "*Quandoque dormitat bonus Homerus*" [Even the good Homer is sometimes caught napping]. But that this is the case is the consequence of the limitation of human powers in general.

The mother of the useful arts is necessity; that of the fine arts superfluity. As their father, the former have understanding; the latter genius, which is itself a kind of superfluity, that of the powers of knowledge beyond the measure which is required for the service of the will.

The nature of man consists in this, that his will strives, is satisfied and strives anew, and so on for ever. Indeed, his happiness and well-being consist simply in the quick transition from wish to satisfaction, and from satisfaction to a new wish. For the absence of satisfaction is suffering, the empty longing for a new wish, languor, *ennui*. And corresponding to this the nature of melody is a constant digression and deviation from the key-note in a thousand ways, not only to the harmonious intervals to the third and dominant, but to every tone, to the dissonant sevenths and to the superfluous degrees; yet there always follows a constant return to the key-note. In all these deviations melody expresses the multifarious efforts of will, but always its satisfaction also by the final return to an harmonious interval, and still more, to the key-note. The composition of melody, the disclosure in it of all the deepest secrets of human willing and feeling, is the work of genius, whose action, which is more apparent here than anywhere else, lies far from all reflection and conscious intention, and may be called an inspiration. The conception is here, as everywhere in art, unfruitful. The composer reveals the inner nature of the world, and expresses the deepest wisdom in a language which his reason does not understand; as a person under the influence of mesmerism tells things of which he has no conception when he awakes. Therefore in the composer, more than in any other artist, the man is entirely separated and distinct from the artist. Even in the explanation of this wonderful art, the concept shows its poverty and limitation. I shall try, however, to complete our analogy. As quick transition from wish to satisfaction, and from satisfaction to a new wish, is happiness and well-being, so quick melodies without great deviations are cheerful; slow melodies, striking painful discords, and only winding back through many bars to the key-note are, as analogous to the delayed and hardly won satisfaction, sad.

The delay of the new excitement of will, languor, could have no other expression than the sustained key-note, the effect of which would soon be unbearable; very monotonous and unmeaning melodies approach this effect. The short intelligible subjects of quick dance-music seem to speak only of easily attained common pleasure. On the other hand, the *Allegro maestoso*, in elaborate movements, long passages, and wide deviations, signifies a greater, nobler effort towards a more distant end, and its final attainment. The *Adagio* speaks of the pain of a great and noble effort which despises a trifling happiness. But how wonderful is the effect of the *minor* and *major!* How astounding that the change of half a tone, the entrance of a minor third instead of a major, at once and inevitably forces upon us an anxious painful feeling, from which again we are just as instantaneously delivered by the major. The *Adagio* lengthens in the minor the expression of the keenest pain, and becomes even a convulsive wail. Dance-music in the minor seems to indicate the failure of that trifling happiness which we ought rather to despise, seems to speak of the attainment of a lower end with toil and trouble. The inexhaustibleness of possible melodies corresponds to the inexhaustibleness of Nature in difference of individuals, physiognomies, and courses of life. The transition from one key to an entirely different one, since it altogether breaks the connection with what went before, is like death, for the individual ends in it; but the will which appeared in this individual lives after him as before him, appearing in other individuals, whose consciousness, however, has no connection with his.

But it must never be forgotten, in the investigation of all these analogies I have pointed out, that music has no direct, but merely an indirect relation to them, for it never expresses the phenomenon, but only the inner nature, the in-itself of all phenomena, the will itself. It does not therefore express this or that particular and definite joy, this or that sorrow, or pain, or horror, or delight, or merriment, or peace of mind; but joy, sorrow, pain, horror, delight, merriment, peace of mind *themselves*, to a certain extent in the abstract, their essential nature, without accessories, and therefore without their motives. Yet we completely understand them in this extracted quintessence. Hence it arises that our imagination is so easily excited by music, and now seeks to give form to that invisible yet actively moved spirit-world which speaks to us directly, and clothe it with flesh and blood, *i.e.*, to embody it in an analogous example. This is the origin of the song with words, and finally of the opera, the text of which should therefore never forsake that subordinate position in order to make itself the chief thing and the music a mere means of expressing it, which is a great misconception and a piece of utter perversity; for music always expresses only the quintessence of life and its events, never these themselves, and therefore their differences do not always affect it. It is precisely this universality, which belongs exclusively to it, together with the greatest determinateness, that gives music the high worth which it has as the panacea for all our woes. Thus, if music is too closely united to the words, and tries to form itself according to the events, it is striving to speak a language which is not its own. No one has kept so free from this mistake as Rossini; therefore his music speaks *its own language* so distinctly and purely that it requires no words, and produces its full effect when rendered by instruments alone.

According to all this, we may regard the phenomenal world, or nature, and music as two different expressions of the same thing, which is therefore itself the only medium of their analogy, so that a knowledge of it is demanded in order to understand that analogy. Music, therefore, if regarded as an expression of the world, is in the highest degree a universal language, which is related indeed to the universality of concepts, much as they are related to the particular things. Its universality, however, is by no means that empty universality of abstraction, but quite of a different kind, and is united with thorough and distinct definiteness. . . . All possible efforts, excitements, and manifestations of will, all that goes on in the heart of man and that reason includes in the wide, negative concept of feeling, may be expressed by the infinite number of possible melodies, but always in the universal, in the mere form, without the material, always according to the thing-in-itself, not the phenomenon, the inmost soul, as it were, of the phenomenon, without the body. This deep relation which music has to the true nature of all things also explains the fact that suitable music played to any scene, action, event, or surrounding seems to disclose to us its most secret meaning, and appears as the most accurate and distinct commentary upon it. This is so truly the case, that whoever gives himself up entirely to the impression of a symphony, seems to see all the possible events of life and the world take place in himself, yet if he reflects, he can find no likeness between the music and the things that passed before his mind. For, as we have said, music is distinguished from all the other arts by the fact that it is not a copy of the phenomenon . . . but is the direct copy of the will itself, and therefore exhibits itself as the metaphysical to everything physical in the world, and as the thing-in-itself to every phenomenon. We might, therefore, just as well call the world embodied music as embodied will; and this is the reason why music makes every picture, and indeed every scene of real life and of the world, at once appear with higher significance, certainly all the more in proportion as its melody is analogous to the inner spirit of the given phenomenon. It rests upon this that we are able to set a poem to music as a song, or a perceptible representation as a pantomime, or both as an opera. Such particular pictures of human life, set to the universal language of music, are never bound to it or correspond to it with stringent necessity; but they stand to it only in the relation of an example chosen at will to a general concept. In the determinateness of the real, they represent that which music expresses in the universality of mere form. For melodies are to a certain extent, like general concepts, an abstraction from the actual. This actual world, then, the world of particular things, affords the object of perception, the special and individual, the particular case, both to the universality of the concepts and to the universality of the melodies. But these two universalities are in a certain respect opposed to each other; for the concepts contain particulars only as the first forms abstracted from perception, as it were, the separated shell of things; thus they are, strictly speaking, *abstracta;* music, on the other hand, gives the inmost kernel which precedes all forms, or the heart of things. . . . To the universal significance of a melody to which a poem has been set, it is quite possible to set other equally arbitrarily selected examples of the universal expressed in this poem corresponding to the significance of the melody in the same degree. This is why the same composition is suitable to many verses; and this is also what makes the *vaudeville* possible. But that in general a relation is possible between a composition and a perceptible representation rests, as we have said, upon the fact that both are simply different expressions of the same inner being of the world. When now, in the particular case, such a relation is actually given, that is to say, when the composer has been able to express in the universal language of music the emotions of will which constitute the heart of an event, then the melody of the song, the music of the opera, is expressive. But the analogy discovered by the composer between the two must have proceeded from the direct knowledge of the nature of the world unknown to his reason, and must not be an imitation produced with conscious intention by means of conceptions, otherwise the music does not express the inner nature of the will itself, but merely gives an inadequate imitation of its phenomenon. All specially imitative music does this; for example, "The Seasons," by Haydn; also many passages of his "Creation," in which phenomena of the external world are directly imitated; also all battle-pieces. Such music is entirely to be rejected.

The unutterable depth of all music by virtue of which it floats through our consciousness as the vision of a paradise firmly believed in yet ever distant from us, and by which also it is so fully understood and yet so inexplicable, rests on the fact that it restores to us all the emotions of our inmost nature, but entirely without reality and far removed from their pain. So also the seriousness which is essential to it, which excludes the absurd from its direct and peculiar province, is to be explained by the fact that its object is not the idea, with reference to which alone deception and absurdity are possible; but its object is directly the will, and this is essentially the most serious of all things, for it is that on which all depends. How rich in content and full of significance the language of music is, we see from the repetitions, as well as the *Da capo,** the like of which would be unbearable in works composed in a language of words, but in music are very appropriate and beneficial, for, in order to comprehend it fully, we must hear it twice.

In the whole of this exposition of music I have been trying to bring out clearly that it expresses in a perfectly universal language, in a homogeneous material, mere tones, and with the greatest determinateness and truth, the inner nature, the in-itself of the world, which we think under the concept of will, because will is its most distinct manifestation. Further, according to my view and contention, philosophy is nothing but a complete and accurate repetition or expression of the nature of the world in very general concepts, for only in such is it possible to get a view of that whole nature which will everywhere be adequate and applicable. Thus, whoever has followed me and entered into my mode of thought, will not think it so very paradoxical if I say, that supposing it were possible to give a perfectly accurate, complete explanation of music, extending even to particulars, that is to say, a detailed repetition in concepts of what it expresses, this would also be a sufficient repetition and explanation of the world in concepts, or at least entirely parallel to such an explanation, and thus it would be the true philosophy.

* [Literally, "again" or "from the beginning"— a musical direction, to turn back to the beginning of the composition and repeat.]

27

AN EXAMINATION OF SUPERNATURALISM *

by

PAUL HENRI THYRY (BARON) D'HOLBACH

(1723–1789)

When we coolly examine the opinions of men, we are surprised to
find that even in those opinions which they regard as the most
essential, nothing is more uncommon than common sense; or, in
other words, nothing is more uncommon, than a degree of judgment sufficient to discover the most simple truths, or reject the most
striking absurdities, and to be shocked with palpable contradictions.
We have an example of it in Theology, a science revered in all times
and countries, by the greatest number of men; an object regarded
by them the most important, the most useful, and the most indispensable to the happiness of society. An examination, however
slight, of the principles upon which this pretended science is founded,
forces us to acknowledge that these principles, formerly judged in-
contestable, are only hazardous suppositions, imagined by ignorance,
propagated by enthusiasm or knavery, adopted by timid credulity,
preserved by custom which never reasons, and revered solely because not understood. "Some," says Montaigne, "make *the world*
think that they believe what they do not; others, in greater number,
make *themselves* think that they believe what they do not, not knowing what belief is.". . . .

Oppressed by the double yoke of spiritual and temporal power,
it has been impossible for the people to know and pursue their happiness. As Religion, so Politics and Morality became sacred things,
which the profane were not permitted to handle. Men have had no
other Morality, than what their legislators and priests brought

* [From *Common Sense* (1772), translated by H. D. Robinson (1856).]

down from the unknown regions of heaven. The human mind, confused by its theological opinions, ceased to know its own powers,
mistrusted experience, feared truth and disdained reason, in order
to follow authority. Man has been a mere machine in the hands of
tyrants and priests, who alone have had the right of directing his
actions. Always treated as a slave, he has contracted the vices of a
slave.

Such are the true causes of the corruption of morals, to which
Religion opposes only ideal and ineffectual barriers. Ignorance and
servitude are calculated to make men wicked and unhappy. Knowledge, Reason, and Liberty, can alone reform them, and make them
happier. But everything conspires to blind them, and to confirm
them in their errors. Priests cheat them, tyrants corrupt, the better
to enslave them. Tyranny ever was, and ever will be, the true cause
of man's depravity, and also of his habitual calamities. Almost always fascinated by religious fiction, poor mortals turn not their
eyes to the natural and obvious causes of their misery; but attribute
their vices to the imperfection of their natures, and their unhappi-
ness to the anger of the gods. They offer up to heaven vows, sacrifices,
and presents, to obtain the end of their sufferings, which in reality,
are attributable only to the negligence, ignorance, and perversity of
their guides, to the folly of their customs, to the unreasonableness
of their laws, and above all, to the general want of knowledge. Let
men's minds be filled with true ideas; let their reason be cultivated;
let justice govern them; and there will be no need of opposing to the
passions such a feeble barrier as the fear of the gods. Men will be
good, when they are well instructed, well governed, and when they
are punished or despised for the evil, and justly rewarded for the
good, which they do to their fellow citizens.

In vain should we attempt to cure men of their vices, unless we
begin by curing them of their prejudices. It is only by showing them
the truth that they will perceive their true interests and the real
motives that ought to incline them to do good. Instructors have
long enough fixed men's eyes upon heaven; let them now turn them
upon earth. An incomprehensible theology, ridiculous fables, impenetrable mysteries, puerile ceremonies, are too fatiguing to be any
longer endured. Let the human mind apply itself to what is natural,
to intelligible objects, sensible truths, and useful knowledge. Let vain
chimeras be banished; and reasonable opinions will of their own
accord enter into heads thought to be destined to perpetual error.

Does it not suffice to annihilate or shake religious prejudice, to
show, that what is inconceivable to man cannot be made for him?
Does it require anything but plain common sense, to perceive, that
a being incompatible with the most evident notions—that a cause

continually opposed to the effects which we attribute to it—that a being, of whom we can say nothing without falling into contradiction—that a being, who, far from explaining the enigmas of the universe, only makes them more inexplicable—that a being, whom for so many ages men have so vainly addressed to obtain their happiness, and the end of their sufferings—does it require, I say, anything but plain, common sense, to perceive—that the idea of such a being is an idea without model, and that he himself is merely a phantom of the imagination? Is anything necessary but common sense to perceive, at least, that it is folly and madness for men to hate and torment one another about unintelligible opinions concerning a being of this kind? In short, does not everything prove, that Morality and Virtue are totally incompatible with the notions of a God, whom his ministers and interpreters have described, in every country, as the most capricious, unjust, and cruel of tyrants, whose pretended will, however, must serve as law and rule to the inhabitants of the earth?

To discover the true principles of Morality, men have no need of theology, of revelation, or of gods: They have need only of common sense. They have only to commune with themselves, to reflect upon their own nature, to consult their visible interests, to consider the objects of society, and of the individuals who compose it; and they will easily perceive, that virtue is advantageous, and vice disadvantageous to such beings as themselves. Let us persuade men to be just, beneficent, moderate, sociable; not because such conduct is demanded by the gods, but because it is pleasure to men. Let us advise them to abstain from vice and crime; not because they will be punished in the other world, but because they will suffer for it in this. . . .

There is a vast empire, governed by a monarch, whose strange conduct is very proper to confound the minds of his subjects. He wishes to be known, loved, respected, obeyed; but never shows himself to his subjects, and everything conspires to render uncertain the ideas formed of his character.

The people, subjected to his power, have, of the character and laws of their invisible sovereign, such ideas only, as his ministers give them. They, however, confess that they have no idea of their master; that his ways are impenetrable; his views and nature totally incomprehensible. These ministers, likewise, disagree upon the commands which they pretend have been issued by the sovereign, whose instruments they call themselves. They announce them differently to each province of the empire. They defame one another, and mutually treat each other as impostors and false teachers. The decrees and ordinances they take upon themselves to promulgate are obscure; they are enigmas, little calculated to be understood, or even divined, by the subjects, for whose instruction they were intended. The laws of the concealed monarch require interpreters; but the interpreters are always disputing upon the true manner of understanding them. Besides they are not consistent with themselves; all they relate of their concealed prince is only a thread of contradiction. They utter concerning him not a single word that does not immediately confute itself. They call him supremely good; yet there is no one who does not complain of his decrees. They suppose him infinitely wise; and under his administration everything appears to contradict reason and good sense. They extol his justice; and the best of his subjects are generally the least favoured. They assert, he sees everything; yet his presence avails nothing. He is, they say, the friend of order; yet throughout his dominions, all is in confusion and disorder. He makes all for himself; and the events seldom answer his designs. He foresees everything; but cannot prevent anything. He impatiently suffers offence, yet gives everyone the power of offending him. Men admire the wisdom and perfection of his works; yet his works, full of imperfection, are short of duration. He is continually doing and undoing: repairing what he has made; but is never pleased with his work. In all his undertakings, he proposes only his own glory; yet is never glorified. His only end is the happiness of his subjects; and his subjects for the most part want necessaries. Those whom he seems to favour are generally least satisfied with their fate; almost all appear in perpetual revolt against a master, whose greatness they never cease to admire, whose wisdom to extol, whose goodness to adore, whose justice to fear, and whose laws to reverence, though never obeyed!

This empire is the world; this monarch *God,* his ministers are the Priests; his subjects mankind. . . .

Metaphysics teaches us, that God is a *pure spirit*. But herein is modern theology superior to that of the savages? The savages acknowledge a *great spirit* for the master of the world. The savages, like all ignorant people, attribute to *spirits* all the effects of which their experience cannot discover the true causes. Ask a savage, what moves your watch? They answer you, *it is a spirit*. Ask our divines, what moves the universe? They answer, *it is a spirit*.

The savage, when he speaks of a spirit, affixes, at least, some idea to the word; he means thereby an agent, like the air, the breeze, the breath, that invisibly produces discernible effects. By subtilizing everything, the modern theologian becomes as unintelligible to himself as to others. Ask him what he understands by a spirit? He will answer you, that it is an unknown substance, perfectly simple, that has no extension, that has nothing common with matter. Indeed, is there anyone, who can form the least idea of such a substance? What then is a spirit, to speak in the language of modern theology, but the absence of an idea? The idea of *spirituality* is yet an idea without model.

Is it not more natural and intelligible to draw universal existence from the bosom of matter, whose existence is demonstrated by all the senses, and whose effects we experience every moment, which we see act, move, communicate motion, and incessantly generate, than to attribute the formation of things to an unknown power, to a spiritual being, who cannot derive from his nature what he has not himself, and who, by his spiritual essence, can create neither matter nor motion? Nothing is more evident, than that the idea they endeavour to give us, of the action of mind upon matter, represents no object, or is an idea without model. . . .

Whence comes man? What is his origin? Is he then the effect of a fortuitous concourse of atoms? Did the first man spring, ready formed, from the dust of the earth? I know not. Man appears to me, like all other beings, a production of nature. I should be equally embarrassed to tell whence came the first stones, the first trees, the first lions, the first elephants, the first ants, the first acorns, etc., as to explain the origin of man. We are incessantly told to acknowledge and revere the hand of God, of an infinitely wise, intelligent and powerful maker, in so wonderful a work as the human machine. I readily confess, that the human machine appears to me surprising. But as man exists in nature, I am not authorized to say that his formation is above the power of nature. . . .

The worshippers of a God find, above all in the order of the universe, an invincible proof of the existence of an intelligent and wise being, who governs it. But this order is nothing but a series of movements necessarily produced by causes or circumstances, which are sometimes favourable and sometimes hurtful to us: we approve of some, and complain of others.

Nature uniformly follows the same round; that is, the same causes produce the same effects, as long as their action is not disturbed by other causes, which force them to produce different effects. When the operation of causes, whose effects we experience, is interrupted by causes, which, though unknown, are not the less natural and necessary, we are confounded; we cry out, *a miracle!* and attribute it to a cause much more unknown than any of those acting before our eyes.

The universe is always in order. It cannot be in disorder. It is our machine alone that suffers when we complain of disorder. The bodies, causes, and beings, which this world contains necessarily act in the manner in which we see them act, whether we approve or disapprove of the effects. Earthquakes, volcanos, inundations, pestilences, and famines are effects as necessary, or as much in the order of nature, as the fall of heavy bodies, the courses of rivers, the periodical motions of the seas, the blowing of the winds, the fruitful rains, and the favourable effects, for which men praise God and thank him for his goodness.

To be astonished that a certain order reigns in the world, is to be surprised that the same causes constantly produce the same effects. To be shocked at disorder, is to forget that when things change, or are interrupted in their actions, the effects can no longer be the same. To wonder at the order of nature, is to wonder that anything can exist; it is to be surprised at one's own existence. What is order to one being, is disorder to another. All wicked beings find that everything is in order, when they can with impunity put everything in disorder. They find, on the contrary, that everything is in disorder, when they are disturbed in the exercise of their wickedness. . . .

It is more than two thousand years, since, according to Lactantius, the sage Epicurus observed: "either God would remove evil out of this world, and cannot; or he can, and will not; or he has not the power nor will; or, lastly, he has both the power and will. If he has the will, and not the power, this shows weakness, which is contrary to the nature of God. If he has the power, and not the will, it is malignity; and this is no less contrary to his nature. If he is neither able nor willing, he is both impotent and malignant, and consequently cannot be God. If he be both willing and able (which alone is consonant to the nature of God) whence comes evil, or why does he not prevent it?" Reflecting minds have been waiting a reasonable solution of these difficulties for more than two thousand years; and our divines tell us that they will be removed only in a future life. . . .

Many people make a subtle distinction between true religion and superstition. They say that the latter is only a base subordinate fear of the Deity; but that the truly religious man has confidence in his God, and loves him sincerely; whereas, the superstitious man sees in him only an enemy, has no confidence in him, and represents him to himself as a distrustful, cruel tyrant, sparing of his benefits, lavish of his chastisements. But, in reality, does not all religion give us the same ideas of God? At the same time that we are told, that God is infinitely good, are we not also told, that he is very easily provoked, that he grants his favours to a few people only, and that he furiously chastises those to whom he has not been pleased to grant them?

If we take our ideas of God from the nature of things, where we find a mixture of good and evil, this God, just like the good and evil which we experience, must naturally appear capricious, inconstant, sometimes good, and sometimes malevolent; and therefore, instead of exciting our love, must generate distrust, fear, and uncertainty. There is then no real difference between natural religion and the most gloomy and servile superstition. If the theist sees God only in a favourable light, the bigot views him in the most hideous light. The folly of the one is cheerful, that of the other is melancholy; but both are equally delirious. . . .

Are not theologians strange reasoners? Whenever they cannot divine the *natural* causes of things, they invent those which they call *supernatural;* such as spirits, occult causes, inexplicable agents, or rather *words,* much more obscure than the *things* they endeavour to explain. Let us remain in nature, when we wish to account for the phenomena of nature; let us be content to remain ignorant of causes too delicate for our organs; and let us be persuaded, that, by going beyond nature, we shall never solve the problems which nature presents. . . .

It is objected against us that materialism makes man a mere machine, which is thought very dishonourable to the whole human species. But will it be much more honourable for man if we should say that he acts by the secret impulses of a spirit, or by a certain *I know not what,* that animates him in a manner totally inexplicable?

It is easy to perceive that the supposed superiority of *spirit* over matter, or of the soul over the body, has no other foundation than men's ignorance of the nature of this soul, while they are more familiarized with *matter,* with which they imagine they are acquainted, and of which they think they can discern the springs. But the most simple movements of our bodies are to every man who studies them, enigmas, as inexplicable as thought.

The high value which so many people set upon spiritual substance has no other motive than their absolute inability to define it intelligibly. The contempt shown for *matter* by our metaphysicians arises only from the circumstance that familiarity begets contempt. When they tell us that *the soul is more excellent and noble than the body,* they only say that what they know not at all must be far more beautiful than what they have some feeble ideas of.

The dogma of another life is incessantly extolled as useful. It is maintained, that even though it should be only a fiction, it is advantageous, because it deceives men, and conducts them to virtue. But is it true that this dogma makes men wiser and more virtuous? Are the nations who believe this fiction remarkable for purity of morals? Has not the visible world ever the advantage over the in-

visible? If those who are intrusted with the instruction and government of men had knowledge and virtue themselves, they would
govern them much better by realities than by fictions. But legislators, crafty, ambitious, and corrupt, have everywhere found it
shorter to amuse nations with fables, than to teach them truths, to
unfold their reason, to excite them to virtue by sensible and real
motives, in fine, to govern them in a rational manner. Priests undoubtedly had reasons for making the soul immaterial; they
wanted souls and chimeras to people the imaginary regions, which
they have discovered in the other life. Material souls would, like
all bodies, have been subject to dissolution. Now, if men should
believe that all must perish with the body the geographers of
the other world would evidently lose the right of guiding men's souls
towards that unknown abode; they would reap no profits from the
hope with which they feed them, and the terrors with which they
oppress them. If futurity is of no real utility to mankind, it is, at
least, of the greatest utility to those who have assumed the office of
conducting them thither.

"But, it will be said, is not the dogma of the immortality of the
soul comforting to beings, who are often very unhappy here below? Though it should be an error, is it not pleasing? Is it not a
blessing to man to believe, that he shall be able to survive himself,
and enjoy hereafter a happiness, which is denied him upon earth?"
Thus, poor mortals! you make your wishes the measure of truth;
because you desire to live for ever, and to be happier, you at once
conclude, that you shall live for ever, and that you shall be more
fortunate in an unknown world than in this known world, where you
often find nothing but affliction! Consent therefore to leave, without regret, this world which gives the greater part of you much more
torment than pleasure. Submit to the order of nature, which demands that you, as well as all other beings, should not endure for
ever. But what will become of me? asketh thou, O mortal! Thou wilt
be what thou wast, millions of years ago. Thou wast then, I know
not what; resolve then to become instantaneously *I know not what,*
which thou wast millions of years ago; return peaceably to the
universal mass, from which without thy knowledge, thou camest in
thy present form, and pass away without murmuring, like all the
beings who surround thee. . . .

The Deist exclaims: "Abstain from worshipping the cruel capricious God of theology; mine is a being infinitely wise and good; he
is the father of men, the mildest of sovereigns; it is he who fills the
universe with his benefits." But do you not see that everything in
this world contradicts the good qualities which you ascribe to your
God? In the numerous family of this tender father almost all are

unhappy. Under the government of this sovereign, vice is triumphant, and virtue in distress. Among those blessings you extol, and which alone your enthusiasm would see, I behold a multitude of evils of every kind, against which you obstinately shut your eyes. Forced to acknowledge that your beneficent God, in contradiction with himself distributes good and evil with the same hand, for his justification you must, like the priest, refer me to the regions of another life. Invent, therefore, another God; for yours is no less contradictory than that of theologians.

A good God, who does evil, or consents to the commission of evil; a God full of equity, and in whose empire innocence is often oppressed; a perfect God, who produces none but imperfect and miserable works; are not such a God and his conduct as great mysteries as that of the incarnation?

You blush for your fellow-citizens, who allow themselves to be persuaded that the God of the universe could change himself into a man and die upon a cross in a corner of Asia. The mystery of the incarnation appears to you very absurd. You think nothing more ridiculous than a God who transforms himself into bread, and causes himself daily to be eaten in a thousand different places. But are all these mysteries more contradictory to reason than a God, the avenger and rewarder of the actions of men? Is man, according to you, free, or not free? In either case, your God, if he has the shadow of equity, can neither punish nor reward him. If man is free, it is God who has made him free; therefore God is the primitive cause of all his actions; in punishing him for his faults, he would punish him for having executed what he had given him liberty to do. If man is not free to act otherwise than he does, would not God be the most unjust of beings, in punishing him for faults which he could not help committing?

The minor, or secondary, absurdities with which all religions abound, are to many people truly striking; but they have not the courage to trace out the source whence these absurdities must necessarily have flowed. They see not, that a God full of contradictions, caprices, and inconsistent qualities, has only served to disorder men's imaginations, and to produce an endless succession of chimeras.

The theologian would shut the mouths of those who deny the existence of a God, by saying, that all men in all ages and countries have acknowledged the government of some divinity or other; that every people upon earth have believed in an invisible and powerful being, who has been the object of their worship and veneration; in short, that there is no nation, however savage, who are not persuaded of the existence of some intelligence superior to human nature. But can an error be changed into truth by the belief of all men? A great philosopher has justly observed, that "general tradition, or the unanimous consent of mankind is no criterion of truth." Another sage had before said, "that a host of learned men were insufficient to alter the nature of error and convert it into truth.". . .

Religion, especially with the moderns, has tried to identify itself with morality, the principles of which it has thereby totally obscured. It has rendered men unsociable by duty, and forced them to be inhuman to every one who thought differently from themselves. Theological disputes, equally unintelligible to each of the enraged parties, have shaken empires, caused revolutions, been fatal to sovereigns, and desolated all Europe. These contemptible quarrels have not been extinguished even in rivers of blood. Since the extinction of paganism, the people have made it a religious principle to become outraged, whenever any opinion is advanced which their priests think contrary to *sound doctrine*. The sectaries of a religion which preaches, in appearance, nothing but charity, concord, and peace, have proved themselves more ferocious than cannibals or savages, whenever their divines excited them to destroy their brethren. There is no crime which men have not committed under the idea of pleasing the Divinity, or appeasing his wrath. . . .

To found morality upon a God, whom every one paints to himself differently, composes in his way, and arranges according to his own temperament and interest, is evidently to found morality upon the caprice and imagination of men; it is to found it upon the whims of a sect, a faction, a party, who will believe they have the advantage to adore a true God to the exclusion of all others.

To establish morality or the duties of man upon the divine will, is to found it upon the will, the reveries and the interests of those who make God speak without ever fearing that he will contradict them. In every religion priests alone have a right to decide what is pleasing or displeasing to their God; we are certain, they will always decide that it is what pleases or displeases themselves. . . .

We are perpetually told that without a God there would be no *moral obligation;* that the people and even the sovereigns require a legislator powerful enough to constrain them. Moral constraint supposes a law; but this law arises from the eternal and necessary relations of things with one another; relations which have nothing common with the existence of a God. The rules of man's conduct are derived from his own nature which he is capable of knowing, and not from the divine nature of which he has no idea. These rules constrain or oblige us; that is, we render ourselves estimable or contemptible, amiable or detestable, worthy of reward or of punishment, happy or unhappy, according as we conform to, or deviate from these rules. The law which obliges man not to hurt himself, is founded upon the nature of a sensible being, who, in whatever way he came into the world, or whatever may be his fate in a future one, is forced by his actual essence to seek good and shun evil, to love pleasure and fear pain. The law which obliges man not to injure, and even to do good to others, is founded upon the nature of sensible beings, living in society, whose essence compels them to despise those who are useless, and to detest those who oppose their felicity.

Whether there exists a God or not, whether this God has spoken or not, the moral duties of men will be always the same, so long as they retain their peculiar nature, that is, as long as they are sensible beings. Have men then need of a God whom they know not, of an invisible legislator, of a mysterious religion and of chimerical fears, in order to learn that every excess evidently tends to destroy them, that to preserve health they must be temperate; that to gain the love of others it is necessary to do them good, that to do them evil is the sure means to incur their vengeance and hatred.

"Before the law there was no sin." Nothing is more false than this maxim. It suffices that man is what he is, or that he is a sensible being, in order to distinguish what gives him pleasure or displeasure. It suffices that one man knows that another man is a sensible being like himself, to perceive what is useful or hurtful to him. It suffices that man needs his fellow-creature, in order to know that he must fear to excite in him sentiments unfavourable to himself. Thus the feeling and thinking being has only to feel and think, in order to discover what he must do for himself and others. I feel, and another feels like me; this is the foundation of all morals.

We can judge of the goodness of a system of morals only by its conformity to the nature of man. By this comparison, we have a right to reject it, if contrary to the welfare of our species. Whoever has seriously meditated religion and its supernatural morality; whoever has carefully weighed their advantages and disadvantages, will be fully convinced that both are injurious to the interests of man, or directly opposite to his nature. . . .

It is asserted that the dogma of another life is of the utmost importance to the peace and happiness of societies; that without it, men would be destitute of motives to do good. What need is there of terrors and fables to make every rational man sensible how he ought to conduct himself upon earth? Does not every one see that he has the greatest interest in meriting the approbation, esteem, and benevolence of the beings who surround him, and in abstaining from every thing by which he may incur the censure, contempt, and resentment of society? However short an entertainment, a conversation, or visit, does not each desire to act his part decently, and agreeably to himself and others? If life is but a passage, let us strive to make it easy; which we cannot effect, if we fail in regard for those who travel with us.

Religion, occupied with its gloomy reveries, considers man merely as a pilgrim upon earth; and therefore supposes that, in order to travel the more securely, he must forsake company and deprive himself of the pleasures and amusements which might console him for the tediousness and fatigue of the road. A stoical and morose philosopher sometimes gives us advice as irrational as that of religion. But a more rational philosophy invites us to spread flowers in the way of life, to dispel melancholy and panic terrors, to connect our interest with that of our fellow-travellers, and by gaiety and lawful pleasures, to divert our attention from the difficulties and cross accidents to which we are often exposed; it teaches us, that, to travel agreeably, we should abstain from what might be injurious to ourselves, and carefully shun what might render us odious to our associates. . . .

Conscience is the internal testimony, which we bear to ourselves, of having acted so as to merit the esteem or blame of the beings with whom we live; and it is founded upon the clear knowledge we have of men, and of the sentiments which our actions must produce in them. The conscience of the religious man consists in imagining that he has pleased or displeased his God, of whom he has no idea, and whose obscure and doubtful intentions are explained to him only by men of doubtful veracity, who, like him, are utterly unacquainted with the essence of the Deity, and are little agreed upon what can please or displease him. In a word, the conscience of the credulous is directed by men who have themselves an erroneous conscience, or whose interest stifles knowledge. . . .

A man of reflection cannot be incapable of his duties, of discovering the relations subsisting between men, of meditating his own nature, of discerning his own wants, propensities, and desires, and of perceiving what he owes to beings who are necessary to his happiness. These reflections naturally lead him to a knowledge of the morality most essential to social beings. Dangerous passions seldom fall to the lot of man who loves to commune with himself, to study, and to investigate the principles of things. The strongest passion of such a man will be to know truth, and his ambition to teach it to others. Philosophy is proper to cultivate both the mind and the heart. On the score of morals and honesty, has not he who reflects and reasons, evidently an advantage over him who makes it a principle never to reason?

28

ME *

by

WILLIAM JAMES
(1842–1910)

The Empirical Self of each of us is all that he is tempted to call by the name of *me*. But it is clear that between what a man calls *me* and what he simply calls *mine* the line is difficult to draw. We feel and act about certain things that are ours very much as we feel and act about ourselves. Our fame, our children, the work of our hands, may be as dear to us as our bodies are, and arouse the same feelings and the same acts of reprisal if attacked. And our bodies themselves, are they simply ours, or are they *us*? Certainly men have been ready to disown their very bodies and to regard them as mere vestures, or even as prisons of clay from which they should some day be glad to escape.

We see then that we are dealing with a fluctuating material. The same object being sometimes treated as a part of me, at other times as simply mine, and then again as if I had nothing to do with it at all. *In its widest possible sense,* however, *a man's Self is the sum total of all that he* CAN *call his,* not only his body and his psychic powers, but his clothes and his house, his wife and children, his ancestors and friends, his reputation and works, his lands and horses, and yacht and bank-account. All these things give him the same emotions. If they wax and prosper, he feels triumphant; if they dwindle and die away, he feels cast down,—not necessarily in the same degree for each thing, but in much the same way for all. . . .

The constituents of the Self may be divided into two classes, those which make up respectively—

[1]　(*a*)　The material Self;
　　　(*b*)　The social Self;
　　　(*c*)　The spiritual Self; and
[2]　(*d*)　The pure Ego.

* [From Ch. X in *The Principles of Psychology* (1890).]

(a) The body is the innermost part of *the material Self* in each of us; and certain parts of the body seem more intimately ours than the rest. The clothes come next. The old saying that the human person is composed of three parts—soul, body and clothes—is more than a joke. We so appropriate our clothes and identify ourselves with them that there are few of us who, if asked to choose between having a beautiful body clad in raiment perpetually shabby and unclean, and having an ugly and blemished form always spotlessly attired, would not hesitate a moment before making a decisive reply. Next, our immediate family is a part of ourselves. Our father and mother, our wife and babes, are bone of our bone and flesh of our flesh. When they die, a part of our very selves is gone. If they do anything wrong, it is our shame. If they are insulted, our anger flashes forth as readily as if we stood in their place. Our home comes next. Its scenes are part of our life; its aspects awaken the tenderest feelings of affection; and we do not easily forgive the stranger who, in visiting it, finds fault with its arrangements or treats it with contempt. All these different things are the objects of instinctive preferences coupled with the most important practical interests of life. We all have a blind impulse to watch over our body, to deck it with clothing of an ornamental sort, to cherish parents, wife and babes, and to find for ourselves a home of our own which we may live in and 'improve.'

An equally instinctive impulse drives us to collect property; and the collections thus made become, with different degrees of intimacy, parts of our empirical selves. The parts of our wealth most intimately ours are those which are saturated with our labor. There are few men who would not feel personally annihilated if a life-long construction of their hands or brains—say an entomological collection or an extensive work in manuscript—were suddenly swept away. The miser feels similarly towards his gold, and although it is true that a part of our depression at the loss of possessions is due to our feeling that we must now go without certain goods that we expected the possessions to bring in their train, yet in every case there remains, over and above this, a sense of the shrinkage of our personality, a partial conversion of ourselves to nothingness, which is a psychological phenomenon by itself. We are all at once assimilated to the tramps and poor devils whom we so despise, and at the same time removed farther than ever away from the happy sons of earth who lord it over land and sea and men in the full-blown lustihood that wealth and power can give, and before whom, stiffen ourselves as we will by appealing to anti-snobbish first principles, we cannot escape an emotion, open or sneaking, of respect and dread.

(*b*) *A man's Social Self* is the recognition which he gets from his mates. We are not only gregarious animals, liking to be in sight of our fellows, but we have an innate propensity to get ourselves noticed, and noticed favorably, by our kind. No more fiendish punishment could be devised, were such a thing physically possible, than that one should be turned loose in society and remain absolutely unnoticed by all the members thereof. If no one turned round when we entered, answered when we spoke, or minded what we did, but if every person we met 'cut us dead,' and acted as if we were non-existing things, a kind of rage and impotent despair would ere long well up in us, from which the cruellest bodily tortures would be a relief; for these would make us feel that, however bad might be our plight, we had not sunk to such a depth as to be unworthy of attention at all.

Properly speaking, *a man has as many social selves as there are individuals who recognize him* and carry an image of him in their mind. To wound any one of these his images is to wound him. But as the individuals who carry the images fall naturally into classes, we may practically say that he has as many different social selves as there are distinct *groups* of persons about whose opinion he cares. He generally shows a different side of himself to each of these different groups. Many a youth who is demure enough before his parents and teachers, swears and swaggers like a pirate among his 'tough' young friends. We do not show ourselves to our children as to our club-companions, to our customers as to the laborers we employ, to our own masters and employers as to our intimate friends. From this there results what practically is a division of the man into several selves; and this may be a discordant splitting, as where one is afraid to let one set of his acquaintances know him as he is elsewhere; or it may be a perfectly harmonious division of labor, as where one tender to his children is stern to the soldiers or prisoners under his command.

The most peculiar social self which one is apt to have is in the mind of the person one is in love with. The good or bad fortunes of this self cause the most intense elation and dejection—unreasonable enough as measured by every other standard than that of the organic feeling of the individual. To his own consciousness he *is* not, so long as this particular social self fails to get recognition, and when it is recognized his contentment passes all bounds.

A man's *fame,* good or bad, and his *honor* or dishonor, are names for one of his social selves. The particular social self of a man called his honor is usually the result of one of those splittings of which we have spoken. It is his image in the eyes of his own 'set,' which exalts or condemns him as he conforms or not to certain requirements that may not be made of one in another walk of life. Thus a layman may abandon a city infected with cholera; but a priest or a doctor would think such an act incompatible with his honor. A soldier's honor requires him to fight or to die under circumstances where another man can apologize or run away with no stain upon his social self. A judge, a statesman, are in like manner debarred by the honor of their cloth from entering into pecuniary relations perfectly honorable to persons in private life. Nothing is commoner than to hear people discriminate between their different selves of this sort: "As a man I pity you, but as an official I must show you no mercy; as a politician I regard him as an ally, but as a moralist I loathe him;" etc., etc. What may be called 'club-opinion' is one of the very strongest forces in life. The thief must not steal from other thieves; the gambler must pay his gambling-debts, though he pay no other debts in the world. The code of honor of fashionable society has throughout history been full of permissions as well as of vetoes, the only reason for following either of which is that so we best serve one of our social selves. You must not lie in general, but you may lie as much as you please if asked about your relations with a lady; you must accept a challenge from an equal, but if challenged by an inferior you may laugh him to scorn: these are examples of what is meant.

(c) By the Spiritual Self, so far as it belongs to the Empirical Me, I mean a man's inner or subjective being, his psychic faculties or dispositions, taken concretely; not the bare principle of personal Unity, or 'pure' Ego, which remains still to be discussed. These psychic dispositions are the most enduring and intimate part of the self, that which we most verily seem to be. We take a purer self-satisfaction when we think of our ability to argue and discriminate, of our moral sensibility and conscience, of our indomitable will, than when we survey any of our other possessions. Only when these are altered is a man said to be *alienatus a se* [estranged from himself].

Now this spiritual self may be considered in various ways. We may divide it into faculties, as just instanced, isolating them one from another, and identifying ourselves with either in turn. This is an *abstract* way of dealing with consciousness, in which, as it actually presents itself, a plurality of such faculties are always to be simultaneously found; or we may insist on a concrete view, and then the spiritual self in us will be either the entire stream of our personal consciousness, or the present 'segment' or 'section' of that stream, according as we take a broader or a narrower view—both the stream and the section being concrete existences in time, and each being a unity after its own peculiar kind. But whether we take it abstractly or concretely, our considering the spiritual self at all is a reflective process, is the result of our abandoning the outward-looking point of view, and of our having become able to think of subjectivity as such, *to think ourselves as thinkers*.

This attention to thought as such, and the identification of ourselves with it rather than with any of the objects which it reveals, is a momentous and in some respects a rather mysterious operation, of which we need here only say that as a matter of fact it exists; and that in everyone, at an early age, the distinction between thought as such, and what it is 'of' or 'about,' has become familiar to the mind. The deeper grounds for this discrimination may possibly be hard to find; but superficial grounds are plenty and near at hand. Almost anyone will tell us that thought is a different sort of existence from things, because many sorts of thought are of no things—e.g., pleasures, pains, and emotions; others are of non-existent things—errors and fictions; others again of existent things, but in a form that is symbolic and does not resemble them—abstract ideas and concepts; whilst in the thoughts that do resemble the things they are 'of' (percepts, sensations), we can feel, alongside of the thing known, the thought of it going on as an altogether separate act and operation in the mind.

Now this subjective life of ours, distinguished as such so clearly from the objects known by its means, may, as aforesaid, be taken by us in a concrete or in an abstract way. Of the concrete way I will say nothing just now, except that the actual 'section' of the stream will ere long, in our discussion of the nature of the principle of *unity* in consciousness, play a very important part. The abstract way claims our attention first. If the stream as a whole is identified with the Self far more than any outward thing, a *certain portion of the stream abstracted from the rest* is so identified in an altogether peculiar degree, and is felt by all men as a sort of innermost centre within the circle, of sanctuary within the citadel, constituted by the subjective life as a whole. Compared with this element of the stream, the other parts, even of the subjective life, seem transient external possessions, of which each in turn can be disowned, whilst that which disowns them remains. Now, *what is this self of all the other selves?*

Probably all men would describe it in much the same way up to a certain point. They would call it the *active* element in all consciousness; saying that whatever qualities a man's feelings may possess, or whatever content his thought may include, there is a spiritual something in him which seems to *go out* to meet these qualities and contents, whilst they seem to *come in* to be received by it. It is what welcomes or rejects. It presides over the perception of sensations, and by giving or withholding its assent it influences the movements they tend to arouse. It is the home of interest,—not the pleasant or the painful, not even pleasure or pain, as such, but that within us to which pleasure and pain, the pleasant and the painful, speak. It is the source of effort and attention, and the place from which appear to emanate the fiats of the will. A physiologist who should reflect upon it in his own person could hardly help, I should think, connecting it more or less vaguely with the process by which ideas or incoming sensations are 'reflected' or pass over into outward acts. Not necessarily that it should *be* this process or the mere feeling of this process, but that it should be in some close way *related* to this process; for it plays a part analogous to it in the psychic life, being a sort of junction at which sensory ideas terminate and from which motor ideas proceed, and forming a kind of link between the two. Being more incessantly there than any other single element of the mental life, the other elements end by seeming to accrete round it and to belong to it. It becomes opposed to them as the permanent is opposed to the changing and inconstant.

One may, I think, without fear of being upset by any future Galtonian circulars, believe that all men must single out from the rest of what they call themselves some central principle of which each would recognize the foregoing to be a fair general description,— accurate enough, at any rate, to denote what is meant, and keep it unconfused with other things. The moment, however, they came to closer quarters with it, trying to define more accurately its precise nature, we should find opinions beginning to diverge. Some would say that it is a simple active substance, the soul, of which they are thus conscious; others, that it is nothing but a fiction, the imaginary being denoted by the pronoun I; and between these extremes of opinion all sorts of intermediaries would be found.

Later we must ourselves discuss them all, and sufficient to that day will be the evil thereof. *Now*, let us try to settle for ourselves as definitely as we can, just how this central nucleus of the Self may *feel*, no matter whether it be a spiritual substance or only a delusive word.

For this central part of the Self is *felt*. It may be all that Transcendentalists say it is, and all that Empiricists say it is into the bargain, but it is at any rate no mere *ens rationis* [a thing of reason], cognized only in an intellectual way, and no *mere* summation of memories or *mere* sound of a word in our ears. It is something with which we also have direct sensible acquaintance, and which is as fully present at any moment of consciousness in which it *is* present, as in a whole lifetime of such moments. When, just now, it was called an abstraction, that did not mean that, like some general notion, it could not be presented in a particular experience. It only meant that in the stream of consciousness it never was found all alone. But when it is found, it is *felt*; just as the body is felt, the feeling of which is also an abstraction, because never is the body felt all alone, but always together with other things. *Now can we tell more precisely in what the feeling of this central active self consists,* —not necessarily as yet what the active self *is*, as a being or principle, but what we *feel* when we become aware of its existence?

I think I can in my own case; and as what I say will be likely to meet with opposition if generalized (as indeed it may be in part inapplicable to other individuals), I had better continue in the first person, leaving my description to be accepted by those to whose introspection it may commend itself as true, and confessing my inability to meet the demands of others, if others there be.

First of all, I am aware of a constant play of furtherances and hindrances in my thinking, of checks and releases, tendencies which run with desire, and tendencies which run the other way. Among the matters I think of, some range themselves on the side of the thought's interests, whilst others play an unfriendly part thereto. The mutual inconsistencies and agreements, reinforcements and obstructions, which obtain amongst these objective matters reverberate backwards and produce what seem to be incessant reactions of my spontaneity upon them, welcoming or opposing, appropriating or disowning, striving with or against, saying yes or no. This palpitating inward life is, in me, that central nucleus which I just tried to describe in terms that all men might use.

But when I forsake such general descriptions and grapple with particulars, coming to the closest possible quarters with the facts, *it is difficult for me to detect in the activity any purely spiritual element at all. Whenever my introspective glance succeeds in turning round quickly enough to catch one of these manifestations of spontaneity in the act, all it can ever feel distinctly is some bodily process, for the most part taking place within the head.* Omitting for a moment what is obscure in these introspective results, let me try to state those particulars which to my own consciousness seem indubitable and distinct.

In the first place, the acts of attending, assenting, negating, making an effort, are felt as movements of something in the head. In many cases it is possible to describe these movements quite exactly. In attending to either an idea or a sensation belonging to a particular sense-sphere, the movement is the adjustment of the sense-organ, felt as it occurs. I cannot think in visual terms, for example, without feeling a fluctuating play of pressures, convergences, divergences, and accommodations in my eyeballs. The direction in which the object is conceived to lie determines the character of these movements, the feeling of which becomes, for my consciousness, identified with the manner in which I make myself ready to receive the visible thing. My brain appears to me as if all shot across with lines of direction, of which I have become conscious as my attention has shifted from one sense-organ to another, in passing to successive outer things, or in following trains of varying sense-ideas.

When I try to remember or reflect, the movements in question, instead of being directed towards the periphery, seem to come from the periphery inwards and feel like a sort of *withdrawal* from the outer world. As far as I can detect, these feelings are due to an actual rolling outwards and upwards of the eyeballs, such as I believe occurs in me in sleep, and is the exact opposite of their action in fixating a physical thing. In reasoning, I find that I am apt to have a kind of vaguely localized diagram in my mind, with the various fractional objects of the thought disposed at particular points thereof; and the oscillations of my attention from one of them to another are most distinctly felt as alternations of direction in movements occurring inside the head.

In consenting and negating, and in making a mental effort, the movements seem more complex, and I find them harder to describe. The opening and closing of the glottis play a great part in these operations, and, less distinctly, the movements of the soft palate, etc., shutting off the posterior nares from the mouth. My glottis is like a sensitive value, intercepting my breath instantaneously at every mental hesitation or felt aversion to the objects of my thought, and as quickly opening, to let the air pass through my throat and nose, the moment the repugnance is overcome. The feeling of the movement of this air is, in me, one strong ingredient of the feeling of assent. The movements of the muscles of the brow and eyelids also respond very sensitively to every fluctuation in the agreeableness or disagreeableness of what comes before my mind.

In *effort* of any sort, contractions of the jaw-muscles and of those of respiration are added to those of the brow and glottis, and thus the feeling passes out of the head properly so called. It passes out of the head whenever the welcoming or rejecting of the object is *strongly* felt. Then a set of feelings pour in from many bodily parts, all 'expressive' of my emotion, and the head-feelings proper are swallowed up in this larger mass.

In a sense, then, it may be truly said that, in one person at least, *the 'Self of selves,' when carefully examined, is found to consist mainly of the collection of these peculiar motions in the head or between the head and throat.* I do not for a moment say that this is *all* it consists of, for I fully realize how desperately hard is introspection in this field. But I feel quite sure that these cephalic motions are the portions of my innermost activity of which I am *most distinctly aware.* If the dim portions which I cannot yet define should prove to be like unto these distinct portions in me, and I like other men, *it would follow that our entire feeling of spiritual activity, or what*

*commonly passes by that name, is really a feeling of bodily activities
whose exact nature is by most men overlooked.*

Now, without pledging ourselves in any way to adopt this hypothesis, let us dally with it for a while to see to what consequences
it might lead if it were true.

In the first place, the nuclear part of the Self, intermediary between ideas and overt acts, would be a collection of activities
physiologically in no essential way different from the overt acts
themselves. If we divide all possible physiological acts into *adjustments* and *executions*, the nuclear self would be the adjustments collectively considered; and the less intimate, more shifting self, so far
as it was active, would be the executions. But both adjustments and
executions would obey the reflex type. Both would be the result of
sensorial and ideational processes discharging either into each other
within the brain, or into muscles and other parts outside. The
peculiarity of the adjustments would be that they are minimal re-
flexes, few in number, incessantly repeated, constant amid great
fluctuations in the rest of the mind's content, and entirely unimpor-
tant and uninteresting except through their uses in furthering or
inhibiting the presence of various things, and actions before consciousness. These characters would naturally keep us from introspec-
tively paying much attention to them in detail, whilst they would
at the same time make us aware of them as a coherent group of
processes, strongly contrasted with all the other things consciousness
contained,—even with the other constituents of the 'Self,' material,
social, or spiritual, as the case might be. They are reactions, and
they are *primary* reactions. Everything arouses them; for objects
which have no other effects will for a moment contract the brow and
make the glottis close. It is as if all that visited the mind had to
stand an entrance-examination, and just show its face so as to be
either approved or sent back. These primary reactions are like the
opening or the closing of the door. In the midst of psychic change
they are the permanent core of turnings-towards and turnings-from,
of yieldings and arrests, which naturally seem central and interior in
comparison with the foreign matters, *apropos* to which they occur,
and hold a sort of arbitrating, decisive position, quite unlike that held
by any of the other constituents of the Me. It would not be surprising, then, if we were to feel them as the birthplace of conclusions and
the starting point of acts, or if they came to appear as what we called
a while back the 'sanctuary within the citadel' of our personal life.

If they really were the innermost sanctuary, the *ultimate* one of all
the selves whose being we can ever directly experience, it would
follow that *all* that is experienced is, strictly considered, *objective;*

that this Objective falls asunder into two contrasted parts, one realized as 'Self,' the other as 'not-Self;' and that over and above these parts there *is* nothing save the fact that they are known, the fact of the stream of thought being there as the indispensable subjective condition of their being experienced at all. But this *condition* of the experience is not one of the *things experienced* at the moment; this knowing is not immediately *known*. It is only known in subsequent reflection. Instead, then, of the stream of thought being one of *con*-sciousness, "thinking its own existence along with whatever else it thinks," (as Ferrier says) it might be better called a stream of *Scious*ness pure and simple, thinking objects of some of which it makes what it calls a 'Me,' and only aware of its 'pure' Self in an abstract, hypothetic or conceptual way. Each 'section' of the stream would then be a bit of sciousness or knowledge of this sort, including and contemplating its 'me' and its 'not-me' as objects which work out their drama together, but not yet including or contemplating its own subjective being. The sciousness in question would be the *Thinker,* and the existence of this thinker would be given to us rather as a logical postulate than as that direct inner perception of spiritual activity which we naturally believe ourselves to have. 'Matter,' as something behind physical phenomena, is a postulate of this sort. Between the postulated Matter and the postulated Thinker, the sheet of phenomena would then swing, some of them (the 'realities') pertaining more to the Matter, others (the fictions, opinions, and errors) pertaining more to the Thinker. But *who* the Thinker would be, or how many distinct Thinkers we ought to suppose in the universe, would all be subjects for an ulterior metaphysical inquiry. . . .

At present, . . . the only conclusion I come to is the following: That (in some persons at least) the part of the innermost Self which is most vividly felt turns out to consist for the most part of a collection of cephalic movements of 'adjustments' which, for want of attention and reflection, usually fail to be perceived and classed as what they are; that over and above these there is an obscurer feeling of something more; but whether it be of fainter physiological processes, or of nothing objective at all, but rather of subjectivity as such, of thought become 'its own object,' must at present remain an open question,—like the question whether it be an indivisible active soul-substance, or the question whether it be a personification of the pronoun I, or any other of the guesses as to what its nature may be.

29

THE LARGER SELF *

by

JOSIAH ROYCE,

(1855–1916)

Idealism has two aspects. It is, for the first, a kind of analysis of the world, an analysis which so far has no absolute character about it, but which undertakes, in a fashion that might be acceptable to any skeptic, to examine what you mean by all the things, whatever they are, that you believe in or experience. This idealistic analysis consists merely in a pointing out, by various devices, that the world of your knowledge, whatever it contains, is through and through such stuff as ideas are made of, that you never in your life believed in anything definable *but* ideas, that, as Berkeley put it, "this whole choir of heaven and furniture of earth" is nothing for any of us but a system of ideas which govern our belief and our conduct. Such idealism has numerous statements, interpretations, embodiments. . . . In this aspect idealism is already a little puzzling to our natural consciousness, but it becomes quickly familiar, in fact almost commonplace, and seems after all to alter our practical faith or to solve our deeper problems very little.

The other aspect of idealism is the one which gives us our notion of the absolute Self. To it the first is only preparatory. . . .

I begin with the first and the less significant aspect of idealism. Our world, I say, whatever it may contain, is such stuff as ideas are made of. This preparatory sort of idealism is the one that, as I just suggested, Berkeley made prominent, and, after a fashion familiar. I must state it in my own way, although one in vain seeks to attain novelty in illustrating so frequently described a view.

Here, then, is our so real world of the senses, full of light and warmth and sound. If anything could be solid and external, surely, one at first will say, it is this world. Hard facts, not mere ideas,

* [The greater part of Lecture XI in *The Spirit of Modern Philosophy* (1892). By kind permission of Houghton Mifflin Co.]

meet us on every hand. Ideas any one can mould as he wishes. Not so facts. In idea socialists can dream out Utopias, disappointed lovers can imagine themselves successful, beggars can ride horses, wanderers can enjoy the fireside at home. In the realm of facts, society organizes itself as it must, rejected lovers stand for the time defeated, beggars are alone with their wishes, oceans roll drearily between home and the wanderer. Yet this world of fact is, after all, not entirely stubborn, not merely hard. The strenuous will can mould facts. We can form our world, in part, according to our ideas. Statesmen influence the social order, lovers woo afresh, wanderers find the way home. But thus to alter the world we must work, and just because the laborer is worthy of his hire, it is well that the real world should thus have such fixity of things as enables us to anticipate what facts will prove lasting, and to see of the travail of our souls when it is once done. This, then, is the presupposition of life, that we work in a real world, where house-walls do not melt away as in dreams, but stand firm against the winds of many winters, and can be felt as real. We do not wish to find facts wholly plastic; we want them to be stubborn, if only the stubbornness be not altogether unmerciful. Our will makes constantly a sort of agreement with the world, whereby, if the world will continually show some respect to the will, the will shall consent to be strenuous in its industry. Interfere with the reality of my world, and you therefore take the very life and heart out of my will.

The reality of the world, however, when thus defined in terms of its stubbornness, its firmness as against the will that has not conformed to its laws, its kindly rigidity in preserving for us the fruits of our labors,—such reality, I say, is still something wholly unanalyzed. In what does this stubbornness consist? Surely, many different sorts of reality, as it would seem, may be stubborn. Matter is stubborn when it stands in hard walls against us, or rises in vast mountain ranges before the path-finding explorer. But minds can be stubborn also. The lonely wanderer, who watches by the seashore the waves that roll between him and his home, talks of cruel facts, material barriers that, just because they *are* material, and not ideal, shall be the irresistible foes of his longing heart. "In wish," he says, "I am with my dear ones, but alas, wishes cannot cross oceans! Oceans are material facts, in the cold outer world. Would that the world of the heart were all!" But alas! to the rejected lover the world of the heart *is* all, and that is just his woe. Were the barrier between him and his beloved only made of those stubborn material facts, only of walls or of oceans, how lightly might his will erelong transcend them all! Matter stubborn! Outer nature cruelly the foe of ideas! Nay, it is just an idea that now opposes him,—just an idea, and that, too, in the mind of the maiden he loves. But in vain does he call this stubborn bit of disdain a merely ideal fact. No flint was ever more definite in preserving its identity and its edge than this disdain may be. Place me for a moment, then, in an external world that shall consist wholly of ideas,—the ideas, namely, of other people about me, a world of maidens who shall scorn me, of old friends who shall have learned to hate me, of angels who shall condemn me, of God who shall judge me. In what piercing north winds, amidst what fields of ice, in the labyrinths of what tangled forests, in the depths of what thick-walled dungeons, on the edges of what tremendous precipices, should I be more genuinely in the presence of stubborn and unyielding facts than in that conceived world of ideas! So, as one sees, I by no means deprive my world of stubborn reality, if I merely call it a world of ideas. On the contrary, as every teacher knows, the ideas of the people are often the most difficult of facts to influence. We were wrong, then, when we said that whilst matter was stubborn, ideas could be moulded at pleasure. Ideas are often the most implacable of facts. Even my own ideas, the facts of my own inner life, may cruelly decline to be plastic to my wish. The wicked will that refuses to be destroyed,— what rock has often more consistency for our senses than this will has for our inner consciousness! The king, in his soliloquy in "Hamlet,"—in what an unyielding world of hard facts does he not move! and yet they are now only inner facts. The fault is past; he is alone with his conscience.

> What rests?
> Try what repentance can. What can it not?
> Yet what can it, when one cannot repent?
> O wretched state! O bosom black as death!
> O limëd soul, that, struggling to be free,
> Art more engaged!

No, here are barriers worse than any material chains. The world of ideas has its own horrible dungeons and chasms. Let those who have refuted Bishop Berkeley's idealism by the wonder why he did not walk over every precipice or into every fire if these things existed only in his idea, let such, I say, first try some of the fires and the precipices of the inner life, ere they decide that dangers cease to be dangers as soon as they are called ideal, or even subjectively ideal in me.

Many sorts of reality, then, may be existent at the heart of any world of facts. But this bright and beautiful sense-world of ours,— what, amongst these many possible sorts of reality, does that embody? Are the stars and the oceans, the walls and the pictures, real as the maiden's heart is real,—embodying the ideas of somebody, but none the less stubbornly real for that? Or can we make something else of their reality? For, of course, that the stars and the oceans, the walls and the pictures have *some* sort of stubborn reality, just as the minds of our fellows have, our analysis so far does not for an instant think of denying. Our present question is, what sort of reality? Consider, then, in detail, certain aspects of the reality that seems to be exemplified in our sense-world. The sublimity of the sky, the life and majesty of the ocean, the interest of a picture,— to what sort of real facts do these belong? Evidently here we shall have no question. So far as the sense-world is beautiful, is majestic, is sublime, this beauty and dignity exist only for the appreciative observer. If they exist beyond him, they exist only for some other mind, or as the thought and embodied purpose of some universal soul of nature. A man who sees the same world, but who has no eye for the fairness of it, will find all the visible facts, but will catch nothing of their value. At once, then, the sublimity and beauty of the world are thus truths that one who pretends to insight ought to see, and they are truths which have no meaning except for such a beholder's mind, or except as embodying the thought of the mind of the world. So here, at least, is so much of the outer world that is ideal, just as the coin or the jewel or the bank-note or the bond has its value not alone in its physical presence, but in the idea that it symbolizes to a beholder's mind, or to the relatively universal thought of the commercial world. But let us look a little deeper. Surely, if the objects yonder are unideal and outer, odors and tastes and temperatures do not exist in these objects in just the way in which they exist in us. Part of the being of these properties, at least, if not all of it, is ideal and exists for us, or at best is once more the embodiment of the thought or purpose of some world-mind. About tastes you cannot dispute, because they are not only ideal but personal. For the benumbed tongue and palate of diseased bodily conditions, all things are tasteless. As for temperatures, a well known experiment will show how the same water may seem cold to one hand and warm to the other. But even so, colors and sounds are at least in part ideal. Their causes may have some other sort of reality; but colors themselves are not in the things, since they change with the light that falls on the things, vanish in the dark (whilst the things remained unchanged), and differ for different eyes. And as for sounds, both the pitch and the quality of tones depend for us upon certain interesting peculiarities of our hearing organs, and exist in nature only as voiceless sound-waves trembling through the air. All such sense qualities, then, are ideal. The world yonder may—yes, must—have attributes that give reasons why these qualities are thus felt by us; for so we assume. The world yonder may even be a mind that thus expresses its will to us. But these qualities need not, nay, cannot resemble the ideas that are produced in us, unless, indeed, that is because these qualities have place as ideas in some world-mind. Sound-waves in the air are not like our musical sensations; nor is the symphony as we hear it and feel it any physical property of the strings and the wind instruments; nor are the ether-vibrations that the sun sends us like our ideas when we see the sun; nor yet is the flashing of moonlight on the water as we watch the waves a direct expression of the actual truths of fluid motion as the water embodies them.

Unless, then, the real physical world yonder is itself the embodiment of some world-spirit's ideas, which he conveys to us, unless it is real only as the maiden's heart is real, namely, as itself a conscious thought, then we have so far but one result: that real world (to repeat one of the commonplaces of modern popular science) is in itself, apart from somebody's eyes and tongue and ears and touch, neither colored nor tasteful, neither cool nor warm, neither light nor dark, neither musical nor silent. All these qualities belong to our ideas, being indeed none the less genuine facts for that, but being in so far ideal facts. We must see colors when we look, we must hear music when there is playing in our presence; but this *must* is a must that consists in a certain irresistible presence of an idea in us under certain conditions. *That* this idea must come is, indeed, a truth as unalterable, once more, as the king's settled remorse in Hamlet. But like this remorse, again, it exists as an ideal truth, objective, but through and through objective *for* somebody, and not *apart from* anybody. What this truth implies we have yet to see. So far it is only an ideal truth for the beholder, with just the bare possibility that behind it all there is the thought of a world-spirit. And, in fact, *so* far we must all go together if we reflect.

But now, at this point, the Berkeleyan idealist goes one step further. The real outside world that is still left unexplained and unanalyzed after its beauty, its warmth, its odors, its tastes, its colors, and its tones, have been relegated to the realm of ideal truths, what do you now *mean* by calling it real? No doubt it *is* known as somehow real, but *what* is this reality *known as* being? If you know that this world is still there and outer, as by hypothesis you know, you are bound to say *what* this outer character implies for your thought. And here you have trouble. Is the outer world, as it exists outside of your ideas, or of anybody's ideas, something having shape, filling space, possessing solidity, full of moving things? That would in the first place seem evident. The sound isn't outside of me, but the sound-waves, you say, are. The colors are ideal facts; but the ether-waves don't need a mind to know them. Warmth is ideal, but the physical fact called heat, this playing to and fro of molecules, is real, and is there apart from any mind. But once more, *is* this so evident? What do I *mean* by the shape of anything, or by the size of anything? Don't I mean just the idea of shape or of size that I am obliged to get under certain circumstances? What is the meaning of any property that I give to the real outer world? How can I express that property except in case I think it in terms of my ideas? As for the sound-waves and the ether-waves, what are they but things ideally conceived to explain the facts of nature? The conceptions have doubtless their truth, but it is an ideal truth. What I mean by saying that the things yonder have shape and size and trembling molecules, and that there is air with sound-waves, and ether with light-waves in it,—what I *mean* by all this is that experience forces upon me, directly or indirectly, a vast system of ideas, which may indeed be founded in truth beyond me, which in fact *must* be founded in such truth if my experience has any sense, but which, like my ideas of color and of warmth, are simply expressions of how the world's order must appear to me, and to anybody constituted like me. Above all, is this plain about space. The real things, I say, outside of me, fill space, and move about in it. But what do I mean by space? Only a vast system of ideas which experience and my own mind force upon me. Doubtless these ideas have a validity. They have *this* validity, that I, at all events, when I look upon the world, am bound to see it in space, as much bound as the king in Hamlet was, when he looked within, to see himself as guilty and unrepentant. But just as his guilt was an idea,—a crushing, an irresistible, an overwhelming idea,—but still just an idea, so, too, the space in which I place my world is one great formal idea of mine. That is just why I can describe it to other people. "It has three dimensions," I say, "length, breadth, depth." I describe each. I form, I convey, I construct, an idea of it through them. I know space, as an idea, very well. I can compute all sorts of unseen truths about the relations of its parts. I am sure that you, too, share this idea. But, then, for all of us alike it is just an idea; and when we put our world into space, and call it real there, we simply think one idea into another idea, not voluntarily, to be sure, but inevitably, and yet without leaving the realm of ideas.

Thus, all the reality that *we* attribute to our world, in so far as *we* know and can tell what we mean thereby, becomes ideal. There is, in fact, a certain system of ideas, forced upon us by experience, which we have to use as the guide of our conduct. This system of ideas we can't change by our wish; it is for us as overwhelming a fact as guilt, or as the bearing of our fellows towards us, but we know it only *as* such a system of ideas. And we call it the world of matter. John Stuart Mill very well expressed the puzzle of the whole thing, as we have now reached the statement of this puzzle, when he called matter a mass of "permanent possibilities of experience" for each of us. Mill's definition has its faults, but it is a very fair beginning. You know matter as something that either now gives you this idea or experience, or that would give you some other idea or experience under other circumstances. A fire, while it burns, is for you a permanent possibility of either getting the idea of an agreeable warmth, or of getting the idea of a bad burn, and you treat it accordingly. A precipice amongst mountains is a permanent possibility of your experiencing a fall, or of your getting a feeling of the exciting or of the sublime in mountain scenery. You have no experience just now of the tropics or of the poles, but both tropical and polar climates exist in your world as permanent possibilities of experience. When you call the sun 92,000,000 miles away, you mean that between you and the sun (that is, between your present experience and the possible experience of the sun's surface) there would inevitably lie the actually inaccessible, but still numerically conceivable series of experiences of distance expressed by the number of miles in question. In short, your whole attitude towards the real world may be summed up by saying: "I have experiences now which I seem bound to have, experiences of color, sound, and all the rest of my present ideas; and I am also bound by experience to believe that in case I did certain things (for instance, touched the wall, traveled to the tropics, visited Europe, studied physics), I then should get, in a determinate order, dependent wholly upon *what* I had done, certain other experiences (for instance, experiences of the wall's solidity, or of a tropical climate, or of the scenes of an European tour, or of the facts of physics)." And this acceptance of actual experience, this belief in possible experience, constitutes all that you mean by your faith in the outer world.

But, you say, Is not, then, all this faith of ours after all well founded? Isn't there really something yonder that corresponds in fact to this series of experiences in us? Yes, indeed, there no doubt is. But what if this, which so shall correspond without us to the ideas within us, what if this hard and fast reality should itself be a system of ideas, outside of our minds but not outside of every mind? As the maiden's disdain is outside the rejected lover's mind, unchangeable so far for him, but not on that account the less ideal, not the less a fact in a mind, as, to take afresh a former fashion of illustration, the price of a security or the objective existence of this lecture is an ideal fact, but real and external for the individual person,—even so why might not this world beyond us, this "permanent possibility of experience," be in essence itself a system of ideal experiences of some standard thought of which ours is only the copy? Nay, must it not be such a system in case it has any reality at all? For, after all, isn't this precisely what our analysis brings us to? Nothing whatever can I say about my world yonder that I do not express in terms of mind. *What* things are, extended, moving, colored, tuneful, majestic, beautiful, holy, *what* they are in any aspect of their nature, mathematical, logical, physical, sensuously pleasing, spiritually valuable, all this must mean for me only something that I have to express in the fashion of ideas. The more I am to know my world, the more of a mind I must have for the purpose. The closer I come to the truth about the things, the more ideas I get. Isn't it plain, then, that *if* my world yonder is anything knowable at all, it must be in and for itself essentially a mental world? Are my ideas to *resemble* in any way the world? Is the truth of my thought to consist in its *agreement* with reality? And am I thus capable, as common sense supposes, of *conforming* my ideas to things? Then reflect. What can, after all, so well agree with an idea as another idea? To what can things that go on in my mind conform unless it be to another mind? If the more my mind grows in mental clearness, the nearer it gets to the nature of reality, then surely the reality that my mind thus resembles must be in itself mental.

After all, then, would it deprive the world here about me of reality, nay, would it not rather save and assure the reality and the knowableness of my world of experience, if I said that this world, as it exists outside of my mind, and of any other human minds, exists in and for a standard, an universal mind, whose system of ideas simply constitutes the world? Even if I fail to prove that there is such a mind, do I not at least thus make plausible that, as I said, our world of common sense has no fact in it which we cannot interpret in terms of ideas, so that this world is throughout such stuff as ideas are made of? To say this, as you see, in no wise deprives our world of its due share of reality. If the standard mind knows now that its ideal fire has the quality of burning those who touch it, and if I in my finitude am bound to conform in my experiences to the thoughts of this standard mind, then in case I touch that fire I shall surely get the idea of a burn. The standard mind will be at least as hard and fast and real in its ideal consistency as is the maiden in her disdain for the rejected lover; and I, in presence of the ideal stars and the oceans, will see the genuine realities of fate as certainly as the lover hears his fate in the voice that expresses her will. . . .

What I have desired thus far is merely to give each of you, as it were, the sensation of being an idealist in this first and purely analytical sense of the word idealism. The sum and substance of it all is, you see, this: you know your world in fact as a system of ideas about things, such that from moment to moment you find this system forced upon you by experience. Even matter you know just as a mass of coherent ideas that you cannot help having. Space and time, as you think them, are surely ideas of yours. Now, what more natural than to say that *if* this be so, the real world beyond you must in itself be a system of somebody's ideas? If it is, then you can comprehend what its existence means. If it isn't, then since all you can know of it is ideal, the real world must be utterly unknowable, a bare x. Minds I can understand, because I myself am a mind. An existence that has no mental attribute is wholly opaque to me. So far, however, from such a world of ideas, existent beyond me in another mind, seeming to coherent thought essentially *un*real, ideas and minds and their ways, are, on the contrary, the hardest and stubbornest facts that we can name. *If* the external world is in itself mental, then, be this reality a standard and universal thought, or a mass of little atomic minds constituting the various particles of matter, in any case one can comprehend what it is, and will have at the same time to submit to its stubborn authority as the lover accepts the reality of the maiden's moods. If the world *isn't* such an ideal thing, then indeed all our science, which is through and through concerned with our mental interpretations of things, can neither have objective validity, nor make satisfactory progress towards truth. For as science is concerned with ideas, the world beyond all ideas is a bare x. . . .

There are problems soluble and problems insoluble in that world of ideas. It is a soluble problem if one asks what whole number is the square root of 64. The answer is 8. It is an insoluble problem if one asks me to find what whole number is the square root of 65. There is, namely, no such whole number. If one asks me to name the length of a straight line that shall be equal to the circumference of a circle of a known radius, that again, in the world of ideas, is an insoluble problem, because, as can be proved, the circumference of a circle is a length that cannot possibly be exactly expressed in terms of any statable number when the radius is of a stated length. So in the world of ideas, problems are definite questions which can be asked in knowable terms. Fair questions of this sort either may be fairly answered in our present state of knowledge, or else they could be answered if we knew a little or a good deal more, or finally they could not possibly be answered. But in the latter case, if they could not possibly be answered, they always must resemble the problem how to square the circle. They then always turn out, namely, to be absurdly stated questions, and it is their absurdity that makes these problems absolutely insoluble. Any fair question could be answered by one who knew enough. No fair question has an unknowable answer. But now, *if* your unknowable world out there is a thing of wholly, of absolutely problematic and inscrutable nature, is it so because you don't *yet* know enough about it, or because in its very nature and essence it is an absurd thing, an *x* that *would* answer a question, which actually it is nonsense to ask? Surely one must choose the former alternative. The real world may be unknown; it can't be essentially unknowable.

This subtlety is wearisome enough, I know, just here, but I shall not dwell long upon it. Plainly *if* the unknowable world out there is through and through in its nature a really inscrutable problem, this must mean that in nature it resembles such problems as, What is the whole number that is the square root of 65? Or, What two adjacent hills are there that have no valley between them? For in the world of thought such are the *only* insoluble problems. All others either may now be solved, or would be solved if we knew more than we now do. But, once more, *if* this unknowable is only just the real world as now unknown to us, but capable sometime of becoming known, then remember that, as we have just seen, only a mind can ever become an object known to a mind. If I know you as external to me, it is only because you are minds. If I can come to know *any* truth, it is only in so far as this truth is essentially mental, is an idea, is a thought, that I can ever come to know it. Hence, if that so-called unknowable, that unknown outer world there, ever could, by any device, come within our ken, then it is already an ideal world. For just that is what our whole idealistic analysis has been proving. Only ideas are knowable. And nothing absolutely unknowable can exist. For the absolutely unknowable, the *x* pure and simple, the Kantian thing in itself, simply cannot be admitted. The notion of it is nonsense. The assertion of it is a contradiction. Round-squares, and sugar salt-lumps, and Snarks, and Boojums, and Jabberwocks, and Abracadabras; such, I insist, are the only unknowables there are. The unknown, that which our human and finite selfhood hasn't grasped, exists spread out before us in a boundless world of truth; but the unknowable is essentially, confessedly, *ipso facto* a fiction.

The nerve of our whole argument in the foregoing is now pretty fairly exposed. We have seen that the outer truth must be, if anything, a "possibility of experience." But we may now see that a *bare* "possibility" as such, is, like the unknowable, something meaningless. That which, whenever I come to know it, turns out to be through and through an idea, an experience, must be in itself, before I know it, either somebody's idea, somebody's experience, or it must be nothing. What is a "possibility" of experience that is outside of me, and that is still nothing *for* any one else than myself? Isn't it a bare x, a nonsense phrase? Isn't it like an unseen color, an untasted taste, an unfelt feeling? In proving that the world is one of "possible" experience, we have proved that in so far as it is real it is one of actual experience.

Once more, then, to sum up here, *if*, however vast the world of the unknown, only the essentially knowable can exist, and *if* everything knowable is an idea, a mental somewhat, the content of some mind, then once for all we are the world of ideas. Your deepest doubt proves this. Only the nonsense of that inscrutable x, of that Abracadabra, of that Snark, the Unknowable of whose essence you make your real world, prevents you from seeing this.

To return, however, to our dilemma. *Either* idealism, we said, *or* the unknowable. What we have now said is that the absolutely unknowable is essentially an absurdity, a non-existent. For any fair and statable problem admits of an answer. *If* the world exists yonder, its essence is then already capable of being known by some mind. If capable of being known by a mind, this essence is then already essentially ideal and mental. A mind that knew the real world would, for instance, find it a something possessing qualities. But qualities are ideal existences, just as much as are the particular qualities called odors or tones or colors. A mind knowing the real world would again find in it relations, such as equality and inequality, attraction and repulsion, likeness and unlikeness. But such relations have no meaning except as objects of a mind. In brief, then, the world as known would be found to be a world that had all the while been ideal and mental, even before it became known to the particular mind that we are to conceive as coming into connection with it. Thus, then, we are driven to the second alternative. The real world must be a mind, or else a group of minds.

But with this result we come in presence of a final problem. All this, you say, depends upon my assurance that there is after all a real and therefore an essentially knowable and rational world yonder. Such a world would have to be in essence a mind, or a world of minds. But after all, how does one ever escape from the prison of the inner life? Am I not in all this merely wandering amidst the realm of my own ideas? *My* world, of course, isn't and can't be a mere x, an essentially unknowable thing, just because it *is my* world, and I have an idea of it. But then does not this mean that *my* world is, after all, forever just *my* world, so that I never get to any truth beyond myself? Isn't this result very disheartening? My world is thus a world of ideas, but alas! how do I then ever reach those ideas of the minds beyond me?

The answer is a simple, but in one sense a very problematic one. You, in one sense, namely, never *do* or can get beyond your own ideas, nor ought you to wish to do so, because in truth all those other minds that constitute your outer and real world are in essence one with your own self. This whole world of ideas is essentially *one* world, and so it is essentially the world of one self and *That art Thou.*

The truth and meaning of this deepest proposition of all idealism is now not at all remote from us. The considerations, however, upon which it depends are of the dryest possible sort, as commonplace as they are deep.

Whatever objects you may think about, whether they are objects directly known to you, or objects infinitely far removed, objects in the distant stars, or objects remote in time, or objects near and present,—such objects, then, as a number with fifty places of digits in it, or the mountains on the other side of the moon, or the day of your death, or the character of Cromwell, or the law of gravitation, or a name that you are just now trying to think of and have forgotten, or the meaning of some mood or feeling or idea now in your mind,—all such objects, I insist, stand in a certain constant and curious relation to your mind whenever you are thinking about them,—a relation that we often miss because it is so familiar. What is this relation? Such an object, while you think about it, needn't be, as popular thought often supposes it to be, the *cause* of your thoughts concerning it. Thus, when you think about Cromwell's character, Cromwell's character isn't just now *causing* any ideas in you,—isn't, so to speak, doing anything to you. Cromwell is dead, and after life's fitful fever his character is a very inactive thing. Not as the *cause,* but as the *object* of your thought is Cromwell present to you. Even so, if you choose now to think of the moment of your death, that moment is somewhere off there in the future, and you can make it your object, but it isn't now an active cause of your ideas. The moment of your death has no present physical existence at all, and just now causes nothing. So, too, with the mountains on the other side of the moon. When you make them the object of your thought, they remain indifferent to you. They do not affect you. You never saw them. But all the same you can think about them.

Yet this thinking *about* things is, after all, a very curious relation in which to stand to things. In order to think *about* a thing, it is *not* enough that I should have an idea in me that merely resembles that thing. This last is a very important observation. I repeat, it is *not* enough that I should merely have an idea in me that resembles the thing whereof I think. I have, for instance, in me the idea of a pain. Another man has a pain just like mine. Say we both have toothache; or have both burned our finger-tips in the same way. Now my idea of pain is just like the pain in him, but I am not on that account necessarily thinking about *his* pain, merely because what I am thinking about, namely my own pain, resembles his pain. No; to think about an object you must not merely have an idea that resembles the object, but you must *mean* to have your idea resemble that object. Stated in other form, to think of an object you must consciously aim at that object, you must pick out that object, you must already in some measure possess that object enough, namely, to identify it as what you mean. But how can you *mean*, how can you *aim at*, how can you *possess*, how can you *pick out*, how can you *identify* what is not already present in essence to your own hidden self? Here is surely a deep question. When you aim at yonder object, be it the mountains in the moon or the day of your death, you really say, "I, as my real self, as my larger self, as my complete consciousness, already in deepest truth possess that object, have it, own it, identify it. And that, and that alone, makes it possible for me in my transient, my individual, my momentary personality, to mean yonder object, to inquire about it, to be partly aware of it and partly ignorant of it." You can't mean what is utterly foreign to you. You mean an object, you assert about it, you talk about it, yes, you doubt or wonder about it, you admit your private and individual ignorance about it, only in so far as your larger self, your deeper personality, your total of normal consciousness already *has* that object. Your momentary and private wonder, ignorance, inquiry, or assertion, about the object, implies, asserts, presupposes, that your total self is in full and immediate possession of the object. This, in fact, is the very nature of that curious relation of a thought to an object which we are now considering. The self that is doubting or asserting, or that is even feeling its private ignorance about an object, and that still, even in consequence of all this, is *meaning*, is *aiming at* such object, is in essence identical with the self for which this object exists in its complete and consciously known truth.

So paradoxical seems this final assertion of idealism that I cannot hope in one moment to make it very plain to you. . . . But what I intend by thus saying that the self which thinks about an object, which really, even in the midst of the blindest ignorance and doubt concerning its object still means the object,—that this self is identical with the deeper self which possesses and truly knows the object,—what I intend hereby I can best illustrate by simple cases taken from your own experience. You are in doubt, say, about a name that you have forgotten, or about a thought that you just had, but that has now escaped you. As you hunt for the name or the lost idea, you are all the while sure that you mean just one particular name or idea and no other. But you don't yet know what name or idea this is. You try, and reject name after name. You query, "Was this what I was thinking of, or this?" But after searching you erelong find the name or the idea, and now at once you *recognize* it. "Oh, that," you say, "was what I meant all along, only —I didn't know what I meant." Did not know? Yes, in one sense you knew all the while,—that is, your deeper self, your true consciousness knew. It was your momentary self that did not know. But when you found the long-sought name, recalled the lost idea, you recognized it at once, because it was all the while your own, because you, the true and larger self, who owned the name or the idea and were aware of what it was, now were seen to include the smaller and momentary self that sought the name or tried to recall the thought. Your deeper consciousness of the lost idea was all the while there. In fact, did you not presuppose this when you sought the lost idea? How can I mean a name, or an idea, unless I in truth am the self who knows the name, who possesses the idea? In hunting for the name or the lost idea, I am hunting for my own thought. Well, just so I know nothing about the far-off stars in detail, but in so far as I mean the far-off stars at all, as I speak of them, I am identical with that remote and deep thought of my own that already knows the stars. When I study the stars, I am trying to find out what I really mean by them. To be sure, only experience can tell me, but that is because only experience can bring me into relation with my larger self. The escape from the prison of the inner self is simply the fact that the inner self is through and through an appeal to a larger self. The self that inquires, either inquires without meaning, or if it has a meaning, this meaning exists in and for the larger self that knows.

Here is a suggestion of what I mean by Synthetic Idealism. No truth, I repeat, is more familiar. That I am always meaning to inquire into objects beyond me, what clearer fact could be mentioned? That only in case it is already I who, in deeper truth, in my real and hidden thought, *know* the lost object yonder, the object whose nature I seek to comprehend, that only in this case I can truly *mean* the thing yonder,—this, as we must assert, is involved in the very idea of *meaning*. That is the logical analysis of it. You can mean what your deeper self knows; you cannot mean what your deeper self doesn't know. To be sure, the complete illustration of this most critical insight of idealism belongs elsewhere Few see the familiar. Nothing is more common than for people to think that they mean objects that have nothing to do with themselves. Kant it was, who, despite his things in themselves, first showed us that nobody really means an object, really knows it, or doubts it, or aims at it, unless he does so by aiming at a truth that is present to his own larger self. Except for the unity of my true self, taught Kant, I have no objects. And so it makes no difference whether I know a thing or am in doubt about it. So long as I really *mean* it, that is enough. The self that *means* the object is identical with the larger self that possesses the object, just as when you seek the lost idea you are already in essence with the self that possesses the lost idea.

In this way I suggest to you the proof which a rigid analysis of the logic of our most commonplace thought would give for the doctrine that in the world there is but *one* Self, and that it is *his* world which we all alike are truly meaning, whether we talk of one another or of Cromwell's character or of the fixed stars or of the far-off æons of the future. The relation of my thought to its object has, I insist, this curious character, that *unless* the thought and its object are parts of one larger thought, I can't even be *meaning* that object yonder, can't even be in error about it, can't even doubt its existence. You, for instance, are part of one larger self with me, or else I can't even be meaning to address you as outer beings. You are part of one larger self along with the most mysterious or most remote fact of nature, along with the moon, and all the hosts of heaven, along with all truth and all beauty. Else could you not even intend to speak of such objects beyond you. For whatever you speak of you will find that your world is meant by you as just your world. Talk of the unknowable, and it forthwith becomes your unknowable, your problem, whose solution, unless the problem be a mere nonsense question, your larger self must own and be aware of. The deepest problem of life is, "What is this deeper self?" And the only answer is, *It is the self that knows in unity all truth.* This, I insist, is no hypothesis. It is actually the presupposition of your deepest doubt. And that is why I say: Everything finite is more or less obscure, dark, doubtful. Only the Infinite Self, the problem-solver, the complete thinker, the one who knows what we mean even when we are most confused and ignorant, the one who includes us, who has the world present to himself in unity, before whom all past and future truth, all distant and dark truth is clear in one eternal moment, to whom far and forgot is near, who thinks the whole of nature, and in whom are all things, the Logos, the world-possessor,—only his existence, I say, is perfectly sure. . . .

Our whole idealistic analysis . . . from the beginning of this discussion, has been to the effect that facts must be facts for somebody, and can't be facts for nobody, and that *bare* possibilities are really impossible. Hence whoever believes, whether truly or falsely, about objects beyond the moment of his belief, is an organic part of a reflective and conscious larger self that has those objects immediately present to itself, and has them in organic relation with the erring or truthful momentary self that believes. . . .

Flee where we will, then, the net of the larger Self ensnares us. We are lost and imprisoned in the thickets of its tangled labyrinth. The moments are not at all in themselves, for as moments they have no meaning; they exist only in relation to the beyond. The larger Self alone is, and they are by reason of it, organic parts of it. They perish, but it remains; they have truth or error only in its overshadowing presence.

And now, as to the unity of this Self. Can there be many such organic selves, mutually separate unities of moments and of the objects that these moments mean? Nay, were there *many* such, would not their manifoldness be a truth? Their relations, would not these be real? Their distinct places in the world-order, would not these things be objects of possible true or false thoughts? If so, must not there be once more the inclusive real Self for whom these truths were true, these separate selves interelated, and their variety absorbed in the organism of its rational meaning?

There is, then, at last, but one Self, organically, reflectively, consciously inclusive of all the selves, and so of all truth. I have called this self, Logos, problem-solver, all-knower. Consider, then, last of all, his relation to problems. In [a] previous lecture we doubted many things; we questioned the whole seeming world of the outer order; we wondered as to space and time, as to nature and evolution, as to the beginning and the end of things. Now he who wonders is like him who doubts. Has his wonder any rationality about it? Does he *mean* anything by his doubt? Then the truth that he means, and about which he wonders, has its real constitution. As wonderer, he in the moment possesses not this solving truth; he appeals to the self who can solve. That self must possess the solution just as surely as the problem has a meaning. The real nature of space and time, the real beginning of things, where matter was at any point of time in the past, what is to become of the world's energy: these are matters of truth, and truth is necessarily present to the Self as in one all-comprehending self-completed moment, beyond which is naught, within which is the world.

The world, then, is such stuff as ideas are made of. Thought possesses all things. But the world isn't unreal. It extends infinitely beyond our private consciousness, because it is the world of an universal mind. What facts it is to contain only experience can inform us. There is no magic that can anticipate the work of science. Absolutely the *only* thing sure from the first about this world, however, is that it is intelligent, rational, orderly, essentially comprehensible, so that all its problems are somewhere solved, all its darkest mysteries are known to the supreme Self. This Self infinitely and reflectively transcends our consciousness, and therefore, since it includes us, it is at the very least a person, and more definitely conscious than we are; for what it possesses is self-reflecting knowledge, and what is knowledge aware of itself, but consciousness? Beyond the seeming wreck and chaos of our finite problems, its eternal insight dwells, therefore, in absolute and supreme majesty. Yet it is not far from every one of us. There is no least or most transient thought that flits through a child's mind, or that troubles with the faintest line of care a maiden's face, and that still does not contain and embody something of this divine Logos.

30

DESPAIR *

by

SØREN KIERKEGAARD
(1813–1855)

I. THAT DESPAIR IS THE SICKNESS UNTO DEATH

A. DESPAIR IS A SICKNESS IN THE SPIRIT, IN THE SELF, AND SO IT MAY ASSUME A TRIPLE FORM: IN DESPAIR AT NOT BEING CONSCIOUS OF HAVING A SELF (DESPAIR IMPROPERLY SO CALLED); IN DESPAIR AT NOT WILLING TO BE ONESELF; IN DESPAIR AT WILLING TO BE ONESELF.

* [From *The Sickness Unto Death* (1849). Taken from Søren Kierkegaard, *Fear and Trembling and The Sickness Unto Death,* trans. with Introduction and Notes by Walter Lowrie (copyright 1941, 1954 by Princeton University Press; Princeton Paperback, 1968): selections from pp. 146–151, 153–154, 212–213, and 216–227. Reprinted by permission of Princeton University Press.]

Man is spirit. But what is spirit? Spirit is the self. But what is the self? The self is a relation which relates itself to its own self, or it is that in the relation [which accounts for it] that the relation relates itself to its own self; the self is not the relation but [consists in the fact] that the relation relates itself to its own self. Man is a synthesis of the infinite and the finite, of the temporal and the eternal, of freedom and necessity, in short it is a synthesis. A synthesis is a relation between two factors. So regarded, man is not yet a self.

In the relation between two, the relation is the third term as a negative unity, and the two relate themselves to the relation, and in the relation to the relation; such a relation is that between soul and body, when man is regarded as soul. If on the contrary the relation relatès itself to its own self, the relation is then the positive third term, and this is the self.

Such a relation which relates itself to its own self (that is to say, a self) must either have constituted itself or have been constituted by another.

If this relation which relates itself to its own self is constituted by another, the relation doubtless is the third term, but this relation (the third term) is in turn a relation relating itself to that which constituted the whole relation.

Such a derived, constituted, relation is the human self, a relation which relates itself to its own self, and in relating itself to its own self relates itself to another. Hence it is that there can be two forms of despair properly so called. If the human self had constituted itself, there could be a question only of one form, that of not willing to be one's own self, of willing to get rid of oneself. This formula [i.e. that the self is constituted by another] is the expression for the total dependence of the relation (the self namely), the expression for the fact that the self cannot of itself attain and remain in equilibrium and rest by itself, but only by relating itself to that Power which constituted the whole relation. Indeed, so far is it from being true that this second form of despair (despair at not willing to be one's own self) denotes only a particular kind of despair, that on the contrary all despair can in the last analysis be reduced to this. If a man in despair is as he thinks conscious of his despair, does not talk about it meaninglessly as of something which befell him (pretty much as when a man who suffers from vertigo talks with nervous self-deception about a weight upon his head or about its being like something falling upon him, etc., this weight and this pressure being in fact not something external but an inverse reflection from an inward experience), and if by himself and by himself only he would abolish the despair, then by all the labor he expends he is only laboring himself deeper into a deeper despair. The disrelationship of despair is not a simple disrelationship but a disrelationship in a relation which relates itself to its own self and is constituted by another, so that the disrelationship in that self-relation reflects itself infinitely in the relation to the Power which constituted it.

This then is the formula which describes the condition of the self when despair is completely eradicated: by relating itself to its own self and by willing to be itself the self is grounded transparently in the Power which posited it.

B. POSSIBILITY AND ACTUALITY OF DESPAIR

Is despair an advantage or a drawback? Regarded in a purely dialetical way it is both. If one were to stick to the abstract notion of despair, without thinking of any concrete despairer, one might say that it is an immense advantage. The possibility of this sickness is man's advantage over the beast, and this advantage distinguishes him far more essentially than the erect posture, for it implies the infinite erectness or loftiness of being spirit. The possibility of this sickness is man's advantage over the beast; to be sharply observant of this sickness constitutes the Christian's advantage over the natural man; to be healed of this sickness is the Christian's bliss.

So then it is an infinite advantage to be able to despair; and yet it is not only the greatest misfortune and misery to be in despair; no, it is perdition. Ordinarily there is no such relation between possibility and actuality; if it is an advantage to be able to be this or that, it is a still greater advantage to be such a thing. That is to say, being is related to the ability to be as an ascent. In the case of despair, on the contrary, being is related to the ability to be as a fall. Infinite as is the advantage of the possibility, just so great is the measure of the fall. So in the case of despair the ascent consists in not being in despair. Yet this statement is open to misunderstanding. The thing of not being in despair is not like not being lame, blind, etc. In case the not being in despair means neither more nor less than not being this, then it is precisely to be it. The thing of not being in despair must mean the annihilation of the possibility of being this; if it is to be true that a man is not in despair, one must annihilate the possibility every instant. Such is not ordinarily the relation between possibility and actuality. Although thinkers say that actuality is the annihilated possibility, yet this is not entirely true; it is the fulfilled, the effective possibility. Here, on the contrary, the actuality (not being in despair), which in its very form is a negation, is the impotent, annihilated possibility; ordinarily, actuality in comparison with possibility is a confirmation, here it is a negation.

Despair is the disrelationship in a relation which relates itself to itself. But the synthesis is not the disrelationship, it is merely the possibility, or, in the synthesis is latent the possibility of the disrelationship. If the synthesis were the disrelationship, there would be no such thing as despair, for despair would then be something inherent in human nature as such, that is, it would not be despair, it would be something that befell a man, something he suffered passively, like an illness into which a man falls, or like death which is the lot of all. No, this thing of despairing is inherent in man himself; but if he were not a synthesis, he could not despair, nor, if the synthesis were not from God's hand, constituted in the right relationship, could man despair.

Whence then comes despair? From the relation wherein the synthesis relates itself to itself, in that God who made man a relationship lets this go as it were out of His hand, that is, in the fact that the relation relates itself to itself. And herein, in the fact that the relation is spirit, is the self, consists the responsibility under which all despair lies, and so lies every instant it exists, however much and however ingeniously the despairer, deceiving himself and others, may talk of his despair as a misfortune which has befallen him, with a confusion of things different, as in the case of vertigo aforementioned, with which, though it is qualitatively different, despair has much in common, since vertigo is under the rubric soul what despair is under the rubric spirit, and is pregnant with analogies to despair.

So when the disrelationship—that is, despair—has set in, does it follow as a matter of course that it continues? No, it does not follow as a matter of course; if the disrelationship continues, it does not follow as a consequence of the disrelation but as a consequence of the relation which relates itself to itself. That is to say, every time the disrelation expresses itself, and every instant it exists, it is to the relation one must revert. Observe that we speak of a man contracting a disease, maybe through carelessness. Then the illness sets in, and from that instant it affirms itself and is now an *actuality*, the origin of which recedes more and more into the *past*. It would be cruel and inhuman if one were to continue to say incessantly, "This instant thou, the sick man, art contracting this disease"; that is, if every instant one were to resolve the actuality of the disease into its possibility. It is true that he did contract the disease, but this he did only once; the continuance of the disease is a simple consequence of the fact that he once contracted it, its progress is not to be referred every instant to him as the cause; he contracted it, but one cannot say that he *is contracting* it. Not so with despair: every actual instant of despair is to be referred back to possibility, every instant the man in despair is *contracting* it, it is constantly in the present tense, nothing comes to pass here as a consequence of a bygone actuality superseded; at every actual instant of despair the despairer bears as his responsibility all the foregoing experience in possibility as a present. This comes from the fact that despair is a qualification of spirit, that it is related to the eternal in man. But the eternal he cannot get rid of, no, not to all eternity; he cannot cast it from him once for all, nothing is more impossible; every instant he does not possess it he must have cast it or be casting it from him—but it comes back, every instant he is in despair he contracts despair. For despair is not a result of the disrelationship but of the relation which relates itself to itself. And the relation to himself a man cannot get rid of, any more than he can get rid of himself, which moreover is one and the same thing, since the self is the relationship to oneself.

C. DESPAIR IS "THE SICKNESS UNTO DEATH"

The concept of the sickness unto death must be understood, however, in a peculiar sense. Literally it means a sickness the end and outcome of which is death. Thus one speaks of a mortal sickness as synonymous with a sickness unto death. In this sense despair cannot be called the sickness unto death. But in the Christian understanding of it death itself is a transition unto life. In view of this, there is from the Christian standpoint no earthly, bodily sickness unto death. For death is doubtless the last phase of the sickness, but death is not the last thing. If in the strictest sense we are to speak of a sickness unto death, it must be one in which the last thing is death, and death the last thing. And this precisely is despair.

Yet in another and still more definite sense despair is the sickness unto death. It is indeed very far from being true that, literally understood, one dies of this sickness, or that this sickness ends with bodily death. On the contrary, the torment of despair is precisely this, not to be able to die. So it has much in common with the situation of the moribund when he lies and struggles with death, and cannot die. So to be sick *unto* death is, not to be able to die— yet not as though there were hope of life; no, the hopelessness in this case is that even the last hope, death, is not available. When death is the greatest danger, one hopes for life; but when one becomes acquainted with an even more dreadful danger, one hopes for death. So when the danger is so great that death has become one's hope, despair is the disconsolateness of not being able to die.

It is in this last sense that despair is the sickness unto death, this agonizing contradiction, this sickness in the self, everlastingly to die,

402 READINGS IN PHILOSOPHY

to die and yet not to die, to die the death. For dying means that it is all over, but dying the death means to live to experience death; and if for a single instant this experience is possible, it is tantamount to experiencing it forever. If one might die of despair as one dies of a sickness, then the eternal in him, the self, must be capable of dying in the same sense that the body dies of sickness. But this is an impossibility; the dying of despair transforms itself constantly into a living. The despairing man cannot die; no more than "the dagger can slay thoughts" can despair consume the eternal thing, the self, which is the ground of despair, whose worm dieth not, and whose fire is not quenched. Yet despair is precisely *self*-consuming, but it is an impotent self-consumption which is not able to do what it wills; and this impotence is a new form of self-consumption, in which again, however, the despairer is not able to do what he wills, namely, to consume himself. This is despair raised to a higher potency, or it is the law for the potentiation. This is the hot incitement, or the cold fire in despair, the gnawing canker whose movement is constantly inward, deeper and deeper, in impotent self-consumption. The fact that despair does not consume him is so far from being any comfort to the despairing man that it is precisely the opposite, this comfort is precisely the torment, it is precisely this that keeps the gnawing pain alive and keeps life in the pain. This precisely is the reason why he despairs—not to say despaired—because he cannot consume himself, cannot get rid of himself, cannot become nothing. This is the potentiated formula for despair, the rising of the fever in the sickness of the self. . . .

Socrates proved the immortality of the soul from the fact that the sickness of the soul (sin) does not consume it as sickness of the body consumes the body. So also we can demonstrate the eternal in man from the fact that despair cannot consume his self, that this precisely is the torment of contradiction in despair. If there were nothing eternal in a man, he could not despair; but if despair could consume his self, there would still be no despair.

Thus it is that despair, this sickness in the self, is the sickness unto death. The despairing man is mortally ill. In an entirely different sense than can appropriately be said of any disease, we may say that the sickness has attacked the noblest part; and yet the man cannot die. Death is not the last phase of the sickness, but death is continually the last. To be delivered from this sickness by death is an impossibility, for the sickness and its torment . . . and death consist in not being able to die.

This is the situation in despair. And however thoroughly it eludes the attention of the despairer, and however thoroughly the despairer may succeed (as in the case of that kind of despair which is char-

acterized by unawareness of being in despair) in losing himself
entirely, and losing himself in such a way that it is not noticed in
the least—eternity nevertheless will make it manifest that his situation was despair, and it will so nail him to himself that the torment
nevertheless remains that he cannot get rid of himself, and it becomes
manifest that he was deluded in thinking that he succeeded. And
thus it is eternity must act, because to have a self, to be a self, is
the greatest concession made to man, but at the same time it is
eternity's demand upon him.

II. DESPAIR IS SIN

CHAPTER I

GRADATIONS IN THE CONSCIOUSNESS OF THE SELF
(THE QUALIFICATION "BEFORE GOD")

Sin is: before God in despair not to will to be oneself, or before
God in despair to will to be oneself. But is not this definition, even
though in other aspects it may be conceded to have advantages (and
among them this which is the weightiest of all, that it is the only
Scriptural definition, for the Scripture always defines sin as disobedience), is it not after all too spiritual? To this one must first
of all make answer that a definition of sin can never be too spiritual
(unless it becomes so spiritual that it does away with sin); for sin
is precisely a determinant of spirit. And in the next place, why
should it then be too spiritual? Because it does not talk about murder, theft, unchastity, etc.? But does it not talk of them? Is it not
also self-assertion against God when one is disobedient and defies
His commandment? But on the other hand, when in talking about
sin one talks only of such sins, it is so easily forgotten that in a way it
may be all right, humanly speaking, with respect to all such things
up to a certain point, and yet the whole life may be sin, the well-
known kind of sin: glittering vices, wilfulness, which either spirit-
lessly or impudently continues to be or wills to be unaware in what
an infinitely deeper sense a human self is morally under obligation to
God with respect to every most secret wish and thought, with respect
to quickness in comprehending and readiness to follow every hint of
God as to what His will is for this self. The sins of the flesh are
the self-assertion of the lower self; but how often one devil is cast
out by the devil's help, and the last state becomes worse than the
first. For so it is with men in this world: first a man sins from frailty
and weakness; and then—yes, then perhaps he learns to flee to God
and to be helped by faith which saves from all sin; but of this we

are not talking here—then he despairs over his weakness and becomes, either a Pharisee who in despair manages to attain a certain legal righteousness, or he despairs and plunges again into sin.

The definition therefore certainly embraces every conceivable and actual form of sin; it certainly throws into relief the decisive fact that sin is despair (for sin is not the wildness of flesh and blood, but it is the spirit's consent thereto), and it is . . . before God. As a definition it is algebraic. In this little work it would be out of place, and an effort moreover which perhaps would not succeed, were I to begin by describing the particular sins. The principal thing here is that the definition like a net must embrace all forms. And that it does, as can be seen when one tests it by setting up the opposite, namely, the definition of faith, by which I steer my course in the whole of this work, as by a sure mariners' mark. Faith is: that the self in being itself and in willing to be itself is grounded transparently in God.

But too often it has been overlooked that the opposite of sin is not *virtue*, not by any manner of means. This is in part a pagan view which is content with a merely human measure and properly does not know what *sin* is, that all sin is before God. No, *the opposite of sin is faith*, as is affirmed in Rom. 14:23, "whatsoever is not of faith is sin." And for the whole of Christianity it is one of the most decisive definitions that the opposite of sin is not virtue but faith. . . .

Christianity teaches that this particular individual, and so every individual, whatever in other respects this individual may be, man, woman, servingmaid, minister of state, merchant, barber, student, etc.—this individual exists *before God*—this individual who perhaps would be vain for having once in his life talked with the King, this man who is not a little proud of living on intimate terms with that person or the other, this man exists before God, can talk with God any moment he will, sure to be heard by Him, in short, this man is invited to live on the most intimate terms with God! Furthermore, for this man's sake God came to the world, let himself be born, suffers and dies; and this suffering God almost begs and entreats this man to accept the help which is offered him! Verily, if there is anything that would make a man lose his understanding, it is surely this! Whosoever has not the humble courage to dare to believe it, must be offended at it. But why is he offended? Because it is too high for him, because he cannot get it into his head, because in the face of it he cannot acquire frank-heartedness, and therefore must have it done away with, brought to naught and nonsense, for it is as though it would stifle him.

For what is offense? Offense is unhappy admiration. It is therefore akin to envy, but it is an envy which is turned against oneself, or, more exactly, envy which is worst of all against oneself. The narrow-mindedness of the natural man cannot welcome for itself the extraordinary which God has intended for him; so he is offended.

The degree of the offense depends upon what passion a man has for admiration. The more prosaic men, devoid of imagination and passion, and who therefore are not apt to admire, they too may be offended, but they confine themselves to saying, "Such a thing I can't get through my head, I let it alone." These are the sceptics. But the more passion and imagination a man has, the nearer he also is in a certain sense (that is, in the possibility) to being able to become a believer—*nota bene!* by adoringly humbling himself under the extraordinary—and with that, all the more passionate is the offense, which at last cannot be contented with less than the expression: annihilated and trodden in the dust.

If one would learn to understand offense, let him study human envy, a subject which I offer as an extra course, pluming myself upon having studied it profoundly. Envy is concealed admiration. An admirer who feels that he cannot be happy by surrendering himself elects to become envious of that which he admires. So he speaks another language, and in that language of his the thing which he really admires is called a stupid, insipid and queer sort of thing. Admiration is happy self-surrender; envy is unhappy self-assertion.

So also it is with offense: that which in the relation between man and man is known as admiration/envy, in the relation between man and God is adoration/offense. The *summa summarum* of all human wisdom is this "golden," or perhaps more properly the gilded, *ne quid nimis* [not anything too much], too much or too little spoils the broth. This is given and taken between man and man as wisdom and is honored by admiration, its quotation never fluctuates, the whole of humanity guarantees its value. So if once in a while there lives a genius who goes a little bit beyond it, he is declared mad . . . by the wise. But Christianity takes a prodigious giant-stride beyond this *ne quid nimis*, a stride into the absurd—there Christianity begins . . . and the offense.

One sees now how extraordinarily (that there might be something extraordinary left)—how extraordinarily stupid it is to defend Christianity, how little knowledge of men this betrays, and how truly, even though it be unconsciously, it is working in collusion with the enemy, by making of Christianity a miserable something or another which in the end has to be rescued by a defense. Therefore it is certain and true that he who first invented the notion of defending Christianity in Christendom is *de facto* Judas No. 2; he also betrays with a kiss, only his treachery is that of stupidity. To defend anything is always to discredit it. Let a man have a storehouse full of gold, let him be willing to dispense every ducat to the poor—but let him besides that be stupid enough to begin this benevolent undertaking with a defense in which he advances three reasons to prove that it is justifiable—and people will be almost inclined to doubt whether he is doing any good. But now for Christianity! Yea, he who defends it has never believed in it. If he believes, then the enthusiasm of faith is . . . not defense, no, it is attack and victory. The believer is a victor.

Thus it stands with Christianity and the offense. The possibility of the offense is quite rightly included in the Christian definition of sin—in this phrase, "before God." A pagan, the natural man, is very willing to admit that sin exists, but this "before God," which really is what makes sin to be sin, is for him too much, it seems to him (though in a different sense from that pointed out here) to make too ᐧmuch of what it is to be a man; a little less, and then he is willing to agree to it—"but too much is too much."

CHAPTER 2

THE SOCRATIC DEFINITION OF SIN

Sin is ignorance. This is the well-known Socratic definition of sin, which, like everything Socratic, is an opinion always worthy of attention. However, with respect to this Socratic position, as with respect to many other Socratic positions, how many men have felt a need of going further? What an innumerable number have felt the need of going further than the Socratic ignorance—presumably because they felt that it was impossible for them to stay there; for in every generation how many men are there that are capable, even for only a month, of enduring and existentially expressing ignorance about everything?

Therefore I do not by any means intend to dispose of the Socratic definition on the ground that one cannot stop with it; but, having the Christian definition *in mente* [in mind], I would make use of it to bring the other out sharply (just because the Socratic definition is so genuinely Greek), so that here as always the hollowness of every other definition which is not in the strictest sense Christian (that is, of every partial definition) may become manifest.

The difficulty with the Socratic definition is that it leaves undetermined how ignorance itself is to be more precisely understood, the question of its origin, etc. That is to say, even if sin be ignorance (or what Christianity would perhaps prefer to call stupidity), which in one sense cannot be denied, we have to ask, is this an original ignorance, is it always the case that one has not known and hitherto could not know anything about the truth, or is it a superinduced, a subsequent ignorance? If it is what the last question implies, then sin must properly have its ground in something else, it must have its ground in the activity with which a man has labored to obscure his intelligence. But also when this is assumed, the stiff-necked and tough-lived difficulty returns, prompting the question whether at the instant a man began to obscure his intelligence he was distinctly conscious of what he was doing. If he was not distinctly conscious of this, then his intelligence was already somewhat obscured before he began, and the question merely returns again. If it is assumed on the contrary that when he began to obscure his intelligence he was distinctly conscious of it, then sin (even though it be unconsciousness, seeing that this was an induced state) would not lie in the intelligence but in the will, and the question which must be raised is about the relation of the intelligence and the will to one another. With such questions as these (and one might continue to augment them for many a day) the Socratic definition does not deal. Socrates was certainly an ethical teacher (the Classical age claims him absolutely as the discoverer of ethics), he was the first one, as he is and remains the first in his class; but he begins with ignorance. Intellecually, it is toward ignorance he tends, toward the position of knowing nothing. Ethically, he understands by ignorance quite a different thing, and so he begins with that.

But on the other hand, as a matter of course, Socrates is not an essentially religious ethicist, still less a dogmatic one, as the Christian ethicist is. Hence he does not really enter into the whole investigation with which Christianity begins, into the *prius* [before] in which sin presupposes itself, and which is Christianly explained by the doctrine of original sin—a dogma to the border of which only we come in this investigation.

Socrates therefore never really gets to the determinant we know as sin, which is surely a defect in a definition of sin. Why is this? For if sin is indeed ignorance, then sin properly does not exist, since sin is definitely consciousness. If sin consists in being ignorant of what is right, so that one consequently does what is wrong, sin does not exist. If this is sin, then it must be assumed, as Socrates also assumed, that the case does not occur of a man knowing what is right and doing what is wrong, or knowing that a thing is wrong and doing the wrong. So then, if the Socratic definition is correct, sin does not exist. But, lo, precisely this is, Christianly understood, just as it should be, in a deeper sense it is quite correct, in the interest of Christianity it is *quod erat demonstrandum* [that which was to be demonstrated]. Precisely the concept by which Christianity distinguishes itself qualitatively and most decisively from paganism is the concept of sin, the doctrine of sin; and therefore Christianity also assumes quite consistently that neither paganism nor the natural man knows what sin is; yea, it assumes that there must be a revelation from God to make manifest what sin is. For it is not true, as a superficial view assumes, that the doctrine of the atonement is the qualitative difference between paganism and Christianity. No, the beginning m··st be made far deeper, with sin, with the doctrine of sin, as Chrisuanity also does. What a dangerous objection therefore against Christianity if paganism had a definition of sin which Christianity must admit is correct!

What determinant is it then that Socrates lacks in determining what sin is? It is will, defiant will. The Greek intellectualism was too happy, too naïve, too aesthetic, too ironical, too witty . . . to be able to get it sinfully into its head that a person knowingly could fail to do the good, or knowingly, with knowledge of what was right, do what was wrong. The Greek spirit proposes an intellectual categorical imperative.

The truth in this definition must by no means be overlooked, and it needs to be enforced in times such as these which have gone astray in so much flatulent and unfruitful knowledge, so that doubtless now, just as in Socrates' age, only much more, it is advisable that people should be starved a little bit. It is enough to provoke both laughter and tears—not only all these protestations about having understood and comprehended the highest thought, but also the virtuosity with which many know how to present it *in abstracto,* and in a certain sense quite correctly—it is enough to provoke both laughter and tears when one sees then that all this knowing and understanding exercises no influence upon the lives of these men, that their lives do not in the remotest way express what they have understood, but rather the contrary. One involuntarily exclaims at the sight of a disproportion at once so sorrowful and so ludicrous. But how in the world is it possible that they have understood it? And is it true that they have understood? Here the ancient ironist and ethicist makes answer: "My dear man, never believe it, for if they truly had understood, their lives also would have expressed it, they would have done what they understood."

To understand/and to understand are therefore two things? Certainly they are; and he who has understood this (but not, be it noted, in the sense of the first sort of understanding) is initiated into all the secret mysteries of irony. It is with this contradiction irony is properly employed. To perceive the comic in the fact that a person is actually ignorant of something means a very low sort of comic, beneath the dignity of irony. There is properly no profound comic in the fact that people once lived who assumed that the earth stands still—when nobody knew any better. The same thing will presumably befall our age in contrast with an age which knows more of physical law. The contradiction is one between two different ages, there is lacking a deeper point of coincidence; such a contradiction is not essential, and hence neither is it essentially comic. No, but that a man stands up and says the right thing . . . and so has understood it, and then when he has to act does the wrong thing . . . and so shows that he has not understood it—yes, that is comic. It is infinitely comic that a man, moved unto tears, so much moved that not only tears but sweat trickle from him, can sit and read, or hear, representations of self-denial, of the nobility of sacrificing one's life for the truth—and then the next instant—one, two, three, slap-dash, almost with the tears still in his eyes—is in full swing, in the sweat of his brow, with all his might and main, helping falsehood to conquer. It is infinitely comic that an orator, with truth in his voice and in the expression of his features, profoundly touched and profoundly touching, can present the truth in a heart-rending way, can tread all evil and all the powers of hell under his feet, with an aplomb in his attitude, an assurance in his glance, a resoluteness in his step, which is altogether admirable—it is infinitely comic that almost at the same moment, almost "with his dressing-gown still on," he can run cowardly and timidly out of the way of the least inconvenience. It is infinitely comic that a man can understand the whole truth about how wretched and petty this world is, etc.—that he can understand this, and then cannot recognize again what he understood; for almost in the same moment he himself goes off and takes part in the same pettiness and wretchedness, takes glory in it and receives glory from it, that is, accepts it. O when one beholds a man who protests that he has entirely understood how Christ went about in the form of a lowly servant, poor, despised, and, as the Scripture says, spat upon—when I see the same man so careful to betake himself thither where in a worldly sense it is good to be, and accommodate himself there in the utmost security, when I see him apprehensive of every puff of wind from right or left, as though his life depended upon it, and so blissful, so utterly blissful, so awfully glad—yes, to make the thing complete, so awfully glad that he is able to thank God for it—glad that he is held in honor by all men—then I have often said to myself and by myself, "Socrates, Socrates, Socrates, can it be possible that this man has understood what he says he has understood?" So I have said, and at the same time I have wished that Socrates might be right. For it seemed to me after all as though Christianity were too severe, nor can I bring it into accord with my experience to treat such a man as a hypocrite. No, Socrates, thee I can understand; thou dost treat him as a wag, as a sort of

merry Andrew, thou dost treat him as a butt for laughter, thou hast
no objection, it has even thine approval, that I prepare and serve
him up as a comic dish—provided I do it well.

Socrates, Socrates, Socrates! Yes, one may well call thy name
thrice, it would not be too much to call it ten times, if that would
do any good. People think that the world needs a republic, and they
think that it needs a new social order, and a new religion—but it
never occurs to anybody that what the world now needs, confused
as it is by much knowing, is a Socrates. But that is perfectly natural,
for if anybody had this notion, not to say if many were to have it,
there would be less need of a Socrates. What a delusion most needs is
the very thing it least thinks of—naturally, for otherwise it would
not be a delusion.

So then, such an ironic-ethical correction might very well be what
our age needs, and perhaps the only thing it really needs; for it is
evident that this is the thing it least thinks of. It is highly important
that, instead of going further than Socrates, we simply return to the
Socratic dictum that to understand/and to understand are two
things—not returning to it as a result [once for all acquired], for
in the end that only helps men into the deepest wretchedness, since
it simply abolishes the distinction between understanding/and understanding, but returning to it as the ethical interpretation of everyday life.

The Socratic definition helps itself out as follows. When a person
doesn't do the right thing; why then, neither has he understood it;
his understanding is a vain conceit, his assertion that he has understood it is a false indication of the way, his repeated assertion that
the devil take him if he has not understood it is a prodigious re-
moteness along the greatest possible detour. But then indeed the definition is correct. If a man does the right thing, then surely he doesn't
sin; and if he doesn't do the right thing, then neither has he understood it; if in truth he had understood it, this would at once have
moved him to do it, would at once make him an echo of his understanding—*ergo* sin is ignorance.

But where does the difficulty lie? It is to be ascribed to a fact of
which the Socratic view itself was aware (though only to a certain
degree) and sought to remedy, that it lacks a dialectical determinant
for the transition from having understood something to the doing of
it. In this transition Christianity makes its start; by proceeding along
this path it proves that sin lies in the will, thus attaining the concept
of defiance; and then, in order to make the end thoroughly fast,
it adjoins to this the dogma of original sin—for, alas, the secret
of Speculation's success in comprehending is just this, of sewing
without making the end fast and without knotting the thread, and

therefore it can marvellously keep on sewing, i.e. keep on pulling the end through. Christianity, on the contrary, fastens the end by means of the paradox.

In pure ideality, where there is no question of the real individual man, the transition is accomplished by necessity (in the System indeed everything comes about by necessity), in other words, there is no difficulty at all connected with the transition from understanding to doing. This is purely in the Greek spirit—yet not Socratic, for Socrates was too much of an ethicist for that. And quite the same thing is really the secret of the whole of recent philosophy: *cogito ergo sum*, to think is to be. The Christian motto, on the contrary, is: As thou believest, so it comes to pass; or As thou believest, so art thou; to believe is to be. So one can see that modern philosophy is neither more nor less than paganism. But this is not the worst, to be akin to Socrates is not the meanest position. But the entirely unsocratic trait of modern philisophy is that it wants to make itself and us believe that it is Christianity.

In the world of reality, on the other hand, where it is a question of the individual man, there is this little tiny transition from having understood to doing it; it is not always *cito citissime* [as quickly as possible], not *geschwind wie der Wind* [fast as the wind], if I may speak German for lack of philosophic terms. On the contrary, here begins a very prolix story.

In the life of spirit, on the other hand, there is no stopping [*Stilstand*] (nor in reality is there any condition [*Tilstand*], everything is actuality): in case then a man the very same second he has known what is right does not do it—well then, first of all, the knowledge stops boiling. And next comes the question how the will likes this thing that is known. If it does not like it, it does not follow that the will goes ahead and does the opposite of that which the intelligence understood, such strong contrasts occur doubtless rather seldom; but the will lets some time pass, there is an interim, that means, "We'll see about that to-morrow." All this while the intelligence becomes more and more obscured, and the lower nature triumphs more and more. For, alas, the good must be done at once— at once, the moment it is known (and hence the transition goes so easily in the pure ideality where everything is "at once"), but the strength of the lower nature consists in dragging a thing out. The will has no particular objection to it—so it says with its fingers crossed. And then when the intelligence has become duly darkened, the intelligence and the will can understand one another better; at last they agree entirely, for now the intelligence has gone over to the side of the will and acknowledges that the thing is quite right as it would have it. And so there live perhaps a great multitude of men who labor off and on to obscure their ethical and religious understanding which would lead them out into decisions and consequences which the lower nature does not love, extending meanwhile their aesthetic and metaphysical understanding, which ethically is a distraction.

However, with all this we have not yet got any further than the Socratic position; for, as Socrates would say, if this comes about, then it only shows that such a man had not understood what is right. That is to say, the Greek spirit had not the courage to assert that a man knowingly does what is wrong, with knowledge of the right does what is wrong; so Socrates comes to its aid and says, When a man does wrong, he has not understood what is right.

Quite correct, and further than that no *man* can go: no man by himself and of himself can explain what sin is, precisely because he is in sin. All his talk about sin is at bottom palliation for sin, an excuse, a sinful mitigation. Hence Christianity begins also in another way, by declaring that there must be a revelation from God in order to instruct man as to what sin is, that sin does not consist in the fact that man has not understood what is right, but in the fact that he will not understand it, and in the fact that he will not do it.

With respect to the distinction between not being *able* to understand/and not being *willing* to understand, even Socrates furnishes no real enlightenment, whereas he is Grand Master above all ironists in operating by means of the distinction between understanding/and understanding. Socrates explains that he who does not do the right thing has not understood it; but Christianity goes a little further back and says, it is because he will not understand it, and this in turn is because he does not will the right. And in the next place, describing what properly is defiance, it teaches that a man does wrong although he understands what is right, or forbears to do right although he understands what is right; in short, the Christian doctrine of sin is pure impertinence against man, accusation upon accusation; it is the charge which the Deity as prosecutor takes the liberty of lodging against man.

But can anyone comprehend this Christian doctrine? By no means —this too is Christian, and so is an offense. It must be believed. Comprehension is conterminous with man's relation to the human, but faith is man's relation to the divine. How then does Christianity explain this incomprehensible? Quite consistently, in an equally incomprehensible way, by means of the fact that it is revealed.

So then, Christianly understood, sin lies in the will, not in the intellect; and this corruption of the will goes well beyond the consciousness of the individual. This is the perfectly consistent declaration, for otherwise the question how sin began must arise with respect to each individual.

Here again we have the criterion of the offense. The possibility of the offense consists in the fact that there has to be a revelation from God to enlighten man as to what sin is and how deep it lies. The natural man, the pagan, thinks thus: "O well, I admit that I have not understood everything in heaven and earth; if there is to be a revelation, let it inform us about the heavenly; but that there should be a revelation to explain what sin is, that is the most preposterous thing of all. I don't pretend to be a perfect man, far from it, but I know and I am willing to concede how far I am from perfection—ought I not then to know what sin is?" But Christianity makes answer, "No, that is what you know least about, how far you are from perfection, and what sin is." Behold, in this sense, in a Christian sense, sin doubtless is ignorance, it is ignorance of what sin is.

The definition of sin which was given in the preceding chapter therefore still needs to be completed: sin is, after having been informed by a revelation from God what sin is, then before God in despair not to will to be oneself, or before God in despair to will to be oneself.

31

THE ETHICS OF SELF-SACRIFICE *

by

FRANCIS HERBERT BRADLEY

(1846–1924)

What are the limits of self-sacrifice? How far and on what principle is a man or a nation to give up welfare or existence? I will try first to state the principle of self-sacrifice, I will point out next some prejudices which obscure this principle, and will then show the general mode of its application.

I shall here assume that self-sacrifice can exist and also may be right. And the question is on what principle is self-sacrifice right, and is there a limit at which it becomes wrong? The general prin-

* [The whole of an article originally printed in the *International Journal of Ethics* (1894). By kind permission of the University of Chicago Press and the editors of *Ethics*.]

ciple is perhaps not hard to lay down. To sacrifice one's self is to destroy or diminish one's personal existence, and this by itself is not good. Mere self-destruction, whether partial or complete, is not desirable. Self-sacrifice is right if the loss is sustained with a view to a greater gain, and otherwise it is wrong. We must assume that what I forgo is of value, for, if it were worth nothing, it could not be a sacrifice. Supposing, then, that I lose it for something worth no more, my action is not right, and if I lose it for something worth less, my action is wrong and may be immoral. This is the principle, and to this there will perhaps be no objection. The conflict of opinion arises in part from difficulties in the application, but it comes mainly, I think, from the interference of moral prejudices. There are one-sided points of view not subordinated to the governing principle, and we must next proceed to see what these are.

I will begin with the self-styled 'Christian' party, who profess to base their morality on the New Testament. But whether it is really more Christian to follow or to ignore the teaching of the Gospels I shall not discuss.

Let us then examine this 'Christian' point of view, and ask if there is here any limit to self-sacrifice. There is no limit whatever. The soul of every man is worth so much that they are all worth the same. They have cost the same price and their value is equal. And there is no end for the individual but to avoid the torment and to gain the bliss both for himself and others, and these two objects emphatically are not two but one. My interest is indivisible from the interest of others, for I can save myself only by seeking to save also my brother. Hence competition disappears; for if I struggled merely for myself, I should lose myself certainly.

This theory is simple, but it is fatally defective. Self-sacrifice seems unlimited, but it really is impossible. A man cannot give up his good where he has no good to give up. The temporal existence which you sacrifice you declare to be worthless; indeed, you naively urge that as a reason for sacrificing it. But apart from this existence you sacrifice nothing. What is the living self-development of an individual or nation? What is the beauty and the good of human being? you have made it all dross, or stumbling-blocks, or means of probation. The end is in the *other* world, and that means it is taken out of this world; and that means that life is worthless or immoral. Where the self is worth nothing, self-sacrifice is surely impossible. And, again, it is only where no man has any value that all men have equal value. When there is an end and a worth in this world men become unequal, for they must realize the end in different degrees. Hence Christianity in the above sense cannot be reconciled with morality; and let us proceed to examine another false point of view. We may call it the doctrine of one-sided patriotism, or national morality.

Worldly existence is here in itself desirable. The life of the individuals in the community and of the community in the individuals, the development of humanity in the organism of the state, is the end. Self-sacrifice of the member is demanded and limited by the good of the body. If the body requires it he develops himself, and if the body requires it he suppresses himself. Thus, self-sacrifice for the good of the state is right, and for any other end is wrong. Outside the state there is no moral self-sacrifice, because outside there is no good. And there is, of course, no international morality.

But human duties cannot be limited to the sphere of the state. And hence this view, like the 'Christian' view, is one-sided and false, nor could either be consistently followed. And yet both creeds to-day own their thoughtless adherents. There is a 'Christian' party and a party of 'British interests.' But the 'Christian' politician never asks whether, if war is contrary to the gospel, politics also are not contrary. And the man who denies international right, and preaches tribal morality, can hardly be consistent. Neither party is in earnest with the principle on which it orders us to act.

But these doctrines are combined and confused in a third view more common than either. I must now examine this, but I confess I do not know what to call it. For the name of 'Humanitarian' is too good to be more than lent for the occasion.

The elements which enter into this creed are (1) the idea of personal and national self-development, (2) the doctrine of universal love and self-sacrifice, and (3) the principle of the value of the individual. It may be said to start with the morality of the state, to widen this so as to take in humanity, and to qualify it further by the idea of unlimited self-sacrifice, adding also a notion of the infinite worth and equality of all men. And the practical conclusion is that nations, like men, all have equal rights, that they should all be governed by law, and none selfishly struggle for advantage, and that neither peoples nor individuals may be exterminated, but in any case must be respected.

This creed is identified with much that is noble; but it is inconsistent, deficient, and in part downright false. It approves of self-development, but it condemns self-assertion, the struggle of competition without which there is no development. It extends the range of state morality, but leaves out one factor of that morality, and it transplants others beyond the conditions of their existence. And, borrowing from religion the value of the individual, it seeks to use that value falsely elsewhere. I will go through these points, and will begin with the worth of the individual.

The equality, or, again, the absolute value of individuals, is not a principle which holds between man and man or nation and nation. On the contrary, the end being the development of human nature, those who have the force, and who judge this course to be conducive to the end, may exterminate or make any use of both men and nations. For the end is superior to the individual, and it is right to act for this end to the best of one's judgement. And, if so, the conclusion must follow as above. The end *does* justify the means, and cannot fail to do so, unless either the means are not essential, or the end itself not desirable or at least not paramount. But the end we are speaking of here is absolute.

There is a sense in which all men have equal and incomparable value, but this sense falls outside the world of morality. The inner moral values of men may not be comparable, but you cannot from this conclude that they are equal. It is only before God that men become equal, and even thus their equality is but partial. As ideally one with the Divine Will they all are equal, but as diverse functions of that Will they become unequal. Where there is a performance there are degrees, and where men come into relation there is an outward performance which can be compared. And religious equality is here no truth, but has become a superstition.

And leaving these abstract considerations, if we take the case of criminals within, or savages without, the community, it surely may be right to abolish their existence. The principle we act on no doubt can be misused by the immoral. It can furnish a pretext for blind persecution or selfish aggrandizement. And the progress of humanity being furthered by the diversity of its elements, it is desirable in general that individuals should develop their natures. And this shows a presumption against the extinction or hindrance of man or nation. But it does not prove that in some cases we are not morally bound to accomplish it.

The early Christians were right to insist on the sacredness of life and on the equality of all men, but for us now these ideas have a subordinate position. To the Christians men were equal, because in the other world their value was infinite and in this world nothing. For the development of human nature was not to them desirable. But for us that development is a good thing and an end in itself. And, this being so, we have left the one ground on which individuals are sacred. In getting a *temporal* value they have acquired a *relative* value, and that relative value, measured by the end, may demand their suppression. It thus, for practical purposes, is wrong to maintain the equal or absolute value of individuals unless we are prepared to hold that human nature in itself is worthless. And with this we pass to the remaining elements of 'Humanitarianism.'

This, we saw, extends national morality to the world. The relations of states are to be those of men in a state; and here we have at once false analogy. This creed, again, ignores the principle of self-assertion which is sanctioned by the state; and here is defective analogy. And, in preaching unlimited self-sacrifice, it runs counter to sound morality.

Beginning with the false analogy, and considering the moral relations of citizens and of states, I will recall some familiar points of difference. In a nation the law is supported by force. There is a sovereign, which by its executive carries out the laws and compels the unwilling. But there is no international sovereign now, and there may never be any. And a nation has courts for the settlement of differences, while international courts seem hardly possible. The absence of an executive would make them idle, and this is not all. A national court is presumed morally to represent its citizens. It stands on the common morality of the litigants, and has no selfish interests. But an international tribunal could not be presumed to be always representative or even disinterested. And it is doubtful if international law can be said really to exist.

I shall be told, no doubt, that the absence of a sovereign, and judicature, and executive, makes no difference to our duties. But surely that must depend on what our duties are. Unless we believe in some *a priori* rights of human beings as such, it is the conditions of our lives which make our duties and rights, and if you remove the conditions the duties are removed. To take men's goods without their consent, we are told for instance, is stealing, and stealing is stealing whether with individuals or nations, and whether you have laws or none. But this is all erroneous. Stealing is an offence against property, but there is no absolute reason why property should exist; and in a communistic state it might not exist. It is in the end the state which decides whether I am to have property, and fixes the conditions on which I am to hold it. And to say that the removal of these circumstances leaves things where they were seems really irrational. Mine is mine, no doubt, and yours is yours; but then, *what* is mine and yours, and how, where there are no laws, can that question be answered? I am not denying here the existence of right between states; but to take the moral rules we find existing between citizens, and, turning these into abstractions, to apply them recklessly everywhere and anywhere, I urge, is indefensible.

Thus we cannot argue in general from civic to international morality, and in particular we cannot transport the duty of self-sacrifice unaltered into the world at large. A man owes a debt to his country, but a nation may feel it owes nothing to some other nation. Duty to one's neighbour remains, but then who is one's

neighbour? Within the community he is another representative of
the same ideas, and I can believe, when I sacrifice myself, that my
life survives in the whole, and that the common spirit gains by my
loss. Can a state say this of a neighbour alien in race and alien in
ideas? Or may not self-sacrifice bring here no advantage, and but
result in fruitless waste?

In such points the analogy from citizens to nations is false. But
this analogy, we have now to see, is also deficient. Within the
state there is a principle opposed to self-sacrifice; and reasoning from
men to nations, we could not say that self-sacrifice is unlimited, for
the self-assertion of the citizen is a moral duty.

The welfare of another, just because it is another's, is not better
than mine, and the consequences which would follow are grossly
absurd. Nor is it much less absurd to teach that self-sacrifice should
stop nowhere, or that the well-being of any one is as good as that
of any one else. Doubtless, the mere fact that he is he, and I am I,
ought to make no difference, and it is foolish indeed in any one to
suppose that it could. But if you mean that *the kind of man he is*
should make no difference, and that he may not, because of this,
get in front of another, you have passed from verbiage to falsehood.
The good of the whole is the end, and the competition of the individuals is a means, for if the best do not come to the front there
is general loss. And so the community sanctions self-assertion, and
it lays down the limits and conditions of self-seeking. You may
not kill or steal, but you may struggle against one another for
existence. To empty a man's till is forbidden, but to bring him to
beggary by competition may often be laudable. 'Unto him that hath
shall be given' and 'reward for merit' are not principles of self-
sacrifice, but, within limits, they are principles approved by the
state.

And the rule of self-assertion must also hold between nations.
Our 'Christian' free-traders forbid us to take the goods of a nation
by force; but to undersell it in its markets, and to drive it out of
its trade, seems one more illustration of the precepts of the gospel.
For, 'this is not selfish, and it will be better for all in the end. In
the pacific contest of free-trade my gain or loss is still one with my
neighbour's and *we* need not raze the commandment "Thou shalt
not covet", for coveting is impossible.'

But even if competition in trade is ultimately for the good of
humanity, it is hard to believe that the advantage must come to every
man. Men and nations take time to find the better trade they have
been compelled to seek. They suffer in the process, and they do not
always survive it. And while their competitor is gaining, he surely

sometimes must gain what they lose, and after all has sought his own at the expense of his neighbour.

Thus, within limits, self-seeking is desirable among nations, and the question is solely about these limits. It is easy to talk of law, and to assert that war between states is to be judged like violence within states; but this is merely to fall into the old false analogy. The state sanctions the principle of self-assertion, and qualifies it to suit with civic conditions. But, conditions being different, the principle of competition may have a different range. If a nation narrows that range and excludes itself from foreign commerce, why should it not do so? But if, again, it carries self-assertion beyond the limits allowed in civil life, once more, is this immoral? It may sound fine to say, 'Competition is one thing and war is another', but it is not easy to draw a distinction in principle.

Selfishness is not wicked, for the state encourages its citizens to be selfish; and violence is not wicked, for the state is violent towards its citizens. War is not *illegal* violence if there is no law which condemns it, and we might even say that such a law must be founded on war. It is here that our 'Humanitarians' make a terrible mistake, for if international law is ever to be real, it must have an executive. But an executive must mean force, and force between nations is war. When a majority have become agreed that on certain points they will compel refractory states, the law of nations will be a reality. And thus, if war goes out, it will surely be by way of war, by an irresistible armed consensus with force in reserve. But what, if so, shall we say to the 'Humanitarian' who cries Peace at any price? Shall we answer, There is but one Humanitarian and one friend of peace—the man who is for war in the name of Humanity?

We have found that the equal value of individuals is an illusion, and that the analogy from the citizen to the nation is invalid. The end is general perfection, and for this end, certainly, self-sacrifice may be required. But duties within the state being specially determined, to extend these beyond their conditions is indefensible; for, like other general truths, the general truths of ethics are conditional. And beside this mistake we found also another. The analogy from civil life does not show that self-sacrifice is unlimited, but it shows, on the contrary, that within limits self-assertion is valid.

But our 'Christian' party, I suppose, will have a word for us. 'You have proved', they may say, 'that self-assertion is recognized by worldly morality, but the morality of the Gospel is the ultimate standard.' And on this point I think we should understand one another. If 'Christianity' is to mean the taking the Gospels as our rule of life, then we none of us are Christians and, no matter what we say, we all know we ought not to be. If Greek morality was one-sided, that of the New Testament is still more one-sided, for it implies that the development of the individual and the state is worthless. It is not merely that it contemns victory over the forces of nature, that it scorns beauty and despises knowledge, but there is not one of our great moral institutions which it does not ignore or condemn. The rights of property are denied or suspected, the ties of the family are broken, there is no longer any nation or patriotism, and the union of the sexes becomes a second-rate means against sin. Universal love doubtless is a virtue, but tameness and baseness—to turn the cheek to every rascal who smites it, to suffer the robbery of villains and the contumely of the oppressor, to stand by idle when the helpless are violated and the land of one's birth in its death-struggle, and to leave honour and vengeance and justice to God above—are qualities that deserve some other epithet. The morality of the primitive Christians is that of a religious sect; it is homeless, sexless, and nationless. The morality of to-day rests on the family, on property, and the nation. Our duty is to be members of the world we are in; to be in the world and not of it was their type of perfection. The moral chasm between us is, in short, as wide as the intellectual; and if it has been politic to ignore this, I doubt if it is politic any longer. We have lived a long time now the professors of a creed which no one consistently can practise, and which, if practised, would be as immoral as it is unreal.

Self-assertion, we have now seen, is as right as self-sacrifice, and at this point we may notice another mistake. It is no true deduction from Mr. Darwin's views if any one maintains the morality of mere national selfishness. For the mere fact of self-assertion and the acting on the principle of self-assertion are, in the first place, not the same. And, further, in the beginnings of morality among gregarious animals this fact of self-assertion itself has visibly suffered a change. The struggle of the community against outsiders plainly holds a place by the struggle of the individuals within the community. And how can we consistently set up tribal morality and a mere struggle between states as ultimate, when within tribal morality the principle of selfishness is not paramount? If there the law of self-assertion has ceased to be supreme, its supremacy, where states are concerned, is the merest assumption. The progress which has limited the struggle of the citizens will limit, we may rather suppose, the struggle of states, and self-assertion will everywhere be reduced to an element in a higher morality.

And here we may take leave of the one-sided ideas we have criticized. The end we take to be the development of human nature. This principle necessitates self-sacrifice, since its way may be through the loss of individuals. And it necessitates self-assertion, since only thus can the end be reached at all. It subordinates both, and their limits can be stated in general. It is possible that a man or a state can develop self best by serving others most, and here the question disappears. Again, a man or state, by giving up private good, may do most for the end; and here self-sacrifice becomes a duty. But if by self-assertion, to the loss or even extinction of others, a man or a state considers that it most profits humanity, there self-sacrifice is immoral.

These truths seem too obvious to require explanation, but they are so constantly misunderstood that I venture to dwell on them. Suppose, first, that we have one single nation; the perfection of human nature within that nation will be the end. The good of each man here for the most part should coincide with that of others, but wholly it cannot and should not coincide. For without competition the community grows effete through the loss of vigorous individuals. The worthless are not pushed aside, and the fittest do not come to the front. And hence, if I am the fittest to have advantage, it is my duty to take it. But on the same principle there are cases where self-sacrifice should be welcomed. Self-sacrifice is an end in general where it results in a greater gain, and it is an end to the loser so far as he identifies himself with that which gains. But in itself self-sacrifice is an evil, and there is always some presumption against it. To give up life or possessions or talents for the sake of others may be immoral.

And the same thing holds between nations. Each gains generally, but not always, by the gain of all. Some competition, and hence self-assertion to the loss of another, may thus at times be right. And at other times, for the sake of humanity, a nation should deny itself. National self-sacrifice, as compared with civic, has a wider object but a narrower exercise. It is hard for a state to judge that its loss is balanced by general gain. And nations differ in value, and there is no organism to ensure that loss of one shall advantage the others. The influence of example is weak where public spirit has hardly an existence. And (sophistic as it may sound) the readiness in a nation for self-sacrifice would be an argument in favour of its self-assertion.

The general principle seems plain, but does not carry us far. A nation must aim at the good of mankind and at peace in the end;

but, as things are, this principle will in some cases justify violence, and even extermination. For, beside the principle which establishes the end, there can be no absolute law; and the means to this end cannot be fixed beforehand. And such means certainly need not always consist in abstinence from war or even from aggression. Our first hope at present is an international executive enforcing the morality of the best; but, if that is to exist, then the best must agree, and must be the strongest. And strength means war in reserve. We may look beyond this possibly to a better state of things, but the first seems the only road to the second. The meek will *not* inherit the earth, and a nation which claims morality must be ready to use force in defence of right.

It is idle to denounce this view as the trumpeting of a bellicose policy or the glorification of blood and pillage. This view necessitates the belief that a war begun thoughtlessly or selfishly is a crime. It is hostile only to the reckless application of one-sided principles. We remind the party of 'British interests' that a cynical self-seeking is immoral, and that a nation which adopts it may lose one source of strength. To the peace-at-any-price manufacturer we remark that a thing may be worth more than what it fetches in the market; and we say to either the 'Christian' politician or the covert Quaker that, while on other points he ignores the teaching of the Gospels, he is a hypocrite if he tries to teach us our duty on this. And we beg the sentimentalist to remember that, after all, force rules the world, and that self-assertion, after all, is a condition of welfare.

It would be a good day if in England we could gain some clearer ideas about selfishness and patriotism; if we could learn to abstain from insincere professions and from sickening cant. We might then, perhaps, remember that, when trade is gone and manufactures perished, the memory of a nation that has strengthened itself, and dared to risk something in the cause of humanity, is not so easily lost.

32

PLEASURE AND HAPPINESS *

by

ARISTOTLE

(B.C. 384–322)

Some people say that the [highest] good is pleasure; others, on the contrary, that pleasure is something utterly bad, whether, as is possible, they are convinced that it really is so, or they think it better in the interest of human life to represent pleasure as an evil, even if it is not so, feeling that men are generally inclined to pleasure, and are the slaves of their pleasures, and that it is a duty therefore to lead them in the contrary direction, as they will so arrive at the mean or proper state.

But I venture to think that this is not a right statement of the case. For in matters of the emotions and actions theories are not so trustworthy as facts; and thus, when theories disagree with the facts of perception, they fall into contempt, and involve the truth itself in their destruction. For if a person censures pleasure and yet is seen at times to make pleasure his aim, he is thought to incline to pleasure as being entirely desirable; for it is beyond the power of ordinary people to make distinctions. It seems then the true theories are exceedingly useful, not only as the means of knowledge but as guides of life; for as being in harmony with facts, they are believed, and being believed they encourage people who understand them to regulate their lives in accordance with them.

Enough then of such considerations; let us review the various doctrines of pleasure.

Eudoxus held that pleasure was the good, because he saw that all things, whether rational or irrational, make pleasure their aim. He argued that in all cases that which is desirable is good, and that which is most desirable is most good; hence the fact of all things being drawn to the same object is an indication that that object is the best for all, as everything discovers what is good for itself in the same way as it discovers food; but that that which is good for all, and is the aim of all, is the good.

* [From Bk. X in J. E. C. Welldon's translation (1892) of the *Nicomachean Ethics*. By kind permission of the Macmillan Co.]

His theories were accepted, not so much for their intrinsic value as for the excellence of his moral character; for he was regarded as a person of exemplary temperance. It seemed then that he did not put forward these views as being a votary of pleasure, but that the truth was really as he said. He held that this truth resulted with equal clearness from a consideration of the opposite of pleasure; for as pain is something which everybody should avoid, so too its opposite is something which everybody should desire. He argued that a thing is in the highest degree desirable, if we do not desire it for any ulterior reason, or with any ulterior motive, and this is admittedly the case with pleasure; for if a person is pleased, nobody asks the further question, What is his motive in being pleased? a fact which proves that pleasure is desirable in itself. And further that the addition of pleasure to any good, e.g. to just or temperate conduct, renders that good more desirable, and it follows that if the good is augmented by a thing, that thing must itself be a good

It seems then that this argument proves pleasure to be a good, but not to be a good in a higher sense than anything else; for any good whatever is more desirable with the addition of another good than when it stands alone. It is by a precisely similar argument that Plato tries to prove that pleasure is not the good. Pleasure (he says) is not the chief good, for the pleasant life is more desirable with the addition of prudence than without it; but if the combination is better, pleasure is not the good, as the good itself cannot be made more desirable by any addition.

But it is clear that, if pleasure is not the good, neither can anything else be which is made more desirable by the addition of any absolute good. What is it then which is incapable of such addition, but at the same time admits of our participating in it? For it is a good of this kind which is the object of our research.

People who argue on the other hand that that which all things aim at is not a good may be said to talk nonsense; for we accept the universal opinion as true, and one who upsets our trust in the universal opinion will find it hard to put forward any opinion that is more trustworthy. If it were only unintelligent beings that longed for pleasure, there would be something in what he says; but if intelligent beings also long for it, how can it be so? It is probable that even in the lower creatures there is some natural principle which is superior to the creatures themselves, and aims at their proper good.

Nor does it seem that these people fairly meet the argument drawn from the opposite of pleasure. They say it does not follow that, if pain is an evil, pleasure is a good, as not only is one evil opposed to another, but both are opposed to that which is neither one nor the other, but a neutral state. This is true enough, but it does not apply to pleasure and pain. For if both pleasure and pain were evil, it would have been a duty to avoid both, and if neither were evil, it would have been a duty not to avoid either, or not to avoid one more than the other; whereas in fact it is clear that people avoid one as an evil, and desire the other as a good. It follows then that pleasure and pain are opposed to each other as good and evil.

Nor again does it follow that, if pleasure is not a quality, neither is it a good, for the activities of virtue are not qualities, nor is happiness.

It is argued too that good is definite, but pleasure is indefinite, as it admits of degrees.

Now if the ground of this opinion is that it is possible to be pleased in a greater or a less degree, the same thing is true of justice and the other virtues. For here it is evident that we speak of persons as possessing the several virtues in a greater or less degree; some people are just and courageous in a greater or less degree than others, and it is possible to act with a greater or less degree of justice and temperance.

If however the meaning is that the indefiniteness resides in the pleasures, this is, I think, not the true explanation, supposing that some pleasures are mixed and others unmixed.

Again, health is definite, yet it admits of degrees; and why should it not be so with pleasure? For health is not the same symmetry or proportion of elements in all people, nor is it always uniform in the same person; it admits of relaxation up to a certain point, and of different degrees, without ceasing to be health. Something of the same kind then may be also true of pleasure.

Again, the opponents of pleasure, looking upon the good as perfect or complete, and the processes of movement and production as imperfect or incomplete, try to prove that pleasure is motion or production. But they are wrong, I think, nor is pleasure a motion at all. For quickness and slowness are characteristic, it seems, of every motion, either absolutely, as of the motion of the universe, or else relatively, but neither of them is a condition inherent in pleasure. It is possible to become pleased, as it is to become angry, quickly, but not to be pleased quickly or relatively, i.e. in comparison with somebody else, as it is to walk or to grow quickly and so on. The transition then, to a state of pleasure may be quick or slow, but the active experience of pleasure, i.e. the state of being pleased, cannot be quick.

In what sense, too, can pleasure be a process of production? It is apparently not the case that anything can be produced out of anything; it is the case that a thing is resolved into that out of which it is produced. Also, pain is the destruction of that of which pleasure is the production. It is said too that pain is a deficiency of the natural state, and pleasure its satisfaction. But this deficiency and this satisfaction are emotions of the body. If, then, pleasure is a satisfaction of the natural state, it follows that the part which is the seat of the satisfaction will feel pleasure, i.e. the body. But this seems not to be the case. We conclude therefore that pleasure is not a satisfaction of the natural state, although one may feel pleasure while the process of satisfaction is going on, as he may feel pain while undergoing an operation.

This view of pleasure, viz. that it is a process of satisfaction, seems to have originated in the pleasures and pains of eating and drinking, as in them we first feel a deficiency and an antecedent pain, and then feel pleasure at the satisfaction. But this is not true of all pleasures; the pleasures of mathematics e.g. have no such antecedent pain, nor among the pleasures of the senses have those of the smell, nor again many sounds and sights, memories and hopes. What is there then of which these will be processes of production? For in them there has been no deficiency to be satisfied.

But if the instance of immoral pleasures be adduced to prove that pleasure is a bad thing, we may answer that these are not really pleasant. They may be pleasant to people who are in a bad condition, but it must not be inferred that they are pleasant except to such people, any more than that things are healthful or sweet or bitter in themselves, because they are so to invalids, or that things are white, because they appear so to people who are suffering from ophthalmia.

Perhaps the truth may be stated thus: Pleasures are desirable, but not if they are immoral in their origin, just as wealth is pleasant, but not if it be obtained at the cost of turning traitor to one's country, or health, but not at the cost of eating any food, however disagreeable. Or it may be said that pleasures are of different kinds, those which are noble in their origin are different from those which are dishonourable, and it is impossible to enjoy the pleasure of the just man without being just, or that of the musician without being musical, and so on. The distinction drawn between a friend and a flatterer seems to bring out clearly the truth that pleasure is not a good, or that there are pleasures of different kinds; for it seems that while the object of the friend in social intercourse is good, that of the flatterer is pleasure, and while the flatterer is censured, the friend for his disinterestedness is praised.

Again, nobody would choose to live all his life with the mind of a child, although he should enjoy the pleasures of childhood to the utmost, or to delight in doing what is utterly shameful, although he were never to suffer pain for doing it. There are many things too upon which we should set our hearts, even if they brought no pleasure with them, e.g. sight, memory, knowledge, and the possession of the virtues; and if it be true that these are necessarily attended by pleasures, it is immaterial, as we should desire them even if no pleasure resulted from them. It seems to be clear then that pleasure is not the good, nor is every pleasure desirable, and that there are some pleasures which are desirable in themselves, and they differ in kind or in origin from the others.

We may regard this as a sufficient account of such views as are held in regard to pleasure and pain.

But the nature or character of pleasure will be more clearly seen, if we resume our argument from the beginning.

It seems that the act of sight is perfect or complete at any time; it does not lack anything which will afterwards be produced, and will make it perfect of its kind. Pleasure appears to resemble sight in this respect; it is a whole, nor is it possible at any time to find a pleasure which will be made perfect of its kind by increased duration.

It follows that pleasure is not a motion; for every motion takes a certain time, and aims at a certain end. Thus the builder's art is perfect or complete when it has accomplished its object. It is complete, either in respect of the whole time which the building took, or in respect of the moment when it was completed. But in the various parts of the time the various processes or motions are imperfect and different in kind from the whole and from one another; for the setting of the stones is different from the fluting of the pillar, and both from the building of the temple as a whole, and whereas the building of the temple is complete, nothing being wanting to the object proposed, that of the basement and the triglyph is incomplete, as each is only the building of a part of the temple. These processes or motions are therefore different in kind, and it is impossible at any time when the building is going on to find a motion which is complete or perfect of its kind. Such a motion, if found at all, will be found only in the whole time.

It is much the same with walking or any other process. For here again, although all locomotion is a motion from one place to another, there are different kinds of locomotion, such as flying, walking, jumping, and the like. And not only so, but walking itself is of different kinds; for the starting-point and the goal are not the same in the whole course, and in a part of it, or in one part of the course and in another; nor is it the same thing to cross one line as to cross another; for it is not only that a person crosses a line, but the line which he crosses is in a certain place, and one line is in a different place from another.

The subject of motion has been accurately discussed in another treatise. Motion is apparently not complete in any and every period of time; on the contrary, most motions are incomplete and different in kind, inasmuch as the starting-point and the goal constitute a difference of kind. Pleasure on the other hand seems to be complete or perfect of its kind in any and every period of time.

It is clear then that motion and pleasure must be distinct from one another, and that pleasure is something which is whole and perfect.

Another reason for holding this view is that motion is impossible except in a period of time, but pleasure is not; for the pleasure of a moment is a whole.

It is clear from these considerations that pleasure is not rightly described as a motion or process of production, for such a description is not appropriate to all things but only to such as are divisible into parts and are not wholes. For there is no process of production in an act of sight or in a mathematical point or in a unit, nor is any one of these things a motion or a process of production. It follows that there is no such process in pleasure, as it is a whole.

Again, every sense exercises its activity upon its own object, and the activity is perfect only when the sense itself is in a sound condition, and the object is the noblest that falls within the domain of that sense; for this seems to be preeminently the character of the perfect activity. We may say that it makes no difference whether we speak of the sense itself or of the organ in which it resides as exercising the activity; in every instance the activity is highest when the part which acts is in the best condition, and the object upon which it acts is the highest of the objects which fall within its domain. Such an activity will not only be the most perfect, but the most pleasant; for there is pleasure in all sensation, and similarly in all thought and speculation, and the activity will be pleasantest when it is most perfect, and it will be most perfect when it is the activity of the part being in a sound condition and acting upon the most excellent of the objects that fall within its domain.

Pleasure perfects the activity, but not in the same way in which the excellence of the sense or of the object of sense perfects it, just as health is the cause of our being in a healthy state in one sense and the doctor is the cause of it in another.

It is clear that every sense has its proper pleasure; for we speak of pleasant sights, pleasant sounds and so on. It is clear too that the pleasure is greatest when the sense is best, and its object is best; but if the sentient subject and the sensible object are at their best, there will always be pleasure so long as there is a subject to act and an object to be acted upon.

When it is said that pleasure perfects the activity, it is not as a state or quality inherent in the subject but as a perfection super-added to it, like the bloom of youth to people in the prime of life.

So long then as the object of thought or sensation and the critical or contemplative subject are such as they ought to be, there will be pleasure in the exercise of the activity; for this is the natural result if the agent and the patient remain in the same relation to each other.

It may be asked then, How is it that nobody feels pleasure continuously? It is probably because we grow weary. Human beings are incapable of continuous activity, and as the activity comes to an end, so does the pleasure; for it is a concomitant of the activity. It is for the same reason that some things give pleasure when they are new, but give less pleasure afterwards; for the intelligence is called into play at first, and applies itself to its object with intense activity, as when we look a person full in the face in order to recognize him, but afterwards the activity ceases to be so intense and becomes remiss, and consequently the pleasure also fades away.

It may be supposed that everybody desires pleasure, for everybody clings to life. But life is a species of activity and a person's activity displays itself in the sphere and with the means which are after his own heart. Thus a musician exercises his ears in listening to music, a student his intellect in speculation, and so on.

But pleasure perfects the activities; it therefore perfects life, which is the aim of human desire. It is reasonable then to aim at pleasure, as it perfects life in each of us, and life is an object of desire.

Whether we desire life for the sake of pleasure or pleasure for the sake of life, is a question which may be dismissed for the moment. For it appears that pleasure and life are yoked together and do not admit of separation, as pleasure is impossible without activity and every activity is perfected by pleasure.

If this be so, it seems to follow that pleasures are of different kinds, as we hold that things which are different in kind are perfected by things which are themselves different in kind. For this is apparently the rule in the works of nature or of art, e.g. animals, trees, pictures, statues, a house, or a piece of furniture. Similarly we hold that energies which are different in kind are perfected by things which are also different in kind.

Now the pleasures of the intellect are different from the pleasures of the senses, and these again are different in kind from one another. It follows that the pleasures which perfect them will also be different.

This conclusion would appear also to result from the intimate connexion of each pleasure with the activity which it perfects. For the activity is increased by its proper pleasure, as if the activity is pleasant, we are more likely to arrive at a true judgment or an accurate result in any matter. It is so e.g. with people who are fond of geometry; they make better geometricians and understand the various problems of geometry better than other people. It is so too with people who are fond of music or architecture or any other subject; their progress in their particular subject is due to the pleasure which they take in it. Pleasure helps to increase activity, and that which helps to increase a thing must be closely connected with it. Where things then are different in kind, the things which are closely connected with them will also be different in kind.

This becomes still clearer when we observe that the pleasures which spring from one activity are impediments to the exercise of another. Thus people who are fond of the flute are incapable of attending to an argument, if they hear somebody playing the flute, as they take a greater pleasure in flute-playing than in the activity which they are called to exercise at the moment; hence the pleasure of the flute-playing destroys their argumentative activity. Much the same result occurs in other cases, when a person exercises his activity on two subjects simultaneously; the pleasanter of the two drives out the other, especially if it be much the pleasanter, until the activity of the other disappears. Accordingly, if we take intense delight in anything, we cannot do anything else at all. It is only when we do not care much for a thing that we do something else as well, just as people who eat sweetmeats in the theatres do so most when the actors are bad.

As the pleasure then which is proper to an activity refines it and gives it greater permanence and excellence, while alien pleasures impair it, it is clear that there is a wide difference between these pleasures. It may almost be said that the pleasures which are alien to it have the same effect as the pains which are proper to it; for the pains which are proper to an activity destroy it, as, when a person finds writing or thinking unpleasant and painful, he does not write or does not think, as the case may be.

The pleasures and pains then which are proper to an activity have opposite effects upon it. I mean by "proper" such as are the consequences of the activity *per se*. But it has been already stated that alien pleasures have much the same effect as pain; they are destructive of the activity, although not destructive of it in the same way.

Again, as the activities differ in goodness and badness, some being desirable, some undesirable, and some neither the one nor the other, so it is with pleasures, as every activity has its proper pleasure. Thus the pleasure which is proper to a virtuous activity is good, and that which is proper to a low activity is vicious. For the desires of what is noble are themselves laudable, the desires of what is disgraceful are censurable; but the pleasures which reside in the activities are more strictly proper to them than the desires, as the latter are distinct from the activities in time and nature, but the former are closely related in time to the activities, and are so difficult to distinguish from them that it is a question whether the activity is identical with the pleasure.

It seems however that pleasure is not the same thing as thought or sensation; it would be strange if it were so; but the impossibility of separating them makes some people regard them as the same.

As the activities then are different, so are the pleasures. Sight is different from or superior to touch in purity, hearing and smell are superior to taste; there is a corresponding difference therefore in their pleasures. The pleasures of the intellect too are different from or superior to these, and there are different kinds of pleasures of the senses or of the intellect. It seems that there is a pleasure, as there is a function, which is proper to every living thing, viz. the pleasure inherent in its activity. If we consider individual living things, we see this is so; for the pleasures of a horse, a dog, and a man are different, and as Heraclitus says, "a donkey would choose a bundle of hay in preference to gold; for fodder is pleasanter to donkeys than gold."

As the pleasures then of beings who are different in kind are themselves different in kind, it would be reasonable to suppose that there is no difference between the pleasures of the same beings. But there is a wide difference, at least in the case of men; the same things give pleasure to some people and pain to others, to some they are painful and hateful, to others pleasant and lovable. This is true of sweet things; the same things do not seem sweet to a person in a fever and to a person in good health, nor does the same thing seem hot to an invalid and to a person in a good physical condition. It is much the same with other things as well.

But in all these cases it seems that the thing really is what it appears to the virtuous man to be. But if this is a true statement of the case, as it seems to be, if virtue or the good man *qua* good is the measure of everything, it follows that it is such pleasures as appear pleasures to the good man that are really pleasures, and the things which afford him delight that are really pleasant. It is no wonder if what he finds disagreeable seems pleasant to somebody else, as men are liable to many corruptions and defilements; but such things are not pleasant except to these people, and to them only when they are in this condition.

It is clear then that we must not speak of pleasures which are admitted to be disgraceful as pleasures, except in relation to people who are thoroughly corrupt. But the question remains, Among such pleasures as are seen to be good, what is the character or nature of the pleasures that deserve to be called the *proper* pleasures of Man? It is plain, I think, from a consideration of the activities; for the activities bring pleasures in their train. Whether then there is one activity or there are several belonging to the perfect and fortunate man, it is the pleasures which perfect these activities that would be strictly described as the *proper* pleasures of Man. All other pleasures are only in a secondary or fractional sense the pleasures of Man, as are all other activities.

After this discussion of the kinds of virtue and friendship and pleasure it remains to give a sketch of happiness, since we defined happiness as the end of human things. We shall shorten our account of it if we begin by recapitulating our previous remarks.

We said that happiness is not a moral state; for, if it were, it would be predicable of one who spends his whole life in sleep, living the life of a vegetable, or of one who is utterly miserable. If then we cannot accept this view, if we must rather define happiness as an activity of some kind, as has been said before, and if activities are either necessary and desirable as a means to something else or desirable in themselves, it is clear that we must define happiness as belonging to the class of activities which are desirable in themselves, and not desirable as means to something else; for happiness has no want, it is self-sufficient.

Again, activities are desirable in themselves, if nothing is expected from them beyond the activity. This seems to be the case with virtuous actions, as the practice of what is noble and virtuous is a thing desirable in itself. It seems to be the case also with such amusements as are pleasant, we do not desire them as means to other things; for they often do us harm rather than good by making us careless about our persons and our property. Such pastimes are generally the resources of those whom the world calls happy. Accordingly people who are clever at such pastimes are generally popular in the courts of despots, as they make themselves pleasant to the despot in the matters which are the objects of his desire, and what he wants is to pass the time pleasantly.

The reason why these things are regarded as elements of happiness is that people who occupy high positions devote their leisure to them. But such people are not, I think, a criterion. For a high position is no guarantee of virtue or intellect, which are the sources on which virtuous activities depend. And if these people, who have never tasted a pure and liberal pleasure, have recourse to the pleasures of the body, it must not be inferred that these pleasures are preferable; for even children suppose that such things as are valued or honoured among them are best. It is only reasonable then that, as men and children differ in their estimate of what is honourable, so should good and bad people.

As has been frequently said, therefore, it is the things which are honourable and pleasant to the virtuous man that are really honourable and pleasant. But everybody feels the activity which accords with his own moral state to be most desirable, and accordingly the virtuous man regards the activity in accordance with virtue as most desirable.

Happiness then does not consist in amusement. It would be paradoxical to hold that the end of human life is amusement, and that we should toil and suffer all our life for the sake of amusing ourselves. For we may be said to desire all things as means to something else, except indeed happiness, as happiness is the end *or perfect state*.

It appears to be foolish and utterly childish to take serious trouble and pains for the sake of amusement. But to amuse oneself with a view to being serious seems to be right, as Anacharsis says; for amusement is a kind of relaxation, and it is because we cannot work for ever that we need relaxation.

Relaxation then is not an end. We enjoy it as a means to activity; but it seems that the happy life is a life of virtue, and such a life is serious, it is not one of mere amusement. We speak of serious things too (for serious things are virtuous) as better than things which are ridiculous and amusing, and of the activity of the better part of man's being or of the better man as always the more virtuous. But the activity of that which is better is necessarily higher and happier. Anybody can enjoy bodily pleasures, a slave can enjoy them as much as the best of men; but nobody would allow that a slave is capable of happiness unless he is capable of life; for happiness consists not in such pastimes as I have been speaking of, but in virtuous activities, as has been already said.

If happiness consists in virtuous activity, it is only reasonable to suppose that it is the activity of the highest virtue, or in other words, of the best part of our nature. Whether it is the reason or something else which seems to exercise rule and authority by a natural right, and to have a conception of things noble and divine, either as being itself divine or as relatively the most divine part of our being, it is the activity of this part in accordance with its proper virtue which will be the perfect happiness.

. . . [Happiness] is a speculative activity, *i.e. an activity which takes the form of contemplation.* This is a conclusion which would seem to agree with our previous arguments and with the truth itself; for the speculative is the highest activity, as the intuitive reason is the highest of our faculties, and the objects with which the intuitive reason is concerned are the highest of things that can be known. It is also the most continuous; for our speculation can more easily be continuous than any kind of action. We consider too that pleasure is an essential element of happiness, and it is admitted that there is no virtuous activity so pleasant as the activity of wisdom or philosophic reflection; at all events it appears that philosophy possesses pleasures of wonderful purity and certainty, and it is reasonable to suppose that people who possess knowledge pass their time more pleasantly than people who are seekers after truth.

Self-sufficiency too, as it is called, is preeminently a characteristic of the speculative activity; for the wise man, the just man, and all others, need the necessaries of life; but when they are adequately provided with these things, the just man needs people to whom and with whom he may do justice, so do the temperate man, the courageous man and everyone else; but the wise man is capable of speculation by himself, and the wiser he is, the more capable he is of such speculation. It is perhaps better for him in his speculation to have fellow-workers; but nevertheless he is in the highest degree self-sufficient.

It would seem too that the speculative is the only activity which is loved for its own sake as it has no result except speculation, whereas from all moral actions we gain something more or less besides the action itself.

Again, happiness, it seems, requires leisure; for the object of our business is leisure, as the object of war is the enjoyment of peace. Now the activity of the practical virtues is displayed in politics or war, and actions of this sort seem incompatible with leisure. This is absolutely true of military actions, as nobody desires war, or prepares to go to war, for its own sake. A person would be regarded as absolutely bloodthirsty if he were to make enemies of his friends for the mere sake of fighting and bloodshed. But the activity of the statesman too is incompatible with leisure. It aims at securing something beyond and apart from politics, viz. the power and honour or at least the happiness of the statesman himself and his fellow citizens, which is different from the political activity and is proved to be different by our search for it as something distinct.

If then political and military actions are preeminent among virtuous actions in beauty and grandeur, if they are incompatible with leisure and aim at some end, and are not desired for their own sakes, if the activity of the intuitive reason seems to be superior in seriousness as being speculative, and not to aim at any end beyond itself, and to have its proper pleasure, and if this pleasure enhances the activity, it follows that such self-sufficiency and power of leisure and absence of fatigue as are possible to a man and all the other attributes of

felicity are found to be realized in this activity. This then will be
the perfect happiness of Man, if a perfect length of life is given it,
for there is no imperfection in happiness. But such a life will be too
good for Man. He will enjoy such a life not in virtue of his humanity
but in virtue of some divine element within him, and the superiority of
this activity to the activity of any other virtue will be proportionate
to the superiority of this divine element in man to his composite
or material nature.

If then the reason is divine in comparison with the rest of Man's
nature, the life which accords with reason will be divine in comparison with human life in general. Nor is it right to follow the
advice of people who say that the thoughts of men should not be too
high for humanity or the thoughts of mortals too high for mortality;
for a man, as far as in him lies, should seek immortality and do all
that is in his power to live in accordance with the highest part of
his nature, as, although that part is insignificant in size, yet in power
and honour it is far superior to all the rest.

It would seem too that this is the true self of everyone, if a
man's true self is his supreme or better part. It would be absurd then
that a man should desire not the life which is properly his own but
the life which properly belongs to some other being. The remark
already made will be appropriate here. It is what is proper to everyone that is in its nature best and pleasantest for him. It is the life
which accords with reason then that will be best and pleasantest for
Man, as a man's reason is in the highest sense himself. This will
therefore be also the happiest life.

33

ULTIMATE RELIGION *

by

GEORGE SANTAYANA

(1863-1952)

Before this chosen audience, in this consecrated place, I may venture to pass over all subsidiary matters and come at once to the

* [The whole of an address read at the Hague during the commemoration
of the tercentenary of Spinoza's birth. Originally printed in *Septimana Spinozana*
(1933), Martinus Nijhoff, the Hague.]

last question of all: What inmost allegiance, what ultimate religion, would be proper to a wholly free and disillusioned spirit? The occasion invites us to consider this question, and to consider it with entire frankness. Great as you and I may feel our debt to be to Spinoza for his philosophy of nature, there is, I think, something for which we owe him an even greater debt; I mean, the magnificent example he offers us of philosophic liberty, the courage, firmness, and sincerity with which he reconciled his heart to the truth. Any clever man may sometimes see the truth in flashes; any scientific man may put some aspect of the truth into technical words; yet all this hardly deserves the name of philosophy so long as the heart remains unabashed, and we continue to live like animals lost in the stream of our impressions, not only in the public routine and necessary cares of life, but even in our silent thoughts and affections. Many a man before Spinoza and since has found the secret of peace: but the singularity of Spinoza, at least in the modern world, was that he facilitated this moral victory by no dubious postulates. He did not ask God to meet him half way: he did not whitewash the facts, as the facts appear to clear reason, or as they appeared to the science of his day. He solved the problem of the spiritual life after stating it in the hardest, sharpest, most cruel terms. Let us nerve ourselves today to imitate his example, not by simply accepting his solution, which for some of us would be easy, but by exercising his courage in the face of a somewhat different world, in which it may be even more difficult for us than it was for him to find a sure foothold and a sublime companionship.

There is a brave and humorous saying of Luther's, which applies to Spinoza better, perhaps, than to Luther himself. When asked where, if driven out of the Church, he would stand, he replied: "Under the sky." The sky of Luther was terribly clouded: there was a vast deal of myth tumbling and thundering about in it: and even in the clear sky of Spinoza there was perhaps something specious, as there is in the blue vault itself. The sun, he tells us, seemed to be about two hundred feet away: and if his science at once corrected this optical illusion, it never undermined his conviction that all reality was within easy reach of his thought. Nature was dominated, he assumed, by unquestionable scientific and dialectical principles; so that while the forces of nature might often put our bodily existence in jeopardy, they always formed a decidedly friendly and faithful object for the mind. There was no essential mystery. The human soul from her humble station might salute the eternal and the infinite with complete composure and with a certain vicarious pride. Every man had a true and adequate idea of God: and this saying, technically justified as it may be by Spinoza's definitions of terms, cannot help surprising us: it reveals such a virgin sense of familiarity with the absolute. There could not but be joy in the sweep of an intelligence that seemed so completely victorious, and no misgivings could trouble a view of the world that explained everything.

Today, however, we can hardly feel such assurance: we should be taking shelter in a human edifice which the next earthquake might shake down. Nor is it a question really of times or temperaments: anyone anywhere, if he does not wish to construct a plausible system, but to challenge his own assumptions and come to spiritual self-knowledge, must begin by abstention from all easy faith, lest he should be madly filling the universe with images of his own reason and his own hopes. I will therefore ask you today, provisionally, for an hour, and without prejudice to your ulterior reasonable convictions, to imagine the truth to be as unfavourable as possible to your desires and as contrary as possible to your natural presumptions; so that the spirit in each of us may be drawn away from its accidental home and subjected to an utter denudation and supreme trial. Yes, although the dead cannot change their minds, I would respectfully beg the shade of Spinoza himself to suspend for a moment that strict rationalism, that jealous, hard-reasoning, confident piety which he shared with the Calvinists and Jansenists of his day, and to imagine—I do not say to admit—that nature may be but imperfectly formed in the bosom of chaos, and that reason in us may be imperfectly adapted to the understanding of nature. Then, having hazarded no favourite postulates and invoked no cosmic forces pledged to support our aspirations, we may all quietly observe what we find; and whatever harmonies may then appear to subsist between our spirits and the nature of things will be free gifts to us and, so far as they go, unchallengeable possessions. We shall at last be standing unpledged and naked, under the open sky.

In what I am about to say, therefore, I do not mean to prejudge any cosmological questions, such as that of free will or necessity, theism or pantheism. I am concerned only with the sincere confessions of a mind that has surrendered every doubtful claim and every questionable assurance. Of such assurances or claims there is one which is radical and comprehensive: I mean, the claim to existence and to directing the course of events. We say conventionally that the future is uncertain: but if we withdrew honestly into ourselves and examined our actual moral resources, we should feel that what is insecure is not merely the course of particular events but the vital presumption that there is a future coming at all, and a future pleasantly continuing our habitual experience. We rely in this, as we must, on the analogies of experience, or rather on the clock-work of instinct and presumption in our bodies; but existence is a miracle, and, morally considered, a free gift from moment to moment. That it will always be analogous to itself is the very question we are begging. Evidently all interconnections and sequences of events, and in particular any consequences which we may expect to flow from our actions, are really entirely beyond our spiritual control. When our will commands and seems, we know not how, to be obeyed by our bodies and by the world, we are like Joshua seeing the sun stand still at his bidding; when we command and nothing happens, we are like King Canute surprised that the rising tide should not obey him: and when we say we have executed a great work and re-directed the course of history, we are like Chanticleer attributing the sunrise to his crowing.

What is the result? That at once, by a mere act of self-examination and frankness, the spirit has come upon one of the most important and radical of religious perceptions. It has perceived that though it is living, it is powerless to live; that though it may die, it is powerless to die; and that altogether, at every instant and in every particular, it is in the hands of some alien and inscrutable power.

Of this felt power I profess to know nothing further. To me, as yet, it is merely the counterpart of my impotence. I should not venture, for instance, to call this power almighty, since I have no means of knowing how much it can do: but I should not hesitate, if I may coin a word, to call it *omnificent:* it is to me, by definition, the doer of everything that is done. I am not asserting the physical validity of this sense of agency or cause: I am merely feeling the force, the friendliness, the hostility, the unfathomableness of the world. I am expressing an impression; and it may be long before my sense of omnipresent power can be erected, with many qualifications, into a theological theory of the omnipresence of God. But the moral presence of power comes upon a man in the night, in the desert, when he finds himself, as the Arabs say, alone with Allah. It re-appears in every acute predicament, in extremities, in the birth of a child, or in the face of death. And as for the unity of this power, that is not involved in its sundry manifestations, but rather in my own solitude; in the unity of this suffering spirit overtaken by all those accidents. My destiny is single, tragically single, no matter how multifarious may be the causes of my destiny. As I stand amazed, I am not called upon to say whether, if I could penetrate into the inner workings of things, I should discover omnificent power to be simple or compound, continuous or spasmodic, intentional or blind. I stand before it simply receptive, somewhat as, in Rome, I might stand before the great fountain of Trevi. There I see jets and cascades flowing in separate streams and in divers directions. I am not sure that a single Pontifex Maximus designed it all, and led all those musical waters into just those channels. Some streams may have dried up or been diverted since the creation; some rills may have been added today by fresh rains from heaven; behind one of those artificial rocks some little demon, of his own free will, may even now be playing havoc with the conduits; and who knows how many details, in my image, may not have been misplaced or multiplied by optical tricks of my own? Yet here, for the spirit, is one total marvellous impression, one thunderous force, confronting me with this theatrical but admirable spectacle.

Yet this is not all. Power comes down upon me clothed in a thousand phenomena; and these manifestations of power open to me a new spiritual resource. In submitting to power, I learn its ways; from being passive my spirit becomes active; it begins to enjoy one of its essential prerogatives. For like a child the spirit is attracted to all facts by the mere assault of their irrational presence and variety. It watches all that happens or is done with a certain happy excitement, even at the most fearful calamities. Although the essence of spirit may be merely to think, yet some intensity and progression are essential to this thinking; thinking is a way of living, and the most vital way. Therefore all the operations of universal power, when they afford themes for perception, afford also occasions for intellectual delight. Here will and intellect, as Spinoza tells us, coincide: for omnificent power flows in part through our persons; the spirit itself is a spark of that fire, or rather the light of that flame: it cannot have an opposite principle of motion. With health a certain euphoria, a certain alacrity and sense of mastery are induced in the spirit; and a natural effect of perspective, the pathos of nearness, turns our little spark for us into a central sun. The world moves round us, and we move gladly with the world. What if the march of things be destined to overwhelm us? It cannot destroy the joy we had in its greatness and in its victory. There may even be some relief in passing from the troubled thought of ourselves to the thought of something more rich in life, yet in its own sphere and progression, untroubled: and it may be easier for me to understand the motion of the heavens and to rejoice in it than to understand or rejoice in my own motions. My own eclipse, my own vices, my own sorrows, may become a subject to me for exact calculation and a pleasing wonder. The philosophical eye may compose a cosmic harmony out of these necessary conflicts, and an infinite life out of these desirable deaths.

Does it not begin to appear that the solitude of a naked spirit may be rather well peopled? In proportion as we renounce our animal claims and commitments, do we not breathe a fresher and more salubrious air? May not the renunciation of everything disinfect everything and return everything to us in its impartial reality, at the same time disinfecting our wills also, and rendering us capable of charity? This charity will extend, of course, to the lives and desires of others, which we recognize to be no less inevitable than our own; and it will extend also to their ideas, and by a curious and blessed consequence, to the relativity and misery of our own minds. Yet this intellectual charity, since it is inspired by respect for the infinite, will by no means accept all views passively and romantically, as if they were equal and not subject to correction; but doing better justice to the holy aspiration which animates them in common, it will rise from them all, and with them all, to the conception of eternal truth.

Here we touch the crown of Spinoza's philosophy, that intellectual love of God in which the spirit was to be ultimately reconciled with universal power and universal truth. This love brings to consciousness a harmony intrinsic to existence: not an alleged harmony such as may be posited in religions or philosophies resting on faith, but a harmony which, as far as it goes, is actual and patent. In the realm of matter, this harmony is measured by the degree of adjustment, conformity, and cooperation which the part may have attained in the whole; in a word, it is measured by *health*. In the realm of truth, the same natural harmony extends as far as do capacity and pleasure in understanding the truth: so that besides health we may possess *knowledge*. And this is no passive union, no dead peace; the spirit rejoices in it; for the spirit, being, according to Spinoza, an essential concomitant of all existence, shares the movement, the *actuosa essentia* of the universe; so that we necessarily *love* health and knowledge, and *love* the things in which health and knowledge are found. In so far as omnificent power endows us with health, we necessarily love that power whose total movement makes for our own perfection; and in so far as we are able to understand the truth, we necessarily love the themes of an intense and unclouded vision, in which our imaginative faculty reaches its perfect function.

Of this religion of health and understanding Spinoza is a sublime prophet. By overcoming all human weaknesses, even when they seemed kindly or noble, and by honouring power and truth, even if they should slay him, he entered the sanctuary of an unruffled superhuman wisdom, and declared himself supremely happy, not because the world as he conceived it was flattering to his heart, but because the gravity of his heart disdained all flatteries, and with a sacrificial prophetic boldness uncovered and relished his destiny, however tragic his destiny might be. And presently peace descended; this keen scientific air seemed alone fit to breathe, and only this high tragedy worthy of a heroic and manly breast. Indeed the truth is a great cathartic and wonderfully relieves the vital distress of existence. We stand as on a mountaintop, and the spectacle, so out of scale with all our petty troubles, silences and overpowers the heart, expanding it for a moment into boundless sympathy with the universe.

Nevertheless, the moral problem is not solved. It is not solved for mankind at large, which remains no less distracted than it was before. Nor is it solved even for the single spirit. There is a radical and necessary recalcitrancy in the finite soul in the face of all this cosmic pomp and all this cosmic pressure: a recalcitrancy to which Spinoza was less sensitive than some other masters of the spiritual life, perhaps because he was more positivistic by temperament and less specifically religious. At any rate many a holy man has known more suffering than Spinoza found in the long work of salvation, more uncertainty, and also, in the end, a more lyrical and warmer happiness. For in the first place, as I said in the beginning, a really naked spirit cannot assume that the world is thoroughly intelligible. There may be surds, there may be hard facts, there may be dark abysses before which intelligence must be silent, for fear of going mad. And in the second place, even if to the intellect all things should prove perspicuous, the intellect is not the whole of human nature, nor even the whole of pure spirit in man. Reason may be the differentia of man; it is surely not his essence. His essence, at best, is animality qualified by reason. And from this animality the highest flights of reason are by no means separable. The very life of spirit springs from animal predicaments: it moves by imposing on events a perspective and a moral urgency proper to some particular creature or some particular interest.

Good, as Spinoza would tell us, is an epithet which we assign to whatsoever increases our perfection. Such a doctrine might seem egotistical, but is simply biological; and on its moral side, the maxim is a greater charter of liberty and justice than ever politician framed. For it follows that every good pursued is genuinely good, and the perfection of every creature equally perfection. Every good therefore is a good forever to a really clarified, just, and disinterested spirit; such a spirit cannot rest in the satisfaction of any special faculty, such as intelligence, nor of any special art, such as philosophy. That the intellect might be perfectly happy in contemplating the truth of the universe, does not render the universe good to every other faculty; good to the heart, good to the flesh, good to the eye, good to the conscience or the sense of justice. Of all systems an optimistic system is the most oppressive. Would it not be a bitter mockery if, in the words of Bradley, this were the best of possible worlds, and everything in it a necessary evil? The universal good by which the spirit, in its rapt moments, feels overwhelmed, if it is not to be a mystical illusion, cannot fall short of being the sum of all those perfections, infinitely various, to which all living things severally aspire. A glint or symbol of this universal good may be found in any moment of perfect happiness visiting any breast: but it is impossible unreservedly to love or worship anything, be it the universe or any part of it, unless we find in the end that this thing is completely good: I mean, unless it is perfect after its kind and a friend to itself, and unless at the same time it is beneficent universally, and a friend to everything else. Pure spirit would be lame, and evidently biassed by some biological accident, if it did not love every good loved anywhere by anybody. These varied perfections are rivals and enemies in the press of the world, where there seems not to be matter or time enough for everything: but to impartial spirit no good can render another good odious. Physically, one good may exclude another: nature and natural morality must choose between them, or be dissolved into chaos: but in eternity the most opposite goods are not enemies; rather little brothers and sisters, as all odd creatures were to St. Francis. And that all these various perfections are not actually attainable is a material accident, painful but not confusing to a free spirit. Their contrariety increases sorrow, but does not diminish love; the very pain is a fresh homage to the beauty missed, and a proof of loyalty; so that the more the spirit suffers the more clearly, when it unravels its suffering, it understands what it loves. Every perfection then shines, washed and clear, separate and uncontaminated: yet all compatible, each in its place, and harmonious. To love things spiritually, that is to say, intelligently and disinterestedly, means to love the love in them, to worship the good which they pursue, and to see them all prophetically in their possible beauty. To love things as they are would be a mockery of things: a true lover must love them as they would wish to be. For nothing is quite happy as it is, and the first act of true sympathy must be to move with the object of love towards its happiness.

Universal good, then, the whole of that to which all things aspire, is something merely potential; and if we wish to make a religion of love, after the manner of Socrates, we must take universal good, not universal power, for the object of our religion. This religion would need to be more imaginative, more poetical, than that of Spinoza, and the word God, if we still used it, would have to mean for us not the universe, but the good of the universe. There would not be a universe worshipped, but a universe praying; and the flame of the whole fire, the whole seminal and generative movement of nature, would be the love of God. This love would be erotic; it would be really love and not something wingless called by that name. It would bring celestial glimpses not to be retained, but culminating in moments of unspeakable rapture, in a union with all good, in which the soul would vanish as an object because, as an organ, it had found its perfect employment.

For there is a mystery here, the mystery of seeming to attain emotionally the logically unattainable. Universal good is something dispersed, various, contrary to itself in its opposite embodiments; nevertheless, to the mystic, it seems a single living object, the One Beloved, a good to be embraced all at once, finally and for ever, leaving not the least shred of anything good outside. Yet I think this mystery may be easily solved. Spirit is essentially synthetic; and just as all the known and unknown forces of nature make, in relation to experience and destiny, one single omnificent power; and just as all facts and all the relations between facts compose for the historical and prophetic mind one unalterable realm of truth; so exactly, for the lover, all objects of love form a single ineffable good. He may say that he sees all beauties in a single face, that all beauties else are nothing to him; yet perhaps in this hyperbole he may be doing his secret heart an injustice. Beauty here may be silently teaching him to discern beauty everywhere, because in all instances of love only the sheer love counts in his eyes: and in the very absoluteness of his love he may feel an infinite promise. His ecstasy, which passes for a fulfilment, remains a sort of agony: and though itself visionary, it may, by its influence, free his heart from trivial or accidental attachments and lead it instead to a universal charity. Beggars in Catholic and Moslem countries used to beg an alms, sometimes, for the love of God. It was a potent appeal; because God, according to the Socratic tradition, was the good to which all creation moved; so that anyone who loved deeply, and loved God, could not fail, by a necessary inclusion, to love the good which all creatures lived by pursuing, no matter how repulsive these creatures might be to natural human feeling.

Thus the absolute love of anything involves the love of universal good; and the love of universal good involves the love of every creature.

Such, in brief, seems to me the prospect open to a mind that examines its moral condition without any preconceptions. Perhaps an empirical critic, strictly reducing all objects to the functions which they have in experience, might see in my meagre inventory all the elements of religion. Mankind, he might say, in thinking of God or the gods have always meant the power in events: as when people say: *God willing*. Sometimes they have also meant the truth, as when people say: *God knows*. And perhaps a few mystics may have meant the good, or the supreme object of love, union with whom they felt would be perfect happiness. I should then have merely changed the language of traditional religion a little, translated its myths into their pragmatic equivalents, and reduced religion to its true essence. But no: I make no such professions: they would be plainly sophistical. The functions which objects have in experience no doubt open to us different avenues to those objects: but the objects themselves, if they exist, are not mere names for those functions. They are objects of faith: and the religion of mankind, like their science, has always been founded on faith. Now there is no faith invoked in the examination of conscience which I have made before you this evening: and therefore, properly speaking, what I come to is not religion. Nor is it exactly philosophy, since I offer no hypotheses about the nature of the universe or about the nature of knowledge. Yet to be quite sincere, I think that in this examination of conscience there is a sort of secret or private philosophy perhaps more philosophical than the other: and while I set up no gods, not even Spinoza's infinite *Deus sive Natura* [God or Nature], I do consider on what subjects and to what end we might consult those gods, if we found that they existed: and surely the aspiration that would prompt us, in that case, to worship the gods, would be our truest heart-bond and our ultimate religion.

If then any of us who are so minded should ever hear the summons of a liturgical religion calling to us: *Sursum corda, Lift up your hearts,* we might sincerely answer, *Habemus ad Dominum, Our hearts by nature are addressed to the Lord.* For we recognize universal power, and respect it, since on it we depend for our existence and fortunes. We look also with unfeigned and watchful allegiance towards universal truth, in which all the works of power are eternally defined and recorded; since in so far as we are able to discover it, the truth raises all things for us into the light, into the language of spirit. And finally, when power takes on the form of life, and begins to circle about and pursue some type of perfection, spirit in us necessarily loves these perfections, since spirit is aspiration become conscious, and they are the goals of life: and in so far as any of these goals of life can be defined or attained anywhere, even if only in prophetic fancy, they become glory, or become beauty, and spirit in us necessarily worships them: not the troubled glories and brief perfections of this world only, but rather that desired perfection, that eternal beauty, which lies sealed in the heart of each living thing.

34

CRITO *

by

PLATO

(B.C. 427–347)

Scene:—The Prison of Socrates.

Socrates. Why have you come at this hour, Crito? it must be quite early.?

Crito. Yes, certainly.

Soc. What is the exact time?

Cr. The dawn is breaking.

Soc. I wonder that the keeper of the prison would let you in.

Cr. He knows me, because I often come, Socrates; moreover, I have done him a kindness.

Soc. And are you only just come?

Cr. No, I came some time ago.

Soc. Then why did you sit and say nothing, instead of awakening me at once?

Cr. Why, indeed, Socrates, I myself would rather not have all this sleeplessness and sorrow. But I have been wondering at your peaceful slumbers, and that was the reason why I did not awaken you, because I wanted you to be out of pain. I have always thought you happy in the calmness of your temperament; but never did I see the like of the easy, cheerful way in which you bear this calamity.

Soc. Why, Crito, when a man has reached my age he ought not to be repining at the prospect of death.

Cr. And yet other old men find themselves in similar misfortunes, and age does not prevent them from repining.

Soc. That may be. But you have not told me why you come at this early hour.

Cr. I come to bring you a message which is sad and painful; not, as I believe, to yourself, but to all of us who are your friends, and saddest of all to me.

Soc. What! I suppose that the ship has come from Delos, on the arrival of which I am to die?

* [The complete dialogue, translated by Benjamin Jowett (1871).]

Cr. No, the ship has not actually arrived, but she will probably be here to-day, as persons who have come from Sunium tell me that they left her there; and therefore to-morrow, Socrates, will be the last day of your life.

Soc. Very well, Crito; if such is the will of God, I am willing; but my belief is that there will be a delay of a day.

Cr. Why do you say this?

Soc. I will tell you. I am to die on the day after the arrival of the ship?

Cr. Yes; that is what the authorities say.

Soc. But I do not think that the ship will be here until to-morrow; this I gather from a vision which I had last night, or rather only just now, when you fortunately allowed me to sleep.

Cr. And what was the nature of the vision?

Soc. There came to me the likeness of a woman, fair and comely, clothed in white raiment, who called to me and said: O Socrates,

"The third day hence to Phthia shalt thou go."

Cr. What a singular dream, Socrates!

Soc. There can be no doubt about the meaning, Crito, I think.

Cr. Yes; the meaning is only too clear. But, Oh! my beloved Socrates, let me entreat you once more to take my advice and escape. For if you die I shall not only lose a friend who can never be replaced, but there is another evil: people who do not know you and me will believe that I might have saved you if I had been willing to give money, but that I did not care. Now, can there be a worse disgrace than this—that I should be thought to value money more than the life of a friend? For the many will not be persuaded that I wanted you to escape, and that you refused.

Soc. But why, my dear Crito, should we care about the opinion of the many? Good men, and they are the only persons who are worth considering, will think of these things truly as they happened.

Cr. But do you see, Socrates, that the opinion of the many must be regarded, as is evident in your own case, because they can do the very greatest evil to any one who has lost their good opinion.

Soc. I only wish, Crito, that they could; for then they could also do the greatest good, and that would be well. But the truth is, that they can do neither good nor evil: they can not make a man wise or make him foolish; and whatever they do is the result of chance.

Cr. Well, I will not dispute about that; but please to tell me, Socrates, whether you are not acting out of regard to me and your other friends: are you not afraid that if you escape hence we may get into trouble with the informers for having stolen you away, and lose either the whole or a great part of our property; or that even a worse evil may happen to us? Now, if this is your fear, be at ease; for in order to save you, we ought surely to run this, or even a greater risk; be persuaded, then, and do as I say.

Soc. Yes, Crito, that is one fear which you mention, but by no means the only one.

Cr. Fear not. There are persons who at no great cost are willing to save you and bring you out of prison; and as for the informers, you may observe that they are far from being exorbitant in their demands; a little money will satisfy them. My means, which, as I am sure, are ample, are at your service, and if you have a scruple about spending all mine, here are strangers who will give you the use of theirs; and one of them, Simmias the Theban, has brought a sum of money for this very purpose; and Cebes and many others are willing to spend their money too. I say therefore, do not on that account hesitate about making your escape, and do not say, as you did in the court, that you will have a difficulty in knowing what to do with yourself if you escape. For men will love you in other places to which you may go, and not in Athens only; there are friends of mine in Thessaly, if you like to go to them, who will value and protect you, and no Thessalian will give you any trouble. Nor can I think that you are justified, Socrates, in betraying your own life when you might be saved; this is playing into the hands of your enemies and destroyers; and moreover I should say that you were betraying your children; for you might bring them up and educate them; instead of which you go away and leave them, and they will have to take their chance; and if they do not meet with the usual fate of orphans, there will be small thanks to you. No man should bring children into the world who is unwilling to persevere to the end in their nurture and education. But you are choosing the easier part, as I think, not the better and manlier, which would rather have become one who professes virtue in all his actions, like yourself. And indeed, I am ashamed not only of you, but of us who are your friends, when I reflect that this entire business of yours will be attributed to our want of courage. The trial need never have come on, or might have been brought to another issue; and the end of all, which is the crowning absurdity, will seem to have been permitted by us, through cowardice and baseness, who might have saved you, as you might have saved yourself, if we had been good for anything (for there was no difficulty in escaping); and we did not see how disgraceful, Socrates, and also miserable all this will be to us as well as to you. Make your mind up then, or rather have your mind already made up, for the time of deliberation is over, and there is only one thing to be done, which must be done, if at all, this very night, and which any delay will render all but impossible;

I beseech you therefore, Socrates, to be persuaded by me. and to do as I say.

Soc. Dear Crito, your zeal is invaluable, if a right one; but if wrong, the greater the zeal the greater the evil; and therefore we ought to consider whether these things shall be done or not. For I am and always have been one of those natures who must be guided by reason, whatever the reason may be which upon reflection appears to me to be the best; and now that this fortune has come upon me, I can not put away the reasons which I have before given: the principles which I have hitherto honored and revered I still honor, and unless we can find other and better principles on the instant, I am certain not to agree with you; no, not even if the power of the multitude could inflict many more imprisonments, confiscations, deaths, frightening us like children with hobgoblin terrors. But what will be the fairest way of considering the question? Shall I return to your old argument about the opinions of men? some of which are to be regarded, and others, as we were saying, are not to be regarded. Now were we right in maintaining this before I was condemned? And has the argument which was once good now proved to be talk for the sake of talking;—in fact an amusement only, and altogether vanity? That is what I want to consider with your help, Crito:—whether, under my present circumstances, the argument appears to be in any way different or not; and is to be allowed by me or disallowed. That argument, which, as I believe, is maintained by many who assume to be authorities, was to the effect, as I was saying, that the opinions of some men are to be regarded, and of other men not to be regarded. Now you, Crito, are a disinterested person who are not going to die to-morrow—at least, there is no human probability of this, and you are therefore not liable to be deceived by the circumstances in which you are placed. Tell me then, whether I am right in saying that some opinions, and the opinions of some men only, are to be valued, and other opinions, and the opinions of other men, are not to be valued. I ask you whether I was right in maintaining this?

Cr. Certainly.

Soc. The good are to be regarded, and not the bad?

Cr. Yes.

Soc. And the opinions of the wise are good, and the opinions of the unwise are evil?

Cr. Certainly.

Soc. And what was said about another matter? Was the disciple in gymnastics supposed to attend to the praise and blame and opinion of every man, or of one man only—his physician or trainer, whoever that was?

Cr. Of one man only.

Soc. And he ought to fear the censure and welcome the praise of that one only, and not of the many?

Cr. That is clear.

Soc. And he ought to live and train, and eat and drink in the way which seems good to his single master who has understanding, rather than according to the opinion of all other men put together?

Cr. True.

Soc. And if he disobeys and disregards the opinion and approval of the one, and regards the opinion of the many who have no understanding, will he not suffer evil?

Cr. Certainly he will.

Soc. And what will the evil be, whither tending and what affecting, in the disobedient person?

Cr. Clearly, affecting the body; that is what is destroyed by the evil.

Soc. Very good; and is not this true, Crito, of other things which we need not separately enumerate? In the matter of just and unjust, fair and foul, good and evil, which are the subjects of our present consultation, ought we to follow the opinion of the many and to fear them; or the opinion of the one man who has understanding, and whom we ought to fear and reverence more than all the rest of the world: and whom deserting we shall destroy and injure that principle in us which may be assumed to be improved by justice and deteriorated by injustice;—is there not such a principle?

Cr. Certainly there is, Socrates.

Soc. Take a parallel instance:—if, acting under the advice of men who have no understanding, we destroy that which is improvable by health and deteriorated by disease—when that has been destroyed, I say, would life be worth having? And that is—the body?

Cr. Yes.

Soc. Could we live, having an evil and corrupted body?

Cr. Certainly not.

Soc. And will life be worth having, if that higher part of man be depraved, which is improved by justice and deteriorated by injustice? Do we suppose that principle, whatever it may be in man, which has to do with justice and injustice, to be inferior to the body?

Cr. Certainly not.

Soc. More honored, then?

Cr. Far more honored.

Soc. Then, my friend, we must not regard what the many say of us: but what he, the one man who has understanding of just and un-

just, will say, and what the truth will say. And therefore you begin
in error when you suggest that we should regard the opinion of the
many about just and unjust, good and evil, honorable and dishonorable.—Well, some one will say, "but the many can kill us."

Cr. Yes, Socrates; that will clearly be the answer.

Soc. That is true: but still I find with surprise that the old argument is, as I conceive, unshaken as ever. And I should like to know
whether I may say the same of another proposition—that not life,
but a good life, is to be chiefly valued?

Cr. Yes, that also remains.

Soc. And a good life is equivalent to a just and honorable one—
that holds also?

Cr. Yes, that holds.

Soc. From these premises I proceed to argue the question whether
I ought or ought not to try and escape without the consent of the
Athenians: and if I am clearly right in escaping, then I will make
the attempt; but if not, I will abstain. The other considerations
which you mention, of money and loss of character and the duty
of educating children, are, as I fear, only the doctrines of the multitude, who would be as ready to call people to life, if they were
able, as they are to put them to death—and with as little reason.
But now, since the argument has thus far prevailed, the only question which remains to be considered is, whether we shall do rightly
either in escaping or in suffering others to aid in our escape and
paying them in money and thanks, or whether we shall not do
rightly; and if the lattter, then death or any other calamity which
may ensue on my remaining here must not be allowed to enter into
the calculation.

Cr. I think that you are right, Socrates; how then shall we proceed?

Soc. Let us consider the matter together, and do you either refute
me if you can, and I will be convinced; or else cease, my dear
friend, from repeating to me that I ought to escape against the wishes
of the Athenians: for I am extremely desirous to be persuaded by
you, but not against my own better judgment. And now please to
consider my first position, and do your best to answer me.

Cr. I will do my best.

Soc. Are we to say that we are never intentionally to do wrong,
or that in one way we ought and in another way we ought not to
do wrong, or is doing wrong always evil and dishonorable, as I was
just now saying, and as has been already acknowledged by us? Are
all our former admissions which were made within a few days to
be thrown away? And have we, at our age, been earnestly discoursing with one another all our life long only to discover that we are

no better than children? Or are we to rest assured, in spite of the opinion of the many, and in spite of consequences whether better or worse, of the truth of what was then said, that injustice is always an evil and dishonor to him who acts unjustly? Shall we affirm that?

Cr. Yes.

Soc. Then we must do no wrong?

Cr. Certainly not.

Soc. Nor when injured injure in return, as the many imagine; for we must injure no one at all?

Cr. Clearly not.

Soc. Again, Crito, may we do evil?

Cr. Surely not, Socrates.

Soc. And what of doing evil in return for evil, which is the morality of the many—is that just or not?

Cr. Not just.

Soc. For doing evil to another is the same as injuring him?

Cr. Very true.

Soc. Then we ought not to retaliate or render evil for evil to any one, whatever evil we may have suffered from him. But I would have you consider, Crito, whether you really mean what you are saying. For this opinion has never been held, and never will be held, by any considerable number of persons; and those who are agreed and those who are not agreed upon this point have no common ground, and can only despise one another when they see how widely they differ. Tell me, then, whether you agree with and assent to my first principle, that neither injury nor retaliation nor warding off evil by evil is ever right. And shall that be the premiss of our argument? Or do you decline and dissent from this? For this has been of old and is still my opinion; but, if you are of another opinion, let me hear what you have to say. If, however, you remain of the same mind as formerly, I will proceed to the next step.

Cr. You may proceed, for I have not changed my mind.

Soc. Then I will proceed to the next step, which may be put in the form of a question:—Ought a man to do what he admits to be right, or ought he to betray the right?

Cr. He ought to do what he thinks right.

Soc. But if this is true, what is the application? In leaving the prison against the will of the Athenians, do I wrong any? or rather do I not wrong those whom I ought least to wrong? Do I not desert the principles which were acknowledged by us to be just? What do you say?

Cr. I can not tell, Socrates; for I do not know.

Soc. Then consider the matter in this way:—Imagine that I am about to play truant (you may call the proceeding by any name which you like), and the laws and the government come and interrogate me: "Tell us, Socrates," they say; "what are you about? are you going by an act of yours to overturn us—the laws and the whole state, as far as in you lies? Do you imagine that a state can subsist and not be overthrown, in which the decisions of law have no power, but are set aside and overthrown by individuals?" What will be our answer, Crito, to these and the like words? Any one, and especially a clever rhetorician, will have a good deal to urge about the evil of setting aside the law which requires a sentence to be carried out; and we might reply, "Yes; but the state has injured us and given an unjust sentence." Suppose I say that?

Cr. Very good, Socrates.

Soc. "And was that our agréement with you?" the law would say; "or were you to abide by the sentence of the state?" And if I were to express astonishment at their saying this, the law would probably add: "Answer, Socrates, instead of opening your eyes: you are in the habit of asking and answering questions. Tell us what complaint you have to make against us which justifies you in attempting to destroy us and the state? In the first place did we not bring you into existence? Your father married your mother by our aid and begat you. Say whether you have any objection to urge against those of us who regulate marriage?" None, I should reply. "Or against those of us who regulate the system of nurture and education of children in which you were trained? Were not the laws, who have the charge of this, right in commanding your father to train you in music and gymnastic?" Right, I should reply. "Well then, since you were brought into the world and nurtured and educated by us, can you deny in the first place that you are our child and slave, as your fathers were before you? And if this is true you are not on equal terms with us; nor can you think that you have a right to do to us what we are doing to you. Would you have any right to strike or revile or do any other evil to a father or to your master, if you had one, when you have been struck or reviled by him, or received some other evil at his hands?—you would not say this? And because we think right to destroy you, do you think that you have any right to destroy us in return, and your country as far as in you lies? And will you, O professor of true virtue, say that you are justified in this? Has a philosopher like you failed to discover that our country is more to be valued and higher and holier far than mother or father or any ancestor, and more to be regarded in the eyes of the gods and of men of understanding? also to be soothed, and gently and reverently entreated when angry, even more than a father, and if not persuaded, obeyed? And when we are punished by her, whether with imprisonment or stripes, the punishment is to be endured in silence; and if she lead us to wounds or death in battle, thither we follow as is right; neither may any one yield or retreat or leave his rank, but whether in battle or in a court of law, or in any other place, he must do what his city and his country order him; or he must change their view of what is just: and if he may do no violence to his father or mother, much less may he do violence to his country." What answer shall we make to this, Crito? Do the laws speak truly, or do they not?

Cr. I think that they do.

Soc. Then the laws will say: "Consider, Socrates, if this is true, that in your present attempt you are going to do us wrong. For, after having brought you into the world, and nurtured and educated you, and given you and every other citizen a share in every good that we had to give, we further proclaim and give the right to every Athenian, that if he does not like us when he has come of age and has seen the ways of the city, and made our acquaintance, he may go where he pleases and take his goods with him; and none of us laws will forbid him or interfere with him. Any of you who does not like us and the city, and who wants to go to a colony or to any other city, may go where he likes, and take his goods with him. But he who has experience of the manner in which we order justice and administer the state, and still remains, has entered into an implied contract that he will do as we command him. And he who disobeys us is, as we maintain, thrice wrong; first, because in disobeying us he is disobeying his parents; secondly, because we are the authors of his education; thirdly, because he has made an agreement with us that he will duly obey our commands; and he neither obeys them nor convinces us that our commands are wrong; and we do not rudely impose them, but give him the alternative of obeying or convincing us;—that is what we offer, and he does neither. These are the sort of accusations to which, as we were saying, you, Socrates, will be exposed if you accomplish your intentions; you, above all other Athenians." Suppose I ask, why is this? they will justly retort upon me that I above all other men have acknowledged the agreement. "There is clear proof," they will say, "Socrates, that we and the city were not displeasing to you. Of all Athenians you have been the most constant resident in the city, which, as you never leave, you may be supposed to love. For you never went out of the city either to see the games, except once when you went to the Isthmus, or to any other place unless when you were on military service; nor did you travel as other men do. Nor had you any curiosity to know other states or their laws: your affections did not go beyond us and our state; we were your special favorites, and you acquiesced in our government of you; and this is the state in which you begat your children, which is a proof of your satisfaction. Moreover, you might, if you had liked, have fixed the penalty at banishment in the course of the trial—the state which refuses to let you go now would have let you go then. But you pretended that you preferred death to exile, and that you were not grieved at death. And now you have forgotten these fine sentiments, and pay no respect to us the laws, of whom you are the destroyer; and are doing what only a miserable slave would do, running away and turning your back upon the compacts and agreements which you made as a citizen. And first of all answer this very question: Are we right in saying that you agreed to be governed according to us in deed, and not in word only? Is that true or not?" How shall we answer that, Crito? Must we not agree?

Cr. There is no help, Socrates.

Soc. Then will they not say: "You, Socrates, are breaking the covenants and agreements which you made with us at your leisure. not in any haste or under any compulsion or deception, but having had seventy years to think of them, during which time you were at liberty to leave the city, if we were not to your mind, or if our covenants appeared to you to be unfair. You had your choice, and might have gone either to Lacedaemon or Crete, which you often praise for their good government, or to some other Hellenic or foreign state. Whereas you, above all other Athenians, seemed to be so fond of the state, or, in other words, of us her laws (for who would like a state that has no laws), that you never stirred out of her; the halt, the blind, the maimed were not more stationary in her than you were. And now you run away and forsake your agreements. Not so, Socrates, if you will take our advice; do not make yourself ridiculous by escaping out of the city.

"For just consider, if you transgress and err in this sort of way, what good will you do either to yourself or to your friends? That your friends will be driven into exile and deprived of citizenship, or will lose their property, is tolerably certain; and you yourself, if you fly to one of the neighboring cities, as, for example, Thebes or Megara, both of which are well-governed cities, will come to them as an enemy, Socrates, and their government will be against you, and all patriotic citizens will cast an evil eye upon you as a subverter of the laws, and you will confirm in the minds of the judges the justice of their own condemnation of you. For he who is a corruptor of the laws is more than likely to be corruptor of the young and foolish portion of mankind. Will you then flee from well-ordered cities and virtuous men? and is existence worth having on these terms? Or will you go to them without shame, and talk to them, Socrates? And what will you say to them? What you say here about virtue and justice and institutions and laws being the best things among men? Would that be decent of you? Surely not. But if you go away from well-governed states to Crito's friends in Thessaly, where there is a great disorder and license, they will be charmed to have the tale of your escape from prison, set off with ludicrous particulars of the manner in which you were wrapped in a goatskin or some other disguise, and metamorphosed as the fashion of runaways is—that is very likely; but will there be no one to remind you that in your old age you violated the most sacred laws from a miserable desire of a little more life? Perhaps not, if you keep them in a good temper; but if they are out of temper you will hear many degrading things; you will live, but how?—as the flatterer of all men, and the servant of all men; and doing what?—eating and drinking in Thessaly, having gone abroad in order that you may get a dinner. And where will be your fine sentiments about justice and virtue then? Say that you wish to live for the sake of your children, that you may bring them up and educate them—will you take them into Thessaly and deprive them of Athenian citizenship? Is that the benefit which you would confer upon them? Or are you under the impression that they will be better cared for and educated here if you are still alive, although absent from them; for that your friends will take care of them? Do you fancy that if you are an inhabitant of Thessaly they will take care of them, and if you are an inhabitant of the other world they will not take care of them? Nay; but if they who call themselves friends are truly friends, they surely will.

"Listen, then, Socrates, to us who have brought you up. Think not of life and children first, and of justice afterwards, but of justice first, that you may be justified before the princes of the world below. For neither will you nor any that belong to you be happier or holier or juster in this life, or happier in another, if you do as Crito bids. Now you depart in innocence, a sufferer and not a doer of evil; a victim, not of the laws, but of men. But if you go forth, returning evil for evil, and injury for injury, breaking the covenants and agreements which you have made with us, and wronging those whom you ought least to wrong, that is to say, yourself, your friends, your country, and us, we shall be angry with you while you live, and our brethren, the laws in the world below, will receive you as an enemy; for they will know that you have done your best to destroy us. Listen, then, to us and not to Crito."

This is the voice which I seem to hear murmuring in my ears, like the sound of the flute in the ears of the mystic; that voice, I say, is humming in my ears, and prevents me from hearing any other.

And I know that anything more which you may say will be vain. Yet speak, if you have anything to say.

Cr. I have nothing to say, Socrates.

Soc. Leave me then, Crito, to follow the intimations of the will o, God.